Y0-BZA-968

THE AROUND AUSTRALIA GUIDE

If you think you can you will.
If you think you can't you most certainly won't.

This book is dedicated to all those of you who do.
STEVE PARISH

Photography by Steve Parish
Text by Rod Howard

Steve Parish™
PUBLISHING

INTRODUCTION

FOLLOWING DREAMS

For any traveller, the "around Australia adventure" is one of the world's most appealing and ambitious journeys. Appealing for the incredible range of experiences and environments the country offers and ambitious for the very same reason.

Australia's scale and diversity is truly awesome — ranging from reef to rainforest, desert to alps and languid outback towns to vivacious cities. The best part is that this adventure can be undertaken by travellers of all ages and budgets in a nation well known for its hospitality and security. What more could the 21st century explorer hope for?

While this book presents the journey around Australia as one continuous trek in an anti-clockwise direction (with a number of long-range detours thrown in for good measure), it was not my intention to create a book offering this route as the only option. An adventure on this scale would take a minimum of 4–5 months — a time frame beyond the scope of many people. The real function of this guide is to help you pick and choose your own start and finish points, trip duration and preferred travel conditions.

I have included seasonal information about the times when you are most likely to see, for example, the country's spectacular wildflowers or migrating whales. Also included are special chapters with tips on how to best photograph your journey and practical information on camping, 4WD essentials, cultural considerations and much more.

To create this book I employed local knowledge and visual material drawn from my own Australian journeys. The subject matter leans heavily towards landscape, flora, fauna, national parks and our fascinating social history — in my opinion, the best aspects of this magnificent country. I worked with Rod Howard, an experienced travel writer, with the objective of creating a narrative that will empower you to make your own discoveries and revel in an adventure unlike any other.

Dive into these pages and hit the open road with an open mind prepared to uncover the many surprising secrets of this inspiring land.

Steve Parish

Ways to Travel

If I look back over my photographic expeditions, I must honestly say that many did not turn out quite as I had expected. I am sure you will agree that there are occasions when the joy of anticipating a long-awaited trip provides more pleasure than the trip itself! This section is about developing ways to help ensure that the expectations you originally form before departing on your expedition are met.

Negative Experiences: There are a range of events that may bring your high hopes crashing down to earth, or even threaten your very wellbeing — things like bushfires, storms, floods, extreme heat, dust, flies, biting insects, endless corrugated roads, bad tour drivers or guides, unfriendly people, schedule delays, the wrong light for a photographic opportunity, or lack of cooperation from your wildlife (or human!) subjects. If you are travelling in a group, a single whinger can destroy morale. Oh, let's not forget a camera breakdown! On any extended journey, these things and more can, and most likely will, occur on your trip. The key is to find how to manage events and turn them around so that you can celebrate life in every single moment.

Inspect Your Expectations: Many people, including photographers, plan their travel according to expectations that are based on prior visual stimulus (from sources such as television, the internet or published images). However, remember that what you see represented on a website or one hour TV program may bear almost no resemblance to what you experience when you visit. The documentary you saw may have taken two years to make; production may well have run through all the seasons; the creators probably used experienced guides to tap the rich veins of local knowledge; and the crew may have been granted special permission to enter private land. The point is that the majority of sequences are stage-managed, and many of the wildlife species featured, and conditions experienced, may never be seen during your trip; even if you stayed in the one place for a year! Equally, that "special" place that your friends or family found so engaging may not hold similar fascination for you. Examine your own motivations for wanting to visit a particular location.

Manage Your Expectations: Over the years I have learnt to manage my expectations. Apart from planning around the likely weather, I try hard to let events unfold as they will. I remind myself that this is my journey to enjoy — my window of time and opportunity. Of course, you will still have expectations — after all, you would not be going if you did not. At the same time, those expectations can be tempered with the reality of the length of time you are able to spend in your selected destinations; and the acceptance that chance occurrences are part of the allure of travelling. Try to glean the most from new opportunities that arise in the face of an unexpected turn of events. I know that, regardless of whether I am in an urban or natural environment, the more time I spend watching, listening and thinking, the more "evolved" my experience of the location (and the resulting photographic images) are likely to be.

Travelling Light

Most people commence their preparations for a journey with the good intentions of only taking with them the minimum required luggage and equipment. But a quick glance at the overloaded vehicles and sprawling campsites at any given location will tell you that such intentions often fall by the wayside. Of course, some of this excess baggage — toolkits, fuel and extra water — is an essential precaution for journeys into Australia's more remote areas. Other items are not so essential. Be honest — how many spare fishing rods, kitchen gadgets and changes of clothing will you really need? More often than not, these items simply become a burden when packing and unpacking vehicles day after day on your trip. Overpacking may even prevent you from venturing to destinations that you would otherwise have visited. Write a list of essential items and resist the urge to try to replicate your home environment on the road — what you require when travelling is different from being at home. If you simply can't live without all the mod cons found in the typical home, perhaps you should re-think travelling altogether!

The Beauty of the Beast

One of the great beauties of Australia is that there are many opportunities to leave modern conveyances behind and take a trek on the back of beasts. This will not only provide a different perspective on the country around you, it will also help you appreciate the experiences of Australia's original explorers, settlers and pioneers.

Retrace the hoof prints left by mountain cattlemen (*above left*) or imagine you are an Afghan camel driver high aboard his "ship of the desert" (*above right*). The extent and mode of your journey is up to you, but the options range from half-hour rambles to month-long guided expeditions camping under the stars of the Southern Cross. Such forays give you an unparalleled opportunity to observe Australia's prolific native animals in their natural environs. The wonder of travelling beyond the reach of roads into the wilderness will never be forgotten.

Bus Coach Tours

Australia is a continent suited to bus coach travel. The long distances often encountered between major towns can make for exhausting stints behind the wheel; so travel by modern passenger coach offers the chance to relax and survey the countryside while someone else does the driving. The affordability and availability of coaches make them a favourite of backpackers (both young and old). Return bus coach tours to specific scenic destinations such as Uluṟu can provide a welcome break from bouts of white line fever.

Campervans

Australia's highways are becoming increasingly populated by a wide variety of campervans. These range from compact but cosy hire vehicles to the huge Winnebagos and re-purposed buses often used by longer term travellers. The reason for their popularity is simple — journeying in your travelling home eliminates the need to set up campsites or tow a caravan. Be aware, though, that many park campsites and roads are unsuitable for this type of vehicle.

Camp Trailers & Caravans

The perennially popular caravan has been joined by camp trailers and collapsibles as the most common form of towed accommodation. Each have their merits, but adventurous travellers may become frustrated by the limitations on towing vans and trailers across many of Australia's outback roads. On-site caravans are available for hire in most large commercial camping parks and are a good compromise for those who crave the occasional creature comfort.

Swags & Tents

Australia is a great place to camp. There are 516 national parks covering over 25 million ha — or over 3% of the continent's surface. Campsites range from the purely barbaric to the luxuriously comprehensive. In addition, there are plentiful commercial operations, particularly along the coasts. In the desert regions, sleeping out under a sky crammed with stars can be a great option — unroll your swag and see how many shooting stars you can count before you nod off.

Resorts & Hotels

If your pockets are deep enough, or if you feel you deserve a few nights of luxury, Australia offers a huge range of resorts. Hotels and backpacker accommodation to suit all budgets also abound. Many cheap hostels are crammed full of character and stories. The choice is yours, but weigh up whether the cost of comfort could be better invested in a longer stay in simpler (and often more social) circumstances.

Travelling With Others: Cooperation is vital when travelling with others. This is very important if you choose for economic or social reasons to travel by bus or on an organised tour where the ultimate decision-making does not rest with you. In such circumstances, a positive way of approaching the situation is to turn it around and use it to your benefit. The distances between locations offer the chance to take a nap or do some research, neither of which is possible if you are driving your own vehicle. The costs of organised tours can often be considerably lower than those of using your own vehicle or hiring one, and these trips can also be a great way to meet other travellers.

Planning Your Journey: If you are planning your first extended trip, remember not to underestimate the size of Australia and the consequent travelling time between destinations. To avoid falling into this trap, I suggest you consult a map of the whole of Australia and mark out areas of particular interest. Having done this, calculate how far apart each pair of localities are, and then estimate the time you will need to move from one region to the next. Ensure you factor in time for unexpected events that may arise along the way. The next important thing to consider is how you are going to travel. This is usually decided by three criteria — available time, budget and knowledge of the local area. See the individual journey sections of this book for detailed information on each region.

Memory Myths: It is interesting to note that the longer the time elapsed since the trip, the blurrier the bad bits become. This is especially true for photographers, whose primary memories are based on the images they keep and like most. I know that, while many of my trips have been physically uncomfortable, the photographic results were so favourable that I have forgotten what I went through to achieve the images. Equally, friends and family (and tourist publications) often omit the bad bits when relating stories of magically discovering that "incredible" isolated stretch of beach, spectacular mountain view or hidden rainforest. In many regions of Australia, some discomfort is unavoidable if you wish to reach the most remote and unspoilt parts. Seek your own experiences rather than attempting to emulate others.

Always remember that it is you who is in charge, and only you can control how your expectations are being met. In fact, the most important things to pack on any trip are acceptance, patience, tolerance and flexibility. Take them with you, and you can bet that you will have many moments of absolute joy, and memories reflective of your state of mind.

Off the Beaten Track

While Australia has densely populated urban areas, the greater part of the continent has a very small population and so there are vast regions of land in which it is possible to find isolation. Escaping the cities to camp, explore, fish or photograph are all popular pastimes of Australians. In fact, there are few places on earth that offer the range of wilderness and outback experiences to be found in Australia. If you are new to four wheel driving or roaming the less-travelled regions, take great care and be sure to do comprehensive research on the destinations you intend to explore before setting out. Some parts of the Australian interior, particularly inland Western Australia and the Northern Territory, are extremely isolated, and thorough precautions should be taken before venturing through these areas.

Finding Solitude

In most parts of Australia, it is not necessary to travel far to escape civilisation. Close to the major cities, solitude can be found in many ways. On endless strips of beach-blessed coastline; by hiking in hinterland mountain retreats; camping in one of the country's numerous national parks; or lazing on a continental island. Getting away from it all does not necessarily mean travelling thousands of kilometres to desert destinations.

Following Dreams

Wandering around Australia can become an addictive recreational pursuit. Once you start, you may well find that you simply don't want to go back home (well, not for a year or so, anyway). In 1982–83, I took off on such a quest, and that was the trip that established the base for my photographic library. You can achieve a similar goal in a number of ways. You may choose to find others of like-mind and form a long-range carpool; or take the plunge and sell up, buying a bus and converting it; or even take a bicycle, horse or camel wagon and drift with the seasons.

While the various shire councils do not generally permit roadside camping, in more remote areas few take the trouble to challenge a wayward camper. Then, of course, there is always the extraordinarily generous hospitality offered by country and outback residents who often enjoy having visitors (however, do heed signs expressing a wish to be left alone).

Hitchhiking was a very popular form of travel some years back, but these days practically all authorities advise strongly against it for personal safety reasons. Although I have never felt threatened in any way during 30 years of wandering, I would only hitchhike in an emergency.

Chartering

Many types of adventure vehicle are simply easier (and cheaper!) to charter or hire rather than supply yourself. Some, like light planes, helicopters and large cruise boats, come with pilots and other expert assistance included. Others, like houseboats, yachts and 4WD vehicles can be hired and steered to destinations of your choice. Chartering is a vast industry in Australia and good research will result in obtaining the best price and experience.

Walking & Cycling

Australia is comprehensively served by walking paths and tracks, which often are the only means of reaching some of the continent's most spectacular locations. Some of the best short walks are highlighted in this book, but comprehensive guides are also available from the various parks authorities. Cycling is an extremely common mode of transport, exploration and recreation — all of Australia's major cities have excellent cycling paths that serve many of their most scenic and popular locations.

Outdoor Adventure Tours

Whether your taste is for hurtling down the rapids in a raft or ballooning high into the dawn sky, there is an outdoor adventure operator ready to satisfy it. On every coast, diving, snorkelling, yachting and sportfishing charters are on offer to suit both the novice and experienced enthusiast. Rock climbing, bushwalking, desert treks and cross-country skiing are just a few of the many experiences that await adventurers in Australia's interior.

Eco Educational Tours

A relatively new but burgeoning industry, ecotourism is characterised by educational excursions into the natural environment. These tours emphasise minimal impact upon the resident fauna and flora. If this sounds boring compared to some of the more highly spruiked tourist offerings, don't be deterred — a nocturnal walk led by expert guides in a wildlife-rich habitat (such as the Daintree rainforest) is one of the most exhilarating travel experiences Australia has to offer.

Touring By Boat & Train

Before the introduction of roads and cars, large tracts of the continental mainland were served by train and boat. Today, some of the world's most memorable rail journeys, including the cross-continental *Ghan* desert train, are enjoyed by thousands of travellers each year. Glass-bottomed boats tour the reefs; historic paddlesteamers creep along the great inland rivers; and cruising yachts track the stunning Kimberley coast in Australia's north-west.

Website Links

Official National Parks

ACT — Environment ACT
www.tams.act.gov.au/live/environment

QUEENSLAND — EPA/QLD Parks & Wildlife
www.epa.qld.gov.au

Great Barrier Reef Marine Park Authority
www.gbrmpa.gov.au

NEW SOUTH WALES — NSW National Parks & Wildlife Service
www.nationalparks.nsw.gov.au

NORTHERN TERRITORY — Department of Natural Resources, Environment & the Arts
www.nt.gov.au/nreta/parks

SOUTH AUSTRALIA — Department for Environment & Heritage, SA
www.parks.sa.gov.au/parks/index.htm

TASMANIA — Parks & Wildlife Service, Tasmania
www.dpiw.tas.gov.au

VICTORIA — Parks Victoria
www.parkweb.vic.gov.au

WESTERN AUSTRALIA — Department of Environment & Conservation, WA
www.calm.wa.gov.au

AUSTRALIA — Department of Environment, Water, Heritage & the Arts
www.environment.gov.au

Photography in National Parks

Australia's national parks offer some of the most photogenic locations and subjects in the world. For the most part, amateur photography and video recording is permitted provided you do not contravene any park regulations or interfere with the environment or wildlife in the course of getting your shot.

There are, however, some important exceptions to this. Many Aboriginal sites and areas of cultural significance are off-limits to photography (out of respect for the laws and beliefs of their original owners). If in doubt, consult a park ranger before taking photos or using a video camera. Commercial photography and video recording in Australia's national parks are governed by strict regulations, and fees apply.

Visiting Australia's National Parks

Over four million people visit at least one of Australia's 516 national parks each year. Most of Australia's sixteen terrestrial World Heritage Areas, including the Daintree, Kakadu and Uluru–Kata Tjuta, are designated as national parks (excluding the World Heritage-listed Sydney Opera House and Royal Exhibition Centre). There are also 145 protected marine areas, including the World's largest coral reef system — the Great Barrier Reef Marine Park. Under the Australian constitution, the creation and management of most national parks is the responsibility of the individual State governments, which in turn have established park authorities to handle their administration and conservation. Comprehensive information regarding each park and its facilities can be obtained by contacting these bodies or visiting their websites (*see list at left*). Key information on walking and camping in the major national parks as well as contact telephone numbers for regional park offices are listed in the relevant destination sections of this book.

National parks play a leading role in conserving and protecting Australia's most precious habitats; native flora and fauna; and important historical, geological and archaeological features. Many national parks, such as Kakadu, also help to protect traditionally owned Aboriginal land and these are cooperatively managed by Aboriginal community representatives and Parks Australia. A wide range of national park regulations are in place to ensure the continued health and amenability of the parks and to protect their wildlife populations. These regulations vary, but it is important when travelling, walking or camping in national parks to observe the rules applying to their use — many of these are established to preserve your own safety. Failing to heed rules may result not only in fines, but in injury or even death. If in any doubt, consult a national park ranger or officer who will assist and advise visitors on all aspects of national park use.

Australia's national parks are the nation's most treasured assets and the natural wonders they contain are countless. Even a casual stroll in most parks will reveal sights and sounds to surprise and delight — it is almost impossible to imagine an extended journey around Australia that would not include a visit to several of its incredibly diverse national parks. While the level of facilities range from minimal to mollycoddling, camping is possible in nearly all of these protected areas. Advance booking of campsites is essential in the more popular parks and site registration is required in most. Walking tracks are also found in nearly all parks, ranging from short, wheelchair-friendly paths that lead to waterfalls and key natural features to multi-day treks that should only be tackled by the most experienced of bushwalkers. Always check guides and consult with rangers to find walks suited to your ability and level of fitness. If you are embarking on a walk that will require you to camp out overnight, or if you are walking a considerable distance, inform a ranger of your intended route and estimated time of return.

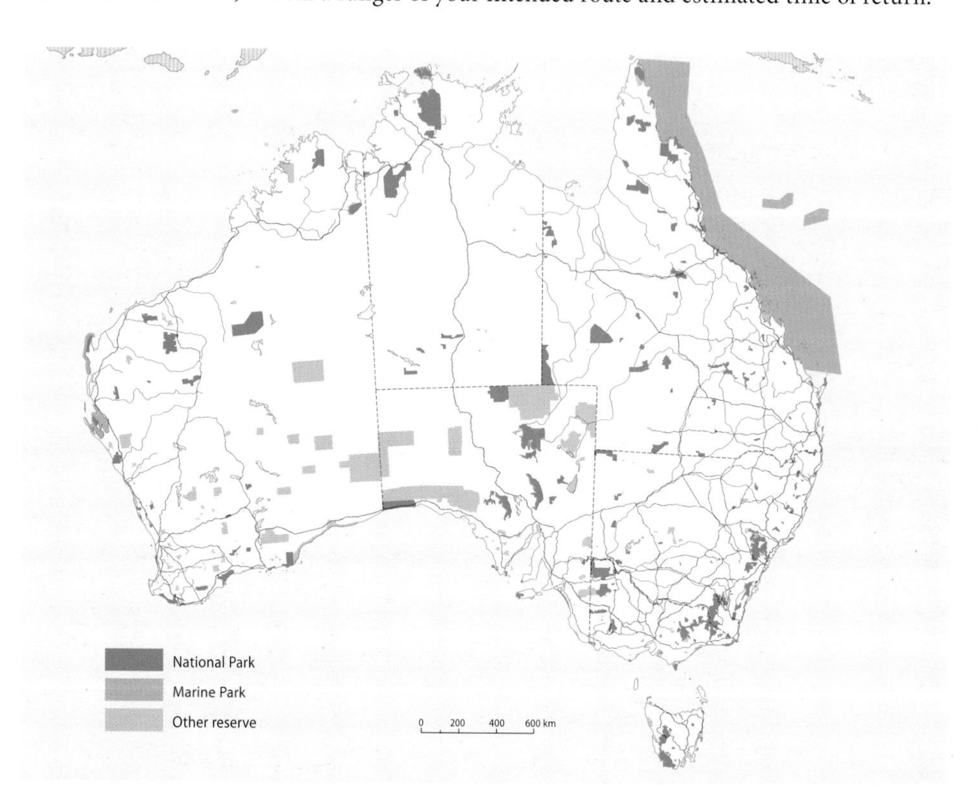

Safety & Responsibility

By their very nature, national parks are areas of rugged and untouched terrain. Great care needs to be taken when visiting, camping and walking in national parks to ensure your own safety. Walking tracks vary widely in difficulty, and weather conditions can change rapidly. Always ensure you are equipped with sufficient water and food; an adequate first aid kit; up-to-date maps; and appropriate clothing before commencing any walk. Inform a ranger if you intend to camp out overnight.

National Park Facilities

Before setting out on any national park visit, familiarise yourself with the facilities provided within the park. Camping is permitted in most, but not all, national parks and the level of comfort varies from bush camps (often just small cleared areas) to fully equipped caravan sites and campgrounds. Comprehensive visitor centres offering maps, guides and educational materials are found in many of the larger national parks. Site booking and registration is also required in many parks.

Commercial Activities in NPs

Access to various geological features, accommodation facilities and locations in some of Australia's national parks is licensed to commercial operators. Some of these (such as tours of Undara Lava Tubes in Queensland) require pre-booking before arrival. Others, like the Scenic Skyway in the Blue Mountains, can be accessed by purchasing tickets in the park itself. Check guides (including this book) and consult the relevant websites to avoid disappointment.

Activities in National Parks

A multitude of outdoor activities are on offer within the country's national parks. Snowskiing, whitewater rafting, canoeing, kayaking, abseiling, rockclimbing, hang-gliding, bushwalking, fishing, diving, snorkelling and swimming are a small selection of the experiences on offer. Each national park has different regulations regarding the use of its waterways, so be certain to check before launching craft, swimming, diving or dangling a rod.

National Park Roads

National Park roads vary with their environment and intended use. Many are 4WD only and are unsuitable for caravans, camp trailers or campervans. Seasonal conditions such as flooding may also cause frequent road closures, particularly in Australia's northern regions (some parks are closed to all access in the wet season). Observe all road use signs and be alert to rapidly changing road and weather conditions.

Encountering Aussies

Australians, or Aussies (according to local vernacular), are a diverse bunch of people. As a photographer who has travelled the length and breadth of the continent meeting and capturing Aussies (on film) over many decades, I have learnt that this is one of the least homogenous species on earth. Since earliest Aboriginal time, Aussies have been travellers — and today there is an enormous level of social mobility between city and bush, and desert and coast. From the time European boats first reached these shores several hundred years ago, there has been a huge influx of peoples from nearly every country on the globe and this has resulted in a cultural mosaic of mind-boggling complexity. There are now more than 20 million Aussies spread across one of the world's most sparsely populated continents and whether you are an Aussie or a visitor there is always something new to discover when travelling and meeting these remarkable people.

Meeting with Aussies

Aussies have a reputation as open, straightforward and friendly people with little patience for pretence. While no glib generalisation can ever properly sum up such a wide range of people, it seems true to me that Aussies respect and gravitate toward people who are willing to be themselves. They also relish curiosity about their lifestyle and take pride in discussing their endeavours. I have met and photographed people from nearly every walk of life in Australia and very rarely have I found them standoffish or unwilling to offer an opinion on everything from sport to politics. While the strong divide that once existed between the urban and the rural Aussie has been diluted by migration in both directions over recent decades, there are still some differences that define these related species. Many of these are directly related to time and space. Country Australia still offers a more relaxed pace than that experienced by city-dwellers and as a result I find it generally true that the country Aussie is still more generous in making time to converse with visitors. The larger cities are similar to any major city around the world, in that they are often frenetically busy places, preoccupied with the business of making a living. That said, their citizens are also enormously expressive, producing an extensive spectrum of artistic, sporting and cultural offerings for visitors to enjoy. Aussies, on the whole, are outdoorsy types and that makes meeting the species relatively easy. Aussies flock to beaches, pubs, sporting events, parks, snowfields, barbecues, wineries and restaurants. Both city and country offer an innumerable number of festivals as contrasting as thong-throwing and prawn-peeling to the internationally acclaimed Adelaide Festival of Arts and Sydney's spectacularly-large, Gay and Lesbian Mardi Gras. The world of the Aussie is an inclusive, multi-dimensional society that rewards lengthy exploration.

Private Property

Australia has one of the greatest ratios of public to private land of any country in the world. Nonetheless, one issue that requires the awareness of both travellers and photographers is that the rights of owners of commercial, residential or Aboriginal lands should always be respected. Overall, the best approach to adopt can be summarised in the timeless golden rule: "do unto others as you would have them do unto you". How would you feel if someone barged into your home and began nonchalantly snapping away with a camera or souveniring personal items?

This is of particular note in country and remote areas where the division between public and private property can be blurry at best. Some land owners advertise at the gate their wish to be left undisturbed, but others do not. Always seek out the owner of the land for permission before taking photographs, fishing in waterways or using private roads as a thoroughfare. Often I have been pleasantly surprised by a generous invitation to stay for tea!

Indigenous communities are the same, although you must gain permission from an elder, not the first person you meet. Always ask permission before photographing Indigenous people, cultural artefacts or ceremonies.

Personal Safety – City & Bush

Australia is a relatively safe place to travel but, as with all places, common sense is your best guard against having a holiday spoiled. Ensure your personal belongings are safely secured — whether you are staying in a city hotel or remote campsite. Be aware of people around you when moving through busy areas, particularly airports, department stores, tourist zones and other high traffic places. Try not to advertise your status as an out-of-towner too loudly in dress or demeanour or you may become the target of pickpockets and scammers. Never walk alone through isolated city or country areas at night and when bushwalking always inform someone where you are going and what time you expect to return.

Not all potential dangers are from other humans. Heed signs and advice regarding the presence of potentially dangerous wildlife and never swim or walk too closely to crocodile-infested waters. While Australia is not quite the land of bestial terrors as is often reported overseas, its wilderness areas and coastal waters are the habitat of creatures such as sharks, snakes and marine stingers, which can be dangerous when people fail to take due caution.

Photographing Children

In urban and rural areas, people are understandably cautious of strangers snapping photographs of their children. Even an inadvertent shot of a child while photographing another subject, scenery or background can lead to suspicion and hostility. If you would like to take a photograph that involves a child, approach the parent first and seek his or her permission. If there is any doubt, simply move on — or frame your shot to exclude the child.

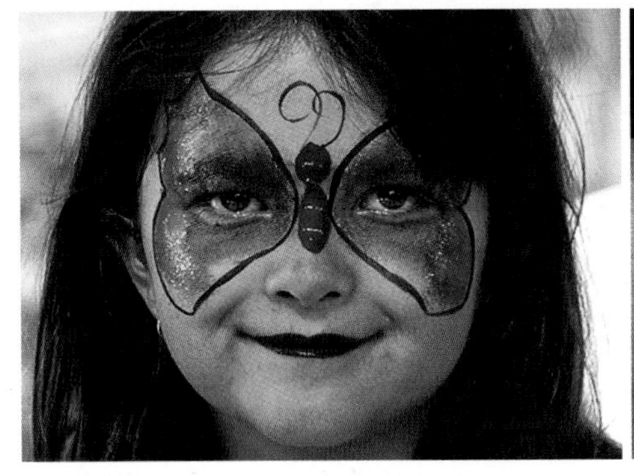

Photography in Public Places

For the most part, it is acceptable to photograph for non-commercial purposes in Australian public places. However, like many countries around the world, Australia now has increased security, which limits photography in certain public places (particularly around government buildings). Ensure you obey any signs forbidding photography or you may find yourself becoming the focus of unwanted interest.

Festive Aussies

There are literally thousands of public outdoor festivals and fairs held throughout Australia each year. Many of these are annual so you should time your journey to coincide with the celebrations of your choice. Festivals can be a superb way of meeting Aussies with similar interests and are a visual feast for lovers of people photography (like myself). Do ask permission before photographing Aboriginal ceremonies or cultural activities that often form part of these festivals.

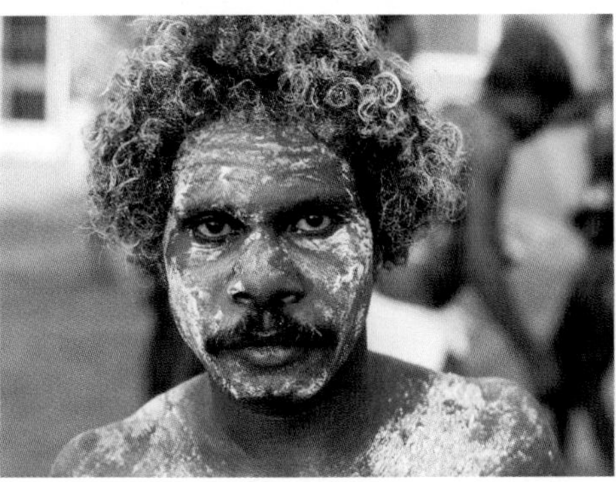

Aussies at Market

Nearly every Australian town has an outdoor market staged nearby at least monthly. These range from modest trash and treasures to sprawling avenues of stalls selling everything you can imagine. Markets can offer a great opportunity to pick up an interesting piece of memorabilia from your trip or commune with the locals. They can also offer a chance to test your haggling skills (but don't be disappointed if a stall owner insists on a set price as profit margins are usually small).

Bush Aussies

The bush Aussie can be hard to define, but all I can say is you will know one when you meet one! They are often defiantly eccentric, itinerant (or reclusive) types who remind you that Australia remains a place strongly connected with its heritage and land. While the "swaggie" (the bush equivalent of a light traveller) may be a dying breed, there are still many Aussies who live life by the rules of the bush and have a swag of yarns to share if you lend them an ear.

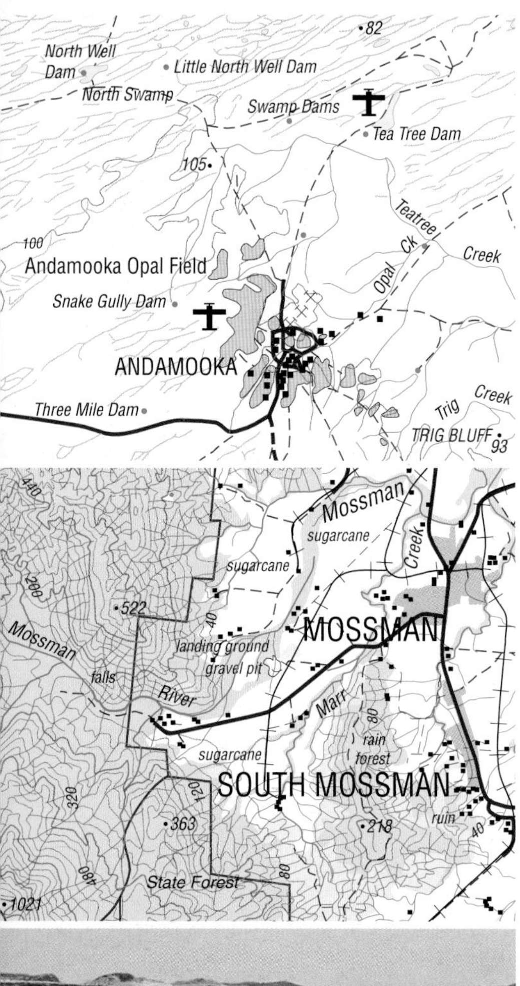

Reading the Topography

One thing that helps make travel particularly exciting is understanding the topography (or elevation of terrain) of an area. I believe that the more I study topographic maps, the more adventuresome my image-making and travel becomes. These days of course we have Google Earth, which enables us to "drop in" and see our landscapes in breathtaking detail. A definite advantage, but I sometimes feel this aid to travel does take something of the mystery out of one's adventures.

Regardless of the method, topographical research is worthwhile for all physical landscape, because topography and climate are interlinked, and together they determine vegetation, wildlife and human associations. Australia is a country of startling contrasts and extremes, and it is these contrasts that often make the scenery even more striking.

Overseas visitors, especially those from densely populated urban areas like Great Britain, Europe, Asia, some parts of the USA, and even urbanised Australian first-time travellers, can be overwhelmed, by the sheer size of Australia. The vast open spaces, enormous distances and time it takes to travel from one place to another can even deter them from making a trip. To enjoy your experience is, I think, merely a matter of attitude and preparation.

Photographers have the advantage over destination-oriented travellers in that they view every kilometre of the space between destinations as mini-goals in their own right. In fact, if I were to look over my favourite images, I would discover that many were taken on the journeys between targeted destinations. For example: the vast distance across the Nullarbor; or from Port Augusta to Alice Springs; or Alice Springs to Darwin; is rich with photographic opportunities. Never should such a stretch be thought of as a tedious, seemingly endless, time-wasting journey. The fact is that roadside discoveries or short detours can present you with unexpected opportunities. The famous Bungle Bungle Range in north-west Western Australia was unknown — except to Indigenous people — until 1983 when a photographer studied a topographic map and took a detour!

I find the space between destinations so valuable that I always factor in extra time into my travel plans, especially during wildflower seasons.

From the Air

While topographic maps give you some idea of what to expect in terms of landscape, they will never be a substitute for actually being on location. Air perspectives of localities, like the towers of "lost cities" of southern Arnhem Land (*below, left to right*); and the unique geological features of Warrumbungle National Park from the air are spectacular (*above, left to right*). However, to be on the ground physically touching the landscape is the real thrill.

Topographical Map

My topographical map suggested that I could expect clearly delineated dune systems in the far central west of Western Australia, near the coast. While the route was a slight detour, I decided to take a look because I knew the area had been flooded some months earlier. My hunch paid off, and the minor detour turned out to take several days while I photographed the explosion of wildflowers on each dune.

Top: A section of the topographical map of the area in the Pilbara. Distinctive dune systems marked on a topographic map. River systems show potential for flooding during cyclonic downpours. (Map copyright © Commonwealth of Australia, Geoscience Australia.) **Above:** I wandered this Pilbara dune system during the July 2000 profusion of wildflowers.

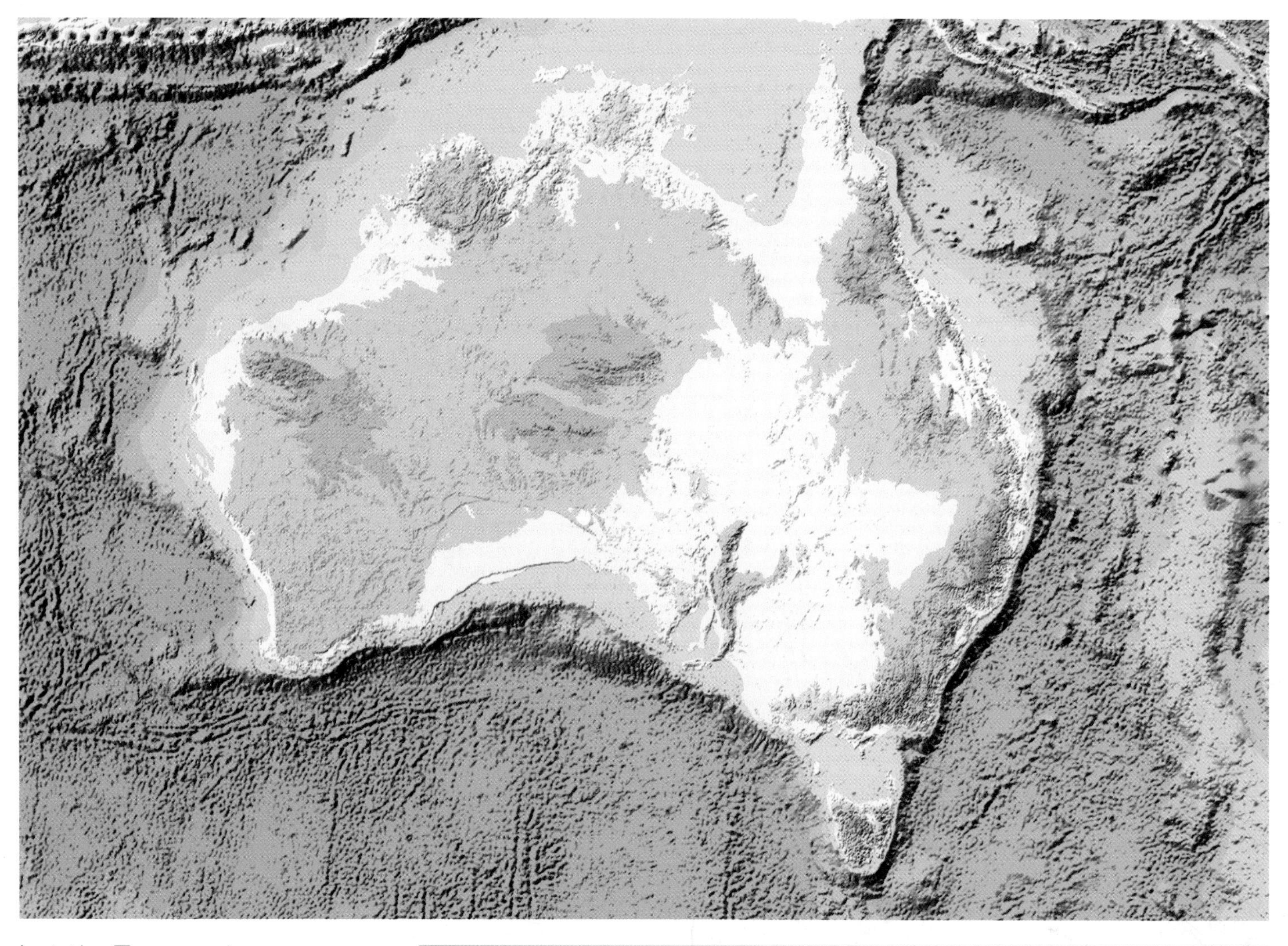

Let the Topography Show You the Way

A map showing the topography is best studied before you take your journey — and the more detailed the map, the better. If you study your intended route, you may find short diversions that will take you into photogenic country that few have visited. Even a basic understanding of the geology, flora and fauna will open doors. Richard Waldendorp, a renowned aerial photographer from Perth, discovered the potential of the now famous Bungle Bungle Range in the northern Kimberley as recently as 1983. He took a flight detour in search of new landscapes; it was his topographic map that laid the bait though.

Above and right: My first experience of the Bungle Bungles was from the air as a result of being lured out by Richard's pictures. It would take many years before roads were constructed to facilitate access on the ground.

Travelling with the Seasons

Australia is so large and its climate so contrasting that it can be difficult to choose the time frame within which to plan your journey, particularly if you intend to travel across remotely dissimilar regions over a period of only several months. There is no single ideal season to travel in both northern and southern Australia. And to complicate matters further, seasonal conditions vary widely between coastal and inland regions, and mountains and plains, as well as from year-to-year. The key is to study each region's climate carefully and leave more detailed scheduling until as late as possible before departure. Even then, you should be prepared to change your plans as the weather dictates. In the tropical north's wet season, dried up creekbeds can turn to swollen, flooding rivers almost overnight, and insufficient planning can result in huge delays or worse. To assist in mapping out your journey, I have listed below some general guidelines to the climatic conditions that are likely in various regions throughout the year.

Wet & Dry Areas

December to late February can be very wet, and roads may become impassable. Abundant water means that wildlife disperses over large areas. Temperatures and humidity will be high and it can rain for days on end. In coastal, savannah and hinterland regions, tropical cyclones can unleash destructive winds and torrential rain. March, April and May can be very pretty — grasses are still green, waterholes are full and lilies are in bloom. Soon humidity and rainfall decrease. June to late August (the early dry season) is the coolest period, and is therefore the peak tourist season. Gradually birds start to congregate around shrinking waterholes and September to December (the hot dry season) is excellent for finding wildlife concentrated in such areas, but conditions can be hot, smoky and dusty.

Arid & Semi-arid Areas

October to March are the warmer months in arid areas — so hot that travel and camping can be most unpleasant. The wildflowers have died off and the vegetation has lost its green lustre. April and May are the earliest months to think of travelling in the dry, hot centre of the arid region. However, June through to September can be the time when wildflowers and wildlife are most abundant — depending on how much rain has fallen in previous months.

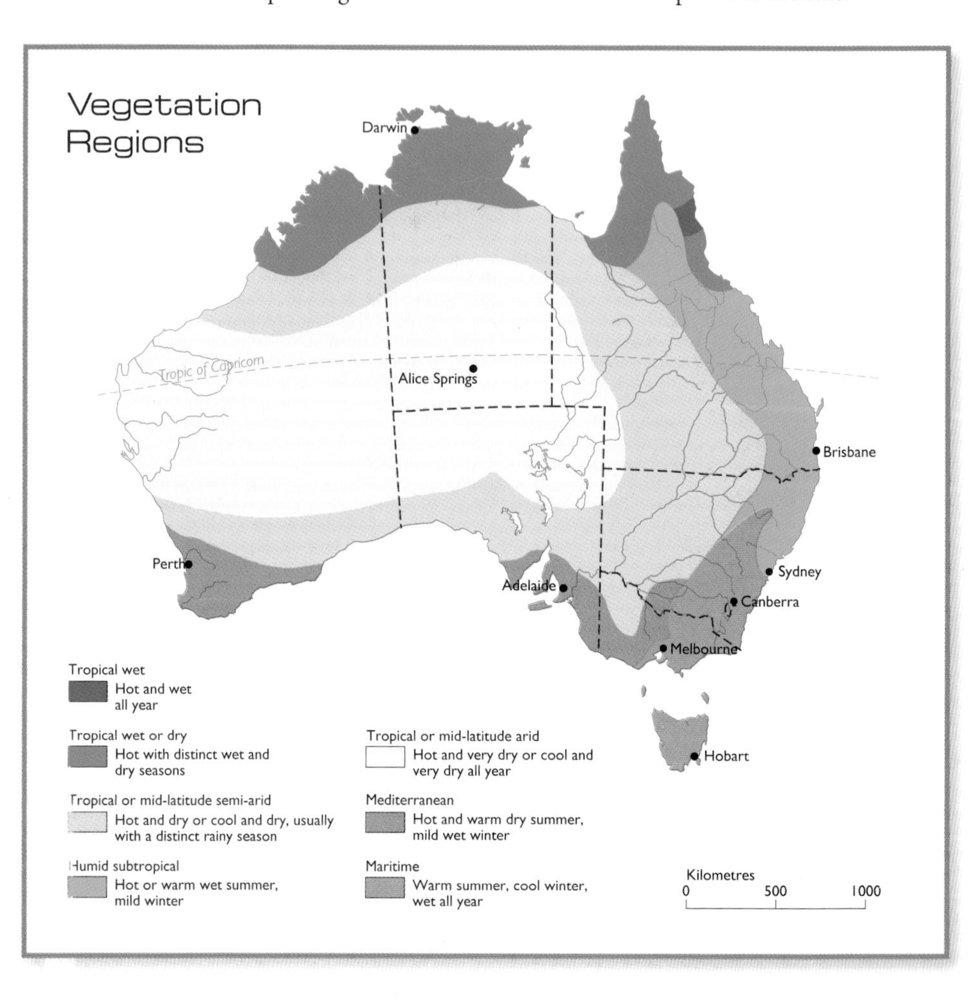

Six Seasons in the Top End

In the upper reaches of the Northern Territory, including Darwin, Kakadu and Arnhem Land, the European model of four seasons in each year, or even a tropical dry and wet season, is not entirely applicable. A more useful guide is the traditional Aboriginal model of six seasons, dictated by both climatic conditions and the changes in habitat that can be observed. Refer to the Kakadu section of this book (*see page 140*) for a more detailed description of each season and the conditions you can expect to encounter.

Travelling In The Wet

No windscreen wipers or all-wheel drive vehicle can overcome the conditions to be found in parts of northern Australia during the wet season. Roads are often washed away or submerged below flooded rivers, sometimes leaving no choice but to retreat to safety.

"Mediterranean" Areas

The "Mediterranean" regions of Australia have hot, dry summers and mild, wet winters. Vast coastal heathlands covered with abundant wildflowers during the spring months of August, September and October are a feature of these regions.

May to July are the cooler, wetter months and the winds can blow endlessly at this time. Late spring (October and November) and late summer (February and March) are wonderful times for general touring, although I always tend to focus on the spring months, because when the wildflowers are out, the animals and birds are most active. These months are favoured by locals for festivals and outdoor activities.

Maritime Areas

This climatic type encompasses Sydney and Melbourne, the most populous areas of Australia. It also includes some of the nation's most picturesque regions, such as: the Blue Mountains; the Australian Alps; and the south-east coastline, which is a big picture postcard from one end to the other. My preferred time for travel is during spring — but if snow or alpine regions are to your liking then the mid-winter months of June, July and August are best. In Victoria, Canberra and the Blue Mountains, and in many country towns, autumn sees non-native trees passing through a swathe of colours. The summer months of December through to February can be very hot, with heat haze and bushfire smoke common, even in the city areas. The weather in the island State of Tasmania, one of the nation's best States for photography, can vary enormously. Not a cloud in the sky at dawn, by midday overcast and raining, and by late afternoon hot and clear again. These fluctuating extremes may not suit every traveller, but variety is the spice of life, particularly for photographers.

Autumn Splendour

As autumn falls in the more southern parts of Australia the changes in colour are a photographer's dream. The main streets of many towns in Victoria, South Australia and New South Wales are bordered by stands of European trees whose leaves ignite in russet tones from March to May.

Snow Seasons

Many overseas visitors are surprised to learn that "the Sunburnt Country" also features mountainous snow regions populated with busy ski resorts. The alpine regions of New South Wales, Victoria and Tasmania attract huge numbers of skiers and snowboarders each year. While the season can be fickle, June to August are generally the best months for skiing in Australia, especially amid the higher peaks of the Australian Alps near Mount Kosciuszko (Australia's highest mountain) in southern New South Wales.

Spring into Life

Spring brings temperate weather to many parts of Australia, making it a comfortable period in which to travel. Another great attraction is the spectacular blooming of native wildflowers throughout many regions, particularly in the southern coastal areas of Western Australia from Geraldton to Perth.

Eastern Spinebill

Appreciating Native Vegetation

Some travellers complain that Australia's landscape and vegetation varies little over great distances, but I find this particular comment usually arises from those who have not bothered to explore their environment in any real detail. It is true that Australia has substantial areas of sandy desert and scrubby plain — the early cross-continental explorers found this terrain the most mentally and physically challenging part of their expeditions. But even within desert regions there is great variation, particularly between seasons. The wet season reveals new life where little had previously been apparent. After the rain, blooms of wildflowers can blanket the desert floor in a spectacular symphony of colour that may last no more than a few days. Some species (such as eucalypts) are spread across the continent, but within the *Eucalyptus* genus there are a huge range of flowering trees and shrubs. Visitors to the tropical and semi-arid regions of the Northern Territory and Western Australia are often surprised by the amount of lush green vegetation and the number of flowing rivers.

During the dry season, hardy *Acacia* species wait out the scorching heat, dropping seeds that will germinate in the fertile ash following bushfires and flourish with the lack of other floral competition. Much of Australia's native flora is not only sparsely, almost abstractly, beautiful, but also highly productive — attracting a riot of insect, bird and mammalian life, some of which is dependent on just a few specialist plants for its survival.

The coastal and inland areas of Australia showcase great botanical variety, from the cold, mountainous forests of Tasmania to the gum-lined rivers of Victoria and the lush rainforest of northern Queensland. The type of vegetation that appeals to you is most likely to be a personal thing — for some it is the uncluttered solitude of the desert, others, like myself, could spend weeks wandering coastal landscapes carpeted with wildflowers. Even the cool, alpine areas hide delightful, dainty secrets such as alpine heath and glistening eyebrights.

Consider what type of vegetation is of greatest appeal when planning your trip and keep an open mind (and lens) to the potential surprises to be found in seemingly familiar or unchanging environments. Often on your travels, but particularly in Western Australia's South West and along the continent's east coast, you may encounter dense forest or a spectrum of wildflowers enlivening the road verges. In the spirit of making the most of your holiday leisure time, be sure you take the time to stop and smell the flowers.

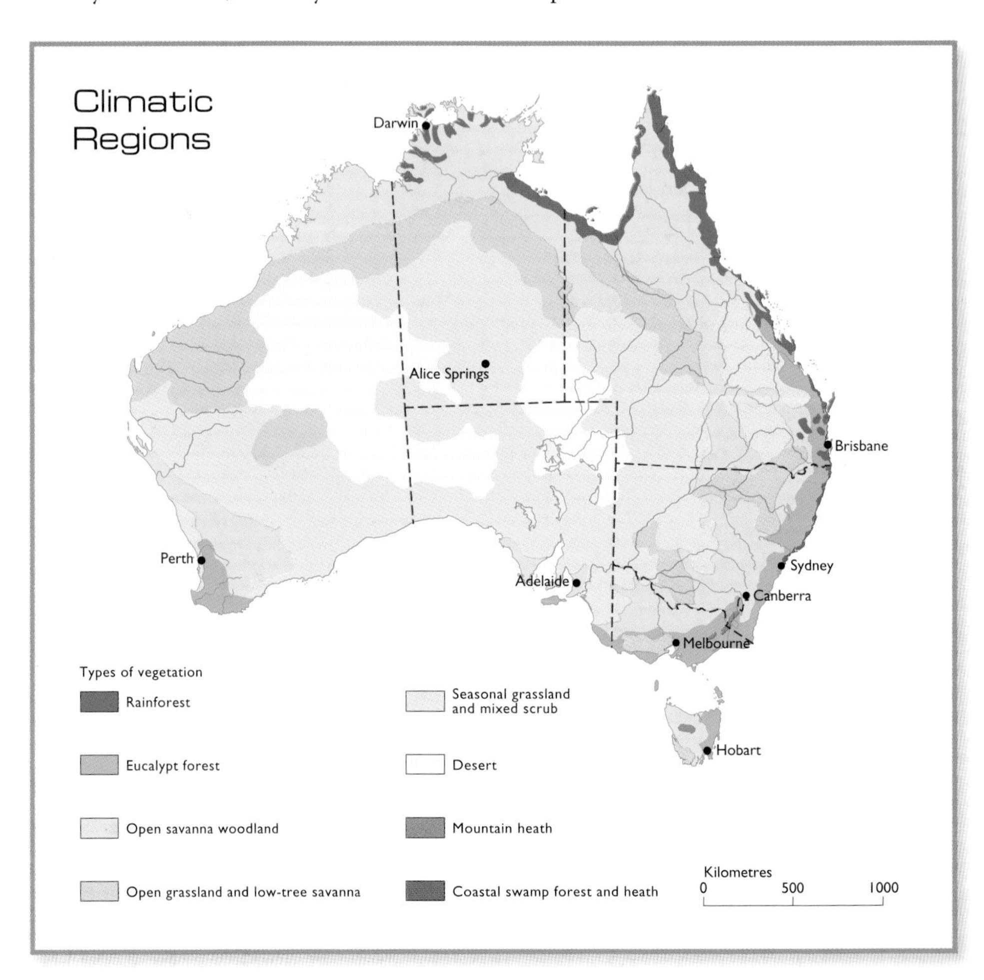

Top to bottom: Australia has more than 700 eucalypt species; Daisies are widely distributed across the country; Wattle species are profuse in Australia.

Unique & Abundant Plants

Australia has an astonishing range of native plants — some 24,000 have been identified to date. Many of these have been known to Aborigines and used for food and medicinal purposes for millennia. On Captain Cook's *Endeavour* voyage of 1770, botanists Joseph Banks and Daniel Solander collected no less than 30,000 specimens.

Some common genera are: *Acacia* (commonly known as wattles); *Eucalyptus* (of which 700 of the world's 712 species are found only in Australia); *Grevillea*, *Melaleuca* (including tea tree, paperbark and honey myrtle trees); *Eremophila* (known as Emu bushes); and *Anigozanthos* (including the distinctive kangaroo paw).

Within Australia's rainforests, ranges and arid zones are relict plants dating back millions of years. Surviving in the gorges of northern Western Australia are ancient cycads and figs. The Blue Mountains are home to the Wollemi Pine, which co-existed with the dinosaurs. The Daintree rainforest contains representatives of twelve of the world's nineteen primitive flowering plant families.

Rainforest

Seasonal grassland with mixed scrub

Eucalypt forest

Desert

Open savannah woodland

Mountain heath

Open grassland and low-tree savannah

Coastal swamp forest and heath

Some Major Terrestrial Vegetation Regions

Australia can be roughly divided into eight major vegetation regions. Desert and seasonal grassland with mixed scrub covers the central, western and eastern inland. The northern region is mostly open savannah/grassland with low-tree savannah, and coastal swamp forest along the northern coast. Rainforest is found along the northern parts of the eastern seaboard while eucalypt forest spreads over the hinterland and ranges of the east, south-east and south-west coasts. Tasmania features a mix of vegetation including mountain heath. For comprehensive information on Australian habitat, *Wild Habitats (right)* is highly recommended.

Meeting the Locals

Whether on a golf course or campsite's mown lawns (which regularly attract wallabies and kangaroos) or in a fauna park or zoo, connecting with Australian animals up close and personal is a popular activity for thousands of people each year. A close encounter often allows for touch, sound and smell to be involved as well as sight, making the experience so much richer. Such meetings and interactions can stimulate a lifetime interest in natural history and wildlife.

Encounters with Animals

Australia's wildlife is one of the greatest natural attractions you are likely to encounter while travelling the country. While some creatures, such as kangaroos, can be found in many different parts of Australia, each region is also home to locally endemic animals, birds and insects that will be found nowhere else in Australia — or even the world. Some of these are threatened species, which may survive only in a small pocket of rainforest, coastal heath, wetland or national park. Since the main continental landmass separated from Gondwana some 55 million years ago, Australia's native wildlife has evolved in isolation, resulting in some of the world's most fascinating creatures. Australia has over 140 species of marsupial, most of which are native to this country. But while the Tasmanian Devil, Platypus and Koala have developed international reputations for their peculiarities and idiosyncracies, there are literally thousands of remarkable Australian creatures to discover. Every animal encounter is unique, and I find wildlife observation to be a thrilling pursuit that reveals something new on each occasion. Australia is a wonderful place to observe animal behaviour and see how habitat, climate and wildlife interact within the incredible theatre that is nature.

Bird & Wildlife Watching

Australia's national parks, conservation areas, state parks and forests offer the chance to view and photograph birds and other animals in their natural environment. A few days or more spent camping or walking in these havens will deliver countless opportunities to observe a wide range of creatures by day and night (*see facing page*). Some parks even offer "hides" from which the quiet observer can discreetly watch the activities of animals without disrupting their natural behaviours or environment. Australia's wetlands are world-renowned and provide refuge for millions of migratory birds, some in transit to destinations as far-flung as Siberia. Thousands of fish species thrive in the country's reefs, lagoons and waterways, from the tiny Stout Infantfish of the Great Barrier Reef to the mighty Barramundi of tropical rivers.

Wildlife Parks & Zoos

The conservation and breeding of Australian wildlife in nature parks and zoos provides the opportunity to observe many creatures in the space of a few hours. State capitals, as well as several regional centres, have zoos featuring both native and exotic wildlife. Complementing these operations are a number of well-run and popular commercial parks such as Australia Zoo on Queensland's Sunshine Coast (home of the late "wildlife warrior" Steve Irwin), Sea World on the Gold Coast and Territory Wildlife Park in the Northern Territory.

Highway Encounters

With such a huge wildlife population, it is perhaps not surprising that many of Australia's creatures frequently stray onto the country's roads, particularly (but not exclusively) in outback regions. Cassowaries, kangaroos, emus and goannas are but a few of the animals that can unexpectedly appear, causing drivers to collide, brake sharply or take evasive measures.

Many cattle stations are unfenced and wayward cattle can also be a real danger. While it is always sad to see an animal killed on the road, remember that it is better to hit an animal than a vehicle coming in the opposite direction. Drive carefully and watch for unbidden wanderers. Where possible, avoid driving in country and remote areas at dawn and dusk.

Nocturnal Camp Raiders

It is not uncommon for park campers to discover that the leftover food they forgot to put away after dinner has disappeared overnight. Covertly devoured by nocturnal creatures who have learnt to lie in wait for such opportunities. Sometimes brazen thieves even snatch meals from distracted diners' plates before they can get fork to mouth.

Daylight Robbery

Animal visitations are not confined to the cover of night. Birds and lizards are particularly good pirates and their tastes are not confined to that slice of bread left over from lunch. Some birds, such as magpies, are very effective at putting items such as tent pegs and rope to use when building nests. Shiny objects, in particular, attract attention. Be careful what you leave unattended, or your own nest may be stripped clean.

Creepy Crawlies

Australia is literally crawling with insects and arachnids. In fact there are over 2900 known spider species in Australia, only a few of which have a potentially fatal bite (but no one in Australia has been known to have died from a spider bite since 1979). Creepy? Perhaps, but there is more to be fascinated by than feared when it comes to Australia's insects and arachnids.

Eek! A Snake!

Snakes are prolific in Australia and can be found in both rural and urban areas. Encounters with snakes in national parks, on farms and in forests, particularly during warmer months, are common. The good news is that most snakes are not particularly interested in humans or hostile by nature and prefer to be left alone. Never approach or touch a snake in the wild and avoid cornering or threatening a snake. Achieve this and you should not have any problems.

The Importance of not Feeding

Deliberately feeding animals or birds in the wild can cause illness, death and can permanently alter their natural habits and behaviour.
Food and beverages that may be completely harmless to humans can be potentially fatal to many creatures. If you wish to experience or photograph the feeding of an animal, there are various sanctuaries around Australia that offer controlled feeding opportunities with specially prepared food.

Deadly & Dangerous Australian Animals

What Is a Dangerous Animal?

Australia has a somewhat unjustified (and highly exaggerated) reputation as a land of deadly creatures, where marauding wildlife crazed with murderous intent roam desert, forest, river and sea. While the nation's diverse range of animals certainly includes many species with the potential to cause harm to humans, such attacks are relatively rare and are often caused only by a lack of proper caution.

Different animals have different ways of defending themselves. Some use their teeth, tusks, claws, horns or antlers; others use venom, poison, acids and other chemicals to protect themselves or to kill their prey. If given a choice, almost all animals will try to escape humans rather than attack. However, any animal that is able to kill, injure or even cause discomfort to a person may be regarded as "dangerous".

The "deadly" group is made up of animals that have caused death by biting, stinging, stabbing, scratching or poisoning people. This can occur during defence, in a deliberate attack, or when eaten. The identity of some of these animals may surprise you, although in some cases the death may have occurred due to a freak accident or allergy, rather than an attempt to kill. The "dangerous" group comprises animals that may injure (or, in very rare cases, even kill) people but usually do so only if threatened. The "harmful" group is made up of animals that cause a painful reaction if stepped on, touched or brushed, and (for animals like the Australian Magpie) those that can harm us if we are in their territory. In other words, these animals are not really doing anything except defending themselves from us. The disease carrying group is made up of creatures that can give people diseases, or that are parasites. Mosquitoes, some flies, flying-foxes, rats, feral pigs and some fish fall into this group.

Apart from (some) sharks and Estuarine Crocodiles, animals do not normally attack people unless provoked. More often than not, it is our behaviour that causes problems with animals — sometimes we may not even notice that we have disturbed an animal in its environment. It is important to understand that just because a certain animal is deadly and can harm or kill someone - doesn't mean it will. For example, the Western Taipan, *Oxyuranus microlepidotus* — by far the most venomous snake in the world — lives in mostly unpopulated areas of the Australian outback where few people ever go. So this snake is very rarely seen and even when it is seen it is shy and moves quickly into hiding.

However, the Eastern Brown Snake, *Pseudonaja textilis*, is found in most parts of the continent, often living close to people in farms and suburbs. It does not take much for this snake to become agitated and aggressive. Despite having short fangs and venom that is less toxic than the Western Taipan's, the Eastern Brown Snake is considered more dangerous to humans. Deadly and dangerous animals are fascinating. By understanding how these animals live and behave, how they attack and the effects of attack, you should find that it is easy to stay safe from these animals while travelling Australia.

Marine Stingers

In summer months, many northern Australian beaches are closed due to the presence of dangerous marine stingers. The most dangerous of these inhabitants of tropical seas, such as the Box Jelly and Irukandji, can cause severe injuries and even death. To prevent this, many northern beaches are closed during the "stinger season", while stinger nets, (which aim to exclude the animals from swimming areas), offer some protection at others. However, these nets cannot guarantee protection: broken tentacles or tiny jellyfishes are often able to penetrate the mesh. One excellent option is to wear a lycra "stinger suit". Observe all warning signs posted at beaches and never swim at a beach that has been closed. In Queensland, surf lifesavers immediately close beaches when deadly marine stingers are sighted or when a swimmer has been stung.

Aside from spiders and snakes, Australia's most feared creatures are almost certainly sharks and crocodiles. Attacks are common enough to warrant caution, but the facts show that sharks and crocodiles are actually responsible for only a tiny proportion of Australia's annual deaths. Both animals are carnivores, but their dietary preferences are normally for creatures other than humans. Even so, extreme care should be exercised when travelling near the crocodile-infested waters of Australia's northern regions.

How Many People Have Died?

It is not an easy task to tell exactly how many people have died in Australia from bites, stings and attacks caused by animals. We can guess that many people were killed by wildlife before European settlement and also that many casualties were not reported from remote communities in the past. Another reason for poor early records was the unreliable identification of animals because the classification system of Australian fauna had only just begun.

Many fatal attacks were assigned to the wrong species or in some cases there were no witnesses to verify the details of the accident. Even in modern times, there is no requirement to keep records of deaths caused by wildlife but the Australian Bureau of Statistics does keep such records.

The figures presented in the table listing the deaths by various animals below, should be interpreted as "at least" statistics rather than absolutes.

Tiger Snake The yellow and black stripes give the Tiger Snake its name. This snake is responsible for 18 deaths in Australia.

	Common Name	Scientific Name	Australia	Worldwide
Mammals	Dingo	*Canis lupus dingo*	2	
	Asian Water Buffalo	*Bubalus bubalis*	1	
Birds	Southern Cassowary	*Casuarius casuarius*	2	
Reptiles	Estuarine Crocodile	*Crocodylus porosus*	17	
	Coastal Taipan	*Oxyuranus scutellatus*	6	
	Common Death Adder	*Acanthophis antarcticus*	5	
	Tiger Snake	*Notechis scutatus*	18	
	Chappell Island Tiger Snake	*Notechis scutatus serventyi*	2	
	Eastern Brown Snake	*Pseudonaja textilis*	19	
	King Brown Snake	*Pseudechis australis*	1	
	Rough-scaled Snake	*Tropidechis carinatus*	1	
	Eastern Small-eyed Snake	*Cryptophis nigrescens*	1	
	Copperhead	*Austrelaps superbus*	1	
	Sea snakes	Various spp.	0	150
Amphibians			0	
Insects	Bee	*Hymenoptera* spp.	38	
	Wasp	*Hymenoptera* spp.	7	
	Bulldog Ant	*Myrmecia* spp.	6	
Arachnids	Sydney Funnelweb Spider	*Atrax robustus*	13	
	Redback Spider	*Latrodectus hasselti*	14	
	Paralysis Tick	*Ixodes holocyclus*	20	
Fish	White Shark	*Carcharodon carcharias*	40	232
	Tiger Shark	*Galeocerdo cuvier*	23	86
	Bull Shark	*Carcharhinus leucas*	10	75
	Hammerhead shark	*Sphyrna* spp.	0	16
	Bronze Whaler Shark	*Carcharhinus brachyurus*	3	15
	Stonefish	*Synanceia* spp.	1	4
	Stingray	Various spp.	3	17
Jellyfish	Box Jelly	*Chironex fleckeri*	67	
	Irukandji	*Carukia barnesi*	2	
Other marine animals	Cone shell	*Conus* spp.	1	15
	Blue-ringed Octopus	*Hapalochlaena maculosa*	2	1

A Bad Reputation

While Australia's Sydney Funnelweb (*left*) and Redback Spiders (*right*) have gained a notoriety far exceeding their size, these headline-grabbing arachnids are very rarely responsible for injury or death. In fact, these spiders have killed just 27 people in 80 years; bees, wasps and ants have caused many more deaths in Australia than these infamous arachnids since record keeping began. Of the 35 species of funnelweb identified to date, only the Sydney Funnelweb Spider (*Atrax robustus*) is known to have caused human death. An estimated 30–40 cases of funnelweb spider bite occur annually, with fewer than 10% of cases requiring antivenom treatment.

SYDNEY

& THE JOURNEY TO BRISBANE

1

The vast majority of Australians are coastal dwellers — over 80% of the nation's 20 million people live within 50 km of the sea. Of that figure, nearly half live in the coastal regions of New South Wales and Queensland — and this journey reveals why. Along this sun-drenched strip lie some of Australia's most alluring destinations. Sydney, Byron Bay, Brisbane and the glittering Gold Coast are internationally famous, but the journey from Sydney to Brisbane reveals a near continuous chain of charismatic coastal towns boasting blue skies and azure seas. However, the appeal of the Hunter Valley and a mass of pristine national parks (including the World Heritage Area of the Blue Mountains) frequently tempts travellers to voyage inland. Here you will find true heritage and character — places set among verdant tablelands and filled with history. Whether you choose to cruise the coast or journey inland (or do both) the trip from Brisbane to Sydney features some of the country's greatest natural assets, as well as the progression and preservation of its European culture.

Waratah

Left: Aerial of Cape Byron, Byron Bay. **Above:** Sydney Harbour, featuring two of the city's most famous landmarks — Sydney Opera House and Sydney Harbour Bridge.

SYDNEY & Surrounds

Sydney & Surrounds
Top Things to Do

1 Explore the historic Rocks district.
2 Spend a morning at Sydney Aquarium, then check out Sydney Wildlife World.
3 Take a dawn walk in the Royal Botanic Gardens — the birds are more active then.
4 Climb Sydney Harbour Bridge and survey Sydney in the late afternoon light.
5 Spend the day on a Sydney Harbour Ferry photographing with a telephoto lens. You will be amazed at the results.
6 Take a dawn cliff-top walk from Bondi Beach along the coastal path to Coogee.
7 Soak up the sun and surf at Manly.
8 Go west. Escape to the Blue Mountains.
9 Go east. Take a trip to Lord Howe Island or historic Norfolk Island.

Blessed by National Parks

The national parks spreading over the northern Sydney region are a bushwalker's paradise. Ku-Ring-Gai Chase National Park, opened in 1894, is one of the most accessible natural getaways for Sydneysiders. Straddling the Pacific Highway, the park's northern boundary is formed by the magnificent Hawkesbury River and it has many miles of meandering creeks, quiet unpopulated beaches and thick forests. The Resolute Track is also one of Australia's best locations to view Aboriginal rock art — a legacy of the original Guringai people.

At Bobbin Head is the park's information centre and close by is the Kalkari Visitor Centre, featuring an Australian wildlife sanctuary and nature trail (enter on Ku-Ring-Gai Chase Road at the south-western tip of the park). One of the park's more unusual features is a 1.5 m high replica of the Great Sphinx. This monument, carved from sandstone by a returned soldier in the 1920s, commemorates the fallen of WWI. It is accessible via the Sphinx Track off Bobbin Head Road, where you can also see Aboriginal middens (shell deposits), burial sites and rock engravings.

Sydney is bounded by pristine national parks and a spectacular coastline, which together promise an abundance of outdoor experiences. The city's geographical layout allows for a multitude of daytrips with recreational possibilities ranging from birdwatching to kiteboarding. Even around the harbour's heartland, a generous amount of space is given over to national park. Whether you choose to delve into the city's fine detail or roam beyond the urban frontier, the region's stunning native beauty will remain a constant and welcome companion on your journey.

Beaches, Bays & Rivers

One of Sydney's best natural assets is its long stretch of northern beaches. Between perennially popular Manly and well-heeled Palm Beach there are bounteous options for sand, surf and sun lovers. Narrabeen Lakes are perfect for a picnic or shoreline ramble. The Coastal Environment Centre, at North Narrabeen, provides detailed information on the region. Self-guided walking brochures are also available. The coastal views are never more jaw-dropping than at Pittwater. The first governor of New South Wales, Arthur Phillip, described it in 1788 as: "the finest piece of water I ever saw." The region later harboured escaped convicts and liquor smugglers but nowadays there's no need to bootleg your own. Forty minutes from the CBD, Sydney's largest waterfront beer garden, the Newport Arms Hotel, has been serving thirsty travellers since 1880 (Kalinya St, Newport, Ph: (02) 9997 4900). This sprawling pub and restaurant complex on the shores of Pittwater is an ideal place to lunch while taking in the sights of Broken Bay, Ku-Ring-Gai Chase, Scotland Island and Church Point that Phillip considered so impressive.

Past Palm Beach, at the tip of the peninsula, the Barrenjoey Lighthouse is a fantastic location for views of the surrounding sea, national parks and rivers. Here the famous Hawkesbury River meets the Pacific Ocean at Broken Bay, creating a landscape of truly astonishing beauty. Ku-Ring-Gai Chase National Park lies to the south, Brisbane Water National Park to the north and Marramarra National Park to the west. Incredibly, this largely unspoilt wilderness is just a short drive (about 40 minutes) from the CBD. Marramarra can also be reached by boat or canoe from the Hawkesbury River, Berowra Creek and Marramarra Creek, via a landing at historic Gentlemans Halt — the final point of Arthur Phillip's Hawkesbury explorations.

Sydney – City of Sand

Sydney's beaches contain only a small proportion of the city's sand. The entire region is supported and shaped by a 200 m thick sandstone basin. The origin of nearly all the visible rocks and cliff faces in Sydney can be traced to Hawkesbury sandstone laid down during the Triassic Period about 200 million years ago.

Its ready availability made sandstone the building material of choice in the first century following European settlement. Numerous sandstone quarries around Sydney (including more than 50 in the inner city Pyrmont area alone) provided a convenient resource for constructing many of the city's early houses and public buildings. Today the streetscapes remain coloured by the sandstone upon which they rest.

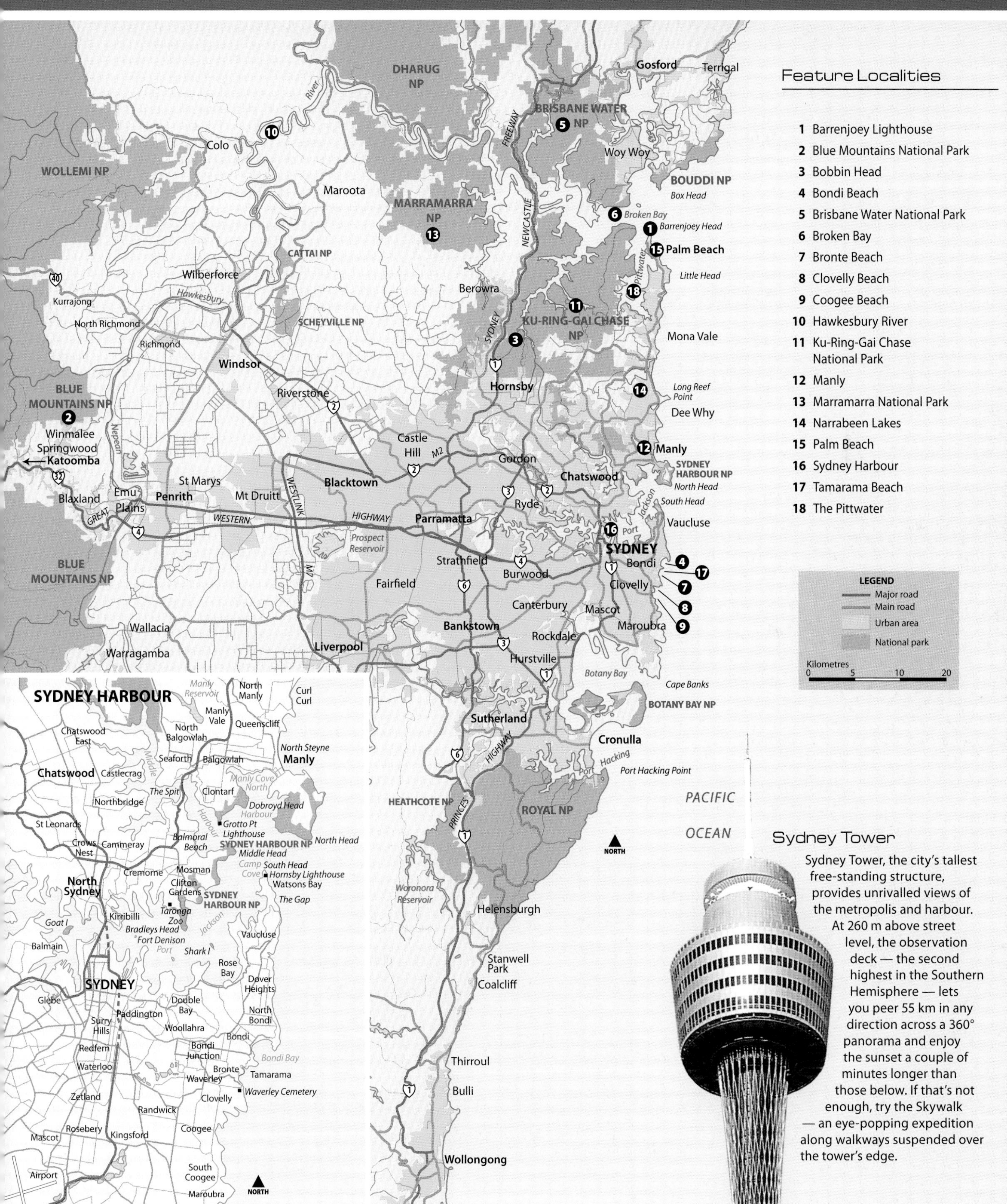

Feature Localities

1 Barrenjoey Lighthouse
2 Blue Mountains National Park
3 Bobbin Head
4 Bondi Beach
5 Brisbane Water National Park
6 Broken Bay
7 Bronte Beach
8 Clovelly Beach
9 Coogee Beach
10 Hawkesbury River
11 Ku-Ring-Gai Chase National Park
12 Manly
13 Marramarra National Park
14 Narrabeen Lakes
15 Palm Beach
16 Sydney Harbour
17 Tamarama Beach
18 The Pittwater

Sydney Tower

Sydney Tower, the city's tallest free-standing structure, provides unrivalled views of the metropolis and harbour. At 260 m above street level, the observation deck — the second highest in the Southern Hemisphere — lets you peer 55 km in any direction across a 360° panorama and enjoy the sunset a couple of minutes longer than those below. If that's not enough, try the Skywalk — an eye-popping expedition along walkways suspended over the tower's edge.

Australia's First Street

George Street, now one of Australia's busiest thoroughfares, was originally a dirt track leading convicts from their camp near The Rocks through bushland to a brick-making site at Cockle Bay (adjacent to Darling Harbour). George Street is the nation's oldest roadway — linking the CBD with Circular Quay and the Sydney Harbour foreshore. It is also home to one of Sydney's most popular shopping complexes — Queen Victoria Building.

Ferries & Monorails

Regular ferries have plied the waters of Sydney Harbour and the Parramatta River since 1861. Despite the construction of major bridges and the Harbour Tunnel, Sydney Ferries remain a desirable form of commuter and tourist transport, transporting more than 14 million passengers per year. Sydney's Metro Monorail, running on a loop from Darling Harbour, serves eight stations throughout the CBD. Use it to visit the Sydney Entertainment Centre, Sydney Aquarium, Paddy's Markets and the Powerhouse Museum, or simply hop on and enjoy the fresh air and passing views.

Sydney City

British explorer James Cook certainly wasn't the first person to appreciate Sydney's enviable location on Australia's eastern seaboard. Founded on a raw harbourside landscape that had sustained the Cadigal people for millennia, the city began its rapid urban evolution as a small penal colony at Sydney Cove in 1788. Despite the region's physical beauty, decades of hardship followed for both the original occupants and transported convicts; however, in just over two centuries Sydney has been transformed from a harsh labour camp into a major world city.

Home to many of the nation's most familiar icons — Bondi Beach, Sydney Opera House and Sydney Harbour Bridge — the city also contains some of Australia's oldest buildings. Sydney is world renowned for its breathtaking harbour setting and brassy, fast-paced lifestyle. Australia's largest city is also its most popular tourism destination, main port and business capital. Colloquially dubbed the "Emerald City" (a nod to both Australian playwright David Williamson's 1987 play and the mythical metropolis in *The Wizard of Oz*), Sydney's thrilling collision of big city infrastructure and natural splendour assures a lasting impact.

Sydney Cove & The Rocks

An excellent starting point for any exploration of Sydney is the historical Rocks area near the southern pylon of Sydney Harbour Bridge on Sydney Cove. Feet are your best mode of transport and walking tours abound. The Rocks area is an engrossing warren of streets lined with original and restored 19th century shops, cottages, hotels, maritime buildings and warehouses stretching down to Circular Quay. It offers excellent elevated vantages for viewing and photographing the city's harbour, its thriving heritage and, of course, the Opera House.

The history of Sydney's first settled district is revealed through the interactive displays and artefacts presented at The Rocks Discovery Museum (housed in a restored sandstone warehouse in Kendall Lane). The Sydney Visitor Centre (corner of Argyle and Playfair Streets, Ph: 1800 067 676) provides a wealth of services including tour, cruise and hotel reservations, as well as maps and information on city events and attractions. Both are open daily (except Good Friday and Christmas Day).

The Rocks Market is staged every weekend beneath a cover of sail canopy. It offers handcrafted Australian goods, art, homewares, street theatre and live music and touts itself as Sydney's leading "lifestyle market" (northern end of George and Playfair Streets, Saturday and Sunday, 10 am – 5 pm). The Rocks area is also home to over 30 galleries, museums and exhibition spaces showing (and selling) Aboriginal and modern art, sculpture, photography, glass works, ceramics and textiles. The Museum of Contemporary Art (MCA), a restored maritime building situated right on the harbour foreshore between the Harbour Bridge and Circular Quay, must boast one of the art world's best addresses (140 George St, open 10 am – 5 pm, daily except Christmas Day). The MCA is Australia's only museum solely dedicated to collecting and exhibiting local and international contemporary art. The site itself is also significant, marking the official landing point of the First Fleet.

City Aspects

The globetrotting British novelist, Anthony Trollope once wrote: "I despair of being able to convey to any reader my own idea of the beauty of Sydney Harbour."

Luckily, with the miracle of modern photography we no longer need to rely on words alone to communicate the power of this magnificent waterway. If you are looking to capture the city through your own digital lens, Sydney's shoreline offers countless opportunities — each delivering a unique perspective and mood. Try Mrs Macquaries Point, Blues Point, Dawes Point Park and Bennelong Point.

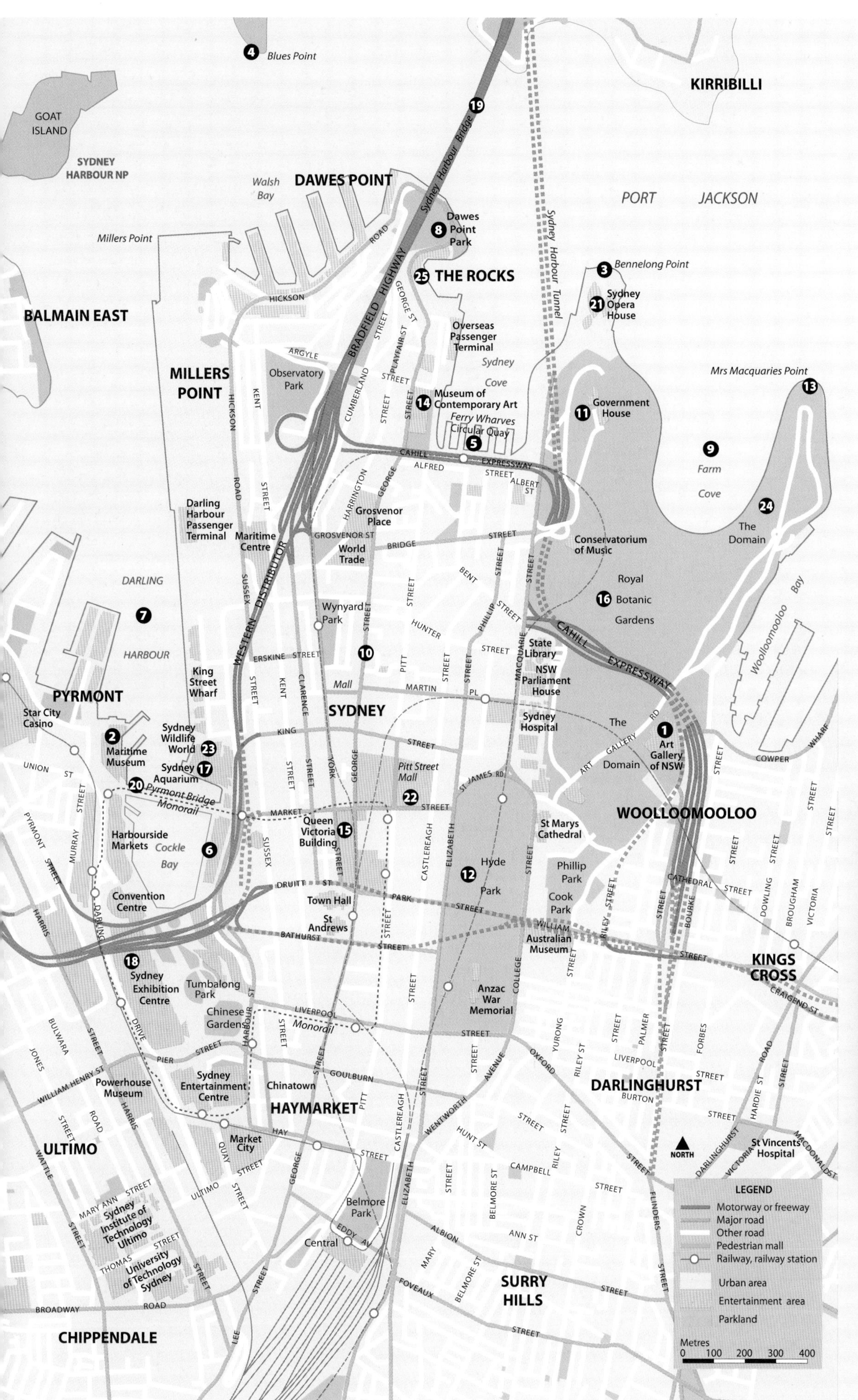

Feature Localities

1 Art Gallery of New South Wales
2 Australian National Maritime Museum
3 Bennelong Point
4 Blues Point
5 Circular Quay
6 Cockle Bay Wharf
7 Darling Harbour
8 Dawes Point Park
9 Farm Cove
10 George Street
11 Government House
12 Hyde Park
13 Mrs Macquaries Point
14 Museum of Contemporary Art
15 Queen Victoria Building
16 Royal Botanic Gardens
17 Sydney Aquarium
18 Sydney Convention & Exhibition Centre
19 Sydney Harbour Bridge
20 Sydney Monorail
21 Sydney Opera House
22 Sydney Tower
23 Sydney Wildlife World
24 The Domain
25 The Rocks

Cultural Celebration

As one of the world's great cosmopolitan cities, Sydney regularly celebrates its cultural diversity. The Greek Festival, Chinese New Year, Loy Krathong, St Patrick's Day and the Darling Harbour Fiesta are just some of the many major dates on the city's festival calendar.

Urban Diversions

The Rocks & Circular Quay

Circular Quay, at the northern end of the CBD, is Australia's busiest commuter port with fleets of ferries and hydrofoils departing for all points of the harbour every few minutes.

Immediately adjacent, The Rocks marks the point of contact for Sydney's first European settlement. Take a stroll through time in this fascinating harbourside enclave of sandstone pubs, restored shops, archaeological sites, colonial cottages and cobbled laneways.

Royal Botanic Gardens

Established at Farm Cove in 1816 (the site of Australia's first farm) and stretching from Bennelong Point to Mrs Macquaries Point is Sydney's extensive Royal Botanic Gardens.

Wander the promenades through this meticulously planned, 30 ha oasis and discover native and exotic plants (including rare and threatened species) among a variety of habitats. Eye-pleasing fountains, sculptures and memorials enhance this historic green space.

Hyde Park & The Domain

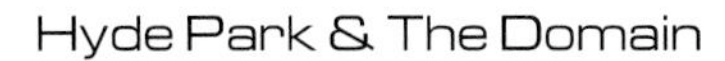

Opposite the Royal Botanic Gardens on the eastern flank of the CBD is The Domain, a spacious reserve that once divided Governor Phillip's residence from the penal colony.

Today its grassy expanse hosts some of Sydney's most popular outdoor events, including the internationally renowned Tropfest short film festival. The impressive Art Gallery of New South Wales is also located in the park. Just south of The Domain is Hyde Park, originally the colony's first racecourse, and now a popular lunchtime retreat for city workers and tourists. It features important war memorials including the Archibald Fountain (*right*) and the Anzac War Memorial.

QVB & Shopping

The Queen Victoria Building (QVB) was built in 1898 and occupies the original Sydney markets site on George Street.

Today the QVB is an elegantly restored hive of over 100 shops and restaurants. Indulge yourself in one of the country's best shopping venues, but be sure to take the time to admire the detail of the building's many grandiose features, including its massive glass dome, glorious stained-glass windows and elaborate stonemasonry.

Darling Harbour

Darling Harbour was redeveloped in 1984 to become a thriving business and leisure hub, which includes such family-friendly attractions as the Australian National Maritime Museum, IMAX Theatre and the Sydney Convention and Exhibition Centre.

Known to the Cadigal people as *Tumbalong* (or a place where shellfish could be found), succulent fresh seafood can still be savoured at Darling Harbour's many waterfront restaurants and cafés.

Sydney's Wild Side

Within close range of Sydney's commercial heartland lies an exhilarating collection of urban wildlife sanctuaries.

Taronga Zoo (at Mosman on the harbour's north shore) is one of Australia's premier animal parks, housing over 340 species. The skylift meets the ferry from Circular Quay and transports you to the top of the park where you can enjoy a leisurely downhill (photographic) safari. Don't miss the daily Free Flight bird show, staged at a clifftop amphitheatre and starring the country's largest raptor — the mighty Wedge-Tailed Eagle.

Taronga Zoo Orang-utans

At Sydney Aquarium, Darling Harbour, 11,500 species, including huge sharks, rays, crocodiles and penguins are on display in both saltwater and freshwater habitats. Travel by ferry from Circular Quay or walk from the CBD to experience one of the world's most spectacular aquariums.

Sydney Wildlife World, located next to Sydney Aquarium, is home to over 6000 Australian animals in nine different habitats. This remarkable inner city menagerie includes a soaring Flight Canyon, Nocturnal House, deadly snake and spider exhibits, and the star attraction of the rainforest habitat — the Southern Cassowary.

Squirrel Glider

Sydney Harbour Bridge

An immediate icon upon its completion in 1932, the Sydney Harbour Bridge took 1400 men, eight years to build. Affectionately known as "the Coathanger", the apex of this famous arch rises some 134 m above sea level.

The Bridge Climb

A trip to the top will refresh your respect for the resilience of Sydney Harbour Bridge builders and reward you with unparalleled views of the city's glittering expanse (the three and a half hour return journey departs from 5 Cumberland Street, The Rocks, Ph: (02) 8274 7777).

Sydney Opera House

Easily Australia's most photographed architectural object, the Sydney Opera House has come to symbolise not only Sydney but the nation entire. Positioned for maximum effect on Bennelong Point, the soaring white shells are adorned with over one million ceramic tiles. Designer, Jørn Utzon originally envisaged a sail-like roof, but the expressionist geometry was the result of a cost-saving initiative — each shell was taken from a different section of the same sphere.

Sydney Harbour & City Beaches

Sydney has evolved a stronger beach culture than any other major Australian city and the reasons why are immediately evident to any visitor. The temperate climate, generous sunshine and abundance of inner city sand and surf makes beachgoing enjoyable year-round.

The nation's two most famous beaches, Manly on the north shore and Bondi to the south-east, always attract a crowd, yet even in the height of summer their spacious shores means you can always stake out a spot on the sand (surfers be warned — slotting into the line-up is somewhat more testing). On any given weekend you may also be lucky enough to witness one of Sydney's regular surf lifesaving carnivals. Grab your camera if you do; these competitions are colourful spectacles that include surfboat races, boardriding, lifesaving and traditional club parades — the archetypical "bronzed Aussie" experience. Travel to Manly from Circular Quay by ferry (30 minutes) or JetCat (15 minutes). Bondi Beach is 20 minutes from the CBD by car, but parking can be difficult. Public transport is often a better option; catch a train to Bondi Junction, then ride the bus (10 minutes) to the beach.

Bondi All-year-round, crowds mass at this legendary 1 km strand. Fortunately, Bondi is the widest beach in the Sydney region and usually has enough space for everyone to find their place in the sun.

Tamarama Beach This protected cove lies immediately south of Bondi. Tama Cafe, adjoining the boardwalk, is a top spot to refuel before undertaking the Bondi to Bronte Coastal Walk (part of the larger Eastern Beaches Coastal Walk).

South of Bondi

Beyond the scarps at the south of Bondi lie the sandy bays of Tamarama, Bronte, Clovelly and Coogee. Each has their own charm and all are well worth exploring. Follow the coastal walking path and cool off in the sea as you go. If waves aren't your thing (rips can be strong, particularly at Bronte), ocean baths are located at Bondi, Bronte, Clovelly and Coogee. Tiny Tamarama, known by locals as "Glamourama", has been popular since the early 1900s when it boasted an amusement park (Wonderland City) complete with roller-coaster. Sadly, the park has long gone but its heyday is recalled in a 13 m mural on the eastern wall of the surf club. On the clifftops 10 minutes walk south of Bronte, Waverley Cemetery's residents lay in tombs with a view. Many notable Sydney personalities and luminaries are interred here — seek out the gravestones of legendary Australian writers Henry Lawson and Dorothea Mackellar.

Sydney Harbour National Park

Many foreshore regions around the harbour are protected and are known collectively as Sydney Harbour National Park. The national park takes in sections of North, South and Middle Head, Bradleys Head (near Taronga Zoo) and Dobroyd Head (along the Manly Scenic Walkway).

Harbour Beaches

Sydney Harbour beaches offer more sedate pleasures than the city's busy ocean strips. Some, like Collins Beach (home to a Little Penguin colony), are peaceful retreats that form part of Sydney Harbour National Park. Others, such as Clontarf and Clifton Gardens, have safe swimming areas and adjacent parks, making them popular with local families. Balmoral Beach is one of Sydney's prettiest harbour beaches. Sheltered by Middle Head, this little "secret spot" has great views across Middle Harbour to North Head.

Manly

Manly actually incorporates several beaches, the main strand comprising Queenscliff, North Steyne and South Steyne, and a shark-meshed harbour beach just west of the ferry wharf. They are connected by a touristy shopping and dining strip known as The Corso, which spans the narrow isthmus separating North Harbour from the sea.

Bondi

Cradled by extending arms of ancient sandstone and quartzite, Bondi Beach is one of Sydney's most fabled and popular seaside destinations. Aboriginal rock carvings may still be found within the cliff walls of Ben Buckler, the beach's northern headland. The grand Bondi to Bronte Coastal Walk begins at the southern end of Bondi Beach.

Watsons Bay & South Head

Lunch at Watsons Bay is a sacred Sydney ritual. Travel by ferry and loll away the afternoon in one of the harbour's most pleasant nooks. Leave time for a walk to The Gap and South Head, where the Hornsby Lighthouse and sweeping Pacific views will reward your efforts. Stop by at Camp Cove — original landing site of the First Fleet.

Manly Scenic Walkway

The Manly Scenic Walkway links Manly to the Spit Bridge (*above*). The tracks along this 9.5 km (4 hr) stroll showcase some of Sydney Harbour's best scenery and beaches. Along the way, illustrated plaques provide information about the local flora. Pack your togs, a picnic and plenty of water and stride out along West Esplanade from Manly Wharf, skirting the Fairlight foreshore. Forty Baskets Beach marks the start of the National Park and the track winds through Reef Beach (clothes optional), Dobroyd Head and Crater Cove. The sandstone outcrop of Grotto Point is graced by a small lighthouse and well-maintained Aboriginal rock engravings. Dusk and dawn views over the harbour from either the Grotto Point Lighthouse or Crater Cove Lookout are brilliant. Continue along the edge of Middle Harbour to Clontarf Beach and enjoy the final 40 minute walk around Sandy Bay and Fisher Bay to the Spit. Those with plenty of gas left in the tank can continue their adventure along the foreshore — it's an invigorating 17 km to Sydney Harbour Bridge!

Fort Denison

This rocky island in the middle of Sydney Harbour has been variously known as *Mattewanye*, Pinchgut and Fort Denison. It was originally used to confine criminals, and the fort was constructed in 1857 amid fears of Russian invasion following the Crimean War. It has since been restored with daily heritage tours available (Ph: (02) 9247 5033).

Clockwise from top left: Manly Cove, with North Head beyond; The world famous strand of Manly Beach; Crater Cove (*centre*), flanked by Sydney Harbour National Park, is a highlight of the Manly Scenic Walkway.

A Day on the Water

Ferries offer the ideal mode of transport for exploring and photographing Sydney Harbour. They are also the perfect way to reflect upon Sydney's transition from raw wilderness to world city. On a brilliant blue day, the views back across the harbour toward the CBD from around South Head, North Sydney or Manly Cove define the city's visual style. Not to be missed.

Blue Mountains

Top Things to Do

1. Soar over the Jamison Valley in the glass-bottomed gondolas of the Scenic Skyway.
2. Photograph the Three Sisters.
3. Enjoy the charm of historic townships like Leura and Mount Victoria.
4. Hike through the Valley of the Waters en route to Wentworth Falls.
5. Celebrate Christmas in winter with Yulefest.
6. Descend through rainforest on the Scenic Railway — the world's steepest railway track.
7. Follow the Six Foot Track to Jenolan Caves and marvel at the incredible limestone formations.
8. Explore the region for local art.
9. Stroll the area's beautiful gardens.

Blackheath

Blackheath, elevated 1000 m above sea level, is the highest township in the Blue Mountains. Its pure air and fertile landscape facilitate the growth of superb rhododendron gardens — the botanical star of an annual November show.

Leura

Leura's carefully manicured gardens and streets have made the township a beloved destination. The cooler climate supports many varieties of flowers and shrubs that are not easily cultivated in metropolitan Sydney.

A Detour West – Blue Mountains

A natural process by which eucalypt oil vapour refracts sunlight (and drenches the surrounding atmosphere in a blue glaze) has helped give the Blue Mountains its name. This vast sandstone plateau, rising 1300 m above sea level, is populated by some of the world's rarest plant and animal species, including the Wollemi Pine — a prehistoric conifer regarded as the world's rarest. The rugged, high-altitude region was considered impenetrable until a 1813 crossing by explorers Blaxland, Wentworth and Lawson which then wrote itself into national folklore.

These pioneers hacked through dense bush for eighteen days in the hope of forging a path through the mountains. With the crossing completed, the mountains were opened up to visitors and the construction of country homes soon followed. A road was cut in 1814 by William Cox and a team of 30 convicts. In a little over three months they had cut 80 km of roadway to Mount York. Within six months they had constructed a further 80 km of road to Bathurst (a major centre for agriculture). Within 20 years, tourism in the area had begun.

Today, the Blue Mountains — part of the Great Dividing Range stretching from Gippsland, Victoria, to the rainforests of northern Queensland — is one of Sydney's most cherished retreats. The ancient rock formations of the area (such as the Three Sisters, Ruined Castle and Pulpit Rock) attract local and international visitors year-round. Katoomba, the Blue Mountain's largest town, is home to the region's main train station and the Three Sisters. Echo Point, 2 km from town, is the best vantage for observing this imposing sandstone marvel.

Echo Point also provides panoramic views of other Blue Mountains' landmarks such as Jamison Valley, Narrow Neck, Falls Reserve and Mount Solitary, as well as walking track departure points. A well-equipped and informative visitor centre is located here.

Photographing the Three Sisters

- A zoom lens is ideal, allowing both tight and panoramic shots (*above, upper right*) that include the impressive surrounds.
- When drifting clouds create shadows on the ground, wait until important elements are lit (*above, lower right*).
- Vertical shots with a very wide lens can be dramatic. This image (*above, left*) has been deliberately underexposed for effect.
- Don't ignore misty or early morning conditions. Silhouettes and shrouds can be very effective (*left, upper and lower*).
- Late afternoon is usually the best time to catch gold-washed hues across the rock (*above, upper right*).

Scenic World

The Scenic Railway (*above right*), the steepest incline railway in the world, provides a 415 m descent through the surrounding rainforest to the start of the Scenic Walkway — an informative 2 km boardwalk that links up with the Scenic Flyway and the Scenic Skyway (*above left*) aerial cable cars. The latter takes its passengers on a 720 m "flight" over the Jamison Valley and has a glass-bottom floor for real heart-in-the-mouth views of the ravines and waterfalls below.

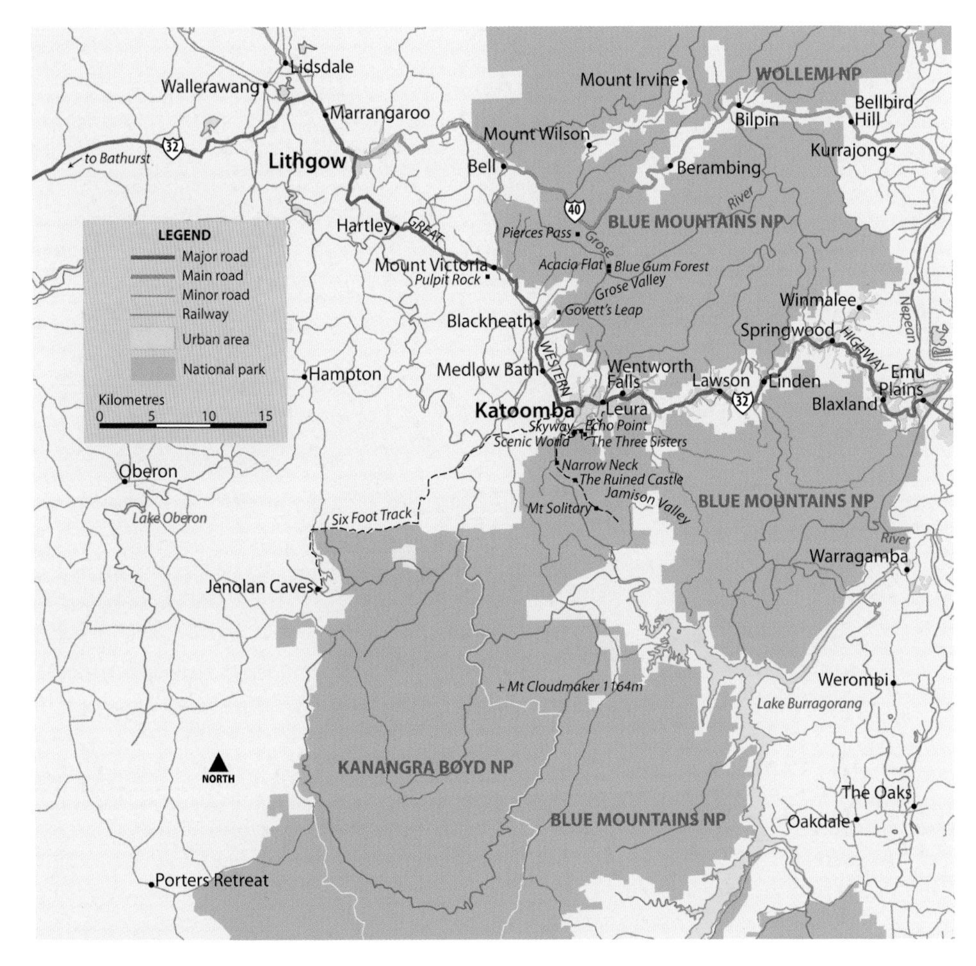

Further Information

- Echo Point Visitor Information Centre
  Echo Point Rd, Katoomba
  (Ph: 1300 653 408)
- Glenbrook Visitor Information Centre
  Great Western Hwy, Glenbrook
  (Ph: 1300 653 408)
- Blue Mountains Heritage Centre
  Govetts Leap Rd, Blackheath
  (Ph: (02) 4787 8877)

City of the Arts

In 1996 the Blue Mountains became New South Wales' inaugural "City of the Arts" — a worthy title for a region whose regular cultural expositions and artistic output complement the spectacular beauty of its landscapes.

The Blue Mountains is home to a large community of highly talented and creative artists practising a wide variety of differing forms — painting, sculpture, multimedia, textiles, jewelry and ceramics (to mention just a few!). A multitude of galleries, museums and antique dealers scattered throughout the region help facilitate the area's art trade.

The Blue Mountains calendar is busy with cultural events. Over summer, the "One Van" International Puppet Festival holds court in Blackheath. Autumn brings three days of folk, jazz and world music to Katoomba with the annual Blue Mountains Folk Music Festival. The crisp months of winter herald the biggest occasions on the arts calendar, including the Winter Magic Festival and Yulefest. Spring is a time to celebrate earthly beauty with the Leura Gardens Festival.

Mount Victoria

Mount Victoria is the most westerly of the Blue Mountains' townships. This small heritage-listed village, originally named One Tree Hill, is home to a number of historic buildings. These include: the Imperial Hotel (1878); St Peter's Anglican Church (1874); the Manor House (1876); and the Old Toll Bar House (1849).

Besides its historic appeal, Mount Victoria also serves as an access point to a number of natural attractions, including Victoria Falls Lookout, Pulpit Rock and Bedes Lookout.

Katoomba

Katoomba was destined to become the Blue Mountains' chief township when industry and tourism converged at around the same time in the 1870s. A crushing plant (supplying raw materials for the railway across the mountains) was already in place when the Katoomba Coal Mine was established. This gave the region one of its trademark attractions. The cable car track cut into the cliff to transport kerosene shale from the Jamison Valley which is now utilised by the Scenic Railway to transport tourists. With the opening of the Great Western Hotel (now The Carrington) in 1882, Katoomba was also emerging as a fashionable holiday resort and its views across the valley have continued to attract visitors over the years. The Three Sisters is its flagship attraction, but if you are feeling energetic you can traverse the 800 steps of the Giant Stairway. A few kilometres west of Katoomba, on the Great Western Highway near the Explorers Tree, are the graves of six unnamed convicts who died while cutting the first road through the Blue Mountains.

Blue Mountains

Walks to Remember

1. Princes Rock Walk (1 km, 1/2 hr, easy).
2. Overcliff–Undercliff Track (4 km, 2 hr, easy).
3. Weeping Rock–Fletchers Lookout Track (1 km, 1 hr, medium).
4. Cliff Top Track (3 km, 1.5 hr, medium).
5. Govetts Leap Descent (1.3 km, 1.5 hr, hard).
6. Perrys Lookdown–Blue Gum Forest (5 km, 5 hr, hard).

Hikers' Cardinal Rules — Don't Forget!

1. Take enough food and water for emergencies.
2. Wear comfortable footwear and take protective clothing for all weather conditions.
3. Never walk alone. Always keep your party together.
4. Take complete first aid equipment.
5. Leave an itinerary with park rangers or with friends.
6. Tread softly. Respect the national park.

Top to bottom: Megalong Valley; Hanging Rock in the Grose Valley; The Three Sisters overlooking Jamison Valley.

Bushwalking in the Blue Mountains

Bushwalking is big in the Blue Mountains. From the many elevated vantage points you can see blue valleys and mountain ranges merging with distant hilltops, rocky outcrops, cascading waterfalls, quiet rivers, mist-shrouded ravines and dense rainforest. Dramatic seasonal changes and a wealth of unique flora and fauna make trekking a popular pastime any month of the year. There are many short tracks of varying difficulty but some Blue Mountains bushwalks take up to a week to complete. Bushwalkers should be prepared for rapid changes in temperature and conditions. The weather fluctuates through extremes greater than those in Sydney.

A topographic map and compass are necessary for serious hikes but one of the park's best walks — the 5 km Grand Canyon Track — only requires casual wear, a bottle of water and a pair of comfortable shoes. The journey culminates in wide sweeping views across Grose Valley. Echo Point, site of the Katoomba Visitors Centre and the Three Sisters lookout, is the departure point of another enjoyable, if steeper, walk — the Federal Pass Track. At a little over 5 km, it is a difficult grade track that takes in many of the Blue Mountains' scenic highlights. Go slow and you will find a lot of life here.

The track weaves its way through some truly majestic wilderness, incorporating immense stone staircases and spectacular streams, waterfalls, rainforests and elevated lookouts. A three-hour round trip returns visitors to Echo Point.

From Govetts Leap Lookout at Blackheath, the Pulpit Rock Track leads walkers on a 6 km adventure to the imposing landmark of Pulpit Rock, a lone pinnacle, standing high against the awesome backdrop of Grose Valley.

The dense outcrop of tall trees at picturesque Blue Gum Forest can be reached after a moderately strenuous, 8 km trek from Pierces Pass. The track travels through a landscape of lush native rainforest and flowing creeks. Fairy Grotto Rainforest gives way to tall trees leading down to the Grose River crossing point. From here there is an easy passage to Blue Gum Forest and the campgrounds of Acacia Flat. These are just a sample of the many fine walks around the Blackheath area.

From the southern side of the Glenbrook Causeway a 6 km walking track leads to Red Hands Cave, so named for the Aboriginal hand stencils on its walls. They were discovered by Europeans in 1913, during a search for a lost child. It is also possible to reach the cave by car by taking the right turn-off at Oaks picnic area near the causeway.

The Prince Henry Cliff Walk is an easy 9 km breathtaking trek that follows the line of the cliff edge from Katoomba Cascades to Gordon Falls (near Leura). Your journey along the track is all about stopping to take in the best of the Blue Mountains' views, so be prepared to set a leisurely pace.

Committed and fit bushwalkers can also tackle the immense Six Foot Track, a three-day, 42 km trek from Katoomba to Jenolan Caves by way of the original horse track (dating back to the 1880s) used for the journey between the two sites. With over 20 major caves in the system, Jenolan Caves are a subterranean fantasy land of deep limestone caverns (arguably Australia's most impressive). Be sure to take a guided tour through any or all of the nine caves open to the public.

For maps and more information about bushwalking in the Blue Mountains, visit the Blue Mountains Heritage Centre (contact details on previous page).

Flora & Fauna in the Blue Mountains

The unique geological evolution of the Blue Mountains, which has occurred over 300 million years, has formed a range of habitats that together support a wide variety of native animals. The Blue Mountains comprises of open eucalypt forests, closed eucalypt forests (trees that are more closely packed together in the cooler, low-lying gullies and slopes), wet and dry heathlands, rainforests and swamps. The Blue Mountains are brimming with wildlife. Over 400 different animal species are attracted to these habitats and several threatened species survive here, including: the Spotted-tailed Quoll; the Long-nosed Potoroo; the Blue Mountains Water Skink; and the Green and Golden Bell Frog.

Birds & Birdwatching

The Blue Mountains are a paradise for both native birds and serious birdwatchers. The differing habitats appeal to a huge range of species and the open eucalypt forests attract the most boisterous characters. High up in the branches, Laughing Kookaburras can be heard competing with vocal flocks of colourful cockatoos, including the Sulphur-crested Cockatoo (*above left*) and Yellow-tailed Black-Cockatoo, which call beside trees full of shrieking rosellas. In the understorey, flowering banksias and grevilleas tempt honeyeaters, silvereyes and other nectar connoisseurs like the Eastern Spinebill. Listen for the ringing ventriloquism of the Crested Bellbird and keep your eyes peeled for some of the smaller species, such as the Scarlet Robin and Red-browed Finch.

In the closed forests, the Pilotbird scratches in the leaf litter for insects, spiders and other invertebrates. The Superb Lyrebird, another resident of the dense forest, is the undisputed master of mimicry, imitating perfectly the calls of other birds and human activity (e.g. mobile phone ringtones).

Flora

Open eucalypt forests are the most common habitat in the Blue Mountains. The many types of gum trees include Black Ash, Red Bloodwood, Scribbly Gum, Sydney Red Gum, she-oaks and stringybarks. Flowering plants, such as wattles and hakeas, are prevalent and it is worth keeping an eye out for the distinctive Mountain Devil and the New South Wales' floral emblem, the Waratah.

The magnificent Blue Gum is the botanical flagship of the cool, closed forests. Blue Gum Forest is an outstanding site for observing its namesake and can be accessed from Grose Valley via Perrys Lookdown or Pierces Pass. Various mosses and fungi grow here, as does the gigantic King Fern. Beautiful flowers, boronias and orchids, add startling colour to these forests. A kaleidoscope of floral colour explodes over the heathlands during spring (a natural spectacle worth seeing). Pea flowers, flannel flowers, conesticks, and guinea flowers flourish in these open areas.

Clockwise from top left: Blue Mountains fauna — Male Red-browed Finch; Scarlet Robin; Common Brushtail Possum; Eastern Pygmy-possums.

Clockwise from top left: Mountain Devil; Blue Gum Forest; Pink Boronia.

Mammals

Mammals abound in the Blue Mountains but it takes patience and a keen pair of eyes to observe them in their natural state. Possums and gliders, as well as bats, bandicoots and carnivorous marsupials (such as the quoll) prefer to forage or hunt for food under the cover of darkness. In the open forests, Short-beaked Echidnas are easily disturbed and, once they have burrowed into the ground, are well-camouflaged. Koalas are immobile, furry lumps for the best part of 20 hours a day and it is hard to spot them high in the treetops of the open forests.

The swamps of the Blue Mountains support ferns and sedges which the Swamp Wallaby relishes as food. This wallaby is more diurnal than most other macropods and may be observed during the day by cautious visitors.

Reptiles & Amphibians

Snakes are common and a number of venomous and non-venomous species enjoy a (mostly) secretive life here. Eastern Blind Snakes (burrowing, worm-like snakes that are extremely sensitive to light and feed on termites and ants) live in the loose soil of open forests. Death Adders use the cover of leaf litter within closed forests to ambush their prey. Wriggling the slim tip of their fat tails, they lure unsuspecting rodents into a deadly trap.

The large (but harmless) Diamond Python (*right*) is another resident regularly encountered.

Lizards, such as the Blue Mountains Water Skink, can be found basking on grassy tussocks in the heaths near Leura, Wentworth Falls and Newnes Plateau. Eastern Water Dragons and Eastern Snake-necked Turtles live around the rivers and waterways. Frogs, too, thrive in these rainforest environments. The Bleating Tree-frog and The Blue Mountains Tree-frog are just two of several frog species that can be heard in natural symphony with the rush of fresh, mountain water.

Lord Howe & Norfolk Islands
Top Things to Do

1. Explore Norfolk Island's superb botanical garden for a day.
2. Take a glass-bottom boat trip across Lord Howe's lagoon.
3. Snorkel at Sylph's Hole — over 450 species of fish have been identified at Lord Howe.
4. Wrangle monster pelagics on a deep sea fishing charter.
5. Climb to the summit of Mount Gower — Lord Howe's highest peak.
6. Inspect the Old Military Barracks at Kingston.
7. Amble among the graves at Norfolk Island's historic cemetery.
8. Cool off at Emily Bay — Norfolk Island's most inviting swimming spot.

A Detour East – Lord Howe & Norfolk Islands

Adventurous souls seeking to stretch the limits of a "typical" Australian journey might just find what they desire overseas — in the unhurried paradise of either Lord Howe or Norfolk Island. These volcanic islands are part of Australia's external territory (though Norfolk is self-governed) and promise visitors an experience unlike anything on the mainland.

Lord Howe is a stunning, vaulted landscape and unique terrestrial ecoregion. Nearly 50% of the island's plant species are endemic (Kentia Palms are an eye-catching botanical feature), while the Lord Howe Woodhen is found nowhere else in the world. The island is surrounded by the world's most southerly coral reef and a profusion of fish (more than 450 species) make their homes in these pristine waters.

Norfolk Island is also blessed by natural splendour, but it is a rich cultural heritage that truly distinguishes the island. The relics of Norfolk's past are well preserved and create an air of quaint, but dignified, charm. Cows graze among the historic buildings and locals still speak in a traditional Pitcairn Island tongue.

Top to bottom: Lord Howe Island, featuring Mt Lidgbird and Mt Gower; Island forest shares species with Australia, New Zealand and New Caledonia; Feeding the fish at Ned's Beach.

Lord Howe Island Marine Park

Ph: (02) 6563 2114

Striped Boarfish

Lord Howe Island was inscribed as a World Heritage Area in 1982, and its ocean environs have been a protected marine park since 1998. The island lies 550 km east of Port Macquarie and was discovered in 1788 but not settled until 1833. Today Lord Howe has a permanent population of around 300 and only 393 visitors can be accommodated on the island at any one time. Approximately 11 km long and 2.8 km across at its widest point, the island is one of a series of ancient volcanic pinnacles rising from an undersea ridge to form the Lord Howe Island Group. Both the island and its surrounding waters support a vast array of ecosystems, and the 46,000 ha marine park protects the world's southernmost coral reef. The relatively shallow coastal seabed allows abundant sunlight to reach the ocean floor, helping to create a huge population of temperate and tropical marine life. There are at least 105 endemic plant species found on the island itself, along with numerous unique animals including 50 species of spider, the flightless Lord Howe Woodhen and the world's rarest insect, the Lord Howe Stick Insect.

Conspicuous Angelfish

Marine Life: Over 450 species of fish have been identified among the coral reefs and waters off Lord Howe Island. Starfish and sea urchins are common sights, as well as a huge variety of crabs. The distinctive yellow and purple marked Swift-footed Rock Crab scuttles along the seashores along with Ghost Crabs and the shell-stealing Hermit Crab. Sea cucumbers, marine snails, marine slugs and a wide range of bivalves are found in Lord Howe's many rockpools. Fourteen species of sea bird, including terns, petrels and shearwaters, flock to these well-stocked waters to nest and breed. Green and Hawksbill Turtles are also found here.

Activities: Snorkelling and diving on the coral reef is an unforgettable experience. Snorkelling is also possible in only a metre of water off Ned's Beach, as well as at Sylph's Hole and North Bay. Chartered cruises are available to many of the outlying islands and rock formations, including Ball's Pyramid, a 551 m high pinnacle 23 km south-east of Lord Howe Island. Sportfishing (but not spearfishing) is a specialist pastime — huge Yellowtail Kingfish are the target species. Simply walking on the beach and investigating rockpools will leave you marvelling at the huge diversity of sea and shorelife to be found on Lord Howe. Walking tracks on the island lead to a variety of beach, rainforest and sightseeing destinations. Guided climbs are available to the summit of the volcanic peak of Mount Gower (at the island's southern end). Snorkelling and diving gear are available for hire.

Access: Via air from Sydney, Brisbane, Coffs Harbour and Port Macquarie. The island's only road runs from the jetty past the airport to Salmon Beach in the south.

Accommodation: There are seventeen accommodation properties on Lord Howe including apartments, holiday units, lodges and chalets. All accommodation must be booked in advance. There are also several licensed restaurants.

Red-tailed Tropicbird

Kingston Old Military Barracks.

Emily Bay One of Norfolk's best swimming areas.

Top to bottom: Norfolk Island Cemetery; Snorkelling at Point Ross; Norfolk Island Pines, some over 50 m in height, tower above the landscape.

Norfolk Island

Tourism Office: +67 232 2147 • National Park Manager: +67 232 2695

While Polynesian travellers are known to have visited Norfolk Island for many centuries, the island was not officially settled until 1788, fourteen years after James Cook landed there and identified its towering Norfolk Island Pines as potentially valuable to the British fleet. An initial convict settlement was abandoned in 1814, but a later convict scheme (established in 1825) persisted for 30 years. After transportation ceased, the island was inhabited by descendants of the infamous *Bounty* mutineers, most of whom left their home on Pitcairn Island to take up life on Norfolk. Today, roughly a third of the island's 1800 people are direct descendants of these settlers and such fabled heritage is one of the island's chief drawcards. Some islanders still speak a local language known as Norfolk. After settlement, whaling, timber and agriculture sustained Norfolk Island's inhabitants, but in modern times tourism has become the island's economic mainstay. Fifteen percent of the island (including the two highest points, Mt Pitt and Mt Bates) is national park managed by the Australian government. The island enjoys a moderate subtropical climate and is an excellent year-round destination.

Location: Norfolk Island is 1610 km north-east of Sydney and 1456 km south-east of Brisbane. The island is 8 km long and 5 km wide. Norfolk Island's major centre is Kingston.

Major Features & Activities: It is impossible to visit Norfolk Island without becoming immersed in its unique and intriguing history. A large number of tours and historic re-enactments are on offer and the major sites to visit are the Old Military Barracks, Kingston's historic museum complex, the Kingston ruins and the fascinating Norfolk Island Cemetery (including the graves and headstones of *Bounty* and First Fleet mutineers). A Captain Cook monument and lookout has been erected at the site of his landing on the northern coast (via Duncombe Bay Rd). Numerous tracks of varying difficulty and length intersect the national park (mostly they are moderate hikes). Walking tracks lead to the summit of Mt Pitt and Mt Bates, with panoramic views across the island to Phillip Island. An easier and shorter track at Palm Glen leads to a lookout (with seating), ideal for sunset views and photography over the southern part of the island. Norfolk Island's superb botanical garden (all 62.7 ha) is worthy of a day's exploration.

Access: Regular flights to Norfolk Island operate from Sydney, Brisbane, Newcastle and Auckland. An Australian or New Zealand Passport or entry visa is required for all visitors. While hiring a car is one of the best ways to get about the island, taxis are also available (but there is no public transport).

Accommodation: Norfolk Island offers a wide range of accommodation from self-catering options to resorts. All accommodation must be pre-booked prior to arrival. Camping is not permitted within the national park.

Norfolk Redcoat

SYDNEY to Brisbane

Sydney to Brisbane
Top Things to Do

1. Experience the superb natural sanctuary of Bouddi National Park.
2. Visit the Australian Reptile Park, near Gosford.
3. Explore the beautiful Lake Macquarie district.
4. Enjoy one of Newcastle's heritage tours.
5. Tour the Hunter Valley's wineries.
6. Head to Nelson Bay and photograph migrating Humpback Whales (June–July).
7. Explore the magnificent coastline from Port Macquarie to Byron Bay.
8. Boot scoot at Tamworth — Australia's country music capital.
9. Camp amid wild rivers and waterfalls in the national parks east of Armidale.
10. Spoil yourself with some Gold Coast glamour.

Whale Watching

In the winter months of June and July, the warm coastal waters of the Pacific Ocean form a major route for the journey of Southern Right and Humpback Whales from Antarctic waters to birthing grounds off the Great Barrier Reef. Pods of whales can be observed from many points along the coast during this time, but some of the most popular viewing locations are:

- Crackneck Lookout (Wyrrabalong National Park).
- Tomaree National Park (Nelson Bay).
- Crowdy Bay National Park (near Taree).
- Solitary Islands Marine Park (Coffs Harbour).
- Dirriangan Lookout (Yuraygir National Park, near Angourie).
- Iluka Bluff (Bundjalung National Park, near Grafton).
- Cape Byron (Byron Bay).

Whether you choose to travel to Brisbane along the coast or via the New England Tableland, the first stage of either trip will take you through the glorious Central Coast region, characterised by a series of huge coastal lakes, national parks and beautiful sandy beaches. Its many natural attractions, mild climate and close proximity to Sydney and Newcastle makes the entire area a popular weekend and holiday destination. Only 80 km from Sydney, and just north of Brisbane Water National Park, the town of Gosford is the Central Coast's major commercial centre and the launching pad to a trove of regional attractions.

Yellow-tailed Black-Cockatoo

Central Coast

A collection of small but captivating sanctuaries, national parks and reserves lie within easy reach of Gosford. The Australian Reptile Park (Ph: (02) 4340 1022) is one of the Central Coast's premier attractions and operates a vital snake and spider antivenom program. South-east of Gosford, beyond the holiday and fishing resort town of Terrigal, is Bouddi National Park. *Bouddi* is the local Aboriginal name for the eastern headland of Maitland Bay and the park contains more than 100 recorded Aboriginal sites, including rock art shelters. The 1898 shipwreck of the PS *Maitland* is another interesting relic, lying at the northern end of Maitland Bay. Campgrounds with excellent facilities close to car parking are available at Putty Beach (near Killcare) and Little Beach. Further north toward Newcastle are two major coastal saltwater lakes — Tuggerah Lake and Lake Macquarie (which is Australia's largest). On the shores of Tuggerah Lake, Wyrrabalong National Park protects the Central Coast's last remaining areas of littoral rainforest. Wyrrabalong Lookout, in the park's southern section, is the highest coastal point between Sydney and Newcastle.

Newcastle

Located at the mouth of the Hunter River, Newcastle is Australia's second-oldest city. Founded as an auxiliary penal colony to Sydney, the early discovery of coal reserves and the establishment of the nation's largest steelworks in 1915 transformed the town into a major industrial centre and port. Today, Newcastle is a lively and charismatic city complemented by attractive stretches of coastline and impressive heritage buildings. Board Newcastle's Famous Tram for an informative 45 minute historical tour of the city (departs from Newcastle Railway Station, weekdays, Ph: (02) 4977 2270). Walking, too, is the perfect way to soak up Newcastle's character. Cooks Hill is just one of six heritage conservation areas in the city and a number of walking trails showcase Newcastle's beauty. City maps and detailed information can be obtained from the visitor information centre (363 Hunter St, Ph: (02) 4974 2999 or 1800 654 558).

Two Routes to Brisbane

The Tablelands

The New England Highway begins at Newcastle and cuts through the Hunter Valley and the country music capital of Tamworth to the New England Tableland. Worth exploring is the chain of superb national parks that lie to the east of Armidale and Glen Innes before heading through Tenterfield and Warwick to Brisbane.

The Coast

The Pacific Highway is the most popular route north to Brisbane and takes in the major towns of Taree, Port Macquarie, Coffs Harbour, Grafton and Byron Bay. To make the most of the trip (and escape the endless traffic), take the time to leave the highway and explore the many smaller towns, beaches and parks along the coast.

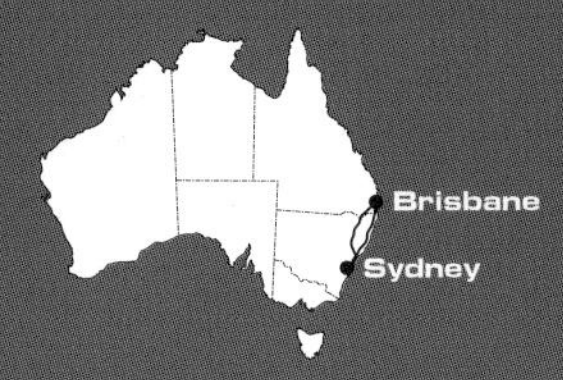

Feature Localities

1 Armidale
2 Barrington Tops National Park
3 Boonoo Boonoo National Park
4 Booti Booti National Park
5 Border Ranges National Park
6 Bouddi National Park
7 Byron Bay
8 Cathedral Rock National Park
9 Coffs Harbour
10 Crowdy Bay National Park
11 Dorrigo National Park
12 Girraween National Park
13 Gold Coast
14 Gosford
15 Grafton
16 Guy Fawkes River National Park
17 Hat Head National Park
18 Hunter Valley
19 Lamington National Park
20 Mount Warning National Park
21 Myall Lakes National Park
22 Nelson Bay
23 Newcastle
24 Nimbin
25 Oxley Wild Rivers National Park
26 Port Macquarie
27 Scone
28 Solitary Islands Marine Park
29 Springbrook National Park
30 Tamborine National Park
31 Tamworth
32 Taree
33 Tomaree National Park
34 Warwick
35 Wollemi National Park
36 Wyrrabalong National Park
37 Yengo National Park
38 Yuraygir National Park

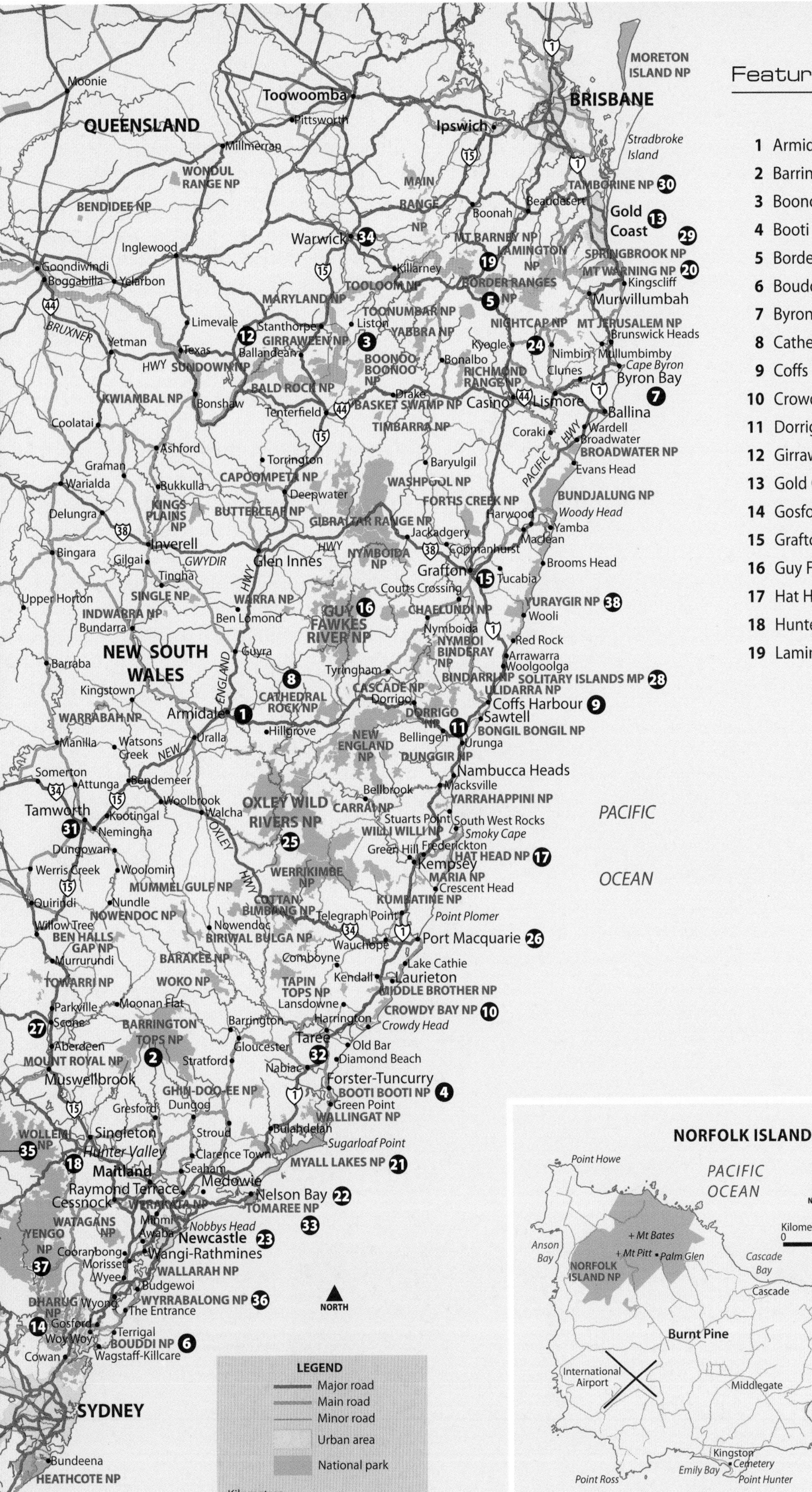

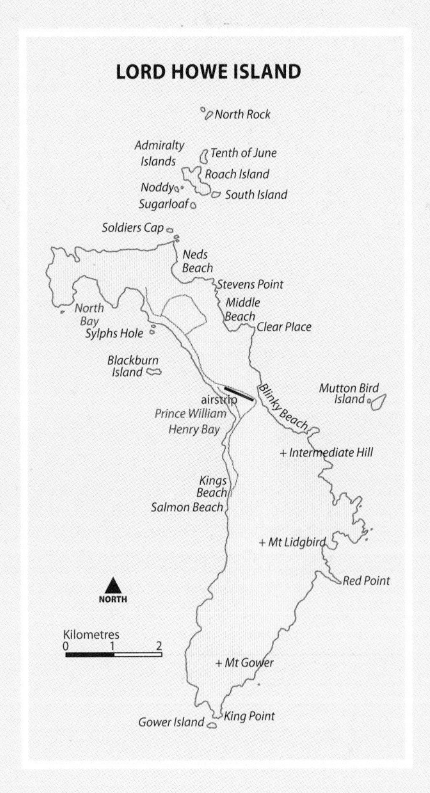

Newcastle

Excellent views of the Newcastle region can be enjoyed from lookouts at King Edward Park, Shepherds Hill and Mt Sugarloaf. Overlooking Nobbys Beach, historic Fort Scratchley now houses a Military Museum. From the beach below, a convict-built pier and breakwater leads to the island known as Nobbys and its pretty lighthouse.

Newcastle to Coffs Harbour

Fifty kilometres north-east of Newcastle is Port Stephens and the holiday centre of Nelson Bay. The bulging headlands, white sandy beaches and pristine blue waters make for scenery of considerable grandeur, best viewed from Tomaree National Park and Inner Head Lighthouse. Up the coast toward Taree are the "twin towns" of Forster and Tuncurry, now really a single resort area located on either side of the entrance to Wallis Lake and linked by a concrete bridge. Brilliant panoramas of this section of coast can be admired from a platform at Cape Hawke, a steep 400 m walk up from Cape Hawke Rd in Booti Booti National Park.

Taree is the main centre of the Manning River Valley. Drivers seeking respite from the road can stretch their legs in Fotheringham Park, north of the bridge on the banks of the river. Nearby Manning Point is an attractive village in an area renowned for oysters — Taree's reputation for the molluscs is honoured by a monstrous "Big Oyster" on the northern town limits (dismissed by many locals as "The Big Mistake"). Hugging the coast en route to Port Macquarie is Crowdy Bay National Park. Walk the beaches and explore the rockpools around Diamond Head or see how many of the 235 animal species you can identify here.

Port Macquarie

From Crowdy Bay a series of coastal reserves and lakes lead the way to Port Macquarie at the mouth of the Hastings River. In the 1890s local writer Louis Becke described it as "the dullest coast town in New South Wales" but its delightful setting, regional importance and a roaring tourist trade have long since rendered the insult redundant. Swimmers can choose from over a dozen surf beaches in close proximity and the kids can enjoy camel rides on Lighthouse Beach (Ph: (02) 6583 7650). The Tacking Point Lighthouse was built in 1879 and is Australia's third-oldest. Australia's only Koala Hospital, in Port Macquarie Nature Reserve near Flynn's Beach, treats 250 sick and injured animals per year and is open to the public (Lord St, Ph: (02) 6584 1522). Also check out Port Macquarie Tourist Information Centre (Ph: (02) 6581 8000).

Mid North Coast

The region between Port Macquarie and Coffs Harbour is a holiday wonderland of coastal and hinterland national parks, expansive beaches and ideally positioned towns. The region is served by the commercial centre of Kempsey. If you tire of the highway and have a 4WD vehicle it is even possible to forego the bitumen for sand and drive up the beach from the Hastings River Punt near Port Macquarie to Crescent Head (permit required, Ph: (02) 6566 3200). Crescent Head is a delightful small seaside village with a big surfing reputation. Surf beaches with names like Racecourse and Big Hill give you an inkling of the type (and scale) of swell to be expected here. A challenging six hole golf course with expansive views offers more relaxed leisure. Protecting the foreshore north is Hat Head National Park. Adjacent South West Rocks is a well equipped getaway near the mouth of the Macleay River that retains much of its old fishing port character. Visit Trial Bay Gaol on Laggers Point (a late 19th century stone prison used to confine internees during World War I), sample the local oysters or take a lunch cruise on the Macleay. Off the highway north, Scotts Head, Grassy Head and Stuarts Point are peaceful beach retreats with a drowsy holiday feel. From here to Coffs Harbour the highway skirts verdant dairy country with the coastal town of Nambucca Heads to the east and artsy Bellingen lying to the west (on the Bellinger River). Above in the mist-shrouded range, the rustic mountain village of Dorrigo and World Heritage — inscribed Dorrigo National Park mark the start of the Waterfall Way.

Seashore Sunrises

The sight of the sun rising over the Pacific along the beaches of the midnorth coast makes early morning shore walks one of the region's great pleasures. You don't have to take a rod (though the surf and rock fishing is some of Australia's best) but a camera is a must.

Clockwise from top left: Myall Lakes National Park; Seal Rocks, looking south along the coast of Myall Lakes National Park; Camping at Myall Lakes National Park; Trial Bay and Hat Head National Park.

Mid North Coast National Parks

Ph: (02) 6586 8300

Myall Lakes National Park

With 40 km of unspoilt coastline, expansive sandy dunes, plenty of fantastic campsites and an interconnected system of natural lakes, it is not hard to fathom the attraction of this national park only an hour's drive from Newcastle. Myall Lakes National Park is listed as a Ramsar site (wetlands of international significance) and any visitor here should prepare themselves for serious aquatic leisure. However, while boating, kayaking, canoeing and sailing are favoured activities, bushwalkers will appreciate the great range of tracks, which take in cultural sites and the park's numerous plant and animal species. The Mungo Track (22 km) is usually undertaken in sections, but provides a good overview of local landforms and the area's ecology. Near Seal Rocks, a village at the northern end of the park, Sugarloaf Point Lighthouse (built in 1875) delivers dramatic views of the coast.

Crowdy Bay National Park

Only 25 km north-east of Taree, Crowdy Bay National Park is another gem in the mid New South Wales coastal bioregion. With its excellent beaches, anglers and surfers will make the most of this destination but wildlife photographers will also revel in the park's heath and remnant littoral rainforest environs. The park's most prominent geological feature, Diamond Head, provides an excellent vantage for surveying the area's cliffs, rockpools (kids will love exploring these at low tide) and beaches. Walks in the park include the 4.8 km Diamond Head Loop Track (linking the Diamond Head and Indian Head campgrounds) and the walk to Kylie's Hut. Built for Australian author Kylie Tennant (and lovingly restored), the hut adds a nice cultural touch to this picturesque area.

Hat Head National Park

Before European settlement, this bountiful national park supported one of New South Wales' highest Indigenous populations. Hat Head's traditional custodians, the Dunghutti people, enjoyed a ready supply of fresh fish and shellfish harvested from nearby estuaries, creeks, wetlands and beaches. And the park contains a number of Aboriginal burial sites, middens and ceremonial areas. Atop a narrow headland at the northern end of the park, Smoky Cape Lighthouse (built in 1891) is a great spot to take in the pristine scenery. Nearby Arakoon State Conservation Area protects the ruins of Trial Bay Gaol (established in the 1870s). The ruins and gaol museum relate a riveting chapter in Australian history.

Magpie

Port Stephens

Port Stephens is actually a drowned valley, resulting from a huge rise in sea levels more than 70,000 years ago. The surrounding volcanic peaks guard a marine haven that is home to a resident population of around 80 Bottlenose Dolphins. Nearby Cabbage Tree Island is the world's only breeding ground of the rare Gould's Petrel.

Taree & Manning River

The Manning River enters the ocean twice, at Harrington and Farquhar Inlet (Old Bar), 12 km south. The two river limbs converge at Taree and the complex estuarine system includes old mangrove stands and nearly 100 km^2 of wetlands — an important breeding ground for a wide variety of shorebirds.

Port Macquarie

Port Macquarie was established in 1821 as a penal settlement and excellent views over the town and the mouth of the Hastings River are available from Gaol Point Lookout (off Stewart St). Construction of the railway in the early 1900s saw the harbour's use decline and today a large marina filled with leisure craft reflects Port Macquarie's recreational focus.

Coffs Harbour

Awarded the title of World's Most Liveable City (population under 75,000) by the United Nations in 2002, Coffs Harbour offers a huge variety of recreational activities and natural attractions. Scuba diving expeditions to the Solitary Islands Marine Park and whale-watching cruises (May to Sept) depart from the Harbour Drive marina.

Coffs Harbour to Brisbane

Captain John Korff found safe haven from storms in this area in 1847, but his place in history was obscured due to a misprint in a government gazette that renamed the location Coffs Harbour. It was once the capital of the nation's prime banana-growing region, explaining the famed Big Banana monument (originally built in 1963) on the left of the highway heading north. The oversized fruit was an instant hit, attracting 30,000 visitors in its first week, and tourism in the Coffs Harbour area has since gone from strength to strength. Sport is also an important part of Coffs' life and the city is the permanent training base for the Australian rugby union team. The harbour and surrounding beaches are quite beautiful and offer diverse pleasures — visit the trendy seaside village of Sawtell a few kilometres south or pretty Sapphire Beach just north. Near Coffs' main jetty, a causeway leads to Muttonbird Island, a protected habitat for breeding Wedge-tailed Shearwaters, and a must-visit location for views back across the harbour, Coffs Coast and the Solitary Islands to the north. The Glenreagh Mountain Railway, 25 minutes drive north of Coffs on the Orara Way, offers a 35 km journey by restored steam train through the hinterland (Ph: (02) 6649 2234).

If you have time, break the journey to Grafton with a detour to Yuraygir National Park, where wildflowers bloom in the coastal heath along the longest strip of undeveloped coastline in New South Wales. Coloured by generous stands of Jacarandas, and straddling the Clarence River, nearby Grafton is a handsomely preserved regional centre. Wander Victoria Street to admire (and photograph) the town's many heritage buildings, including the Classical Revival style Court House and Christ Church Anglican Cathedral. In Fitzroy Street, one of the city's finest residences has been converted into Schaeffer House Museum (Ph: (02) 6642 5212).

Grafton

Known as the "Jacaranda City", Grafton is home to 6500 carefully planted trees and 24 parks. The Jacaranda Festival (Australia's oldest flora festival) is held in the last week of October and a Jazz and Blues Festival at Easter. Susan Island, in the Clarence River near Memorial Park, is home to the Southern Hemisphere's largest colony of flying-foxes.

North to Byron Bay

The highway north passes through several surprisingly multicultural townships celebrating their European heritage. Maclean, with its tartan-decorated telegraph poles and Gaelic street signs, has been proclaimed "Australia's First Scottish Town". New Italy's impressive museum complex tells the unusual story of a group of Italian immigrant settlers who survived an ill-fated journey to Australia to develop the region. On the coast, Evans Head lays claim to having been Australia's first prawning port and a large fishing fleet moors at the mouth of the Evans River. Nearby Razorback Lookout offers views north to Cape Byron Lighthouse.

Ballina began life as a timber cutting town on the Richmond River populated by Irish immigrants. It became a major fishing centre and boasts a Big Prawn to complement Coff's Big Banana. The Big Scrub, by contrast, is not a large washcloth but the name locally given to the lush subtropical rainforest that once covered the area. Visit Victoria Park Nature Reserve west of Ballina (near Alstonville) to see how it all looked before logging altered the landscape.

Just south of Cape Byron is the pretty village of Bangalow — its main street lined with brightly restored shopfronts, cafés and antique stores. Once a sleepy whaling station, then a mecca for "alternative lifestyles", neigbouring Byron Bay is the energetic epicentre of tourism on the north coast. It retains many reminders of its past incarnations, but is now definitely more luxury resort than retreat. The town centre offers as large a variety of retail options and restaurants as many small cities, but the surf beaches south and north have lost none of their original allure. Arts festivals, including the legendary Blues and Roots Festival (Easter) and Byron Bay Writers Festival (August), attract international megastars and huge crowds.

Nimbin

New age, hippie, bohemian, call it what you will, but Nimbin has something different on show along a psychedelic strip surrounded by some of New South Wales' most beautiful subtropical countryside. Take a (historic) trip through the community's counter-culture at the delightfully eccentric Nimbin Museum.

Mount Warning & Tweed Caldera

Twenty kilometres south-west of Murwillumbah is the great magma plug of an ancient volcano. Named Mt Warning by James Cook — to alert mariners to dangerous reefs offshore — the Bundjalung people originally knew the twin peaked formation as *Wollumbin* ("Fighting Chief of the Mountains"). The volcano's last eruption was around 20 million years ago but the basalt rock formed from its cooling lava flows is found as far south as Lismore, north to Mt Tambourine and east to Tweed Heads.

The original volcano was twice the current height of Mt Warning. The Tweed Valley is a caldera formed by its collapse and erosion and, at over a kilometre deep, is the largest of its kind in the Southern Hemisphere.

Solitary Islands Marine Park

Even hardened lighthouse keepers once thought South Solitary Island an isolated place. Impossible to reach in rough weather, the island is now part of a marine park stretching 75 km along the coast opposite Yuraygir National Park, north of Coffs Harbour.

The park is rich in fish and invertebrate species due to its location midway between temperate and tropical waters. The water is usually clear and warm, perfect for year-round diving and underwater photography (depending, of course, on the ocean conditions). Unlike much marine life in southern NSW waters, underwater attractions are in relatively shallow water so bottom time can be extended.

Diving Charters

The five islands of the marine park and their aquatic realms cater for all levels of diving experience, from beginner to expert. There are literally hundreds of dive sites, from 12 m shallow reefs to 30 m deep reef walls positively teeming with marine life. Coffs Harbour's dive shops and the PADI five-star-rated Jetty Dive Centre on Harbour Drive all operate extensive dive charters on weather-friendly days. Dive Quest at Mullaway (30 km north of Coffs near Woolgoolga) runs excellent dives at North Solitary Island.

Spectacular Fish Life

This is one of the best regions south of the Great Barrier Reef to observe and photograph marine creatures. The reefs around North Solitary Island boast the largest numbers of anemones and clown fish (think Nemo) in the world. The marine park is home to Greynurse Sharks, Manta Rays, large pelagic fish, sea turtles and tropical fish.

South Solitary Island

Byron Bay & Cape Byron

The windswept Cape Byron (*left*) is Australia's most easterly point and home to the nation's most powerful lighthouse. The first settlement here was originally known by the area's Indigenous name of *Cavvanbah* before changing to Byron Bay (*far left*) with the opening of the railway in 1894.

Byron to the Tweed

North of Byron Bay, the Pacific Highway tracks the coast to Tweed Heads. For a vision of Byron Bay before mass tourism set in, visit Brunswick Heads, an excellent swimming and surfing spot set on the Brunswick River.

Murwillumbah, on the Tweed River at the foothills of the McPherson Ranges just south of the Queensland border, was rebuilt in 1907 after a fire devastated the burgeoning town. It is now a busy commercial and tourist centre. Views of Mt Warning can be seen from the main bridge over the Tweed (*left*).

Australian Pelican

Golden Miles

The Gold Coast has something for everyone — the glamour of Surfers Paradise, Broadbeach's luxurious lifestyle, a surfeit of shopping, wide sun-drenched beaches, verdant hinterland, thrilling theme parks and wonderful wildlife.

Shoppers' Paradise

There is no lack of options for the determined shopper on the Gold Coast. Fashion boutiques showcase designer labels from the world's catwalks, while large shopping complexes (such as Pacific Fair) house specialty shops and department stores under one roof. Weekend markets are awash with an endless array of holiday souvenirs.

Thrill City

Theme parks like Sea World and Movie World have proliferated on the Gold Coast since the opening of Ski Gardens in 1958. There is now a galaxy of "worlds" guaranteed to energise even the most world-weary visitor. One of the biggest hits among a multitude of thrillingly inventive rides and whacky distractions is Dreamworld's resident troupe of Bengal Tigers.

The Tweed to Brisbane

Once merely a string of sleepy resort towns, the Gold Coast has become a premier holiday destination for both Australian and international visitors. Over a century ago, the location was already important in linking Australia with the rest of the world. The nation's first trans-Pacific cable, laid in 1902 and traversing the oceans to Canada, terminated here at a hut on Main Beach. Today the hut is gone and the beach is lined with skyscraping hotels and apartment towers, which stand as testimony to the Gold Coast's lofty ambitions and perpetual growth. The region takes in 57 km of coastline from Coolangatta to the Broadwater. Despite the scale of development, the Gold Coast remains an enticing destination for its long beaches, clear ocean and ever-shining sun. A head-spinning range of entertainment options add dazzle to your downtime — eight theme parks, wall-to-wall shops, restaurants, cafés, nightclubs aplenty, a casino and several excellent wildlife sanctuaries.

Surfers Paradise & Surrounds

At the heart of it all is Surfers Paradise, which includes a busy shopping and leisure precinct centred around Cavill Avenue. The city on the sand continues to rise ever upwards and now boasts Australia's tallest structure — a 323 m apartment tower branded Q1. The design was inspired by the 2000 Sydney Olympic Games torch, and you can see both the original torch and the phenomenal vistas (up to 80 km on a clear day) by visiting the public observation deck (Hamilton Ave, Surfers Paradise, Ph: (07) 5630 4700). Each October, the streets north of Cavill Avenue are barricaded to form the racetrack for one of Australia's biggest motorsport events — the Indy 300. Neighbouring Main Beach runs north from Surfers Paradise to Southport and the Spit. Now the Gold Coast's prime commercial centre, Southport was the region's original holiday mecca, attracting the patronage of the Queensland Governor and Brisbane's social set from as early as the 1890s. Behind Surfers and Broadbeach, the tributary creeks of the Nerang River have disappeared beneath a labyrinthine system of artificial canals. What were once swamp lands have been replaced by luxurious waterside homes, many with jetties for mooring private boats.

Green Behind the Gold

Expansive plains give way inland to the rugged, rainforested McPherson and Darlington Ranges. Here, in the lush Gold Coast hinterland, exceptional natural treasures form part of the World-Heritage-listed Gondwana Rainforests of Australia (formerly known as the Central Eastern Rainforest Reserves) — Lamington, Springbrook, Tamborine and Border Ranges National Parks.

Wild Places

Just over the Queensland border at fauna-rich Springbrook National Park, glow-worms huddle in a cavern below a fascinating ancient rock formation known as Natural Bridge (*right*). While the scenery is remarkable at any time, the glow-worms are best viewed at night during summer months. Springbrook also has an abundance of spectacular waterfalls and cascades. Excellent camping facilities are available at The Settlement (off Carricks Road).

West of Springbrook, Lamington National Park features an extensive system of high-quality walking tracks. There is a choice of either a resort or camping at Green Mountains, Binna Burra or O'Reilly's — the latter being particularly good for birdwatching. Watch out for the rare Albert's Lyrebird (a mesmerising songster) on the rainforest tracks. Local lookouts provide dramatic views over the Gold Coast and Northern New South Wales.

North-west of Nerang, Tamborine National Park (*right, bottom*) is extremely popular with daytrippers and hikers. The park habitat is characterised by Piccabeen Palm groves, tall Flooded Gums, Bracken Fern, strangler figs and woodland. Many easy to moderate grade walks wind through the park (the Witches Falls circuit is popular). Camping is not permitted in the park.

Gold Coast Wildlife Viewing

With a number of well-loved and long-lived wildlife and marine parks, the Gold Coast remains strongly connected to the natural world. Since 1925, these sanctuaries have given holidaymakers the opportunity to observe and interact with a diverse range of animals. The Gold Coast's major wildlife attractions include Currumbin Wildlife Sanctuary, David Fleay Wildlife Park, Dreamworld and Sea World.

Currumbin Sanctuary

Currumbin Wildlife Sanctuary has been delighting visitors for over six decades providing the opportunity to get up-close and personal with local birdlife. Scaly-breasted and Rainbow Lorikeets descend from the trees to feed from visitors' hands (*left*). The sanctuary also provides safe haven for over 1400 native animals including kangaroos, wombats and crocodiles.

Location: Tomewin Street (off Gold Coast Highway), Currumbin.
Opening Hours: Daily (except Christmas Day), 8 am – 5 pm.
Ph: 1300 886 511

David Fleay Wildlife Park

David Fleay Wildlife Park, south-west of Burleigh Heads, was established in 1951 by Dr David Fleay, an acclaimed naturalist and the first man to successfully breed the Platypus in captivity. The park is now managed by the Queensland Government as an environmental education, breeding and research centre. Tour the sanctuary (*left*) and meet the 1500 native inhabitants via 2 km of winding boardwalk.

Location: West Burleigh Rd, Burleigh Heads.
Opening Hours: Daily (except Christmas Day), 9 am – 5 pm.
Ph: (07) 5576 2411

Dreamworld

The Australian Wildlife Experience at Dreamworld features over 800 native animals and offers everything from Koalas (*left*) to close inspections of crocodiles and kangaroos. The experience showcases a variety of simulated habitats, from Daintree Rainforest to Kakadu Wetlands, as well as a Sunset Safari (which includes encounters with the Bengal Tigers of Tiger Island) and an outback spotlighting adventure.

Location: Dreamworld Parkway, Coomera.
Opening Hours: Daily (except Christmas Day), 10 am – 5 pm.
Ph: (07) 5588 1111 or 1800 073 300

Sea World

Sea World's extensive Animal Adventures programme gives you the chance to swim with dolphins, dive with sharks and snorkel on tropical reefs. Shark Bay is the world's largest artificial lagoon system for sharks and provides spectacular underwater and above-water viewing of some of the world's largest marine predators. Two orphaned Polar Bear cubs rescued from the Canadian wilds, Hudson and Nelson, are the star residents of Polar Bear Shores — a meticulously re-constructed Arctic environment.

Location: The Spit, Main Beach.
Opening Hours: Daily (except Christmas Day), 10.00 am – 5.30 pm.
Ph: (07) 5588 2205

Coolangatta

At the Gold Coast's southern end is Coolangatta, almost imperceptibly separated from its "twin" city Tweed Heads by the Queensland border. Atop Point Danger headland is an 18 m high memorial to James Cook crafted from iron ballast jettisoned from Cook's own ship, the *Endeavour*. The area boasts some of the region's best surf and beaches. Places like Kirra, Greenmount and Snapper Rocks are iconic point breaks.

Surfers Paradise

In 1925, keen-eyed entrepreneur James Cavill built a hotel (complete with private zoo) at a seaside village known as Elston and dubbed it Surfers Paradise. In response to Cavill's lobbying, the village later also adopted the exotic title, which succeeded in conjuring up images of a utopian, sun-kissed life and lured swarms of travellers to the Gold Coast.

Broadwater Boating

A busy anchorage for South East Queensland's many boating enthusiasts, the sheltered Broadwater provides safe harbour close to wharfside shops and restaurants as well as easy access to the ocean for diving and offshore game and reef fishing.

Newcastle to Brisbane (via the Tablelands)

If you wish to take the New England Tableland route to Brisbane, there are several options. Each offers its own reward and all bring you within reach of the enchanting wilderness areas east of Armidale. Your choice will be dictated by time and the length of coast you wish to travel before heading inland. Alternatively, some of these regions (such as the Hunter Valley) can be explored as daytrips before continuing up the coast road to Brisbane.

Newcastle to Armidale (via New England Highway)

Leaving the coast at Newcastle, the New England Highway leads north-west through Hunter River country to the township of Branxton. From here Wine Country Drive leads south to the bacchanalian pleasures of the lower Hunter Valley and its "capital" Cessnock. To the north is the Upper Hunter and the heritage towns of Singleton, Muswellbrook, Scone and Murrurindi. Here agriculture, thoroughbred horse studs, and cattle and merino sheep farms combine to create a vibrant rural culture. Several excellent national parks lie just to the west of Singleton, including Yengo and Wollemi (via the Golden Highway and Putty Road) and Barrington Tops (84 km north). The New England Highway continues north to Tamworth, an important rural centre serving one of the nation's biggest pastoral communities.

Port Macquarie to Armidale (via Oxley Highway)

Travelling west from Port Macquarie will bring you to a region of quaint towns with splendid period architecture, pretty rural scenery and old-growth wet eucalypt forests. Aim for an early departure to allow enough time to enjoy the cascading waters of Stoney Creek, Tia and Apsley Falls west of the ranges of Cottan-Bimbang National Park. Tia Falls, 7 km of gravel road south of the highway at the head of a spectacular gorge, is particularly impressive following heavy rain and several short walking tracks access different lookouts. The Oxley Highway continues through sheep and cattle country to the small town of Walcha, before joining the New England Highway 65 km south of Armidale.

Coffs Harbour to Armidale (via Waterfall Way)

Perhaps the most spectacular route to Armidale commences from just south of Coffs Harbour on the Waterfall Way. Depart in the early morning and allow at least six hours for the drive (excluding stopovers). From the Pacific Highway at Raleigh, the road west leads to Bellingen, a fashionable village lined with heritage buildings and an extraordinarily creative regional centre for music, arts and crafts. Ahead the road climbs steeply up the escarpment between Bellinger River National Park and Dorrigo National Park to Dorrigo. Turn right just before town to access the national park and visit the Dorrigo Rainforest Centre, where there is a Skywalk into the rainforest canopy. The park contains many excellent walking tracks and falls. Waterfall Way continues through gorge country past Dorrigo to Ebor and Wollomombi, which (together with Point Lookout between them) offer breathtaking Great Escarpment views. Wollomombi Falls, where the Macleay River plunges 220 m in a single drop, is the highest in New South Wales. Fifteen minutes east of Armidale is Hillgrove, the abandoned ghost of a mining town once powered by one of Australia's first hydro-electric schemes.

Armidale to Brisbane (via New England Highway)

Armidale is the commercial and educational centre of the New England Tableland. The city and its surrounds are resplendent in historic buildings and churches, monuments, museums and well-preserved pastoral homesteads. The region is world-renowned for wool and beef production and there are numerous farm-stay options in the area between here and Guyra for those seeking a true taste of country life. The highway to the Queensland border passes through the towns of Glen Innes, which celebrates its Celtic roots at a major festival each January, and Tenterfield — "Birthplace of Our Nation", where Sir Henry Parkes delivered his famous federation speech in 1889. Over the border en route to Brisbane are the "Granite Belt" towns of Stanthorpe and Warwick, home of Australia's most famous rodeo carnival.

Roadside Encounters

While travelling along the Waterfall Way, you will find opportunities aplenty for wildlife spotting and photography. The national parks that fringe the road abound with native fauna, including one of the most widespread, but reclusive, Australian animals — the Short-beaked Echidna (*below*).

Hunter Valley

The verdant Hunter Valley is the headquarters of the New South Wales wine industry. Many internationally acclaimed vineyards lattice the landscape of Australia's oldest wine-producing region. The valley is broadly divided into seven main centres, including beautiful Cessnock, Pokolbin and Mount View. Other places of interest include Lovedale, Broke Fordwich, Wollombi Valley and Rothbury.

Scone

Scone is a timeless rural town based around agriculture and racehorse breeding. As the second-largest breeding region in the world (after Kentucky, USA), Scone hosts several major festivals each year. A highlight is the much-loved Scone Horse Festival each May, with its parades, rodeo and keenly contested horse races (including the coveted Scone Cup).

Tamworth

This lively rural centre has a deserved reputation as Australia's "Nashville". Each January the town's population of 35,000 more than doubles in celebration of the Southern Hemisphere's biggest country music festival. Many of Australia's brightest country stars, including Troy Cassar-Daley and Kasey Chambers, have cut their musical teeth performing on the streets and stages of Tamworth and been awarded the Festival's highest honour, the Golden Guitar.

The Top National Parks

Consistent rainfall in the high climes between the coast and the tablelands creates a spectacular wilderness of surging rivers, dramatic gorges and cascading waterfalls.

Oxley Wild Rivers National Park

Ph: (02) 6738 9100

Walks in the Park: There are easy walking tracks to all major waterfall viewing points from car parks and campgrounds. The Bicentennial National Trail traverses the park, offering more challenging bushwalking experiences.
Access: The park's major sections and waterfalls can be reached via Walcha (Oxley Highway), Wollomombi or Armidale (Waterfall Way).
Camping: Campgrounds with good facilities are available at Wollomombi Gorge, Apsley Falls (*top, left*), Dangar Falls and Tia Falls. Accommodation is also available at Kunderang East Homestead (via Wollomombi on the Kempsey Road).

Cathedral Rock & Guy Fawkes River National Park

Ph: (02) 6657 2309

Walks in the Park: The huge sculpted boulders and soaring Wedge-tailed Eagles of Cathedral Rock make it a superb area for photography. Follow the Cathedral Rock Track, a leisurely three hour circuit, or take the medium grade Woolpack Rocks Walk. The 115 m stepped Ebor Falls (*left*) are in the adjacent Guy Fawkes River Nature Reserve (there are three excellent viewing platforms).
Access: Cathedral Rock NP — 60 km west of Dorrigo off Waterfall Way. Guy Fawkes River NP — off Waterfall Way just south of Ebor.
Camping: Cathedral Rock NP — basic car-accessible facilities available at Barokee (near Round Mountain Rd) and Native Dog campgrounds (on Guyra–Ebor Rd). Guy Fawkes River NR — limited picnic and camping facilities at Ebor Falls.

Dorrigo National Park

Ph: (02) 6657 2309

Walks in the Park: The elevated boardwalks running through the rainforest are brilliant for birdwatching and photography. The longer Casuarina Falls Walk and the Rosewood Creek Track from the Never Never picnic area provide excellent views of the escarpment, still rainforest pools and various waterfalls, such as Crystal Falls (*left*).
Access: The park turnoff is just before Dorrigo on Waterfall Way.
Camping: There is bush camping only in remote areas of the park.

Girraween National Park

Ph: (07) 4684 5157

Walks in the Park: Girraween (*left*) features precariously balanced granite boulders strewn throughout the park's rocky landscape. Granite Arch is an easy walk through blackbutt forest, while the Pyramid and Balancing Rock Walks are longer and more strenuous hikes but provide exhilarating views.
Access: Turn off the New England Highway 26 km south of Stanthorpe.
Camping: Facilities are available at Bald Rock Creek and Castle Rock (bookings are mandatory).

Armidale

As the cultural heart of the New England Tableland, Armidale has a lively selection of institutions to sate artistic appetites. The New England Regional Art Museum holds 1200 works, including paintings by Tom Roberts and Arthur Streeton. The University of New England also has several interesting collections, including the Museum of Antiquities.

Warwick & Surrounds

Stanthorpe and Warwick are the easternmost towns of Queensland's Darling Downs, famous for beef and agricultural production. Warwick is the state's second-oldest city, and Stanthorpe is its coldest — a fact celebrated during the town's annual Brass Monkey Festival (held in July).

Darling Downs

This inland region of fertile plains and moderate rainfall stretching north from the Queensland border supports a variety of crops including grapevines, sunflowers and wheat. North of Warwick off the New England Highway, the Darling Downs Zoo breeds and exhibits a wide range of exotic animals from Australia, Asia, Africa and South America.

Lamington National Park – A World Heritage Area

Within easy reach of Brisbane and the Gold Coast on Queensland's southern border, Lamington National Park is one of the world's most outstanding subtropical rainforest areas. It is divided into two sections — the Green Mountains region to the west and Binna Burra to the east. Allow approximately 80 minutes to drive between the two sections.

Superb Lyrebird

Lamington National Park – Green Mountain Section

Ph: (07) 5544 0634

Walks in the Park: There is a large choice of walks in this section of Lamington National Park, ranging from 30 minute strolls to multiple day treks. The medium grade Python Rock (1 hour) and Moran Falls Tracks (1.5 hours) climb through rainforest to panoramic views over surrounding peaks and waterfalls. Both walks commence close to the visitor information centre.

Access: Travel 36 km south along Lamington National Park Road from Canungra.

Camping: Green Mountains Campground is a large scale camping site with excellent facilities (including luxurious hot showers). Campervans (but not caravans) are permitted, and bookings are advised at all times. Remote bush camping is possible from February to November but permits are essential. O'Reilly's Rainforest Retreat is a commercial rainforest resort that has been operating at Lamington National Park for over 80 years. It provides a variety of accommodation options, comprehensive facilities and guided rainforest tours (Ph: 1800 688 722 for bookings).

Lamington National Park – Binna Burra Section

Green Catbird

Ph: (07) 5533 3584

Walks in the Park: Many of the walks in this section radiate out from the Border Track. The visitor information centre at the park entrance has self-guided walking maps.

Access: Drive 28 km south of Canungra via Beechmont.

Camping: There are no park-operated campgrounds in this section, but remote bush camping is possible from February to November. Binna Burra Mountain Lodge offers canvas cabins, powered caravan sites and tent spaces (Ph: 1800 074 260).

Lamington National Park Is the world's largest area of protected subtropical rainforest and supports an astonishing variety of flora and fauna.

McPherson Range The cooler temperatures and high rainfall of McPherson Range and Lamington National Park create surroundings in dramatic contrast to the sand and surf of the neighbouring Gold Coast.

Top: Guests at O'Reilly's Rainforest Retreat entertain the local Crimson Rosellas. **Top row, left to right:** Eastern Yellow Robin; Australian King-Parrot; Male Regent Bowerbird. **Centre row, left to right:** Red-necked Wallaby; Brush-tailed Phascogale; Common Brushtail Possum. **Bottom row, left to right:** Freckled Monitor; Carpet Python; Orange-eyed Tree-frog.

A World Class Habitat

The significance of the subtropical rainforests, wet sclerophyll forests and woodland habitats of north-eastern New South Wales and South East Queensland have been recognised with World Heritage-listings. Known as the Gondwana Rainforests of Australia, they include the most extensive areas of subtropical rainforest in the world, large areas of warm temperate rainforest and nearly all of the planet's Antarctic Beech cool temperate rainforest. More than 200 rare or threatened plant and animal species survive here. The rainforests on either side of the border are a particularly rich area for wildlife, with the highest concentration of frog, snake, bird and marsupial species in Australia.

Birds & Birdwatching

The region is home to several bird species that have Gondwanan ancestry (before the Australian land mass separated from South East Asia). These include the Logrunner and thornbills and scrubwrens. Other significant conservation species include the Rufous Scrub-bird, Wompoo Fruit-Dove, Marbled Frogmouth, Paradise Riflebird, Eastern Bristlebird, Black-breasted Button-quail and the Coxen's Fig-Parrot. The vulnerable Albert's Lyrebird, one of only two species of lyrebird in existence, is found exclusively in the border rainforest. From the coastal woodlands to the rainforest and ranges, this is a superb region for birdwatching.

Mammals

Seventy-five species, constituting 30% of Australia's terrestrial mammals, have been identified in this region. These include two monotreme species, over 30 marsupial and bat species and 10 rodent species. The subtropical rainforest and wet sclerophyll forest alone are home to some 30 species of mammal. Some of the mammals that may be sighted include the Parma Wallaby, Yellow-bellied Glider, Hastings River Mouse, Golden-tipped Bat, Short-beaked Echidna, Platypus, Spotted-tailed Quoll (*below*), Red-necked Pademelon and Red-legged Pademelon. Evening walks will reveal numerous species of bandicoots, possums, gliders and flying-foxes.

Reptiles & Amphibians

The Gondwana Rainforests of Australia boast 110 reptile species and 45 frog species. Pythons, tree snakes and Lace Monitors are found even in the more southern areas of the reserve, including Dorrigo National Park. Fat Lace Monitors (which can grow up to 2 m in length) often frequent park camping areas in search of leftover food scraps. Prehistoric-looking Eastern Water and Southern Forest Dragons are also prolific and can be spied around waterways on rocks and the branches of trees. Common frog species include the Pouched Frog, Giant Barred Frogs and Mountain Stream Tree-frog.

BRISBANE

& THE JOURNEY TO CAIRNS

2

Blackback Anemonefish

For two decades during the 19th century, Brisbane was feared as one of Australia's most brutal penal settlements. The cessation of convict transportation and opening of the region to free settlers in 1842 saw the eventual development of Queensland's first city on the banks of the Brisbane River. Since that time, Queensland's capital, Brisbane has evolved into a vibrant, modern city that capitalises on glorious natural surrounds. From here north, the coast is dressed in brilliant hues of azure, green and gold. Names speak for themselves — the Coral Coast and Sunshine Coast conjure images of an aquamarine Arcadia and showcase places where holiday ideals are frequently realised. The World-Heritage-listed Fraser Island, the world's largest sand island is an essential detour. So too the Whitsundays, where palm-fringed beaches melt into an island-studded blue Pacific — a vision almost too travel-brochure-perfect to be true. Some of the most captivating sights lie below the surface — diving and snorkelling the Great Barrier Reef is one of the world's great travel experiences. Between these gems are regional towns rich in local character and alive with the legendary "Queenslander" spirit.

Opposite: The journey to Cairns offers some of the world's most pristine beaches. Here, on Heron Island, early morning walks around the island before breakfast are popular with visitors.

BRISBANE & Surrounds

Brisbane & Surrounds

Top Things to Do

1. Take in the views of Greater Brisbane and the Brisbane River from Mount Coot-tha Lookout.
2. Explore South Bank Parklands and the Queensland Cultural Centre including the Gallery of Modern Art (GoMA).
3. Enjoy the sights along Brisbane's RiverWalk.
4. See the River City by boat — use the CityCat to travel around Brisbane's city reaches.
5. Look for something different at the city's colourful weekend markets.
6. Hike, mountain bike or camp in Brisbane Forest Park.
7. Book a twilight climb of the Story Bridge.
8. Visit Moreton Bay's incredible sand islands.

River Plain

The Greater Brisbane region stretches from western hills, rising to nearly 600 m, east to the coast. The serpentine curve of the Brisbane River shapes the city and its flat floodplain forms its foundations. Brisbane has always been susceptible to severe flooding — in 1974 more than 8000 houses were inundated.

Queensland's Queenslanders

Since the 1820s, "Queenslander" houses have developed in different styles and sizes, but all are designed to maximise air flow and create cool living spaces. Key features of the Queenslander's architectural style are its corrugated iron roof, timber construction and open verandahs. Fine lacework and other details are lovingly restored.

The region now known as Brisbane is the traditional home of the Turrbal and Jagera people, who call it *Mian-jin* or "place shaped like a spike". In 1823, the New South Wales Surveyor-General John Oxley navigated into Moreton Bay, on Queensland's south-east coast seeking a suitable location for the establishment of a new penal settlement. In fact, three escaped convicts from Sydney had already beaten him there and, upon their chance meeting with Oxley, alerted him to the existence of a large river snaking inland from the bay. This subtropical paradise formed the backdrop to a harsh penal outpost until 1842. The region was then opened to adventurous free settlers who, in a remarkably short time helped transform Brisbane's squalid shanty atmosphere into a thriving town. In 1859, Brisbane became the capital of the new colony of Queensland.

City on the Rise

Today Brisbane is one of Australia's fastest growing cities — a sprawling metropolis with a population of nearly two million people (and rising rapidly by the week). Many of these new Brisbanites hail from the southern states, lured by sunshine, a lower cost of living and job opportunities. Shining "Brisvegas", once derided for a perceived lack of urban sophistication, now basks in the glory of booming tourism, business investment and a riverside renaissance that have seen it become one of Australia's most dynamic 21st century cities. Its suburbs spread across a coastal floodplain, reaching east to Moreton Bay and west toward the Great Dividing Range. Close to the city centre are the hills of Mount Coot-tha and Mount Gravatt. The ubiquitous "Queenslander", a distinctively designed timber house set high (usually) on stumps and featuring generous verandahs, give many suburbs their homely charisma.

The best way to come to grips with Brisbane's layout is to observe it from altitude. Mount Coot-tha Lookout provides panoramic views (best in the late afternoon) of the city's expansion across the floodplains to the coast and north to the foothills of the Glasshouse Mountains. One of the first things you will notice is the welcome proportion of green spaces spreading out from the river and surrounding the city. Brisbane's subtropical climate of mild winters and hot, humid summers supplies the ideal conditions for cultivating different plant species.

Mt Coot-tha Lookout

First climbed by European explorers in 1828, Mt Coot-tha is part of the Taylor Range. It was originally dubbed "One Tree Hill" after scrub clearing left a lone gum tree at the top. In 1880, it became a public reserve and was renamed Coot-tha, reflecting the peak's Aboriginal name — "place of honey".

A kiosk was built in 1918 to cater to the large numbers of visitors attracted by the sweeping views of the city and river. Since that time, the kiosk has continually evolved, along with the main lookout platform area. The summit's structures and landscaped gardens are recognised as an important part of Brisbane's heritage. Sir Samuel Griffith Drive leads to the lookout and a series of walking tracks radiate out through the park. The terraced Summit Restaurant is open daily for lunch and dinner.

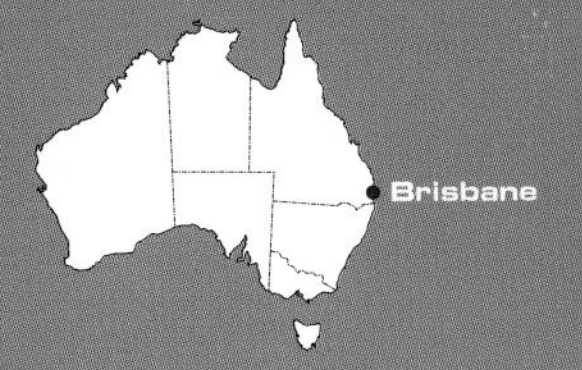

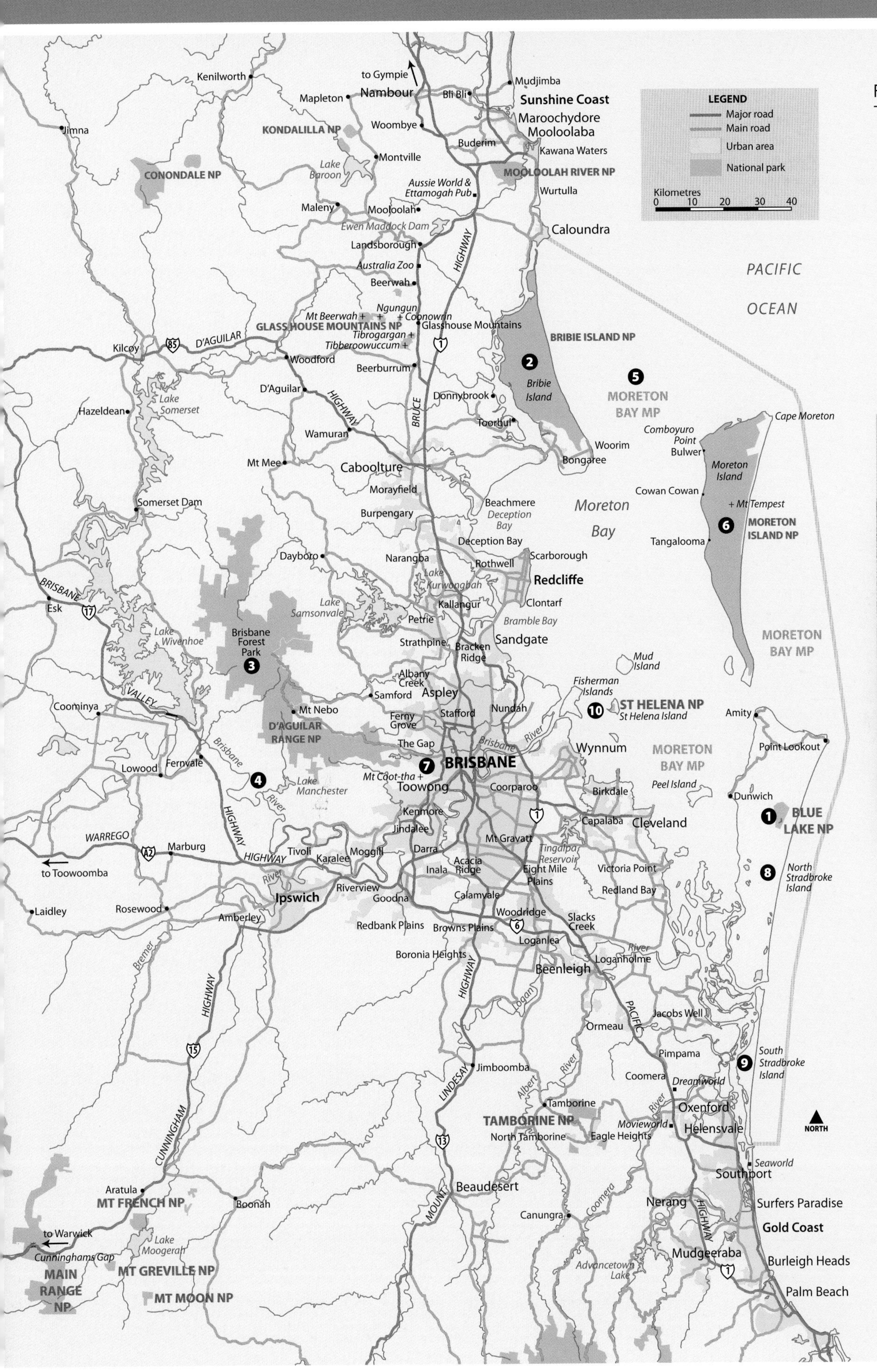

Feature Localities

1. Blue Lake National Park
2. Bribie Island
3. Brisbane Forest Park
4. Brisbane River
5. Moreton Bay Marine Park
6. Moreton Island
7. Mt Coot-tha
8. North Stradbroke Island
9. South Stradbroke Island
10. St Helena Island

The Jacaranda Season

It is a strange quirk that such a parochial city as Brisbane should adopt a South American plant as its floral mascot. However, one glance at New Farm Park (*above*) in spring bloom will quickly convince anyone that the Jacaranda is a tree worth celebrating.

The first specimen was collected in 1864 by Walter Hill, original director of the Brisbane Botanic Gardens. It remained a feature of the City Botanic Gardens until slain by a storm in 1980. *Jacaranda* is an enduring genus — many of the purple-flowered trees in New Farm are around 100-years-old.

Story Bridge

Traversing the Brisbane River from Kangaroo Point to Fortitude Valley is the 777 m long, steel cantilever Story Bridge.

This proud iron-grey structure frames some of the city's best views and stands as a monument to the enterprise and vision of Brisbane citizens during the Great Depression. Upon its opening in 1940, some 600,000 people walked over the river. Its appeal remains today. The experience has been heightened with the addition of a walkway across the upper span of the bridge, providing stunning views by day and night.

Cultural Festivals

Brisbane's abundance of outdoor spaces and its passion for the arts regularly come together in the form of major cultural festivals.

The annual River*festival* runs for ten days at the start of September and is the city's signature event. River*festival* attracts masses of residents and visitors to riverside venues, showcasing theatre, dance, music and visual arts. River*fire*, a massive pyrotechnics display staged on the river during the festival, attracts the biggest crowds of any event held in the city. Its sister celebration, the biennial, multi-arts Brisbane Festival, also fires the community's spirit and imagination.

Brisbane City

Brisbane today is a vibrant blend of colonial heritage and newly defined modernity. Nestled in the river's major bend, the city streets combine pedestrian malls and civic spaces, shopping centres and commercial districts. The CBD radiates from Queen Street Mall, running from historic George Street to the bustle of Edward Street, and is home to the city's largest department stores, retail complexes and landmark arcades. The CBD's fringing suburbs (West End, Spring Hill, New Farm and the Valley) each harness a local style of their own.

Historic Brisbane

Brisbane's sassy postmodern facelift is balanced by a respect for its sandstone heritage. Carefully preserved buildings such as Customs House, with its superb stonemasonry and verdigris copper dome, and the classically inspired City Hall co-exist with their more contemporary incarnations. Get a snapshot of Brisbane history by walking the city's heritage trail, which commences at City Hall (King George Square) and takes in Brisbane's oldest building — the convict-constructed (and powered) Old Mill at Wickham Terrace. The sandstone structure was erected in 1828 to grind flour and maize for the penal colony and later converted to use as a signal station. Many great buildings can be seen along George Street, including Queensland's original Government House near the City Botanic Gardens.

Riverside Renaissance

In and around the CBD, expansive parks and gardens meet the riverfront at numerous points. Along the river, bike trails, walking paths, cafés and markets create an enticing leisure zone. South Bank Parklands is also home to many of the city's major cultural institutions. Facing the river and linked by a common public plaza are the State Library of Queensland, Queensland Art Gallery, Gallery of Modern Art (GoMA) and the Queensland Museum. Next door is the Queensland Performing Arts Centre (QPAC), Brisbane's premier performance venue housing the Lyric and Cremorne Theatres, Playhouse and 1800 seat Concert Hall. All are only a five minute walk from the city across Victoria Bridge. To get a proper sense of the river's central role in Brisbane life, jump aboard a CityCat hydrofoil ferry from South Bank (terminals are located along the riverside's Clem Jones Promenade).

Naldham House Built in the late 1870s and used for over a century as a shipping office, Naldham House is distinguished by its octagonal tower with cupola at the river end.

Queensland Art Gallery The State's largest collection of art (over 11,000 objects) have been exhibited in this contemporary riverside complex since 1982.

Alfresco City

Encouraged by a climate offering year-round sunshine, Brisbane is, at its heart, an outdoor city.

Open city spaces and long riverside paths make outdoor recreation an integral part of Brisbane life. More than 500 km of cycle paths, including the Bicentennial Bikeway, wind through the city.

Following the river's sinuous course from the CBD to Toowong, bikeways and walking paths are one of the city's best means of travel, exercise and discovery — as well as offering some of the best vantage points for photography.

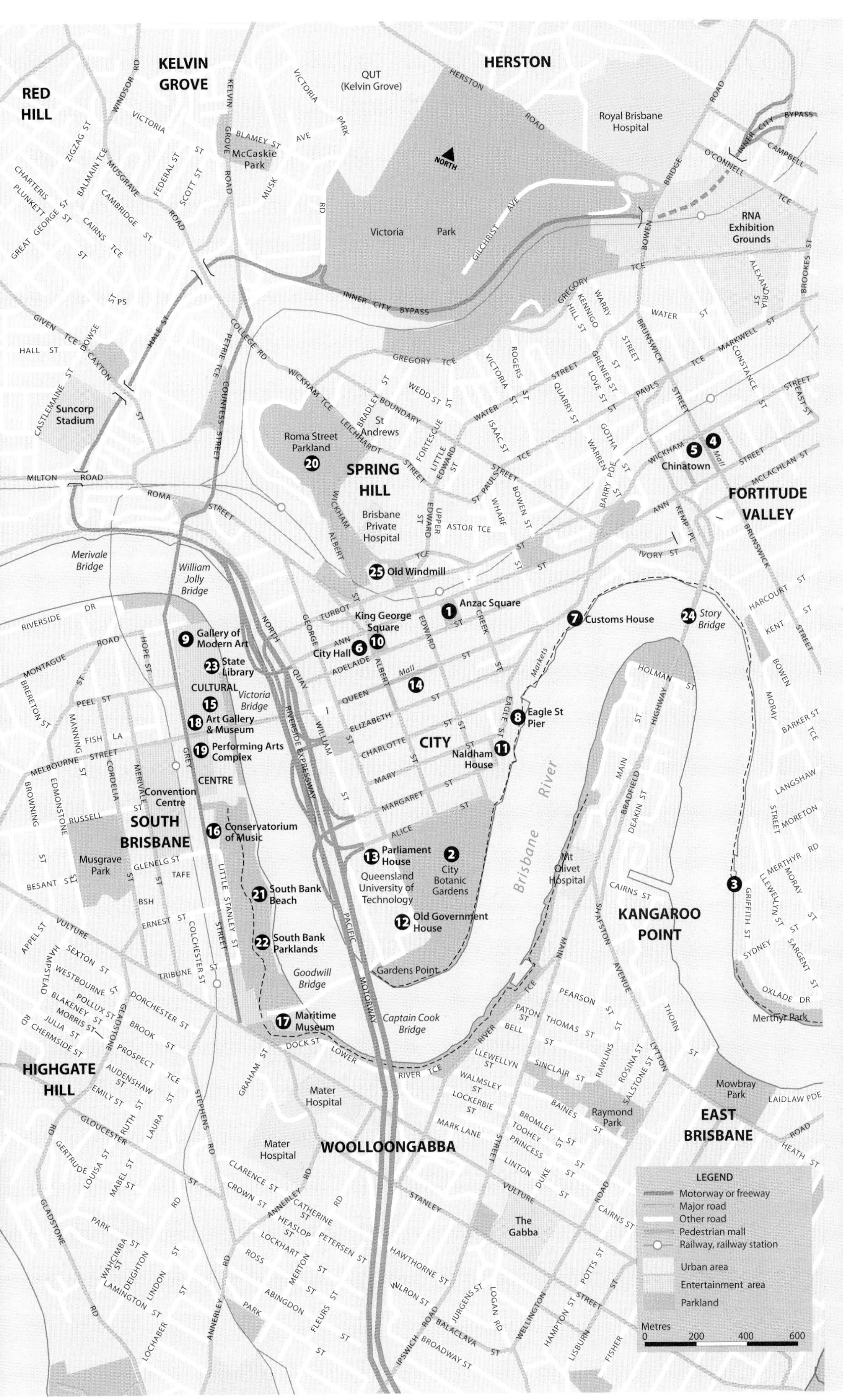

Feature Localities

1 Anzac Square
2 Brisbane Botanic Gardens
3 Brisbane RiverWalk
4 Brunswick Street Mall
5 Chinatown
6 City Hall
7 Customs House
8 Eagle Street Pier
9 Gallery of Modern Art
10 King George Square
11 Naldham House
12 Old Government House
13 Parliament House
14 Queen Street Mall
15 Queensland Art Gallery
16 Queensland Conservatorium of Music
17 Queensland Maritime Museum
18 Queensland Museum
19 Queensland Performing Arts Complex
20 Roma Street Parkland
21 South Bank Beach
22 Southbank Parklands
23 State Library of Queensland
24 Story Bridge
25 Wickham Terrace Windmill

Around Town

Performing Arts Complex

The Cremorne Theatre, Lyric Theatre, Playhouse and Concert Hall (*top*) offer year-round shows (including major comedies, operas, ballets, dramas, singers and musicals). The venue's facilities and location (*above*) are on a par with any in the world.

Queensland Cultural Centre

A pleasant walk from the mall across Victoria Bridge leads to the Queensland Cultural Centre — a campus of modern buildings that form the hub of Brisbane's art world.

The Performing Arts Complex stages a variety of theatrical and artistic extravaganzas in its three theatres. Queensland Art Gallery shows Australian and international works of art. Nearby, the Queensland Museum displays a range of exhibits from the Dinosaur Garden (*below*) to *Mephisto* — the only remaining German tank from WWI.

The Cultural Centre also houses the State Library, Queensland Conservatorium of Music and the Queensland Gallery of Modern Art Australia's largest modern art gallery.

City Hall

Forming the southern boundary of King George Square, Brisbane's City Hall was completed in 1930 and was once the tallest structure in the city. It houses the Brisbane City Council Chambers, the Museum of Brisbane and six classy function rooms. The main auditorium (*right*) with its sky dome ceiling, high galleries and ornate sculpturing exudes a stately elegance that makes it one of Brisbane's finest venues.

King George Square

Located between Ann and Adelaide Streets, Brisbane's main civic square is a flowing space of lawn and stone featuring an eclectic range of statues, sculptures and fountains. Presided over by the impressive clock tower and neo-classical facade of City Hall, the square is a popular meeting place and a traditional venue for public gatherings, exhibitions, and markets.

Anzac Square

Further north along Ann Street is Anzac Square, a popular public space commemorating those fallen in war. Carefully spaced Bottle Trees commemorate the Queensland Light Horse Regiments' efforts during the Boer War.

Overlooking the gardens and walkways are the Shrine and the Eternal Flame of Remembrance. The Shrine's eighteen columns represent the year of peace following WWI (1918). The square is the focal point for Brisbane's annual Anzac Day tributes on April 25.

Fortitude Valley

The lively inner city suburb of Fortitude Valley is renowned for its dining and nightlife. The Valley is located a kilometre from the CBD at the northern end of Ann Street and is also popular for its weekend markets and hip fashion boutiques. Also located in Fortitude Valley is Chinatown — with its own colourful weekend market and a range of well-stocked Asian grocery shops and specialty importers.

Maritime Museum

Featuring a Torres Strait pearl lugger, 19th century naval cannons and a 1940s Royal Australian Navy Frigate, the Queensland Maritime Museum offers visitors a fascinating voyage of discovery. The museum is located on the Brisbane River at the southern end of the Goodwill Bridge at South Bank Parklands.

River Bridges

The Brisbane River is spanned by no less than twelve bridges, from the Gateway Bridge in the east to Centenary Bridge at Jindalee. The major city bridges are the William Jolly Bridge (*far left*), Story Bridge, Victoria Bridge, Captain Cook Bridge and Goodwill Bridge (*left*), a popular cycling and pedestrian link that crosses the river from Gardens Point to South Bank.

Brisbane Markets

You will find occasional and permanent markets in a wide variety of locations throughout the city. At the Riverside Centre on Eagle Street, a weekly Sunday market offers everything from abstract art to zucchinis. South Bank Markets, with over 150 stalls, kicks off on Friday night and runs over the weekend (in Stanley Street Plaza). With live music and oodles of character, the Green Flea Community Market (Davies Park, West End) and Valley Markets (Brunswick St Mall) project a true market vibe.

Brisbane RiverWalk

The RiverWalk is a connecting series of pedestrian pathways running for nearly 20 km along, and above, the Brisbane River. You can access the RiverWalk at many points throughout the city and inner suburbs.

The city to New Farm section provides perhaps the most novel walking experience, featuring an 850 m path elevated on floating pontoons 35 m out from the river bank. The floating walkway rises and falls with the tide, can open to allow boats access to private moorings and boasts spectacular views (and photographic perspectives) back across the river to the Story Bridge and CBD.

From New Farm (and other points along the way) you can board a CityCat for the journey back to the city or continue your RiverWalk exploration through New Farm Park on your way to the Brisbane Powerhouse.

River Boats

Travelling the river by boat is one of the most relaxing ways to see the city and environs. Your options include luxuriating aboard the three-tiered reproduction paddlewheelers *Kookaburra River Queen I & II*, built for Brisbane's World Expo in 1988.

CityCats and ferries are available from 21 terminals positioned throughout the city on both sides of the river. Guides and timetables are available at the Brisbane Ferry Information Centre (Riverside Ferry Terminal, Eagle St, Ph: 13 12 30), onboard the vessels or online (www.translink.com.au).

South Bank Parklands

Created on the Expo '88 site, South Bank Parklands are now the city's premier leisure and recreation destination. This 17 ha river precinct is linked with the Brisbane CBD via the Goodwill and Victoria Bridges and comprises many unique features including a magnificent steel-tentacled arbour draped in vivid bougainvillea (*above*), a hand-carved Nepalese pagoda (*below, centre*) and a 2000 m^2 lifeguard-patrolled artificial beach (*bottom*). Clem Jones Promenade (*below, top*) runs alongside the river and is the setting for public events like the annual River*festival*.

Roma Street Parkland

Labelled the world's largest urban subtropical garden, Roma Street Parkland lies just west of the CBD, directly adjacent to Roma Street Train Station. Composed of distinct precincts displaying a range of plants from rainforest ferns to succulents and coastal species, the garden also features a large lake and performance amphitheatre. The Spectacle Garden (*above*) is one of the parkland's most popular precincts and includes a Topiary Maze, lilly-pillies and an extensive collection of herbs. Barbecues are dotted throughout the grounds and a licensed café is located in the Carriage Shed on Parkland Boulevard. The parklands are accessible by train, bus, car or foot from Albert or Roma Streets.

City Botanic Gardens

Occupying an enviable position adjoining the CBD on the river bend south of Alice Street, the City Botanic Gardens offer both tranquillity and water views. Lose yourself in the Bamboo Grove or visit the Mangrove Boardwalk, a 380 m path constructed of platforms raised above the river mud.

Even if you're not peckish it is worth visiting the delightful City Gardens Cafe, set in a heritage-listed "cottage" originally built as the curator's residence in 1903. On the gardens' fringe are Queensland's Parliament House, the Old Government House and Queensland University of Technology.

Mt Coot-tha Botanic Gardens

The Brisbane Botanic Gardens at Mt Coot-tha are a 52 ha paradise only 7 km from the city centre. Built on this elevated site to escape river flooding, the gardens feature representative plants from every Australian region.

Within the artificial climate of a beguiling Tropical Display Dome (*right*) thrives a spectacular array of tropical plants. A Fern House has also been constructed to display more than 80 different species of fern. Situated near the large Bamboo Grove is a picturesque lagoon — a great habitat for birds, lizards, eels and turtles. Eastern Water Dragons and Sulphur-crested Cockatoos are common sights.

One of the garden's most popular attractions is the Sir Thomas Brisbane Planetarium. Named for the astronomer (and NSW governor) who undertook the first extensive mapping of the southern skies. The planetarium features a Cosmic Skydome theatre offering regular digital presentations and an observatory where you can stargaze with resident astronomers (bookings required). The gardens are open daily from 8 am and entry is via Mt Coot-tha Road. Vehicles are allowed to drive through the gardens on weekdays (roads closed on weekends).

Maiala National Park Part of Brisbane Forest Park in the D'Aguilar Ranges.

Brisbane Forest Park

Phone Ranger: 1300 723 684

Brisbane Forest Park occupies part of the D'Aguilar Range only 12 km north-west of Brisbane. The park protects 28,500 ha of bushland and mountain range and incorporates numerous national parks, state forests and reserves. Most of the park, with Mount Nebo village at its centre, is eucalypt woodland with moist gullies and rock outcrops. There is also superb subtropical palm and vine rainforest, especially at Mount Glorious. There are many picnic areas, walking tracks and lookouts within the park, and regular nature interpretation activities are held. Visit the Brisbane Forest Park Information Centre (60 Mt Nebo Road, The Gap) for further details.

Walks in the Park: A network of graded walking trails from Class 2 (easy) to Class 4 (caution required), leads through the park. At Mount Glorious there is an excellent walk along the Maiala Track to Greene's Falls. Take this walk in the early morning or late afternoon — it can be teeming with bird and reptile fauna. A dusk or evening wander is likely to produce encounters with frogs, geckoes, spiders and possums.

Access: Via Mount Nebo Road. A bus service operates from Brisbane to the park's information centre, but you will require your own transport to access most of the walking trails.

Camping: The Mount Nebo "back country" section provides bush camping (no facilities, walking access only, fees and permits apply). There is also a range of holiday accommodation at Mount Glorious.

Top to bottom: Wivenhoe Outlook; Maiala National Park; Jolly's Lookout.

Lace Monitor

Wild Walks

1. Golden Boulder Track (Class 3) — a 40 minute, 1 km circuit leads past historic gold mines (steep in parts).
2. Morelia Walking Track (Class 4) — a 6 km return track leads from Manorina car park through eucalypt forest to a lookout with superb views of Samford Valley and Moreton Bay.
3. Egernia Circuit (Class 3) — an excellent short (1.5 km) circuit (great for morning birdwatching) near the car park at Jolly's Lookout.
4. Rainforest Circuit (Class 3) — a 1.1 km track leads from Boombana picnic area into subtropical rainforest featuring strangler figs, palms, vines and ferns.

The Wildlife of Brisbane Forest Park

Brisbane Forest Park is an outstanding location for wildlife observation and photography. Both mountain and forest provide rich, diverse habitats. Giant Barred Frogs and Orange-eyed Tree-frogs populate the range tops (particularly after summer rains). Eastern Long-necked Turtles are found in the waterways and Yellow-bellied Gliders and owls are active at night.

Walk-About Creek Wildlife Centre

Within the park, Walk-About Creek Wildlife Centre features recreated natural environments for many native animals, including wallabies, pademelons and a Platypus (*above*), a night house for viewing nocturnal creatures, and a walk-through aviary. The unique Lungfish (*top*) — of ancient ancestry and likely a descendant of the fish which evolved into land animals — is here too. It is native to South-East Queensland's Mary and Burnett Rivers, and has been introduced into the Brisbane River (open daily, 9 am – 4.30 pm).

Moreton Bay & Islands

Nineteen kilometres east of Brisbane's CBD, the Brisbane River empties into the broad, shallow basin of Moreton Bay. The region was originally home to many Aboriginal clans and was first mapped by maritime explorer Matthew Flinders in 1799. Flinders' brief but volatile encounter with the Indigenous residents of Bribie Island is memorialised in the name Skirmish Point. Moreton Bay stretches 160 km south from Caloundra to the Gold Coast and is punctuated by over 360 islands. Its calm waters are the result of the presence of two of the world's largest sand islands, Moreton Island and North Stradbroke Island, whose protective bulk buffer the mainland from the swells of the Pacific Ocean. The bay and islands have also created an important ecological environment where Humpback Whales, Bottlenose Dolphins, Dugongs and many other marine species thrive in safety.

The coastal suburbs along the Moreton Bay shoreline served as holiday retreats as far back as the late 19th century. Manly and Wynnum were especially popular (and remain so to this day). Visit the "Great Wall of Manly" (in Falcon Street), built by workers during the Great Depression and featuring moulded concrete images of human faces and native animals. Survey the bay from atop Manly Hill before leaving shore to explore the islands.

Major Islands & Access

The forests, lakes, swamps and beaches of Moreton Island are an astonishingly rich habitat and support a large variety of native flora and fauna. Migrating wading birds flock to the island's sandflats between September and April, and nesting Green and Loggerhead Turtles occasionally come ashore in summer. The adjacent bay waters and reefs (a paradise for divers and snorkellers) are protected within Moreton Bay Marine Park.

There are three small settlements on Moreton (vehicle access is by 4WD track only and permits are required) and a resort at Tangalooma. A proper exploration of the island's natural attractions will take at least several days and national park campgrounds with good facilities are available in a variety of locations, including specific sites along the beach. Other accommodation and supplies are available at Kooringal (south-east tip) and Bulwer (on the north-west coast).

Nearby North Stradbroke Island is more tourist-oriented but development has had minimal impact upon the island's wilder residents, which include birds-of-prey like high-wheeling Brahminy Kites, Ospreys and White-bellied Sea-Eagles. A popular surfing and fishing spot, "Straddie" is serviced by vehicular ferries and water taxis operating from Cleveland.

Forty-five minutes cruise from Manly Harbour is St Helena Island, an infamous penal colony from 1867 to 1932. Tours are available of the extensive prison ruins, including the stockade, workshops and bakery. Once covered by vine forests the island is now a national park, with an intriguing mix of remnant gardens, moor-like lawns and former prison crops.

Bay of Plenty

The luminous blue, resource-rich waters of *Quandamooka* (Moreton Bay) are a sanctuary that long sustained the coastal Aborigines prior to European settlement. During the Great Depression, many of Brisbane's jobless took refuge in the region, building shelters and surviving off the bay's natural harvest.

Diving & Snorkelling

Moreton Bay's appeal goes beyond its sparkling surface. On Moreton Island, locations such as the Tangalooma Wrecks (*above*), an artificial reef of fifteen scuttled vessels, teems with sealife and are a popular diving and snorkelling site.

Backyard Boating

Moreton Bay's natural and artificial harbours provide mooring for thousands of recreational boats and fishing fleets. On the mainland, bayside suburbs like Raby Bay (*above*) provide deepwater moorings for luxury vessels. Many of the bay's islands have also undergone residential and resort development.

Safe Harbour

Although Moreton Island was once a major whaling station, the surrounding bay is now a safe resting place for migrating Humpback Whales on their journey north each year.

The bay is also home to a large population of wild Bottlenose Dolphins, inquisitive creatures that will approach close to shore to investigate humans. At Tangalooma Resort on Moreton Island, visitors learn about and interact with the dolphins in their natural environment (*top right*). The bay and its crucial seagrass beds also nurture a significant Dugong population.

However, not all of the bay's residents enjoy human interaction. The barnacled disguise of the stonefish (*bottom right*), sometimes seen in the sandy shallows and mudflats, camouflages a highly venomous (and excruciating) sting. Its thirteen hidden spines can penetrate the soles of shoes.

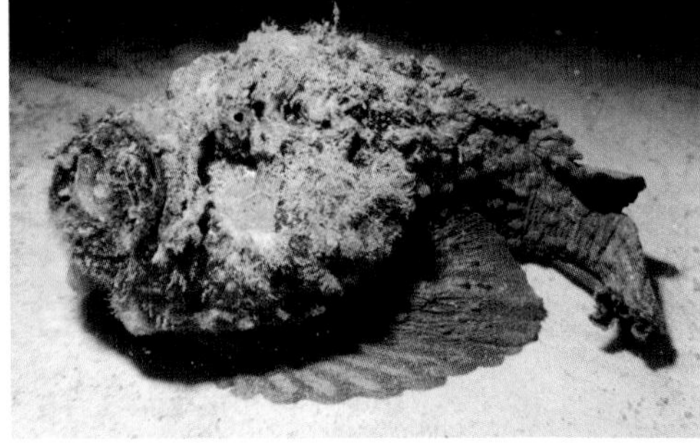

Moreton Island National Park

Phone Ranger: (07) 3408 2710

Moreton Island, or *Moorgumpin* in the language of the local Ngugi people, is 37 km long with a total area of 17,000 ha. At its centre is Mount Tempest, a 280 m high dune recognised as the world's tallest permanent coastal sandhill. Even in busy holiday periods, the island's size makes it easy to find solitude, except, of course, for the constant company of any of about 180 bird species. The distinctive Cape Moreton Lighthouse, 8 km from Bulwer, was the first built in Queensland (erected in 1857).

Walks in the Park: There are many walking trails leading you through the varied landscapes. Depending on your energy levels, try either the trudge up Little Sandhills or Big Sandhills. There are also numerous freshwater lakes — including Blue Lagoon, south of Cape Moreton, which offers superb swimming in clear water surrounded by fine white sand (if you prefer your sand in other hues, a coloured "desert" lies behind Tangalooma). Some tours also offer the chance to test your sandboarding and tobogganing skills on some of Australia's steepest dunes.

Access: Regular ferry services operate to Moreton Island and the journey takes approximately two hours. If you wish to take your car, the *Micat* vehicular ferry departs from Lytton for Tangalooma (Ph: (07) 3903 3333) and the *Combie Trader II* travels to Bulwer from Scarborough (Ph: (07) 3203 6399). Passenger-only ferries run from Holt Street in Pinkenba and Redlands Point.

Camping: Camping is available at Blue Lagoon, North Point, Ben-Ewa, The Wrecks or Comboyuro as well as specific sites along the beach. Check with rangers before camping along the beach. The Christmas, New Year and Easter holiday periods are extremely busy. Supplies are available at the settlements of Bulwer and Kooringal. Freshwater is available at the Big Sandhills (western beach), Rous Battery Track (eastern beach), North Point and the campgrounds at Blue Lagoon, North Point, Eagers Creek, Comboyuro Point, The Wrecks and Ben-Ewa. Boil water before drinking.

Left to right: Built in 1857, the Cape Moreton Lighthouse is the oldest operating lighthouse in Queensland; Backpackers hike along the beach below Cape Moreton, Moreton Island.

North & South Stradbroke Islands

A single island when first sighted by James Cook, tidal erosion eventually divided North and South Stradbroke Islands in 1896. Both are a hybrid of protected park areas, and residential and resort development. Blue Lake National Park on North Stradbroke features a superb freshwater lake of crystal blue accessed by a walking trail through wallum (banksia) woodlands.

Bribie Island

The northernmost island of Moreton Bay can be reached by road bridge near Ningi. Bribie Island Recreation Area occupies much of the island and a large range of coastal camping experiences are possible. Bribie has excellent walking, swimming and fishing. The southern end has been developed for residential and holiday accommodation, including caravan parks.

BRISBANE to Mount Isa

While the majority of Queensland's tourism promotion spruiks its spectacular coastal attractions, there is just as much (some might even say more) colour and character to be found in the State's outback. A journey from Brisbane north-west along the Warrego and Matilda Highways may not offer much by way of beaches or snorkelling, but you'll enjoy just as many golden sunsets and fishy tales along the way. And there are still reefs to be found — the mining centres of Cloncurry and Mount Isa were built on them.

Brisbane to Matilda Highway

Around 130 km west of Brisbane is the Darling Downs capital of Toowoomba. Clinging to the edge of the Great Dividing Range 700 m above sea level, the "Garden City" is renowned for its picturesque landscapes and annual Carnival of Flowers (first week of September). The city also features many fine buildings and art galleries. Pause to admire the restored Art Deco Empire Theatre in Neil Street, the Italian Renaissance style railway station or the views over Table Top Mountain and the fertile Lockyer Valley from Picnic Point parklands.

From Toowoomba, the Warrego Highway continues north-west through Dalby and Chinchilla to Roma. Roma's early days of oil and gas exploration are remembered by a display of old rigs and relics at the Big Rig Complex but the town is now more famous for staging the biggest cattle sales in the Southern Hemisphere. The town of Mitchell (87 km west of Roma) is named for the explorer Thomas Mitchell who first surveyed this region. Thirty minutes north of town (on Forest Vale Road), the Major Mitchell campsite and monument on the Maranoa River commemorates the spot where his expedition rested. An hour or so further west is Morven, where you will need to choose between travelling the slightly longer route via Charleville, or the more direct road to the Matilda Highway at Augathella.

Toowoomba Toowoomba's annual Carnival of Flowers celebrates its status as Queensland's, "Garden City".

Dalby The distinctive pot-bellied forms of Bottle Trees are a feature along the town streets of Dalby and Roma.

Classic Outback Buildings

The distinctive colonial flavour of the hotels, railway stations and public buildings of Queensland's outback towns is one of the most interesting facets of travelling the region. Broad timber verandahs, like those at the School of Arts Hotel in Roma (*above*), provide shelter from the often relentless sun and occasional torrential rains that typify Australia's volatile outback climate. These classic outback structures make brilliant photographic subjects and provide a refreshing break from the long haul across open highway.

Brisbane to Mount Isa
Top Things to Do

1. Check out the spring Carnival of Flowers in Queensland's, "Garden City", Toowoomba.
2. Visit explorer Thomas Mitchell's old campsite on the Maranoa River, near Mitchell.
3. Stay on a working cattle station.
4. Tour the historic outback towns of Charleville, Longreach and Cloncurry.
5. Visit the Australian Stockman's Hall of Fame and Qantas Outback Museum in Longreach.
6. Take an underground mine tour in Mount Isa.
7. Marvel at the fossilised dinosaur stampede at Lark Quarry Conservation Park.
8. Explore the stark expanse of Simpson Desert National Park.
9. Savour a cold beer at the Birdsville Hotel.

Mustering

Since Thomas Mitchell first explored these parts in 1845 cattle grazing has become a major commercial industry. Queensland now accounts for over 45% of Australia's cattle population. Take the opportunity to tour (or stay on) one of the many working cattle stations in the region.

Outback Scenes

The Queensland outback offers a surprising mix of scenery — from desert in the south through flooding Channel Country and the vast cattle stations west of the Darling Downs to the ore-rich hills of Mount Isa.

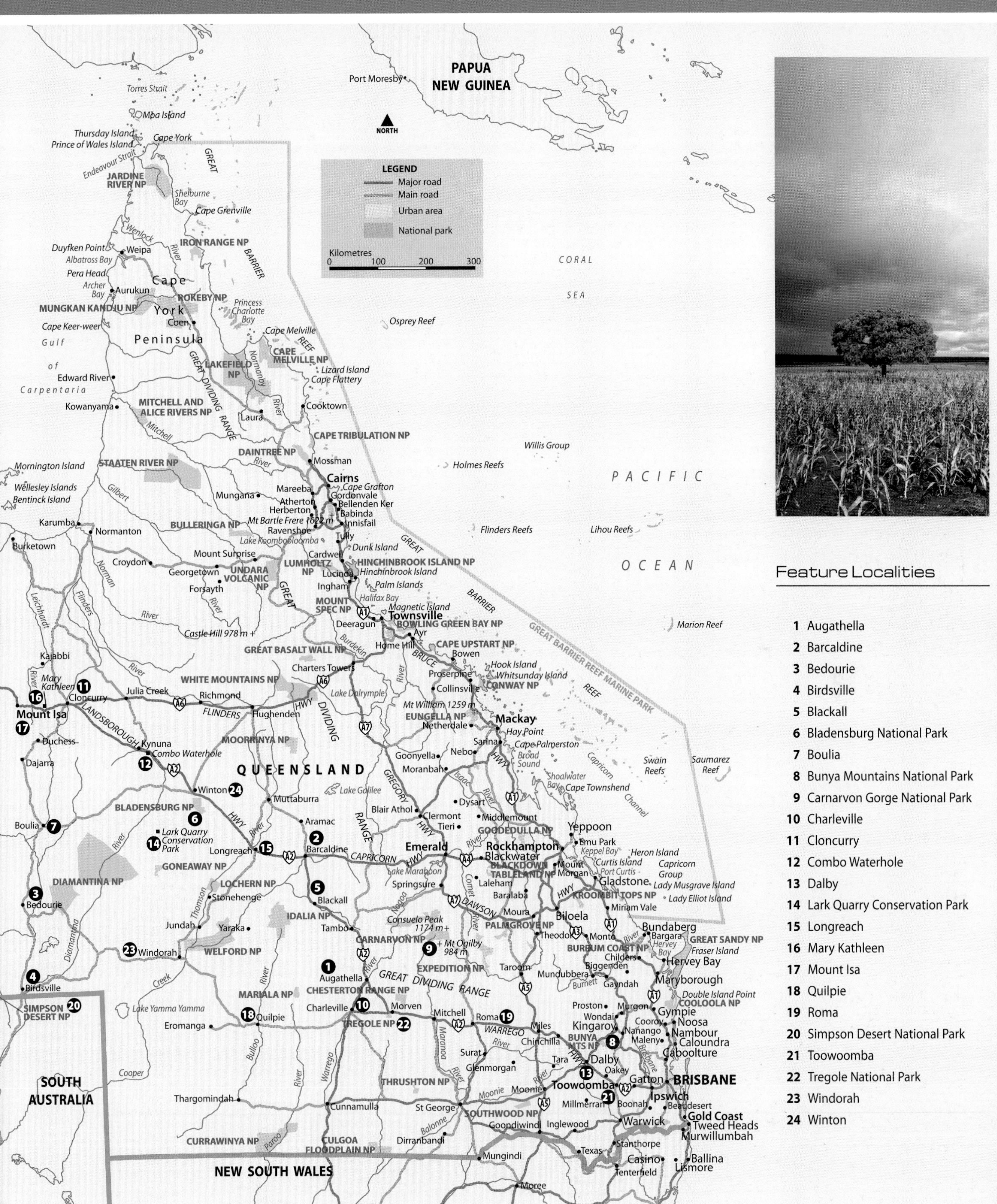

Feature Localities

1 Augathella
2 Barcaldine
3 Bedourie
4 Birdsville
5 Blackall
6 Bladensburg National Park
7 Boulia
8 Bunya Mountains National Park
9 Carnarvon Gorge National Park
10 Charleville
11 Cloncurry
12 Combo Waterhole
13 Dalby
14 Lark Quarry Conservation Park
15 Longreach
16 Mary Kathleen
17 Mount Isa
18 Quilpie
19 Roma
20 Simpson Desert National Park
21 Toowoomba
22 Tregole National Park
23 Windorah
24 Winton

Australian Stockman's Hall of Fame

One of rural Australia's biggest museums and tourist attractions, the Australian Stockman's Hall of Fame (at Longreach) overflows with pioneer memorabilia, multimedia exhibits and Aboriginal artefacts. Allow several hours to explore the multitude of displays on show (Ph: (07) 4658 2166, open daily from 9 am – 5 pm).

Qantas Outback Museum

The Qantas Founders' Outback Museum is located in the original Qantas Hangar at Longreach airport (adjacent to the Australian Stockman's Hall of Fame). See original Qantas mail and passenger planes as well as taking a "wing walking" tour of a retired 747 VH-EBQ jumbo jet (Ph: (07) 4658 3737, open daily from 9 am – 5 pm).

Charleville

Located in the heart of "Mulga Country", historic Charleville was once a centre for the building of Cobb & Co. coaches. The town's captive Bilby breeding program plays an important role in protecting the endangered marsupial (*below*). "Meet a Bilby" tours are available from April to October (National Parks & Wildlife Service, Ph: (07) 4654 1255).

Charleville to Mount Isa

(via the Matilda Highway)

Charleville, the largest of south-west Queensland's towns is famed as the departure point for the very first mail flight of Qantas airlines, which left for Cloncurry in 1922. The clear outback skies also make it a perfect location for the Cosmos Centre, an observatory and interactive exhibition devoted to stargazing (Qantas Drive, Ph: (07) 4654 7771). The Great Matilda Camel Races and Festival are staged at Charleville each July and, in true outback style, the action puts unlikely contestants to the test with both goat and yabby races. Look for the Steiger Vortex Gun in the Bicentennial Park at the southern entry to town, the legacy of a bizarre rainmaking experiment staged in Charleville in 1902.

Augathella, on the road north, has taken as its mascot the Meat Ant — an omnivorous and prolific local insect you are likely to meet while picnicking on the Warrego River. Despite its name, which means "river of sand", the waterway once sustained thirsty droving teams and has, on occasion, caused major floods in Augathella and Charleville. From here, the Matilda Highway traces a north-west route through cattle and sheep stations to Blackall and Barcaldine. If you've ever wondered just where the "black stump" is, you'll find it in the main street of Blackall. Although the stump itself is a replica and more brown than black, the original was used by surveyors in 1887 as a sturdy base for their measuring equipment, giving rise to the colloquial description of a remote place — "beyond the black stump".

In Spring, Barcaldine's wide streets are attractively enhanced by bougainvillea gardens and wildflowers but, like Blackall, it is a tree that really put the town on the map. In 1891, striking shearers gathered in the shade of an old Ghost Gum outside the railway station to protest their working conditions. The event became known as the "Great Shearer's Strike" and is considered to have laid the foundations for the Australian Labor Party. The Australian Workers Heritage Centre in Ash Street was built to mark the centenary of the strike, and in 2007 the "Tree of Knowledge" (as the famous eucalypt is known) was uprooted for preservation and transformed into a permanent monument.

Longreach to Mount Isa

Once no more than a large waterhole on the Thomson River, Longreach grew rapidly after the continuation of the rail line from Barcaldine and is now a major commercial centre and home to the Australian Stockman's Hall of Fame and Qantas Founders' Outback Museum.

Further north in "Dinosaur Country", Winton claims strong links with Australia's unofficial national anthem, *Waltzing Matilda*. Seventeen kilometres to the town's south is Bladensburg National Park, a region of sandstone ranges and flat-topped mesas featuring views of the surrounding grass plains. The park has a huge variety of wildlife including Brolgas, Emus, wallaroos and dunnarts (marsupial mice). Further south is one of Australia's oldest opal mining areas, with operations focused on the (aptly named) town of Opalton. After chequered beginnings, Cloncurry grew to become the biggest (and wildest) town in the Queensland outback. At the turn of the century it was also known as a "Ghantown" after its large population of Afghan camel drivers. The fascinating Mary Kathleen Memorial Park includes original town buildings and more than 18,000 mineral exhibits. Between Cloncurry and Mount Isa the landscape is dotted with spinifex and Ghost Gums.

Mount Isa is one of the world's great mining cities. Mount Isa Mine is the largest underground mine in Australia with 1000 km of tunnels burrowing some 1800 m into the rock. Lead and silver were discovered here in 1923 and it has since become one of the planet's most important ore-producing areas with a daily output of 30,000 tonnes. Underground mine tours are available, or else visit the extensive Outback at Isa complex (19 Marian Street, Ph: 1300 659 660) to get a first-hand experience of mining life.

Tree of Knowledge & Water of Life

Before it was uprooted for permanent preservation, the Tree of Knowledge (*left*) owed its survival to a vast subterranean water supply known as the Great Artesian Basin, which stretches from Lake Eyre to Cape York and east to the Great Dividing Range. The basin underlies over one-fifth of the continent and its groundwater is the life blood of inland Australia.

A Song Is Born

Poet A B "Banjo" Paterson wrote the lyrics to Australia's unofficial national anthem, *Waltzing Matilda* while on a visit to Dagworth Station, north-west of Winton, in 1895.

Combo Waterhole (south of the highway near Kynuna) is believed to have been the site of the incident that inspired the song. It describes the misfortunes of an itinerant 1890s shearer who leapt into a "billabong" (waterhole) to avoid capture by police following the burning down of a woolshed on Dagworth Station. A museum complex devoted to the song and a statue of the "jolly swagman" are located in Elderslie Street, Winton.

Land of the Giants

Australia's once-largest dinosaur was discovered in 1999 when a grazier near Winton hit a bump on his quad bike. Further investigations showed the bump to be part of the 100-million-year-old femur bone of a giant saurapod palaeontologists dubbed "Elliot". Since then, even larger specimens have been found. The area around Winton is rich territory for dino-hunters. At Lark Quarry Conservation Park, (113 km south-west of town on the Jundah Road) you can view an amazing trail of 95-million-year-old footprints — a permanent imprint of a stampede of small ornithopods and theropods fleeing a large and hungry carnosaur (Ph: (07) 4657 1466).

Cloncurry The scenic drive from Cloncurry is best undertaken either early in the morning or late in the afternoon when the outback hues are at their richest.

Lake Moondarra A popular recreation site east of Mount Isa.

Clockwise from top left: Mount Isa Mine, with the 270 m exhaust stack towering above the lead smelter; Central Hotel, Cloncurry; Aboriginal rock art near Mount Isa; Outback at Isa mining displays.

Mining Country – Cloncurry to Mount Isa

Fortuitous mineral strikes are responsible for much of the growth in towns of Queensland's far north-west. The discovery of copper near Cloncurry in 1867 by a pastoralist named Ernest Henry gave rise to a rich mineral boom that has continued into the 21st century. Close to Mount Isa is the abandoned uranium mining township of Mary Kathleen, whose underground riches were discovered in 1954 by a prospector whose vehicle had broken down in a nearby creek bed.

About 10% of Mount Isa's population of 23,500 people is employed by the town's massive silver, copper, lead and zinc mine. Located on the Leichhardt River and surrounded by ruddy, spinifex-covered hills, the town is north-west Queensland's commercial and industrial centre.

The region was first inhabited by the Kalkadoon people. Today their descendants host tours retelling their history at the Kalkadoon Tribal Centre (in Centenary Park, Marian Street). The region's ancient history is illuminated by displays and exhibits at the Riversleigh Fossil Centre in the Outback at Isa complex.

The Amazing Outback

The journey from Birdsville to Mount Isa may appear somewhat bereft of attractions on a map but it is an adventure full of surprises. This is true outback Australia, coloured by unlikely characters in dusty, historic pubs (like Bedourie's Royal Hotel) regaling sceptical travellers with local legends such as the mystery of the Min Min Light.

The Desert Comes to Life

The rains that make all the rivers run in the Channel Country around Windorah also transform the red sands and rocky gibber plains of south-western Queensland. Dormant desert wildflowers bloom almost instantaneously after even the smallest amount of precipitation. Some species remain visible for only hours, others endure for weeks or even months. These hardy natives are the desert's true survivors.

Charleville to Mount Isa (via Birdsville)

If you have plenty of time, a reliable vehicle and want to experience one of Australia's most absorbing outback journeys, you can divert west from Charleville to Birdsville then north to Mount Isa via Bedourie and Boulia. The payoff is in experiencing the real outback and Birdsville itself — a one pub pioneer town on the desert edge that roars to life during the famous Birdsville Races held on the first Saturday of September each year (*see box below*).

The route to Birdsville follows the old railway line 210 km west from Charleville to Quilpie before heading north-west to Windorah and the unsealed Birdsville Developmental Road. The development of the railway from Charleville to Quilpie in 1917 created several trading post towns around stations and sidings, which now resemble ghost towns rising out of the dusty red earth. Cooladdi, 90 km west of Charleville, has a general store and motel known as the Cooladdi Foxtrap (those trustworthy enough may be enlightened with the origins of the name). Camping, fishing and swimming is also possible on nearby Quilberry Creek. Further down the line at Cheepie, 74 km from Quilpie, there is also a pleasant creek but the town that once boasted a police station, butcher shop, hotel and bakery now has a population of just two. Quilpie is set on the banks of the Bulloo River in the midst of western Queensland's famous Channel Country. Internationally known for its boulder opal mining industry (*see facing page*), it is surrounded by some of the State's oldest pastoral districts.

The 248 km trek to Windorah along the Diamantina Developmental Road is notable for its lack of towns, but several stations in the area offer farmstay accommodation. Windorah derives from an Aboriginal word meaning "big fish" and if you manage to land a fat Yellowbelly from one of the many channels of Cooper Creek you'll understand why (*see facing page*). A deep current of outback history runs through Windorah and several walks around the district's buildings and ruins provide insights to its early development. Take the 12 km nature drive or head out west to see and photograph mountainous red sandhills.

The final leg of the journey to Birdsville (*see box below*) involves a 277 km dawdle through gibber plains down the Birdsville Developmental Road. Be wary of animals (including cattle) wandering on to the track at any time. Break the journey with a stop at the tiny "township" of Betoota (population zero) if you like, but don't try to buy a drink at the pub — it closed in 1987. Both Betoota and Birdsville were established in the 19th century as border "toll" towns exacting taxes from passing drovers — you won't need to fork out any cash today as the laws were abolished with federation, consigning the towns to economic doom.

Birdsville to Mount Isa

The trip from Birdsville to Mount Isa is punctuated by only three main towns — Bedourie, Boulia and Dajarra. Bedourie lies on Eyre Creek and was once an important drover's watering stop — the historic Royal Hotel at Bedourie's heart has traded continuously since 1886. There is also a motel, caravan park and an aquatic centre, which offers the delightfully unexpected relief of a 22-person therapeutic spa fed by an artesian bore (Herbert Street). Boulia, on the Burke River, is bigger and has even stranger attractions. The irregular appearance of the mysterious Min Min Light (*see above left*) has perplexed residents and visitors for nearly a century. The town is the venue for the Boulia Camel Races, staged annually on the third Friday of July. While in Boulia, visit the Old Stone House Museum (cnr Pituri & Hamilton Sts), which exhibits a collection of fossils, photographs and some unusual Aboriginal artefacts. Dajarra, 155 km south of Mount Isa, was once a huge cattle trucking depot that served drovers from as far afield as Western Australia and is rich in Aboriginal heritage.

Birdsville

If one town has come to symbolise the isolation of Australia's outback it is Birdsville. Isolated it may be, but boring it ain't. Each September, 6000 visitors from far and wide arrive for the running of the Birdsville Cup. And to enjoy the associated entertainment, including Fred Brophy's traditional tent boxing troupe. Just east of town on the Diamantina River is a Coolabah tree reputed to have been marked by explorers Burke and Wills on their ill-fated trek north. Take your camera 40 km west to the biggest dune in the Simpson Desert — *Nappanerica* or "Big Red".

Simpson Desert National Park

Phone Ranger: (07) 4656 3272

Running north from the South Australian border along the Northern Territory–Queensland border is Queensland's biggest national park. It protects one of the world's largest (and youngest) parallel dune deserts. The reddish dunes rise to 20 m high and lie around 1 km apart. The regions between the dunes are characterised by gibber-ironstone flats, spinifex grass, claypans, saltpans and sand drifts.

Walks/Drives in the Park: There are no walking tracks in the park. Visitors should remain close to their cars at all times and walking any distance is not advised. Instead, follow the self-guided drive with ten signposted sites on the track from the eastern park boundary to Poeppels Corner.

Access: A 4WD vehicle is required. Travel 165 km west from Birdsville on the QAA line. Queensland Parks and Wildlife Service advise that travellers should only visit Simpson Desert National Park during April to October as roads are impassable during the wet. Only experienced, self-sufficient visitors should explore the Simpson Desert. Leave a copy of your travel plans (including precise time of return) with your family or a responsible authority. Travel in two-vehicle parties and stay on the track. Take a two-way radio and plenty of food, water, fuel and spare parts for your vehicle. Be prepared for extremely hot days and freezing nights.

Camping: No camping facilities but visitors may bush camp within 500 m of the QAA line.

Simpson Desert The visually arresting colours and textures of the Simpson Desert. In photos its captivating beauty belies an extremely remote and inhospitable environment of searing temperatures, dust storms and freezing nights. Despite this, over 180 bird species survive in the desert — from small wrens to large birds-of-prey. Reptiles also make their homes here, as does the Mulgara — a small, fast marsupial carnivore and vulnerable native species.

Quilpie

Quilpie is the largest producer of boulder opal in the world. Much of the town's boulder opal is exported but there are three opal shops in the main street of Quilpie, as well as an unusual opal altar at the local church. Aside from its rich lode of gems, Quilpie is an unusually multi-faceted outback town. Its main street is a gallery of public murals and sculpture. The signposted Bulloo River Walk is a great way to discover the birdlife and flora of the area. Nearby Lake Houdraman (6.5 km north) is a popular picnicking, swimming and fishing spot. Baldy Top Hill Lookout is a fine place to photograph the region, particularly at sunrise or sunset.

Fishing the Channels

Cooper Creek's remarkable network of channels and creeks supports a huge variety of terrestrial, avian and aquatic wildlife and, in times of flood, can flow all the way to Lake Eyre in South Australia (arriving nine to ten months after the deluge). The Channel Country is reputed to be the only place in the world where two rivers (Thomson and Barcoo) merge to become a creek. Fishing the channels is remarkably rewarding and the main species caught include Yellowbelly (*below*), Freshwater Catfish and yabbies. The fish survive times of drought by huddling in the few remaining permanent waterholes.

Australian King-Parrot

A Detour North from Dalby – Bunya Mountains National Park

Phone Ranger: (07) 4668 3127

Bunya Mountains has been recognised as a unique mountain retreat since the 1860s and was the first large area of Queensland to be declared a national park (in 1908). Mountain peaks rise to 1100 m in height and the national park is covered in no fewer than nine different types of rainforest. Skyscraping Bunya Pines, trees whose ancestry extends back to before the dinosaurs, are found on the upper slopes and range top. Bottle Trees are spread throughout the vine thickets below. An astonishing 119 species of native grass (growing in clearings known locally as "balds") are also found here. Until the late 19th century, the Bunya Mountains region was an important meeting, hunting and feasting ground for Aborigines. Large gatherings of peoples from as far afield as Wide Bay and Northern New South Wales would seasonally congregate for the *bonyi bonyi* festival, at which the delectable seeds of the Bunya Pine were harvested.

This precious environment is a refuge for wildlife and supports 120 bird species and a profusion of mammals, frogs and reptiles. Over 30 rare and threatened species found in the park include Sooty Owls, Powerful Owls, Black-breasted Button-quails and a number of mammals. Mountain Brushtail Possums and the region's own ringtail possums feed on the rich fruits, flowers and leaves of forest trees, including Hoop Pine seeds.

Walks in the Park: There are 35 km of walking trails in the park of varying difficulty, many of which commence (and/or end) at the various camping areas. From Dandabah, there is an easy 500 m loop winding through Bunya Pine forest. The longer Scenic Circuit (4 km return) takes in rock pools and Festoon and Tim Shea Falls, and leads to superb South Burnett views from Pine Gorge Lookout. There are a series of walks along the western cliffs near the Westcott camping area, some of which can be abbreviated by arranging to leave a car or be picked up at road exit points. Contact park office for further walk details.

Access: From Dalby, travel 25 km to Kaimkillenbun and then 30 km to Bunya Mountains. All roads are sealed, but caravans and trailers are not recommended on this steep and winding road into the mountains.

Camping: There are three camping areas — Dandabah, Westcott and Burton's Well. Dandabah has coin-operated barbecues, hot showers and toilets. Westcott and Burton's Well are suitable for tents only and have toilets and fireplaces. Westcott has no showers, but Burton's Well has "boil your own water" bush showers. Bookings are advised for holiday periods (Ph: 13 13 04). A wide variety of accommodation options are available in the district surrounding the park (contact South Burnett Visitor Information Centre, (Kingaroy, Ph: (07) 4162 6272).

Clockwise from top left: Bunya Pine silhouetted by the setting sun, Bunya Mountains National Park; Bottle Tree, Bunya Mountains; Native grasses abound in Bunya Mountains National Park, with nearly 120 different species.

Clockwise from top left: Bunya Mountains form a refuge for Red-necked Wallabies; Crimson Rosellas frequent the camping areas; Dense areas of rainforest and eucalypt forest cover the lower ranges.

Clockwise from top: Carnarvon Creek meanders below surrounding gorge faces; Remnant rainforest at Carnarvon Gorge gives the area a prehistoric atmosphere; White sandstone cliffs are a feature of Carnarvon Gorge National Park.

Clockwise from top: Aboriginal rock art (such as these hand stencils) is an important cultural feature of Carnarvon Gorge National Park; The serenity of the Moss Garden; The Amphitheatre is known for its beautiful acoustics.

A Detour North from Roma – Carnarvon Gorge National Park

Phone Ranger: (07) 4984 4505

Carnarvon Gorge National Park is like a sampler of the best aspects of national parks found anywhere in Queensland. Spectacular white sandstone gorges, plunging waterfalls, large regions of rainforest, caves and stunning Aboriginal rock art make this a brilliant destination to spend time walking and camping. Carnarvon Creek weaves its way through the bottom of the gorge and the world's tallest fern, the King Fern, reaches for light through the forest canopy. The wide range of Aboriginal art found at Balloon Cave, Cathedral Cave and the Art Gallery includes rock engravings, ochre stencils and freehand paintings.

The park's diverse wildlife includes 173 species of birds. Platypuses, Whiptail Wallabies and Common Brushtail Possums are seen here as well as Yellow-bellied and Greater Gliders in the evening. A walk along the Nature Trail may provide keen-eyed hikers with a glimpse of a Platypus.

Walks in the Park: Carnarvon Gorge is an easily accessible place to walk with most tracks commencing from near the visitor car park area. The Balloon Cave Walk (500 m, 30 min return), Mickey Creek Gorge Walk (1.5 km, 1 hr return), the Rock Pool Walk (2 km, 1–1.5 hr return) and the Nature Trail (1 km circuit, 30 min) are all excellent walks for anyone of basic fitness.

The walk to the Art Gallery (5.4 km, 3–4 hr return) is well-rewarded by the fascinating examples of Aboriginal rock art to be seen here. The Boolimba Bluff Walk (3.2 km, 2–3 hr return) offers excellent views across the park. The Moss Garden Walk (3.4 km, 2–3 hr return) leads to an otherworldly glade where moss and lichen cling to every surface, fed by a natural spring.

Longer treks for more experienced and properly equipped bushwalkers include Cathedral Cave (9 km, 5–6 hr return) and Battleship Spur (14 km, 8–10 hr return).

Access: From Roma, travel 90 km north to Injune and then 160 km along the Carnarvon Developmental Road.

Camping: Camping in the Carnarvon Gorge visitor areas is permitted only during the Easter, June–July and September–October Queensland school holidays. Bookings are essential. Use fuel stoves only — fires are not permitted. There is a hike-in bush camp (toilet only, treat water before drinking) at Big Bend, 9.6 km from the information centre.

Local accommodation is also available at Takarakka Bush Resort (4 km from visitor centre, Ph: (07) 4984 4535) and Carnarvon Gorge Wilderness Lodge (3 km from visitor centre, Ph: (07) 4984 4503). Takarakka Bush Resort stocks basic supplies.

Platypus

BRISBANE to Rockhampton

Brisbane to Rockhampton

Top Things to Do

1. Cruise the beaches of the Sunshine Coast.
2. Search for domestic treasures at the famous Eumundi Markets.
3. Camp, fish and 4WD drive on Fraser Island.
4. Take a whale watching cruise in Hervey Bay.
5. Visit the Conondale Ranges.
6. Dive or snorkel off Heron Island.
7. Camp offshore on the islands of the Capricorn–Bunker Group.
8. Tour the famous Bundaberg Rum Distillery.
9. Explore Maryborough's Victorian heritage.
10. Savour a juicy slab of prime beef in Rockhampton — Queensland's cattle capital.

For most travellers, the Queensland experience focuses on the coast — the long, white sandy beaches and the invitingly warm waters of the Coral Sea. Not far north of Fraser Island, the wonders of the Great Barrier Reef begin at a collection of islands known as the Capricorn–Bunker Group. Like the reefs further north, the entire area is marine national park and the diversity of habitat and life must be seen to be truly believed.

Northern Delights

Close to Brisbane, the Sunshine Coast's pleasures beckon holidaymakers — the upmarket beach culture of Noosa, the coloured sand cliffs of Rainbow Beach and Eumundi's famous markets. From Hervey Bay, it is only a short cruise to Fraser Island, one of the world's defining national park experiences. To the north is Bundaberg on the Burnett River — one of Australia's great sugar-producing centres. Just outside Bundaberg is Mon Repos Conservation Park, a vital mainland nesting site for sea turtles. A little further on, seaward from Seventeen Seventy (*see box below*), Lady Elliot Island marks the start of the Capricorn–Bunker Group and gives north-bound visitors their first taste of the magical reef. Gladstone, the port for the central Queensland coalfields, is built around a natural deepwater harbour and is home to the world's largest alumina plant. Further north-west is Rockhampton, Australia's beef capital on the Tropic of Capricorn.

Fraser Island The world's greatest sand island, in Hervey Bay, is also a microcosm of the great Australian holiday — sun, sand, surf and extraordinary nature.

Heron Island This resort island in the Capricorn–Bunker Group north-east of Gladstone is actually a coral cay famed for its incredible diving and snorkelling.

Coral Coast

The Coral Coast stretches north from Bundaberg to Rockhampton. This section of the 2000 km long Great Barrier Reef features Capricornia Cays National Park and the idyllic tourist resort of Heron Island. The area is characterised by some of the world's most precious marine habitats.

Cattle & Cane

The twin pillars of Queensland's rural economy, cattle farming and cane growing, are readily visible from the Sunshine Coast north. Canefields reach to the edge of the Bruce Highway and Rockhampton is surrounded by some of Australia's finest cattle grazing country.

Cook's Tour

Fifty-five kilometres east of Miriam Vale on the Bruce Highway is the Town of Seventeen Seventy. You are correct in guessing the town was named in honour of the year Captain Cook came ashore here from his barque *Endeavour*. You may not know that Bustard Bay on which it is perched refers to Cook and his crew's dinner — an Australian Bustard they surprised and shot on the beach. Given that Cook's men were the first Europeans ever to set foot on the Queensland coast, this was one unlucky bustard indeed.

Close by at Round Hill Head is Joseph Banks Conservation Park, where a stone monument honours the voyagers. The conservation park and bordering Eurimbula National Park are excellent for bird and wildlife viewing. Look up for Peregrine Falcons (which hunt at speeds of over 180 km/h) and the White-bellied Sea-Eagle, Australia's second-largest (and perhaps most striking) bird-of-prey. From December to March look down for adult and hatchling Green, Flatback and Loggerhead Turtles which nest at Bustard Beach (but don't handle or touch them). The southernmost islands of the Great Barrier Reef Marine Park lie to the north-east of Seventeen Seventy.

Top to bottom: Round Hill Head; Lady Musgrave Island, north-east of Seventeen Seventy.

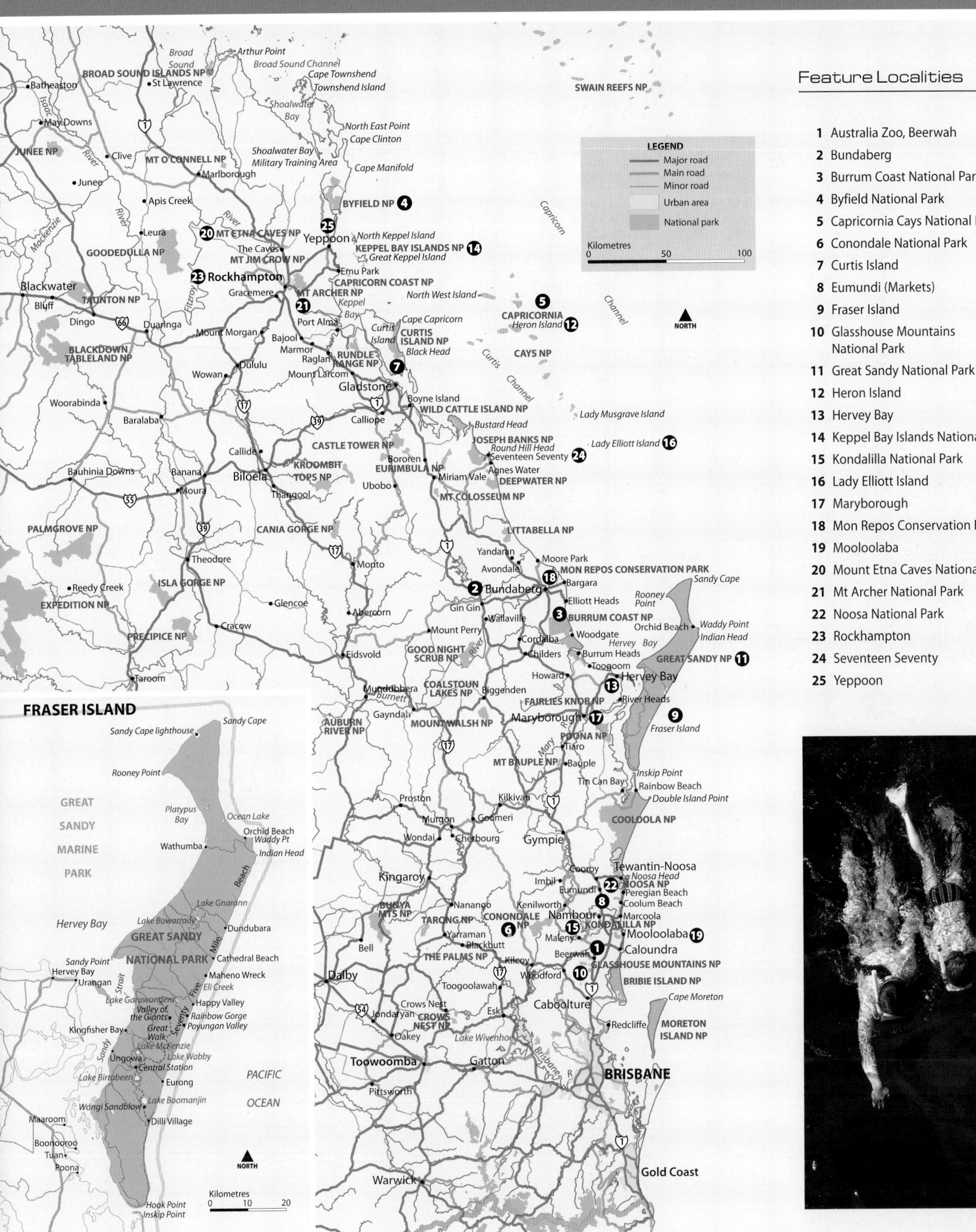

Feature Localities

1 Australia Zoo, Beerwah
2 Bundaberg
3 Burrum Coast National Park
4 Byfield National Park
5 Capricornia Cays National Park
6 Conondale National Park
7 Curtis Island
8 Eumundi (Markets)
9 Fraser Island
10 Glasshouse Mountains National Park
11 Great Sandy National Park
12 Heron Island
13 Hervey Bay
14 Keppel Bay Islands National Park
15 Kondalilla National Park
16 Lady Elliott Island
17 Maryborough
18 Mon Repos Conservation Park
19 Mooloolaba
20 Mount Etna Caves National Park
21 Mt Archer National Park
22 Noosa National Park
23 Rockhampton
24 Seventeen Seventy
25 Yeppoon

The Sunshine Coast

The Sunshine Coast's endless strips of beach and glorious climate could convince you that the locals lead a fairly leisurely brand of life. In fact, the region is a hive of activity from field to foreshore. The sun-drenched climate is ideal for cultivating tropical produce and the hinterland is full of orderly rows of pineapples and trees laden with avocados, bananas and macadamia nuts. Nambour has long been associated with pineapple production and the inland towns of Buderim and Yandina are famed for their ginger industries. At Eumundi Markets, smaller scale local production is on show every Wednesday and Saturday when over 500 stalls offer everything from goji berries to plate armour. Keeping the hectic tourism trade going is also a major source of regional employment and investment. Just watching all that work going on will make you feel like a little R&R and, happily, the Sunshine Coast's many beach resorts, forests, waterways, golf courses and restaurants serve this urge perfectly.

Beaches & Attractions

It all starts an hour north of Brisbane at Caloundra, where a long ribbon of golden beach reaches south from the apartment-topped headland of Wickham Point. Many of Caloundra's swimming and surfing spots, including popular Kings Beach, are lifeguard-patrolled. Just south of Caloundra on the Glass House Mountains Tourist Drive near Beerwah is Australia Zoo — pride and joy of the internationally famous "Crocodile Hunter", the late Steve Irwin. Aside from crocodiles, the zoo exhibits a large range of reptiles, native marsupials and mammals as well as exotic animals such as tigers and Galapagos Tortoises.

Mooloolaba, a coastal settlement at the Mooloolah River mouth, is known for its lively and convivial atmosphere. It is the finish line for the Auckland–Mooloolaba and Sydney–Mooloolaba yacht races, which attract droves of sailing enthusiasts. Check out Mooloolaba Wharf on the river mouth, grab some fresh prawns off the trawlers, visit the 25,000 marine creatures at Underwater World or bodysurf at one of the superb beaches nearby.

The busiest town on the Sunshine Coast is Maroochydore, on the estuary of the Maroochy River. The town is a holiday centre with modern shopping complexes and a long strip of high-rise apartments running along the foreshore, and has an airport serving the coastal resorts and northern islands. The large-scale development that has occurred here since the 1950s is offset by the preservation of green parklands and picnic spaces along the river. Near Eudlo Creek you can experience how the first European travellers to this coast might have felt — in a lagoon near Maroochy River Resort floats a two-thirds scale model of James Cook's *Endeavour*, which you can board and tour (off David Low Way, Ph: (07) 5476 8391).

Continuing north almost 15 km to Noosa National Park is an unbroken stretch of sand leading past the seaside (and golfing) resort of Coolum and the village of Peregian Beach. The holiday destination of Noosa, on Laguna Bay, is the pearl of the Sunshine Coast — a shiny sliver of protected beach, flanked by green and laden with quality dining, accommodation and shopping options. Walking in Noosa National Park is one of the best (and cheapest) excursions — the ocean views are far superior to those from the swanky resorts. Keep an eye out for Koalas and Glossy Black-Cockatoos. Camping is not permitted, but a little further north across from Tewantin, at Great Sandy National Park, the facilities are excellent — as are the high dunes, wide beaches and coloured sand cliffs.

Majestic Mountains

The Sunshine Coast begins north of Brisbane where the dramatic shape of the Glass House Mountains loom over the plains. The peaks are volcanic plugs of rhyolite and, depending on your choice of story, were either named by James Cook after the glass furnaces in his native Yorkshire or for the way the glassy rocks reflected sunlight.

Noosa Lifestyle

Once a quiet coastal settlement, Noosa's natural and commercial attractions have made it a magnet for tourists. Some like the climate, shopping and food so much that they choose to stay and permanently adopt the Noosa lifestyle.

Rural Retreats

Along the Blackall and Conondale Ranges lie a string of charming and laid-back hinterland villages filled with craft shops, galleries and restaurants (promoting fresh local ingredients) to tempt you away from the sun and sand of the coast. Maleny, Montville (*above*) and Mapleton are favourite retreats. The ridge-top roads offer superlative views of the coast and countryside.

Hinterland Parks

Amid the Sunshine Coast's sprawling development there remain many pristine tracts of wilderness to explore. Several state forests and national parks have been declared in the upper Mary Valley. A 90 minute scenic drive commences at the park office at Kenilworth State Forest and traverses the ranges of Conondale National Park. Conondale includes pockets of subtropical rainforest that once covered much of the Sunshine Coast. These forests are now a refuge for rare and endangered native animals such as the Yellow-bellied Glider. In Kondalilla National Park (4 km north of Montville), Skene Creek plunges 90 m at the spectacular Kondalilla Falls (*left*) into rainforest below.

Conondale National Park

Phone Ranger: (07) 5446 0925

Conondale National Park (*left*) adjoins Kenilworth Forest Reserve in the Conondale Ranges. The main walking trails and camping facilities lie within Kenilworth but the entire region is blessed with picturesque forests, waterfalls and creeks. Booloumba Gorge, at the junction of Peters and Booloumba Creeks, features scenic cascades and rock pools.

Walks in the Park: There are many trails including several from Booloumba campground. The Gold Mine Walk is a steep 5.2 km trek through riparian rainforest to a disused mine. It incorporates views of the creek and surrounding gorge. Commencing off the forest drive in the southern section of Conondale, the Booloumba Falls trail is a 3 km return moderate grade walk.

Access: Via the Eumundi–Kenilworth Road, off the Bruce Highway. Kenilworth is about 28 km from the highway. The turnoff to Charlie Moreland is about 7 km past Kenilworth and the turnoff to Booloumba Creek and Conondale National Park is a further 500 m.

Camping: Three campgrounds at Booloumba Creek and one at Charlie Moreland. One of the Booloumba sites is suitable for caravans and large groups. There is a neighbouring enclosed paddock for horses.

Noosa National Park

Phone Ranger: (07) 5447 3243

Noosa National Park (*above, left and right*) includes the scenic headland at Noosa Heads, parts of Lake Weyba, Emu Mountain and the coastal lowlands towards Coolum. The Noosa Headland section is one of the Sunshine Coast's most popular bushwalking areas. The park is home to Koalas as well as threatened species including the Glossy Black-Cockatoo, Ground Parrot, Red Goshawk, Wallum Froglet, Swamp Orchid and Christmas Bell.

Walks in the Park: Beginning near the picnic area in the Noosa Headland section, the Palm Grove Circuit is a 1 km walk through rainforest featuring Hoop Pines and Piccabeen Palms. The Coastal Track is 5.4 km return over several headlands and takes in picturesque coves such as Tea Tree Bay. There are several lookouts along the track, which leads to a high bluff at Hell's Gates. Take care when the track weaves close to cliff edges and keep children under close supervision. At Peregian Beach, a boardwalk leads through paperbark swamp and sedgelands down a sandy track to heathland and She-oak forests. The Emu Mountain Summit Walk is short and steep, but offers spectacular views. The East Weyba section has no marked tracks, and vehicle tracks should be followed if walking here — unexploded ordnance may still be present in the area (a legacy from its days as a World War II training camp).

Access: The Noosa Headland section is at the end of Park Road in Noosa Heads. It can also be reached via Sunshine Beach, Parkedge Road and Viewland Drive. Access to the Peregian, East Weyba and Emu Mountain sections is from David Low Way south of Noosa.

Camping: Not permitted in the park.

Mooloolaba

Walk out to the breakwater or lighthouse at Point Cartwright for sweeping views of the river, coast and ocean. The 32 m lighthouse was constructed in 1978 when high-rise beach development obscured the former signal light at Caloundra.

Eumundi

Twice a week the former timber and railway town of Eumundi is transformed by the Eumundi Markets. Stalls selling local crafts, original artwork, clothes and organic food fill the grounds. In true bazaar style, performance artists and buskers add an upbeat vibe to the trading.

Great Sandy National Park

This protected region of bush-fringed beach, lakes and rivers extends along the coast from Noosa north to Fraser Island (*see following page*). The southern section features the Noosa River and Lakes Cootharaba, Como and Cooloola. 4WD vehicles can access the national park by ferry from Tewantin, and beach driving is permitted at low tide to Double Island Point (road rules apply). Some great walking tracks allow you to absorb the full magnificence of the park's natural features. The coloured sands and cliffs of Teewah and Rainbow Beach are a perennial attraction, as are the numerous sandblows and dunes.

The Fraser Coast

The coast of the Wide Bay–Burnett district, extending north from the peaceful shores of Tin Can Bay to Hervey Bay is also known as the Fraser Coast. It is named for Captain James Fraser and his wife Eliza who sought refuge on the region's largest island in 1836 after the shipwreck of their vessel, the *Stirling Castle*. They were taken in by Fraser Island's Indigenous inhabitants, the Butchulla people, who had occupied the island they knew as *K'gari* (meaning "paradise") for more than 5000 years. By the 1930s none of the Aborigines remained — disease, dispossession and other effects of European settlement and industry had rendered Fraser a paradise lost. Logging and sand mining continued to damage the environment over the next 50 years but today the entire island is national park and its restoration and ongoing preservation as a natural haven is a fiercely defended ideology.

Covering 1840 km^2, Fraser Island is the world's largest sand island and lies just off the coast at Hervey Bay. The region's popularity is inextricably tied to the presence of the island, and the bay's marina and piers serve as departure points for a huge fleet of cruise and charter boats. While a daytrip will give you a brief taste of Fraser Island, its sheer size and ecological diversity can only be properly appreciated through more extensive exploration.

Fraser Island's wilderness is truly exceptional. Over half the world's dune lakes occur here, and the 200 ha Lake Boomanjin is the world's largest perched lake. Boomerang Lakes, at 120 m above sea level, are some of the world's highest. At Rainbow Gorge and Cathedral Beach, iron-rich minerals in the sand have painted spectacularly coloured cliffs in mustard, rust and brown shades. Immense sand dunes rise to 240 m and the beaches are many and varied. The largest is 75 Mile Beach on the island's eastern side (also a registered highway for vehicles). Birds (over 350 species) and other wildlife make their home on Fraser Island in habitat ranging from wallum to rainforest. There are also archaeological sites and remains from the Butchulla people's residence that record thousands of years of island history.

Fraser has numerous small townships including Kingfisher Bay, Eurong, Orchid Beach, Happy Valley and Cathedral Beach. All offer various supplies and services. Accommodation, ranging from camping facilities to self-contained cabins and fully serviced resorts, is spread about the townships, lakes and trails. Due to the presence of wild Dingoes on the island, campers with children under the age of fourteen are advised to use one of the five fenced campgrounds available (bookings are required for most campsites). A range of commercial adventure tours are on offer, including charter flights, guided walks, 4WD tours and horseback treks. Maps and guides are available at the Great Sandy Information Office (Tewantin) and the three national park offices on the island (at Eurong, Dundubara and Waddy Point).

Hervey Bay

What were once five separate villages — Urangan, Torquay, Scarness, Point Vernon and Pialba — have gradually been linked by coastal development to form the city of Hervey Bay. The area is a magnet for tourists and much of the foreshore region has been annexed for caravan park grounds. Holiday apartments and hotels are also in plentiful supply. A good sense of the coastal region can be gained by strolling part or all of the 15 km Scenic Walkway, commencing from central Hervey Bay. Dayman Park is named for one of the *Stirling Castle* survivors, and there is a memorial here to the maritime explorer Matthew Flinders, who first mapped much of this coast in 1802. South at Dundowran Beach, Arkarra Lagoons is a 12 ha nature sanctuary featuring walking trails around wetland lagoons inhabited by waterbirds, goannas, turtles and other native wildlife.

Fraser Island Ecotourism

Fraser Island supports complex habitats where a mix of tall rainforest trees, eucalypt forest, mangroves, ferns and wallum grow in the moving sands and provide homes for many animals (some of them rare). This fragile ecosystem was inscribed as a World Heritage Area in 1992. In keeping with this concern for Mother Nature's welfare, many ecotourism options are available to tourists, each designed to bring people close to nature (with minimal harm to it), while fostering a greater understanding of Fraser's environmental significance.

Humpback Hotel

The northern end of Fraser Island forms the eastern boundary of Hervey Bay, providing an aquatic resort for Humpback Whales. These mighty mammals may be seen frolicking in the waters here from July to November. A number of whale-watching cruises operate from Hervey Bay.

Land of Sand

Over 700,000 years the immense volume of sand that constitutes Fraser Island has been continually shifted and shaped, swept by coastal currents and waves from the Tasman Sea. The island's sand dunes, including some mammoth peaks over 200 m high, are still moving today, pushed slowly across the island and sculpted by onshore winds.

Pure Nature

Fraser Island's isolation means that some of its wildlife has not been altered through interbreeding. Fraser Island's Dingoes (*above*) are believed to have one of the purest bloodlines in Australia and so are probably the closest living links with their likely predecessor, the Indian Wolf.

Wild Walks

1 Lake Wabby — 3 km return, 1.5 hr, moderate.

2 Valley of the Giants — 2.6 km return, 1.5 hr, moderate.

3 Kingfisher Bay to Dudonga Creek — 3.3 km return, 1.5 hr, moderate.

4 Dilli Village to Wongi Sandblow — 8.4 km return, 3–4 hr, moderate to hard.

Walking on Fraser – Don't Forget

1 Choose walks that suit your fitness and time.

2 Dingoes and other dangerous wildlife (including venomous snakes) live on the Island.

3 Carry first aid supplies and enough water.

4 Never walk alone.

5 Stay with your children at all times.

Fraser Island – Great Sandy National Park

Phone Ranger: (07) 5449 7792

Fraser Island's streams flow through dense rainforest past incredibly pure perched, barrage and window lakes. There are over 100 freshwater lakes, including the paperbark-fringed Lake McKenzie, where aquamarine waters spread over white sand. Some of Fraser's freshwater is so pure that it cannot sustain life. Lake Wabby, the deepest lake on the island, lies at the advancing edge of the Hammerstone Sandblow. Drive around Cornwell's Break Road up to the ridge above the lake, where a short walk takes you to a splendid lookout offering a view of this barrage lake and the sandblow that is slowly engulfing it. At least 354 bird species have been recorded on the island, including the endangered Ground Parrot, which is found among the wallum heathlands. Fraser Island and the Great Sandy Strait are important resting places for migratory waders on epic flights between southern Australia and their Siberian breeding grounds.

Walks in the Park: Central Station, once the timber industry's headquarters, is now the centerpiece of a beautiful rainforest walk that follows Wanggoolba Creek. The Fraser Island Great Walk is a 90 km wilderness trail broken by overnight camps that takes in many of the island's key natural attractions. Complementing this are many other destination-specific walks to beaches, lakes, waterfalls and other natural features. Complete walking guides are available from the Queensland Parks and Wildlife Service and on Fraser Island.

Access: Passenger and vehicular barge services (4WD only) to Fraser Island operate from Hervey Bay (Urangan Boat Harbour) to Moon Point and from River Heads (east of Maryborough) to Kingfisher Bay and Wanggoolba. The journey is approximately 30–50 minutes, depending on weather conditions. Barges also operate daily from Inskip Point, 15 minutes drive from Rainbow Beach (east of Gympie) to Hook Point (a quick 10 minute journey). Vehicle permits are essential and must be bought prior to driving on the island (Ph: 13 13 04).

Camping: Fenced campgrounds for travellers with children under the age of fourteen are available at Lake Boomanjin, Central Station, Dundubara, Waddy Point (top campground) and Dilli Village (commercially operated). Other campgrounds include Waddy Point beachfront, Ungowa and Wathumba. All campgrounds have water and toilets and most have gas barbecues, dishwashing sinks and information displays. Beach camping areas with no facilities are located behind the dunes on the eastern beach. Camp only within signposted areas and always at least 50 m from watercourses. There are also bushwalking camps along the Fraser Island Great Walk at Jabiru Swamp, Lake Boomanjin, Lake Benaroon, Central Station, Lake McKenzie, Lake Wabby, Valley of the Giants, Lake Garawongera and Dilli Village (privately operated, Ph: (07) 4127 9130).

Top to bottom: Lake Wabby and the Hammerstone Sandblow; Wanggoolba Creek, showing a section of Fraser's Island's subtropical rainforest habitat; Indian Head, on the eastern side of Fraser Island.

Scientific National Park

Six islands in the Capricornia Cays are considered "scientific" national parks and are off limits to the public. These include East and West Fairfax Islands (*above*), only a few metres above water but vital nesting sites for sea birds and turtles.

Maryborough

Maryborough was a small river port before major gold finds around Gympie in 1867 brought wealth and population to the area. The city then rapidly established itself as an engineering, timber, sugar and immigration centre. The city has many fine Victorian buildings, restored "Queenslander" homes and a historic precinct along Wharf Street.

Bundaberg

The city of Bundaberg, founded in 1870, sits astride the Burnett River. Well known for sugarcane processing, the city also boasts many fine parks and surrounding beaches. Poincianas, figs and bauhinias, which flower in spring and summer, bring colour to "Bundy's" wide streets.

The Coral Coast

Maryborough, on the Mary River, is a beautifully preserved city and port that has long been the centre of Queensland's rail engineering industry. Each Thursday at the Heritage Market in Queens Park you can ride a replica of the State's first steam locomotive along the river to the marina. The city is also the birthplace of P L Travers — author of the *Mary Poppins* series of children's books. A 1.5 m statue of the magical, umbrella-powered nanny now stands outside the former Union Bank building (corner of Richmond and Kent Streets), once managed by Travers' father. A little further north lies Childers, another town of heritage interest, boasting well-restored 19th century shops, some excellent local museums and a historical complex. The main street is shaded by unusual Brazilian Leopard trees.

Much of the coast between here and Bundaberg is protected by Burrum Coast National Park, which is split into three sections. The south features the Burrum River and its mangrove-lined banks, (access from Burrum Heads Road); a central section showcases coastal heathlands, melaleuca swamp and palm forests (access via Woodgate Beach township); and the northern Kinkuna section is dominated by dunes (4WD access only). Camping facilities are available at Burrum Point (central section) and bush camping is permitted in designated areas of the Kinkuna section. Just north of the park is Elliott Heads, a pretty, secluded village on the estuary of the Elliott River that has golden swimming beaches and great fishing.

The Coral Coast begins at Bundaberg, Australia's premier sugar industry town and gateway to the Great Barrier Reef. Daily tours of the famous Bundaberg Rum Distillery established in 1888 (Whittred Street, East Bundaberg) are available and there are many other historical attractions including the home of pioneer aviator Bert Hinkler (in the Bundaberg Botanical Gardens) and the Fairymead House Sugar Museum (Thornhill Street).

Heron Island A languid mid-afternoon settles over Heron Island.

Capricorn-Bunker Group

The "first lady" of the Great Barrier Reef, Lady Elliot Island, is a coral cay that first appeared above sea level approximately 3500 years ago. Today it is an eco-friendly resort island serviced by regular flights from Bundaberg Airport (around 30 minutes flying). Daytrips by air are also possible from Bundaberg and Gladstone. Lady Elliot is small — it is possible to walk the length of the island in 15 minutes — but her attractions are many (including glass-bottom boat tours, reef walking, fish feeding, diving, snorkelling and more). The cay's wild residents include giant Manta Rays, lurid tropical fish and, of course, the living coral reef itself.

Lying east of Gladstone are the major islands of the Bunker Group, the southernmost of which is Lady Musgrave Island. This cay is a national park and there is no resort but camping is possible (*see facing page*). Its central Pisonia forest and the surrounding reef waters form a fabulously rich habitat for sea birds and Green Turtles. As a low-key introduction to the wonders of the reef, Lady Musgrave Island is ideal. Access to the island is by charter boat and cruises from Seventeen Seventy, Bundaberg and Gladstone. If you plan on camping you will need to take your own freshwater and supplies. A sense of solitude is guaranteed, with a maximum of 40 people allowed to camp on the island at any one time.

Heron Island in the Capricorn Group is the region's major reef holiday destination. Accommodation on the island is at the low-rise Voyages Resort (Ph: 1300 134 044) which offers boat and helicopter transfers from Gladstone Marina. An array of reef exploration opportunities are available (the diving is sensational) and regular sightings of rays, reef sharks and turtles are just some of Heron's multitude of underwater attractions.

Camping is permitted on North West Island and Masthead Island in the Capricorn Group, and both are accessible by boat from Gladstone (permits and fees apply, (Ph: (07) 4971 6500). North West is the largest Green Turtle nesting site on the southern Great Barrier Reef.

Heron Island

Heron Island is surrounded by 24 km of reef, which in many places lies only metres from the beach. Guests can swim straight from the sandy white shore into a spectacular coral garden crowded with tropical fish. Heron boasts more than 30 separate dive sites, half of which are only 15 minutes from the beach.

The original holiday resort on the island was established in 1932 by Captain Christian Poulson, whose family continued to operate it until 1977. Daytrippers are not permitted on the island, allowing Heron to retain a private resort flavour. The island is also the headquarters for The University of Queensland marine science research team and nest site to a huge population of sea birds (including terns, noddies, shearwaters and the island's namesake).

Lady Elliot Island

Guano mining stripped Lady Elliot Island of virtually all its vegetation until replanting by conservationist and aviator Don Adams in 1967 revived life on the cay. Diving in the surrounding waters offers some of the best visibility of the entire reef system. If you'd prefer to stay above water, it is possible at low tide to walk the entire distance from the island's lagoon to the reef edge.

Capricornia Cays National Park – Camping Adventures

Phone Ranger: (07) 4971 6500

Capricornia Cays is the southernmost national park of the Great Barrier Reef World Heritage Area and comprises eight coral cays — Lady Musgrave, North West, Masthead, Wilson, Broomfield, Erskine and Tryon Islands and the eastern part of Heron Island. These low-lying islands rise only several metres from the Coral Sea. Heron Island was named for the colonies of Reef Herons that make their home in its environs. In 1943, it became one of the first Great Barrier Reef islands to be declared a national park.

Island Walks: There are short walking tracks across North West and Lady Musgrave Islands through Pisonia forest. Walking is also permitted on the surrounding reefs but be sure to walk in the sand channels and never on live corals, which are easily damaged (and can cause nasty cuts). Do not stir up sand and remember that collecting any corals, rocks or reef creatures is not permitted. The protected lagoon on Lady Musgrave is an ideal introduction to the addictive art of reef snorkelling.

Access: Cruises, tours and charter vessels operate from Gladstone, Bundaberg and Seventeen Seventy. It is also possible to access the islands on private vessels.

Camping: Camping is only permitted on Lady Musgrave, North West and Masthead Islands. Camping periods are restricted and capacity limits apply. Bookings can be made up to 11 months in advance. The camping area on Lady Musgrave Island is 400 m from the east end of the island and camping is permitted from the start of the Easter school holidays until the end of the summer school holidays in January (capacity limit — 40 people). Camping on Masthead Island is permitted from the start of the Easter school holidays to 15 October each year (capacity limit — 50 people. The camping area is in the north-west corner but no facilities are provided. Camping on North West Island is permitted from the start of the Easter school holidays until the end of the summer school holidays in January (capacity limit — 150 people). Composting toilets, fuel storage and a compressor bunker are provided. Daytrips or picnics on North West and Lady Musgrave Islands are permitted all year, and at Masthead or Erskine Islands from the start of the Easter (Queensland) school holidays until 15 October.

Red and Black Anemonefish

Biters & Stingers

The tropical beaches, waters and islands off the Queensland coast are home to the greatest diversity of marine life in the world. It is a miracle of adaptability, rather than malicious intent, that causes some of the reef's denizens to harm humans from time-to-time. Venomous marine animals, such as the Box Jelly, Irukandji, Cone Shell, Reef Stonefish, Blue-ringed Octopus and Common Lionfish, can cause serious injury and (in some cases) death.

To reduce the risk, swim only at patrolled beaches between the flags and observe warning signs. Wearing protective clothing can also help, as can entering the water slowly (most species will simply swim away). Stinger-free enclosures operate on many Queensland beaches between the months of November and May, but these are stinger-resistant rather than stinger-proof so care still needs to be exercised. If stung, seek immediate medical assistance. For further information contact Surf Lifesaving Queensland (Ph: (07) 3846 8000 or see www.marinestingers.com).

Blue-ringed Octopus (*above left*); Common Lionfish (*top*); Cone Shell (*above right*).

What about Sharks?

Sharks in a range of sizes and species are present in all Australian waters, but in most conditions it is uncommon for them to venture close to shore. Most Australians will not see a shark during the course of their lifetimes (other than in an aquarium). Nevertheless, sharks will occasionally visit warmer inshore waters in pursuit of fish.

Of course, fatal attacks do very occasionally occur (about one every year on average), but if you are swimming on lifeguard-patrolled beaches between the flags the risk is almost zero. Do not swim alone or at night (when sharks are likely to be feeding closer to shore) and avoid swimming near the mouths of rivers or in canals.

Bull Shark

Snorkelling

One of the greatest pleasures of visiting Queensland's magnificent coast is the opportunity to snorkel amid coral reefs teeming with tropical fish and other marine oddities. If you have never snorkelled before or are not a strong swimmer, don't be deterred. Many cruises and island resorts offer extensive snorkelling training and the chance to snorkel in shallow waters or off family-friendly reef pontoons.

Scuba Diving

The Great Barrier Reef is recognised as one of the world's best diving destinations. All diving gear can be hired and world-accredited PADI training is offered in most locations. Dive cruises and charters cater to all levels of experience, including beginners. Although diving can be a strange (and often disconcerting) experience at first, new divers soon become enthralled at the sense of weightlessness and the compelling life forms they encounter underwater.

Reef Walking

Many coral cays and islands are surrounded by encircling reef, which means that you can observe spectacular coral gardens and a kaleidoscope of fish and invertebrate species by simply walking a few metres off the beach. Observe the rules of reef walking — wear sturdy, protective footwear and sun-safe clothing, walk along sand channels and avoid stepping on live coral. Look but don't touch; never remove any animals, shells or coral and be aware of the incoming tide.

Guided Educational Tours

Many coastal reserves, as well as larger islands and cays, can be explored through guided beach and reef walks and ecotours. With knowledgeable guides these are often the best possible introduction to the marine and coastal ecology and a great way to discover resident wildlife that you may not otherwise encounter. Both commercial operators and parks authorities offer educational experiences in various locations around the Coral Coast.

Underwater Tours

In an environment as vast and varied as the Great Barrier Reef, it can be almost impossible to know where to start your underwater explorations. Dive and snorkel charters abound, but if you want to engage this incredible marine world without getting your feet wet, glass-bottom boat, semi-submersible and underwater observatory tours are also available.

Wildlife of the Capricorn-Bunker Group

The Capricorn-Bunker Group, at the southernmost tip of the Great Barrier Reef, presents visitors with a superb snapshot of the life of one of the world's greatest natural wonders. Exploring the reef is not only about venturing underwater to observe an incredible array of corals and fish species, but is also about education. The reef is a huge inter-related ecosystem of plants and animals that exist in and above the ocean and depend on each other in complex ways. The richness of life to be found not only in the water, but on the land and in the skies as well, forms an eye-opening and humbling experience for many visitors.

Harlequin Tuskfish (*top*) and Masked Bannerfish.

Fish & Marine Mammals

Over 1500 bony fish species live in the warm waters around the Capricornia Cays. There are also some 30 whale and dolphin species that rely on these waters along with four turtle species. Seagrass meadows support large communities of Dugongs. Along with the ubiquitous Clown Anemonefish, there are large pelagic predators such as sharks, barracudas and mackerels. Other fish are less conspicuous — cave-dwelling fish like the squirrelfish, and camouflaged species like gobies and seahorses are present in large, if less visible, numbers. The vivid corals of the reef provide camouflage for many inhabitants whose colours conceal them in an environment where, in an instant, just about anything can become prey.

Above: Spotted and Painted Sweetlips.

Birds & Birdwatching

The Capricornia Cays form both temporary and permanent homes to large communities of birds. Between October and April, hundreds of thousands of migrating sea birds visit to breed and nest. North West Island alone provides a breeding ground for 70% of the Wedge-tailed Shearwaters on Australia's east coast. They are readily recognised by their tube-nosed bill and distinctive call, or howl, which can often be heard at night. Common and Black Noddies also nest in the Pisonia trees that populate the cays, providing excellent opportunities for observation. In winter, White-bellied Sea-Eagles breed on six of the islands. Take care not to disturb nests and observe signs and protected areas. Some birds, such as Black-naped and Roseate Terns, nest on exposed beaches and in the crevices of rocks. The beaches and reef flats are also home to a wide variety of birds including boobies, oystercatchers, gulls and egrets. Migrant waders include Whimbrels, Ruddy Turnstones, Mongolian Plovers and Bar-tailed Godwits. In terms of land birds, these cays are home to a separate race of Silvereye, which happens to be the largest race.

Left to right: Black Noddy with chick; Reef Herons.

Invertebrate Parade

By far the most populous class of creature found in the reef regions is the marine invertebrate. On average, a new species is identified every month and they constitute nearly 95% of all the animals that live within the Great Barrier Reef Marine Park. From the coral polyps that form the very basis of reefs to clams, octopuses, sea jellies, sponges, seastars, cuttlefish and crabs, an amazing congregation of the world's invertebrates are on display. Their variation in size, shape and colour is near infinite, from the single-celled protozoa to large cephalopods such as squid and octopus. Some, like coral polyps and the hermaphroditic sea squirt, are so immobile as to be readily mistaken for plants. Yet, while apparently inactive, the sea squirt plays an important role on the reef, filtering the water and helping to keep it clear. When you are diving or snorkelling in these pristine waters don't forget to offer a silent thanks to the humble sea squirt.

Above: Invertebrate species are most prolific on reefs of the Capricorn-Bunker Group.

Coral Cay Flora

Nearly every type of plant found on the cays of the Capricorn-Bunker Group owes its existence to the guano (droppings) of visiting sea birds that has fertilised the ground and dispersed seed. Consequently, coral cays support only a few tree and plant species in comparison to continental islands. The predominant vegetation is Pisonia (*Pisonia grandis*) and 70% of the total Pisonia rainforest in Australia is found on the Capricornia Cays. Growing around the islands' fringes are Coastal She-oaks, Octopus Bushes, native grasses and Pandani. On North West Island, strangling figs and Native Elms grow within the Pisonia forest, along with Native Mulberries, Sandpaper Figs and Lantern Bushes.

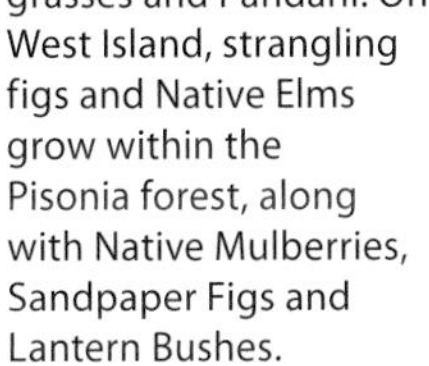

Coral Cod (*top*) and Blue Tang are just two of many colourful reef fish species.

Above: Pandanus is a characteristic plant species of coral cays.

Rockhampton & Surrounds

More than simply a departure point for the reef, Gladstone is Queensland's industrial powerhouse. Its port handles 18% of Australia's coal exports, the city boasts the State's largest coal-fired power station and it is home to the nation's biggest aluminium smelter. It also plays host to Australia's annual One Arm Raw Prawn Peeling Championship each September (although, as the local joke goes, one-armed prawns can be hard to find). There are also two nearshore islands worthy of exploration that are often overlooked in the rush to visit their more glamorous distant cousins. Facing Island, aptly facing the town in the outer harbour, is mostly a sand island with some notable rock and reef formations, good beaches, a campground and picnic facilities. To reach the island, catch a ferry from Gladstone Marina. The same ferry transports visitors to the larger Curtis Island, just to its north, and the small settlement of South End. Much of Curtis Island is wilderness, creating many excellent opportunities for bushwalking, beach lazing, wildlife viewing and shutter snapping.

Rockhampton

Located just above the Tropic of Capricorn on the Fitzroy River, Rockhampton is a gracious city of broad streets and classic old Queensland buildings. As the commercial capital of the State's beef industry, it prides itself on being the place where "country meets city". Regular rodeo events are staged in a 2000-seat undercover arena in a hotel owned by Australian country singing star Lee Kernaghan in the heart of town (Great Western Hotel, Stanley St, Ph: (07) 4922 1862). The city is even built on a former cattle run, established in 1855 by the region's first European settlers, the Archer brothers, for whom nearby Mount Archer is named. If you need more convincing of the importance of cattle to the local economy, life-size bull statues are scattered throughout the streets. Rockhampton's non-bovine attractions are of no lesser interest. The acclaimed botanic gardens in Spencer Street are a magnificent sight in any season (this is the tropics, after all) and include a free zoo featuring koalas, cassowaries and a pair of chimpanzee brothers named Cassie and Ockie. If you are looking to cool off without driving the 28 km to the coast, Rockpool Waterpark (Berserker Street) offers pools, water slides and other such slippery amusements.

Mount Archer National Park forms a picturesque backdrop to Rockhampton and protects dry rainforest and woodland on the Berserker Ranges. Two easy, short walks from the summit picnic area provide elevated views of the city, coast and surrounding peaks.

Yeppoon

Yeppoon is Rockhampton's closest beach resort. Rising out of the landscape on the road east are ancient volcanic plugs, the largest of which are Mount Jim Crow and Mount Hedlow. Yeppoon is an unassuming but well-serviced holiday town with a range of accommodation options. On the headland at Emu Park, 15 minutes south, is a soaring white sculpture and wind chime known as the *Singing Ship* — a musical monument to James Cook (*left, top*). A short drive west at Coowonga there is also a working crocodile farm offering daily tours (Koorana Saltwater Crocodile Farm, Ph: (07) 4934 4749). There are some excellent beaches along the Scenic Highway south of Yeppoon, including Kinka and Mulabin. Wreck Point Lookout and the coastal walk at Kemp's Beach offer superb views of the outlying islands of Keppel Bay. Thirty minutes north of Yeppoon is Byfield National Park, an area of towering dunes on Corio Bay (*see facing page*).

Passenger ferries and cruises to nearby reef islands (*see facing page*) depart from Rosslyn Bay just south of Yeppoon. The most popular of these is Great Keppel Island, which boasts seventeen beaches and a huge range of aquatic and reef-based activities. A broad range of accommodation options are available, from camping to luxury resorts.

The Capricorn Coast

The region from Gladstone to Byfield National Park, with Rockhampton in between, is known as the Capricorn Coast. It includes the Great Barrier Reef islands of Keppel Bay, many of which are in close proximity to the mainland shore. The touristy Great Keppel Island can be reached by ferry, charter boat or private vessel from Rosslyn Bay near Yeppoon, east of Rockhampton.

Rockhampton

Rockhampton's historic architecture (*top*) is a feature of the city. The original Customs House in Quay Street (*above*) is now a tourist hub, information centre and exhibition space for the "Spirit of Rockhampton". The city's yesteryear has been recreated at the Rockhampton Heritage Village, an active township museum (Bruce Highway past Yeppoon turn-off).

Mount Etna Caves National Park

Some of Australia's rarest bats can be seen in their natural cave habitat at Mount Etna Caves National Park, 26 km north of Rockhampton. The limestone caves support 80% of the nation's population of Little Bent-wing Bats and a colony of endangered Ghost Bats (*left*).

The park was once below sea level — its rocky landscape and chambers have been formed by limestone from ancient coral reefs. Ranger-guided tours to the bats' roosting and feeding areas at Bat Cleft are available from December to February (Ph: (07) 4936 0511).

Keppel Bay Islands National Park

Murex shell

Phone Ranger: (07) 4933 6595

Fifteen islands lying off the Capricorn Coast, with the exception of Great Keppel, constitute Keppel Bay Islands National Park. North Keppel and Humpy Island are the most popular camping destinations. North Keppel was originally inhabited by the Woppaburra people who were sustained for many thousands of years by the rich marine life of the surrounding reefs and sea.

Island Walks: There are three easy to moderate walks on North Keppel Island. Mazie Bay Track (3.5 km return) passes mangrove forests through woodland to the one-time Aboriginal camp of Mazie Bay. Keppel Bay Lookout Track (3.1 km return) branches off the Mazie Bay Track to the lookout. It is possible to continue past the lookout on an island circuit track that winds along the eastern side of the island, giving spectacular views of ocean, islands and coast. Stroll the Ridgetop Trail on Humpy Island (1.9 km return) for magnificent views of surrounding reefs, islands and marine life. Reef walking is possible at Mazie Bay, Olive Point (Middle Island), Miall and Humpy Islands.

Access: Island access is by boat. Launch facilities and charters are available from Rosslyn Bay Harbour. It is also possible to arrange charters to camping islands from Great Keppel Island.

Camping: Camping is permitted on seven of the islands with maximum capacity limits ranging from 6–75 people. The islands with camping facilities are North Keppel Island (75 people), Humpy Island (60), Middle Island (18), Miall Island (6), Conical Island (6), Divided Island (6) and Pelican Island (6).

Top to bottom: While outside of the national park, Great Keppel Island combines tourist activities and facilities with stunning natural surrounds; Sapphire waters surround the lush green, sand-fringed islands in Byfield National Park.

Top to bottom: North Keppel Island is a national park paradise; Great Keppel offers luxury accommodation.

Byfield National Park

Phone Ranger: (07) 4936 0511

The sweeping coastline of Byfield National Park overlooks Corio Bay. Huge dunes and sandblows in the south reach up to 6 km inland. The bay and Waterpark Creek are important breeding grounds for prawns and fish.

Walks: The Five Rocks Track is an easy 500 m walk from the visitor area that follows Findlay's Creek down to the beach between Stockyard Point and Five Rocks headland. This walk is best at low tide as Three Rivers Beach is cut off at high tide. There is a walking track to the coast from the car park at Sandy Point.

Access: Via Byfield State Forest, 9.8 km east of the Waterpark Creek visitor area. A 4WD vehicle is required from this point to traverse the 15 km soft sand track to the coast. Sandy Point car park is accessible in conventional vehicles.

Camping: The Five Rocks camping and picnic ground is accessible by 4WD only. Beach camping is permitted at Nine Mile Beach. If you have a boat, you can also camp at the little cove off Waterpark Point.

ROCKHAMPTON to Townsville

Rockhampton to Townsville Top Things to Do

1. Appreciate the incredible botanical diversity on display along the Mackay Highlands Great Walk.
2. Check out the region's shipping infrastructure at Hay Point.
3. Stroll through the lowland rainforest of Eungella National Park.
4. Kick up your heels in cosmopolitan Airlie Beach.
5. Take in the island views from Conway National Park.
6. Cruise the Whitsunday Passage and find your own deserted isle.
7. View Aboriginal rock art at Nara Inlet on Hook Island.
8. Check out Townsville's Strand and the views over Cleveland Bay from Castle Hill.
9. Find your very own slice of solitude on the beaches and bays of Magnetic Island.

Beyond Rockhampton, the highway leads through a series of small rural sugarcane towns north to Mackay, but the real interest lies eastward. From here the inner islands and cays of the Great Barrier Reef Marine Park form a closely linked chain. The mostly uninhabited Duke Islands, Percy Isles and Northumberland Islands all lie south-east of Mackay, where the splendour and sparkle of the Whitsunday Coast begins. Inland is a sea of sugarcane, producing nearly a third of Australia's sugar. To the north and west are several outstanding national parks including Cape Hillsborough and Eungella, bastions for the region's original lowland rainforest and vine forest habitat. At the northern end of the Whitsunday Coast is Bowen, famous for mango cultivation. Deep into the tropics, Townsville, the self-proclaimed capital of north Queensland, looks out across Cleveland Bay to Magnetic Island.

Island Pleasures

The Whitsunday Islands are famed as one of the greatest sailing and cruising grounds in the world. Seventy-four islands provide both safe anchorage and some of the most glorious ocean scenery you will ever see — pure silica sands, fringing coral reefs and uninhabited landscapes. Bustling Airlie Beach, located between Mackay and Bowen, is the main departure point for resort islands whose names are deeply ingrained in Australia's folklore of ideal tropical escapes — Daydream, Hayman, Lindeman, Hamilton and Hook. Yet within this high traffic holiday zone, 96% of the total island land mass remains protected from human development.

Brampton Island The mountainous terrain of Brampton Island in the Cumberland Group of the Whitsundays.

Emperor Angelfish The Great Barrier Reef Marine Park is a vital habitat for some of the world's most striking creatures.

Continental Isles

The Whitsundays are continental islands — the peaks of mountain ranges (formerly connected to the mainland) that were submerged when sea levels rose at the end of the last Ice Age. Dark green forests plunge down these steep-sided isles to stop abruptly at snow-white beaches fringing the land. The ocean shades from deepest peacock blue to pale turquoise (where sandbars lie close to the surface in shallow water).

Great Walks of Queensland

The Mackay Highlands Great Walk is a 56 km route through the hinterland rainforest, dense palm groves (*right*) and unforgettable mountain scenery linking Eungella and Homevale National Parks inland from Mackay. The entire walk takes around five days to complete, but is broken into small sections for those wanting just a taste of this unique Central Queensland landscape.

The walk commences at Pine Grove in the Eungella township and finishes at either Moonlight Dam or Mount Britton. The walk will appeal to everyone, but no doubt holds a particular attraction for lovers of botany. Over 860 plant species are represented — including towering Red Cedar and magnificent Mackay Tulip Oak. Walking in the park is best between April and September (in order to avoid climatic extremes). Four walkers' camps with basic facilities lie at different points along the track (bookings apply, Ph: 13 13 04).

Townsville
Rockhampton

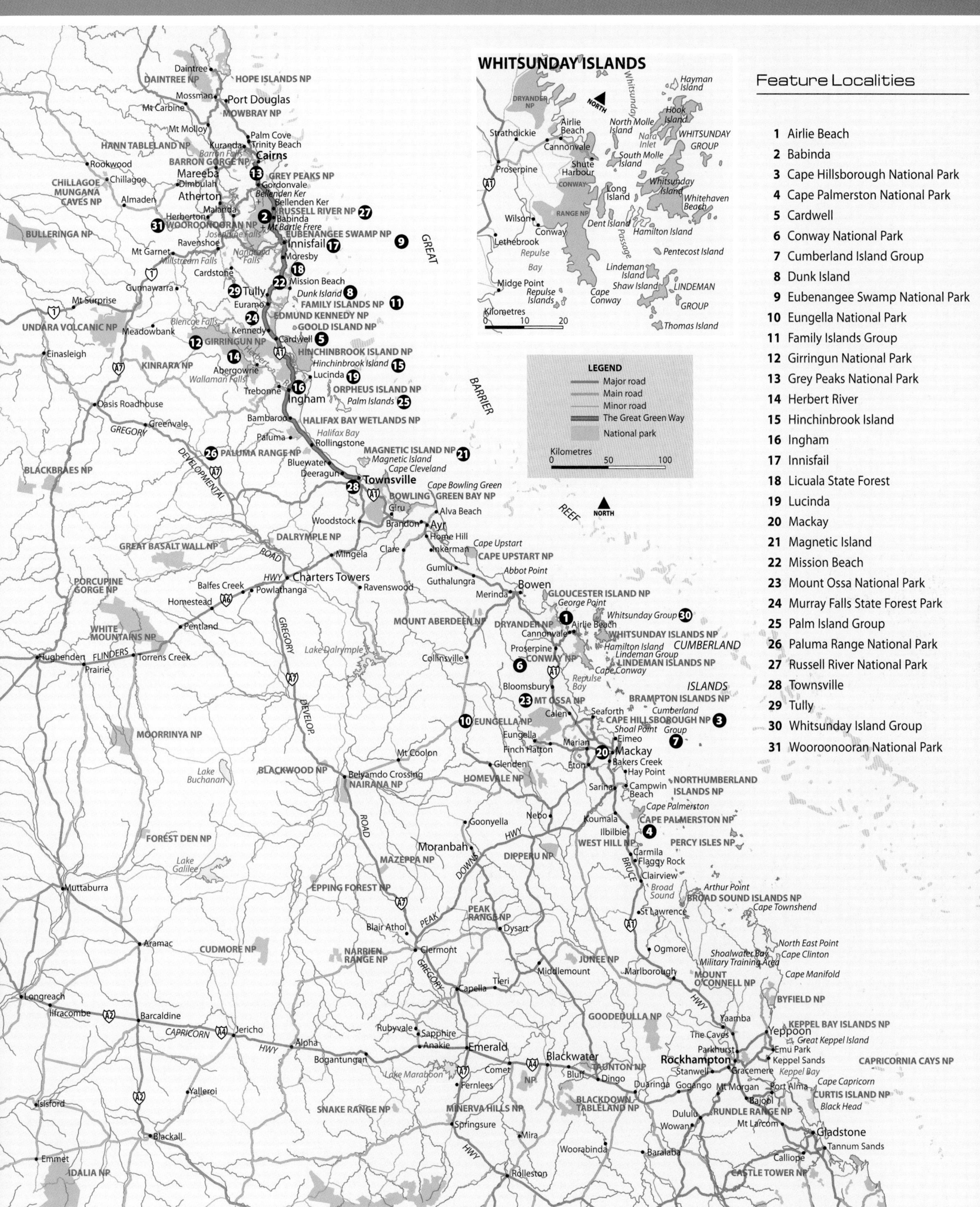
WHITSUNDAY ISLANDS
LEGEND
Major road
Main road
Minor road
The Great Green Way
National park
Kilometres
0 50 100
NORTH
Feature Localities
1 Airlie Beach
2 Babinda
3 Cape Hillsborough National Park
4 Cape Palmerston National Park
5 Cardwell
6 Conway National Park
7 Cumberland Island Group
8 Dunk Island
9 Eubenangee Swamp National Park
10 Eungella National Park
11 Family Islands Group
12 Girringun National Park
13 Grey Peaks National Park
14 Herbert River
15 Hinchinbrook Island
16 Ingham
17 Innisfail
18 Licuala State Forest
19 Lucinda
20 Mackay
21 Magnetic Island
22 Mission Beach
23 Mount Ossa National Park
24 Murray Falls State Forest Park
25 Palm Island Group
26 Paluma Range National Park
27 Russell River National Park
28 Townsville
29 Tully
30 Whitsunday Island Group
31 Wooroonooran National Park

Into the Tropics

Beyond Rockhampton and the Capricorn Coast, the distinct character and colours of tropical Queensland emerge. There is a relaxed air to the area's towns and cities, which provide a welcome contrast with the region's busy tourism trade. Of course, the stunning natural environs have a little to do with this — gazing out upon a glittering aquamarine ocean or walking through verdant coastal rainforest does tend to induce a languid and welcoming calm.

Airlie Beach

Whether you are treating yourself to a luxurious rest stop en route to the reef or craving the social buzz brought on by a fraternity of local and international travellers, Airlie Beach exudes both a lazy tropical ambience and energetic nightlife that is difficult to resist.

This cosmopolitan town looks out over the waters of Pioneer Bay, dotted with yachts, to the islands of the inner reef. Airlie is great for shopping (the foreshore is the setting for the local Saturday markets) and its huge artificial lagoon makes a top swimming spot in summer.

Mackay & Surrounds

From Rockhampton the Bruce Highway tracks the coast north-west. Don't expect ocean views though, as the Torilla Peninsula north of Byfield National Park is predominantly occupied by the restricted Shoalwater Bay Military Training Area, and over the next 300 km to Mackay the road only nears the coast again in a short stretch around Clairview. In between are a series of small rural and railway towns developed over the past century to service the sugar industry. Clairview is a pleasant fishing and crabbing town with unspoiled beaches, a caravan park and camping facilities. A little further up the road, Carmila and Carmila Beach offer similar amenities. The Exotic Fruit Garden and Ice Creamery, set on a small lagoon at Flaggy Rock, is a popular spot for a refreshing pause from the rigours of highway travel.

South of the sugar town of Sarina is Cape Palmerston National Park, a favourite of anglers and birdwatchers. This protected region of coast features rocky headlands, rainforest, swamps, dunes and Estuarine Crocodiles! Access is by 4WD vehicle only and basic bush camping is available. There are excellent views of the Northumberland Islands from Cape Palmerston. Further up the coast at Hay Point (21 km north of Sarina), is one of the world's biggest coal export ports — worth visiting just to gape at the wharves, stretching nearly 4 km out to sea, which operate around the clock loading bulk carriers with Queensland coal.

Shute Harbour

As the major launching pad to the Whitsundays, Shute Harbour is reputed to be Australia's second-busiest commuter port after Circular Quay (in Sydney). Ferries, cruises and charter vessels are not your only option for offshore exploration — each day helicopters and seaplanes also depart Shute Harbour to the islands beyond.

Mackay

Established on the traditional land of the Yuibera people, this tropical city's handsome heritage buildings are the remarkable survivors of a devastating 1918 cyclone that sent 2.7 m high waves surging down the main streets. Cattle, coal and cane are the city's economic lifeblood, but Mackay also offers some unique cultural attractions. The multi-million dollar Artspace Mackay (Gordon Street) boasts an international-standard exhibition gallery, while the Central Queensland Conservatorium of Music, and Mackay Entertainment Centre (Gordon Street) present a broad variety of musical performances. This range of arts is perhaps unsurprising given that Dame Nellie Melba, one of the world's great operatic stars, lived near Mackay for a time after her father purchased a sugar mill at Mirani. The house in which she lived after marrying the mill's manager is open to the public (Eungella Road, Mirani). Immediately north of town are some excellent beaches, including Harbour Beach, Lamberts Beach (with a fine lookout) and the 6 km long Blacks Beach (lined with tropical gardens). Bucasia Beach (20 minutes north) has stinger-protection enclosures for year-round swimming and great views to the North Cumberland Islands and Dolphin Heads. Eimeo's clifftop Pacific Hotel has a beer garden with panoramas of the Coral Sea and Sunset Bay.

Proserpine & Airlie Beach

The highway to Proserpine passes below the eastern edge of Eungella and Mt Ossa National Parks. The beautiful Cape Hillsborough National Park (*see facing page*) can be accessed from Seaforth Road or Mt Ossa Road (partly unsealed). Proserpine is enveloped by dense canefields — the first European explorer in this region, George Dalrymple, was so impressed with its agricultural potential he named the valley for the Greek goddess of fertility. The town's many commercial facilities are the mainstay of local rural industry and Whitsundays tourism.

Driving into Airlie Beach you may wonder why many visitors only use it as a transit point for the reef islands. This idyllic holiday village may well tempt you to stay on the mainland with its seemingly endless accommodation, dining and nightlife options, bustling foreshore markets and stinger-free swimming at the capacious Airlie Lagoon. If you can drag yourself away, Shute Harbour, 8 km down the road through wooded Conway National Park (*see facing page*), is your embarkation point for the glorious Whitsundays.

Top to bottom: An example of Eungella National Park palm forest; Platypus.

Eungella National Park

Phone Ranger: (07) 4944 7800

High mountain peaks, rugged escarpments, deep gorges, abundant birdlife and plenty of lush vegetation distinguish this unique reserve on the Clarke Range about 80 km west of Mackay. Eungella marks a convergence point between subtropical and tropical ecology.

Walks in the Park: With more than 20 km of walking tracks (including the starting section of the 56 km Mackay Highlands Great Walk), Eungella National Park is a bushwalker's dream.

Access: From Mackay drive 80 km west on the Mackay–Eungella Road to Picnic Grove. The steep Clarke Range is not suitable for caravans.

Camping: Set in a serene patch of rainforest, Fern Flat lies on the western side of the Broken River picnic area (accessible by hikers only).

Cape Hillsborough National Park

Phone Ranger: (07) 4944 7800

Dusk often brings kangaroos to the mesmerising shorelines of Cape Hillsborough National Park. The park's forested wetlands and rocky headlands, strewn with boulders from ancient volcanic eruptions, are also major attractions.

Walks in the Park: Walk on the beaches, explore tidal rockpools, follow the boardwalk through mangrove forest or learn about Aboriginal plant use on the Yuibera Plant Trail. There are also great coastal vistas from the Beachcomber Cove and Andrews Point Tracks.

Access: Via Seaforth Road (20 km north of Mackay off the Bruce Highway); keep driving for another 20 km to reach the Cape Hillsborough turn-off and a further 10 km to reach the park.

Camping: A small bush camp at Smalleys Beach has toilets and town water.

Top to bottom: Cape Hillsborough National Park; Kangaroo sunset at Cape Hillsborough.

Conway National Park

Phone Ranger: (07) 4936 0511

Immediately south of Airlie Beach off the Shute Harbour Road is the largest coastal national park in Queensland, covering 22,500 ha. Leave your car at Conway picnic ground, Mount Rooper car park or Coral Beach car park and explore this huge region of lowland rainforest and coast via one of the excellent walking paths. The park's diverse native fauna includes mound-building birds — the Australian Brush-turkey and the Orange-footed Scrubfowl.

Walks in the Park: The 2.4 km climb up Mount Rooper reveals excellent scenic views of the coast and islands from Mount Rooper Lookout.

Access: Follow Shute Harbour Road south-east from Airlie Beach. From Airlie, the Conway picnic ground is only a 6.5 km drive.

Camping: A basic walk-in bush camp is provided 2.1 km from Mt Rooper car park at Swampy Bay (overlooking Daydream Island).

Shute Harbour Shute Harbour, gateway to the Whitsundays. Conway National Park provides a beautiful backdrop.

Mackay

The town's palm-fringed main street has a grand array of historic buildings. The area is also rich in natural assets — the cool, rainforest-clad refuge of Eungella National Park lies to the west; the blue water of the Pioneer River runs through the city's heart; and the Whitsundays beckon offshore to the north-east. Mackay's busy marina is a pleasant place to dine and watch the world sail past.

Proserpine

On winter nights, when pre-harvest burning takes place, the sugarcane plantations of the Proserpine Valley paint an archetypical vignette of regional Australia. Proserpine's airport serves the major resort islands of the Whitsundays and its streets are enlivened by original Art Deco buildings and pubs.

Bowen Beaches

The beaches north of Bowen are some of mainland Australia's best. The sultry and relaxed atmosphere offers something different from the classic surf beaches of southern Queensland and there is superb snorkelling and diving to be experienced on the reef hugging this coast. Check out Murrays Bay, Greys Bay and Rose Bay.

The Whitsundays

Globally revered as a top-shelf tropical destination, there has always been more to the Whitsundays than meets the eye. While the Whitsundays' glamorous and heavily promoted resort destinations take centre stage, most of the region's 74 islands hold special appeal as uninhabited national parks. Large parts of the developed islands are also protected as wilderness areas, which preserves their sense of remoteness and provides excellent opportunities to escape to nature. While sailing through the Whitsunday Passage in 1770, James Cook observed members of one of Australia's earliest recorded Aboriginal groups, the Ngaro, on island beaches. The Ngaro people inhabited both the Whitsundays' coast and islands, and their rock art sites, cave paintings, stone quarries and middens are found throughout the region — notably at Nara Inlet on Hook Island.

The Whitsundays stretch from the resort island of Brampton Island (technically part of the Cumberland Group) to Hayman Island north-east of Airlie Beach. The shortest distance by boat from Shute Harbour are South and North Molle Islands and Daydream Island. But even the most remote of the resort isles (Hayman) is only 45 minutes away from Hamilton Island's airport, while Brampton Island is but a 10 minute flight from Mackay. The biggest of the group is the largely pristine Whitsunday Island, directly east of Airlie Beach.

Major Resorts

The first holiday getaway ever developed in the Whitsundays was a thatched hut run by the Nicholson family on Lindeman Island in 1923. That primitive hut has evolved into the 225-room Club Med that proudly claims to be the first reef resort to receive accreditation under Australia's National Ecotourism Accreditation Program. It also has all the usual Club Med accoutrements — ultra-organised activities, a range of kids' clubs and an army of superfit, tanned stewards to attend to the every desire of its "gentils membres" (as guests are rather quaintly called). It is reached by launch from Hamilton Island or Shute Harbour. Direct flights from Proserpine land at the island's airstrip. Beyond the resort, Lindeman has seven beaches and 20 km of bushwalking tracks spread over nearly 700 ha of National Park.

Hamilton Island, Lindeman's northern neighbour, is the most keenly promoted of the group and boasts the most comprehensive facilities. This is a small-scale tropical city with its own major airport and myriad shops, bars and restaurants. There is even a local church (lest a romantic holiday leads to spontaneous betrothal). The resort offers a wide range of accommodation options, from child-free luxury to family-friendly beachside bures. Remarkably, amid all this development, over 80% of the island remains in its natural state.

Perhaps the most luxurious resort is Hayman Island, a five-star splurge of silver service, ocean-view restaurants and celebrity-style penthouses — even the bushwalking tracks are regularly graded. It was developed as a resort in the 1940s by airline tycoon Sir Reginald Ansett. If your wallet extends to extravagance, begin in style and arrive by seaplane from Proserpine Airport. South Molle Island's resort is more low-key and family-oriented. It was developed over 60 years, and has been re-built since Cyclone Ada struck in 1970. The leisurely pace is enhanced by a variety of excellent walks to the island's many hills and secluded beaches. Daydream Island was once known by the decidedly less poetic name of West Molle. It is the smallest of the resort islands but still offers the full gamut of tropical island activities.

Camping & Cruising

A huge choice of resorts means that camping on the Whitsunday Islands is often overlooked. However, Whitsundays camping is probably the closest you'll come to a true tropical castaway experience. As many of the islands provide safe anchorage, camping can also be readily combined with a chartered or self-skippered cruise. Book camping sites well in advance, as capacity limits apply on all islands. Numerous commercial tour operators package camping and cruising holidays.

The Queensland Parks and Wildlife Service lists 33 official camping sites. The main destinations are Whitsunday Island, Gloucester Island, Hook Island, Shaw Island and South Molle Island. Planton Island and Denman Island offer the most secluded, Crusoe-like adventures (bookings and permits are required for all camping sites, Ph: (07) 4946 7022).

Emerald & Azure

Seen from the air, the islands of the Whitsunday Passage are a long broken chain of white fringed, hilly green outcrops in a sea of perfect azure. On the more heavily touristed islands, the resorts are visible but commercial development is still heavily outweighed by miles of pristine woodland and beach. The Whitsundays' reefs harbour the full spectrum of tropical marine life.

Island Wildlife

The Whitsundays form part of the route navigated annually by migratory Humpback Whales. Dugongs, turtles, dolphins and rays are also often seen close to island shores and large birds-of-prey (including Brahminy Kites (*above*) and Ospreys) can be spied in the skies overhead. Whitsunday and Gloucester Islands teem with wildlife, including rock-wallabies, Beach Stone-curlews (*below*), bats and monitors.

Hook Island

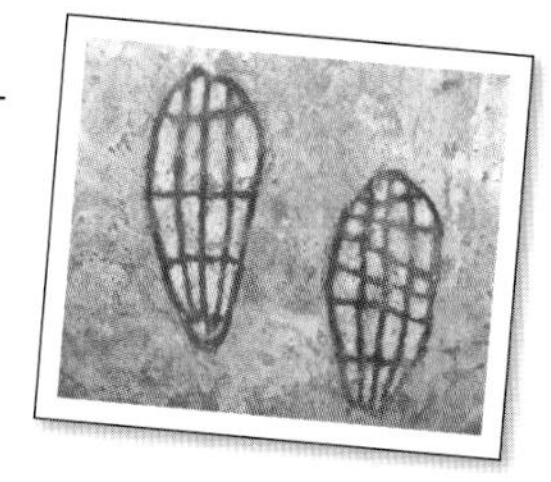

Separated from Whitsunday Island by a narrow, deep passage, Hook Island combines a "wilderness" styled resort and camping facilities with soul-refreshing forest walks, pure blue waters and white silica beaches. The Aboriginal rock art at Nara Inlet, created by the original Ngaro people, is also superb.

Camping: There are five separate camping sites set on the beaches of Hook Island with capacity limits ranging from 12–36 people.

Hamilton Island

If it's mod cons you crave, Hamilton Island boasts the most. From the time of your arrival at the airport with the hordes of sunseekers from Australia's southern states, Hamilton can supply everything you require. All you need is time to explore the exhausting list of leisure options — oh, and a healthy holiday slush fund, of course.

Camping: There are no public camping areas on Hamilton Island.

Lewin's Honeyeater

Hayman Island

One of the Whitsunday Group's closest islands to the Great Barrier Reef, Hayman Island has for many years been seen as the archetypal Whitsundays experience. Luxury, leisure and long sunny days lazing by lagoon, pool or ocean — if you've ventured that far from your five-star suite.

Camping: There are no public camping areas on Hayman Island.

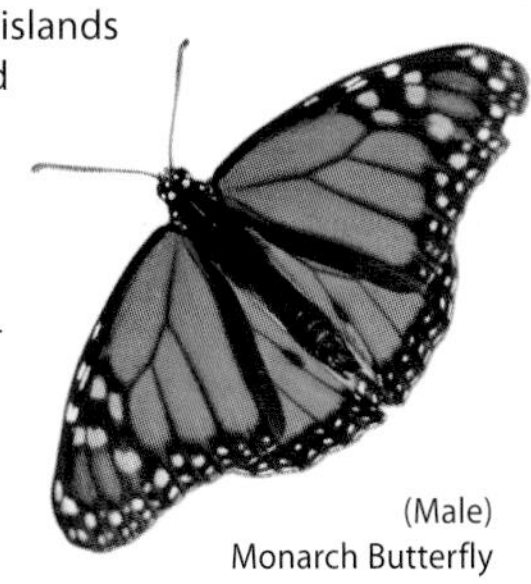

(Male) Monarch Butterfly

Whitsunday Island

While it may not have the celebrity status of its neighbours, nor a resort to call its own, Whitsunday Island attracts increasing numbers of visitors looking to explore deserted island wilderness. The island features a number of excellent walks, beautiful beach campsites and the long ribbon of Whitehaven Beach — possibly the most unspoilt strip of sand in the entire Whitsunday region and one of the whitest beaches you are ever likely to see.

Camping: There are eight separate campsites on Whitsunday Island with capacity limits ranging from 6–60 people.

Dive, Snorkel, Sail & Fish

Hook, Border and Langford Islands are among the best Whitsunday locations for snorkelling and diving, but at high tide snorkelling almost anywhere over the reef is worthwhile. In calm weather conditions, the water is clearest at the northern ends of outer islands.

The Whitsunday Passage is also one of the world's premier sailing destinations and many a mariner has spent extended periods adrift exploring the isles. Be sure to use public mooring areas (as anchorage regulations now apply in the Whitsundays to minimise reef damage). Fishing is also restricted but permitted in some zones (Ph: (07) 4946 7022 for detailed information before your departure).

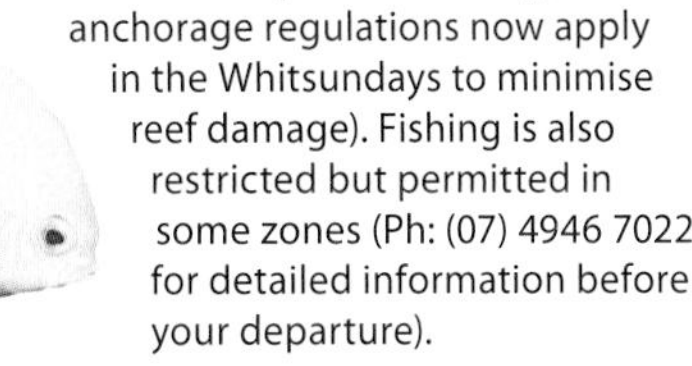

Damselfish

Townsville & Surrounds

The two main towns that break the 200 km journey between the Whitsundays and Townsville are Bowen and Ayr. Bowen sits in the northern crook of Edgecombe Bay, a tidy old-fashioned town with exceptional beaches to its north. Bowen's industry includes coal exporting and fish processing, but the surrounding hinterland is also a major fruit and vegetable growing area, with tomatoes and mangoes its key crops. Accordingly there is, of course, a Big Mango gracing the entrance to the Bowen Visitor Information Centre on the Bruce Highway south of town. Bowen's history is depicted in an expansive series of murals that decorate the town's main business area. The story is also told through a huge collection of memorabilia and relics on display at the excellent Bowen Historical Museum (22 Gordon Street).

Murals are also a feature of Collinsville, situated south-west of Bowen in a region that has a long history of opal and coal mining. North of Bowen, the Bruce Highway crosses the mighty Burdekin River via the "Silver Link" — a 1 km bridge built in 1958 to prevent the town of Ayr being cut off by flood. On the southern side of the bridge is Ayr's twin town Home Hill where, while there is no hill, there are more murals to be found depicting bucolic scenes. Ayr is a peaceful rural town 10 km inland from pretty Alva Beach, which has a growing reputation among kiteboarding enthusiasts. Tropical sportfish are also avidly pursued in these parts.

Townsville

Townsville is Australia's largest tropical city, the capital of the north, and home to one of northern Australia's largest commercial ports. During World War II, Townsville was an important base for allied forces and the population boomed. The city was bombed three times and the Post Office's stone clock tower was removed to prevent it becoming a target (as had Darwin's). Located in Flinders Street, the historic post office is now a boutique brewery under which a red brick tunnel was discovered in 2002 leading to the Customs House on The Strand. Rumour has it that this and several other tunnels discovered under Townsville had some strategic military purpose. Discover more about Queensland's wartime experience in the North Queensland Military Museum at Jezzine Barracks on Kissing Point and at the Cape Pallarenda Conservation Park (the 2 km Forts Track has fantastic views over Cleveland Bay).

With a real heartland feel, Townsville is a welcoming, busy city that does not depend on tourism for its existence. Nocturnal activity is concentrated around historic Flinders Street East in North Ward (on one side of Ross Creek) and Palmer Street in South Townsville (on the opposite bank). The Strand, a palm-fringed promenade stretching along the foreshore of Cleveland Bay, is an extremely popular spot for walking and cycling. It features 2.5 km of landscaped gardens, public sculptures, restaurants and cafés. Close by, the attractive Queens Gardens stretch seaward from the base of Castle Hill just north of the CBD. Reef HQ (on Flinders Street East) boasts the largest living reef in captivity, nurtured in a huge outdoor coral aquarium complex. Next door is the Museum of Tropical Queensland. Presiding over Ross Marina at the southern end of The Strand are Jupiters Casino and the Townsville Entertainment and Convention Centre. For all its shrewd development, the city still enjoys a close communion with the nature of the tropics. Flying-fox colonies emerge at twilight and Freshwater Crocodiles enjoy lotus-fringed habitats in Ross River's upper reaches. The Town Common (6 km north of the city) protects remnant wetland habitats and plenty of birdlife.

Crowned by Hill

Castle Hill (*above*) rises 286 m above Townsville, providing the city with a dramatic pink granite backdrop. A lookout at the summit can be reached either by car or foot and provides sweeping views of Townsville, Cleveland Bay and Magnetic island. Two kilometres south of Townsville, the 585 m Mount Stuart delivers an even more dramatic geographical layout.

Blessed by Bay

Flanked by Cape Pallarenda (west) and Cape Cleveland (east), Cleveland Bay is protected from prevailing breezes. The bay is shallow (about 50% is less than 5 m deep) and its seagrass beds support many Dugongs — hence the bay has been declared a "class A" Dugong sanctuary.

On the Waterfront

Along Townsville's beloved Strand are a number of interesting historical sites. Stop for a swim near the marina at the famous Tobruk Pool where many Australian swimming stars, including Dawn Fraser, trained in preparation for the Melbourne Olympics of 1956. At the Strand's northern end is the Rock Pool, a picturesque enclosure situated below the headland at Kissing Point. Flushed by ocean tides and free of marine stingers, it remains a favourite swimming spot all-year-round.

Arthur Bay Pine-fringed beaches provide secluded relaxation on Magnetic Island.

Magnetic Island National Park

Phone Ranger: (07) 4778 5378

Known as "Maggie" to its friends and thought by James Cook to be the home of "magnetic" rocks that played havoc with his compass, Magnetic Island lies 8 km off Townsville across Cleveland Bay. Its prime attractions are quiet beaches, sheltered bays and shaded walking tracks through the island's curious boulder-strewn landscape. Mount Cook rises to 497 m at its centre. A large portion (just over half) of Maggie is national park. The island has a resident population of 2500 and tourist accommodation ranges from backpacker hostels to more upmarket resorts. The island's relatively shallow waters and close-to-shore submerged wrecks make for excellent diving and snorkelling. It is also home to Australia's largest colony of wild Koalas (*left*).

Walks in the Park: The most popular walking tracks commence in the eastern section of the island. From Picnic Bay, an easy 1.2 km track leads to the top of a large boulder on Hawking Point with views across the bay to Townsville. A much longer (but easy grade) 16 km track leads along the coast to West Point. From Nelly Bay you can follow a 5 km track across the ridge to Arcadia, or branch off north to Horseshoe Bay. From the Forts Walk car park on Horseshoe Bay Road, tracks lead to Arthur Bay, Radical Bay and Florence Bay (the fringing reef at Florence Bay provides excellent snorkelling).

Access: Passenger ferries depart from Breakwater Terminal and the car ferry leaves from the opposite side of the creek. The relatively calm waters of Cleveland Bay make the island easy to reach with your own boat.

Camping: Not permitted, but private operators offer a full range of accommodation options.

Top to bottom: Allied Rock-wallaby — one of Maggie's native marsupials; Nelly Bay, Magnetic Island.

Clockwise from top: Paluma Range rainforest; Jourama Falls section, Paluma Range National Park; Little Crystal Creek Bridge.

Paluma Range National Park

Phone Ranger: (07) 4722 5224

Paulma Range National Park is split into two sections — the Jourama Falls section (in the foothills of the Seaview Ranges) and the Mount Spec section (straddling the Paluma Range escarpment). Tropical rainforest, woodland and clean waterfalls are features of both sections. Nearly 75% of the park lies in the Wet Tropics World Heritage Area.

Walks in the Park: In the Mount Spec section, a track leads through rainforest from McClelland's Lookout to Witt's Lookout (1.5 km one way) and to Cloudy Creek (2 km one way). The track to Jourama Falls lookout is 3 km return. All tracks are moderate grade.

Access: Mt Spec section is 61 km north of Townsville via the old Bruce Highway. Jourama Falls section is 91 km north of Townsville.

Camping: There are well-equipped campgrounds with both tent and caravan sites at Big Crystal Creek in the southern section and Jourama Falls in the northern section.

Some Special Dive Trips

1 Dive the SS *Yongala* wreck off Cape Bowling Green.

2 Go jaw-to-jaw with reef sharks at Scuba Zoo.

3 Test your limits. Drift-dive plummeting walls and canyons around Flinders Reef.

4 Embark on a multi-day, outer reef dive expedition aboard a fully equipped cruiser.

Coral Sea Diving from Townsville

The warm waters of the Coral Sea offer ideal year-round diving conditions for every level of diver. In many locations it is unnecessary to descend to great depths to experience some of the world's most remarkable diving experiences. The outlying reefs (actually the tips of ancient mountains) are frontier territory for recreational divers. Numerous live-aboard vessels offer multi-day diving adventures complete with gear, food, beverages and entertainment. Some of the most popular dive sites in the Coral Sea off Townsville include Wheeler Reef, China Wall, Pelagic Lookout, Scuba Zoo, Anemone City and the highly rated wreck of the SS *Yongala*. The coral reefs, pinnacles, caves, canyons and undersea gullies teem with marine life and provide magnificent opportunities for photography. The encyclopaedic range of marine creatures you can encounter include barracuda, tuna, wrasse, groupers, trevally, sharks, cuttlefish, rays, sea hares and morays. Visibility in the Coral Sea is superb, often exceeding 30 m.

Wreck Diving

The 115 m SS *Yongala* was a passenger steamer that disappeared in a cyclone off Cape Bowling Green near Townsville in 1911. One hundred and twenty-two souls were lost and despite extensive searches, the wreck was not located until 1947. Today, the *Yongala* has become a marine haven. Metre for metre, it is one of the world's most biodiverse reef environments in the world. A stunning array of fish can be seen here, including Napoleon Wrasse, Cobia, Shovelnose Rays, Bull Sharks and Coral Trout. The *Yongala's* coral-covered upper deck is only 15 m below the surface, making this one of the planet's best and most accessible wreck dives.

Scuba Zoo

Renowned as one of the country's top shark dives, Scuba Zoo offers the chance to dive with more than 30 sharks and from within custom-built cages anchored to the sea floor, safely observe these awesome beasts devouring their dinner.

Anemone City

Coral beds blanketed with anemones (and resident anemonefish) and populated by a huge range of reef fish are the key attractions of Anemone City off Townsville.

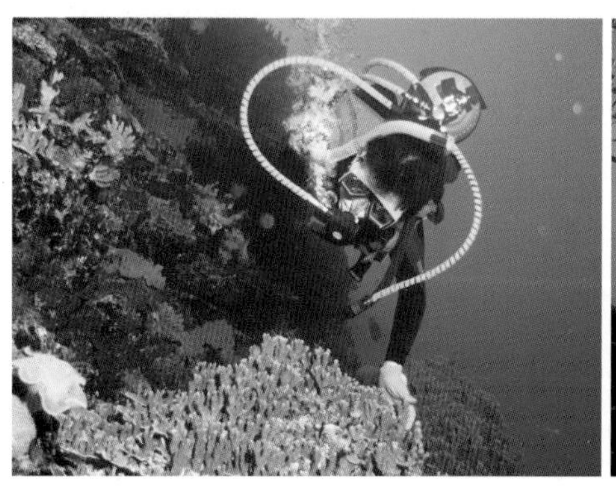

Wall Dives

The Coral Sea offers an amazing range of spectacular plunging walls, labyrinthine caves and seemingly bottomless underwater canyons.

For experienced divers, the shelving drop-off of China Wall (which plummets to depths in excess of 1000 m) exhilarates with its schools of Grey Reef Sharks and other hefty pelagics cruising alongside the steep slopes covered with an amazing selection of fan corals and marine invertebrates.

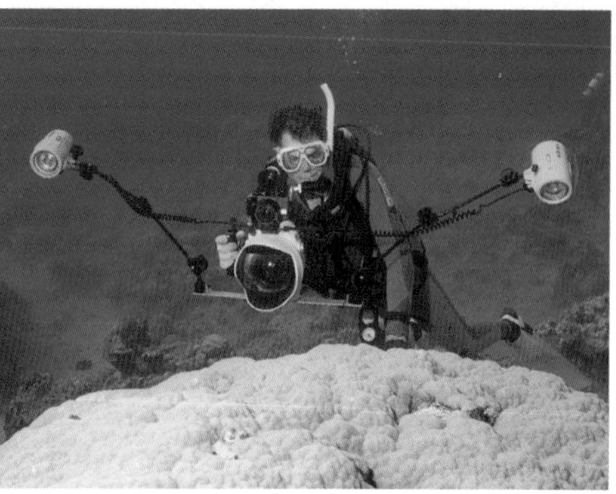

Ideal for Photography

The warm, clear waters of the Coral Sea provide unrivalled conditions and superb visibility for underwater photography. Flinders Reef, Wheeler Reef (perfect for beginner divers), Anemone City and the wreck of the SS *Yongala* are some of the most popular dive photography sites.

Photographic equipment, including cameras and protective gear, are available for hire in Townsville. Underwater photography training and tutorials are also available from major dive centres.

Cruising the Queensland Coast

There are literally thousands of different types of cruises departing from nearly every marina and port from Brisbane to Port Douglas. These range from hour long jaunts along inner reefs to week or even month long expeditions to remote outer reefs. You can explore many of the more popular islands in the space of a day — others are more distant (and more adventurous). Remote reef and island cruises are often longer and more expensive, but gift you with an opportunity to see parts of the Great Barrier Reef and Coral Sea inaccessible to island resort guests and daytrippers. Exploring the Whitsunday region on a chartered boat or yacht has become one of the world's most coveted travel experiences. It is also possible to travel the entire distance between Brisbane, Cairns and Port Douglas on one of the larger passenger ships that regularly cruise these waters. Travel time varies according to operator but some vessels make the return trip in a week, stopping at several ports and anchorages (often including isolated Willis Island) along the way.

Some Special Things to Do

1. Learn to dive or snorkel while staying along the coast.
2. Surf the breaks off the outer reef.
3. Set sail for untouched Willis Island.
4. Cruise the Queensland coast from Brisbane to Port Douglas — unforgettable!

Training & Safety

For many, travelling along the Queensland coast represents their first opportunity to snorkel and dive. Training and safety courses, from beginner to advanced levels (including globally accredited PADI dive training), are widely available. Snorkelling tutorials are often offered as part of a charter or cruise, and every creditable dive operator will check your level of certification before taking your booking for a dive. Never undertake dives for which you are not qualified. Basic water safety and lifesaving courses are also available to help make your reef induction both thrilling and safe.

Lonely Cays & Islands

Willis Island (*far left*), 450 km east of Cairns, is a popular anchorage for many larger cruise ships. A true "desert" isle, Willis Island has hosted a manned meteorological and cyclone warning station since 1921. It is also home to a huge community of sea birds, marine turtles and crabs. Percy Island, 122 km south-east of Mackay, was described by Matthew Flinders in 1802 as "one of the prettiest places imaginable" and has become a legendary stopover for yachts cruising the reef. It features a shack-like "shrine" to passing mariners who make offerings with a variety of nautical artefacts (*left*).

A Surfeit of Sea Birds

Innumerable sea birds (both resident and migratory species) cruise the skies, fish the waters and nest on the islands of the Great Barrier Reef and Coral Sea. Among the most prevalent species are Ospreys, boobies, terns, kites, herons, noddies and shearwaters.

In many cases, sea birds are responsible for the vegetation of Coral Sea cays, which grows from seed transported within and fertilised by guano.

Sail, Scuba or Surf – the Choice is Yours

Such is the popularity of cruising the Queensland coast that operators offer a seemingly endless array of options from which to choose. Snorkel and dive charters are available from every reef port and resort island but there are also sea kayaking tours, sportfishing expeditions, yachting adventures, surf trips, glass bottom and submersible boat tours and more. The high level of commercial competition means you can usually find a trip to suit your budget, but it may be helpful to solicit the opinion of "salty" travellers before making a final decision.

The Rush West

The discovery of gold west of Townsville at Ravenswood and Charters Towers in the late 1800s precipitated a huge influx of hopeful prospectors that laid the foundations for the region's development. While Ravenswood became a virtual ghost town after its rich mineral seams were exhausted, Charters Towers continued to prosper and is now a commercial centre for graziers and miners of the north-west.

Trail of the Overlanders

The expansive grazing areas of Queensland's north-west attracted a hardy breed of settlers willing to tolerate a sapping climate and isolation in their quest for pastoral wealth. The regions west of Charters Towers were first opened up by explorers such as William Landsborough (who surveyed much of the area while searching for explorers Burke and Wills). The subsequent establishment of cattle stations led to "overlanders" driving cattle from the Queensland outback to the coast and across the Barkly Tableland to the Territory.

Charters Towers

The central precinct of Charters Towers, known as the "One Square Mile", has a wealth of heritage buildings including City Hall (*above*), making it the state's most beautifully preserved city.

Townsville to Darwin (via Overlanders Way)

If you've had your fill of reef and are itching to get to the Top End, it is only a short 2500 km hop across the outback and the desert from Townsville to Darwin. Sections of this journey may be undertaken as separate trips and are covered in the following chapters of this book, but the route from Townsville to Cloncurry and Mount Isa to Three Ways in the Northern Territory is of interest here. The entire drive to Darwin can be made on sealed road via the Flinders, Barkly and Stuart Highways, and is considerably more comfortable than the horseback journeys undertaken by the overlanders of Australian history.

Townsville to Charters Towers

The Flinders Highway heads south out of Townsville through Woodstock (the location of several historic World War II sites) and Calcium, which is named for the limestone found (and once mined) in the area. Mingela's wetlands are a natural resort for itinerant wading birds and this otherwise quiet one-pub town stages a rowdy rodeo festival in April.

A fascinating detour from the highway leads to Ravenswood (38 km south of Mingela), a National Trust gold-mining town replete with ghost stories. The highway passes over the Burdekin River at Macrossan, where a marker indicates the ominous heights the river previously reached in this notoriously flood-prone region — the record is a remarkable 21.79 m in 1946. In Macrossan Park, a photogenic historical railway bridge stands near its modern (and decidedly less photogenic) incarnation.

Within 25 years of gold being discovered in the Charters Towers region, Charters Towers had grown to become Queensland's second-largest city and was nicknamed "The World" (a reference to the claim that every race on the planet, indeed everything, could be found here at the time). Today the city has slightly more modest aspirations, but the sobriquet is remembered in the World Theatre, an impressive conversion of the original Bank of Commerce building in Mosman Street to a cinema and performing arts complex. Visitors can receive a good introduction to both the layout and history of Charter Towers by visiting the Venus Gold Battery (a historical site featuring an original ore-crushing plant 5 km east of town) and continuing on to Towers Hill Lookout, with its fine views, interpretative displays and amphitheatre cinema. The visitor information centre is in the original wooden National Bank building in Mosman Street, which has been relocated four times since construction.

West of Charters Towers (a region that includes Richmond and Hughenden), history becomes prehistory in dinosaur country — celebrated for some of Australia's most legendary fossil finds. The last significant settlement before Cloncurry is the rural service and supply town of Julia Creek — the "Gateway to the Gulf", as it became known when a bitumen road through to Normanton was constructed in 1964. The town has the distinction of lending its name to one of Australia's most endangered marsupials, the tiny, carnivorous Julia Creek Dunnart, which inhabits an area of around 100 km around the township. For road-weary travellers with an interest in savouring the outback experience, the corrugated iron Eddington Arms pub at Gilliatt, south of the highway, is worth a detour for a taste of authentic early Queensland (and a frosty lager).

Mount Isa to the Territory

A highlight of the trek from Mount Isa to the Northern Territory border is Camooweal Caves National Park, 24 km south of Camooweal. You can also take a detour north of Mount Isa to Boodjamulla (Lawn Hill Gorge) National Park, comprising a series of lush oases tucked amid gorges, and the World-Heritage-listed Riversleigh Fossil Fields.

Over the border and into the Territory, the highway crosses the elevated cattle-grazing plains of the Barkly Tableland to meet the Stuart Highway at Three Ways, where the journey north to Darwin begins. Huge Northern Territory properties (such as Austral Downs, which covers approximately 469,200 ha) have been in operation since the 1880s. Austral Downs still has the original stone dams (built by 19th-century Chinese workers) and a rocket shelter that was part of the Woomera Space Program.

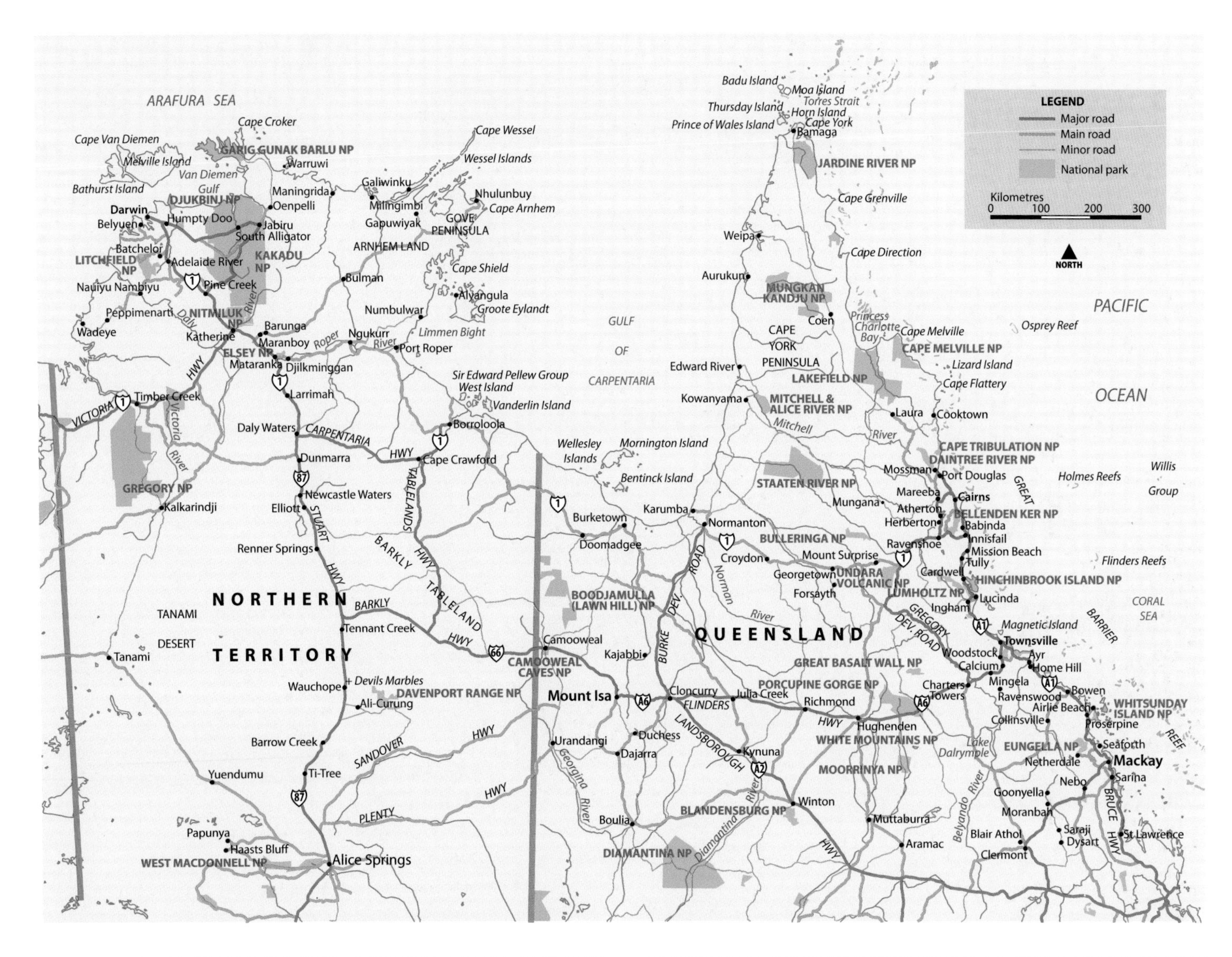

Ravenswood

Stand in the main street of Ravenswood outside the ornate Edwardian facade of the Imperial Hotel and try to imagine a town teeming with over 4000 people (and 50 hotels) at the frenzied height of the goldrush. Visit the Courthouse Museum in Macrossan Street for an insight into the area's fascinating history. At nearby White Blow Environment Park the outback sun strikes 300-million-year-old white quartz outcrops, and views across to the Leichhardt Range give the landscape an unquenchable scope.

Cloncurry

Originally occupied by the Mitakoodi, Kalkadoon and Pitta Pitta Aboriginal people, the Cloncurry region was visited by Burke and Wills in 1861, and settled by pastoralist Ernest Henry in 1868. The discovery of copper and gold in the area transformed Cloncurry into the Queensland outback's biggest (and toughest) town. Cloncurry is a more welcoming place today, but the mineral wealth that put it on the map remains a focus for some of Australia's largest mining operations.

The Dinosaur Way – Hughenden to Riversleigh

At the edge of an ancient inland sea that once extended from the Gulf of Carpentaria to South Australia, the Hughenden area is famous for the discovery of the fossilised skeletal remains of the gigantic *Muttaburrasaurus langdoni* dinosaur.

From Hughenden, the "Dinosaur Way" (Gregory Developmental Road) leads south-west through fossil-rich country to Winton. Hughenden, Richmond and Winton form a triangle that is world renowned for paleontological discoveries. Nearly 3000 fossils found in the Flinders Shire have been registered with the Queensland Museum.

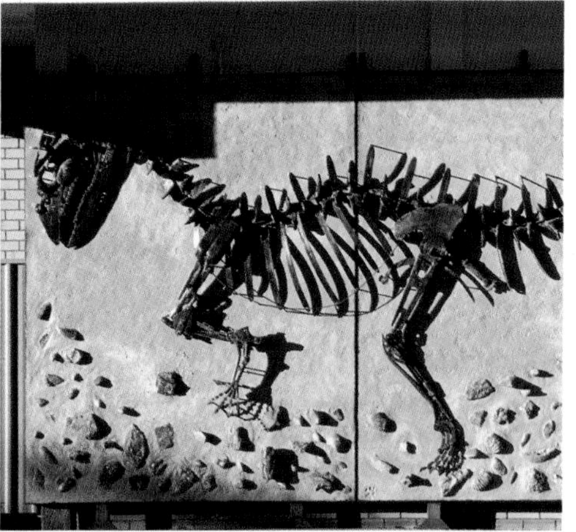

Hughenden

A 3.5 m high, life-size reproduction of the *Muttaburrasaurus* skeleton is displayed at the Flinders Discovery Centre in Gray Street and a statue of the creature welcomes visitors to town at the corner of Gray and Stansfield Streets. Other dinosaur remains found in the region include the 22 m long Hughenden sauropod as well as icthyosaurs (marine reptiles) and an *Anhungurea* — one of only two flying pterosaurs found in Australia.

Richmond

Several major paleontological finds have been made in the Richmond region, including bones of the 120-million-year-old *Kronosaurus* and the crocodile-like Richmond Pliosaur. Near complete skeletons and other remnants are on display at the Richmond Marine Fossil Museum at Kronosaurus Korner (look for the gaping pliosaur jaws) on Goldring Street. The biennial Fossil Festival is staged in even-numbered years and features the world's only moon rock throwing competition. The local Lions Park has a display of these strangely smooth, spherical geological wonders, which are found throughout the region.

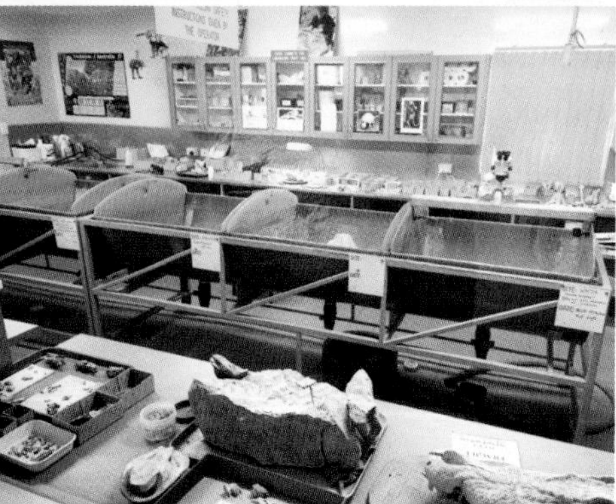

Riversleigh Fossil Centre

If you've ever wanted to experience the heady thrill of prehistoric bones being revealed for the first time, your chance awaits at Riversleigh Fossil Centre in Mount Isa.

Part of the award-winning Outback at Isa mining museum complex, the Riversleigh Fossil Centre offers laboratory tours where visitors can observe real paleontologists in action, hunting out the remnants of prehistoric creatures in rocks gathered from the nearby Riversleigh fossil fields.

The rocks are placed in vats of acetic acid, which dissolves the limestone and exposes the fossils within. Once freed from their rocky bondage, the fossils help theme the dioramas and displays that provide a dramatic insight to the world of fossil and dinosaur hunting.

This rich fossil area is world famous for the vital contribution it makes to academic and scientific research — particularly in the field of megafauna (comparatively large species that roamed Australia until their extinction around 50,000 years ago). Riversleigh fossils are prehistoric "snapshots", but also give important clues to the development of Australia's megafauna over the past 30-million-years.

National Parks between Townsville & Northern Territory Border

From ancient volcanic formations to spectacular gorges and subterranean caverns, the national parks between Townsville and the Northern Territory border present a wild conglomeration of varied landscapes.

Top to bottom: Great Basalt Wall National Park; White Mountain National Park; Porcupine Gorge National Park.

Great Basalt Wall & Dalrymple National Parks – a Dirt Road Detour North

Phone Ranger: (07) 4722 5224

Running parallel to the highway north of Charters Towers is the Great Basalt Wall, a 120 km long, 8 km wide formation that resulted from 13,000-year-old volcanic lava flows. The Great Basalt Wall spans an untamed area of national park intermittently closed to the public, but Dalrymple National Park on its eastern edge is accessible and also features basalt flows, Burdekin River woodlands and the old Dalrymple township site.

Walks in the Park: Rough trails follow the Burdekin River. Longer trails to Mount Keelbottom should only be attempted by experienced, fit and well-equipped hikers.

Access: Drive 42 km north of Charters Towers (via Gregory Developmental Rd). From the south, turn right off the highway onto unsealed track at Fletcher Creek Crossing (4WD needed).

Camping: Beautiful campsites at Burdekin River and Fletcher Creek (permits required).

White Mountains National Park

Phone Ranger: (07) 4722 5224

White Mountains National Park is a rugged outback wilderness of white sandstone gorges and bluffs. Incredibly, the park contains headwaters of streams that flow south-west to Lake Eyre, north to the Gulf of Carpentaria and east to the coast (when there is any water flowing at all).

Walks in the Park: No walking tracks in the park. Burra Range Lookout is along the highway.

Access: Travel 80 km north-east of Hughenden on the Flinders Highway.

Camping: Canns Camp Creek, 11 km west of the Burra Range Lookout, is the only campground in the park. Only a toilet is provided, and visitors need to bring their own water and fuel stoves. A 4WD vehicle is recommended and the road to the campground can be closed during the Wet Season (October to April).

Porcupine Gorge National Park – North of Hughenden

Phone Ranger: (07) 4722 5224

Porcupine Gorge is a dramatic rock incision descending 120 m to waterholes. The gorge features superbly coloured sandstone cliffs and sections of vine forest.

Walks in the Park: The 2.4 km return Gorge Walk (1.5 hr) commences at the Pyramid campground and descends into the gorge. Walk upstream (or down) along a rock platform.

Access: Travel 45 km north of Hughenden on the unsealed Kennedy Developmental Road, which runs along the western edge of the gorge. The Gorge Lookout is another 15 km up the road, the campground and Gorge Walk another 9 km north (Note: The road may be closed to conventional vehicles and caravans following rain).

Camping: Pyramid campground is suitable for tents, caravans and campervans. There are basic toilet facilities, but water should be brought in and no generators are permitted. Camping permits are required (Ph: 13 13 04 or the national parks office).

Camooweal Caves National Park

Phone Ranger: (07) 4722 5224

Located in a semi-arid corner of the Barkly Tableland, Camooweal Caves are a series of sinkholes caused by water rising up through 500-million-year-old layers of soluble dolomite. The process has caused the formation of caverns linked by vertical shafts up to 75 m deep. Tread carefully; their surface openings can be difficult to see amongst the spinifex woodland and Mitchell Grass plains and entry to the caverns is not permitted. They are home to Ghost Bats as well as owls who feed on the park's small mammals, such as the Long-haired Rat. Above ground, monitors and lizards scamper around the rocky outcrops and the seasonal waterhole attracts a surprising variety of waterbirds (including cormorants and spoonbills).

Walks in the Park: There are no walking tracks in the park.

Access: Drive 24 km south of Camooweal on the Urandangi Road (4WD recommended). Travel should not be attempted to the park in (or shortly after) wet weather.

Camping: Basic bush camping site at Caves Waterhole, 14 km from the park entrance (no water or showers).

TOWNSVILLE to Cairns

SEE MAP PAGE 97

Townsville to Cairns
Top Things to Do

1. Enjoy the Cardwell Forest Drive with its spectacular views to Hinchinbrook Island.
2. Take the plunge and try whitewater rafting on the rampaging Tully River.
3. Fish for Barramundi in Hinchinbrook Channel.
4. Snorkel off Orpheus Island.
5. Visit towering Wallaman Falls in gorgeous Girringun National Park.
6. Check out the toothy grins at Johnstone River Crocodile Farm.
7. Get stranded for a few days at Mission Beach. Keep your eyes peeled for the elusive Southern Cassowary.
8. Go bushwalking on Dunk Island.
9. Immerse yourself in the rainforest of Wooroonooran National Park.
10. Climb to the summit of Mount Bartle Frere — Queensland's highest peak.

Top to bottom: Preparing to kayak from Mission Beach around Dunk Island; Winding through the mangroves on Hinchinbrook Island; Sailing, one of the greatest ways to explore the Cassowary Coast.

The route from Townsville to Cairns, known as the Great Green Way, passes through canefields, tropical orchards and lush forests as it runs up the coast through the towns of Ingham, Cardwell, Tully and Innisfail. The region is dubbed the Wet Tropics with good reason — towns like Tully and Babinda have the highest annual rainfalls in Australia. To the east the long chain of reef islands continues, with magnificent Orpheus Island National Park lying offshore from Ingham. From the coast at Cardwell the most dramatic views are of the mountainous peaks of Hinchinbrook Island, with mangroves and forest landward and sandy beaches seaward. Rainforest-cloaked Dunk Island is only 4 km offshore from the popular holiday resort of Mission Beach.

Green Treasures

This is a region of uninhibited natural splendour. West of the highway is an almost unbroken series of national parks protecting the Cardwell Range and Tully Gorge environs. Tully River is one of Australia's premier whitewater rafting destinations. Just west of Tully Gorge, 92 km from Innisfail, is Ravenshoe, the highest town in Queensland, perched above the Atherton Tableland and surrounded by rainforest and waterfalls. North of Innisfail the road separates Wooroonooran and Davies Creek National Parks from the superb coastal parks of Ella Bay, Eubenangee Swamp, Russell River and Grey Peaks. Fifty kilometres south of Cairns is Bartle Frere, Queensland's highest mountain. Travel slowly and take your time to explore — the region rewards those who apply the traveller's maxim: "It's the journey, not the destination."

Great Walks of Queensland – Tropical North

Thorsborne Trail – Hinchinbrook Island

As one of Australia's earliest national parks (protected since 1932), Hinchinbrook Island provides visitors with an unforgettable wilderness experience. Every year over 1000 hikers trek the world-famous Thorsborne Trail — a 32 km track that follows the island's east coast (*above*).

Generally taking three to five days, walkers experience stunning topographic variety and a range of native plant communities. Beaches (both sandy and rocky), headlands, swamps, rainforest, waterfalls, river crossings, mountains and valleys combine to make this the walk of a lifetime. Bookings should be made six months in advance (Ph: (07) 4046 6600).

Misty Mountains Walking Trail – Cardwell Range Track

The Misty Mountains Trail network comprises over 130 km of walking tracks, many of them following pathways established by the area's traditional custodians — the Jirrbal and Ma:Mu people. These routes connected the tablelands (*gambilbara*) with the coastal plain (*yabulmbara*). Other tracks follow in the footsteps of early timber pioneers.

You can access the western end of the Cardwell Range Track (26.7 km one way) from Ravenshoe (via Cockram/Gold Coast Road, off Tully Falls Road). Traversing the hills of the Cardwell Range, the hike takes about two days to complete and along the way you will pass through untouched highland rainforest with clean creeks, waterfalls, rugged ridge-line topography and magnificent views. The best time to undertake your Misty Mountains journey is from March to October. You'll need a permit to camp overnight and a special Wet Tropics permit to travel along Maple Creek Road (between Hinson and Gorrell Trailheads), (contact QPWS for more info, Ph: (07) 4046 6600).

Warning – Estuarine Crocodiles Inhabit This Area

Northern Australia has the world's greatest population of Estuarine (or Saltwater) Crocodiles. Growing up to 7 m long (although 5 m is normal for a male), the Estuarine Crocodile is our planet's largest and most physiologically advanced living reptile. It is also a highly successful and enduring predator — its longevity and mobility complemented by unnerving stealth and incredible power.

How Dangerous Are Estuarine Crocodiles?

The name suggests that these giant reptiles are restricted to saltwater, but the truth is, they are just as much at home in freshwater and regularly move between salt and fresh. This means that caution must be taken in any north Australian water bodies. Most Estuarine Crocodiles will avoid humans, but there are occasionally those individuals, which, for a variety of reasons, will attack. Aboriginal people have co-existed with "salties" in Australia for thousands of years because they know and respect the ways of these giant reptiles. Today we are guided by warning signs and rules, but occasional attacks still occur, mainly through ignorance. With a good natural food supply crocodiles are less likely to trouble humans.

Finding & Watching Salties

In the right circumstances, Estuarine Crocodiles are not difficult to locate and are fascinating animals to observe. They are surprisingly tolerant of humans and will usually go about their business once they have determined that you mean them no harm. Like all wild animals, they need their personal space, so it is not advisable to approach too closely.

Unlike mammals or birds, crocodiles are great energy conservers. These cold-blooded creatures spend a lot of time doing nothing but basking in the sun. Crocodiles are most active during the night, and behavioural activity can usually best be observed early or late in the day when these creatures move into the shadows after having warmed up in the early sunlight.

Most wild crocodile viewing is undertaken from the safety of boats. Many of Australia's tropical national parks now offer wetland boat cruises specifically for viewing aquatic wildlife, including crocodiles.

You Are Now Entering Cassowary Country

The Southern Cassowary — a grand, flightless bird measuring up to 1.7 m high — is unique to the lowland rainforests, woodlands and swamps of Tropical North Queensland and New Guinea. Its coarse black plumage, large beak, prominent helmet-like casque, brightly coloured wattle and stout, plus scaly legs give this magnificent creature a somewhat prehistoric appearance. Although adults can weigh up to 85 kg, males average 38 kilograms and the slightly larger females weigh in around 47 kg.

Male and female Southern Cassowaries are usually difficult to distinguish outside their breeding season. Generally shy, solitary and territorial, they tolerate each other for several weeks during courtship and mating. The male assumes full parental responsibility, incubating the large, dark green eggs for 50 days and often going without food and water for long periods. He then cares for his clutch of cream and brown striped chicks for a further nine to twelve months. A chick's plumage slowly loses its stripes and darkens as the wattle and casque develop. Cassowaries are sexually mature at three-years-of-age.

Although they eat fungi, flowers and a variety of small forest animals, Southern Cassowaries forage predominately on fallen fruit. Their droppings contain a cache of rainforest seeds, ready to germinate, and many large-fruited rainforest trees depend on these birds for their successful regeneration.

Herbert River

Just north of Ingham the Herbert River flows in deceptive serenity to the ocean. This wild river's 340 km journey begins a couple of hours north-west in the high country of the tablelands. Its upper catchment supports cattle grazing and the lower catchment cane farming. The middle reaches pass through gorges of national parks.

Lucinda

The southern end of Hinchinbrook Island is clearly visible from Lucinda across Hinchinbrook Channel — a mangrove-lined waterway famed for the quality of its Barramundi and home to a healthy Dugong population. Water taxis, tours and charters to Hinchinbrook Island depart from the wharf at Dungeness.

Cardwell

Murals adorning buildings in Cardwell (*above*) celebrate its status as a launching point for the exploration of Hinchinbrook Island and Hinchinbrook Channel.

Townsville to Misson Beach – The Cassowary Coast

The journey north from Townsville provides many opportunities for rainforest walks or strolling secluded beaches. The scenic Mt Spec Tourist Road, painstakingly hand-built by labourers during the Great Depression, leaves the highway 40 km south of Ingham and passes over picturesque stone arch bridges as it climbs the Paluma Range. At the top is Paluma, originally an isolated tin mining settlement and now a quaint mountain village with tearooms and craft shops. It was once known as Cloudy Clearing for the mists that enshroud the forest canopy in the late afternoon. Nearby walking tracks radiate through the ranges and rainforest on their way to lookouts and waterfalls.

Ingham & Surrounds

Ingham is surrounded by sugarcane fields linked by a vast network of narrow gauge railways or "tramways" that deliver harvested cane to mills for crushing. Ingham's Victoria Mill is Australia's largest (Forrest Beach Road, daily tours available during crushing season between July and November). En route to the mill on Sir Arthur Fadden Drive is the Ingham Cemetery, distinguished by its impressive array of ornate Italian mausoleums, reflecting the region's heritage. Over 60% of the town's citizens are of Italian descent and Ingham's annual Australian Italian Festival is staged each May. Take a look at the Sicilian Clock, a gift from the local community, near the Rotary Park. Twenty kilometres east of town, stinger-protected swimming is possible at the humble holiday village of Forrest Beach. A short drive north-east on the coast at Lucinda is the world's largest sugar loading facility with a jetty that protrudes an astonishing 5.76 km into the ocean.

At the northern entrance to Hinchinbrook Channel is Cardwell, a small beachside town providing facilities for anglers and island visitors. Take an enjoyable detour from the Bruce Highway along the 26 km Cardwell Forest Drive to Cardwell Lookout with its expansive views out to Hinchinbrook Island. Along the way Attie Creek, Dead Horse Creek and the Spa Pool provide birdsong-blessed settings for picnicking and safe swimming. Another great lunch location in the area is the stunning Murray Falls (turn off at Bilyana, halfway between Cardwell and Tully on the Bruce Highway).

The Torrents of Tully

The rural town of Tully receives 4.4 m of rainfall per year and celebrates its waterlogged climate with the Golden Gumboot Festival each August. The Big Gumboot (*below*) erected on the highway at the southern end of the main street stands 7.9 m high, representing the record-setting annual rainfall received in 1950. Tully's torrential downpours are largely due to its location on a narrow coastal plain between Mount Tyson and Mount Mackay, which act as magnets for rain clouds drawn across the Coral Sea. Cyclones and monsoonal conditions make January to April the soggiest months to visit.

While the abundance of precipitation makes gumboots standard issue dress for the locals, it also provides the Tully to Innisfail region with a spectacular Wet Tropics environment. Nowhere is this better illustrated than at Tully Gorge, where the Tully River rushes over rocks and boulders at breakneck speed, forming an ideal whitewater rafting course and creating a series of spectacular cascades. The river also provides the power for the Tully–Millstream Hydro-electric Scheme and the moist climate delivers perfect conditions for the cultivation of tropical crops including bananas, lychees and melons.

Palm Islands

Located off the coast east of Ingham, the Palm Islands are a group of granitic continental islands encircled by well-developed reef. While the islands make an unforgettable cruising destination, Orpheus Island is the only one of the group to offer resort accommodation. As a protected coastal marine park, the snorkelling here is exhilarating — over 1100 species of fish, 340 different varieties of coral and giant clams can be observed.

Top to bottom: Hinchinbrook Island; Wallaman Falls; Tully River; Murray Falls.

Hinchinbrook Island National Park

Phone Ranger: (07) 4066 8601

At approximately 40,000 ha, Hinchinbrook is Australia's largest island national park. The island's major resort is at Cape Richards, but the remainder is untouched by development. Hinchinbrook Island was occupied for many thousands of years by the Bandyin people. Its mangrove forests are some of Australia's richest and most varied marine breeding grounds.

Walks in the Park: The Thorsborne Trail, acclaimed as one of the world's great walks, is a 32 km (2–5 day) trek traversing the east coast of Hinchinbrook Island. Walking its entire extent is recommended only for fit, experienced bushwalkers but parts of the track can be walked in smaller return sections.

Access: The island is 8 km east of Cardwell. Access is via commercial water taxi from Cardwell or Dungeness (Lucinda).

Camping: There are numerous campsites along the Thorsborne Trail as well as at Macushla and The Haven (picnic areas and toilets at The Haven).

Girringun NP – Wallaman Falls Section

Phone Ranger: (07) 4066 8601

Walks in the Park: The park is primarily tropical rainforest with 110 km of walking tracks. Begin with the 45 minute Bangguru Walk along Stony Creek for an easy introduction to the wonders of the area. Look out for Eastern Water Dragons, Platypuses and Saw-shelled Turtles. Cassowaries also inhabit the park. The Jinda Walk (2–3 hr) from Wallaman Falls Lookout passes through mossy vine-thicket rainforest before emerging at the base of the falls.

Access: Drive 51 km south-west of Ingham along Abergowrie Road via Trebonne.

Camping: Camping is permitted at Stony Creek near Wallaman Falls. Picnic facilities, barbecues and a shower are provided.

Girringun NP – Blencoe Falls Section

Phone Ranger: (07) 4066 8601

Walks in the Park: Blencoe Falls take a truly spectacular staggered dive to the bottom of the gorge 320 m below. The 5 km return track to Blencoe Falls Lookout travels through rugged dry country populated by kangaroos, Emus and Laughing Kookaburras.

Access: Turn west from Kennedy (11 km north of Cardwell) and travel via the Kirrama Range Road. The journey includes steep, unsealed winding road and takes approximately two hours.

Camping: Camping is permitted at Stony Creek near Wallaman Falls. Picnic and shower facilities are provided.

Tully Gorge National Park

Phone Ranger: (07) 4046 6601

Walks in the Park: Tully Gorge National Park rewards Wet Season visitors with fast-flowing river rapids and dramatic falls. Surrounded by rock and rainforest, the Tully River plunges 300 m down the gorge. The best view is from the Tully Gorge Lookout above the falls. There is also an excellent butterfly walk, best taken between September and February. Watch for the Cairns Birdwing, a behemoth of the butterfly world. If you want to ride the rapids you will need to take an organised tour (available either at Tully or via a travel agent in any of the major centres). The swirling, surging waters of the Tully River are an intoxicating sight as they catapult whitewater rafters downstream at Tully Gorge. If you would rather stay dry and watch others get wet, Flip Wilson Lookout and the boardwalk at Cardstone Weir are excellent photographic vantage points.

Access: Travel 25 km from Ravenshoe on the Tully Falls Road.

Camping: Camping is not permitted in the park.

Murray Falls State Forest Park

Phone Ranger: (07) 4066 8601

Walks in the Park: Located in the foothills of the Kirrama Range, Murray Falls State Forest Park protects a region of rainforest concealing the pretty Murray Falls. This stepped cascade down sculptured rock into crystal pools has a charm all its own. There are two short walks in the vicinity of the falls — a 1.8 km rainforest and lookout circuit and a short 10 minute boardwalk stroll along the creek.

Access: The park turn-off is at Bilyana, 20 km north of Cardwell on the Bruce Highway.

Camping: Tent and caravan camping is permitted at Murray Falls.

Mission Beach to Cairns

Only 20 km north-east of Tully is the palm-trimmed curve of Mission Beach. Its sun-soaked aspect and island views are in stark contrast to the cool, mountainous Wet Tropics wilderness that lies immediately to the west. The coastal villages of Garners Beach, Bingil Bay, North and South Mission Beach and Wongaling are set amid rainforest and mangroves that provide habitat for the region's unique fauna. This is the heart of the Cassowary Coast, and the gangling flightless bird for which it is named furtively wanders the local fan palm forests.

Less than 5 km offshore from Mission Beach are the distinctive green humps of Dunk Island. The isle is the largest of the Family Group — a cluster of continental islands extending 14 km along the coastline. Dunk Island's first white resident, E J Banfield (also known as Rob Crusoe), attracted international interest to the area in the early 1900s with the books he wrote describing island life and ecology, including *The Confessions of a Beachcomber* and *My Tropic Isle*. His promotion of the island as a sanctuary and his insistence that its natural treasures should be protected were largely responsible for preserving the pristine state of Dunk Island until the development of a holiday resort after World War II. Today, a careful balance is maintained between the demands of nature and recreation. All of the island beyond the single resort remains national park. Descendants of the original Djiru and Bandjin people, who once commuted between the islands by bark canoe to hunt and fish, now participate in managing the Family Islands Group.

Mission Beach

Mission Beach is actually a collection of small villages set among some of the region's most gorgeous natural scenery. Long, golden beaches arc round the sparkling Coral Sea with views out to nearby continental islands.

Licuala Fan Palms

Licuala State Forest, located off Mission Beach Road, contains the largest number of Licuala Fan Palms in Australia. Walk along rainforest tracks in the shade of their symmetrical green foliage, learn about the palm and other native plant species and watch out for the elusive Southern Cassowary.

Mission Beach

Once the location of an Aboriginal mission destroyed in the 1918 cyclone, Mission Beach is now a modern tourism centre flanked by palm trees and inviting tropical ocean shores. It is reached via Cassowary Drive from El Arish on the Bruce Highway — a scenic loop that passes through the rainforest home of wallabies, parrots and enchanting butterflies. Numerous guided treks through the surrounding rainforest are on offer, but the Mission Beach Wet Tropics Visitor Information Centre on the foreshore at Porter Promenade also provides walking trail maps (Ph: (07) 4068 7099). The adjacent Environment Centre has cassowary displays and a rainforest plant nursery. The Mission Beach area is almost entirely holiday-oriented and local operators entice visitors with a huge menu of adventure activities (from reef cruises and diving to kayaking and parachuting). Ferries travel to Dunk Island from Clump Point and North Mission Beach (approximately 40 minutes) and water taxis are available from South Mission Beach and Wongaling (10 minutes). Commercial flights also operate direct to Dunk Island's airfield from Cairns and Townsville.

Dunk Island

First known as *Coonanglebah*, Dunk Island (*top and above*) is the largest of the Family Islands. Its hilly terrain is clad in rainforest that creates a vibrant habitat. Among the many species that thrive in this tropical idyll is the beautiful blue-winged Ulysses Butterfly (*left*), the island's faunal emblem. Over 100 bird species call the island home and Dugongs can be seen feeding on seagrass in shallow waters between islands.

Dunk Island

Dunk Island's luxury resort accommodates over 400 people and the full spectrum of leisure facilities, reef visits and water activities are laid on for guests. There is also a small artist's colony on the island (featuring work by resident and visiting Australian artists). Daytrips are popular and camping is permitted (facilities include showers and toilets, Ph: (07) 4068 8199). Supplies are available at the resort and Mission Beach.

Dunk is a great bushwalking destination with 13 km of relatively easy tracks giving visitors an insight of the island's habitat and fascinating past. A track from the resort crosses a suspension bridge and leads past the grave site of Edmund Banfield and his wife Bertha. Further on, you can enjoy panoramic views to Mission Beach and the neighbouring islands of the Family Group from the lookout at Mount Kootaloo (Dunk's highest point). The 10 km Island Circuit takes in beaches, reef flats, rainforest and mangrove habitats. Basic bush camping is also possible on Wheeler and Combe Islands off Tully Heads (group numbers limited). Bedarra and Thorpe Islands, south of Dunk in Rockingham Bay are both privately owned, with a resort on Bedarra.

Top to bottom: Nandroya Falls; Josephine Falls; Walking the Mount Bartle Frere Trail; Eubenangee Swamp National Park.

Wooroonooran National Park

Palmerston Section

Phone Ranger: (07) 4061 5900

Walks in the Park: There are over 500 species of rainforest tree in this section of Wooroonooran, but you may be too busy gaping at the spectacular waterfalls, wild rivers and gorges to notice them all. Several easy walking tracks commence at Goolagan's and Henrietta Creek camping ground. The 7.2 km Nandroya Falls Walk begins just north of Henrietta Creek. Other scenic tracks are the Tchulpa Falls Walk (1.1 km return).

Access: Via Palmerston Highway, 33 km west of Innisfail.

Camping: Tent and caravan sites in the rainforest at Henrietta Creek.

Josephine Falls Section

Phone Ranger: (07) 4067 6304

Walks in the Park: The beautiful Josephine Falls is fed by rainfalls near the summit of Mount Bartle Frere. The track to the main viewing decks is an easy 1.2 km (return) and commences at the car park off the Miriwinni Road. Beware of flash flooding around the falls in wet weather.

Access: Turn off the Bruce Highway 2 km south of Miriwinni.

Camping: No camping permitted.

Mt Bartle Frere

Walks in the Park: The Mount Bartle Frere Trail, starting at Josephine Falls, is no walk in the park. The 15 km track to the summit is spectacular but climbs some 1500 m through the Bellenden Ker Range and should only be attempted by experienced, extremely fit bushwalkers. Most walk the trail over two days.

Access: From Josephine Falls.

Camping: Four established bush camping sites (no facilities).

Eubenangee Swamp National Park

Phone Ranger: (07) 4067 6304

Walks in the Park: This is one of the premier wetland areas on the tropical coast and supports a variety of rare plant species as well as waterbirds, frogs and Estuarine Crocodiles. It is a brilliant location for wildlife observation and photography. A 1 km walking track winds along the Alice River through Eubenangee from the Cartwright Road entrance. At the top of a grassy hill there are excellent views of the floodplain and Mt Bartle Frere. Stay "crocodile safe" by keeping away from the water's edge and do not enter the water.

Access: From the Bruce Highway at Miriwinni follow the national park signs east along the Bramston Beach Road. Turn south into Cartwright Road to the car park.

Camping: Camping not permitted.

Innisfail

A close rival for Tully's "wettest town" status, Innisfail is a busy cane centre at the junction of the North and South Johnstone Rivers. The broad blue expanse of waters running through the town's heart provide a generous choice of rejuvenating riverbank walks. Innisfail's Art Deco buildings, constructed after the cyclone of 1918, give the town a colourful retrospective appeal.

Babinda

Taking its name from the local Yidinji word for waterfall, *bunna binda*, Babinda is nestled in farmland and tropical rainforest at the base of Mount Bartle Frere and the Bellenden Ker Range. It is only several minutes drive to the popular swimming hole at The Boulders — a place of Indigenous spirituality.

Queensland's Tallest Peaks

Queensland's two highest mountains, Mount Bartle Frere (1622 m) and Mount Bellenden Ker (1592 m) are located within Wooroonooran National Park. Known to the Ngadjon Aboriginal people as *Chooreechillum*, Mt Bartle Frere has a long tradition of spiritual significance.

CAIRNS

& THE JOURNEY TO DARWIN

3

The tropical city of Cairns, with its easy proximity to superb beaches, reef, islands and the justly famous wonders of the Daintree rainforest, has become one of the globe's most treasured holiday destinations. In fact, the region boasts so many ready-made natural attractions that most visitors do not venture much further north or west. This is a pity, for I think that the trip to the tip (Cooktown to Cape York) and across the Savannah Way to Kakadu and Darwin rank among Australia's best journeys. And if you've travelled all the way to Cairns, what are a few more kilometres? Granted, the road to Cape York can be rough in spots, but if you don't wish to do it solo you can always join a 4WD safari tour, fly or even cruise by sea. The Savannah Way (really a network of roads and tracks that reach from Cairns across the top of the continent) must be driven, but the rewards for effort are plentiful. Explore the ancient lava tubes of Undara, hunt for ghosts and gold in old mining towns, ride the historic *Gulflander* motor rail or get wet and wild at the outback oasis of Lawn Hill Gorge. Beyond the Queensland border at Hell's Gate lie the natural pleasures of the Northern Territory, among them Kakadu and Katherine Gorge, two of Australia's most breathtaking locations.

Southern Cassowary

Opposite: Twin Falls, Kakadu National Park. **Above:** Darwin Festival.

CAIRNS & Surrounds

The Cairns region has become one of Australia's most popular destinations, with over 1.5 million people visiting each year. Such heavy tourism is easily explained by the region's natural riches. Cairns is the gateway to the Great Barrier Reef, the Daintree and the wilds of Cape York. On its doorstep are the palm-lined beaches of Palm Cove and Port Douglas, beautiful Kuranda and the lush Atherton Tableland. Just offshore lie the marine havens of Green Island and Fitzroy Island. There is literally something for everyone here, be they birdwatchers, beachcombers, snorkellers, divers or hikers. Accommodation ranges from backpacker hostels to some of the world's most luxurious resorts, and friendly tour operators offer every conceivable means of exploring reef, range and rainforest. Cairns city is busy year-round, yet escape from the friendly, tourist-driven clamour can still be found in the hinterland, rivers and islands beyond.

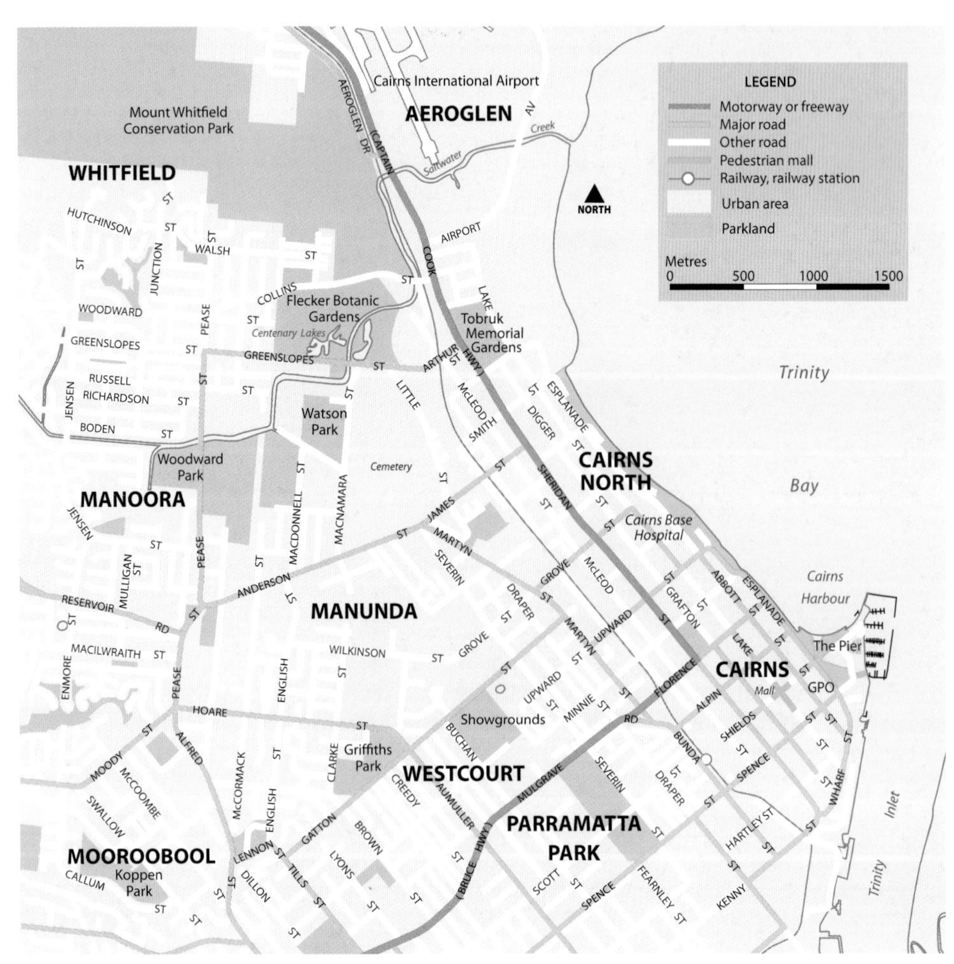

Cairns & Surrounds
Top Things to Do

1. Dive and snorkel the continental islands and cays of the Great Barrier Reef — including Michaelmas and Upolu Cays, and Green and Fitzroy Islands.
2. Immerse yourself in the world's most beautiful rainforest in the Daintree.
3. Explore the historic townships of the Atherton Tableland.
4. Ride the Scenic Railway or Skyrail to Kuranda and check out the historic village markets.
5. Laze on the palm-shaded sands of Port Douglas.
6. Take a trip to Cooktown and explore the town on a heritage walk.
7. Stand at the tip of Cape York Peninsula.
8. Scuba dive at the famous Cod Hole off Lizard Island.

Between Range & Reef

Greater Cairns stretches 30 km along the northern beaches and 60 km south. It is the principal commercial and administrative centre for Tropical North Queensland, with a seaport that handles a huge cargo, exporting goods to the Gulf of Carpentaria and beyond. It is also the country's busiest cruise port with over 200 domestic and international ships visiting each year.

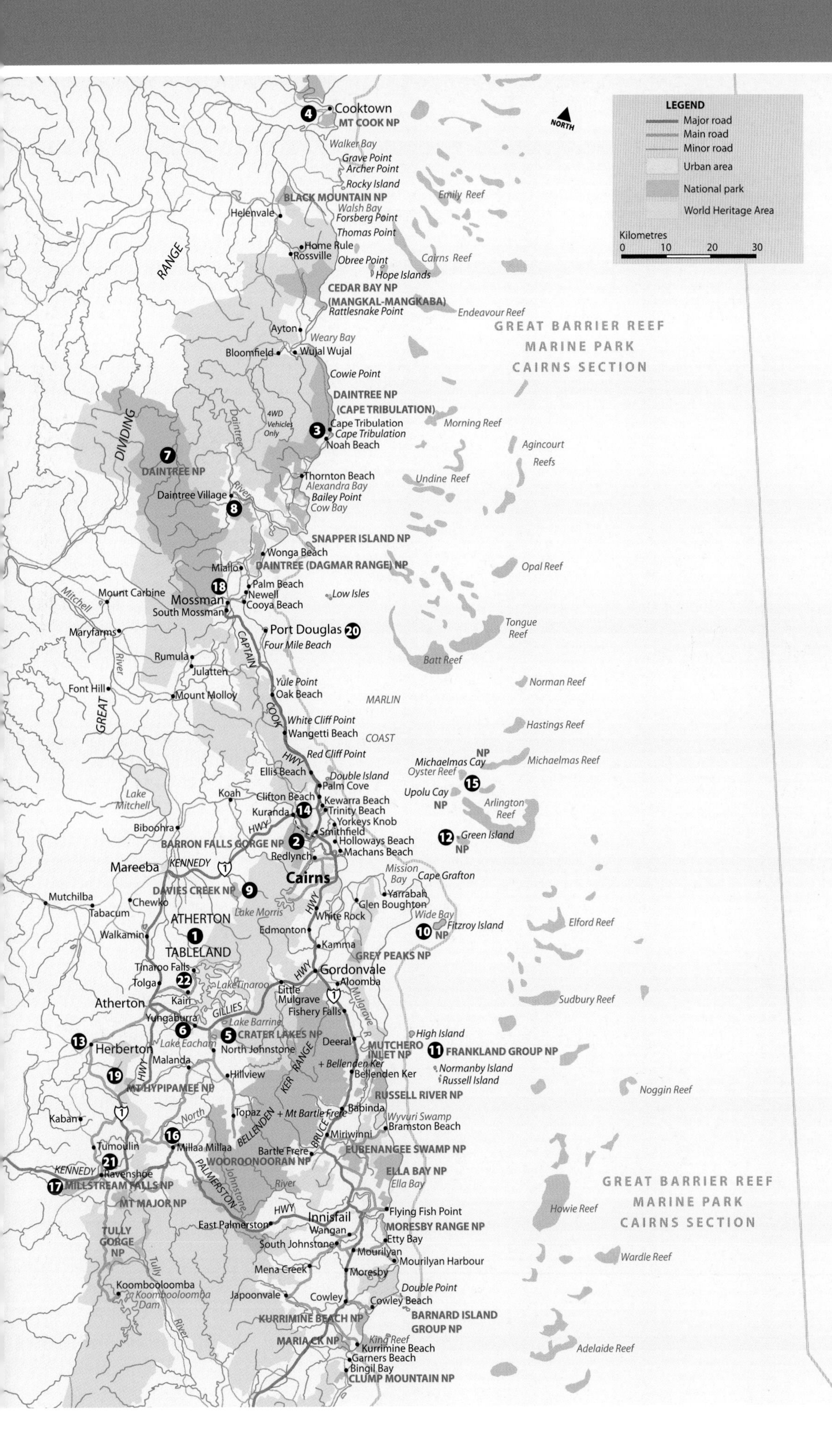

Feature Localities

1. Atherton Tableland
2. Barron Falls
3. Cape Tribulation
4. Cooktown
5. Crater Lakes National Park
6. Curtain Fig, Yungaburra
7. Daintree National Park
8. Daintree Village
9. Davies Creek National Park
10. Fitzroy Island
11. Frankland Islands Group
12. Green Island
13. Herberton
14. Kuranda
15. Michaelmas and Upolu Cays National Park
16. Millaa Millaa Falls
17. Millstream Falls
18. Mossman
19. Mt Hypipamee National Park
20. Port Douglas
21. Ravenshoe
22. Tinaroo Dam

Cairns City

Top Things to Do

1 Explore the old Cairns Port precinct and history of the Barbary Coast.
2 Stroll the balmy breeze-kissed paths of the Esplanade.
3 Swim across Queensland at the Cairns Lagoon.
4 Mingle with Australian wildlife at the Cairns Wildlife Dome.
5 Shop with bay views at Cairns Pier Marketplace.
6 Walk among mangroves on the Jack Barnes Bicentennial Mangrove Boardwalk.
7 Visit the Flecker Botanic Gardens.
8 Take a daytrip to Green Island.
9 Find tropical trinkets at Cairns Night Markets.

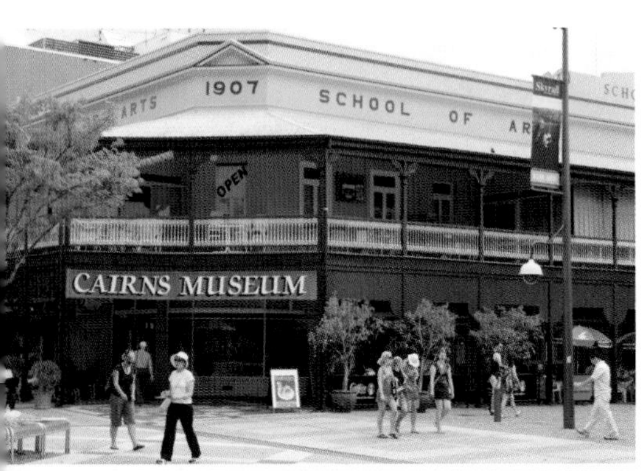

A Past Still Present

Much of Cairns' charm derives from its eclectic blend of architecture. Colonial shops and grand public buildings stand alongside country-style pubs and modern hotels. The hot climate has bred wide streets lined with awnings and broad covered walkways designed for outdoor living.

Cairns City

With its tropical climate and bayside location, Cairns is a city of welcoming natural ambience. Situated beside Trinity Inlet on the flat coastal plain between the reef-laden Coral Sea and the Great Dividing Range, it is surrounded by some of the prettiest scenery in Australia. Only an hour west are the rainforests, rocky peaks and fertile plateaus of the Atherton Tableland. The region's natural resources supported Aboriginal people for millennia, but Cairns itself was only established after much of the region had already been settled by farmers, timber cutters and prospectors chasing riches in the gold rushes around the northern Queensland rivers. Its sheltered bay was deemed suitable for use as a local port but the construction of a railroad servicing the tin mines and timber industries of the Tableland gradually transformed Cairns from a tough frontier town into a prosperous city. Its strategic importance as a military base during World War II, and growing awareness of the marvels of the Great Barrier Reef, consolidated its early growth and assured its development into a modern tourism capital. Today it is served by an international airport and offers a choice of accommodation that rivals all but Australia's biggest cities.

City Centre

Cairns' business and shopping district was once scrub and swamp. The Esplanade, running along the harbour, was the first street surveyed in Cairns (in 1876) and has today been rejuvenated to form a focus for Cairns-life. Some of the city's most interesting heritage buildings stand within the old port precinct at the Esplanade's southern end. The area was once known as the Barbary Coast, a strip of waterfront hotels on Wharf and Lake Streets notorious for the bawdy, brawling behaviour of ship-liberated sailors. The precinct has since been tamed by modern retail and apartment development, but you can still buy a tot of rum and reminisce on the wide verandahs of the old Barrier Reef Hotel (near Cairns Yacht Club on Wharf Street). Reef cruises depart from the piers of busy Marlin Marina in front of Fogarty Park. The park's Ergon Soundshell is a unique outdoor performance amphitheatre. Behind Fogarty Park are the permanent undercover clothes outlets and gift stores of Pier Marketplace.

On the northern side of the main pier is Cairns Lagoon, a 4800 m^2 saltwater swimming zone designed in the shape of the State of Queensland. The lagoon's sparkling, filtered waters are patrolled by lifeguards and bounded by sandy shores, landscaped gardens, a kiosk and picnic facilities. The Esplanade Markets are staged each Saturday, near the lagoon. To the north is Cairns Foreshore Promenade with its inviting shaded lawns and suspended boardwalks overlooking Trinity Inlet. The city side of the Esplanade is a popular tourist and nightlife destination lined with hotels and restaurants.

The modest towers of Cairns CBD rise up behind the Esplanade. The main shopping area, as well as Cairns Museum and Library, are located in a compact grid of streets around City Place mall (between Grafton and Abbott streets). Cairns Central shopping centre, an air-conditioned plaza featuring over 170 specialty shops, food outlets, department stores and cinemas, is located next to Cairns Railway Station on Bunda Street.

Cairns Lagoon

With many beaches off-limits for swimming in the hot summer months (due to the presence of stingers), Cairns' artificial lagoon provides the perfect place to cool off. The lagoon, with its distinctive galvanised steel fish, is adjacent to Trinity Bay and blends easily with the natural environs. It features beach, parkland, picnic areas and playgrounds.

Esplanade, Parks & Gardens

The shaded, open spaces of Cairns' splendid collection of parks and gardens provide relief from the city's muggy, tropical climate.

Hugging the shores of Cairns Harbour north of Trinity Inlet is the Esplanade, an extensive foreshore parkland (*above*). With its spacious promenade, fresh sea breezes and magnificent harbour views, it is much loved by residents and a natural hub for the city's recreational life. Coconut palms line the popular walking paths and lawns of this leisure retreat bordering the city. Each day, below the suspended boardwalk, the receding tide reveals the Cairns mudflats, a prized birdwatching area frequented by Australian Pelicans, ibis and gulls. It is an excellent site for dawn and dusk photography.

Flecker Botanic Gardens (located in Collins Avenue, Edge Hill) are the only botanical gardens in the Wet Tropics, featuring thousands of native tropical plants and tropical exotics. Extending over 300 ha, the gardens include tropical rainforest, a fernery, orchid house, an Aboriginal plant-use trail and collections of bamboos and tropical fruits. For a peek into coastal habitat, Jack Barnes Bicentennial Mangrove Boardwalk (Airport Drive) provides an engaging elevated journey through dense mangrove swamp.

Clockwise from top left: Flecker Botanical Gardens; Jack Barnes Bicentennial Mangrove Boardwalk; Australian Pelicans on the foreshore mudflats; Views across Trinity Inlet.

Pier Precinct

Located at the entrance to Cairns Harbour is Cairns Pier Marketplace, a comprehensive retail complex featuring restaurants and shops spread over two levels. The precinct boasts expansive views over Marlin Marina, Trinity Bay and the mountains beyond.

Night Markets

With over 130 market stalls offering a huge range of items from pearls to crocodile skins, Aboriginal art to tropical tattoos; Cairns' permanent Night Markets are located at the base of the Royal Harbour Hotel on the Esplanade.

Cairns Wildlife Dome

The glass-domed atrium sitting atop the Cairns Reef Hotel Casino is the unlikely (but nonetheless impressive) home to a diverse collection of Australian wildlife, including Koalas, kookaburras, Spectacled Flying-foxes, parrots, pythons and crocodiles. Tours and presentations are offered daily.

Captain Cook Highway

The scenic Captain Cook Highway skirts the eastern foothills of the McAlister Range along the coast, affording breathtaking views of palm-treed shores, secluded coves and the Coral Sea.

Trinity Beach

The languid waters of Trinity Beach lie sheltered between headlands and are a perennial favourite with Cairns residents who come here to soak up the sun and enjoy an afternoon barbie.

Palm Cove

Set below green hinterland ranges, the magnificent palm and melaleuca-shaded beach of Palm Cove also boasts an ocean horizon punctuated by inviting reef isles (including nearby Double Island).

Close to Cairns

The beaches and islands around Cairns are some of the nation's best. The Captain Cook Highway, one of Australia's most scenic drives, commences at Cairns and tracks this superb stretch of coast beyond Port Douglas to the Daintree.

Northern Beaches

For 25 km, a string of immensely popular resort beaches reach north of Cairns along Trinity Bay. Most are equipped with stinger-free enclosures but it is always advisable to check first in these regions before entering the water. Close to the city, Machans Beach and Holloways Beach are relaxed seaside suburbs with an unpretentious character and excellent swimming, boating and picnic facilities.

Yorkeys Knob lies just north of Holloways across a narrow channel and sand bar. During winter, Yorkeys is one of Australia's premier kite-surfing destinations. Without doubt the most popular of all Cairns' beaches is Trinity Beach. Linking two headlands, the beach is a narrow island-style strip of sand lined with luxuriant palms. This egalitarian resort attracts huge numbers of locals and visitors and offers a range of accommodation, dining and leisure activities to suit all tastes and budgets.

The lavishly appointed village of Palm Cove is the most stylish among these northern beaches. Luxury apartments, five-star resorts, restaurants and beachfront cafés sidle up to its incomparably beautiful leafy shores. Reef cruises and charters depart daily from the Palm Cove jetty. Double Island, an exclusive resort just off the coast, is also an important dreaming site for the local Yirrganydji people who know it as *Wangal Djungay* and believe it to be the resting place of *Gudjugudju*, the Rainbow Serpent. Close to Palm Cove are several wildlife sanctuaries including Cairns Tropical Zoo, Cairns Night Zoo and Hartley's Crocodile Adventures (10 km north at Hartleys Creek).

Fitzroy Island Close to the mainland south of Cairns is Fitzroy Island, a submerged continental mountain peak that once formed part of the Malbon Thompson Range.

Cairns reef cruises A huge range of cruises depart from Cairns for reef, cay and island destinations. Many packages include snorkel gear and instruction.

Crocodile Encounters

Hartley's Crocodile Adventures on Hartleys Creek north of Palm Cove features a unique journey into croc country aboard specially constructed riverboats. See and learn about Estuarine Crocodiles while cruising the lagoon. The park also has elevated boardwalks (winding through wetland and rainforest habitat) for viewing wildlife. Regular snake shows, as well as Southern Cassowary and Koala feedings are also a feature (open daily, 8.30 am – 5 pm, Ph: (07) 4055 3576).

Coral Cays & Reefs Close to Cairns

Twenty-seven kilometres north-east of Cairns lies the coral cay of Green Island and its fringing reefs (*see right*). Composed of sand and coral debris deposited by wind and waves, the cay was then colonised by nesting birds and plant life. It is only 12 ha in size but is encircled by 710 ha of reef. The island's shallow lagoon brings human visitors into close contact with marine residents in their own saltwater environment.

Other major coral cays near Cairns include Michaelmas Cay (*see right*) and neighbouring Upolu Cay. Michaelmas Cay is a protected area 40 km north-east of Cairns at the western end of MIchaelmas Reef. The cay is an important seabird breeding ground — up to 30,000 birds nest here in summer, including Sooty Terns and Common Noddies. Because of the way they form, cays are constantly shifting — Michaelmas is moving north at rates of up to 1 m per year. The proximity of cays to their reefs means snorkelling is often possible straight from the beach.

There are many ways to explore reefs and cays. A huge range of cruise options and regular scenic flights from Cairns take in Michaelmas Reef and Arlington Reef as well as the various cays.

Crimson Soldierfish (*right*) and Trumpetfish (*below*)

Green Island

The crystal clear, placid waters of Green Island (*left*) are perfect for swimming, snorkelling, diving and photography. If you don't feel like getting wet, an underwater observatory is located at the end of the main jetty. A small aquarium and crocodile habitat branded Marineland Melanesia also operates on the island. While there is a well-equipped resort, Green Island is also close enough to Cairns and Palm Cove to visit as a day-trip. Camping is not permitted on Green Island.

Michaelmas Cay

Day cruises and sailing adventures to Michaelmas Cay (*left*) are available from Cairns and Palm Cove. If you wish to take your own vessel, there are also public moorings located near the cay's northern channel. The surrounding reef, which is home to a huge population of marine life (including giant clams), is a great diving and snorkelling destination. There is no accommodation or camping on the cay and access is restricted to a roped off area of beach in order to protect the large communities of nesting seabirds.

Reef Pontoons

Large-scale pontoons have been established In various locations on the outer Great Barrier Reef to allow ease of exploration. These moored platforms are family-friendly installations that can include underwater observatories, wading pools, marine touch tanks, snorkelling tutorials, shower facilities and more. The pontoons are serviced by cruise boats and in some cases, helicopter and sea plane transfers from Cairns are also available.

Fitzroy Island

Located 29 km south-east of Cairns, Fitzroy Island (*left and far left*) offers an inviting blend of unspoilt environs with modern resort facilities. The vast majority of the island is national park, protecting regions of rainforest, woodland, mangroves and coral beaches. The well-equipped resort is comparatively inexpensive for a reef holiday destination. You may also visit the island as a daytrip, or camp, and there is an extensive network of walking tracks ranging from 30 minutes to 3 hours return. Ferries travel to the island daily from Cairns (Ph: (07) 4030 7907).

Frankland Islands

The Frankland group (*left and far left*) comprises five uninhabited islands only 10 km off the coast south of Cairns. The islands — High, Normanby, Round, Russell and Mabel — form the Frankland Group National Park. Visitors can circumnavigate any of the islands by foot, but the only formal walking trail is on Normanby Island (1 km circuit, 20 minutes). The fringing reefs are alive with marine creatures and the best snorkelling is off Normanby and Russell Islands.

A haven for seabirds
The Frankland Islands form a natural breeding ground for seabirds including terns, gulls and White-bellied Sea-Eagles (*left*).

Camping on the Continental Islands Close to Cairns

Camping is not possible on Fitzroy, Normanby, Round or Mabel Islands but there are camping facilities on Russell Island and High Island (bookings and a permit are required. High Island, Ph: 13 13 04; Russell Island, Ph: (07) 4046 6600). Maximum capacity limits apply to camping on the islands, and water and fuel stoves must be carried on. First aid equipment must also be carried.

Frankland Islands Cruise and Dive are the only private operator servicing the Frankland Group and can drop and pick up campers on Russell Island (daily departures from Deeral Point, including transfers from Cairns, Ph: (07) 4125 2343). High Island can only be reached by private boat and public moorings are available at Normanby, Russell and High Islands. Guided island walks on Normanby Island and guided snorkelling tours are offered by the cruise operator (for further details, Ph: (07) 4125 2343).

Kuranda Village

Known as *Ngoonbi* to its traditional custodians, the Djabugay people, the village of Kuranda is a sensory delight. Historic buildings house art galleries, restaurants and cafés where you can sample tropical treats and unwind with a cup of locally grown tea or coffee. Accommodation ranges from camping and rainforest cabins to a gothic-styled riverside resort.

Kuranda Markets

Kuranda Heritage Markets are open daily and showcase a range of produce, craft and unusual souvenirs from Emu eggs to shark jaws. In the main street of the village, market stall operators also offer Aboriginal artefacts, handmade goods, woodcraft and jewellery. Street entertainers add further life to the tropical shopping experience with performances including didgeridoo playing and Indigenous dance.

Cairns to Kuranda

Just 20 km north-west of Cairns, but high in the hinterland ranges, Kuranda began its life in the late 1870s as Middle Crossing, an important route over the Barron River for gold prospectors. After the Cairns Range Railway was opened in 1891, Kuranda became a popular retreat for Cairns residents seeking to escape coastal humidity. Nevertheless, it remained quiet until the Kuranda Range Road was completed in 1942. In the late 1960s and 1970s, a steady stream of idealists seeking an alternate lifestyle arrived and established Kuranda as a centre for arts and crafts. Today, Kuranda is known as "the village in the rainforest", and its vibrant, multicultural community enjoys an enviable tropical existence.

The exceptionally photogenic journey by Scenic Railway or Skyrail to Kuranda is an automatic inclusion on most Cairns visitors' itineraries (*see facing page*). The Kuranda Scenic Railway departs each morning from a dedicated platform at Cairns Central Railway Station and from Freshwater Connection (in the Cairns suburb of Freshwater) where a museum and railcar restaurant pay tribute to railway pioneers (Ph: (07) 4036 9333). Skyrail's Caravonica Terminal is located at the corner of Cairns Western Arterial Road and Cook Highway, Smithfield, 15 minutes drive north of Cairns city. (Skyrail runs daily from 8.15 am – 5.15 pm (Ph: (07) 4038 1555). The Skyway, railway and local wildlife attractions can be combined through a selection of tour packages on offer.

An alternative is to take the 20 minute drive up the scenic Kuranda Range Road from Smithfield through the McAlister Range. The road winds past views of coast and ocean below an arch of rainforest trees. A lookout near the top of the range provides an impressive panorama of the coastal plain and Coral Sea.

Kuranda Wildlife Attractions

Around the Kuranda region are located a number of excellent wildlife attractions including Kuranda Koala Gardens, Birdworld Kuranda and the Australian Butterfly Sanctuary (*see box below*). These three attractions are clustered virtually next door to one another near the Kuranda Heritage Markets (off Rob Vievers Drive at the opposite end of town from the railway and Skyway stations). The Kuranda Koala Gardens also feature crocodiles and numerous other native creatures. Birdworld is a free-flight aviary offering great bird feeding and photography opportunities with 25 different species of rainforest bird.

Australian Butterfly Sanctuary

The Wet Tropics World Heritage Area is home to 60% of Australia's butterfly species. A stunning array of psychedelically adorned butterflies light up the forest as they dance from flower-to-flower. The Australian Butterfly Sanctuary in Kuranda gives you the chance to interact with thousands of rare and native butterflies.

Kuranda Scenic Railway & Skyrail

Getting to the picturesque mountain retreat of Kuranda Village, 380 m above sea level, is an unforgettable adventure in itself. The historic Scenic Railway offers breathtaking views and a sense of pioneer spirit as it climbs through the Kuranda Range. The century-old railway commences at Cairns Central Railway Station and travels the 34 km to Kuranda through 15 tunnels and over 36 bridges. This impressive engineering feat began when the tin miners of Herberton were isolated by flood in 1882, emphasising the need for a reliable route from the coast to the Tableland. Construction commenced in 1886 and five years of back-breaking toil by workers equipped only with simple tools, dynamite and old-fashioned ingenuity saw the railway reach the present day site of Kuranda in 1891.

Travelling through the air in a suspended gondola was probably not a viable option then, but today the 7.5 km Skyrail Rainforest Cableway is an equally exhilarating alternative. Whether gliding over the Wet Tropics rainforests or exploring them on foot from the Skyrail's mid-route stations at Red Peak (545 m above sea level) and Barron Gorge, this is a very special rainforest experience that offers superb photographic opportunities. Both travel options give spectacular views of the Barron Gorge and Barron Falls. This is no place to forget (or drop) your camera.

Skyrail Rainforest Cableway It hangs over rainforest.

The Skyrail View over the Cairns Highlands.

Kuranda Railway Station The historic station opened in 1915, nestles among fern and forest.

Barron Falls

Barron Falls, or *Din Din*, holds special significance for the Djabugay people, as the place to celebrate the birth of *Bulurru*, the Creator Spirit and Rainbow Serpent.

Over the past century, travellers have been inspired by these magnificent falls, which are the largest in the Wet Tropics and a spectacular sight in full flow during the wet season. Such a huge volume of water surges over the falls that it is not uncommon for visitors to be enveloped in a cloud of mist. Walking to the falls from the Skyrail is the perfect way to experience the wonder of the rainforest, see wildlife and learn about Djabugay culture. A 570 m elevated boardwalk from Barron Falls car park descends to a lookout and railway platform with spectacular views over the falls.

Doongal Aboriginal Art

Showcasing the work of local Aboriginal artists, Doongal is a distinctive ark-shaped gallery in the heart of Kuranda. Doongal exhibits and sells a wide range of Indigenous art and craft, (including bark paintings and boomerangs) and lays claim to the largest and most diverse collection of didgeridoos in the world. This fabled instrument comes in a plethora of plain and painted styles.

The Atherton Tableland

The Atherton Tableland combines regions of awe-inspiring scenery with rural tranquility. At the top of the steep escarpment behind Cairns, the Tableland is between 600 and 1100 m above sea level and enjoys milder weather than the coast. Rainforest remnants thriving on the area's rich volcanic soils survive within a patchwork of farmlands. In this area of high rainfall rise the headwaters of many of tropical Queensland's largest waterways, including the once gold-bloated Palmer River. Further west from Atherton is the mineral and fossil-rich region of Chillagoe, where you can see ancient coral reefs from a long-vanished sea.

The traditional country of at least six separate Aboriginal peoples including the Ngadjonji, the Tableland was settled by timber getters, miners and pastoralists in the 1870s and soon became scattered with thriving townships. Long a popular holiday destination for Cairns residents, the Tableland experienced a tourism boom in the 1930s and 1940s. Guided tours and accommodation houses sprang up, and many of the area's historic hotels and buildings date from this period. Many artists have found inspiration in the Tableland, and the area is known for its markets and galleries.

Atherton & Surrounds

The Gillies Highway from Gordonvale to Atherton passes between Wooroonooran National Park and Crater Lakes National Park to reach the town of Yungaburra, once the Tableland's prime tourist destination. It may have been superseded by the region's natural attractions but this rural retreat has lost none of its charm. Quaint timber buildings house a range of art galleries, craft shops, accommodation and eateries. In Atherton, the former Chinatown area is of particular interest. Dating from 1903, the Hou Wang Chinese Temple is one of few remaining in north Queensland, despite the integral role Chinese played in the history of the region. Tinaroo Dam, at Tinaroo near Atherton, is a favourite destination for camping, fishing and watersports and is renowned for breeding the world's biggest Barramundi. The Atherton region can also be reached via the Kuranda Range Road and Kennedy Highway via the town of Mareeba. Near Atherton is Tolga, a tiny village that once reverberated with the sound of working timber mills and now has a fascinating museum.

A little west of Atherton is Herberton, a former tin mining town that features a historic railway and many colonial-era buildings. South of Yungaburra en route to Millaa Millaa is Malanda, the heart of dairy country and one of the Tableland's busiest locations.

Southern Tableland

The southern Tableland is an area of outstanding diversity. The region includes Ravenshoe (Queensland's highest town) and the spectacular Millstream Falls. It is also a main access point for the Misty Mountains Walking Trail (a network of long-range walking tracks). Closer to the coast on the Palmerston Highway, Millaa Millaa is a verdant dairying area. The name derives from an Aboriginal word for "plenty of water" and the region, which includes iconic Millaa Millaa Falls and the waterfall circuit (*see box below*), lives up to its title.

The Curtain Fig

Situated on the outskirts of Yungaburra amid beautiful rainforest is a huge strangler fig, fondly named the Curtain Fig Tree (*above*). This long-time tourist attraction, protected by Curtain Fig National Park, bears testimony to the tenacity of nature. The fig's roots hang approximately 15 m to the forest floor and the unusual formation is caused by one host tree falling against another.

Atherton

Named after one of the Tableland's renowned pioneers, John Atherton, the township of Atherton was established in the 1880s to serve farming, mining and timber industries in the area.

The Waterfall Circuit

The thirteen falls on the Waterfall Circuit commence with the classic straight vertical drop of Millaa Millaa Falls (*above left*). This remarkable cavalcade of cascades takes only an hour to walk and includes Zillie Falls, Mungalli Falls and the Elinjaa Falls (*above right*). Millaa Millaa Falls are popular for swimming on hot days. The circuit begins at Millaa Millaa township.

Davies Creek Falls The falls tumble over Tinaroo granite.

Lake Eacham Crater Lakes National Park.

Top to bottom: Explosion crater, Mt Hypipamee National Park; Dinner Falls, Mt Hypipamee National Park.

Davies Creek National Park

Phone Ranger: (07) 4046 6600

Davies Creek National Park, a traditional ceremonial area for the Djabugay, is the closest national park to Cairns. It features falls descending 75 m over granite boulders.

Walks in the Park: The Davies Creek Falls Circuit Walk is a 1.1 km easy trail commencing at the car park and leading to a lookout over the falls. The return journey follows the creek bank through paperbark trees and banksia to a sandy creekside picnic area.
Access: Turn off onto the Kennedy Highway from Captain Cook Highway and travel through Kuranda to Davies Creek Road.
Camping: There is a basic campground with toilets near Davies Creek (no pre-booking needed).

Crater Lakes National Park

Phone Ranger: (07) 4066 8601

Formed some 10,000 years ago by massive explosions of superheated groundwater — later colonised by rainforest and filled with water — Lake Barrine and Lake Eacham are important environments. Their clear waters teem with fish, turtles, eels, crayfish and freshwater life. Taking Devonshire tea at the Lake Barrine Tea House is a long-standing tradition, as is wildlife spotting while cruising on Lake Barrine or walking around the lakes.

Walks in the Park: The Lake Eacham Circuit walk is an easy 3 km stroll that includes two lake-viewing platforms. The circuit walk around Lake Barrine takes approximately two hours. There is also a short walk to the base of two giant 1000 year old Kauri trees from the lower car park at Lake Barrine and a 10 minute rainforest walk from the entrance road. Cruises operate from the Lake Barrine Tea House. Private non-motorised watercraft are also permitted on both lakes.
Access: Lake Barrine is 60 km along the Gillies Highway via Gordonvale from Cairns. Lake Eacham is a further 8 km down the road.
Camping: Camping is not permitted in the park. A commercial caravan and camping ground is located near Lake Eacham.

Mount Hypipamee National Park

Phone Ranger: (07) 4046 6600

Secluded and eerie, particularly at night, Mount Hypipamee is the ideal place to experience the Tableland's volcanic landscape. The explosion crater is set amid beautiful high-altitude rainforests that are remarkably different from tropical rainforests found elsewhere on the Tableland.

Walks in the Park: The track leading to the viewing platform over the explosion crater is an easy 800 m return walk. From the crater a 1.2 km walk leads you to Dinner Falls on the upper Barron River before returning to the car park.
Access: Adjacent to the Kennedy Highway 25 km south of Atherton.
Camping: Camping is not permitted in the park.

Herberton

Herberton, so named for its position near the headwaters of the Herbert River, was once the site of the richest tin mining field in Australia. Many of the town's original buildings remain intact today.

Ravenshoe

At 920 m above sea level, Ravenshoe is Queensland's highest town. The *Millstream Express* steam train travels from Ravenshoe along the Millstream River to Tumoulin each weekend from April to January.

Millstream Falls

Just west of Ravenshoe, national park protects the broad plunging waters of Millstream Falls. This mini-Niagara pours over an ancient basalt lava flow and is Australia's widest waterfall during the full flood of the wet season.

Port Douglas to the Daintree

The relaxed atmosphere of Port Douglas belies its shambolic origins. First known as Island Point, the town roared to life in the late 1870s as an ad hoc port and trading centre for the Palmer River and Hodgkinson River goldfields. When the rivers of gold dried up a decade later, Port Douglas soon shrank into an isolated fishing village. It was not until a century later that it began to take on the vibrant holiday air it exudes today. Since the 1980s, burgeoning tourism has fuelled a continuing real estate boom and Port Douglas, with its world class marina and easy access to reef and rainforest, has become the primary tourism centre north of Cairns. Along with the obligatory luxury resorts, Port Douglas has also become a golfing capital boasting numerous meticulously manicured courses. But even in the face of this surging development, the town has not lost its charm. Its historic buildings and natural environment have been well preserved and palms, bougainvillea and tropical flora camouflage holiday accommodation and hotels.

Sunday markets are staged in the shade of poincianas and figs at Anzac Park on the harbour foreshore of Dicksons Inlet — one of the town's most picturesque sites. Most of the town's restaurants, shops and visitor services congregate along busy Macrossan Street. From the glistening white shores of Four Mile Beach and the green-lined waterfront you can see cays and islands of the Coral Sea and the lower Daintree rainforest. You can also enjoy excellent views of the Port Douglas environs from Flagstaff Hill (follow the signs from the main street). On the historic wharf (once a sugar train terminus) is Ben Cropp's Shipwreck Museum, exhibiting all manner of salvaged flotsam and jetsam from various wrecks. At the junction of Captain Cook Highway and Port Douglas Road is Rainforest Habitat Wildlife Sanctuary, a nature "immersion" experience that permits close interaction with the 1600 animals in residence, including Koalas, the Southern Cassowary, crocodiles and birds.

To the north-east are the Low Isles, two small coral cays on the inner edge of the Great Barrier Reef Marine Park, which may be visited as a day trip. The site of the world's first extensive coral reef studies in 1928, the isles are covered in tropical vegetation and offer superb unspoilt waters for swimming and snorkelling. The original 1878 lighthouse and keepers' cottages on Low Isle are now used as a weather and research station. Tours, dive charters, sailing and game fishing cruises depart daily for the Low Isles and neighbouring reefs.

Mossman

The boom that transformed Port Douglas has had negligible impact on its near northern neighbour Mossman. Looking across the town's low-rise streetscapes of timber buildings to forest and cloud-covered mountains, it is easy to imagine its original incarnation as a gold mining and sugar settlement of the 1890s. In harvesting season, sugar cane trains still run through the main street. As the last major town before the Daintree, Mossman's primary function today is as a service centre for the flocks of visitors lured by the glories of gorge and rainforest. Five kilometres west of Mossman along Johnston Road in the southernmost section of Daintree National Park is Mossman Gorge (*see facing page*).

Port Douglas

A vibrant resort town situated at the end of a wide peninsula (*top*), Port Douglas is flanked by the popular sands of Four Mile Beach on one side and a harbour and marina on the other. It has beaches to die for and the Rainforest Habitat Wildlife Sanctuary (*above*).

Gateway to the Daintree

Only a short drive from exuberant Port Douglas, the more modest rural town of Mossman prepares visitors for the botanical mystique of Daintree National Park.

The Evolution of the Daintree

The Daintree has entered international consciousness as a region of treasured rainforest and inaccessible wilderness. Here, in the world's oldest living rainforest, species that have survived for millions of years provide a glimpse of processes that have shaped life on Earth. Over 200 million years, the Daintree has remained relatively unscathed despite periods of volcanic activity, rising sea levels and climatic changes. Its forests protect thirteen primitive plant species that are relics from the original land mass of the super-continent of Gondwana.

The Daintree is home to an astonishingly high proportion of Australia's flora and fauna. The mangrove forests that line its waterways are among the most complex and diverse in existence. The significance of the Daintree was recognised in 1988 as part of the 894,000 ha Wet Tropics World Heritage Area.

Mossman River Begins at 1300 m altitude and flows just 30 km to the sea.

Daintree Forest National Park – Mossman Gorge Section

Phone Ranger: (07) 4046 6600

Mossman Gorge is the perfect introduction to the unparalleled splendour of the Daintree. Easily reached by road a short distance from Mossman, this majestic region of rainforest, rock and river is the focus of many ancient legends for its Kuku Yalanji custodians, some of whom now act as tour guides through the area. Mount Demi, or *Manjal Dimbi*, is the protecting spirit, and *Wundu* (Thornton Peak) plus *Wurrumbu* (the Bluff) also have spiritual significance.

In the surrounding rainforest, life is rich and abundant. The magnificent Ulysses Butterfly, with its electric blue wings, is conspicuous as it flits around the forest paths. From vantage points overlooking the Mossman River, Buff-breasted Paradise-Kingfishers, Pied Imperial-Pigeons and a variety of turtles and freshwater fish, including Jungle Perch, may be seen. In quieter reaches Platypus (*above*) might be spied. In the forest, the distinctive calls of Wompoo Pigeon, Spotted Catbirds and Noisy Pittas are often heard. As dusk falls, watch for White-rumped Swiftlets and Grey Fantails snatching insects hovering over river pools.

Over millennia the Mossman River, fed by high rainfall on the ranges, has carved the steep-sided valley of Mossman Gorge. Here, torrents of foaming water rush over granite boulders washed down from the overlooking peaks by flood. Lowland rainforest — the home of tree-kangaroos, Musky Rat-kangaroos and endangered Spotted-tailed Quolls — grows to the water's edge. Inhabiting this forest are strangler figs, the predator of the Daintree plant world, which begin life high in the rainforest canopy and reach with thick, twining roots toward the ground, slowly weighing down and squeezing the life from their host trees. Lawyer Vines and other climbing plants travel in the opposite direction, using the trees as stairways to the sunlight high above the rainforest canopy. On the circuit track, a variety of reptiles including Boyd's Forest Dragons can be observed climbing trees, sunbaking on rocks and moving through the ferny undergrowth. The non-venomous Scrub Python, which grows to 8 m in length, is also sometimes seen on walking tracks (but should not be approached).

Walks in the Park: Starting from the car park, follow the 400 m River Circuit Walk alongside the Mossman River. From here, you may either return via the forest or continue to the lookout. Further on, via the scenic Rex Creek suspension bridge, the Rainforest Circuit Walk (2.7 km return) climbs to the *Manjal Dimbi* lookout and an access track to Wurumbu Creek. The local indigenous community also operate Kuku Yalanji Dreamtime Walks (Ph: (07) 4098 2595) — guided tours through the Daintree rainforest over community land.

Access: Via Johnston Road from Mossman. Drive slowly and with care when passing the Mossman Gorge Aboriginal Community on the way to the park.

Camping: Camping is not permitted in the Mossman Gorge section of Daintree Forest National Park. Toilets and picnic tables are provided at the car park.

Red-legged Pademelon

Top to bottom: Mossman Gorge; A guided Daintree walk; Rex Creek.

The Daintree to Cape Tribulation

The 62 km sealed road north from Mossman to Cape Tribulation through the eastern flank of the Daintree is accessible by conventional vehicle. In normal conditions the trip takes around two hours (including crossing the Daintree River by vehicle ferry), but with a tropical garden of earthly delights at every turn there's no reason to hurry. En route to the ferry crossing are the small village of Newell Beach and the old timber settlement of Miallo. Newell Beach, situated between the Mossman River and Saltwater Creek, offers a generous expanse of sandy shoreline and is also popular as a boating and fishing base.

Near Miallo, in the pretty Whyanbeel Valley, is the Karnak Playhouse, a unique 500-seat open air amphitheatre established by Australian actor Dianne Cilento that presents seasonal plays, contemporary dance and musical events. The venue also features a bar and restaurant (Upper Whyanbeel Road, Ph: (07) 4098 8144). Nearby, on Old Forestry Road, is High Falls Farm, another restaurant and tropical fruit plantation enveloped by rainforest (restaurant open Saturday to Tuesday, 9 am – 3 pm, Ph: (07) 40 988231).

From Miallo, the road diverts to the coast and follows the shore around Rocky Point to Wonga Beach. Take the short detour down to the water where you will be greeted by a classic coconut-palmed beach resort at the northern end of Trinity Bay with various accommodation options (including a beachfront caravan park). Wonga Beach was once used as the backdrop for the re-make of the movie *South Pacific*. If you can drag yourself away from this romantic setting and back to the main road, it is only a short distance to Daintree Village and the Daintree River ferry. On the way is the Daintree Mangroves Wildlife Sanctuary, a commercial operation featuring a huge range of native fauna endemic to the area, as well as poolside B&B accommodation and a restaurant (Ph: (07) 4098 7272). A few kilometres north, the cable ferry over the Daintree River transports 16 vehicles at a time and operates between 6 am and midnight daily. While the crossing itself only takes five minutes, be wary of long queues in school holiday periods.

Daintree Village

West of the ferry crossing is Daintree Village, the region's historic centre and a great base for river exploration. In fact, prior to the construction of the road from Mossman in 1933, access to Daintree was only possible via the river. Continue past the ferry turn-off up through the Dagmar Range to this one-time timber-cutting village located on the banks of the Daintree River. There are several good lookouts, including Humbug Reach, along the last 4 km as you approach town. Daintree has a permanent population of only two hundred but its natural attractions, tours, village cafés, craft galleries and guesthouses ensure it is always busy. Daintree Village Natural Walk, commencing at the Pioneers Park off Stewarts Creek Road, provides great views over the village and river.

The Daintree River

From its source in the Great Dividing Range behind Port Douglas, the Daintree River flows down through rainforest and mangroves to its delta near Cape Kimberley. An important waterway for exploration of the region since the 19th century, the river provides the ideal means for seeing and photographing the habitat and creatures of the Daintree.

A large range of river cruises (including dawn wildlife tours and the Daintree River Train) depart from the Daintree Village jetty. In winter, crocodiles can occasionally be seen from here sunbaking on the far side of the river. Along with croc-spotting, Barramundi fishing is also popular on the Daintree, as celebrated by the Big Barramundi overlooking the main street. River fishing tours run by experienced guides provide a safe and satisfying means of getting the most from angling in the Daintree. Other boat tours specialise in birdwatching and nature photography. Private river boat hire is also possible but proper caution must be exercised when travelling these crocodile-infested waters (*see box at right*).

Cape Tribulation

After crossing the Daintree River, the road to Cape Tribulation passes through the picnic spot of Jindalba overlooking Cow Bay, and Thornton Beach, a laid-back cluster of holiday shacks at the mouth of Cooper Creek. Watch out for Cassowaries ambling across the road, particularly in early mornings. The distinctive pyramidal apex of Thornton Peak drifts in and out of view and on either side of the main road is the Cape Tribulation section of Daintree National Park (*see facing page*). The cape was named by James Cook to mark the point where his barque *Endeavour* ran on to the reef. Today Cape Tribulation is brimming with backpacker, camping and resort accommodation and is the popular departure point for an enticing variety of tours and self-guided ventures into the adjoining national park.

What about Crocs?

Both Freshwater and Estuarine (or Saltwater) Crocodiles are found in large numbers in the Daintree. While the "salties" *(lower right)* grow to the largest size and are by far the most dangerous to humans, "freshies" can also attack if they feel threatened or are disturbed during breeding season. These majestic prehistoric creatures are a major attraction for visitors but should be treated with due caution — never approach a croc, stay away from water edges and river banks, do not swim in rivers and keep a safe (large!) distance from crocs when travelling in small craft.

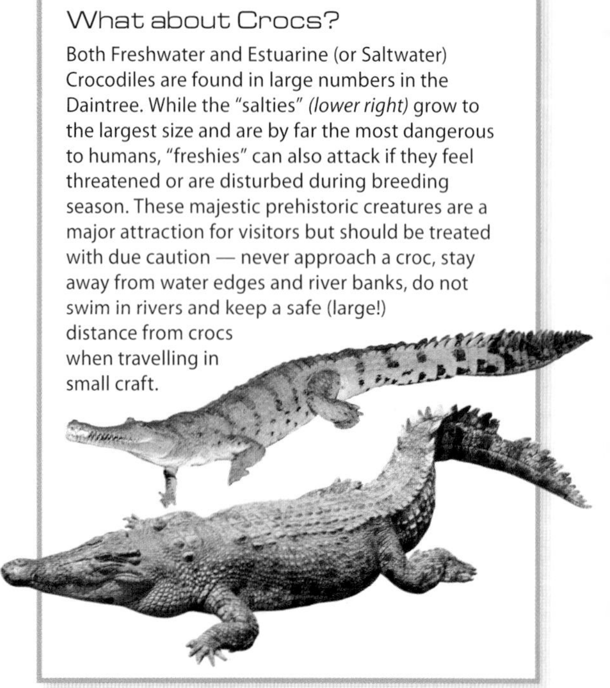

Top to bottom: Driving the Daintree; Secluded beach at Cape Tribulation; View from the Marrdja Boardwalk.

Daintree Forest National Park – Cape Tribulation Section

Phone Ranger: (07) 4098 0052

The Cape Tribulation section of Daintree National Park reaches from the Daintree River north to the Bloomfield River and is characterised by lowland rainforest and near impenetrable forested ranges reaching down to the coast. Some flora and fauna are native to this region alone. Found near Cape Tribulation are rare primitive plants including the ancient flowering Ribbonwood tree, *Idiospermum australiense*, re-discovered in 1972. Bennett's Tree-kangaroo, which lives and sleeps in the tree canopy, is found only in the rainforest between Daintree River and Cape Tribulation. Southern Cassowaries (*below*) play an essential role in the local ecology as the only birds capable of eating the larger tropical rainforest fruits and dispersing their seed. The Kuku Yalanji people are the traditional custodians of this area and their forebears were sustained by the abundant sources of food found in the coastal lowlands, including native fowl, Daintree River Ringtail Possums (*above right*) and Spectacled Flying-foxes (*above left*).

Walks in the Park: While much of the northern Daintree remains inaccessible mountain and forest, there are some excellent short walks on well-maintained boardwalk paths near Cape Tribulation. From Jindalba on the Cape Tribulation road there is a boardwalk that descends through the tropical lowland rainforest. Cassowaries and tree-kangaroos may be seen en route. At Marrdja, near Olivers Creek, an extensive 1.2 km walk affords easy viewing and photography of the mangrove forests, waterway and tropical plant life. The Dubuji boardwalk loop, near a well-equipped picnic area with barbecues and toilets at Myall Beach, takes 45 minutes and includes informative signage. A 800 m return trail from the Kulki visitors area near Cape Tribulation leads to a platform with views over the coast below. Myall Beach is a short walk from the Kulki car park.

A much longer, vastly more difficult, trek is the Mt Sorrow Ridge Walk. This 7 km trail commences at Bloomfield Road, 150 m north of the turn-off to the Kulki day-use area. The walk includes steep ascents and should not be undertaken alone or in hot and humid or wet conditions as the trail can become very slippery. Inform your accommodation operator if you intend to take this walk (and of your estimated time of return), as walkers have become lost on this trail.

Access: Via the Daintree River ferry crossing to Cape Tribulation. Much of the region north of Cape Tribulation to the Bloomfield River is inaccessible by vehicle but there is a crude 4WD track.

Camping: There are seventeen campsites at Noah Beach campground, 8 km south of Cape Tribulation. The sites are only 50 m from the beach in the shade of the forest canopy. Several sites are designed specifically for smaller campervans but caravans and larger vehicles are not permitted. There are toilets and tap water (boil first before consumption), but no fires are allowed. Maximum stay of seven nights. Permits and fees apply.

Wildlife of the Wet Tropics Rainforests

As a bioregion, the rainforests of Queensland's Wet Tropics are famous for their almost unrivalled diversity of wildlife. The Daintree World Heritage Area covers over 12,000 km² and includes the largest single region of tropical rainforest in Australia. Rainforest was once found throughout much of the continent, but climate change over many millennia has reduced it to relatively small pockets. Places like the Daintree are now crucial refuges for wildlife that can only survive in this ecosystem.

Research has confirmed the region as home to 36% of Australia's mammal species, 25% of the country's frog and reptile species, 40% of its freshwater fish species and over 75% of Australia's butterfly species. Over 50% of the total bird species in Australia can be found within the Wet Tropics of north Queensland.

Birds & Birdwatching

The Daintree is one of the best birdwatching locations on the planet. Many international "twitchers", ornithologists and photographers come to the region purely to capture a glimpse of the unique species that reside here. The Wet Tropics are home to thirteen bird species found here and nowhere else, including the Lesser Sooty Owl, Macleay's Honeyeater, Pied Monarch and Victoria's Riflebird.

The Daintree region is also an important breeding ground for many migratory birds, including the Buff-breasted Paradise-Kingfisher, Pied Imperial-Pigeon, Channel-billed Cuckoo, Metallic Starling, Papuan Frogmouth and Great-billed Heron. The endangered Southern Cassowary is often seen north of the Daintree River. Over 30 species of bird frequent the Daintree Village area alone, including Black Bitterns, Double-eyed Fig-Parrots, Wompoo Fruit-Doves and Spotted Catbirds, which eat the fruit of the local Blue Quandong (native pear) tree.

Mammals of the Night

There are over 110 species of mammal to be found in the Wet Tropics, including thirteen found nowhere else in Australia — the highest number of endemic mammal species in any one region of the continent. Many of the mammals of the Wet Tropics are nocturnal, including four types of endemic possum — the Herbert River Ringtail, the Lemuroid Ringtail, the Green Ringtail and the Daintree River Ringtail. Gliders, bats and possums are present in large numbers, particularly in upland regions, and include the black and white Striped Possum and also Squirrel; Greater, Yellow-bellied and Sugar Gliders. The critically endangered Mahogany Glider was re-discovered here in 1989 after an absence of more than a century. There are also many species of fruit, blossom and tiny insectivorous bats. Lumholtz's and Bennett's Tree-kangaroos can sometimes be seen moving about high in the rainforest canopy.

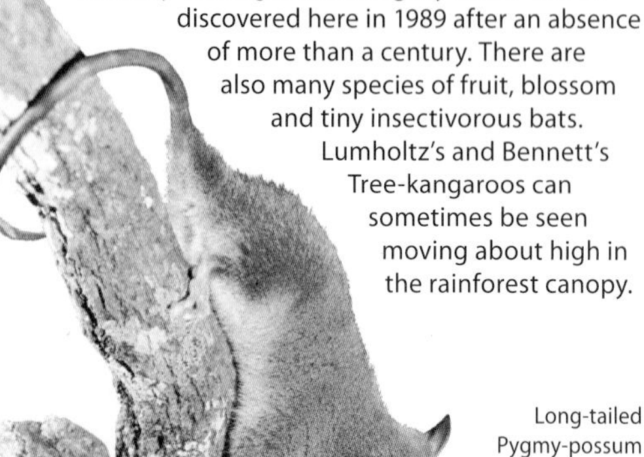

Long-tailed Pygmy-possum

Top: Birdwatching at Daintree Discovery Centre. **Top row, left to right:** Spotted Catbird; Rose-crowned Fruit-Dove; Australian King-Parrot. **2nd row, left to right:** Golden Bowerbird; Noisy Pitta; Victoria's Riflebird. **3rd row, left to right:** Striped Possum; Green Ringtail Possum; Yellow-bellied Glider. **Bottom row, left to right:** Red-legged Pademelon; Little Red Flying-fox; Lumholtz's Tree-kangaroo.

Top row, left to right: Green Tree Python; Boyd's Forest Dragon; Saw-shelled Turtle. **2nd row, left to right:** White-lipped Tree-frog; Stony-creek Frog; Ornate Burrowing Frog. **3rd row, left to right:** Red Lacewing; Cairns Birdwing; Ulysses Butterfly. **Bottom row, left to right:** Saratoga; Purple-spotted Gudgeon; Barramundi.

Daintree Discovery Centre Exploring the rainforest canopy from the Daintree Discovery Centre's tower and elevated boardwalk is a spectacular means of developing your understanding of the rainforest environment.

Reptiles

Over 150 species of reptile are found in the Wet Tropics, eighteen of which are endemic. Dangerous creatures such as crocodiles and death adders attract the most publicity, but there is also an equally fascinating, and less fearsome, range of lizards, pythons, freshwater turtles and geckoes. The Scrub Python is Australia's largest snake, growing up to 8 m long, and is a frequently seen inhabitant of the Wet Tropics. More diminutive, but no less impressive, is the prehistoric-looking Boyd's Forest Dragon.

Frogs

The northern rainforests are home to 54 species of frogs, ranging from the native tree-frogs to the pestiferous Cane Toad. The White-Lipped Tree-frog is amongst the largest known to live here and can reach up to 13 cm in length. Stony-creek Frogs are often seen on roads at night but shyer varieties such as the Northern Barred Frog and the Ornate Burrowing Frog can be more difficult to spot due to their habits, habitat and clever camouflage techniques (which can include changing colour when disturbed).

Butterflies

Butterflies are so common in the Wet Tropics that it is nigh impossible to take a walk through the rainforest without seeing at least two or three species. The most spectacular of these species are the Ulysses Butterfly (sporting brilliant blue wings), the Cairns Birdwing (Australia's largest with a wingspan of over 16 cm), the Red Lacewing and the black and white Orchard Butterfly. Moths are also present in large numbers. Spotting the difference between moths and butterflies? Butterflies are active during the day while moths fly by night.

Freshwater Fish

Many rainforest waterways act as aquariums by holding their freshwater residents captive between plunging waterfalls and salty estuaries, and this isolation leads to the evolution of many unique species. The Bloomfield River Cod, for example, is found only in that watercourse and is believed to have survived relatively unchanged for some 60 million years. Not all of the Wet Tropics' species have yet been identified, but rainbowfish and Pacific Blue-eye are both common. Recreational fishing is hugely popular due to the presence of large Barramundi, Jungle Perch, Sooty Grunter and Mangrove Jack.

Daintree Discovery Centre

Ten kilometres north of the Daintree River ferry is the Daintree Discovery Centre. This award-winning ecotourism facility features aerial walkways winding through the surrounding rainforest. A 23 m tower ascends into the canopy, providing bird's eye views from five viewing platforms. Many of the Daintree's most famous residents, including the Scrub Python, Ulysses Butterfly and Giant Green Tree-frog, live within the reserve. The display centre is equipped with interactive exhibits providing comprehensive information on Daintree habitats (open daily, 8.30 am – 5 pm, Ph: (07) 4098 9171).

COOKTOWN to Cape York

Cooktown to Cape York
Top Things to Do

1. Enjoy historic views on the Cooktown Scenic Rim Walking Trail.
2. Visit the James Cook Historical Museum.
3. Spend an afternoon walking in Black Mountain National Park.
4. Visit Quinkan Aboriginal rock art sites near Laura.
5. Camp by the Normanby River in Lakefield National Park.
6. Watch wildlife and waterbirds at Mungkan Kandju National Park.
7. Stand at the tip of Cape York and have someone photograph you!
8. Dive with gigantic Potato Cod off Lizard Island.
9. Sail from Cairns to Cape York.
10. Take a 4WD safari through Cape York.
11. Hop on a ferry to Thursday Island.

Cairns to Cape York by Sea

Travelling to Cape York by ocean is also an option — Sea Swift operates a Cairns to Cape York service on its vessel, MV *Trinity Bay*. The voyage takes three days and departs from Cairns on Friday afternoon, travelling via Horn Island and Thursday Island and arriving at Seisia (the closest coastal point to Bamaga) on Monday morning (Ph: 1800 424 422).

The 2000 km return trip to the tip — from Cooktown through Lakefield National Park to Cape York — is a journey of intense beauty, unique ecology and deep cultural history. This is not an easy drive — all roads are dirt so be prepared for bumps and clouds of dust during the drier mid-year months, river crossings and floods in others. Much of the road is impassable in the wet season. Australia's far north-east is isolated, rough country and experience with 4WD vehicles is essential. Alternatively, there are plenty of commercial 4WD safaris on offer, or you could fly into Bamaga and explore the region on locally chartered trips.

Cooktown & Surrounds

It is possible to reach Cooktown in a standard 2WD vehicle as the inland route (via the Peninsula–Cooktown Developmental Road) deviates west around the Daintree from Cairns through open tropical savannah and is completely sealed. The Bloomfield Track from Cape Tribulation through the upper Daintree is 4WD only.

After James Cook's *Endeavour* came to grief on the reef east of Cape Tribulation in 1770, the damaged barque limped up the coast to the mouth of Endeavour River — a harbour known as *charco* to the local Guugu Yimithirr people. It was here that Cook made the first record of the use of the Aboriginal word *kangaru* to identify Australia's iconic native marsupial.

A century later, Cook's safe haven would become a port servicing the region's goldfields. The town was almost completely wiped out by cyclones in 1907 and 1949 but, despite these events, the Cooktown area remains steeped in history — much of it related to its namesake. The James Cook Historical Museum, once a late 19th century convent, contains many artefacts relating to Cook's unscheduled stopover, including an anchor and cannon from the *Endeavour* (cnr Helen and Furneaux Streets, Ph: (07) 4069 5386). Nature's Powerhouse, with its remarkable collection of botanical illustrations by acclaimed artist Vera Scarth-Johnson, is located within Cooktown Botanic Gardens (Ph: (07) 4069 6004). Finch Bay, one of Cooktown's best beaches, is a short walk through the gardens. At Grassy Hill (eastern end of Hope Street) you can take in the same panoramic views of the harbour and ocean Cook used to identify a navigable passage through the reef. South of Cooktown, Black Mountain National Park protects the northernmost section of the Wet Tropics World Heritage Area. This superb bushwalking region is defined by piles of huge black granite boulders (rocks coated in blue-green algae).

North to the Tip

Around Laura, the cultural heritage of the Aboriginal peoples who have inhabited the Cape York region for over 40,000 years is visible in some of the world's most significant rock art sites. Known as the Quinkan Galleries for the spirits believed to reside within the sandstone bluffs, the Split Rock and Giant Horse sites should not be missed. Guided tours can be arranged at the Quinkan and Regional Cultural Centre in Laura (Ph: (07) 4060 3457). The town is also the venue for a centerpiece of Aboriginal celebration, the biennial Laura Festival.

Cape York's national parks are separated by large distances, but are a major feature of the region. Twenty-seven kilometres north of Laura is Lakefield National Park and a mere 300 km up the track, via the supply township of Coen (*see facing page*), is Mungkan Kandju National Park. From Mungkan Kandju it is only a further 335 km dust-ridden jaunt up the centre of the peninsula to the sandstone ridges and wild rivers of Jardine River National Park (*see following pages for park details*). Bamaga's Injinoo Airport is the arrival point for flights from Cairns. Facilities are limited but there is camping and accommodation at both Bamaga and Seisia. Ferries to Thursday Island (*see facing page*) depart daily from Seisia Wharf and tours are available to Horn Island and Badu Island. From Bamaga, yet another 32 km of dirt road will allow you to lay claim to having finally made it to the top.

Coen

Just over midway from Cairns to the tip is the old gold mining village of Coen, set near the banks of the Coen River. The town was the location of a overland telegraph station (now a museum known as Cape York Heritage House) and expanded with the establishment of the Great Northern Mine in 1892, the ruins of which are still visible today. The Wunthulpu Arts Centre offers information on the region, its Indigenous culture and history (Ph: (07) 4060 119). Horse races are staged in Coen each August. Fuel, accommodation, camping facilities and supplies are available.

Weipa

Originally the location of a 19th century Aboriginal mission, Weipa is today the site of the world's largest bauxite mine. The town itself was built at Rocky Point in 1965 to accommodate workers. It now has a population of over 3500 people and diverse facilities. Tours of the huge mine, operated by aluminium producer Comalco, are available (contact Weipa Town Office, Hibberd Centre, Rocky Point, Ph: (07) 4030 9400). Fishing and camping are major drawcards of the Weipa area, particularly around the mouth of the Pennefather River and surrounding beaches.

View from the Tip

If you've driven the entire distance from Cairns or Cooktown, you won't go away satisfied until you've reached Australia's northernmost point. Of course, you can't literally drive all the way to the tip — the last 700 m or so entails a walk through a patch of rainforest and over rocky terrain to the water. Here you will find a rather too modest sign acknowledging your remarkable feat. Opposite lie two small uninhabited islets, York Island and Eborac Island (*above*). From the tip of Cape York it is approximately 140 km directly across Torres Strait to Papua New Guinea.

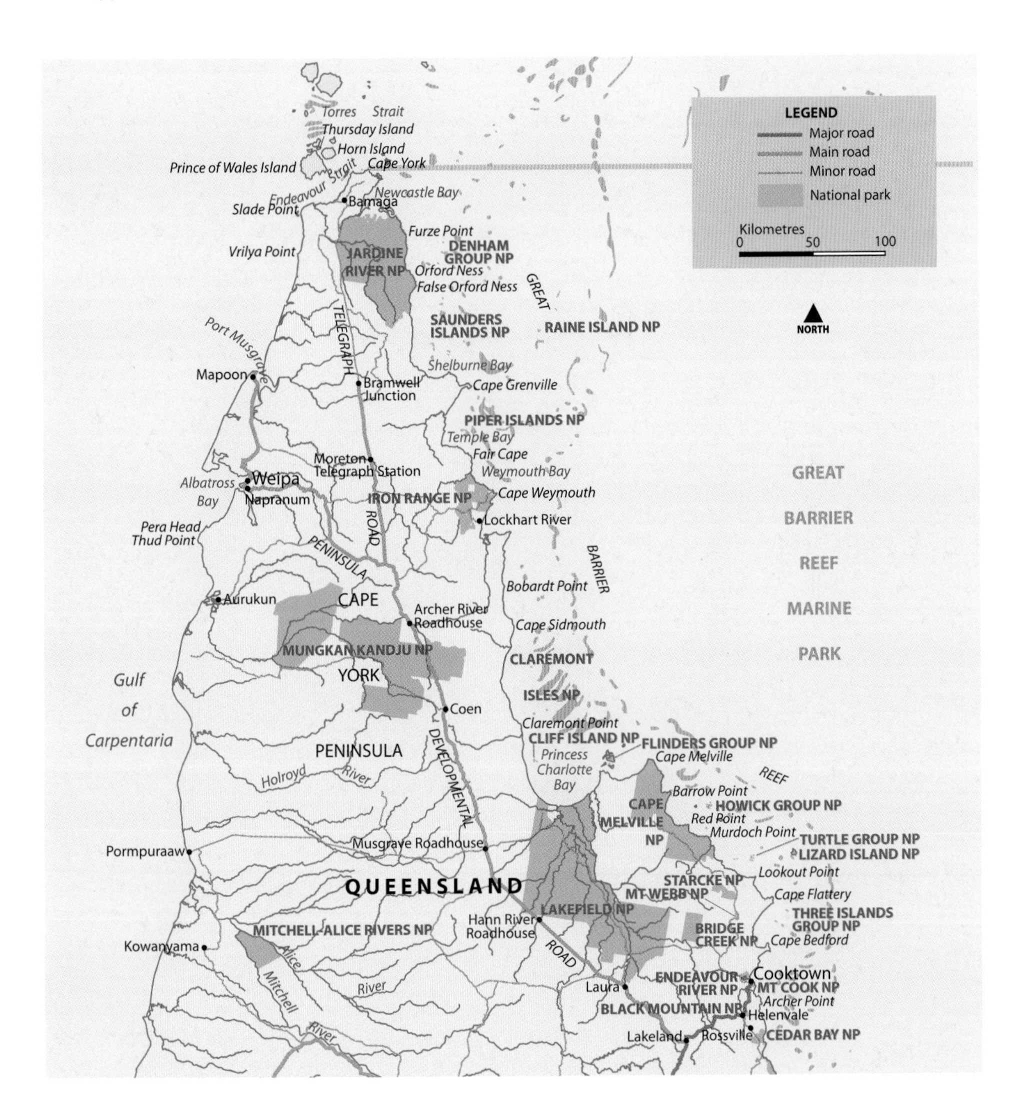

Thursday Island

Traditionally known as *Waiben*, or "dry place", in reference to the lack of available fresh water, Thursday Island (also called TI) is home to the largest community in Torres Strait. Located only 35 km north-west of Cape York, Thursday Island has a typically tropical climate of only two seasons — wet and dry. The island was at the centre of a major pearling industry in the 1880s and during World War II was used as the primary military base in Torres Strait for Allied Forces. Accordingly, Thursday Island has many fascinating historical sites, including Green Hill Fort, a maritime museum and a cemetery for Japanese pearl divers.

Top to bottom: Dancing Brolgas at Lakefield National Park; Lakefield National Park; Iron Range National Park; Mungkan Kandju National Park; Jardine River National Park.

Lakefield National Park

Phone Ranger: (07) 4060 3271

The rivers, wetlands, coastal estuaries, swamps and lagoons of Lakefield National Park are a refuge for wildlife (including the critically endangered Speartooth Shark). The park is bounded to the north by the mangrove systems and reefs of Princess Charlotte Bay. To the south are sandstone hills and escarpments. On the main road, 8 km north of Lakefield ranger station, are White and Red Lily Lagoons with their brilliant coverings of lotus lilies. Breeza, set on a lagoon lined with century-old mango trees, was once the site of a homestead breeding horses for use on the Palmer River goldfields. Old Laura Homestead, off Battle Camp Road, is the remains of one of lower Cape York's earliest cattle ventures.

Walks in the Park: There is a 4 km walking track in the shade of Weeping Paperbark trees along the Normanby River from Kalpowar Crossing. A 7 km return track follows the river from Hann Crossing a little further north.
Access: The Lakefield turn-off is 2 km beyond Laura on the Peninsula Developmental Road. From there it is around 45 minutes to the New Laura ranger station and a further 45 minutes to Lakefield ranger station.
Camping: There are six camping grounds within the park and all are close to permanent waterholes or rivers. Kalpowar Crossing, 3 km from the Lakefield ranger station, has excellent facilities including toilets and showers. Several campgrounds also offer boat access to the national park's Barramundi-filled waterways.

Iron Range National Park

Phone Ranger: (07) 4060 7170

This protected wilderness on the north-east of Cape York Peninsula contains the largest area of lowland rainforest in Australia. There are exceptional views from the beaches and headlands and the park is a unique refuge for bird species, many of which are found only in this region and Papua New Guinea. There is also a large population of nocturnal mammals and reptiles including the Green Tree Python. Palm Cockatoos and Double-eyed Fig-Parrots are seen around the camping areas. Crocodiles are present in the park waterways, so exercise proper caution around rivers and do not swim or use canoes/kayaks.

Walks in the Park: A single 10 km return walking trail (easy grade), commencing at Rainforest campsite and leading through rainforest and woodland along the Old Coen Track, offers superb birdwatching and photographic opportunities. There is also a viewing platform 80 m from Mount Tozer car park and it is possible to walk 5 km along Chili Beach to the mouth of Chili Creek.
Access: Via Peninsula Developmental Road to Portland Roads Road turn-off, 20 km north of Archer River Roadhouse. It is a further 110 km (three to five hours drive) to the park's ranger station. Roads are impassable during the Wet and visits to Iron Range are recommended between April and September. 4WD vehicles access only, at all times.
Camping: Basic campsites are available at Rainforest, Gordons Creek, Cooks Hut and Chili Beach camping areas but there are only toilets at Chili Beach and Cooks Hut. Carry drinking water, a fuel stove and mosquito nets. No generators. Permits are required and fees apply. The ranger station has excellent facilities, including toilets and showers.

The Green Tree Python An arboreal resident of Iron Range National Park.

Mungkan Kandju National Park

Phone Ranger: (07) 4060 1137

This remote wilderness region of woodland, waterholes, lagoons and melaleuca swamp around the Archer and Coen Rivers protects a diverse range of wildlife and is of great significance to its traditional Aboriginal owners.

Walks in the Park: There are no formal walking tracks but you may explore (with due caution as crocs are present) around campsites and along the waterholes and rivers. Recreational fishing is permitted in all waterways with the exception of Peach Creek.
Access: Via Coen to the Rokeby access road turn-off and then west to Rokeby ranger station — taking 1.5 to 2 hours. 4WD vehicles (in good mechanical condition) only.
Camping: Bush camping is possible at marked sites near waterholes (consult ranger). There are no camping facilities in the park.

Jardine River National Park

Phone Ranger: (07) 4060 3271

Known as the "wet desert" to early explorers for its abundance of fresh water and lack of suitable animal feed, Jardine River National Park protects a region of ancient sandstone, heathland, grassland, rainforest and woodland around the Jardine River catchment.

Walks in the Park: There are three short and easy (maximum 15 minute return) tracks from the Eliot Falls campground leading to waterfall, creek and woodland views.
Access: Via Telegraph Road (50 km north of Coen) and then Southern Bypass Road. The major camping and walking areas on the banks of the Jardine River and at Eliot Falls in the park's northern section can also be accessed by 4WD from Bamaga to the north (contact ranger, Ph: (07) 4069 5777).
Camping: Eliot Falls has excellent camping facilities for tents and campervans, including toilets, showers, fireplaces and drinking water. Bush camping is also possible at Captain Billy Landing and at designated sites along the banks of the Jardine River.

Clockwise from top: A diver tickles the chin of a friendly Potato Cod at the famous Cod Hole north of Lizard Island; Snorkelling the outer reef; Crystal clear water reveals innumerable marine creatures around Lizard Island's nearby reefs.

Great Barrier Reef Marine Park – Northern Section

In many places, the northern section of the Great Barrier Reef is at least equally as spectacular as the reefs south of Cairns. The major difference from a traveller's perspective is that there are not so many coastal settlements in Far North Queensland (and they are more widely spaced) and there are far fewer coral cays and continental islands within easy reach. This is, of course, a great asset of the reef's northern section. The remoteness means that numbers of visitors, cruises and dive boats are likely to be much lower — even in the most popular areas. Even the northern section's most heavily promoted destination, Lizard Island, maintains an air of seclusion and serenity that can be hard to find south of Cooktown.

Snorkelling, diving, cruising and photographing the northern section of the Great Barrier Reef Marine Park invariably involves travelling longer distances by road and/or sea. The Flinders Group of islands, 340 km north of Cairns near Cape Melville, comprises seven islands that are sometimes visited by cruise ships departing Cairns (and by private yachts and cruising boats). Camping is possible on Flinders Island, which is an excellent base for exploration of the fringing reef. Nearby Stanley Island has impressive Aboriginal rock art shelters and an interpretive heritage trail.

Clockwise from top: View from Cooks Look, taking in Blue Lagoon and South and Palfrey Islands; Mangrove boardwalk; Boulder-strewn bays of Lizard Island.

Lizard Island National Park

Phone Ranger: (07) 4060 3271

Although most people are only familiar with Lizard Island itself, there are in fact five neighbouring continental islands in the national park. They lie 27 km off the coast, 93 km north-east of Cooktown. A diverse variety of seabirds, native mammals and reptiles are present on the islands. The Sand Monitor (*below*) is a conspicuous native, and is the lizard for which Captain James Cook named the main island.

Walks in the Park: Lizard Island enjoys a wide choice of walking trails, and snorkelling among the giant clam gardens of Watsons Bay plus the stunning corals of the Blue Lagoon is also popular.
Access: Regular flights to Lizard Island operate from Cairns, charter flights from Cairns and Cooktown and charter vessels from Cairns, Port Douglas and Cooktown.
Accommodation/Camping: Bush camping is permitted on Lizard Island at Watsons Bay (toilets and gas barbecue burners are provided). There is a luxury resort (Ph: 1300 134 044) which offers a broad range of recreational activities (including reef diving, snorkelling and glass-bottomed boat tours — children under 15 years of age are not permitted at the resort). Campers are allowed to use the resort restaurant but no other supplies are available.

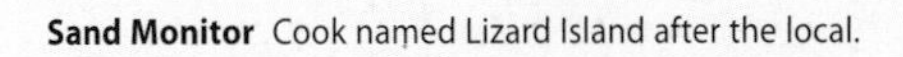

Sand Monitor Cook named Lizard Island after the local.

CAIRNS to Darwin

Cairns to Darwin
Top Things to Do

1. Take a tour of the unique Undara Lava Tubes.
2. Ride the *Gulflander* motor rail from Normanton to Croydon and back.
3. Wander the historic gold mining village at Croydon.
4. Have a cool drink in the cartoon-festooned bar of the Purple Pub in Normanton.
5. Photograph the Gulf of Carpentaria from Karumba Point.
6. Explore the amazing outback oasis of Boodjamulla (Lawn Hill) National Park.
7. Watch the dawn skies over Burketown for the arrival of the incredible Morning Glory cloud formations.
8. Visit the northernmost campsite of explorers Burke and Wills.
9. Match wits against huge Barramundi in the waters of the Gulf of Carpentaria.
10. Fossick for topaz near Mount Surprise.

Gulf Country

The wide, spreading plains of the Gulf are tough, hot country speckled with scrubby bush and saltpans. It is dotted with isolated small towns, Aboriginal communities and cattle stations. Tidal rivers flow into the massive arc of the Gulf of Carpentaria — crocodile country fringed with mud and mangrove. During the wet season, most of the roads are cut and, if supplies run out, air freight is the only reliable way to get goods in.

No less memorable and revealing than the trip to the tip is the epic journey across the Carpentaria "Gulf country" from Cairns to Darwin. This magnificent north Australian adventure follows a series of roads known as the Savannah Way. The entire trek is only possible in the dry season, and some of the track west of Normanton to the Carpentaria Highway in the Territory is traversable only by 4WD.

Cairns to the Gulf

The journey commences with the climb up through the ranges behind Cairns to the Atherton Tableland (*see page 116*). West of Ravenshoe on the Gulf Developmental Road, Undara Volcanic National Park is famous for its long cylindrical caverns (known as lava tubes), formed by the outpouring of lava through rock many thousands of years ago. Georgetown, 147 km west, marks the beginning of the real adventure into less-travelled territory.

Croydon, a historic gold town, is also the railhead for the *Gulflander*, a venerable motor rail, now primarily a tourist attraction, which makes the 150 km trip to Normanton once a week. Normanton is the eastern point of Gulf country, where cattle roam the parched landscape and stock horses remain crucial for mustering and working the most rugged parts of vast stations. Karumba, just north of Normanton (where the Norman River runs into the Gulf), is known for its great fishing and even greater crocodiles. It is also the heart of the Gulf of Carpentaria's lucrative prawn fishing industry. The Gulf's shores and plains are home to Australian Pelicans, wallabies and wallaroos and the coast is a promised land for anglers and birdwatchers. Burketown, 220 km west of Normanton on the Albert River, is the last main town before the Northern Territory border. It lies in the northernmost region explored by cross-continental pioneers Burke and Wills before their ill-fated return journey south.

From Burketown it is possible (with a reliable 4WD vehicle and experienced driver) to travel the 220 km south-west to spectacular Boodjamulla (Lawn Hill) National Park. Here an ancient gorge occupied by Aborigines for over 35,000 years has been carved out by subterranean waterways, creating a lush and unlikely oasis. Also within the park is Riversleigh, one of two Australian Fossil Mammal Site World Heritage Areas. Here, the fossilised remains of carnivorous kangaroos, marsupial lions and huge carnivorous birds that lived over 30 million years ago have been discovered.

Territory to Top End

The Northern Territory section of the journey beyond the remote service towns of Borroloola and Cape Crawford includes famous Katherine Gorge and Kakadu National Park, making this trip an unforgettable tour of some of Australia's most glorious and best-preserved habitat. At road's end is Darwin, the capital of the Top End and a city wherein historical interest and cultural importance far outweigh its geographical size.

Gulf Towns

The few towns that punctuate the journey below the Gulf each have their own distinct character. At Normanton, visitors and drovers alike are drawn to the bar of the Purple Pub (*above left*), a famed local watering hole formally known as The Albion with humorous cartoons adorning the bar room walls. Arriving in town on the nostalgic *Gulflander*, a motor rail that shuttles the short distance between Normanton and Croydon, is a rite of passage in these parts (*above right*).

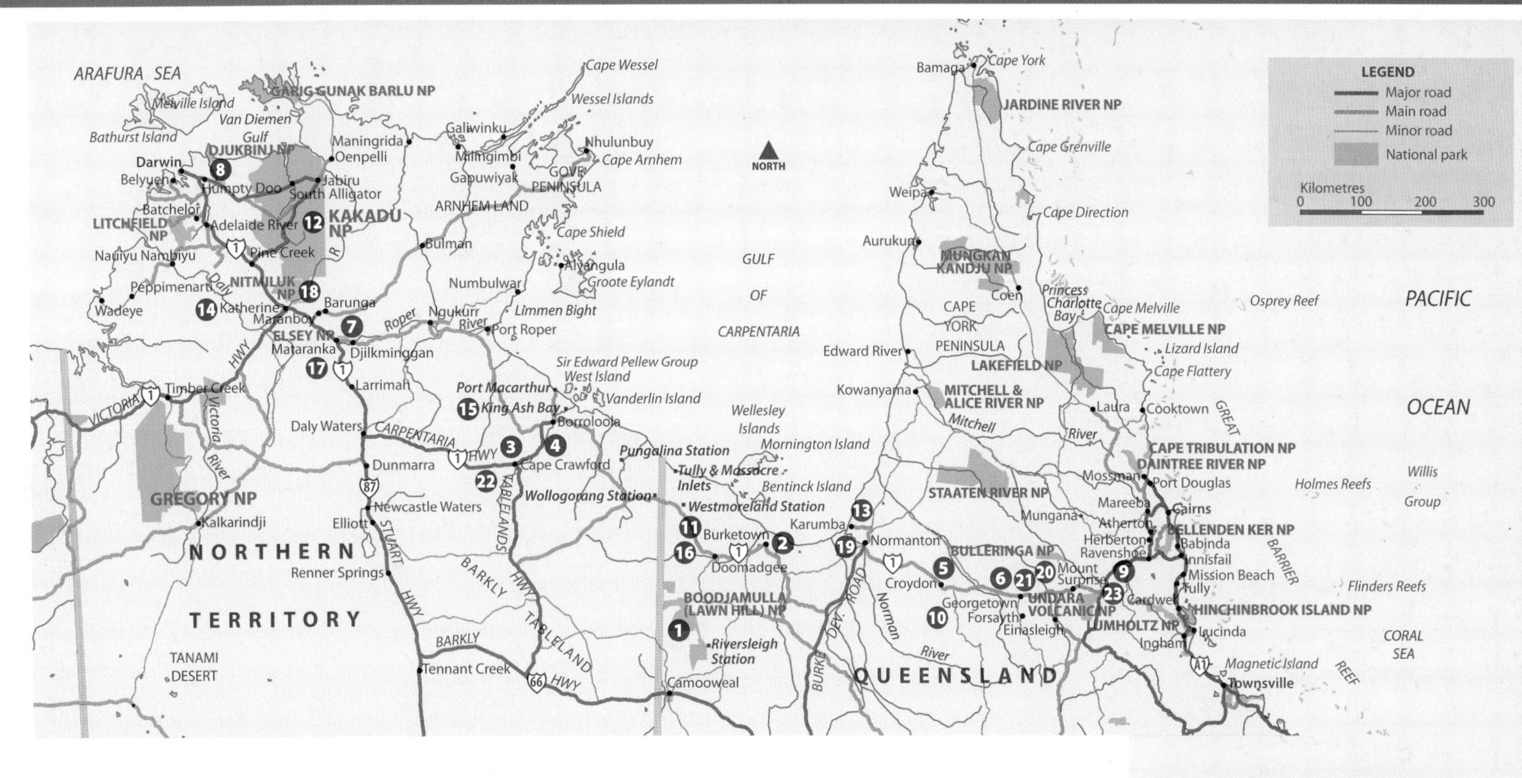

Undara Volcanic National Park

Phone Ranger: (07) 4097 1485

Undara Volcanic National Park protects a series of lava flows formed during volcanic eruptions about 190,000 years ago. *Undara* (from the Aboriginal name meaning "a long way") lava flow is 160 km long — the planet's longest lava flow from a single volcano. Flowing down riverbeds, the lava cooled quickly on the edges but its molten centre continued to flow. The resultant hollow tunnels were subsequently colonised by a specialised group of plants and animals.

With its rich basalt soils, seasonal grasses define the savannah landscape. At the entrances to some caves, a damp, sheltered aspect has allowed vine thickets to thrive while collapsed tubes have nurtured patches of dry rainforest.

Walks in the Park: There is a 2.5 km circuit walk around the rim of the impressive Kalkani Crater. Wildlife includes over 120 species of bird, plus Ghost Bats (*below*), Sugar Gliders, rock-wallabies and wallaroos. Paths and stairways lead down into the lava tubes, but access is only possible through commercial tour operators (contact Bedrock Village, Ph: (07) 4062 3193; Cape Trib Connections, Ph: (07) 4053 3833; Undara Experience, Ph: 1800 990 992).

Access: Enter from Gulf Developmental Road, 17 km west of its junction with Kennedy Highway.

Camping: Camping is not permitted in the park. A range of accommodation, including restored railway carriages, is available at nearby Undara Lava Lodge (Ph: 1800 990 992).

Feature Localities

1 Boodjamulla (Lawn Hill) National Park
2 Burketown
3 Cape Crawford
4 Caranbirini Nature Reserve
5 Croydon
6 Cumberland Chimney
7 Elsey National Park
8 Fogg Dam
9 Forty Mile Scrub National Park
10 Georgetown
11 Hell's Gate
12 Kakadu National Park
13 Karumba
14 Katherine
15 King Ash Bay
16 Kingfisher Camp
17 Mataranka Thermal Pools
18 Nitmiluk National Park
19 Normanton
20 O'Briens Creek Gemfields
21 Tallaroo Hot Springs
22 The Lost City
23 Undara Volcanic National Park

Undara to Lawn Hill National Park

The Kennedy Highway leads south from Ravenshoe to Forty Mile Scrub National Park, a protected remnant of dry rainforest with a huge variety of flora. Here, Black-striped Wallabies may be seen along the short, signposted circuit trail from the picnic area. Only 17 km west along the Gulf Developmental Road are the unique geological marvels of Undara Volcanic National Park. For millions of years, Undara was an active shield volcano until it spewed its molten contents onto the surrounding landscape (at a rate of around 1000 cubic metres every second). The national park now contains the longest lava tube system in existence. Over 35 cave-dwelling species including bats and owls nest in this vast cave system. Access to the Undara lava tube caves is only possible by joining a tour and it is best to book before arrival (*see previous page*).

Around the small town of Mount Surprise are several worthwhile side trips. Forty-two kilometres to the north-west are O'Brien's Creek Gemfields, where fossickers can unearth their own lump of topaz. En route to Georgetown, a turn-off leads north to the Tallaroo Station Hot Springs, an area of natural thermal waters open to the public (daily between April and September). A memorable way to travel the region is aboard the *Savannahlander* — a distinctive silver train that runs from Cairns to Mount Surprise and also offers shorter forays south of Mount Surprise to the old mining districts of Einasleigh and Forsayth. The journey is considered one of the world's most unique train trips (Ph: (07) 4053 6848).

Georgetown to Normanton

Located on the banks of the Etheridge River, Georgetown was once the commercial centre of an area dubbed the "poor man's goldfields", where nuggets could be collected close to the surface without the use of expensive equipment. Today Georgetown is a base for exploration of the gemfields and old mining ghost towns to the south. The Cumberland Chimney, 20 km west of town, is the remains of an ore-crushing plant built by Cornish masons near a lagoon now frequented by waterbirds. Croydon, another former mining boomtown, is the railway terminus for the historic *Gulflander.* The motor rail is affectionately dubbed the "Old Tin Hare" — a train that goes from "nowhere to nowhere". In fact, it travels once a week to Normanton on a track ingeniously constructed with metal sleepers to withstand fire and flood. Unless you wish to spend a week in Normanton awaiting the train's return to Croydon, it is best to catch it from Normanton on a Wednesday morning, get a room at the historic Croydon Hotel and return from Croydon the next day (Ph: (07) 4036 9333).

Normanton is the closest thing to a big town you will encounter along this length of the Savannah Way. With a population of 1300, it's not exactly a bustling metropolis, but it has a fascinating past that reads like a precis of Australia's European exploration. The Norman River on which it is located was first sighted by Dutch explorer Abel Tasman in 1644 and Matthew Flinders landed in the region while circumnavigating Australia in 1802. The enigmatic Ludwig Leichhardt passed through the area on his way to Port Essington from the Darling Downs and it was only 26 km from here that Burke and Wills finally reached the Gulf (or, more accurately, the mangrove swamps at its edge). The exact place of their northernmost camp is marked by plaques on a short 1.5 km detour from the Normanton–Burketown Road. The Barramundi fishing is great, as is the wildlife spotting, with the wetlands region between Normanton and Karumba forming a migratory destination for nearly a third of Australia's waterbirds (including the Brolga and the Sarus Crane). You don't have to venture further than Normanton's main street to be wowed by this Gulf town. Here is an 8.63 m life-size replica of the biggest croc ever captured — Krys the Savannah King.

Croydon

This former gold town is chock full of character (*above, top to bottom*) — a fact evidenced by its carefully conserved historic precinct, which includes the original jail and courthouse, mine warden's office, hospital and town hall. Nearby Lake Belmore is the Gulf's largest body of freshwater in the Gulf savannah.

Normanton

Normanton was once the main river port for the goldfields to the east. Gold and goods for export were once transported by rail from the goldfields to Normanton before being ferried up river to the Gulf by barge. The Normanton Railway Terminus, a charming timber and corrugated iron construction, is a heritage-listed building.

The Gulf of Carpentaria

Dense mangrove fringes, swamps, saltpans and river deltas extending up to 30 km inland characterise the southern reaches of the Gulf of Carpentaria. The Dutch explorer Captain Jan Carstenszoon was the first European to map this stretch of Australia's coast (in 1623), naming it after Pieter de Carpentier, the Dutch Governor-General in Batavia.

Karumba

Situated at the Norman River's mouth, 70 km north of Normanton, Karumba is the only town right on the southern shores of the Gulf of Carpentaria (settlement has been prevented on most of the Gulf's coastline by impenetrable, crocodile-ridden mangroves). Once a stopover for Empire Flying Boats travelling from Sydney to England, Karumba is now sustained by the Gulf's large prawning industry and a port that services regional zinc mining operations. The recreational fishing is world-class and there are superb views of the Gulf from Karumba Point, particularly at sunset.

Burketown to Boodjamulla National Park

The small settlement of Burketown on the Albert River was originally established as the site of a factory for processing local beef for export. Here, if you are lucky, you may witness one of Australia's most unusual natural splendours, the Morning Glory. These are a wave of dark, cigar-shaped clouds that occasionally roll in at great speed off the Gulf in the early dawn hours. The clouds, which are famous among gliding and soaring pilots, can reach lengths of 1000 km and heights of more than 3000 m, but their precise origin remains a mystery. As does their timetable — according to locals, the conditions are right for the appearance of the Morning Glory when the glass in the beer fridge of the local pub frosts up (but that may just be an excuse to pass the time waiting for it to happen at the bar). For more reliable natural wonders, it is only 220 km south-west on unsealed road via Gregory Downs to Boodjamulla (Lawn Hill) National Park, an area of outstanding natural beauty featuring the fertile oasis of Lawn Hill Gorge (*see box below*).

Boodjamulla National Park

– a Detour south-west from Burketown

Phone Ranger: (07) 4722 5224

Boodjamulla protects two timeless features — Lawn Hill Gorge and the World Heritage fossil site at Riversleigh. Around the gorge are a phenomenal range of creatures, including the rare Purple-crowned Fairy-wren, Great Egrets, cormorants, Olive Pythons and Northern Snapping Turtles. The Riversleigh region in the south of the park is home to fossils of ancient mammals preserved in limestone and dating back 25 million years. Here, palaeontologists have found the skeletal evidence of native megafauna including marsupial lions, carnivorous kangaroos, diprotodontids, huge pythons, crocodiles and bats.

Walks in the Park: Six walking tracks commence close to the Lawn Hill Gorge campground. The Wild Dog Dreaming Walk takes in Waanyi rock art shelters as well as the lower gorge. The 3.8 km Indarri Falls Loop Walk offers excellent opportunities for swimming and photography. Canoeing is also a great way to tour the gorge and canoes are available for hire at nearby Adels Grove.
Access: From Burketown it is 220 km south-west via Gregory Downs. Roads may be impassable during the wet season.
Camping: Close to Lawn Hill Gorge with toilets and showers (booking required from Easter to October). Nearby Adels Grove is a well-equipped, privately operated camping retreat in exotic botanical garden surroundings (Ph: (07) 4748 5502).

Wildlife and Habitat of the Savannah Way

The Savannah Way passes through tropical savannahs covering 1.9 million km^2 or nearly a quarter of mainland Australia. This incredibly diverse landscape includes grasslands, woodlands and scattered trees, stony escarpments and gorges, mangrove swamps and mudflats, floodplains, billabongs, wetlands and riverine catchments. The tropical savannah habitats are an important wildlife refuge comprising nineteen distinct bioregions. The lush regions of coastal north-east Queensland give way to outback plains known as the Mitchell Grasslands, reaching west to the Northern Territory border. To the north, much of Cape York is clad in savannah woodlands. The southern shores of the Gulf of Carpentaria are typified by riverland, mangrove swamps and mudflats. Further west are the stony escarpments and woodlands of Western Arnhem Land, Kakadu and Katherine Gorge.

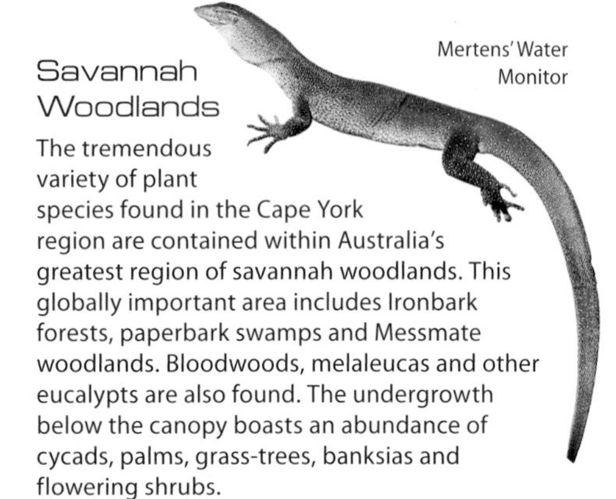
Mertens' Water Monitor

Savannah Woodlands

The tremendous variety of plant species found in the Cape York region are contained within Australia's greatest region of savannah woodlands. This globally important area includes Ironbark forests, paperbark swamps and Messmate woodlands. Bloodwoods, melaleucas and other eucalypts are also found. The undergrowth below the canopy boasts an abundance of cycads, palms, grass-trees, banksias and flowering shrubs.

The skies above the savannah are the realm of hawks, eagles, owls and bats. Below roam lizards, ranging from impressively sized monitors to skinks and geckoes. Pythons and tree snakes doze in the filtered sunlight or covertly slither about in search of prey. Northern Quolls, Brush-tailed Phascogales, dunnarts and Common Planigales can also be found. Some bird species (like the Golden-shouldered Parrot and the Red Goshawk) are endangered. Magnetic termite mounds are also a common sight on the savannah.

River Life

The rivers and streams of the Gulf savannah region are renowned for their plentiful species of fish. The Norman and Mitchell Rivers in particular are target-rich sportfishing destinations with Barramundi, Threadfin Salmon, trevally, bream, Mangrove Jack, Golden Snapper, Grey Mackerel, Queenfish and grunter. These have made the region a magnet not only for recreational anglers, but for a vast range of birds. There are 20 wetlands in the Gulf region and the Gulf lies on the migratory path for a large number of bird species. The area around Normanton alone is host to approximately one-third of Australia's migratory wading birds (such as the Brolga and Sarus Crane). Also look for ibises, herons, terns and ducks. The country's largest raptor, the Wedge-tailed Eagle, is also found throughout the Savannah region — often feasting on highway roadkill.

A Frilled Lizard Darling of the Australian reptile world, poses for a passing photographer.

Clockwise from left: Great Bowerbird; Tornier's Frog; Northern Death Adder.

Clockwise from left: Yellow-billed Spoonbill; Archerfish; Pig-nosed Turtle.

Clockwise from left: Black-necked Stork (or Jabiru); Comb-crested Jacana; Rainbowfish.

Clockwise from left: Short-eared Rock-wallabies; Rock Ringtail Possum; Giant Cave Gecko.

Clockwise from left: Estuarine Crocodile; Mud Crab; Mudskipper.

Floodplains

Huge floodplain wetlands (including melaleuca and mangrove swamps) are found throughout the coastal regions of northern Australia.

These areas are home to large populations of aquatic animals.

Northern Australia attracts vast congregations of waterfowl, particularly Magpie Geese (*left*), in floodplains and other wetlands. Late in the dry season, when water is rare in other parts of the surrounding country, these gatherings on the floodplains can reach truly massive proportions, making a spectacular sight for visitors. The birds comprise both native Australian species and tropical cousins from lands to the nation's north.

Stony Escarpments

The vast sandstone plateaus, isolated rock outcrops and stony escarpments of the savannah regions provide some of the most interesting landscapes and populous wildlife habitats of northern Australia. While much of the stony region of Arnhem Land is too rugged to allow easy access; Kakadu National Park and the incredible gorges of the Katherine River give you the opportunity to explore a sandstone region blessed with an enormous wealth of animals and plant life. Rodents, well-suited to life here, are commonly found, as are marsupials — including kangaroos and wallabies, bandicoots, possums and dasyurids (quolls, dunnarts, phascogales and antechinuses). Warm rocks and sheltered recesses also support an exceedingly diverse number of lizard species — many of which are endemic to these regions.

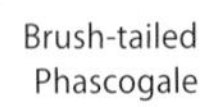

Brush-tailed Phascogale

Mangroves & Mudflats

Much of the savannah coast is characterised by vast mangrove forests and mudflats. The tidal mudflats are home to many terrestrial and mud-dwelling crustaceans such as crabs, prawns and lobsters. Within the mangroves and surrounding seagrass areas are birds, Estuarine Crocodiles, Dugongs and marine turtles. Mangroves are an essential element of the Savannah's coastal ecosystem, fringing the intertidal zone coastal rivers, estuaries and bays. Mangrove forests vary widely, ranging from 2 to 30 m in height, depending upon their environment. Twelve species of mangrove can be found in the Gulf savannah region alone. Mangroves reduce the speed of currents, trapping sediments and helping to reduce siltation in adjacent marine habitats. The "upside down" roots of mangroves reach upward from the water into the air and evolved to compensate for the low levels of oxygen found in the coastal mud.

Rufous Night Heron

Burketown to Katherine
Top Things to Do

1. Photograph Dill Dill Rocks (near Hell's Gate).
2. Experience authentic outback life. Spend a night or two on one of the Gulf region's vast cattle stations.
3. Camp at King Ash Bay, on the McArthur River near Borroloola.
4. Take a helicopter flight over the stone citadel of The Lost City.
5. Stop for a cool drink in the famous bar of the Daly Waters Hotel.
6. Mix it with the locals at Larrimah.
7. Study the sandstone spires of Caranbirini Conservation Reserve.
8. Relax and revitalise at the thermal springs around Elsey National Park.
9. Visit the Cutta Cutta Caves south-east of Katherine.
10. Explore the incredible oasis of Nitmiluk National Park.

The Lost City

The "Lost City", an incredible metropolis of sandstone skyscrapers up to 25 m tall, was discovered by drover Lindsay Crawford near the Abner Ranges in 1880. These clustered, towering formations — the eroded bedrock of an ancient inland sea — spread across an area of around 8 km^2 just south of Cape Crawford.

Burketown to Katherine

Travelling beyond Burketown along the Savannah Way will take you through the Indigenous community at Doomadgee on the Nicholson River. Kingfisher Camp, a shaded campground on a 5 km long waterhole on the Nicholson River, is situated on the boundary of nearby Bowthorn Station. From Doomadgee it is 80 km to Hell's Gate Roadhouse — the last stop before the Northern Territory border.

In the 19th century, the gap in the low rocky escarpment that the road now passes through signified entry into a potentially deadly unknown, giving rise to the name Hell's Gate. To this point, travellers came under the protection of the Native Police at nearby Corinda Station — after Hell's Gate, you were on your own. It is a decidedly less daunting location today and the friendly roadhouse offers fuel, supplies and accommodation (including campsites). Tours of historic Westmoreland Station, 17 km up the road (*see map on page 129*), provide insight to life on the old frontier and there is also an old Afghan camel drivers' camp in the vicinity.

Hell's Gate to Cape Crawford

Just across the border, accommodation, camping facilities and meals are available at Wollogorang Station (*see map on page 129*). Tours can also be organised from here to the fishing and camping destinations of Tully and Massacre Inlets directly north on the Gulf coast. Nearby Redbank Mine is a small-scale open-cut copper mine. Adjacent to Wollogorang, 64 km north of the Savannah Way, is the slightly smaller but equally hospitable Pungalina Station (*see map on page 129*) on the Calvert River. Pungalina now promotes itself as an "outback remote eco-wilderness safari camp", which translates into well-managed tours through the coastal gorges, limestone caves and rivers of the region (Ph: (03) 9882 4236). A little further up the Savannah Way is a pleasant camping site on the banks of the Robinson River, but Borroloola, on the McArthur River close to the coast, is the first main town on the Territory side. Nearby King Ash Bay and the Port McArthur region remain enormously popular Barramundi fishing destinations.

Borroloola has a long history as a rough and ready river port, with a cast of dubious characters (including cattle duffers and rum smugglers) to match. Explore the stories, artefacts and photographs in the local museum (housed in the old police station, which once doubled as the town library). The road to Cape Crawford passes Caranbirini Conservation Reserve, where it is worthwhile pausing to walk amid the sandstone spires and lunch by the waterhole. The curiously named Cape Crawford is neither on coast nor cape, but millions of years ago stood at the shores of an inland sea. The local pub is known as Heartbreak Hotel, a title harking back to the difficulties experienced by the original owner in constructing the building. His heartbreak continued when his wife later ran off with a local ringer. If Elvis was ever here, he has now left the building, but you can stay and take a helicopter or land-based tour of the fascinating Lost City (*see bottom left*).

Cape Crawford to Katherine

The sealed Carpentaria Highway from Cape Crawford leads through several more huge tableland cattle stations to its intersection with the Stuart Highway — 269 km east at Daly Waters. The pub here, one of the oldest buildings in the Northern Territory, is famous for its colourful bar and hearty plates of barbecued beef 'n' barra. Further up the highway is the historic town of Larrimah — once a World War II staging camp for more than 3000 servicemen, recalled by a memorabilia exhibit at the old police station. Mataranka's hot springs (74 km north of Larrimah) are a great place to revive, shed the dust from your skin and soothe tired muscles. Once refreshed, it is only another 105 km further north to Katherine — a busy regional tourist town and service hub south of Darwin. Its most spectacular asset, the magnificent Nitmiluk (Katherine Gorge) National Park, is only 30 km north-east of town (*see pages 136–37*).

Katherine

The Katherine region, with its superb river and gorge, is a traditional meeting place for peoples of the Jawoyan, Walpiri, Dagaman and Wardiman clans. Named by explorer John McDouall Stuart for one of his patron's daughters, Katherine first came to prominence as a station on the Overland Telegraph Line established in 1872. The town and surrounds lie over a natural limestone cave system. Cutta Cutta Caves, 27 km south-east of Katherine on the Stuart Highway, is home to colonies of rare Orange Horseshoe Bats and blind shrimp. Daily tours are conducted on the hour (but may not be possible during the wet season).

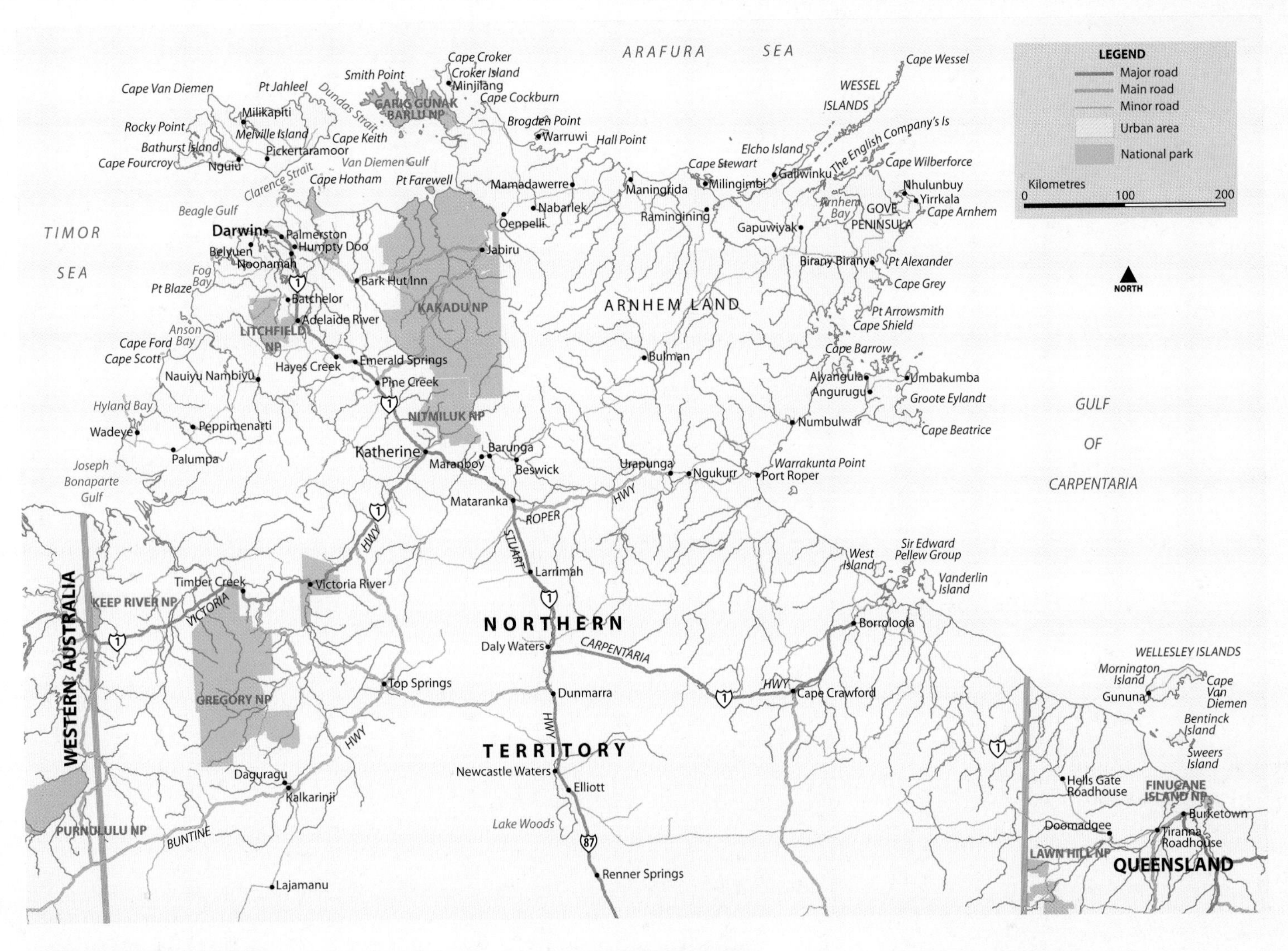

Elsey National Park

Phone Ranger: (08) 8973 8888

The natural springs of Elsey National Park are the source of the Roper River. The spring waters are also the park's main attraction, seeping out of the ground at a temperature of 34 °C to form picturesque (and muscle-relaxing) thermal pools surrounded by glades of forest and fern (*left*). Mataranka Thermal Pools are situated in a region made famous by Jeannie Gunn's 1908 outback novel, *We of the Never Never*.

Walks in the Park: Take the 1.5 km Botanical Walk off John Hauser Drive access road. There is also an 8 km return walk to Mataranka Falls from the 12 Mile Yards campground.

Access: Access the main thermal pool from Homestead Road (1.5 km south of Mataranka on the Stuart Highway). Springs can also be reached from John Hauser Drive (off Homestead Road 4 km from the Stuart Highway). To get to Bitter Springs follow the sealed road from Mataranka township.

Camping: The main campground is located at the 12 Mile Yards campground, which has hot water, grassy areas and ablution areas. Tents and caravans are permitted but there are no powered sites. There are also commercial camping grounds and accommodation at Mataranka.

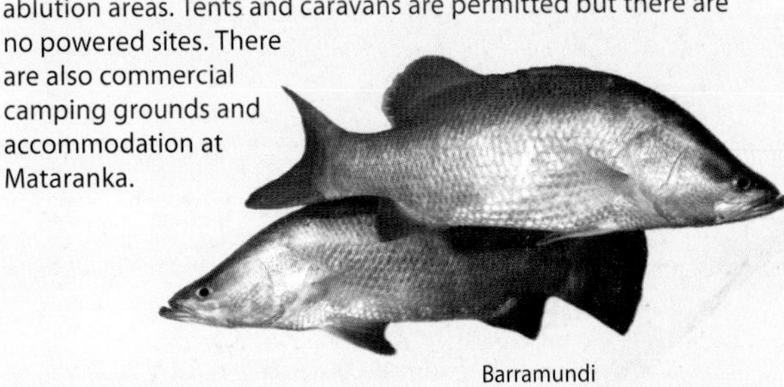

Barramundi

Nitmiluk National Park

Top Things to Do

1 Canoe the Katherine River.

2 Cruise the gorges on a commercial charter. Two-hour trips or half-day safaris are available.

3 Swoop over the Arnhem Land Plateau on a scenic helicopter flight.

4 Take a trip to Edith Falls.

5 Go bushwalking. There are ten marked trails ranging in length from 1.5 km to 66 km.

6 Flick lures for freshwater Barramundi.

7 Take a guided tour and learn about Nitmiluk's natural and cultural history.

8 Pack a picnic and have a swim, or else camp overnight.

9 Capture this incredible oasis on film.

Top: Cruises on the Katherine River reveal the mysteries of life in the Never Never. **Above, left to right:** Vegetation differs dramatically — from spacious eucalypt woodlands to thick Pandanus and paperbark groves lining waterways beyond.

Left and above: The Katherine River cleaves through the Arnhem Land Plateau, creating a series of stunning gorges.

Katherine Gorge The Territory's best canoeing destination.

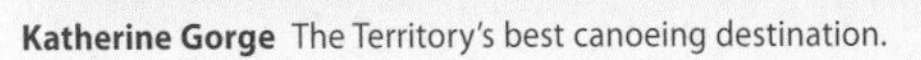

Nitmiluk National Park Boulder rapids punctuate the park's system of gorges.

Nitmiluk National Park & Katherine Gorge

Phone Ranger: (08) 8973 8888

The Katherine River snakes through the middle of Nitmiluk National Park in a series of long, deep reaches beneath high cliffs of magnificent sandstone. In fact, this world-famous region comprises thirteen spectacular gorges (Katherine Gorge being the most famous), separated by boulder rapids. The many possible means of touring the park include boat cruises, canoeing, bushwalking and helicopter flights. The high, jagged walls of the gorge system were slowly carved from the surrounding sandstone-conglomerate plateau by the Katherine River over millions of years. Aboriginal art can be seen along the base of the sandstone escarpment as you travel the Katherine River and there is other evidence of the original Jawoyn people's activities throughout the park. Freshwater Crocodiles bask on exposed rock slabs and sandbanks. Breaches in the gorge walls reveal narrow canyons headed with waterfalls and brimming with palms, figs and paperbarks.

Walks (& Cruises) in the Park: The numerous walking tracks include riverbank strolls, overnight walks and a five-day trek from Katherine Gorge to Edith Falls. Overnight walkers are required to register with the Parks and Wildlife Commission at the Nitmiluk Centre. Nitmiluk Tours operate a variety of boat tours in the Gorge system ranging from the popular two hour cruise, to half-day and full-day safaris incorporating multiple gorges. All tours depart from the main boat ramp. Freshwater crocodiles are harmless unless provoked.

Access: 30 kilometres north-east of Katherine via sealed road from the Stuart Highway.

Camping: Permanent campgrounds are established at the Gorge and Edith Falls. Some Gorge campsites are powered, and car parking and caravan sites are available at both campgrounds. There are also a variety of bush camping sites throughout the park for canoeists and walkers.

The Katherine River The region has been a home to the Jawoyn people for many millennia.

Kakadu National Park
Top Things to Do

1. Take a tour of Ubirr — the location of Kakadu's most famous rock art galleries.
2. Learn about Aboriginal culture on a cruise of the East Alligator River.
3. Photograph the phenomenal range of birdlife at Mamukala Wetlands (Sept–Oct).
4. Marvel at the spectacular waterfalls of the Jim Jim Area.
5. Learn more about Kakadu and its peoples at the info-rich Bowali Visitors Centre.
6. See Ghost Bats, Echidnas and native geckoes at Merl.
7. Contemplate the archetypical Kakadu view of Burrunggui (Nourlangie Rock) over Anbangbang Billabong.
8. Cruise Yellow Water Wetlands. Keep your eyes open for semi-submerged crocs.
9. Camp and swim at Gunlom.
10. Visit the Warradjan Cultural Centre.

Cosmic Sunsets

Kakadu National Park is famous for its emotive and absorbing sunsets. Once the sun goes down, your friends and family can be forgiven for waxing lyrical about the great realm of nature. For many, a Kakadu sunset is deeply spiritual. Be sure to bring an open mind as well as your camera.

Kakadu National Park

Kakadu National Park occupies a vast 19,804 km^2 swathe of the Top End from Nitmiluk National Park in the south to Van Diemen Gulf in the north. It incorporates the West and East Alligator Rivers region and the entire catchment of the South Alligator River. Approximately half of Kakadu is owned by Indigenous people and most of the remaining area is under Aboriginal land claim. This phenomenally rich region is an Aboriginal cultural landscape and internationally famous World Heritage Area. The name Kakadu derives from anthropologist Baldwin Spencer's 1911 record of the word used to describe the dominant Indigenous language of the region. Traditional owners are active partners in managing Kakadu and the park comprises several language groups and a diverse and complex Aboriginal society. There is evidence within Kakadu, including some magnificent rock art, that suggests that Aboriginal people have lived continuously in the area for more than 50,000 years.

The first European explorer to traverse the region was Ludwig Leichhardt, who commented in his diary on the friendly Bininj people and the amazing proliferation of wildlife in all directions as he and his party passed along the South and East Alligator Rivers in 1845. Kakadu today is home to nearly a quarter of Australia's total freshwater fish species, a third of all bird species and over 1000 different plant types.

The presence, nature and behaviour of the region's species are totally interrelated with seasonal conditions. Kakadu's Aborigines long ago learned to read the signs that indicate when seasonal changes will occur; such changes dictated food harvesting and territorial migration schedules. Keep in mind the types of animal, insect and plant life you encounter on your Kakadu adventure are entirely dependent upon the times you visit. A range of habitats make up the national park. Tropical woodland constitutes more than 75% of Kakadu's habitat (mangroves and monsoon forest are the least prevalent). River, floodplains, billabongs and paperbark swamps become one entity during the wet season, linked by floodwater and sharing the same species. These are known collectively as wetlands. In the dry months, however, they become isolated and are frequented by different sets of animals.

The range of natural features within Kakadu make it a spectacularly exciting region to behold (and photograph). The major geological feature is the Arnhem Land Plateau — an ancient sandstone formation that takes up about a third of Arnhem Land. This imposing plateau and escarpment is part of the "stone country" and it is here, on the eastern side of the park, that Kakadu's most unusual plant and animal life can be found.

There are two main roads leading into, and through, the park. Kakadu Highway commences at Pine Creek, 91 km north of Katherine, and enters the park's south-west corner at the Mary River Roadhouse (access through the park via this route may not be possible during wet seasons). The Arnhem Highway branches off the Stuart Highway 35 km south of Darwin and enters the mid-northern region of Kakadu. Both highways lead to Jabiru near the park's eastern border. Flights also land at the airstrip near Jabiru.

Rock Art of Kakadu

In the sandstone galleries of Kakadu is a rock art heritage of global importance — one of the oldest and best-preserved records of human history. The styles range from the ancient hand prints and dynamic stick-figures typical of the Pre-estuarine Period (8000–50,000 years before the present), to the more descriptive "X-ray" style of animal images depicted during the Estuarine/Freshwater Periods (*above*) and the relatively recent drawing of introduced objects (such as sailing ships and exploration parties) from the Contact Period. Although most of the art in Kakadu is not accessible to the public, all styles and periods are well represented in the stunning galleries on view.

South Alligator River

South Alligator River is the largest waterway in Kakadu. Flowing over 300 km south from Van Diemen Gulf through habitat including swamp, mangrove, floodplain, stone country and woodland, it meets the Arnhem Highway 38 km east of Jabiru. An incredible range and huge number of birds seasonally inhabit the South Alligator's wetland areas. There are no alligators, only crocodiles — the name was given to the region's rivers by early maritime explorer Phillip Parker King who (while trying to keep a safe distance) understandably confused the species.

East Alligator River

Forming the majority of the boundary between Kakadu National Park and Arnhem Land, is East Alligator River. Its upper reaches are densely populated with Estuarine Crocodiles, and much of the river corridor is monsoon forest. Just west of the river, close to Jabiluka, is Ubirr — Kakadu's most famous region of Aboriginal rock art sites. The area supported a large population of Bininj people over thousands of years and the galleries of naturalistic images that adorn the sandstone outcrops are a priceless cultural legacy.

Kakadu National Park
Special Walks

1. Mamukala Wetlands — 3 km return, easy (South Alligator Area).
2. Gu-ngarre Monsoon Forest Walk —3.6 km, easy (South Alligator Area).
3. Bowali Bike/Walking Track — 4 km return, easy (Jabiru Area).
4. Iligadjarr Walk —3.8 km, easy (Jabiru Area).
5. Ubirr Track — 1.5 km, easy (East Alligator Area).
6. Bardedjilidji Walk — 2.5 km return, easy (East Alligator Area).
7. Nanguluwurr Art Site Walk — 3.5 km, easy (Nourlangie Area).
8. Mirrai Lookout Walk — 3.6 km return, moderate/difficult (Nourlangie Area).
9. Gun-gardun Walk — 2 km circular, easy (Yellow Water Area).
10. Mardugal Billabong Walk — 1 km return, easy (Yellow Water Area).
11. Yurmikmik Walks — 21 km of connected tracks, easy/moderate (Mary River Area).
12. Twin Falls Plateau — 6 km return, moderate (Jim Jim Area).

Top to bottom: Ubirr, East Alligator Area; Aerial view of the East Alligator Area.

Exploring Kakadu

Phone Ranger: (08) 8938 1120

Kakadu's diverse habitat undergoes enormous change from season-to-season, meaning that the right time to explore the park depends on what you wish to see. In *Gudjewg* (December/January to March), the wet season's, heavy rains wash across the Arnhem Land Plateau — overflowing the Alligator River systems and flooding the low-lying coastal plains. During *Banggerreng* (April/March to May) the skies clear, but violent, windy storms lash the land. As rains replenish the wetlands, countless waterbirds begin their mating rituals. By *Yegge* (May to mid-June), raging waterfalls slow to silver arcs descending to permanent rock pools and the waterbirds retreat from the drying plains to crowd the edges of shallow billabongs and swamps. In the drier seasons of *Wurrgeng* (mid-June to mid-August) and *Gurrung* (mid-August to mid-October), the cool shade of the monsoon forest offers refuge for animal species from other habitats. The monsoon build-up occurs during *Gunumeleng* (mid-October to late December) and thereafter the whole six-season cycle repeats itself. Such is Kakadu's scale that even within the one season there is an expansive selection of wildlife and habitat to explore. It can be a huge challenge just knowing where to start.

Kakadu National Park The mud and mangrove coast of northern Kakadu National Park.

South Alligator Area

Red Crab

This area lies in the very heartland of Kakadu and contains examples of all eight habitats to be found in the park. The best time to visit this area is during the late dry season (September to October).

Walks in the Park: Seven kilometres east of the river crossing are the Mamukala Wetlands, a floodplain area that attracts a variety of birdlife, particularly in the drier seasons. Once a traditional hunting area, it attracts more migratory Magpie Geese than anywhere else in Australia. The area has an easy 3 km circuit walk as well as a viewing platform and several excellent bird hides. Near the Aurora Kakadu Resort is the Gu-ngarre Monsoon Forest Walk. This foliage-shaded 3.6 km trail is ideal for the hotter parts of day, and the forest wildlife you may see includes Agile Wallabies, Orange-footed Scrubfowls and Yellow-spotted Monitors.
Access: Via Arnhem Highway from Pine Creek or Jabiru.
Camping: Basic camping sites (no drinking water) are available at Two Mile, Four Mile Hole, Red Lily Billabong, Bucket Billabong, Alligator Billabong and Waldak Irrmbal (West Alligator Head). Campsites are accessible by 4WD vehicle only.

East Alligator Area

This area takes in the western catchment of the East Alligator River, extensive floodplains and the superb Ubirr rock art sites. Its eastern boundary is shared with Arnhem Land.

Walks in the Park: The highlight of the East Alligator Area is the magnificent galleries of ancient rock art on view at Ubirr. A 1 km circular track leads to five unique sites featuring wide-ranging examples of wildlife motifs, sorcery art and Contact Period art. Rangers provide tours and talks during dry seasons. An additional 250 m moderately steep climb to the lookout is rewarded by superb 360° views over the Nardab floodplain and sandstone outliers to the north. Photograph it at sunset. The Bardedjilidji Trail is a great 2.5 km walk through fine-layered sandstone outliers. It commences at the car park 500 m from the upstream boat ramp. There is also an easy and pleasant walk (1 hr) through monsoon forest that starts near the downstream boat ramp and includes viewing platforms along the river. Guided boat tours are available on East Alligator River and Magela Creek (Ph: (08) 8979 2411).
Access: Via Arnhem Highway from Pine Creek or Jabiru.
Camping: Excellent camping at Merl, within walking distance of the river. Located in rich woodland surrounded by sandstone outliers, the campground at Merl will bring you into close proximity with many of Kakadu's myriad creatures. The Kakadu Hostel (behind the Border Store) also offers budget accommodation with kitchen facilities and a pool (Ph: (08) 8979 2232).

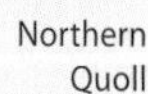

Northern Quoll

Nourlangie Area

This area occupies the central area of the park and primarily comprises the Nourlangie Creek catchment.

Walks in the Park: There are several great walks around Burrunggui (Nourlangie Rock) — a spectacular sandstone outlier south of Jabiru. Attractions here include the numerous viewable rock art galleries and the Anbanbang occupation site, which traces over 20,000 years of Indigenous culture through periods of environmental change. A 1.5 km circular walk includes several art sites and, at its end, a moderately steep walk to Gun-warddehwardde Lookout provides views of Burrunggui. An easy 1.5 km walk from near the first road after leaving the car park leads to pretty Anbangbang Billabong and its local Agile Wallabies, Yellow-spotted Monitors and Northern Long-necked Turtles. The 600 m Nawurlandja Lookout Walk is off the second road after leaving the car park and offers great views of the surrounding outliers and escarpment.
Access: Via Arnhem Highway or Kakadu Highway.
Camping: Muirella Park, east of Kakadu Highway, 7 km after the Burrunggui turn-off, offers toilets, showers and a generator zone.

Jabiru Area

This is one of Kakadu's most civilised districts, offering a range of services and comfy accommodation. The beautifully styled Bowali Visitor Centre contains all the information you need for a Kakadu adventure.

Walks in the Park: The Iligadjarr Walk, near the Malabanjbanjdju and Burdulba camps, is a 3.8 km circular track across a grassy floodplain to Burdulba Billabong.
Access: Via Kakadu Highway or Arnhem Highway.
Camping: Bush camping with basic facilities (no drinking water) available at Malabanjbanjdju and Burdulba. Otherwise treat yourself to the bush bungalows of Lakeview Park (Ph: (08) 8979 3144), cabins at Kakadu Lodge (Ph: (08) 8979 2422) or a hotel room at Gagudju Crocodile Holiday Inn (Ph: (08) 8979 2800).

Nourlangie Rock The Rock seen across Anbangbang Billabong, Nourlangie Area.

Jim Jim Area

Of particular interest here is Jim Jim Creek and its spectacular waterfalls. Access is by 4WD only.

Walks in the Park: Sixty kilometres along the Jim Jim Track is a 2 km walking track through monsoon forest and over rocks to Jim Jim Falls Plunge Pool. The plunge pool and waterfalls are surrounded by 150 m high cliffs (Jim Jim Falls only flows in the wet season). A further 10 km down the road you will find the 2 hour walking track to Twin Falls.
Access: Via Kakadu Highway from Pine Creek or Jabiru. Jim Jim Falls and Twin Falls are both accessed via Jim Jim Track, off Kakadu Highway 50 km south-west of Jabiru.
Camping: Garnamarr campground is located on the main track close to Jim Jim Falls and is equipped with showers and toilets.

Mary River Area

This area is known to its Jawoyn custodians as "sickness country". It is bordered by the stunning Mary River and is home to powerful creation ancestors.

Walks in the Park: From Gunlom campground, a steep 2 km (return) climb leads to Gunlom Falls and lookout. There is also a 2 km return walk to Murrill Billabong.
Access: Via Kakadu Highway from Pine Creek or Jabiru. Main walking section is reached via the eastern turn off near the Mary River ranger station.
Camping: Gunlom camping area, near the Gunlom Plunge Pool, has showers and toilets. The turn-off to Gungurul camping and picnic area is 40 km north of the ranger station on the Kakadu Highway near the South Alligator River.

Brolga

Yellow Water Area

Magnificent wetlands are the key feature of this central Kakadu area. Commercial boat tours are a fantastic way to view this part of the South Alligator floodplain.

Walks in the Park: The Mardugal Walk (1 km return) follows Mardugal Billabong.
Access: Turn north-west off the Kakadu Highway 50 km south of Bowali Visitor Centre.
Camping: Showers and toilets at Mardugal campsite. Motel rooms at Gagudju Lodge Cooinda (Ph: (08) 8979 0145).

Walking in Kakadu
Don't Forget!

1 Be croc safe — always be vigilant around creeks, rivers and on water craft and heed instructions on park signs.
2 Wear comfortable footwear and protective clothing — weather conditions can change rapidly in Kakadu.
3 Never walk alone. Always keep your party together and leave an itinerary with park rangers or with friends.
4 Pack a complete first aid kit.

Top to bottom: Yellow Water; Jim Jim Falls; Mary River.

Kakadu to Darwin
Top Things to Do

1. Photograph wetland birds at Bird Billabong, a magnet for avian life during the dry season.
2. Hire a tinnie at Shady Camp and explore the beautiful Mary River.
3. Embrace stunning sunsets at Couzen's Lookout.
4. Explore the numerous 4WD tracks intersecting the Mary River catchment.
5. Enjoy wetland walks skirting the edges of Fogg Dam and a stroll across the dam wall.
6. Marvel at the wild leaping crocodiles of Adelaide River.
7. Learn about local Aboriginal history and the native environment at Windows on the Wetlands Visitor Centre, Beatrice Hill.
8. Watch wildlife on the Marrakai Plains in Djukbinj National Park.
9. Enjoy a peaceful picnic lunch at Leaning Tree Lagoon Nature Park.

Top to bottom: Fogg Dam bush; Birdwatchers spy a pair of Brahminy Kites; Hovercrafting in the wetlands.

Kakadu to Darwin

Leaving the splendour of Kakadu may be one of the toughest challenges during your Top End adventure, but plenty of other attractions lie in wait at the end of the road (actually, the edge of the continent) in colourful Darwin. Fortunately, there are also ample diversions along the way.

The 219 km drive from Jabiru to Darwin is a progression of wild attractions from jumping crocodiles to award-winning wildlife reserves. Your journey passes through part of the lower Adelaide River and Mary River catchments — two of several connected catchment areas that form vital wetland habitats around Darwin's rural fringe. These are places of international significance — important havens for wildlife and also recognised for their cultural value to local Aborigines. With so much life and colour on display, it is no wonder the Arnhem Highway east of Darwin is also a popular stretch for city residents (anglers, birdwatchers, bushwalkers, photographers and assorted outdoor enthusiasts) seeking a fast track to nature on their weekends.

Mary River National Park

Phone Tourism Top End: (08) 8936 2499

The aim of this (currently proposed) national park is to unite a dozen existing reserves and conservation areas located within the greater Mary River catchment. Tropical freshwater billabongs as well as melaleuca woodland and monsoon forests are features of the proposed national park. A great way to explore this stunning area is by following either the Hardies 4WD Track (5 km west of Mary River) or Wildman 4WD Track (linking Rockhole and Wildman Roads). Despite most areas being accessible to 2WD, many roads are unsealed. The catchment area is perfect crocodile habitat and consequently swimming is not recommended.

Walks in the Park: A turn-off just west of the Mary River crossing brings you to the walking track and viewing platform at Bird Billabong (a natural sanctuary for wetland birds during the dry season). The short walk to Couzen's Lookout (from the campsite near the Mary River) is best undertaken in the late afternoon. The sunsets over the catchment are inspirational. At the northern edge of the park (Point Stuart Coastal Reserve), a 5 km return walk leads from the day use area to a cairn memorial honouring famous inland explorer John McDouall Stuart.

Access: The Mary River crossing is 150 km east of Darwin. Access roads to the main feature areas branch off from the Arnhem Highway.

Camping: Couzen's Lookout camping area offers quiet camping near the Mary River, while Annaburroo Billabong is a scenic camping spot near Bark Hut Inn (which itself has caravan sites). With its boat ramp, dingy hire, picnic facilities and toilets, Shady Camp (north of the Arnhem Highway on Point Stuart Road) is a popular retreat with Darwin's anglers.

Fogg Dam Conservation Reserve

Phone Parks & Wildlife: (08) 8999 4555

Fogg Dam was built by the RAAF Airfield Construction Squadron in the 1950s as an irrigation source for plantations of the short-lived Humpty Doo Rice Project. The dam has since become a lush wetland area brimming with wildlife. Birds are particularly attracted to this environment (especially in the dry season), but Estuarine Crocodiles, Water Pythons and various mammals can also be seen here. The dam wall, extending for 500 m across the wetland, provides an excellent vantage point for surveying the area and photographing wildlife. Be prepared for squadrons of savage mosquitoes (especially early in the morning or late in the afternoon). Also, due to the presence of Estuarine Crocodiles, swimming is not permitted at Fogg Dam.

Walks in the Park: A handful of easy, well-signposted walks reveal the best aspects of the Fogg Dam wetlands. The Woodlands to Waterlily Walk (2.2 km, easy, 45 minutes) meanders through forest fringing the floodplain. A number of lookout points are to be found on the way to a boardwalk leading up to the dam. The Monsoon Forest Walk (3.6 km, easy, 2 hr) leads onto the floodplain through paperbark and monsoon forest. Although it is possible to drive across the dam wall, most people prefer to take their time and stroll across. The Dam Wall Walk (2.2 km return, easy, 45 minutes) is wheelchair-accessible and features shaded viewing platforms along the way. For a more elevated scope of the wetlands, try the Pandanus Lookout Walk (2.5 km return, easy, 1 hr) — a gorgeous location at sunrise and sunset. Guided walks of the area are worth exploring. The Limilngan Cultural Guided Walk gives visitors an understanding of the country's importance to its traditional custodians, while the Nocturnal Walk uncovers a different wetland world to that seen during the day.

Access: With all weather access, and only 65 km east of Darwin via the Arnhem Highway, Fogg Dam is an attractive destination all year round.

Camping: Camping is not permitted.

Top to bottom: A Pandanus grove flaps in the breeze at Fogg Dam; A typical Top End freshwater billabong; Egrets revel in the wetlands of the Mary River catchment area; Flat wetland expanse at Fogg Dam.

Window on the Wetlands Visitor Centre – Beatrice Hill

Beatrice Hill is one of the highest points in the Adelaide River catchment area as was named on 6 June 1864 by two naval officers surveying the river aboard the HMS *Beatrice*.

Standing atop Beatrice Hill is the tastefully designed and award-winning Window on the Wetlands Visitor Centre. For anyone interested in gaining a deeper understanding of the Top End's coastal wetlands, this is a site well worth visiting. The centre provides handy information on tours, regional feature locations and accommodation. Interactive displays educate visitors on wetlands ecology, seasonal changes to the environment and the unfortunate threats posed by noxious plant and animal species. Before embarking on a wetlands expedition, visitors can also brush up on their knowledge of native plants and animals and learn about local Limilngan-Wulna Aboriginal culture. The visitor centre's touchscreen computers make research a breeze.

The views of the floodplain from the top floor are sensational, particularly with the rising and setting of the sun, and it is a great place to safely observe the Top End's ferocious lightning storms later in the year (open daily, 8 am – 7 pm, Ph: (08) 8988 8188).

Jumping Crocodile Cruises

Watching fully grown Estuarine Crocodiles performing sudden vertical launches from the murky brown of the Adelaide River is one of the Top End's most thrilling tourist attractions.

Jumping Crocodile Cruises has been an Territory institution since the mid-1980s (when *Crocodile Dundee* captured the imagination of the film-going world). Responding to the thrill of something primeval, travellers flock from far and wide to see well-trained (but completely wild) crocs leaping up for hunks of meat dangled above the water (Ph: (08) 8988 8144).

Djukbinj National Park

Covering part of the Adelaide River catchment and drainage, Djukbinj National Park (78 km east of Darwin) forms a portion of the ecologically vital Marrakai Plains.

Following the wet season, these swampy grasslands remain inundated for up to three or four months. The park is a nesting and feeding site for birds — Brolgas, Magpie Geese and many other native species flock here. Asian Water Buffalo also roam the landscape. The treeless environment has created a perfect grazing habitat for this introduced bovine. Be sure to keep a safe distance from these massive wild animals.

Leaning Tree Lagoon Nature Park

Situated approximately 70 km east of Darwin, this 100 ha reserve is a picturesque camping, picnicking and canoeing spot. Like other Adelaide River wetland areas, it is also a valuable wildlife refuge. Waterfowl (such as the Green Pygmy-Goose) and other wetland bird species are conspicuous and welcome residents.

Leaning Tree Lagoon Nature Park is also an important cultural area. Aboriginal grinding holes (traditionally used for crushing seeds and, in other cases, for crushing pastes used in rock paintings) have been located here.

DARWIN

& THE JOURNEY TO BROOME

4

Once no more than a frontier trading post, Darwin grew in importance and size with the construction of the Overland Telegraph Line in the 1860s. Its strategically important position made it a target of enemy bombings in WWII before nature wreaked its own devastation with Cyclone Tracy in 1974. Much of the city's architectural heritage was lost, but it has since been fastidiously (and sturdily) re-built. First-time visitors are often surprised by Darwin's cosmopolitan nature — Indigenous, Asian and European influences are all represented in the city's cuisine, culture and numerous extroverted festivals. Darwin is also the starting point for one of my favourite journeys — the trek through the colossal Kimberley region to Broome on Australia's west coast. The Kimberley cannot be over-rated — each return visit leaves me in greater awe of the landscape and wildlife. If you're up for a real adventure, take the Gibb River Road — an old droving track that rides roughshod through the Kimberley heartland. The easier course from Kununurra is via the Great Northern Highway, which also offers outstanding opportunities to experience the grandeur of this remote region. Easier still is to take a cruise along the towering northern Kimberley coast — a place that can only be properly appreciated from sea or air.

Opposite and above: The Pentecost Range lies at the eastern end of the Gibb River Road — a famous track for exploration of the incomparable Kimberley landscape.

DARWIN & Surrounds

Darwin & Surrounds

Top Things to Do

1. Visit the original Government House on Darwin's harbour foreshore.
2. Tour the city's new Parliament House and Supreme Court buildings in State Square.
3. Sunsets over Fannie Bay can be spectacular — pack a picnic hamper and head to one of the city's fine beaches.
4. Take a sunset cruise on Darwin Harbour.
5. Photograph the view from Daly Street Lookout with a telephoto lens. You will be amazed at the results.

City Centre

Darwin's city centre combines creatively designed modern structures with historical stone buildings and a relaxed retail precinct. In keeping with the climate, the city offers numerous air-conditioned arcades and sun-sheltered zones. Smith Street Mall is the city's main shopping district.

Boats & Bay

At first glance Darwin's major marinas, Cullen Bay and Tipperary Waters, appear to shelter a boat for each of the city's residents. The tropical capital's connection with the water and lands beyond is deeply felt. Pearling and fishing industries have flourished in the seas off the Northern Territory coast since the late 19th century.

Australia's most remote capital has survived the devastation of war and cyclone to evolve from a small outpost into a modern city. Darwin's port was first surveyed in 1839 by the captain of Charles Darwin's famous vessel, the HMS *Beagle*. Yet the city may never have endured had it not been for the establishment of Australia's Overland Telegraph Line in 1870. The strand of wire that connected the southern colonies with Port Darwin and from there via submarine cable with Britain, gave permanence to the city. It also brought Chinese immigrants — line workers — to settle in the fledgling town. Largely by virtue of the city's proximity to Asia (it is closer to Jakarta than to Canberra), Darwin's multicultural roots have since flourished. Some residents originate from further afield — remarkably, nearly 10% of the city's present day population hails from the Greek island of Kalymnos, now a sister city to Darwin. The region's traditional occupants, the Larrakia people, also play a prominent role in the community.

The Tropical City

Darwin is consistently hot and a typically tropical climate induces a less formal style in both city and citizen. During the Wet, Darwin is swathed in green, and intense tropical thunderstorms can produce spectacular lightning displays in the northern skies. In the Dry, Darwin takes on a festive air, with outdoor entertainment that includes sporting events, open-air markets and sunset picnics. At Mindil Beach, the weekly sunset market serves up food from 20 different cultures and boasts over 200 craft and produce stalls (Thursday nights, May to October). Nightcliff Markets (Nightcliff Shopping Centre) and sunset jazz concerts (on the lawns of the Skycity Casino at Mindil Beach) are held every Sunday. The parkland across the Esplanade from Parliament House is the venue for the Deckchair Cinema — an outdoor theatre that operates during the Dry.

Walking is a great way to see the city. Trails wind along the Esplanade, Mindil Beach, East Point and the scenic northern suburbs foreshore. An Esplanade stroll taking in neighbouring Bicentennial Park will reveal several interesting historical features, including the Cenotaph war memorial, Lyons Cottage (the city's first stone building) and a memorial to the USS *Peary* (bombed and sunk in Darwin Harbour during WWII). At the opposite end of Bicentennial Park is Aquascene (28 Doctors Gully Rd), where fish can be fed by hand. Within the city centre, the ruins of the old Darwin Town Hall (Smith St) have been preserved as a memorial to the tragedy of Cyclone Tracy, which took 65 lives and left tens of thousands homeless.

The Rebuilt City

Darwin's buildings, ravaged by World War II bombing before falling victim to the destructive force of Cyclone Tracy on Christmas Eve, 1974 are now predominantly low-rise structures, lending the city a relaxed ambience. Darwin's original Government House, one of the few historic buildings to defy both cyclone and war, is known as the House of Seven Gables and stands amid tropical gardens on the harbour foreshore (*at bottom of picture above*). Behind it, in State Square, stand the distinctively modern Northern Territory Parliament House and Supreme Court buildings.

Tropical Gardens

Darwin's tropical parks and gardens garland the city in green. The 42 ha George Brown Darwin Botanic Gardens are located just north of the CBD (bordering Fannie Bay) and contain over 400 species of palm tree. East Point Reserve, once the location of strategic military installations, offers magnificent sunset vistas and picnic areas on Dudley Point. The reserve incorporates Lake Alexander — a reclaimed saltwater marsh that is now a popular safe-swimming destination.

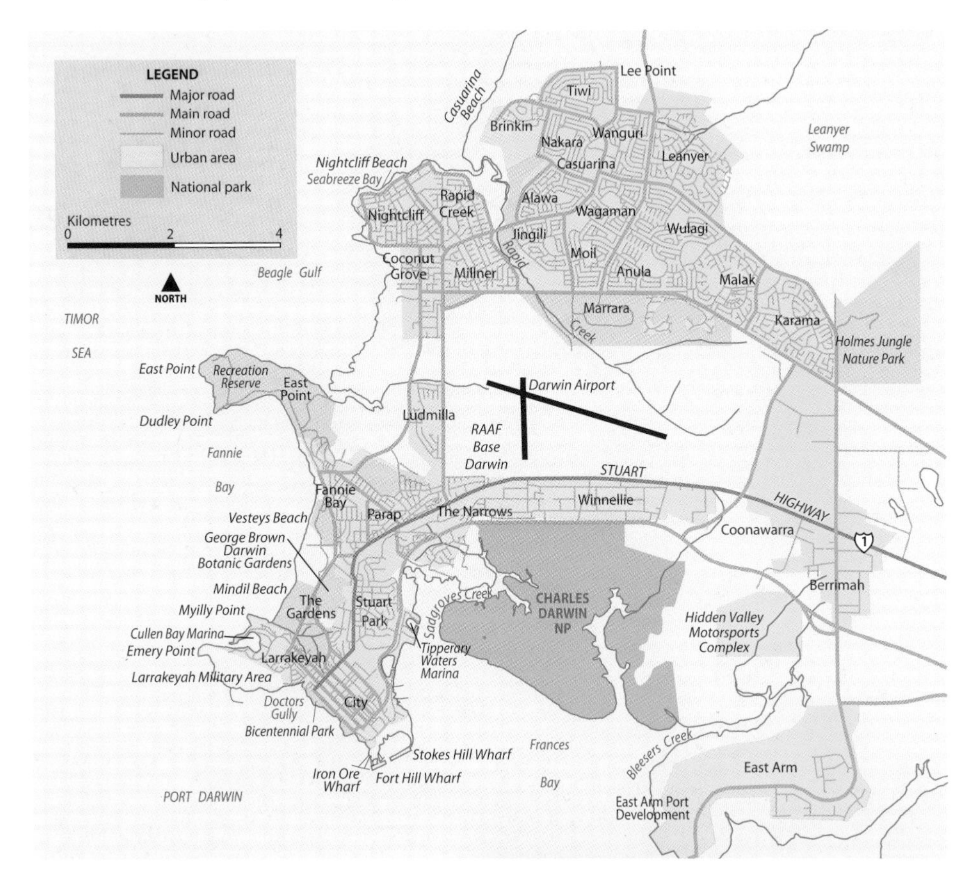

Festive Darwin

Darwin celebrates its multicultural origins and status as the capital of the Top End with a variety of vibrant annual festivals. The popular Darwin Festival (*right*), staged in August each year is a showcase for performing arts, including music and dance from Indigenous, Indonesian and Pacific Island communities.

On the Queen's Birthday weekend in June, Darwin's Hellenic community celebrates with the lively Greek Glenti Festival.

The famous Darwin Beer Can Regatta is held at Mindil Beach each July and features a boat race battled out by vessels entirely constructed of — you guessed it — empty beer cans.

Coves & Beaches

Darwin's suburbs curl around the coast, providing easily accessible beaches on the shores of the Timor Sea and Fannie Bay. Casuarina Beach is the most popular northern suburbs family destination, while the 2 km long Nightcliff Beach provides the setting for the Seabreeze Festival — a colourful annual arts and music festival.

Historic Darwin

While many of Darwin's older buildings have been destroyed, a few important examples of early Darwin life survive to this day. The Old Police Station, Court House and Cell Block on the Esplanade have been restored. The Christchurch Cathedral's historical porch (*above*), built in 1902, was all that remained standing in the wake of Cyclone Tracy.

DARWIN to Kununurra

Darwin to Kununurra

Top Things to Do

1. Visit Crocodylus Park and the nearby Holmes Jungle Nature Park.
2. Go walking around the waterfalls in Litchfield National Park.
3. Camp, walk or fish in Gregory National Park.
4. Explore the superb Aboriginal sites in Keep River National Park.
5. Photograph the wildlife and scenery of Lake Argyle — Australia's largest dam.
6. Explore the waterways of the Ord River Irrigation Scheme.

All the Rivers Run

During the wet season, the north-west region of the Northern Territory takes on a face at odds with its image as Australia's aridlands.

The permanent watercourses of the Victoria, Fitzmaurice and Keep Rivers drain northward into the Joseph Bonaparte Gulf, spreading across floodplains, drowning roads and providing fertile habitat for a huge spectrum of native wildlife. Ninety percent of the region's rainfall falls between December and March, but such is the volume of water that pours from the sky that some rivers continue to run throughout the remaining months of the year.

One of the best ways to get a real feel for the Top End is to make the 860 km journey from Darwin across the West Australian border to Kununurra. In the Dry, it is a relatively comfortable trip on sealed roads through regions of both flat desert plain and mountainous landscape. Litchfield, Gregory and Keep River National Parks are natural oases of green; rippling with rivers and swimming holes. In the Wet, however, the journey may not be possible at all (due to flooding). Kununurra, 35 km over the border, takes its name from an Aboriginal word meaning "meeting of the big waters". The town lies at the centre of the impressive Ord River Irrigation Scheme.

South on the Stuart

The first leg of the journey on the Stuart Highway leads to Litchfield National Park, 113 km south of Darwin. While it can't compete with Kakadu for size, Litchfield protects an extensive range of Top End habitats, and its geological features are no less impressive. Within its boundaries are numerous waterfalls cascading off a sandstone plateau called the Tabletop Range, as well as tall termite mounds and weathered sandstone towers. Litchfield has several excellent camping grounds located close to the main waterfalls and walking tracks. The park's eastern corner meets the Stuart Highway further south at the township of Adelaide River, but most of its more easily accessible attractions and trails are located in the northern section.

West to Kununurra

Leading south-west from Katherine to Kununurra, the Victoria Highway is an extension of the Savannah Way tourist route traversing northern Australia from Cairns to Broome. The main feature of the Northern Territory section is Gregory National Park, a vast 13,000 km^2 protected wilderness of gorges and waterways around the Stokes Range. The Victoria River flows through the park en route to its mouth at Joseph Bonaparte Gulf. Along the highway are the supply stops of Victoria River and Timber Creek. The park offers countless camping, walking and fishing possibilities.

Near the Western Australian border is Keep River National Park — a region containing significant Indigenous cultural sites. Here comfortable walks from well-equipped campsites allow exploration and viewing of Aboriginal middens, art galleries and stone structures. A short drive over the border after leaving the park is Kununurra, a decidedly modern but laid-back town that only came into existence in the late 1950s (as the construction base for the Ord River Irrigation Scheme). The further development of the scheme in 1972 created Australia's largest dam — Lake Argyle — 72 km south of Kununurra.

Nature Parks

Close to Darwin are several excellent places to view and photograph wildlife. Crocodylus Park (*above and right*) overlooks the Holmes Jungle Nature Reserve (just 15 minutes from the CBD) and offers encounters with not only crocodiles but also primates, mammals and big cats. With beautiful Palm Creek coursing through its centre, the nearby Holmes Jungle Nature Park (off Vanderlin Dr) protects an area of dense monsoon forest and a huge number of mammals, reptiles and birds.

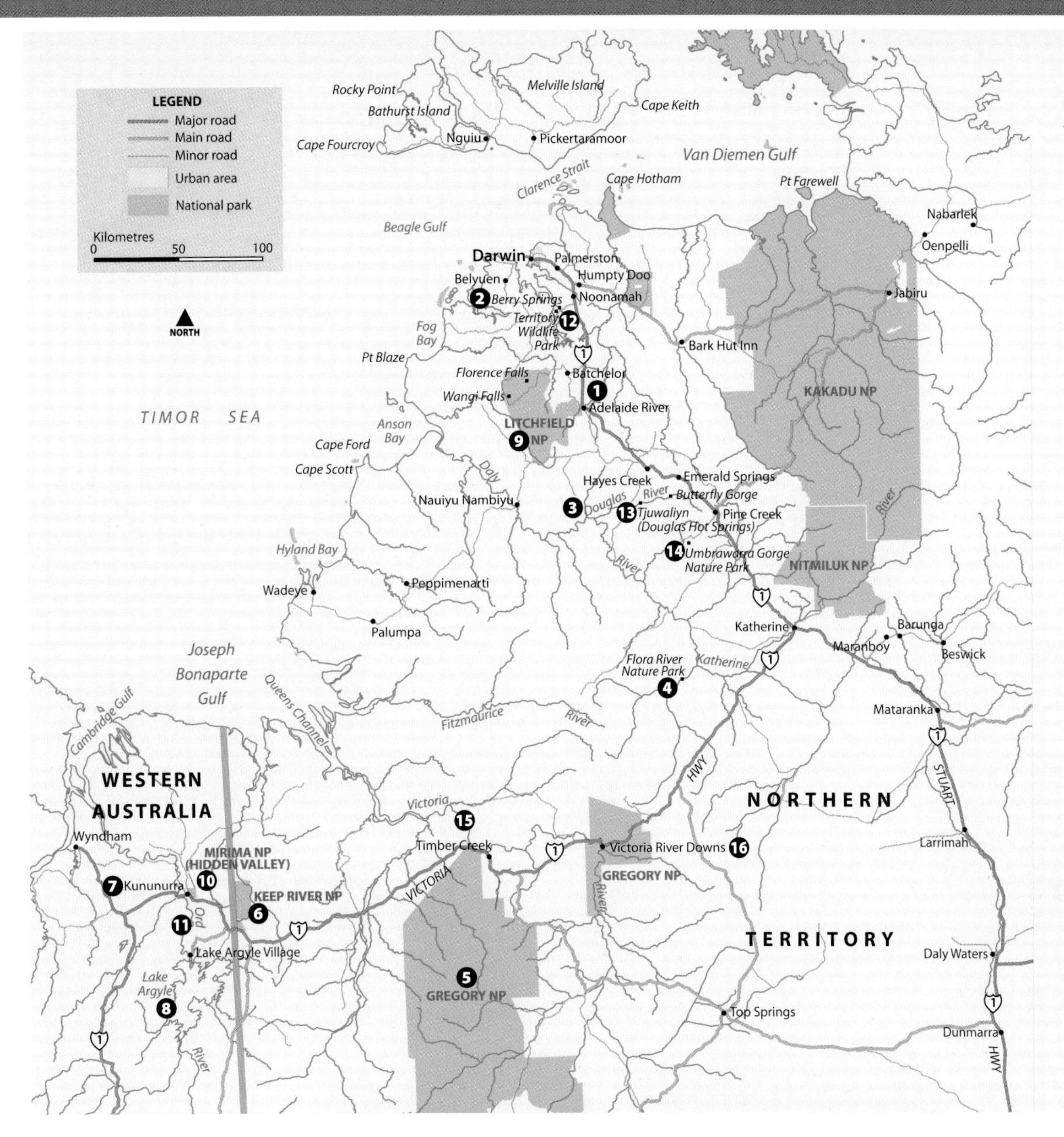

Feature Localities

1. Adelaide River
2. Berry Springs
3. Douglas River
4. Flora River Nature Park
5. Gregory National Park
6. Keep River National Park
7. Kununurra
8. Lake Argyle
9. Litchfield National Park
10. Mirima National Park
11. Ord River
12. Territory Wildlife Park
13. Tjuwaliyn
14. Umbrawarra Gorge Nature Park
15. Victoria River
16. Victoria River Downs

Wandjina Rock Art Style

Wandjina art (*right*) is one of the most visually arresting examples of Indigenous art on display in Australia. Colourful examples of the "naturalistic" or "figurative" paintings from this period can be seen throughout the Kimberley and portray ancestral beings known as Wandjina.

For the Unggumi, Ngarinyin, Wunambal and Worora people; Wandjina art represents the creator spirits that shaped the landscape and seasons, also giving life to animals and plants and dictating laws to live by. Typically, Wandjina figures are drawn with a human shape — a key feature being their large, haunting eyes and the absence of a mouth.

Birdwatching

While the illegal international bird trade has significantly reduced its population, the Gouldian Finch (*above*) can still be found near rivers and waterholes in subcoastal northern Australia. Although small, it is one of the country's most brightly plumed birds, with a green back, yellow belly and a purple breast (with a red, black or yellow face).

Top Things to Do

1. Don't miss out on visiting the magnificent Territory Wildlife Park.
2. Spend a few days exploring Litchfield National Park — its outstanding features rival those of Kakadu.
3. Camp at Wangi Falls (Litchfield National Park).
4. Picnic at Florence Falls (Litchfield National Park).
5. Stop and cool off at Berry Springs.
6. Take to the thermal waters of Tjuwaliyn (Douglas) Hot Springs.
7. Listen for the call of Wagiman ancestors at Butterfly Gorge.
8. Swim, rock-hop and walk through Umbrawarra Gorge Nature Park.
9. View ancient rock art on the walls of Umbrawarra Gorge.
10. Visit the Adelaide River war cemetery.

Swimming in Nature

The diverse nature parks south of Darwin including Howard Springs, Tjuwaliyn (Douglas) Hot Springs, Berry Springs, and Umbrawarra Gorge feature some of the Territory's best natural swimming areas.

Darwin to Victoria Highway

On the outskirts of Darwin lie several excellent parks and natural springs that offer hiking, wildlife viewing and water-based recreation. Berry Springs, 47 km south of Darwin on the Cox Peninsula Road, is a popular place for swimming and, believe it or not, snorkelling. Strap on your goggles and snorkel; enter one of the pools along Berry Creek and you'll be surprised at just how many fish are sharing the warm waters with you. Binoculars (and a camera) are a worthwhile accessory for viewing birdlife on the forest and woodlands loop track. Berry Springs was originally developed as a recreational camp for armed forces personnel during World War II and the remains of original huts can still be seen around the main pool. One kilometre further down the road is the Territory Wildlife Park (*see facing page*), while continuing along Cox Peninsula Road will lead you to the northern entry to Litchfield National Park (the road may be closed in the Wet). Alternatively, you can access the park via the Batchelor turn-off 39 km south on the Stuart Highway. Batchelor was established in 1949 to provide housing for workers on the nearby (but now defunct) Rum Jungle uranium mine. Various local legends have been advanced in explanation of the mine's name, but needless to say, all involve the pouring of vast quantities of rum down desert-dry throats.

Litchfield National Park

Litchfield provides the perfect Top End nature experience for those who don't wish to hike endless kilometres in search of the best waterfall, view or geological formation. Well-marked roads and trails place the park's most outstanding features, including beautiful natural swimming pools within easy reach. Just inside the park border, on Litchfield Park Road, are a series of 2 m high mounds sculpted by magnetic termites. These social insects have ingeniously aligned their homes in a north–south orientation to keep themselves cool. Further on, a turn-off leads north to the magnificent twin cascades of Florence Falls. A few more kilometres ahead on the main road, another track diverts south to the Lost City — a maze of unusual eroded sandstone pillars. Litchfield Park Road continues on past Tolmer Falls and Tjaetaber Falls to the park's most popular destination — the idyllic, monsoon forest surrounded Wangi Falls and its neighbouring kiosk, picnic spots and campground. In the northern section of the park is the camping and swimming area of Walker Creek.

Adelaide River

Beyond the turn-off to Litchfield, at Adelaide River, is an interesting World War II cemetery that protects the graves of army personnel who served in these parts when Adelaide River hosted a military base. While most visitors to the area seem more interested in the well-promoted Jumping Crocodile river tour further upstream at the Arnhem Highway, Tjuwaliyn or Douglas Hot Springs Nature Park, is a popular tourist destination on the route south. Take the Old Stuart Highway scenic route from Adelaide River and take a plunge in the thermal springs that rise up in this part of the Douglas River. But take care also — the Wagiman women who manage this traditional area warn that the waters can become hot enough to burn. The safest places to swim are in the cooler pools 200 m upstream and downstream from the main pool. Swimming is not permitted in the sacred site area, but camping is allowed in designated areas. The striking sheer rock faces, creek walks and swimming areas of Butterfly Gorge lie 17 km upstream (via a 4WD track).

River of Memory

The region around the Douglas River is of vital cultural importance to the Wagiman people. The Wagiman women have long conducted women's business ceremonies in the area now incorporated into Tjuwaliyn Nature Park, and there are several sacred sites within its grounds. The park is sometimes closed in order for the Wagiman women to conduct private ceremonies. The Wagiman people believe their ancestors reside within nearby Butterfly Gorge — they say if you walk quietly around the gorge you may even hear them calling.

Umbrawarra Gorge Nature Park

Located 35 km south-west of Pine Creek, Umbrawarra is an impressive isolated gorge with steep red cliffs. The gorge walls are also a gallery for the ancient rock art of the Wagiman people. When the creek is flowing in early to mid-dry season, Umbrawarra is a brilliant place to swim, rock-hop and walk. The walking track by the creek leads to a large pool with a small sandy beach. There is also a basic camping ground (no water) near the park entrance.

Litchfield National Park

Ph: (08) 8976 0282

Walks in the Park: The waterfalls are all close to camping and picnic areas. Well-signed walking tracks between 1 km and 3 km in length start from the major campsites. Lookouts above Florence and Wangi Falls provide excellent views. Near Florence Falls is Buley Rockholes, a series of spa-like pools and waterfalls. More adventurous (and experienced) bushwalkers can tackle the Tabletop Track, a 39 km circuit bushwalk, which can be accessed from Florence Falls, Greenant Creek, Wangi Falls and Walker Creek.

Access: Via the town of Batchelor from the Stuart Highway, 74 km south of Darwin. Access is also possible at the northern end of the park via Cox Peninsula Road during the dry season.

Camping: The park's main campgrounds are at Wangi Falls, Buley Rockholes and Florence Falls. The camping areas at Tjaynera Falls (Sandy Creek), Surprise Creek Falls and downstream from Florence Falls are accessible by 4WD in the dry season only. There are also walk-in camping sites at Walker Creek (dry season only). A kiosk is located at Wangi Falls and there are shaded picnicking areas at Florence Falls, Tabletop Swamp, Greenant Creek, Wangi Falls and Walker Creek.

Florence Falls Litchfield National Park.

Clockwise from top left: Waterhole at Florence Falls; Stoic sandstone formations of the Lost City; Wangi Falls — a popular picnic site and swimming lagoon.

Territory Wildlife Park

Located next door to Berry Springs Nature Park, and operated by the Parks and Wildlife Commission, the Territory Wildlife Park (*above, top to bottom*) is one of the Northern Territory's best wildlife viewing attractions.

Six kilometres of walking tracks lead visitors past an array of tropical wildlife and plants in habitats including lagoons, woodlands, monsoon forest and wetlands. A huge aviary, an aquarium and a nocturnal house complete the scene. A free shuttle train operates continuously through the park, delivering you to the entrance of each major exhibit open daily (Ph: (08) 8988 7200).

Katherine to Kununurra

The 510 km journey on the Victoria Highway to Kununurra commences at Katherine. The present highway evolved from a series of rough tracks (linking the region's massive cattle stations) and passes through only two small settlements en route to the Western Australian border. It does, however, lead to some of the Territory's most dramatic and interesting landscapes, particularly around the Victoria River and its tributaries in Gregory National Park.

Victoria River Downs

The famous Victoria River Downs, known colloquially as the "Big Run", was once the world's largest cattle station. It is located 114 km south of the Victoria Highway (on Buchanan Highway) and was established in the early 1880s with 20,000 head of cattle overlanded by the legendary drover Nathaniel Buchanan. The station was later purchased by a syndicate that included cattle king Sidney Kidman. After a local malaria epidemic in 1922, a hospital was built on the station by Royal Flying Doctor Service pioneer, John Flynn. The original homestead and the hospital are now heritage-listed, but the station continues to operate.

Shipwreck at Timber Creek

Gregory National Park is named for the explorer Augustus Gregory who first surveyed these parts after travelling to the Victoria River from Sydney in 1855 in a boat loaded with 200 sheep. Their mission was to search for the lost explorer Ludwig Leichhardt and find potential pastoral country. The expedition vessel, *Tom Tough* became "shipwrecked" near Timber Creek on Victoria River and the campsite used by Gregory while repairs were being made is close to the present-day township. The arrival and departure dates Gregory carved in a large Boab Tree at the site are still visible today. Gregory's dreams of establishing a separate Australian colony in the fertile area (to be named Albert, after Queen Victoria's husband) were quashed when South Australia annexed the Northern Territory in 1863.

Top and bottom: Take time out to enjoy the subtle beauty of tropical woodlands as you make your way to Kununurra.

Keep River National Park

Ph: (08) 9167 8827

Just prior to the Western Australian border is Keep River National Park — a small area of large geological and cultural interest. This is an excellent location for photography— volcanic activity in the region has left its chaotic design in a series of eye-catching sandstone formations. Home to the Miriwoong and Gadjerong people for thousands of years, Keep River is also rich in painting sites (*left*) and features unique Aboriginal stone structures. The park entrance is 3 km east of the border, and tracks to the major campgrounds, Aboriginal sites and rock formations all branch off the main park road.

Walks in the Park: The 200 m Ginger's Hill Walk is notable for the Aboriginal stone structure on the hill. Some of the park's superb sandstone formations can be toured on a 2 km walk that starts at the Gurrandalng campground. The Jinumum Walk follows the bed of the Keep River to a site once used by the Mirriwoong people as a wet season shelter. From the Jarnem campground, a complete loop taking in both the Nganalam rock art site and an excellent lookout, can also be broken into two shorter sections.

Access: The park entrance is 3 km east of the WA/NT border off the Victoria Highway.

Camping: Gurrandalng is situated 15 km from the entrance and Jarnem is 13 km further along the Park road.

Flora River Nature Park

Flora River Nature Park, 122 km south-west of Katherine, protects 25 km of the Flora River (*left bottom*) as well as the neighbouring savannah woodlands and floodplain. There are several sites sacred to the Wardaman people near Flora River and songs, stories and ceremonies connecting clans and ancestors are traditionally performed along a "singing trail" that crosses the park. The river is naturally dammed at numerous points by unique tufa walls (formed by the aggregation of calcium carbonate on rock and plant debris). Boating, fishing and canoeing are all popular recreations and a launching facility for small boats and canoes is located 4.3 km from the Djarrung campground. Canoe portages are also provided over the tufa dams. The Pig-nosed Turtle, once thought to be found only in Papua New Guinea, lives in this park. Be warned — both Estuarine and Freshwater Crocodiles are known to inhabit the river (swimming is not recommended).

Gregory National Park

Ph: (08) 8975 0888

Eastern Section

This region is the highlight of the journey to Kununurra and well worth visiting even if you do not intend to continue beyond the border. Gregory National Park is divided into an eastern section around Victoria River Roadhouse and a western section south of Timber Creek. In between lie the community lands of the Ngaliwurri and Nungali peoples. Rock art galleries are a feature of the park. Sixty kilometres south of Timber Creek, historic Bullita Homestead and stockyards are another fascinating remnant of the region's pastoral history.

Victoria River Roadhouse has camping sites, accommodation, meals, telephones, fuel and limited supplies. During the Wet, the river frequently floods in this area, sometimes rising over the bridge and rendering the road impassable. From Kuwang Lookout, 57 km to the west of Victoria River, there are excellent views of the Stokes Range and interpretative displays relating the Aboriginal history of the region.

Walks in the Park: There are great views of the Victoria River and surrounding escarpment from a 3 km return walk that commences at the highway 2 km west of Victoria River Roadhouse. You can avoid the steeper sections by walking only to Garrarnawun Lookout and back again (1 km, easy). At Joe Creek picnic area, 10 km west of Victoria River Roadhouse, there is a relatively difficult 1.7 km track that climbs to an Aboriginal art site and has excellent views along the escarpment. If you want the views without the effort, stop at the Kuwang Lookout further up the Victoria Highway.

Access: Via the Victoria Highway.

Camping: The main campsite is at Sullivan Creek, just off the Victoria Highway 17 km before you reach Victoria River Roadhouse. Camping and accommodation are also available at Victoria River Roadhouse.

Western Section

There are many interesting historical sites, geological features and walking opportunities in the western section of Gregory National Park. Visit Gregory's Tree tour and photograph the stromatolite formations of Limestone Gorge or explore the historic Bullita Homestead. The township of Timber Creek, once a river port servicing the pastoral stations, is now a supply centre with extensive facilities for tourists and local communities.

Walks in the Park: Gregory's Tree is an easy 500 m return walk from the road. The tree itself is surrounded by a boardwalk and there are views of the Victoria River as well as information on Gregory's expedition. From Limestone Gorge campground you can swim in Limestone Creek billabong or enjoy spectacular views of the East Baines River valley on the Limestone Ridge Loop Walk (1.8 km, moderate). Two kilometres before the campground, the Calcite Flow Walk gives you views of the nearby limestone formations (600 m return, easy).

Access: Via the Victoria Highway. The 3 km unsealed road to Gregory's Tree is 9 km west of Big Horse Creek campground. Bullita Homestead is reached via the Bullita Access Road, 10 km east of Timber Creek (dry season only).

Camping: Big Horse Creek campground is 10 km west of Timber Creek on the Victoria Highway. It is equipped with a boat ramp, toilets and fireplaces. Camping is also possible at Bullita campground, on the banks of the Baines River near the homestead. Limestone Gorge campground is 60 km south of Timber Creek along the Bullita Access Road. Accommodation is also available at Timber Creek.

Top to bottom: Gregory River; A freshwater billabong; The road through Gregory National Park; Boab Trees and limestone ridges — scenic features of Gregory National Park.

KUNUNURRA to Broome

Kununurra to Broome
Top Things to Do

1. Photograph the rivers of the Cambridge Gulf region from Five Rivers Lookout.
2. Photograph birdlife at Lake Argyle, Australia's largest dam.
3. Spend a night or more in Purnululu National Park amid the awe-inspiring Bungle Bungles.
4. See some of the eastern Kimberley's best art at Warmun (Turkey Creek).
5. Visit the ruins of a historic gold mining town at Old Halls Creek.
6. Head south on the Tanami Road to Wolfe Creek Meteorite Crater.
7. Explore the Devonian Reef National Park's largest dam.
8. Explore Wyndham, the Kimberley's first port.
9. Photograph wildlife in the King Leopold Ranges.
10. Spend a few days lazing on the brilliant beaches of Broome.

El Questro Wilderness Park

Easily accessible from either the Gibb River Road or the Great Northern Highway near Kununurra, El Questro is a fascinating mixture of working cattle station, luxury retreat and self-imposed wilderness area.

The 405,000 ha property extends 80 km into the Kimberley and features captivating rivers and gorges, waterfalls, thermal springs and caves. Ranger and self-guided tours are available, along with helicopter tours, boat cruises, horse riding treks and wildlife encounters.

El Questro Wilderness Park also features its own station township with restaurant and store, as well as accommodation ranging from riverside camping and cabins to the luxury homestead resort. 4WD vehicles are recommended for reaching the park. Plane and helicopter transfers are available from Kununurra (Ph: (08) 9169 1777).

Taking in 423,000 km^2 of far northern Western Australia, the Kimberley is a spectacular ancient wilderness that was considered a land of plenty by its Aboriginal inhabitants. For countless generations, this was home to over 30,000 people speaking up to 50 different languages. In the mid-19th century, the first European explorers and settlers were lured across spinifex-ridden desert and treacherous ocean by the prospect of pasture, pearls and gold. Their quest gave rise to the gold rushes around Halls Creek (in the mid-1880s), huge pastoral interests and a pearling industry that persists to this day. The region's natural resources continue to be exploited and the Argyle Diamond Mine, south of Kununurra, produces nearly a third of the world's diamonds. Yet the Kimberley remains a sparsely settled area — Kununurra, Derby and Broome are the only northern towns with a population exceeding 2000 people and the majority of the region is untouched wilderness.

Mountains, Marvels & Monsoons

The Kimberley's dramatic landscape features folded ranges, wide plains, limestone fossil reefs and drowned valleys. In the wet season, dry river beds are transformed into gushing rivers and wildlife communities migrate from one region to another in tune with the tropical monsoon climate. The rugged country around Geikie and Windjana Gorges, the King Leopold Ranges and Purnululu National Park harbours an amazing number of native creatures. The Bungle Bungle Range, with its distinctive striped sandstone domes is one of the continent's natural wonders.

East to West

Kununurra and Wyndham are the major towns of the eastern Kimberley region. Wyndham, located on the southern reaches of the Cambridge Gulf, was the Kimberley's first port. From here, you must choose to take the high road or the low road (*see box below*). Gibb River Road offers a bumpy, tyre-stripping frontier adventure through gorge country, including King Leopold Range, Philips Range, Barnett Range, Gibb Range, Mosquito Hills, Mitchell Plateau and the Cockburn Range. The highlights of the more suspension-friendly Highway One include the Bungle Bungles, Halls Creek, Geikie Gorge and Fitzroy Crossing. Tackling either track will eventually lead to the same reward — the sparkling tropical resort of Broome on Roebuck Bay. Of course, if you have sufficient time you could always travel both roads in one giant loop — the grand tour takes in 1775 km of unforgettable Australian countryside.

Two Routes from Kununurra to Broome

There are only two roads traversing the Kimberley from east to west, and one of them is only accessible by 4WD. The most travelled route is the sealed Great Northern Highway (Highway One), which tracks south from Wyndham to Halls Creek and then heads west across the lower Kimberley to Broome. The Gibb River Road carves a path straight through the heart of the Kimberley, across the King Leopold Ranges to Derby on the east coast. Sections are often closed during the Wet. Much of the Kimberley is inaccessible by road in any season, but light aircraft and helicopter charters abound, providing opportunities to enjoy unforgettable views of Australia's north-west.

Left to right: Bell Gorge (Gibb River Road feature); The Bungle Bungles (Great Northern Highway feature).

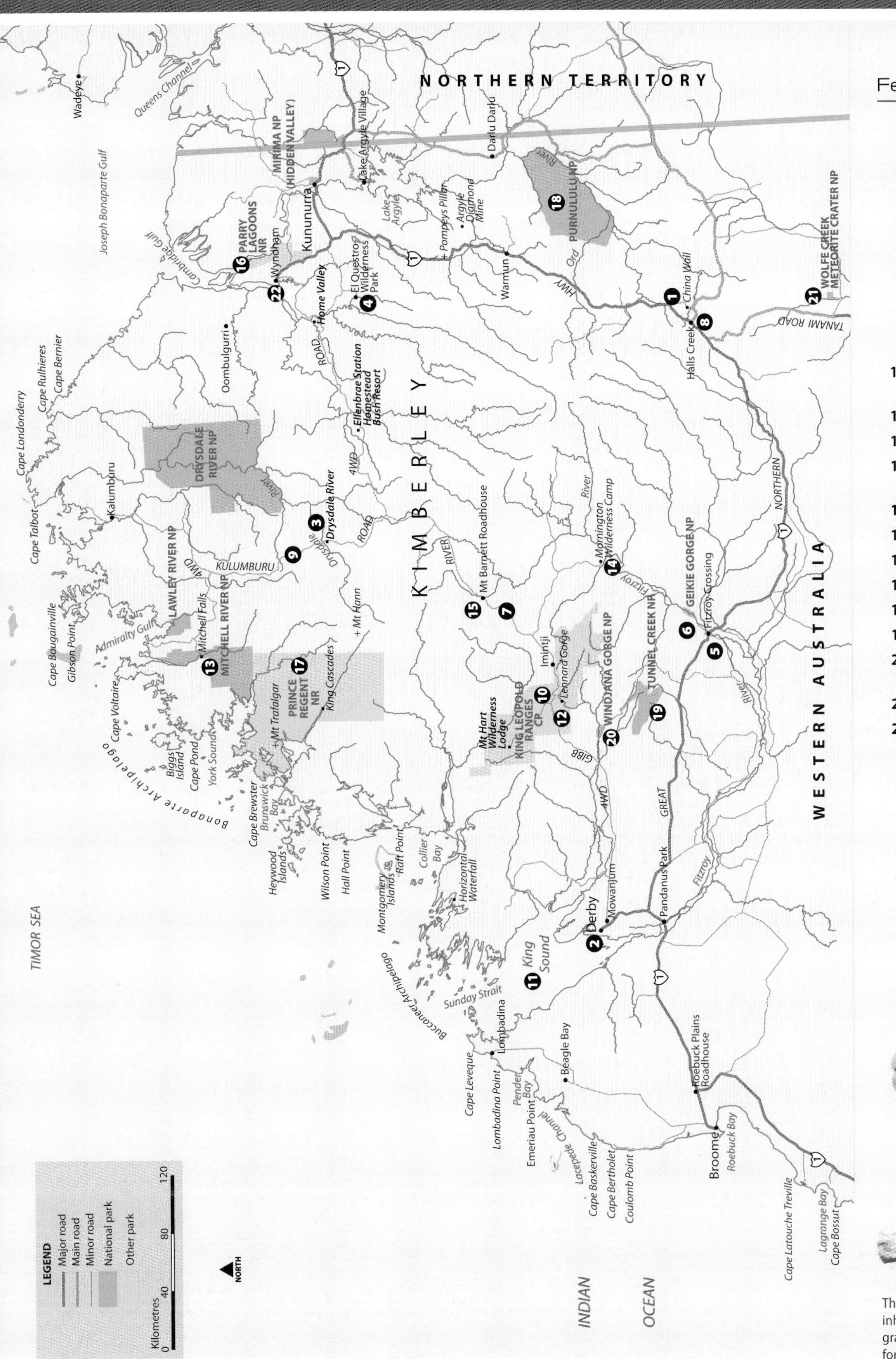

Feature Localities

1 China Wall
2 Derby
3 Drysdale River
4 El Questro Wilderness Park
5 Fitzroy Crossing
6 Geikie Gorge National Park
7 Gibb River Road
8 Halls Creek
9 Kalumburu Road
10 King Leopold Ranges Conservation Park
11 King Sound
12 Lennard Gorge
13 Mitchell Falls, Mitchell River National Park
14 Mornington Wilderness Camp
15 Mount Barnett
16 Parry Lagoons Nature Reserve
17 Prince Regent Nature Reserve
18 Purnululu National Park
19 Tunnel Creek National Park
20 Windjana Gorge, Windjana National Park
21 Wolfe Creek Crater National Park
22 Wyndham

The Red-winged Parrot inhabits open woodlands, grasslands and monsoon forest of the Kimberley region.

Lake Argyle

Early explorers once sought in vain for Australia's inland sea. Such a sea didn't exist so, of course, someone had to invent it.

Lake Argyle (*above*) was created by the damming of the Ord River (*top*) in the Carr Boyd Ranges. While it could fill Sydney Harbour nine times over, legend has it that it only took a single wet season to fill. Mountain peaks now poke above its surface as islands and form homes for wallabies, kangaroos, lizards, snakes and multitudes of birds.

There are numerous ways to view Lake Argyle's breathless magnitude — from cruises commencing at Lake Kununurra to canoeing safaris and scenic flights.

Land of the Ord River Irrigation Scheme

The town of Kununurra and the vast Lake Argyle to its south were created to serve the needs of the Ord River Irrigation Scheme (ORIS). Initiated by the Western Australian government in 1958, the revolutionary irrigation plan demanded harnessing the Ord River to provide the huge volumes of water necessary to coax crops from arid plains. Despite the failure of the first crops due to climatic conditions and pests, the ORIS now successfully produces a bountiful harvest of tropical fruits and vegetables, including sugar cane, melons and bananas. Lake Argyle lies 35 km south of the highway (the turn-off is just over the border) — climb Lake Argyle Lookout to get a true sense of the dam's grandeur. Nearby Argyle Homestead is a partial re-construction of the one-time home of pastoral pioneer Patsy Durack (whose story was told by grand-daughter Mary Durack in the popular Australian book, *Kings in Grass Castles*). The remainder of the original homestead and property is now submerged by the dam.

Kununurra was built to accommodate workers on the scheme and has since evolved into a busy tourism and rural service centre. From here, scenic flights can be chartered over the Ord River region and the western Kimberley. Two kilometres north of the town is Mirima National Park (also known as Hidden Valley) — a region of spectacular twisted sandstone, deep gorges and natural rock sculptures.

Lake Kununurra Sleeping Buddha in the glow of twilight.

Kununurra – Gateway to the Kimberley

Kununurra is the gateway to the Kimberley, a base from which to explore the many outstanding natural features of the region. The town's proximity to the Bungle Bungles, Lake Argyle and the northern gulf region makes it a fascinating destination. Kununurra has also played an important cultural role for the world-renowned Indigenous artists of the east Kimberley region; much of their work first came to prominence through the community-owned Waringarri Aboriginal Arts Centre (Speargrass Road, Ph: (08) 9168 2212).

Mustering cattle Kimberley style.

Kununurra Agricultural activity in the region.

Hidden Valley The valley with Kununurra in the background.

The Kimberley by Air

Australia's far north-west is traversed by only a few roads, most of which are impassable in the Wet. Many of its most striking natural features are surrounded by near impenetrable wilderness, making a flight over the region one of the best ways to experience the Kimberley.

Chartered helicopter flights, fixed-wing aircraft tours and multi-day safaris are available. Some even combine land, sea and air adventures. Tours departing Broome, Halls Creek and Kununurra include all major sites in the Kimberley, such as: Ord River and Lake Argyle; Windjana and Geikie Gorges; King Leopold Ranges; the Bungle Bungles; Fitzroy River; Prince Regent Nature Reserve; and the spectacular waterfalls of Mitchell Plateau.

Purnululu National Park Stone mysticism — seen from the air.

Clockwise from top: Mount Trafalgar, Prince Regent Nature Reserve; Fitzroy River; Raft Point.

Air Charter & Air Safari Websites

1. Broome Air Services, www.broomeairservices.com.au/tours.asp
2. Slingair Heliwork WA, www.slingair.com.au
3. Kimberley Wilderness Adventures, www.kimberleywilderness.com.au
4. Kimberley Safari Centre, www.kimberleysafari.com
5. Alligator Airways, www.alligatorairways.com.au/kimberley.asp
6. East Kimberley Tours, www.eastkimberleytours.com.au
7. King Leopold Air, www.kingleopoldair.com.au

The Kimberley (via Great Northern Highway)

The Great Northern Highway begins at Wyndham — Western Australia's northernmost port. Developed to service boatloads of gold-hungry prospectors bound for Halls Creek, Wyndham outlasted the brief rush by re-purposing its port to serve the pioneer cattle industry. By 1919, a major meatworks was established, bringing prosperity and crocodiles. The meatworks outflow attracted a mass of hungry crocs, which then thrived and bred in the wharf area. There are still a few about today, although they are best viewed in the safety of the nearby Wyndham Crocodile Farm (Port Barytes Road, Ph: (08) 9161 1124). This old frontier town is divided into two sections, Wyndham Port and the newer district of Wyndham Three Mile, appropriately situated about three miles inland. The tourist information centre has self-guided tour maps (Great Northern Highway, Ph: (08) 9161 1281). The Three Mile district boasts a charming outdoor cinema (with deck chairs, naturally) as well as Warriu (Dreamtime Park), an ever-evolving tribute to Aboriginal culture devised by local community leader Reg Birch and featuring huge statues, artwork and memorials. Take your camera and head up to Five Rivers Lookout on Mount Bastion just behind the town — named for its brilliant views of the Forrest, Pentecost, King, Durack and Ord Rivers.

Wyndham to Halls Creek

Wyndham is home to many excellent examples of the strange but beautiful Boab Tree, whose bulging trunk is perfectly designed to store water. Three Mile Caravan Park features a particularly portly specimen (with a girth of nearly 25 m) locally known as "the largest Boab in captivity". Off King River Road is another titan labelled the "Prison Tree", whose hollowed trunk was used in the early 1900s to house overnight prisoners. The Boab Tree's flowering is said to signal the commencement of the wet season. Heading south from Wyndham, the eastern side of the highway is bordered by Parry Lagoons Nature Reserve (*see left*). The Cockburn Range to the west is characterised by photogenic flat-topped sandstone mesas rising 600 m from the plains. Thirty kilometres south is the Grotto, a permanent pool and swimming hole at the bottom of a deep chasm that is accessible via a long rock stairway. Argyle Diamond Mine, the world's largest, is located 122 km south of Kununurra (but is not visible from the road or open to the public). The nearby community of Warmun (formerly Turkey Creek) has attracted international interest over the last 20 years due to the work of its artists, including Rover Thomas and Queenie McKenzie. The Warmun Art Centre is housed in the Old Post Office and exhibits many fine examples of traditional ochre paintings produced by east Kimberley artists; a verbal permit is required to enter the Warmun Community (Ph: (08) 9168 7496). The turn-off to Purnululu National Park and the Bungle Bungles is 52 km south (*see box below*).

Parry Lagoons Nature Reserve

The chain of lagoons and billabongs that form the wetlands of this protected sanctuary are a vital feeding and breeding area for many local and migratory birds. Species include Purple Swamphens, spoonbills (*above*), cranes, Magpie Geese, Australian Pelicans, Brolgas and ducks. It is considered a wetland of international significance. The reserve is open during the dry season and walking tracks are well signposted. Historic sites, such as remnants of the Old Halls Creek Road and the ruins of Telegraph Hill (a World War I naval communications installation), are also found in the reserve.

Purnululu National Park

Phone Kununurra Office: (08) 9168 4200

The Bungle Bungles are one of Australia's most striking geological phenomena. These huge orange and dark grey striped beehives of rock have been formed by uplift and erosion over the last 20 million years. The range rises more than 200 m above the surrounding woodland and plain. In the southern part of the park, at Cathedral Gorge and Piccaninny Gorge, the range is broken into spectacular ridges, natural amphitheatres and domes. Purnululu means "sandstone" in the local Kija language. Scenic flights are available from Halls Creek, Kununurra and Warmun.

Walks in the Park: All walks in the southern section commence at Piccaninny Creek car park. The relatively easy 3 km (return) trail to Cathedral Gorge is the most popular walk. There is also a brief detour (the Domes Track) along the way. It is possible to explore more of the gorges by taking the Piccaninny Creek Track, which follows the dry creek bed. Parts of this walk are not easy, but the views are sensational. Walk a small section or camp out overnight, but remember to register at the park visitor centre beforehand if this is your intention. A short way along the Piccaninny Creek Track there is a turn-off to Sunset Lookout. The lookout is around 35 minutes walk and late afternoon is the best time to absorb the views. The amazing sandstone domes are exclusive to the park's southern section, but the northern area is not wanting for attractions of its own. There are two excellent walks through boulder and Livistona Fan Palm gorges, which commence around 12 km down the 4WD track from the Kurrajong campground. The Mini Palms Walk is 3 km (return) and offers beautiful views over a palm-filled valley. The shorter Echidna Chasm Walk leads deep into an impossibly tall and skinny gorge.
Access: Turn off from the highway 250 km from Kununurra (108 km before Halls Creek). Access is by 4WD only.
Camping: Camping is permitted at Walardi (on Bellburn Creek) or Kurrajong (off the 4WD track to Echidna Chasm). Both sites have toilets and water.

Geikie Gorge National Park

Phone Broome Office: (08) 9192 1036

The jagged limestone peaks of the Oscar Range are actually the top of an ancient reef that formed during the Devonian Period prior to the evolution of mammals and reptiles. At their junction with the Geikie Ranges, the floodwaters of the Fitzroy River have carved a 30 m gorge from the rock. At the river's edge stand Pandanus trees, native reeds, mangroves and eucalypts and the entire area is alive with waterbirds. The Local Bunaba people call the gorge *Darngku*. A guided Aboriginal heritage cruise departs Geikie Gorge Dock daily at 8.15 am.

Walks in the Park: A 3 km (return) Reef Walk along the base of the gorge wall commences at the picnic and information area. The shorter stroll along the riverbank to the popular swimming and fishing spot at the sandbar takes 20 minutes.

Access: The park is 20 km north-east of Fitzroy Crossing. Entry restricted from December to March when the Fitzroy River is in flood.

Camping: Not permitted in the park.

Halls Creek to Fitzroy Crossing

Halls Creek, on the edge of the Tanami Desert, was named for prospector Charles Hall, whose discovery of gold in the region precipitated Western Australia's first rush in 1885. Over 15,000 men from every part of the continent (and beyond) converged on Halls Creek, but only three years later the gold was gone and the town left to decay. A few hardy types stayed on, but in 1949, after constant flooding, the residents of Old Halls Creek relocated to higher ground. Today, in the "new" town, the pioneers of old are remembered by a statue of "Russian Jack", located outside the shire offices in the main street. Jack was actually a prospector by the name of Ivan Fredericks whom local legend claims pushed an ill friend in a wheelbarrow to Wyndham for medical help (*above right*). Adjacent to the tourist information centre on the highway is the Yarliyil Art Centre, which exhibits and sells locally created Aboriginal art. The ruins and cemetery at Old Halls Creek are 15 km south along the Duncan Road. On the way, pause to admire the China Wall, a natural white quartz formation that extends across the landscape in miniature imitation of its great Asian namesake. An even greater astonishment, the Wolfe Creek Meteorite Crater, lies 145 km south of the main highway along the Tanami Road (*see right*).

The highway to Fitzroy Crossing passes through country dotted with cattle stations and numerous Aboriginal communities, with the Mueller, Sparke and Pillarra Ranges lying to the north. The Fitzroy River rises north-west of Fitzroy Crossing in the King Leopold Ranges and travels in a 700 km south-west arc to King Sound near Derby. It is the Kimberley's longest river and, when in flood, is the second-fastest flowing river in the world after the Amazon. Like Halls Creek, the town of Fitzroy Crossing also has a historic "double" — the old town was superseded when a bridge was built across the Fitzroy River further downstream in 1935. Visit the Crossing Inn, the Kimberley's oldest hotel, built in 1897 at the original crossing point. Fitzroy Crossing is a popular base from which to explore the spectacular Devonian Reef National Parks of Geikie Gorge, Tunnel Creek and Windjana Gorge. Boat cruises and Aboriginal Heritage cruises at Geikie Gorge can be booked at the Fitzroy Crossing Tourist Bureau (cnr Great Northern Highway and Forrest Rd, Ph: (08) 9191 5355).

From Fitzroy Crossing, Highway One continues 210 km west to the Derby turn-off. Alternatively, if you are bored with the bitumen (and 4WD equipped), you could continue north from Windjana Gorge National Park and conclude your Kimberley crossing with a brief jaunt down the Gibb River Road. This will let you explore the superb gorges of King Leopold Ranges Conservation Park before venturing on to Derby and Broome.

China Wall

The China Wall is a natural white stone wall formed by a sub-vertical quartz vein that projects above the surrounding rocks. Geologists believe the China Wall to be a section of the largest single fault of its type in the world. Situated 6 km north of Halls Creek above a beautiful creek, it makes a delightful picnic spot.

The wall can be seen to wind its way over some tens of kilometres, appearing like the remnants of a miniature Great Wall of China — the inspiration for its name.

Wolfe Creek Crater

The huge Wolfe Creek Meteorite Crater, familiar to local Aboriginal people for millennia but only discovered by Europeans in 1947, is the second largest in the world. Located south of Halls Creek along the Tanami Road, the crater is 880 m in diameter and surrounded by a 60 m high rim. About 300,000 years ago the 50,000 tonne meteorite that caused this enduring scar crashed to Earth at a speed of 54,000 km/h.

Kununurra to Broome
Top Things to Do

1 Spend time exploring the Cockburn Ranges from El Questro Wilderness Resort.
2 Visit Drysdale River Station.
3 Explore the superb gorges near Mt Barnett and around the King Leopold Ranges.
4 Walk through the cave at Tunnel Creek National Park.
5 Fly over the Buccaneer Archipelago and northern Kimberley coast.
6 Revitalise at the famous Mitchell Falls, Mitchell River National Park.

Top to bottom: Drysdale River National Park; Indigenous rock art site, King Edward River; Mitchell Falls.

Detour to Mitchell Falls

If you are keen to see the northern Kimberley but don't wish to drive the Kalumburu Road, charter flights over the Prince Regent River and Mount Hann to the north-east coast are available from Drysdale River Station. The stunning multi-level Mitchell Falls are one of the highlights of the flight. If you choose to drive to Mitchell River National Park, you can still enjoy the view from above — helicopter tours operate from Mitchell Falls car park (Ph: (08) 9168 1811).

The Kimberley (via Gibb River Road)

The Gibb River Road ranks with trips to the tip of Cape York Peninsula and the Birdsville Track as one of a handful of truly iconic Australian adventures. The 700-odd kilometres of corrugated gravel and dirt on this old stock route is not for the faint-hearted nor the non-4WD equipped. It includes many creek and river crossings (only some of which are paved) and the complete journey across the Kimberley is normally only possible in the Dry. From Gibb River Road you can also divert north on the Kalumburu Road, which covers the entire 263 km across the Mitchell Plateau to the Aboriginal community of Kalumburu on the northern coast. "Tag-along" and convoy 4WD tours operate on both this and the Gibb River Road. There are no towns on Gibb River Road and only two roadhouses (at Imintji Aboriginal Community and Mt Barnett). Diesel fuel and food are available at both, but unleaded petrol is only available at Mt Barnett and on the Kalumburu Road at Drysdale River Station. Tyre repairs are possible at Imintji, Drysdale River and Home Valley Station. Public telephones are available at roadhouses and some homesteads.

Eastern Kimberley

The Gibb River Road (or track, as most of it should more correctly be called) commences 48 km south of Wyndham, cutting across the foothills of the Cockburn Range and past roads leading to the wilderness resorts of El Questro and Emma Gorge. The first of many river crossings lies only 400 m west of the intersection with King River Road (where the Pentecost River breaches the track). Home Valley Station, 8 km down the road, offers camping, accommodation, 4WD tours and horse riding trails on 283,280 ha of pastoral property. The station is owned by the local Balanggarra people (Ph: (08) 9161 4322). One hundred and eight kilometres further on, between the Durack River crossing and the Dawn Creek crossing, is Ellenbrae Station Homestead Bush Resort with campsites nestled between shaded billabongs. B&B accommodation and meals are also available (Ph: (08) 9161 4325). Another 70 km on, past the Russ Creek crossing, is the junction with the Kalumburu road. Cool off and de-dust in the shady swimming spots here along the Gibb River. Even if you don't wish to take the option of travelling all the way to the coast or Mitchell River National Park (*see bottom left*), it's worth journeying the 60 km up Kalumburu Road to Drysdale River. The station offers accommodation, camping, a bar and dining facilities (Ph: (08) 9161 4326, no campsite bookings permitted). Nearby Miners Pool is a large camping ground located on a pleasant (and swimmable) waterhole.

Clockwise from top left: Crossing the Pentecost River; Boab Trees; Roadside billabong; Typical tropical woodland during the dry season.

The Gibb River Road

Once traversed by only the most intrepid of stockmen, the Gibb River Road now attracts a large number of travellers — over 20,000 people make the trip each dry season. Be prepared for camping sites, station facilities and natural attractions to be very busy and, wherever possible, book your accommodation in advance.

Gorging Out

The Gibb River Road gives you the chance to experience Australia's most remote country. This rough bush track takes you into a special part of the Kimberley commonly known as "gorge country". Extensive riverine systems have carved spectacular (and inviting) gorges from the ancient landscape (the geology of which is more than 350-million-years-old). A scattering of national parks protect marvels such as Bell and Windjana Gorges.

Clockwise from top left: Bell Gorge; Manning Gorge; Lennard River Gorge; Galvans Gorge.

Mornington Wilderness Camp

Fifty-three kilometres west of Mt Barnett Roadhouse, a road leads south via Mt House Station to the Mornington Wilderness Camp. This 3000 km^2 tropical sanctuary and retreat comes complete with serviced safari tents and is set on the upper reaches of the Fitzroy River. Simpler styles of camping are also possible (bookings essential, Ph: 1800 631 946). Owned and managed by the non-profit Australian Wildlife Conservancy, Mornington Wilderness Camp provides refuge for over 200 bird species and a healthy mix of other natives. Walk, canoe or fly around nearby Sir John Gorge and Diamond Gorge or dine under the stars at the bush restaurant.

Mt Barnett to Derby

There are several working cattle stations offering accommodation and campsites around Mt Barnett, including Mt Elizabeth Station (turn-off 39 km east of the roadhouse, Ph: (08) 9191 4644) and Charnley River (turn-off 49 km west, Ph: (08) 9191 4646). There are also three must-see gorges in the region — Barnett River Gorge, Manning Gorge and Galvans Gorge. Excellent camping facilities are available at Manning Gorge along with tranquil swimming pools and guided tours of the Aboriginal rock art galleries (camping fees and tour bookings through the roadhouse, Ph: (08) 9191 7007). Imintji Roadhouse, 88 km west of Mt Barnett, is located near the boundary of the King Leopold Ranges Conservation Park (*see following page*). This remarkable area contains some of the Kimberley's most impressive gorges and scenery. Mount Hart Wilderness Lodge, a homestead-style retreat on a former pastoral lease, is located in the north of the park (no camping available, Ph: (08) 9191 4645).

West of the park, at the Lennard River crossing, the Fairfield–Leopold Downs Road leads south to the wonders of Windjana Gorge and Tunnel Creek National Parks (*see following page*). From the crossing it is 124 km to Derby (the last 84 km being sealed road). Derby is a fascinating old-time pastoral, mining and pearling port at King Sound. It stands on the edge of long tidal mudflats that experience the highest tides in Australia. While it no longer operates as a commercial port, the remnants of the huge livestock loading facility can still be seen around the jetty area.

Derby was the first major settled township in the Kimberley and the town's historic buildings include the old wool shed and the original gaol in Loch Street. A 1500 year old Boab prison tree, similar to that found near Wyndham, stands next to the highway 7 km south. Nearby Myall's bore once fed water to the neighbouring 120 m long cattle trough, reputed to be the world's longest. Derby's unusual history can be explored in detail at the Centenary Pavilion (at the jetty) and Wharfingers House Museum (corner of Elder and Loch Streets). Flights are also available to view the thousand islands and natural features of the Buccaneer Archipelago, including the astounding horizontal reversible waterfall at Talbot Bay (bookings through Derby Visitor Centre, Clarendon Street, Ph: (08) 9191 1426).

Top to bottom: King Sound sunrise; Main street in Derby.

King Sound

The first records of exploration of King Sound were made by English maritime explorer and privateer William Dampier, who sailed aboard the *Cygnet* to these waters in 1688. Dampier's reports on the Kimberley and its inhabitants were so dismal that it was nearly 200 years before European settlement took place. Pearlers discovered rich oyster grounds around King Sound and pastoralists exploited the neighbouring hinterland, giving rise to the township and port of Derby.

King Leopold Range Conservation Park

Ph: (08) 9191 1426

Declared in the year 2000 over land once contained within the former Mt Hart pastoral lease, the park protects a section of the King Leopold Ranges and features some of the Kimberley's most magnificent gorges, including Bell Gorge and Lennard Gorge.

Walks in the Park: A 2 km return walk leads from the Bell Gorge car park to spectacular elevated views of the gorge and waterfall. Be advised, the short walking track to Lennard Gorge is steep and rocky. You will need to take care.

Access: Silent Grove and Bell Gorge are reached via a track heading north from Gibb River Road in the southern corner of the park. The turn-off to Lennard Gorge is approximately 20 km further along Gibb River Road.

Camping: Camping is permitted at Bell Gorge and there are campsites with toilets and showers at Silent Grove. No camping at Lennard Gorge.

Clockwise from top left: Bell Gorge waterhole; Isdell River, King Leopold Conservation Park; Bell Gorge.

Windjana Gorge National Park

Ph: (08) 9192 1036

The 3.5 km long Windjana Gorge has been carved through the limestone reef of the Napier Range by the Lennard River. The river flows only in the wet season but small pools surrounded by trees and frequented by Freshwater Crocodiles remain during the Dry.

Walks in the Park: A 7 km return walk explores the entire length of the gorge. Another short trail leads to examples of fossilised marine life embedded in the gorge walls. Nearby are the ruins of the Lillimilura Homestead, which was constructed from limestone in 1887.

Access: Twenty kilometres off the Gibb River Road via Fairfield–Leopold Downs Road.

Camping: There is a well-equipped camping ground with toilets, showers and a portable generator use area at the gorge.

Clockwise from top left: Windjana Gorge; Windjana Gorge from the air at sunset; Stone formations inside Windjana Gorge.

Tunnel Creek National Park

Ph: (08) 9192 1036

As the name suggests, the major feature of the park is a creek that flows 750 m through a rock tunnel. The tunnel (or cave) has been created by water seeping through cracks and joints in the limestone over millions of years. Stalactites descend from the cave roof and it is home to at least five different bat species.

Walks in the Park: It is possible to walk through the cave in the dry season, but carry a torch and be prepared to get wet (and possibly cold). Water pools remain in the cave even in the dry.

Access: Fifty-five kilometres off the Gibb River Road via Fairfield–Leopold Downs Road.

Camping: Not permitted in the park.

Left to right: Tunnel Creek; Rock formations and Boab Tree near Tunnel Creek.

The Kimberley Coast by Sea

From Darwin, Wyndham, Derby and Broome, there are ample opportunities to board a boat and tour Australia's majestic north-west coast. Early Australian travel writer and author Ernestine Hill described the coast in the 1930s as "split into a thousand fiords breathtaking in their colour and beauty ... far and away the loveliest in Australia". Nothing has changed since. Cruises visit coastal highlights such as Raft Point and explore the numerous bays, islands and rivers, including: Doubtful Bay; Buccaneer Archipelago; Prince Regent River; and the spectacular King Cascades. Choose from five day adventures to three week luxury cruises.

Left to right: Mitchell Falls; Prince Regent Nature Reserve.

Left to right: Adventures ashore by tender; King Gorge Falls — one of the Kimberley's most dramatic cascades.

Cruises Websites

1. Kimberley Discovery Cruises — depart from Broome or Derby, www.kimberleydiscoverycruises.com.au
2. AAT Kings Tours — depart Darwin, www.aatkings.com
3. Adventure Associates — depart Darwin and Broome, www.adventureassociates.com
4. Coral Princess Cruises — depart Darwin and Broome, www.coralprincess.com.au
5. Kimberley Safari Centre — depart Darwin and Broome, www.kimberleysafari.com
6. Kimberley to Ocean — depart Broome and Wyndham, www.kimberleycruise.com.au
7. Orion Cruises — depart Broome and Darwin, www.orioncruises.com.au

Clockwise from top left: Beach landing for a day's adventure; Exploring a Kimberley Indigenous rock art gallery; Discovering Prince Regent River; Helicopters are thrilling onboard accessories for some of the Kimberley's tourist boats; Visiting King Gorge Falls; Tourists inspect a marine turtle at Talbot Bay.

BROOME

& THE JOURNEY TO PERTH

5

The journey between Broome and Perth along Australia's western coast does not attract the same level of tourism as the eastern seaboard. This is a boon for travellers, as the West's coral reefs and beaches, dazzling native flora and astonishing geological features are mostly free of crowds. In spring, the entire coast is transformed by wildflowers. Inland, the ore-filled mountains of the Pilbara have become one of the world's richest mining centres. Ningaloo Marine Park and Shark Bay (famous for the gregarious dolphins of Monkey Mia) are havens for marine life. Much of the northern section of coast remains untouched by commerce, but if you are craving company, the old pearling port of Broome is brimming with beautiful beaches and leisure options that attract plenty of holidaymakers. But even here, the unsullied wilds are never far away — the nearby Broome Bird Observatory ranks among the top four locations in the world for viewing shorebirds and waders. The national parks of the west coast all demand exploration. I can't imagine making the trip south to Perth without days and nights spent amid the waterfalls and wildflowers of Karijini or wandering among the Pinnacles — surreal limestone giants that stand watch over the sands of Nambung.

Sturt's Desert Pea

Opposite: Shark Bay, François Peron National Park. **Above:** Karijini National Park — the epitome of Western Australia's weather-beaten and mesmerising Pilbara landscape.

BROOME & Surrounds

Broome & Surrounds

Top Things to Do

1. Visit the Broome Historical Museum and walk the town's heritage trail.
2. Catch a movie at Sun Pictures — the world's longest running outdoor cinema.
3. View the sunset over Cable Beach from the back of a camel.
4. Spend a day (and night) at Broome Bird Observatory.
5. Photograph the eroded rock formations at Gantheaume Point.

Pearl of the North

Known unofficially as the Port of Pearls, the town of Broome was proclaimed in 1883 when the fevered hunt for the "gold of the deep" was at its height. The revolutionary technique of helmet diving had been introduced to the region three years earlier and the lustrous mother-of-pearl found in the huge local oyster, *Pinctada maxima*, soon became famous around the world. While the pearling frenzy lasted, Broome rapidly expanded, with thousands of pearl luggers and their crews basing operations around Roebuck Bay and King Sound to its north. White pearling masters drove Aboriginal and Asian divers ever deeper and the constant hazards of illness, sharks and tropical cyclones took many lives. By 1914, Broome supplied up to 80% of the world's mother-of-pearl, but the industry soon fell into a decline precipitated by war and depression. In the 1950s the introduction of cultured pearls would revive the town's fortunes. Today, Broome is a world leader in pearl farming.

Broome, a colourful Western Australian outpost and cultural melting pot, is a town rich in history. In the late 19th century, pearlers seeking their fortune risked lives on ramshackle luggers along this tortuous stretch of coast. In contrast, now Broome's airport fills daily with holidaymakers. What amazes most people upon their arrival is not that the promise of glorious white sun-soaked beaches is no hoax, but that Broome has so much else to offer. The town has not so much hidden its dramatic past from view as left it untouched for the curious visitor to discover.

Historical Broome

Broome's pearling history can be thoroughly explored at the Broome Historical Society Museum (cnr Saville and Hamersley Sts, Ph: (08) 9192 2075) and Pearl Luggers — a permanent exhibition featuring two fully restored pearling vessels and other memorabilia (tours daily, 31 Dampier Tce, Ph: (08) 9192 2059). There are a number of memorials to pearl divers located around the old port area at the northern end of Carnarvon Street, which also features several original town stores. Nearby Chinatown, with its authentic Asian and colonial architecture, offers some fascinating glimpses of Broome's early years. The original Streeter's Jetty, at the end of Dampier Terrace near Short Street, remains in use today. Japanese divers were once considered the masters of the deep and the Japanese Cemetery off Port Drive is the resting place of over 700 divers who once worked the waters off Broome. The Pioneer Cemetery at Apex Park near Mangrove Point also has graves dating back to the early 1880s.

In Bedford Memorial Park (overlooking Roebuck Bay on Hamersley Street) stands an Anzac memorial, the remains of Broome's first diving decompression chamber and a replica of early maritime explorer and buccaneer, William Dampier's trunk.

Outdoor Broome

Entertainment in Broome centres around its many beaches (*below right*), but once again, there is more than first greets the eye. The monthly Staircase to the Moon markets (staged in the Town Beach Reserve) celebrate the reflection of the full moon in the tidal mudflats, which creates the picturesque illusion of a stairway climbing to the heavens. From the same beach on very low tides, Broome's wartime experience is revealed by the wrecks of three Dutch flying boats sunk at their moorings by Japanese aircraft in 1942.

Sunset camel rides on Cable Beach have become a famous symbol of the town's escapist nature (*see facing page*), but if twilight movies are more your style, take a seat at Broome's historic Sun Pictures. Opened in 1916, it is the world's longest running open-air cinema (Carnarvon St, Ph: (08) 9192 1077).

Gantheaume Point

The sculpted sandstone formations (*above left*) on the headland dividing Roebuck Bay and Cable Beach provide a distinctive exclamation point to the long white strip of Cable Beach. The rugged red cliffs are also home to a feature known as Anastasia's Pool — the story of which a cynic might suspect was concocted by tourist authorities to enhance Broome's romantic repute. This circular ditch in the rock, which fills with water at high tide, is said to have been originally carved by a lighthouse keeper as a pool for his arthritic wife to bathe in. Even more astounding are the 120-million-year-old dinosaur footprints, which can be seen in low-lying rock when the tide falls below 1.5 m.

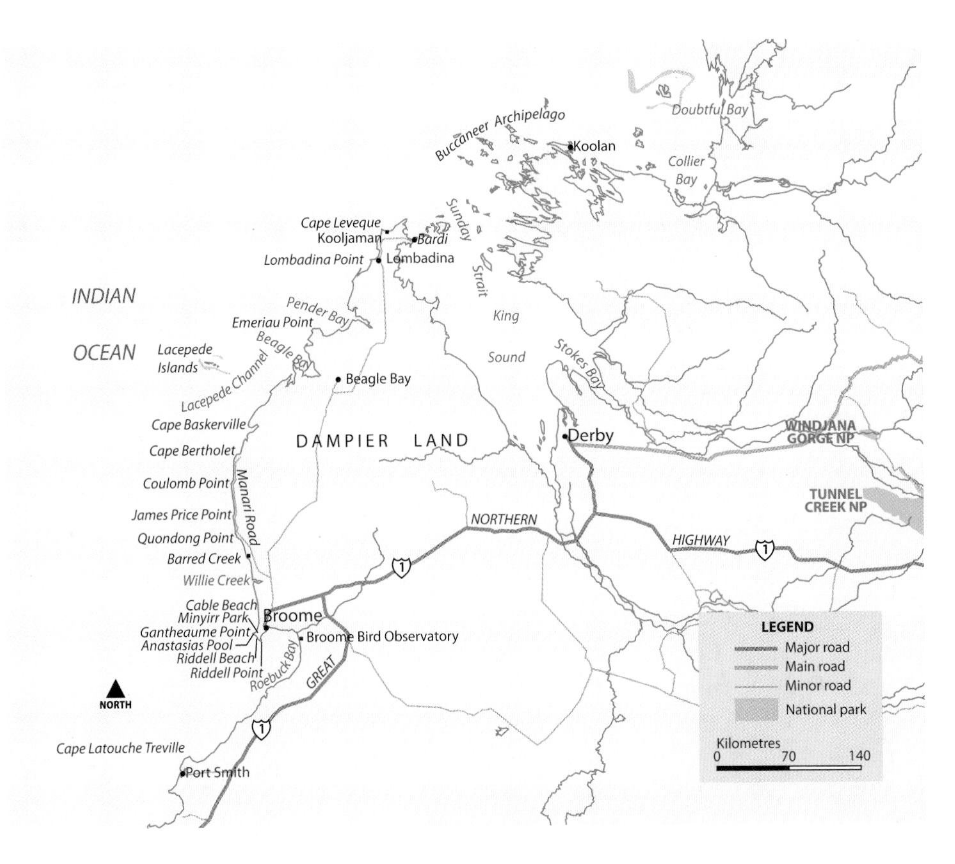

Cable Beach

Named for the Overland Telegraph Cable Station built in Broome in 1883, Cable Beach is the town's premier resort area. Its white sands stretch 22 km north of Gantheaume Point, ensuring you can find your slice of solitude even in peak holiday periods — barring the regular Dromedary processions. The image of camel "trains" transporting visitors along the Cable Beach shoreline is now synonymous with Broome. In the dunes behind Cable Beach, known as Minyirr Park, there are 22 km of walking tracks leading around Gantheaume Point to Riddell Beach. *Minyirr* means "birthplace" and many Indigenous people recognise this region as the place where Aboriginal people were first created.

Surrounding Beaches

While Cable Beach hogs the spotlight, there are plenty of other beaches around Broome worth exploring. Eight kilometres from town, between Gantheaume Point and Riddell Point, lies Riddell Beach — a rocky foreshore studded with pools set against red pindan cliffs. To the north of Broome (via Manari Road) are a series of quiet beaches including Barred Creek, Quandong Point, James Price Point and Coulomb Point. A 4WD vehicle is necessary to access the northern beaches but bush camping is free and the views are spectacular. Willie Creek, 32 km north of Broome, is the location of the town's major pearl farm (Willie Creek Pearl Farm, Ph: (08) 9192 6300).

North to Cape Leveque

Cape Leveque is situated on the tip of the Dampier Peninsula, 220 km north of Broome. The coastal scenery around the area is one of stunning contrasts — brilliant blue seas, brick-red earth and white sands. Access is via 4WD, but a number of scenic flights operate in the area and are a great way to see this incredible place.

Kooljaman (Ph: (08) 9192 4970), an Aboriginal-owned, multi award-winning wilderness camp; provides a stress-free, low-impact environment for exploring the cape's natural delights. Fishing, snorkelling, boating and swimming are popular, as are trips to nearby Sunday Island (where you can take a reef-walk or see the ruins of the old Bardi mission).

Broome Bird Observatory

The Broome region is considered one of the world's top four sites for viewing shorebirds. With more than 800,000 waders visiting the area annually, the region has the greatest diversity of shorebirds on Earth. More than 300 bird species (including 22 of Australia's 24 raptor species) have been recorded in and around Broome.

On the coast of Roebuck Bay, 25 km south of Broome, is the acclaimed Broome Bird Observatory. It was established in 1988 by the non-profit conservation group Birds Australia. The installation provides birdwatching tours, courses, self-guided trails and a natural history library and multimedia displays. A range of accommodation from camping to chalets is also available (Crab Creek Road, Ph: (08) 9193 5600).

BROOME to Shark Bay

Broome to Shark Bay

Top Things to Do

1. Camp near the pink sandstone cliffs of Cape Villaret at Barn Hill.
2. Go crabbing at Port Smith.
3. Spend a few days beachcombing or fishing at Eighty Mile Beach.
4. Cool off in Australia's hottest town with a swim below the famous "marble" bar.
5. Visit the abandoned mining settlements on the edge of the Pilbara.
6. Take a tour of the massive iron ore port and processing plant at Port Hedland.

Marble Bar

Located in the rusty red ranges of the eastern Pilbara, Marble Bar has long held the official record as Australia's hottest place. In 1926, the town endured no less than 161 consecutive days of furnace-like heat — the temperature never dropped below 33.7 °C (100 °F).

The town's name is a misnomer — the reef of marble that prospectors thought they had discovered 5 km west of here at the Coongan River turned out to be a type of quartz known as jasper. The jasper reef can still be seen, while the local waterhole located enticingly below is popular for swimming. Marble Bar was originally founded in 1888 by miners seeking gold after the Kimberley rush began to wane. A museum at the old Comet Goldmine offers daily underground mine tours (7.5 km from town via the Hillside-Marble Bar Road, Ph: (08) 9176 1015).

The Great Northern Highway tracks the Indian Ocean coast south of Broome to Port Hedland, but if you remain on the highway you could believe you were closer to the centre of Australia than its western edge. The ocean remains out of view of the road for nearly all of this 605 km journey and the scrubby flat plains of the Great Sandy Desert to the east offer little by way of conventionally picturesque scenery. However, there are rewards to reap by travelling the short distance to the coast at several different points. About 300 km from Broome, Eighty Mile Beach is a popular location for fishing, birdwatching and shell collecting. A little further south, Cape Keraudren Coastal Reserve is a beachside haven for marine and terrestrial animals and also provides excellent camping opportunities. Be wary of wildlife (including Emus, kangaroos and Dingoes) suddenly appearing on the highway along this entire stretch — particularly in early morning and late afternoon.

Broome to Port Hedland

At the southernmost point of Roebuck Bay are the sandstone cliffs of Cape Villaret, where an ecotourism resort offering comfortable accommodation, dining, nature tours and cruises has been established (Eco Beach Retreat, 130 km south of Broome, Ph: (08) 9192 4844). Just south of the Cape is Barn Hill, a more modest but no less enticing arrangement close to the beach with camping sites and a few chalets (Great Northern Hwy, Ph: (08) 9192 4975).

Western Grey Kangaroo

Another 63 km down the highway is a track leading to Port Smith Lagoon Caravan Park (Ph: (08) 9192 4983). Port Smith Tropical Gardens and Bird Park is 400 m from the camping area and there is also a nine hole bush golf course on site. Crabbing is another favourite recreation in these parts and some super-sized crustaceans have been nabbed around Port Smith.

Between here and Port Hedland there are two well-equipped highway roadhouses — Sandfire Roadhouse (292 km north of Port Hedland, Ph: (08) 9176 5944) and Pardoo Roadhouse (153 km north, Ph: (08) 9176 4916). Both offer fuel, food, supplies, camping/caravan sites and limited accommodation. The palm-shaded Eighty Mile Beach Caravan Park also has a mini-supermarket (open 7 days, 7 am – 7 pm), powered/unpowered sites and cabins (turn off 45 km south of Sandfire Roadhouse, Ph: (08) 9176 5941).

Fifty kilometres south of Port Hedland is the turn-off to one of Australia's hottest towns — Marble Bar (*see below left*). You can reach Marble Bar via an off-road track commencing near Pardoo Roadhouse and leading through a series of abandoned mining settlements originally established in the 1960s at the height of the region's nickel and iron boom.

Once a small pearling port, Port Hedland surged to life in 1965 when it became the major centre for processing and shipping the Pilbara's vast iron ore reserves. Today it boasts the largest annual tonnage of any Australian port and monstrous iron ore carriers are almost always present in the harbour. On your way into town, take note of the huge white pyramids next to the road. These are mountains of salt produced by the local Leslie Salt Company.

Port Hedland

There are two port facilities on opposite sides of Port Hedland's harbour — Nelson Point and Finucane Island. They are linked by a 1.4 km under-harbour tunnel conveyor and railways that service the inland mines. The huge stockpiles of ore held at the facility each contain about 200,000 t and are 15 m high. Over 500 ships are loaded each year — the largest are up to 230 m long and carry up to 260,000 t of ore. Daily tours of the BHP Billiton facility commence from the visitor centre in Wedge Street.

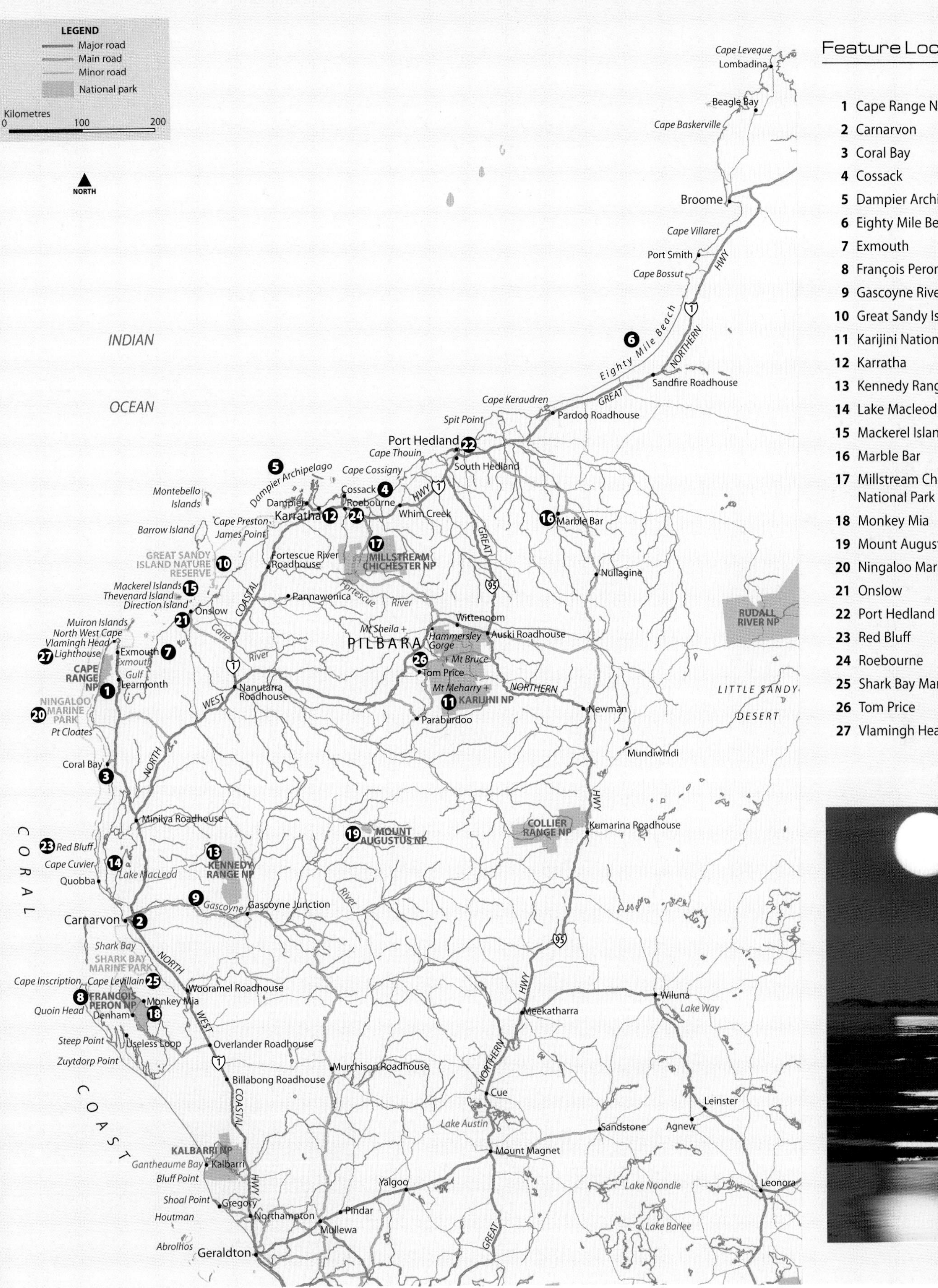

Feature Localities

1 Cape Range National Park
2 Carnarvon
3 Coral Bay
4 Cossack
5 Dampier Archipelago
6 Eighty Mile Beach
7 Exmouth
8 François Peron National Park
9 Gascoyne River
10 Great Sandy Island Nature Reserve
11 Karijini National Park
12 Karratha
13 Kennedy Range National Park
14 Lake Macleod
15 Mackerel Islands
16 Marble Bar
17 Millstream Chichester National Park
18 Monkey Mia
19 Mount Augustus National Park
20 Ningaloo Marine Park
21 Onslow
22 Port Hedland
23 Red Bluff
24 Roebourne
25 Shark Bay Marine Park
26 Tom Price
27 Vlamingh Head Lighthouse

Pilbara & Karijini

Top Things to Do

1. Treat yourself to a scenic flight over the Hamersley Range.
2. Walk among the gorges of Karijini National Park — particularly when the wildflowers are in bloom.
3. Take an open cut mine tour at Tom Price.
4. Drive to the summit of Mount Sheila and photograph the magnificent Hamersley Range panoramas.
5. Camp along the waterholes and springs of Millstream–Chichester National Park.

Ancient Life of the Pilbara

The inland region of the eastern Pilbara is a quintessentially Australian landscape that literally dates back to the dawn of life on Earth.

Local Aborigines knew this place as *Bilybarra* or "dry country". Remarkably, the Pilbara's arid, ore-rich ranges also conceal green oases and water-filled gorges of enormous beauty.

Deep in the rock of this ancient region geologists have identified fossilised oxygen-producing organisms called stromatolites that lived 3.5-billion-years-ago when the planet itself was in its infancy.

The discovery of stromatolites has divided the scientific world, with plenty of research and multiple theories based around the phenomenon.

The Pilbara & Karijini National Park

After the long haul from Broome to Port Hedland, it may be tempting to forge on straight down the coast, but doing so will deny you one of this journey's most interesting experiences. If you have a few days, even a brief excursion to the Hamersley Range and Karijini National Park will provide an unforgettable snapshot of one of Australia's oldest and most distinctive regions. If you also have a 4WD vehicle, exploration of the eastern Pilbara can be achieved without the need to backtrack. The return road will bring you back to the North West Coastal Highway just east of Roebourne via Millstream–Chichester National Park (*see facing page*). From Tom Price you can also travel on the sealed Nanutarra–Wittenoom Road to Nanutarra, east of Exmouth. Alternatively, it is possible to forego the coastal experience altogether and continue south on the Great Northern Highway beyond Newman through Meekatharra and Mount Magnet all the way to Perth — the journey covers 1186 km on sealed road through the mid-west and wheatbelt regions.

The Hamersley Range

Forty-two kilometres south of Port Hedland, the Great Northern Highway diverges due south through the Yandeyarra Aboriginal community and over the Chichester Range to the north-eastern section of Karijini National Park (*see facing page*). The Yandeyarra region played an important role in modern Aboriginal history; it was the location of a widely supported pastoral strike in 1946, which significantly improved conditions for Aboriginal workers (some of whom had only previously received food and clothing for their labours). Regulated wages were later introduced and the Yandeyarra cattle station was eventually handed over to Aboriginal community operation in 1972.

The Hamersley Range region contains Western Australia's tallest peaks. The virtually inaccessible Mount Meharry in the south of Karijini National Park is the State's highest at 1253 m. It has entered national folklore that the vision of exposed fire-red rock on the Hamersley Range from the window of mining magnate Lang Hancock's plane in 1952 induced further investigation of the area's mining potential. It was an astute hunch — geological surveys would reveal that Mount Tom Price and many of the surrounding slopes were composed nearly entirely of iron ore. By 1970, nine new towns had been developed and today the extraction and export of minerals from the eastern Pilbara remains one of Australia's most important industries.

Access to both Karijini National Park and Tom Price is via Karijini Drive, which meets the Great Northern Highway 35 km south of Munjini Roadhouse.

Tom Price

Situated at the base of Mount Nameless and bankrolled by iron ore, Tom Price is a clean and modern mining town with an abundance of services. No matter how uninterested you think you might be in the art of shovelling rock, a tour of the open cut mine at Tom Price will leave you open-mouthed at the sheer immensity and ingenuity of these operations. This is a toddler's sandpit magnified a million-fold — the gargantuan machinery has gouged more than a billion tonnes of ore out of the face of the earth at Tom Price alone (tour bookings at the Tom Price Visitor Centre, Central Rd, Ph: (08) 9188 1112). Nearby Mount Bruce has three walking trails (from 500 m to 9 km) with views over the Marandoo Mine site. The 4WD journey to Mount Sheila leads all the way to the summit and an incredible 360° panorama of the region (approximately 150 km return). A little further north is Hamersley Gorge, a spectacular wave of rock rising above an attractive swimming hole and natural spa. Walking 1 km beyond the spa will bring you to the Grotto — a fern-lined chasm etched from the side of gorge.

Pilbara Mining

The Pilbara's ranges are rich in iron and the mining ventures that have flourished in the Hamersley area since the 1960s have generated enormous wealth. They have also spawned large company towns like Tom Price and Paraburdoo to accommodate mine workers. The resulting network of roads has made it possible to journey through rocky ranges and spinifex-studded desert that early European explorers found nigh impassable.

Top to bottom: Hamersley Gorge; Hamersley Range; Dales Gorge, Karijini National Park; Joffre Falls, Karijini National Park.

Karijini National Park

Ph: (08) 9189 8121

Taking its name from the original Banyjima word for the Hamersley Ranges, Karijini is the second-largest and probably the most surprising national park in the State. The park's incredible range of habitat, steep, shaded gorges and cool watercourses defy its location in one of Australia's hottest regions. After rain, a botanist's catalogue of wildflowers burst into bloom across Karijini and soften the ruddy, rugged terrain. In winter, nights can be cold and even frosty. The park's north has some of Australia's most striking gorges. Dales Gorge is a vision of streams, waterfalls and weathered cliff faces. Weano, Red, Hancock and Joffre Gorges converge in a maze of banded rock at Oxers Lookout. The park visitor centre, a sheer, steel-walled contemporary structure on Banyjima Drive, is also a revelation — its design mimics a goanna moving through country. Talk to the Aboriginal hosts to learn more of the fascinating history of this area.

Walks in the Park: Firstly, take care — walking in Karijini's gorges can be hazardous due to loose rock, steep inclines and narrow ledges. Some are easier than others — try the 1.2 km return Gorge Rim and Circular Pool Lookout at Dales Gorge, or the 30 minute return walk to the shaded pool at the bottom of Kalamina Gorge. The rewarding walk down into, and along the base of, Dales Gorge is 3 hours (return). The Fortescue Falls Walk from the car park off Dales Road is only 800 m but the trail descends to the park's only permanent waterfall and will take approximately 2 hours (return).
Access: Via Karijini Drive off the Great Northern Highway 35 km south of Munjina Roadhouse.
Camping: The park's main camping sites are at Savannah campground (10 km south of Weano) and Dales camping area (off Dales Road near the gorge). Toilets are provided and caravans are permitted at both sites. Note: there are no camping areas, roads or trails in the southern section of Karijini.

Top to bottom: The Fortescue River runs through Millstream–Chichester National Park; Pool in Millstream–Chichester National Park.

Millstream-Chichester National Park

Ph: (08) 9184 5144

The traditional home and meeting place of the Yinjibarndi people, the region was taken over as a pastoral station in the early 1860s. The original homestead now serves as the park visitor centre. The Fortescue River flows through the southern corner of the park and the oasis-like area known as Millstream includes the verdant tropical spring of Chinderwarriner Pool. Native and exotic palms introduced by settlers flourish around this part of the park.

Walks in the Park: There are several excellent short informative walks from the visitor centre. Also try the 20 minute walk from Crossing Pool car park to Python Pool — a permanent waterhole at the base of the Chichester escarpment.
Access: Via the Roebourne–Wittenoom Road. The park's two entrances are on Snappy Gum Drive off Millstream–Yarraloola Road.
Camping: The park's campgrounds are at Deep Reach Pool and Crossing Pool off Snappy Gum Drive.

Pilbara Coast

In contrast to the sparsely populated stretch of land between Broome and Port Hedland, the mid-Pilbara coast includes a cluster of six towns within 50 km of each other. Roebuck and Cossack were pastoral towns first established in the 1860s while Dampier, Karratha and Wickham were constructed a century later to support the booming Hamersley mining industry. Like Port Hedland, Dampier is a major export point for iron ore and salt.

The Pilbara's rich resources do not end at the coast. Beyond are the islands of the Dampier Archipelago and the vast oil and gas deposits of the North West Shelf. The construction of the massive North Rankin natural gas platform and the 130 km pipeline connecting it to Dampier in 1980 was Australia's largest engineering project — employing over 4500 people and costing around $12 billion.

Cossack & Roebourne

Originally established as Mount Welcome Station in 1863, Roebourne quickly developed into the main administrative centre for the mining, pastoral and pearling industries of the north-west. Today, its many fine colonial buildings include the old hospital and post office (1887), the court house, gaol and police barracks, and the Union Bank (1889).

Thirteen kilometres north, at the mouth of the Harding River, Cossack (*above*) was the base for a large pearling fleet. After local reefs were fished out the town dwindled and by the 1950s had been virtually abandoned. A large-scale restoration project has brought the town's buildings back to life and it is now one of Western Australia's best preserved historical towns.

Karratha to the Coral Coast

Top Things to Do

1. Wander the convict-built buildings of old Port Gregory.
2. Tour historic Northampton.
3. Explore the Houtman Abrolhos Islands by sea or air.
4. Photograph wildflowers in the national parks and reserves south of Geraldton.
5. Walk among the amazing Pinnacles.
6. Revisit the life of the old west in historic Greenough.

The Cyclone Coast

The central Pilbara coast around Onslow is notorious for tropical cyclones, which visit this region on a regular basis. Since 1910, no fewer than eight severe cyclones have struck Onslow, resulting in the frequent re-building of the town's infrastructure and residences. Associated storm swells up to 5 m high have reshaped the coastline and inundated the town. The jetty has been destroyed five times and even Onslow's weather reporting station has been lost on several occasions. The most likely period for cyclone activity is between the months of December and March. Severe events such as Tropical Cyclone Vance (in 1999) can cause widespread damage and cut the highway.

Spring Has Sprung

The native flora of the Pilbara region is specially adapted to hot, arid conditions broken only by violent cyclonic deluges in summer.

For budding botanists, any time from July to September is a great time to visit the Pilbara and witness the magnificent spectacle of blooming wildflowers set against the backdrop of deep red earth. The iconic mulla mulla, Sturt's Desert Pea and over 65 species of wattle are just some of the region's multitude of flowering plants.

Karratha to the Coral Coast

After Karratha, Highway One farewells the coast once more and does not revisit the Indian Ocean again until Carnarvon, 647 km south. This is partially explained by the fact that this region is the most cyclone-prone section of the entire Australian coast (*see left*). For much of the journey, the western Pilbara landscape is alluvial, spinifex-studded plain relieved only by red sand hills, tall ant mounds and frequently dry river beds. The highway winds its way up to 100 km inland, but there are several coastal detours worth your time and fuel. About 60 km south of the Karratha Roadhouse, a track diverts a short way east to James Point. Camping is possible at this popular fishing and mud crabbing spot situated near the mouth of the Fortescue River bordering the Great Sandy Island Nature Reserve. Offshore are the gas and oil facilities of Barrow Island. The Montebello Island group to the north-west were used as a British atomic bomb testing site from 1952 to 1956.

Back on the highway, supplies and accommodation are available at the Fortescue River Roadhouse (Ph: (08) 9184 5126). From there it is 121 km to Cane River Conservation Park and the turn-off to the historic town of Onslow. The conservation park includes the contrasting sandstone ranges and granite outcrops of the Parry Range.

Northern Coral Coast

Western Australia's Coral Coast features a unique range of natural marine attractions to rival Queensland's Great Barrier Reef. The Coral Coast stretches from Exmouth to beyond Geraldton, offering magnificent reef viewing, diving and camping experiences. Several of the northern Coral Coast's offerings are world renowned — visitors from around the globe come to swim with Whale Sharks, the world's largest fish at Ningaloo Marine Park.

Onslow & Mackerel Islands

The original settlement of Onslow near the mouth of the Ashburton River was abandoned in 1925 due to regular flooding and a new town was established near Beadon Creek. Unfortunately re-location did not solve the problem — a seasonal battery of cyclone-driven winds and surging walls of water have assaulted the town ever since. The town was also the most southerly town bombed by Japanese forces during WWII when it was used as a US submarine refuelling base. Despite these provocations of war and nature, Onslow has retained a peaceful character and offers relaxed fishing and holiday facilities. The surviving ruins of the original town to the south-east include the stone (and thus cyclone-resistant) police station, gaol, post office and hospital.

Twenty-two kilometres offshore from Onslow is the sportfishing, diving and marine haven of the Mackerel Islands. These northern islands of the Coral Coast showcase pristine reefs and give visitors the chance to observe an abundance of marine life. Mackerel fishing tournaments are staged seasonally. An ex-mining camp has been remodelled as a holiday retreat on Thevenard Island and neighbouring Direction Island also has a single cabin for hire. Boat and light plane transfers are available from Onslow (Ph: (08) 9184 6444).

Exmouth

The Exmouth turn-off is 125 km south of the Nanutarra Roadhouse. The journey is 164 km via the small town of Learmonth — the site of a WWII air defence base used by the RAAF. Learmonth now also hosts the commercial airport for Exmouth and the Coral Coast. Exmouth itself was only constructed in 1964 as a support town for the nearby American naval communications station, but its establishment opened up the region's magnificent natural attractions to adventure tourism. The spectacular gorges and beaches of Cape Range National Park and the superb coral reefs of adjoining Ningaloo Marine Park are within easy reach of the town (*see facing page*). Whale and shark watching, coral viewing, diving and fishing tours can all be booked at the Exmouth Visitor Centre (Murat Road, Ph: (08) 9949 1176). Within the town there is a good selection of retail, dining and accommodation facilities.

Nineteen kilometres north of Exmouth on North West Cape stands Vlamingh Head Lighthouse, which once warned passing sailors of the treachery of the reef (tours available, Ph: 0407 970 647). The drive to the tip of the coastal range at Vlamingh Head provides sweeping views of the coast (including the town of Exmouth and the naval communications station sprawled out below the range). The soaring radio towers are still used to monitor the movement of US warships in the Indian Ocean and the western Pacific. Camping is possible at nearby Lighthouse Caravan Park (Ph: (08) 9949 1478) and Yardie Creek Homestead (Ph: (08) 9949 1389).

Top to bottom: Turquoise waters lap at the shores of Cape Range National Park; Diving with a Whale Shark at Ningaloo Marine Park; Teeming marine life offshore from Coral Bay.

Top to bottom: The stark and rugged plateaux of Cape Range National Park; Yardie Creek, Cape Range National Park.

Ningaloo Marine Park

Ph: (08) 9949 1676

Loggerhead Turtle

The Ningaloo Marine Park adjoins Cape Range National Park and comprises 300 km of pristine coastline and reef. The huge protected coral reef is Western Australia's largest. It is composed of 250 species of hard and soft corals and is a diving and snorkelling paradise. White beaches meet turquoise waters in one of the State's best coastal regions.

Coral Bay, in the southern section of the Ningaloo Marine Park is the perfect place to view the incredible phenomenon of mass coral spawning. This event occurs with remarkable punctuality each March and April, a week after the full moon. The corals simultaneously release millions of pink egg and sperm bundles, which float to the surface of the water and create a floating slick of coral spawn.

Reef Experiences: At Coral Bay, there are coral gardens an easy snorkel from shore, which may also be toured by glass-bottomed boat. Whale watching tours are available from Exmouth and Coral Bay from August to October. Turquoise Bay, 65 km, south of Exmouth is a favoured site for divers of all experience levels due to its ease and the reef's proximity to shore. At Pilgramunna Ledges, there are beautiful corals and masses of colourful reef fish thriving only 10 m offshore.

From March to June each year visitors from all over the world visit Ningaloo to enjoy an unforgettable marine experience — swimming or diving with the mighty Whale Shark, the planet's largest fish. This is the only easily accessible place in the world where Whale Sharks return in large numbers on a regular basis. These placid leviathans can grow to more than 12 m long and weigh in at over 11,000 kg.

Access: From Exmouth, Cape Range National Park and Coral Bay.

Manta Ray

Cape Range National Park

Ph: (08) 9949 1676

The elevated plateaux of Cape Range rises to heights of 314 m. The rugged limestone scarps reach down to the sea at Ningaloo Marine Park, providing a striking contrast between the range and reef environments. The park includes the high-walled ancient gorges of Yardie Creek and Mandu Mandu. Below the range lies a network of caves and tunnels that are home to a unique subterranean animal community. At Mangrove Bay, boardwalks, hides and shaded seating provide ideal vantage points for birdwatching and wildlife photography. Look out for kangaroos, Galahs, Emus, cockatoos and corellas. The best time to visit the park is between April and September. Milyering Visitor Centre is located 51 km from Exmouth on Yardie Road.

Walks in the Park: There is a half hour walk along Yardie Creek Gorge, which may be extended by following the trail along the northern side of the gorge. The Mandu Mandu Gorge Walk is approximately 3 km (2 hr return). Beach walking is possible at many points. Walking in Cape Range is not advised in summer when temperatures can become extreme.

Access: The coastal attractions of the park can be accessed along Yardie Road. The eastern side of the range can be accessed via the Charles Knife and Shothole Canyon Roads, south of Exmouth on the Minilya-Learmonth Road.

Camping: There are eight camping areas in the coastal section of the national park from Boat Harbour to Ned's Camp. All drinking water should be carried in and no fires are permitted. Gas barbecues are provided.

Flora from Broome to Perth

Despite its extensive deserts, Western Australia has amazing floral diversity. Each spring wildflower blooms begin in the north-west, spreading southwards along the coast to the South Western Botanical Province. In the north, many groups of plants are adapted to growing in poor soil and in arid regions. Their nectar-rich flowers are pollinated with the assistance of birds, insects and small mammals.

The coastal heathland is a vision of colour after good winter rain. A particularly stunning region for viewing and photographing wildflowers is the 180,000 ha Kalbarri National Park. Masses of feather flowers, daisies, mulla mulla, orchids and other ephemeral plants carpet the sandy soils beneath the branches of grevilleas, banksias, melaleucas and mulga. The dune systems beside Highway One from Nanutarra to Barradale also boast eye-grabbing wildflower displays in season. Inland regions are studded with spinifex, a tough spiky desert shrub that became the bane of early European explorers and their pack animals.

Inset: Heart-leaved Flame Pea. **Left to right:** Flame peas growing wild; Shark Bay wildflowers.

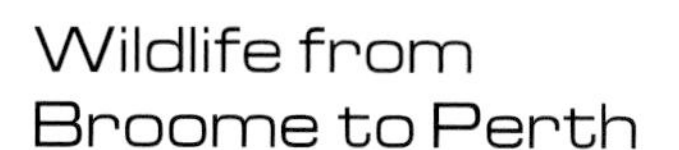

Wildlife from Broome to Perth

The State's native animals are equally hardy. Many inland species are adapted to survive long periods of drought, reproducing when rains bring renewed life to the desert. The coastal waters are also home to some of Australia's most magnificent, and viewer-friendly, wildlife. The pristine waters of Ningaloo Marine Park are superb for observing visiting Whale Shark and Humpback Whales and Shark Bay World Heritage Area is equally famous for the resident Bottlenose Dolphins of Monkey Mia.

Wildlife of Scrublands & Grasslands

Wild marsupials are readily seen grazing on the coastal scrub and grasslands from Broome to Perth. Imperious Red Kangaroos, smaller Euros and wallabies are among the many inhabitants of these regions. At Karijini National Park, in the spinifex-ridden Hamersley Range, kangaroos, Euros and Dingoes can often be seen around waterholes and creeks at dawn and dusk. The Peron Peninsula, in the Shark Bay World Heritage Area, and nearby islands are also sanctuaries for some of the State's rarer native animals, including the endangered Western Barred Bandicoot, the Shark Bay Mouse, Western Quoll (Chuditch), Mulgara, Malleefowl and Rufous Hare-wallaby. Project Eden was established within François Peron National Park to provide a safe haven for native creatures. An electric fence barrier deters introduced predators such as foxes.

Wildlife of Freshwater Habitats

The freshwater habitats found in the coastal and western inland regions are particularly well-populated with wildlife. Wetlands, billabongs, waterholes and creeks provide a relatively dependable source of food for pythons, frogs, lizards and birds — including an assortment of pigeons, wrens and finches.

Clockwise from left: Red Kangaroo; Australian Bustard; Mulgara.

Clockwise from left: Red-necked Avocet; Darter; Mertens' Water Monitor.

Clockwise from left: Brown Honeyeater feeding on a Red and Green Kangaroo Paw; Little Wattlebird; Featherflowers.

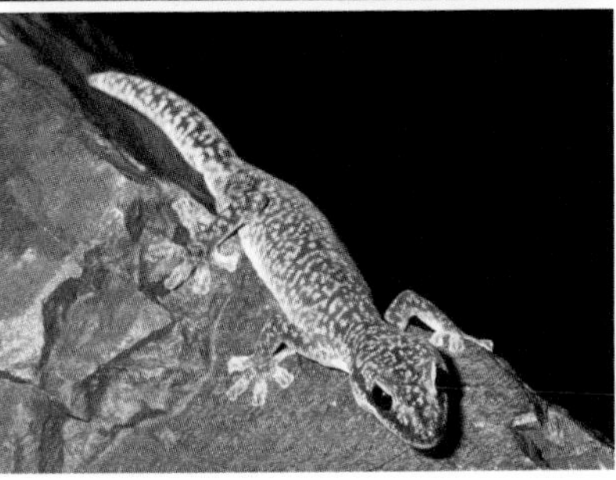

Clockwise from left: Black-footed Rock-wallaby; Magnificent Tree-frog; Marbled Velvet Gecko.

Clockwise from left: Pied Oystercatcher; Shore crab; Western Barred Bandicoot.

Wildlife of Coastal Heathlands

The low heathland common to many of the coastal regions south of Broome erupts into flower after winter rain, providing a smorgasbord of delights for a large range of nectar-eating birds. These are also rich nesting and breeding grounds. Nambung National Park and Kalbarri National Park are excellent wildlife and birdwatching areas. Kalbarri's wildflowers are a magnet for a huge variety of birds from late July to early summer. Many types of honeyeater are easily seen. Numerous native mammals at Kalbarri are nocturnal, but Western Grey Kangaroos and Emus graze in daylight hours. The inimitable Thorny Devil can also sometimes be seen moving around in the undergrowth. Watch also for the White-browed Scrubwren.

Wildlife of Ranges & Scarps

The stark plateaux, slopes and valleys of the Pilbara region may appear harsh and dry but summer cyclones and sporadic winter rains bring a flush of wildflowers; and run-off floods the dry creek beds and gorges. As the surrounding countryside quickly dries, life within the gorges remains comparatively lush. Ferns and mosses grow where moisture trickles over rock ledges, while permanent rockpools and stands of River Red Gums and paperbarks line the gorge floors. This creates a habitable environment for many different animals, but most species avoid the daytime heat. Reptiles shelter among the rocks and tall mounds protect grass-eating termites. The Pebble-mound Mouse retreats to tunnels concealed by stones it has heaped. Other tiny mammals hide under spinifex tussocks. Kangaroos, Euros and Dingoes (*above*) are also inhabitants of the rocky terrain; feeding and drinking at waterholes and creeks. Frogs and lizards live around rocks and mossy creek banks.

Wildlife of Coast & Islands

The coastal waters and islands from Broome to Perth are some of the country's best wildlife and marine animal observation areas. At Shark Bay World Heritage Area, along with the people-friendly dolphins of Monkey Mia, there are: marine turtles; Dugongs; Manta Rays; sharks; and Humpback Whales to be seen. Ningaloo Marine Park encompasses 260 km of coral reefs — home to a vast array of algae, fish, molluscs, crustaceans and other marine life. The mass spawning of reef corals after the March and April full moons coincides with a seasonal algal bloom that attracts plankton-feeding Manta Rays and Whale Sharks. These giant but harmless creatures congregate around Tantabiddi and Mangrove Bay. The Burrowing Bettong (*below*) has been extinct on mainland Australia since the early 1960s, but now survives on four islands off the coast of Western Australia — Bernier, Dorre, Barrow and Boodie.

Carnarvon

The coastline around Carnarvon was first known to the Dutch from 1616 as Eendrachsland in honour of Dirk Hartog's vessel, the *Eendracht*. William Dampier also visited the region in 1699, observing a healthy population of sharks and christening the surrounding waters Shark Bay.

Fruit of the Gascoyne

Although it may appear empty for much of the year, the Gascoyne River continues to flow under the sand. Around the hinterland, over 160 tropical fruit plantations tap its plentiful underground aquifers to produce avocados, macadamia nuts, mangoes, pineapples, melons, pecans, tomatoes and paw paws. Fresh fruit can be purchased direct from the many plantation stalls and sheds in the area.

Meet the Locals

The friendly wild dolphins of Monkey Mia have become the most famous of Western Australia's tourist attractions. In holiday periods, up to a thousand people per day line the shore at Monkey Mia in the hope of brushing shoulders with these marine celebrities. In the 1960s, a local woman named Mimm Watts first handfed the Bottlenose Dolphins that followed her husband's fishing boat and they have been coming back for more ever since.

Carnarvon & Shark Bay

South of Coral Bay, the highway crosses the Tropic of Capricorn. Everything about this part of the coast is wrought large, from 170 m cliffs to massive dunes. Lake MacLeod stretches almost the entire distance between road and ocean to Carnarvon. The 2075 km² shallow lake has been mined for salt and gypsite since 1965 and in places the mineral salt can reach up to 6 m deep. If you would like to take a closer look at the Lake MacLeod salt mining facility and loading port at Cape Cuvier, turn off the highway about 20 km north of Carnarvon (tours can be booked through the Carnarvon Visitor Centre, 11 Robinson St, Ph: (08) 9941 1146). En route, on the other side of the coastal dunes, are the Blowholes — a series of rock fissures and cavities that capture the ocean waves and send huge volumes of water shooting into the sky. The jets of spume can reach 20 m high. Freak or "king" waves are also known to occur here, so heed the signs warning of the dangers present.

North of the blowholes, Quobba Station has been converted into a family holiday retreat offering camping as well as chalets set in the dunes (Ph: (08) 9941 2036). On a cliff near the homestead there is a cairn dedicated to Australia's greatest wartime naval loss, the sinking of the HMAS *Sydney* and its crew of 645 men in a sea battle with the German raider *Kormoran* in 1941. Neither vessel has ever been located, but two lifeboats from the *Kormoran* came ashore here and legend has it that gold bullion and other relics from the ship are stashed somewhere in the dunes. If you are settling in for a long search, camping is possible at several locations along the coast road, including Red Bluff — a popular surfing destination where swells can rise to 6 m. The Herculean power of this coast is also demonstrated by the wreck of the *Korean Star*, still visible at the base of the Cape Cuvier cliffs. The salt cargo vessel was awaiting loading in 1988 when Cyclone Herbie struck, whipping up massive swells and dashing the *Korean Star* onto the rocks, breaking her in half.

Carnarvon

Broad streets, wildflowers and tropical plants characterise this refreshing town set on the mouth of the Gascoyne River. The 40 m wide main drag owes its existence to the huge turning circle once required by camel teams and is enhanced by palms, bouganvillea and hibiscus. Seasonal wildflowers, including mulla mullas, starflowers and Ashburton Pea, bloom throughout the region. One of the best ways to see Carnarvon is to take a historic train from the centre of town to the end of One Mile Jetty (built in 1897) just a few kilometres west. If you prefer to walk, a trail with interpretative signage runs parallel to the tramway. At 1493 m, the jetty is the longest in the north-west and there is a museum explaining its heritage on the shore nearby. Several of Carnarvon's tropical fruit plantations offer tours, including the Westoby Banana Plantation (500 Robinson Street, Ph: (08) 9941 8003).

Carnarvon also has a proud place in the history of space exploration. The town's tracking station and dish played a crucial role in communications with the Apollo moon missions, relaying live pictures and speech (including pioneer moonwalker Neil Armstrong's famous "giant leap for mankind" declaration) around the world. The installation ceased operations in 1987, but the dish, known locally as the "sugar scoop", now houses a museum in its base (open by request, contact Carnarvon Visitor Centre, Ph: (08) 9941 1146). The site also offers excellent views of Carnarvon and its tropical surrounds.

While much of Carnarvon's tourism is generated by its proximity to Shark Bay and Monkey Mia (*see left*), the inland region also rewards exploration. One hundred and sixty kilometres east, the Kennedy Range rises out of the Gascoyne river plains. The southern section of the range is national park and is rich in fossils (*see facing page*). Further east, (and accessible only by 4WD during the dry season), Mt Augustus outdoes Uluṟu as the world's largest single rock (*see facing page*).

Shark Bay

South of Carnarvon, the highway runs parallel to Shark Bay Marine Park (*see facing page*) along Disappointment Reach. The obvious disillusionment of an early surveyor, Captain Henry Denham, is reflected in other names around Shark Bay including Hopeless Reach, Useless Loop and Useless Inlet. It evokes no such reaction today. This World Heritage Area is one of Western Australia's most beautiful coastal regions and includes: François Peron National Park (*see facing page*); the Dugong community of Eagle Bluff; peculiar "living fossil" formations at Hamelin Pool; and the dolphin feeding grounds of Monkey Mia. Access to all of these natural attractions is via the Peron Peninsula Road from Overlander Roadhouse on the North West Coastal Highway.

Shark Bay Marine Park

Ph: (08) 9948 1366

Shark Bay's picturesque inlets and island shallows host a huge community of aquatic life that includes turtles, whales, sea snakes and, of course, sharks. Corals, sponges and other invertebrates are also present, together with a unique mix of tropical and temperate fish species. At the heart of Shark Bay's thriving ecosystem is seagrass — in fact, it has the largest area (and most species) of seagrass recorded anywhere in the world. Healthy seagrass habitats are crucial to the Dugong's (*above*) survival.

Marine Experiences: Commune with wild Bottlenose Dolphins at Monkey Mia. The dolphins visit the shallows voluntarily up to three times a day and rarely fail to appear. Morning is the most reliable time to see them. The park's superb diving and snorkelling sites include Monkey Rock, Broadhurst Corals and the wreck of the *Gudrun*. At Hamelin Pool, ancient microbacterial organisms cluster together at the water's edge to create fascinating formations known as stromatolites. South of Denham are the Dugong community (at Eagle Bluff) and the shell-carpeted Shell Beach.

Accommodation: A full range of accommodation is available at Denham and Monkey Mia on the shores of the marine park. Camping is possible at the old repeater station at Hamelin Pool.

Access: Travel 330 kilometres from Carnarvon via the township of Denham on the Peron Peninsula. Monkey Mia is 22 km from Denham. Commercial flights are also available to Shark Bay.

Kennedy Range National Park

Ph: (08) 9948 1208 or CALM (08) 9941 3754

After rain, this rugged wilderness area of raised sandstone comes alive with wildflowers (including fields of everlastings). Steep gorges, cliffs and ancient dune fields make for a memorable camping experience. Aboriginal ceremonial sites and engravings record a history of occupation lasting more than 20,000 years.

Walks in the Park: The 1 km trail from the northern visitor area runs into a gorge, waterfalls (during wet season) and pool. The trail from the campground leads deep into the gorge.

Access: Travel 150 km east of Carnarvon via Gascoyne Junction.

Camping: There is a basic bush camping area off the main park track.

François Peron National Park

Ph: (08) 9948 1208

Once a pastoral station, this national park is named for the French zoologist who travelled to this coast as part of Nicolas Baudin's 1801 scientific expedition. The old sheep station homestead in the park's southern section is open for inspection and accessible by 2WD vehicle. However, a 4WD is required to access the park's coastline where Shark Bay's incredible range of marine life can be observed. Dotted around the park are gypsum claypans known as birridas. Some, like Big Lagoon, have been breached by the sea to form inlets.

Walks in the Park: Beach walking is possible at many points and there is a 45 minute walking trail around the homestead and outbuildings. Walking in François Peron National Park is not advised in summer when temperatures can be extreme.

Access: The park entrance is 10 km from Denham.

Camping: Bush camping areas with toilets and barbecues are available at Gregories, Cape Peron, Bottle Bay, Herald Bight and Big Lagoon. Camps are only accessible by 4WD vehicle.

Mount Augustus National Park

Ph: (08) 9948 1208

The solitary rock of Mt Augustus rises 717 m over a dry, scrubby sand plain. Mt Augustus is about 8 km long and covers an area of 4,795 ha — twice the size of Uluru.

Walks & Drives in the Park: There are numerous walks and drives around Mt Augustus offering different perspectives on the rock.

Access: Travel 490 km from Carnarvon via Gascoyne Junction.

Camping: No camping in the park, but camping accommodation, meals and supplies are available at Mt Augustus Outback Tourist Resort (Ph: (08) 9943 0527) and Cobra Station (Ph: (08) 9943 0565).

SHARK BAY to Perth

Zuytdorp Cliffs

The Dutch ship *Zuytdorp* was bound for Batavia from Holland in 1712 carrying 250 people and cargo that included 250,000 guilders in newly minted coins. The voyage ended in tragedy at the hand of these unforgiving, jagged cliffs south of Shark Bay. In 1927 artefacts such as coins, broken bottles and breech blocks were found by a local stockman, Tom Pepper, who was working above the wreck. The vessel's remains were later discovered in the treacherous waters below. It is not conclusively known whether any of the passengers or crew survived.

Grim History

The name of the coastline around Geraldton recalls one of the most gruesome incidents in maritime history. It occurred after the Dutch East India Company vessel *Batavia* was shipwrecked on a reef in the nearby Houtman Abrolhos Islands in 1629. The ship's captain, Francisco Pelsaert, took a longboat and set sail for Java to seek assistance. On his return he discovered that 125 of the crew and passengers left in the islands had been tortured and murdered by a band of sadistic mutineers. Two of these men were left marooned on the Australian mainland near the mouth of the Hutt River as punishment, becoming Australia's first "settlers". They disappeared without trace and their eventual fate is unknown.

The journey from Geraldton to Perth takes in an enormously varied region of coastline, much of which is protected by national park and nature reserves. Midway between Shark Bay and Geraldton, the powerful Murchison River meets the ocean at Gantheaume Bay in Kalbarri National Park. West of Geraldton are the fascinating Houtman Abrolhos Islands — the site of one of maritime history's most grisly episodes. Further south the Pinnacles — troops of limestone pillars, rise out of Nambung National Park — forming one of the world's most unusual landscapes.

Shark Bay to Geraldton

From the Australian mainland's most westerly point at Steep Point, an unbroken stretch of cliffs pounded by Indian Ocean swells extend 160 km to Gantheaume Bay. These imposing rock walls rise to a height of nearly 170 m and are named the Zuytdorp Cliffs for a Dutch trading vessel that broke up on a nearby reef in the early 18th century (*see left*). Today much of this coast is inaccessible by road, but scenic flights can be chartered from Kalbarri over the Zuytdorp Cliffs and the Murchison gorges.

Kalbarri National Park protects the lower reaches of the Murchison River as it carves its way through spectacular red and white banded gorges to the ocean. The road to the Kalbarri township is sealed and the main park roads are suitable for all vehicles. The Kalbarri Rainbow Jungle Parrot Breeding Centre is a beautifully landscaped sanctuary featuring the largest free flight parrot aviary in Australia (Red Bluff Road, Ph: (08) 9937 1248). The Kalbarri Wildflower Centre (882 Kalbarri-Ajana Road, Ph: (08) 9937 1229) has over 140 wildflower species spread over 16 ha. Guided tours offer a great chance to identify and learn about the huge variety of native flowers to be seen while travelling this section of the State. Kalbarri's river and ocean setting also makes it a brilliant destination for watersports, including canoeing, waterskiing, yachting and rowing. Camel rides, horse treks, abseiling and rock climbing are also on offer.

Kalbarri National Park

Ph: (08) 9937 1104

The distinctive rock formations, gorges and cliff faces of Kalbarri National Park provide inspiring views and photographic opportunities for its visitors. There is also a stunning number of wildflowers in the park (which bloom from July onward) and plentiful fauna (including Emus, wallabies and the fearsomely armoured but harmless Thorny Devil). Camping is not permitted in the park.

A 2 hour nature trail at Mushroom Rock offers a self-guided introduction to the region's coastal geology and plant life. The huge headland of Red Bluff overlooks a fantastic swimming and surfing beach. At Rainbow Valley, compacted minerals in sand and silt have created multi-coloured layers of rock. Panoramic views of the coast can be seen from the Pot Alley car park and Eagle Gorge. The remnant cliff formations at Shellhouse and Grandstand are highly photogenic, as are Island Rock and Natural Bridge. There is an excellent half day (8 km) clifftop walk between Eagle Gorge and Natural Bridge.

The northern section of Kalbarri National Park has several outstanding natural features around the Loop — where the Murchison River doubles back and changes course (a 7 km walk leads down to the Loop and back up again). Admire the wonderfully framed river scene through the rock arch of Natures Window. In the southern section, Hawks Head, Ross Graham Lookout and Z Bend provide superb gorge walks and views.

Top to bottom: Natures Window; Murchison River.

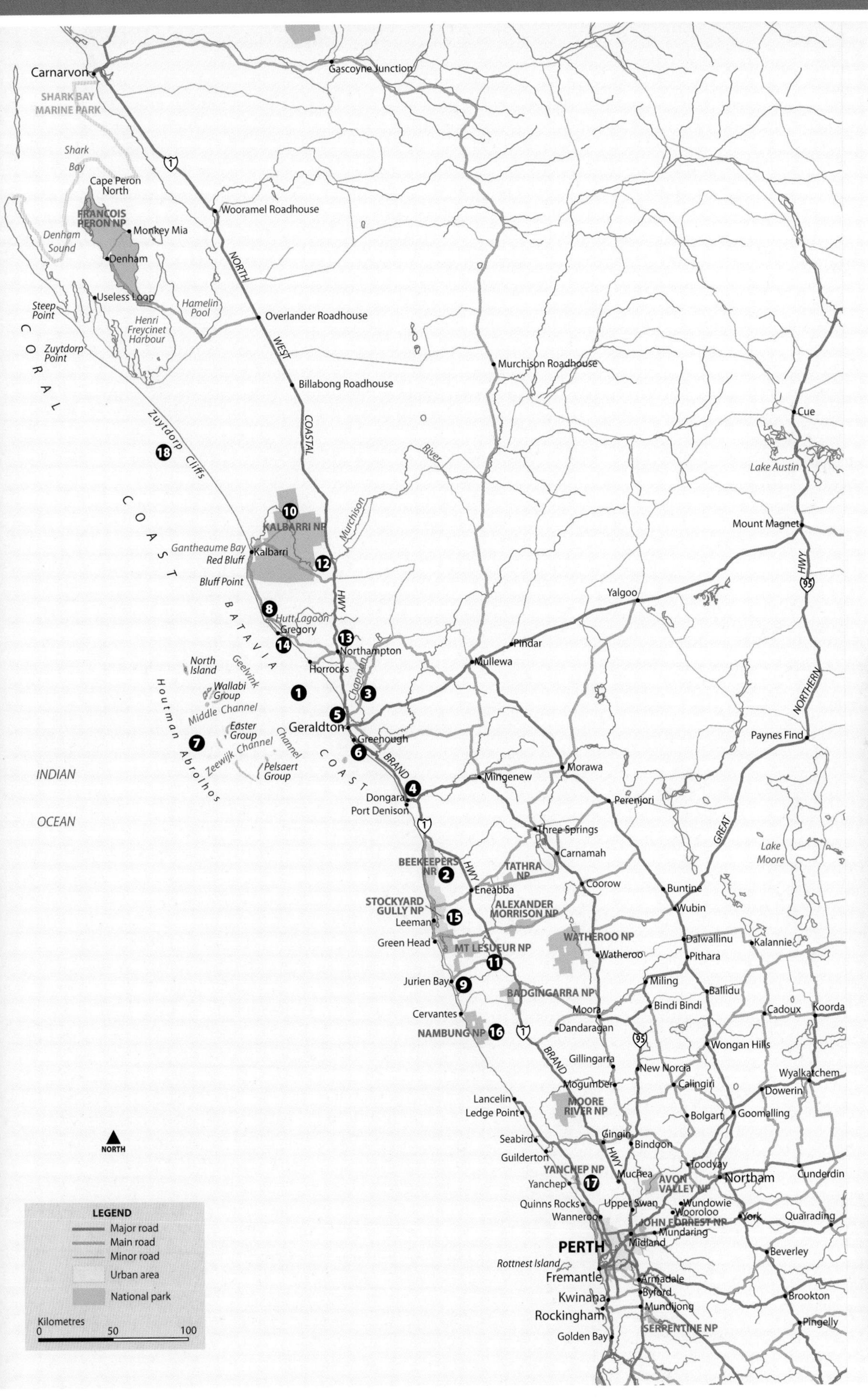

Feature Localities

1 Batavia Coast
2 Beekeepers Nature Reserve
3 Chapman River Valley
4 Dongara
5 Geraldton
6 Greenough
7 Houtman Abrolhos Islands
8 Hutt Lagoon
9 Jurien Bay
10 Kalbarri National Park
11 Mount Lesueur National Park
12 Murchison River & Gorges
13 Northampton
14 Port Gregory
15 Stockyard Gully National Park
16 The Pinnacles, Nambung National Park
17 Yanchep National Park
18 Zuytdorp Cliffs

Geraldton to Perth
Top Things to Do

1. Wander the convict-built buildings of old Port Gregory.
2. Explore historic Northampton.
3. Tour the remote Houtman Abrolhos Islands by sea or air.
4. Photograph wildflowers in the national parks and reserves south of Geraldton.
5. Walk among the amazing Pinnacles.
6. Revisit the life of the old west in historic Greenough.

Houtman Abrolhos Islands

The Houtman Abrolhos are a chain of 122 islands reaching south from North Island to the Pelsaert Group, separated from the coast by the Geelvink Channel. They lie 60 km west of Geraldton and once formed part of the Australian mainland. The islands are rich in birdlife and marine mammals including Australian Sea-lions (*above centre*). They also boast spectacular coral gardens perfect for diving and snorkelling.

Accommodation is restricted to a colony of professional lobster fishermen who have established bases on a number of the islands (*above*). Scenic flights, ecotours and both diving and snorkelling charters operate from Geraldton. It is also possible to dive on the wreck of the *Batavia*, which lies in 4–6 m of clear water off the Pelsaert Group.

Geraldton to Perth

South of Kalbarri, the road follows the coast past the magnificent seascapes of Red Bluff and Bluff Point before reaching the captivating old port village of Gregory. The region was first noted by George Grey in 1839 on his epic walk back to Perth after the loss of his boats on an expedition to the North West Cape. Later exploration by Augustus Gregory revealed prospective farming land and the presence of lead ore in the Murchison River. His brother Francis Gregory returned to the area in 1852 with a group of 60 convicts to be hired out as labourers to the pioneer miners and pastoralists. A hiring depot was established at nearby Lynton and over three years the men constructed a settlement. Despite suffering from scurvy, the quality of their masonry was such that the limestone buildings still exist today. The structures, including the superintendent's house, are near the shores of Hutt Lagoon — a lake distinguished by its bright pink waters (attributable to the presence of beta-carotene, which is now mined for use in food colourings).

Aside from the strange properties of its lagoon, the Hutt River has achieved a sort of infamy in Australian history for two reasons. It is thought to be the place where Captain Pelsaert dumped two of the *Batavia* mutineers on the Australian mainland in 1629, thus creating Australia's first European residents. The Houtman Abrolhos, where the mutiny took place, lie directly west of the coast (*see below left*). The region is also where a farmer dubbing himself Prince Leonard declared his secession from Australia in 1970, establishing the Sovereign State of Hutt River Province and creating his own visas and currency. Despite a complete lack of legal status, the self-exiled prince has successfully milked the principality's tourism potential and today it includes gift shops, tea rooms, a post office and camping facilities.

Geraldton & Surrounds

The highway to Geraldton passes through Northampton, a historically interesting village on the edge of the wheatbelt, which was once a centre for the region's lead and copper mining industry. On the second Saturday of October each year it now hosts one of Australia's most peculiar festivals — the Airing of the Quilts. This is not, as you might imagine, a communal display of dirty doonas but a colourful exhibition of the art of patchwork quilt making (accompanied by much merriment and street parades). To the east, on the outskirts of Geraldton, are the farms and wineries of the Chapman River Valley. Located on Champion Bay, Geraldton has evolved from its origins as a 19th century mining port to a modern commercial centre that retains its maritime flavour. At the start of November each year Geraldton celebrates the opening of the lobster fishing season with a festive "blessing of the boats" at Fisherman's Wharf. The Batavia Coast Marina incorporates boardwalks, residential and restaurant facilities as well as the state of the art WA Museum, Geraldton. A replica of the *Batavia* longboat used by Captain Pelsaert floats on the waters in front of the museum (open daily, 1 Museum Place, Ph: (08) 9921 5080). Geraldton's generous array of white sandy beaches, including St George's Beach and Sunset Beach, are famous among windsurfers.

South to Perth

The Brand Highway leads through the historic Greenough (*see facing page*) to Dongara, a lobster port and holiday town. The scale of the lobster industry on this coast is reflected by the marina storage facility which has a capacity of 35,000 kg of live lobster.

South of Port Denison, the coast is protected by a string of nature reserves and national parks that reach much of the way to Perth. The most famous is Nambung National Park, which features the remarkable Pinnacles (*see facing page*), but all are worth exploring and the Indian Ocean Drive provides easy access. The vast range of wildflowers that grow from Beekeepers Nature Reserve to Lancelin (nearly 200 km south) makes this region the highest honey producing area in the State. At Stockyard Gully National Park near Leeman, subterranean caverns created by an underground river system are home to colonies of bats (4WD access only). Adjoining Mount Leseur National Park offers an 18 km scenic drive with signed roadside stops enabling viewing of some of the park's 820 species of shrubs and plants. To its south, the popular but secluded resort town of Jurien Bay is a magnificent base for viewing the huge diversity of marine creatures that reside in these waters. Charter a cruise to view Australian Sea-lions, dive the reefs or explore islands off the coast. Excellent private boating facilities are also available.

It is possible to continue down the coast to Yanchep and Perth, but the 75 km track linking Nambung National Park to Lancelin is 4WD only. Yanchep National Park is located only 51 km north of Perth and features tours of Crystal Cave and Lake Wagardu.

The Pinnacles The sensational shifting sandscapes of the Pinnacles, Nambung National Park.

Nambung National Park – The Pinnacles

Ph: (08) 9652 1911

The surreal, statuesque limestone formations known as the Pinnacles are irresistible to anyone with a camera. Found in the Nambung National Park, 245 km north of Perth, literally thousands of these marvels of natural erosion rise up to 4 m out of yellow sands, creating an other-worldly landscape.

Over time the Pinnacles have been periodically covered over and then once more revealed by the wind-driven sand. Evidence suggests that they were visible some 6000 years ago at the time of Aboriginal occupation of the area and later submerged until their re-appearance only a few hundred years ago. See and photograph them now before they disappear once more! Dawn and dusk, when the spires cast their long and mysterious shadows in the rippling sand, is the best time for photography.

Walks in the Park: It is possible to go for a 2–3 hour walk into the coloured desert areas, however the walks are not signposted so talk with a ranger first. An adequate supply of water, a compass, good walking shoes and a hat are essential. Picnic areas and barbecues are provided at Kangaroo Point and Hangover Bay, which also has an excellent swimming beach. Dolphins and Australian Sea-lions are sometimes seen from Hangover Bay.

Access: Via the town of Cervantes.

Camping: No camping is permitted in the park but a variety of accommodation and facilities are available at Cervantes.

Greenough

South of Geraldton on the Brand Highway is Greenough, one of Australia's best preserved historical towns. Settled in 1856 on the promise of the region's ideal wheat farming conditions, Greenough thrived. But by the turn of the century, a combination of cyclones, floods and plant disease ravaged the area's farms and saw the township virtually abandoned. Greenough seemed destined to disappear completely until a dedicated restoration program was implemented in the 1980s. A heritage trail through this museum town leads to no less than 36 charming stone buildings, including the original hotel — the Hampton Arms. Greenough Hamlet, a collection of 11 buildings administered by the National Trust, is open daily.

Geraldton

A 34 m tall, red and white striped lighthouse stands on Point Moore (*right*) and has become an icon for the town of Geraldton. The Geraldton region's close connection with the life of the sea has been present since Dutch explorers first sailed these waters in the 17th century.

PERTH

& THE JOURNEY TO ADELAIDE

6

Southern Hairy-nosed Wombat

The city of Perth developed in isolation from its eastern counterparts, expanding from convict-built beginnings to a trading port before harvesting wealth from the goldfields of Kalgoorlie and Coolgardie. The Swan River provides a postcard-perfect setting for this relaxed, green-fringed city. Beyond lies the over-sized splendour of the South West — Indian Ocean beaches sporting towering cliffs and gargantuan waves, hectares of high-yield vineyards and some of the world's tallest trees. Near Esperance, the Fitzgerald Biosphere protects a huge region overflowing with the richest assortment of flora species on the planet. Much fauna too, although often inconspicuous, is undeterred by the dry woodlands of the south and the coast of the Bight. The endangered Southern Hairy-nosed Wombat and the Numbat are both residents of this stretch of wilderness. Although seemingly empty, the Nullarbor conceals its own bounty of secrets — hidden limestone sinkholes have preserved fossilised remains of Australia's prehistoric megafauna. For many, crossing the plain still ranks as a rite of passage for coming to terms with the sheer scale of the continent. At Head of Bight, nursing Humpback Whales cruise close to shore. On the other side of the desert, the Eyre Peninsula and Flinders Ranges beckon. Drink your fill of these natural delights but leave room for a glass of wine in the famous Barossa Valley on your way to Adelaide.

Left: The Cape Leeuwin Lighthouse.

PERTH & Surrounds

Bordering the Indian Ocean on the continent's south-west edge is Australia's most isolated State capital. That its residents do not speak Dutch is due only to unfavourable reports made to the government in Amsterdam by Captain Willem De Vlamingh after his explorations of the region in 1696. De Vlamingh's expedition followed those of compatriots Willem Janszoon (1606), Dirk Hartog (1616) and Abel Tasman (1644), the first Europeans to map coastal parts of the Great Unknown South Land. De Vlamingh arrived on his ship the *Duyfken* in mid-summer when the landscape was at its driest — it has been suggested that if he had arrived in mid-winter, his observations of a temperate port with a broad river whose banks were ablaze with wildflowers may have encouraged the Dutch to stake the land as their own. Instead, it was the British who would eventually lay claim to these shores and establish Australia's last penal colony on the Swan River in 1829.

A Natural Boom Town

Developed on land first occupied by the Nyoongar people, Perth's slow early growth was accelerated by gold mining booms in the desert plain settlements of Coolgardie and Kalgoorlie in the early 1890s. Seventy-five years later a further boom in this resource-rich State transformed a large country town into a modern commercial centre. Blessed with environs that founder Captain James Stirling thought to be "as beautiful as anything of this kind I have ever witnessed", Perth remains a city of natural splendour. The glistening waters of the Swan River sweep by en route to the ocean, providing a stunning foreground to the CBD. Across the river, the wildflower-carpeted bushland and botanic gardens of Kings Park invite visitors to appreciate the city from a different perspective.

Perth is home to most of Western Australia's sparsely developed population, but many who live here have roots overseas. Over half of Perth's million-strong population were either born, or have at least one parent who was born, in another country. Many emigrated from Great Britain and Europe, seeking employment opportunities during the early post-World War II period; but there is also a high proportion of citizens with South African, Indian and Asian backgrounds. The importance of their cultural contribution is readily apparent. Mediterranean and European-influenced architecture abounds, from inner city churches and residences to the restaurants of the busy entertainment precinct of Northbridge.

Much of the region's early history is still in evidence at Fremantle, once Western Australia's major city and Perth's original port. Twenty kilometres downstream from Perth, many of Fremantle's magnificently preserved old town buildings and warehouses have been cleverly transformed into hotels, museums, galleries, restaurants and shops.

Matilda Bay And the Swan River, looking north to Perth's CBD.

Perth & Surrounds
Top Things to Do

1. View Perth and its environs from the green expanses of Kings Park.
2. Cruise the Swan River by day or night.
3. Follow one of four themed walking trails through the city of Perth.
4. Sound the Swan Bells in Barrack Square by the river's edge.
5. Wander the streets of Fremantle — Western Australia's first port.
6. Explore Rottnest Island.
7. View the kangaroos on Heirisson Island.

Perth's Climate

In winter, Perth has a temperate climate that is the envy of much of Australia. But in summer temperatures soar to such feverish heights that they are only relieved with the breath of the Fremantle Doctor. This famous breeze sweeps in across the city on many a hot summer afternoon, instantly reducing temperatures.

Swan Bells

At Barrack Square is one of Perth's most striking monuments — Swan Bells. Within the glass spire you will find the original bells of London's St Martin-in-the-Fields, which once heralded the homecoming of Captain James Cook. Ascend the tower or try your hand at tintinnabulation.

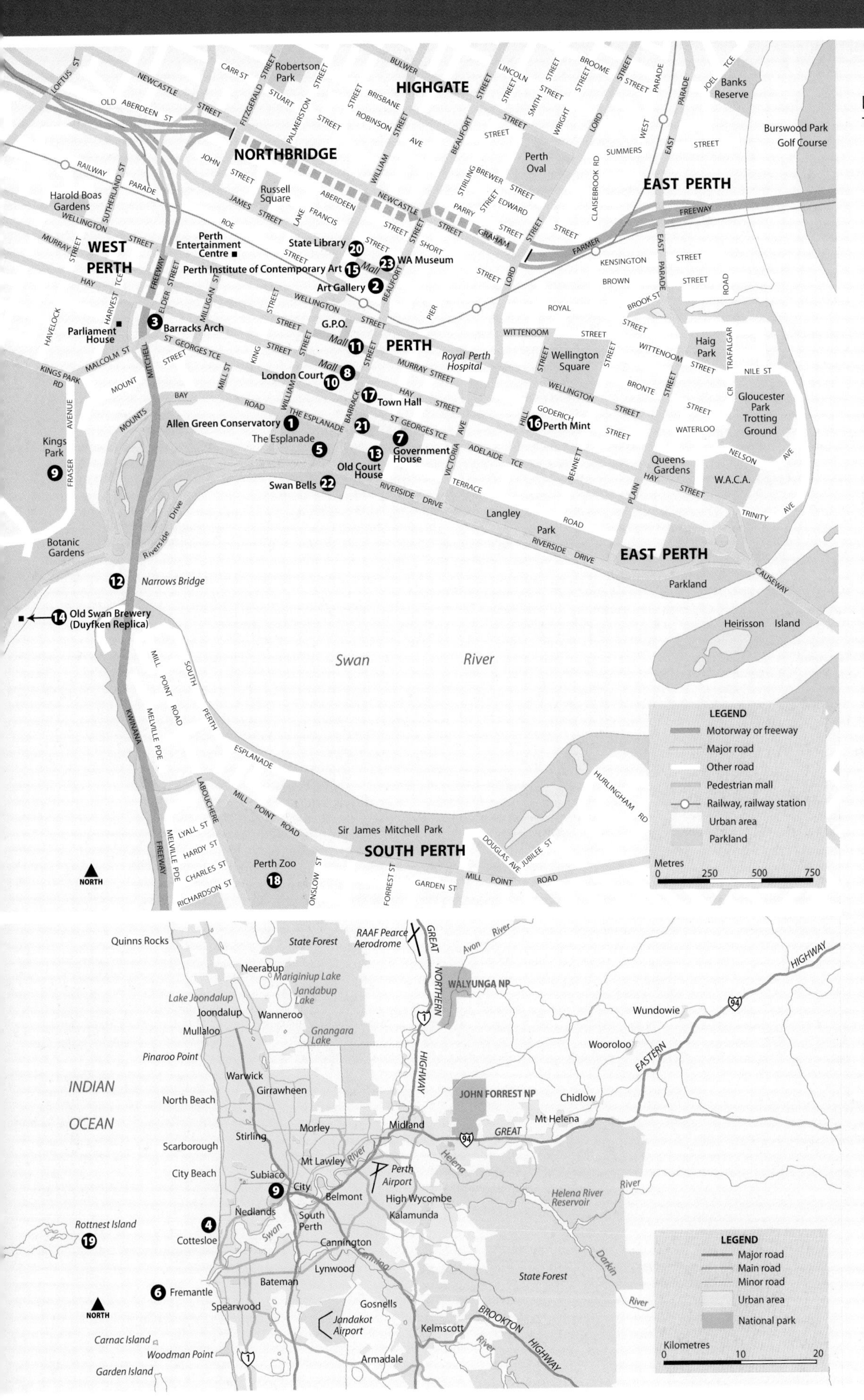

Feature Localities

1 Allen Green Conservatory
2 Art Gallery of Western Australia
3 Barracks Arch
4 Cottesloe Beach
5 Esplanade Reserve
6 Fremantle
7 Government House
8 Hay Street Mall
9 Kings Park
10 London Court
11 Murray Street Mall
12 Narrows Bridge
13 Old Court House
14 Old Swan Brewery (*Duyfken* Replica)
15 Perth Institute of Contemporary Art
16 Perth Mint
17 Perth Town Hall
18 Perth Zoo
19 Rottnest Island
20 State Library
21 Stirling Gardens
22 Swan Bells, Barrack Square
23 Western Australian Museum

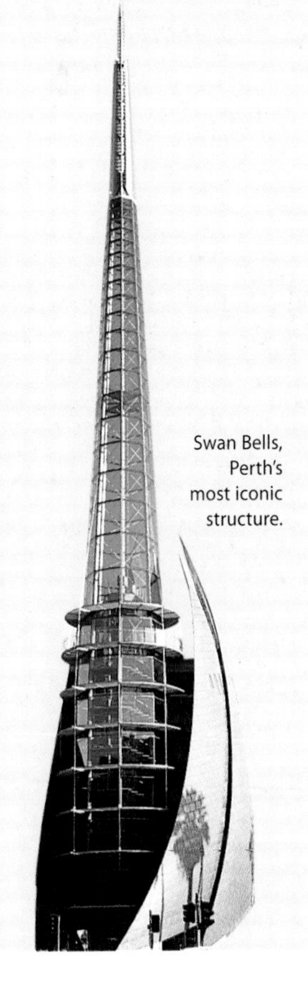

Swan Bells, Perth's most iconic structure.

Perth City

Top Things to Do

1. Tour Perth Mint.
2. Photograph Barracks Arch.
3. Explore the river parklands on the southern edge of the CBD.
4. Dine out in Northbridge.
5. Visit the galleries, museums and exhibition spaces of Perth Cultural Centre.
6. Travel through time to "ye olde" England in London Court.

Perth – Past & Present

Prosperity born of abundant natural resources has seen Perth grow from modest colonial beginnings to a multi-towered contemporary city. A commitment to creating structures of elegant permanence has been evident since first European settlement. Today, Perth's heritage buildings tastefully maintain their place in the midst of a modern metropolis.

Perth City

Perth is one of Australia's best cities to explore on foot. For a great introduction to the city's heritage and layout, follow one of the four City Walking Trails. These themed walks may be taken with a guide (departing from the i-City information kiosk on Murray Street Mall near Forrest Place) or as self-guided tours. Blue Central Area Transit (CAT) buses connect with the trails at various points and also provide a continuous free service around Perth's major landmarks, cultural centres, inner city suburbs and historical sites of interest.

Many of Perth's best heritage buildings are open to the public. At Perth Mint, the oldest operating mint in Australia, you can view Australia's largest collection of gold nuggets and watch gold ingots being poured (corner Hay and Hill Streets, East Perth, Ph: (08) 9421 7222). The restored former police courts are now a wing of the Art Gallery of Western Australia and house the gallery's heritage collection. The city's most elderly surviving building is the Old Court House that stands in the Supreme Court Gardens in Barrack Street — it was erected in 1836. Perth Town Hall, the only civic building of its type in Australia to have been built by convicts, was once used as a camel stable (corner Barrack and Hay Streets, tours by appointment, Ph: (08) 9461 3444). On the corner of Malcolm and Elder Streets is an interesting freestanding tower known as Barracks Arch — all that remains of a guards' barracks that once housed officers appointed to protect the public from convict crime. Public outcry saved the historic arch from demolition in 1966.

Perth's liveliest urban area is Northbridge, which attracts hordes of diners and dancers to its many bars, restaurants, hotels and nightclubs. Northbridge also offers a rich mix of cultural fare — the art gallery and its near neighbours: the Western Australian Museum; Perth Institute for Contemporary Arts (PICA); Blue Room Theatre; and State Reference Library are situated in a precinct adjacent to Perth Train Station and James Street Mall, dubbed the Perth Cultural Centre.

Narrows Bridge, once Australia's longest bridge, crosses the region of the Swan River known as Perth Water and links the city with the parklands, restaurants, and shops of South Perth. The impressive Perth Zoo, which includes two rescued Cambodian Sun Bears, is on the banks of the river only five minutes walk from the ferry terminus at Mends Street Jetty (Perth Zoo is open daily, 20 Labouchere Street, Ph: (08) 9474 0444). A regular public ferry service departing from the Barrack Street Jetty crosses the river to South Perth (Ph: 13 62 13). Commercial boats also operate from here offering river and Rottnest Island cruises. Adjoining Barrack Square is home to the Swan Bells (open daily except Good Friday and Christmas Day, Ph: (08) 9218 8183).

Open Shopping Spaces

The relaxed, car-free zones of Hay Street Mall (*above left*) and Murray Street Mall provide a spacious shopping zone in the heart of Perth. Linked by historic arcades, the malls are lined with chain stores, fashion boutiques, restaurants and cafés. On weekends, street entertainers and artists transform the malls into public performance spaces.

London Court, linking Hay Street Mall and the commercial precinct of St Georges Terrace, is a unique recreation of Elizabethan London (*above right*). This fascinating step back in time was built in 1937 by wealthy goldfields businessman Claude Albo de Bernales. At each end are replica Tudor clocks that mark the hour with miniature mechanised recreations of a jousting tournament and St George slaying the dragon. Lining the court are tiny shops with ornate facades, balconies and window boxes. Even the rubbish bins are decorated with lions and unicorns.

Life on the Swan

Named for the Black Swans seen by Willem De Vlamingh upon its banks, the mighty Swan River links Perth with the Darling Ranges to the north and the Indian Ocean to the south. The river provides Perth with its extraordinarily beautiful waterfront setting and offers an abundance of recreational opportunities. Cruising the Swan River under azure skies by ferry, motorboat, sail or oar is an integral part of Perth life (and the ideal way to get a feel for the city). Despite the constant traffic, you might glimpse a pod of dolphins venturing upriver in search of fish. Waterbirds, including the famous Black Swan, are seen along the waterways and banks. The swans so impressed De Vlamingh in 1696 that he attempted to take two live specimens back to Holland to parade before the Royal Dutch Court. The swans did not survive the journey, but a replica of his boat (the *Duyfken*) is moored at the Old Swan Brewery on Mounts Bay Road (*above left*).

Riverside Gardens

Occupying riverland reclaimed in the 1880s, the Esplanade Reserve was the site of the proclamation of Western Australian self-government in 1890. Its 4.8 ha of public gardens define the southern edge of the CBD and are the venue for Perth's annual Anzac Day parade. It has also been the traditional rallying point for public protest marches. The Allen Green Conservatory (*above*) was established in the reserve to celebrate the State's 150th anniversary of foundation. The conservatory's glass pyramid nurtures numerous tropical and exotic plant species.

The neighbouring Stirling Gardens are the oldest in Perth and feature several interesting works of public art, including Joan Walsh-Smith's and Charles Smith's bronze kangaroos bounding along the St Georges Terrace border (*below*) and historic buildings (including the Old Court House). East along the river is Langley Park — the site of Perth's first aerodrome.

Kings Park

Set on 400 ha directly adjoining the Swan River and overlooking Perth's CBD are the broad green expanses of Kings Park, incorporating Perth Botanic Gardens. Here on the gentle slopes of Mount Eliza, nature's offerings are unrestrained by city streets. Each spring, the Kings Park Wildflower Festival delivers a glorious celebration of colour and scent.

Stirling Gardens One of several inviting green spaces around the Perth CBD.

Fremantle & Perth Coast
Top Things to Do

1. Relax with a coffee on Freo's South Terrace — "Cappuccino Strip".
2. Take a ferry to Rottnest Island, hire a bike and circumnavigate the coast.
3. View the relics of Australia's earliest shipwrecks at the Shipwreck Gallery.
4. Check out the Fremantle Markets.

A Taste of History

Affectionately known as the "Cappuccino Strip", Fremantle's South Terrace is the city's premier dining and leisure precinct. From early morning to the late evening hours, outdoor cafés and restaurants attract crowds of locals and visitors to sip, sup and survey the passing pedestrian traffic. For some, relaxing here with a coffee below ornate 19th century verandahs is a way of life.

Fremantle Markets' 150 stalls are housed in an original market building built over a century ago and are a mandatory Freo experience (cnr South Tce and Henderson St). A recent addition to Fremantle's many shopping options are the E Shed Markets on the waterfront at Victoria Quay. The old cargo store houses an eclectic range of crafts, furniture and souvenir stalls as well as international eateries, outdoor cafés and children's amusements.

The Round House

Perth's original convicts built the imposing 5 m stone walls of the colony's first prison in 1831. It is the oldest building in Western Australia and was designed by civil engineer, H W Reveley. Below the Round House is a tunnel — constructed in 1837 to provide bay whalers with access from the original port at Bathers Beach to the town. The Round House is open daily and tours are conducted by volunteer guides (10 Arthur Head, Ph: (08) 9336 6897).

Fremantle & Perth Coast

There is no better place in Western Australia to gain an appreciation of the State's maritime past than Fremantle or "Freo" as the locals call it. Walking streets lined with restored stone buildings and taking in the historic port waterfront provides a fascinating insight to Perth's early development. Located only 20 minutes south of the city near the mouth of the Swan River, Fremantle is known as *Manjaree* to local Aborigines. Captain Charles Howe Fremantle raised the Union Jack on Arthur Head in 1829, pre-empting French annexation and claiming possession of Australia's west coast for Britain. His action opened the way for convict transportation and colonial development. Only a month later, Captain James Stirling arrived with the first European settlers aboard the *Parmelia*. The distinctive twelve-sided prison erected two years later stands on the headland at the western end of High Street and is known as the Round House (*see bottom left*). While Perth was established as a farming community, Fremantle became the Swan River colony's first port and many of the original convict-built structures can still be seen today.

Much of Fremantle's architectural heritage fell into dilapidation before a flurry of renovation (prior to the America's Cup yachting challenge in 1987) saw the city's rich past revived. Over the ensuing decades hotels, restaurants and shops have flourished and many former warehouses and port buildings have been reincarnated as museums, galleries and artist studios. More than 120 buildings in central Fremantle are heritage-classified. Today, Fremantle is a bustling cultural centre with a festive spirit that sets it apart from a more sedate atmosphere in Perth. The port is also the place many Western Australians first set foot on Australian soil and this cultural diversity is reflected in Fremantle's cuisine, arts and sporting endeavours. The Welcome Walls at the Western Australian Maritime Museum on Victoria Quay (*see facing page*) are a permanent tribute to the contribution made by immigrants to the State's development. Fremantle remains the capital's major port and is the main departure point for Rottnest Island — a leisurely, 30 minute cruise by ferry.

Fremantle Town

The port is so awash with sightseeing possibilities it can be difficult to know where to start. A ride on the free local CAT bus service provides an excellent overview of Fremantle's layout and major attractions. The bus runs every 10 minutes; there are 26 stops throughout the town and maps of the route are available at the Fremantle Visitor Centre on Kings Square in High Street. The town centre spreads out from the old port area at Arthur Head, with the main café strip of South Terrace leading to Fremantle Market. High Street Mall and Kings Square form the heart of the town with the impressive Fremantle Town Hall facing King's Square. Just west of the CBD on The Terrace is Old Fremantle Prison. Since it was finally closed in 1991 after 140 years of service, doing time within this vast edifice has become a Fremantle favourite. If you fancy being locked up, cruising submerged passageways or walking by torchlight among the ghosts of convicts past, then this is the place for you. Numerous tours of Australia's last and most intact convict-built prison are available daily (The Terrace, Ph: (08) 9936 9200).

Festive Fremantle

Fremantle celebrates its cultural heritage with a variety of annual festivals. The largest and oldest of these is the Fremantle Festival, first staged in 1905. Held in November each year, the festival traditionally opens with a free family concert in Kings Square featuring music, dance, comedy and theatre. Ten days of artistic performance and revelry follow, culminating in a street parade at festival end. Fremantle's streets also come alive in Easter with the Street Arts Festival, which features buskers and performance artists from around the world. The port's streetscapes themselves are celebrated with the Fremantle Heritage Festival, staged in the last week of May. It features tours, talks, exhibitions and displays focusing on Fremantle's buildings and social history.

Maritime Museum

Perth's seafaring heritage is on display at the Western Australian Maritime Museum (*right*). Spread over three sites in Fremantle, the museum incorporates the Shipwreck Galleries, showcasing relics and remnants from Australia's earliest wrecks (Cliff Street); the New Maritime Museum complex (Victoria Quay); and the neighbouring decommissioned navy submarine HMAS *Ovens*. The America's Cup winning yacht, *Australia II*, is also on display. The Victoria Quay complex includes permanent exhibitions exploring every facet of Western Australia's maritime history, including immigration and defence. Board an old Swan River ferry or Fremantle's first steam pilot boat; inspect the conning tower of a World War I sub or dive deep in the ocean in the interactive submarine simulator. At the Shipwreck Galleries, a reconstructed section of the ill-fated *Batavia* and numerous artefacts from the ship are on permanent display (the museum sites are open daily from 9.30 am – 5 pm, Ph: (08) 9431 8444).

Rottnest Island

When seafarer Willem De Vlamingh stumbled upon the mobs of Quokkas (*far right*) on this island 19 km west of Fremantle in 1696, he mistook the native marsupials for rats. His error is forever preserved in the island's name, which derives from the Dutch for "rat's nest". The island was later used as an Aboriginal prison and the summer retreat of Western Australia's first governors. It was declared a public reserve in 1917. Despite its chequered history and somewhat unappealing moniker, "Rotto" has since become one of Perth's favourite destinations. During peak periods holiday accommodation is so coveted that a ballot system is employed to determine who will enjoy an island sojourn (Ph: (08) 9372 9732). Rottnest is less crowded at other times and accommodation options abound from campsites to bungalows, hotels and lodges. Daytrips are always possible and ferries depart from the Fremantle terminal (Victoria Quay), North Fremantle (at Rous Head) and Hillarys Boat Harbour in Perth. An air taxi also services Rottnest from Jandakot Airport in Perth.

Once on the island, there is much to explore. The 63 beaches and surrounding waters are a spectacular place to snorkel, scuba dive, surf, sail and swim. Self-driven glass-bottom watercraft, sea kayaks and catamarans are also available. Tours of Rottnest Island's natural and historic attractions are on offer throughout the year (including free guided walking tours) or you might hire a bike and pedal the island's 24 km coast at leisure. Visit the Wadjemup Lighthouse, take the Oliver Hill train to the old gun battery, visit Brett Heady's Family Fun Park, explore Rottnest Museum or go Quokka-spotting. Restaurants and cafés entice or you can even take in a movie at the Picture Hall.

City Beaches

There are nineteen beaches within metropolitan Perth. Cottesloe, located fifteen minutes west of the city, is Perth's most famous seaside suburb. The beach is sheltered from onshore winds by a rocky groyne to the south while Indian Ocean waves crash on white sands to the north. A historic bathing pavilion dominates the beachfront, flanked by convenient grassy slopes on which to laze and take in the view. Along Marine Parade is the iconic Ocean Beach Hotel and an extensive strip of cafés, bars and shops. The beach has been a popular place to cool off since the early 1900s and lifesavers have been keeping visitors safe since 1908.

City Beach is the closest strip of sand to the CBD and offers excellent swimming and bodyboarding conditions between two artificial groynes. Adjacent Floreat Beach is linked to City Beach via a pedestrian path and a dune boardwalk that leads from the northern car park at City Beach to the car park at the southern end of Floreat Beach. With an early offshore breeze, Scarborough, further north, becomes a vision of white and turquoise (*right*).

The Aquarium of Western Australia – AQWA

On Perth's northern coastline is Hillarys Boat Harbour (*far right*), with its sheltered beach and marina, fashionable shops and cafés. Adjacent to the marina is the Aquarium of Western Australia (AQWA), which features spectacular displays of the State's diverse marine environments from the coral reefs of the tropical north to the cold Southern Ocean. Five habitats are represented — the Great Southern Coast, Perth Coast, Marmion Marine Park, the Shipwreck Coast and the Far North.

Australia's largest underwater aquarium tunnel allows visitors to view turtles, sharks, rays and fish from every angle (*right*). Living coral reefs and seals are also on exhibit. The AQWA offers guided snorkelling and dive experiences (including shark encounters) in the Indian Ocean aquarium. Ocean safaris are also available from October to December and include whale, sea-lion and dolphin watching. (Open daily, 10 am – 5 pm, Ph: (08) 9447 7500).

PERTH to the Goldfields

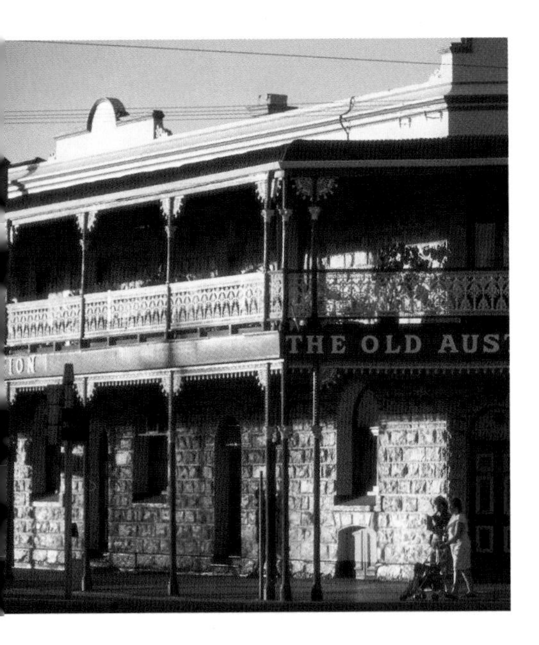

The journey from Perth to the goldfields of Coolgardie and Kalgoorlie retraces the path of prospectors who crowded this trail on horseback and foot over a century ago. The Great Eastern Highway follows much of their original route through the eastern wheatbelt. Today Kalgoorlie can be reached from Perth in 6.5 hours by car and a little less by train (Westrail, Ph: 13 10 53). The road trip begins at Greenmount on the Perth outskirts with a steep 3 km climb through the heart of the Darling Range to an ancient granite plateau. The Jarrah forests that line the highway along the plateau's edge were once the focus of a timber felling operation at Sawyers Valley. John Forrest National Park protects the northern part of the Hills Forest area and provides magnificent vistas of the Swan Valley coastal plain and unique wildlife (*see bottom left*). The nearby town of Mundaring was established in 1898 to accommodate workers on the Mundaring Weir, built to feed a water pipeline running the entire distance to the goldfields (*see left*).

Northam, on the pretty Avon River, was one of the first towns surveyed in Western Australia, but it was not until the construction of the goldfields railway through the region that the town began to flourish. It was used as a military hospital and training base during WWII and became the first Australian home for many post-war refugees and immigrants. A number of the town's earliest buildings have survived, including Morby Cottage, the home of Northam's founder John Morrell (open Sundays, Old York Road, Ph: (08) 9622 2100). Northam grabbed the spotlight on the world stage in 2002 when adventurer-aviator Steve Fossett launched the first solo round-the-world balloon flight in the *Spirit of Freedom* from the town.

Until 1968, Meckering was a busy wheatbelt centre. Then at 10.58 am on 14 October the earth moved, destroying 59 of the town's 78 buildings (including its attractive old bank and hotel). Remarkably, no-one was killed, but some of the ruptures caused by one of Australia's most powerful earthquakes can still be seen and a fault line runs under the highway just west of town. A display in the Meckering parkland features information on the quake and its effects, as well as part of the buckled railway line and a damaged section of the water pipeline. At Cunderdin Museum, formerly a pipeline pump station, you can step inside the interactive Earthquake House to see how it might feel to experience a quake. This large museum also features one of Australia's biggest collections of farming equipment.

The highway continues past soaring wheat silos through the regional farming towns of Tammin and Kellerberrin. A heritage walking trail starting at the Folk Museum in Kellerberrin takes in many of the town's best preserved buildings. The wheatbelt's largest town, Merredin, originated as a waterhole serving passing prospectors but with the advent of the railway and pipeline evolved into an important rural centre. The town's charming Cummins Theatre was constructed in 1928 from bricks salvaged from the demolition of Coolgardie hotels. Westonia, just north of the highway between Walgoolan and Bodallin, was the most westerly goldfields' town, and recreated shopfronts in the main street recall the heady days that followed the discovery of gold in the area in 1910. The larger town of Southern Cross was named for the constellation that led Thomas Risely and Mick Toomey to discover gold there in 1888. The town's streets are also named for constellations, as is the nearby salt lake. The local Yilgarn History Museum provides an excellent journey through the pioneering days on the land and goldfields. At the height of the gold rush more than 20 trains per day ran between Southern Cross and Coolgardie.

Golden Pipeline Heritage Trail

The prospectors who flooded east from Perth in the late 19th century were to discover that while the region was rich in gold, water was in desperately short supply. After many had died of thirst and disease, the Western Australian government implemented one of history's most ambitious water schemes — the construction of a 650 km steel pipeline to carry water from Mundaring Weir in the Perth hills through the wheatbelt east to Kalgoorlie and Coolgardie.

The pipeline still operates and the Golden Pipeline Heritage Trail follows its path along routes once trudged by miners and heritage towns established during the time of the great rush east. The trail is signposted along the Great Eastern Highway and features information panels and walking trails in the main heritage areas.

John Forrest National Park

Only 30 minutes from Perth, this park has been a popular bush retreat for city residents since the early 1900s. Many paths, ornamental gardens and swimming areas were constructed by sustenance workers during the Great Depression. You can trudge along an old railway track, and walk or cycle through the State's only true railway tunnel (now disused). Other walking trails lead to tearooms, waterfalls (including the renowned Hovea Falls) and tranquil pools. Granite outcrops are also an excellent place to see and photograph native fauna, including the Bungarra Lizard.

The Western Brush Wallaby, from the south-west of WA, may be seen in John Forrest National Park.

Wave Rock

The wheatbelt features several massive, isolated granite outcrops (known as tors). The most famous of these is Wave Rock at Hyden. Rising 15 m above the ground, it is forever poised to crash down into the dry earth below. It has taken around 300 million years of weathering to score out the wave's face beneath the overhang.

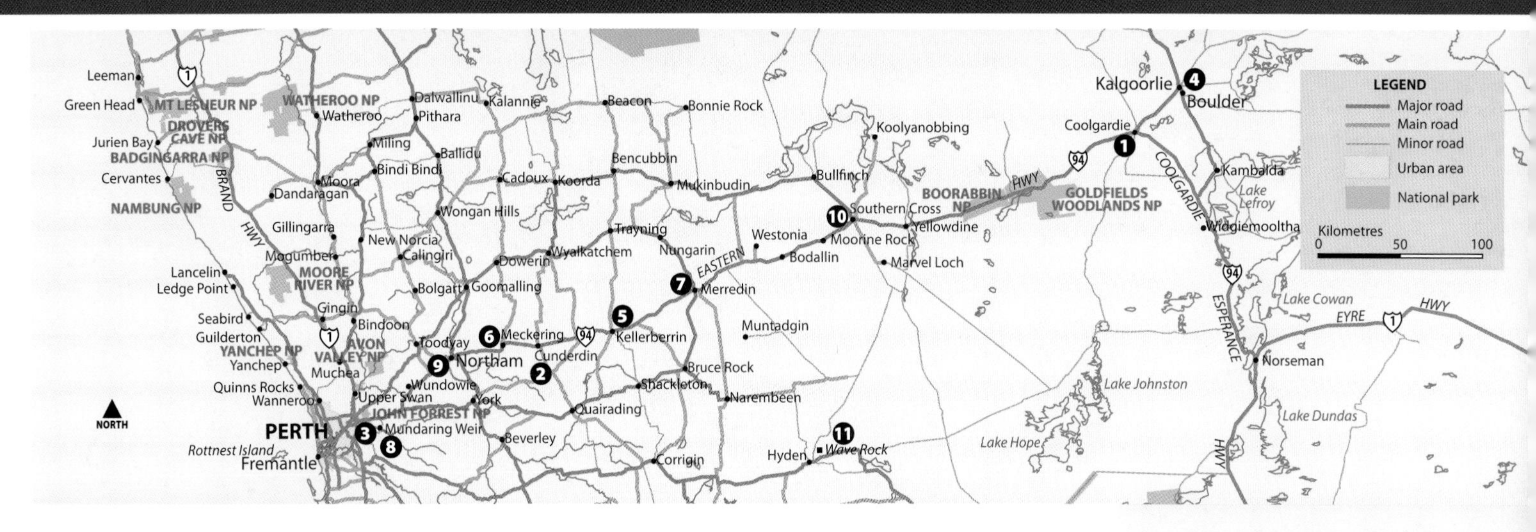

Kalgoorlie

Australia's best known gold town is also one of its most remote. Perched on the western edge of the Nullarbor Plain, Kalgoorlie *(left and centre left)* has outstripped most of it peers in reputation, longevity and output. It all began when three Irish prospectors based at Coolgardie discovered alluvial gold near Mt Charlotte in 1893. Ten years later, the town supported a population of 30,000, with 93 hotels and eight breweries. When the surface gold had been exhausted, investment in deep reef mining at nearby Boulder began to pay dividends. The area became known as the Golden Mile and was thought to contain the world's richest square mile of gold reserves. The Golden Mile has since expanded into a massive 8 km^2 open cut mining operation dubbed the Super Pit. A viewing platform providing panoramas of the mine is accessible via the Outram Street exit from the Goldfields Highway. Photograph the pit around midday when the shadows are shorter.

As you might expect, most of Kalgoorlie's visitor attractions revolve around gold and the life of the prospectors. The Western Australian Museum of Kalgoorlie–Boulder is entered below a towering headframe from the old Ivanhoe mine. A walk down Kalgoorlie or Boulder's main streets, with their many fine period buildings, will instantly transport you to the roaring days of the goldfields. Climb to the top of Mt Charlotte for superb views over the town and environs. Take a guided Indigenous tour of the area or join a prospecting adventure (Kalgoorlie Goldfields Visitor Centre, corner Hannan and Wilson Streets, Ph: (08) 9021 1966).

Coolgardie

In 1892, roving prospectors Arthur Bayley and William Ford discovered gold at Fly Flat — 185 km east of Southern Cross — sparking a huge rush that gave rise to the town of Coolgardie (*left*). Within a decade it was Western Australia's third-largest town and the prospectors' original mine, Bayleys Reward, delivered riches for the next 70 years.

Today Coolgardie is a magnificently preserved slice of goldfields history. For an in-depth tour of Coolgardie's past, visit the Goldfields Exhibition Museum, housed in the Wardens Court Building in Bayley Street (Ph: (08) 9026 6090). From Lions Lookout you can take in the same view of Flys Flat that greeted Bayley and Ford when they rode into town. The head frame of their original mine now stands at the site. The Coolgardie Cemetery has many interesting graves including that of Australia's courageous explorer Ernest Giles — the first man to cross Western Australia's inland desert from east to west. Visit the old Coolgardie Railway Station (now a museum), Warden Finnerty's residence (the 1895 home of Coolgardie's first magistrate, John Finnerty) and Ben Prior's Open Air Museum. Check out the Coolgardie Visitor Centre for more information (Bayley Street, Ph: (08) 9026 6090).

Feature Localities

1 Coolgardie
2 Cunderdin Museum, Cunderdin
3 John Forrest National Park
4 Kalgoorlie
5 Kellerberrin
6 Meckering
7 Merredin
8 Mundaring Weir
9 Northam
10 Southern Cross
11 Wave Rock

PERTH to Adelaide

Perth to Adelaide
Top Things to Do

1. Follow in the footsteps of 19th century prospectors to the gold mining towns of Coolgardie and Kalgoorlie.
2. Discover the giant Karri forests of the magical South West.
3. Surf the world famous swells of Margaret River.
4. Watch migrating whales along the coast.
5. Drive the Nullarbor Plain.
6. Walk in Wilpena Pound.
7. Ride the old *Ghan* railway.
8. Cycle through the Clare Valley.
9. Quaff premium Australian wines in the Barossa Valley.
10. Cruise the Spencer Gulf from Port Augusta.

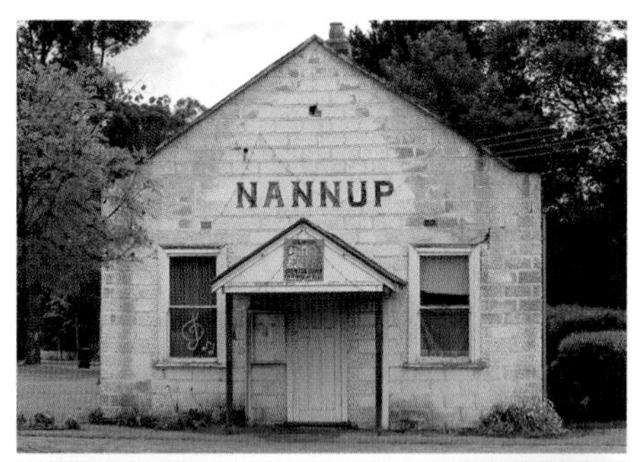

What's up with up?

You will notice that the names of many towns in the South West, such as Myalup, Manjimup, Binningup, Nannikup and Yallingup, end in an -up suffix. These are all Aboriginal words and the "up" simply means "the place of". Yallingup is said to mean "the place of love".

The journey east from Perth to Adelaide has it all — blue oceans and red desert, giants of the sea and forest, wrecks, ruins, mines and wines. The only challenge is how to choose between the many alternative routes, each of which boast a host of fascinations.

A Journey of Possibilities

If you are travelling by car, the 3000 km journey from Perth to Adelaide could be achieved in less than a week, but might just as easily be stretched out to a month or more. The first choice that you must make is whether to travel directly east in the tracks of 1890s fortune-seekers (via the goldfields) or via the woodlands, wineries and waves of the State's magnificent South West. Each adventure is equally absorbing and if you have enough time, they can be combined by following the coast to Esperance before heading north to Coolgardie and Kalgoorlie. One thing, however, is certain — in order to get to Adelaide you must at some point cross the vast expanse of the Nullarbor Plain. No matter which route you travel, all roads eventually lead to Norseman. From here Highway One commences the trek to the South Australian border and around the Great Australian Bight.

After watching whales cruise almost close enough to touch at the Head of Bight, you might be tempted by a detour around the spectacular wilds and seaside idylls of the Eyre Peninsula. At the historic transport hub of Port Augusta more options arise. North to the Red Centre via the "underground" town of Coober Pedy? Perhaps a shorter jaunt to the Flinders Ranges and wonderful Wilpena Pound? Or a journey through history to Lake Eyre and Oodnadatta, tracing the tracks of the old *Ghan* railway line? If you choose instead to head directly south to Adelaide, there are still more possibilities. Several days could be spent exploring the Mid North and Clare Valley before heading south to wine and dine in the famous Barossa. Alternatively, the Yorke Peninsula offers wrecks, ruins, holiday-ready beaches and a superb coastal national park. And at the end of it all lies the reward of Adelaide, one of Australia's most elegant cities. Whichever way you choose to go, this is one of Australia's most remarkable journeys.

Above, top to bottom: It may be flat, but it's long, and crossing the mighty Nullarbor gives many cyclists a tremendous sense of achievement; Great Australian Bight, stretching over 1000 km from Western Australia to South Australia.

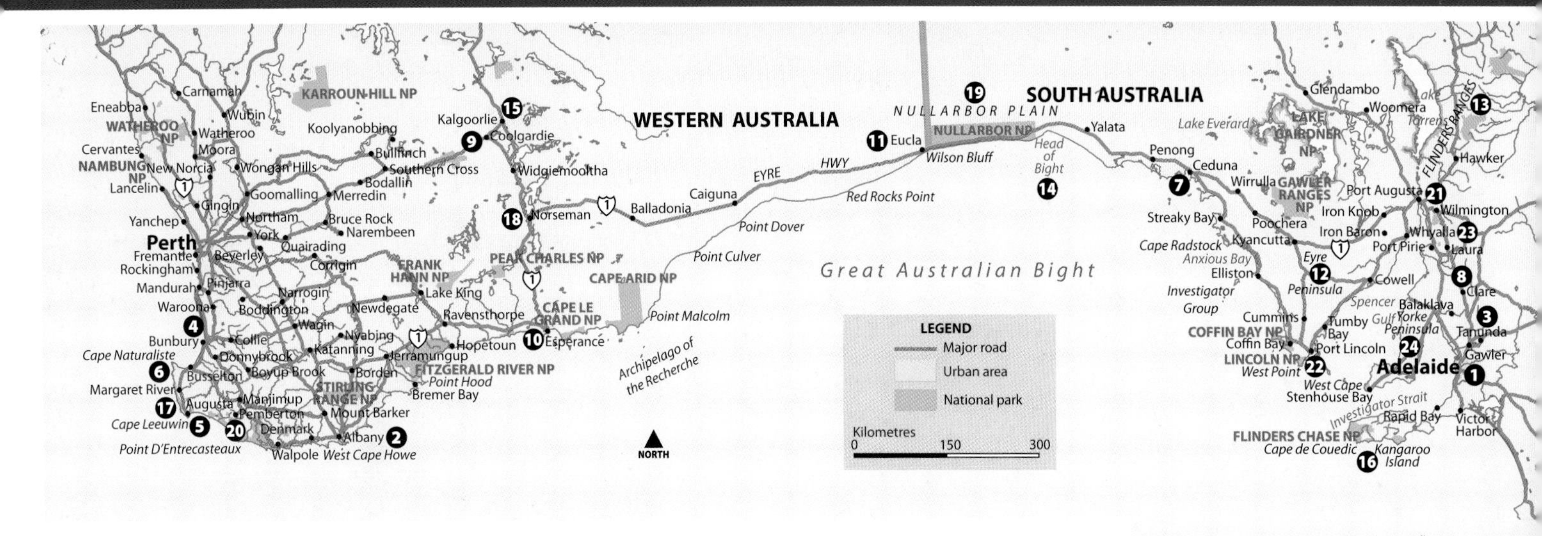

Journey of Discovery

If travel is history come to life, the trip from Perth to Adelaide presents the story of Australia's origins and settlement in living colour. On the Nullarbor Plain, the skeletal remains of some of Australia's most ancient megafauna — including a marsupial lion, wombats the size of ponies and a giant horned kangaroo — have been discovered by paleontologists in limestone sinkholes and subterranean caverns. The creatures had been entombed for up to 1.5 million years. Superb Aboriginal paintings and rock art, evidence of Australia's habitation over more than 20,000 years, are protected in national parks from the South West to the Flinders Ranges in South Australia.

In 1622, Dutch seafarers aboard the vessel *Leeuwin* became the first Europeans to set eyes on the south-west Australian coast, paving the way for 180 years of maritime exploration (culminating in 1801 when Matthew Flinders charted Australia's southern coastline). Sealers and whalers soon established Southern Ocean ports in Albany and Esperance. Following the settlement of the Swan River Colony in 1829, the search for pasture and gold drove exploration of the southern inland. Vast stands of giant eucalypts were discovered in the South West, spawning a timber industry that continues in a more sustainable manner today. In the 1890s, gold strikes at Kalgoorlie and Coolgardie made tiny desert outposts magnets for tens of thousands of prospectors from around the globe. Lucrative mineral deposits were also discovered throughout South Australia in the 19th century, delivering wealth that financed a boom in public works. With the construction of the famous *Ghan* railroad from Port Augusta to Australia's centre, trains replaced camels as the means of breaching the vast isolation of the outback. The entire coastal region from Perth to Adelaide is a natural wonderland with an exhibition of flowers lining the coast at every turn. The UNESCO-recognised Fitzgerald Biosphere near Esperance protects an incredible diversity of plants and wildlife, many of which are found nowhere else in the world.

Right: The endangered Numbat, faunal emblem of Western Australia, inhabits Dryandra National Park.

Feature Localities

1 Adelaide
2 Albany
3 Barossa Valley
4 Bunbury
5 Cape Leeuwin
6 Cape Naturaliste
7 Ceduna
8 Clare Valley
9 Coolgardie
10 Esperance
11 Eucla
12 Eyre Peninsula
13 Flinders Ranges
14 Head of Bight
15 Kalgoorlie
16 Kangaroo Island
17 Margaret River
18 Norseman
19 Nullarbor Plain
20 Pemberton
21 Port Augusta
22 Port Lincoln
23 Whyalla
24 Yorke Peninsula

PERTH to Albany (via Cape Leeuwin)

Perth to Albany
Top Things to Do

1. Follow the snorkelling trail at Shoalwater Islands Marine Park.
2. Swim with the dolphins at Koombana Beach near Bunbury.
3. Walk the 2 km long jetty at Busselton.
4. Visit Wonnerup House near Busselton.
5. Follow the Tuart Forest Scenic Drive.
6. Marvel at the thrombolite structures in Yalgorup National Park.
7. Explore the caves around Yallingup.
8. Tour the vineyards of Margaret River.
9. Birdwatch at Sugarloaf Rock.
10. Stand on the continent's south-west tip at Cape Leeuwin.

Yalgorup National Park

Phone Ranger: (08) 9539 1067

This coastal park lies 50 km south of Mandurah on the western edge of the Swan Valley coastal plain and protects a chain of ten lakes, bordering wetlands and woodlands. The lakes lie in depressions between coastal dunes.

Walks in the Park: An observation walkway at Lake Clifton provides views of the mineralised structures built by primitive micro-organisms (known as thrombolites). These were the only form of life on earth from 3500–650 million years ago. Walking trails at Lake Hayward and Lake Preston protect large communities of frogs and waterbirds.

Access: Via Mandurah on Highway One.

Camping: Camping is permitted at various sites within the park. There are also plentiful commercially operated campgrounds and accommodation options in the Mandurah region.

A journey to Western Australia's South West is a must, particularly during spring months. The sandy heathlands support the largest number of flowering plants found anywhere in the world, the seascapes are breathtaking and the rural towns and landscapes are full of charm. Some of the world's best surf, caves, vineyards, coastal wilderness and eucalypt forests are found here.

Rockingham & Mandurah

Rockingham is only a short distance from Fremantle on the shores of Cockburn Bay and its sheltered north-facing beaches attract visitors all-year-round. The town is named for a ship chartered by Thomas Peel in 1830 to bring English settlers to Australia. The boat sank upon arrival, but the passengers survived and the remains of the *Rockingham* now lie lost in waters off the coast a short distance north. On the Esplanade Road there is also a maritime memorial dedicated to the story of the *Catalpa*, a whaleboat that sailed from America to Rockingham in 1875 to successfully facilitate the escape of six Irish political prisoners incarcerated in Fremantle's prison. A unique feature of the area is a snorkelling trail at Shoalwater Islands Marine Park near Cape Peron which provides a 60 m underwater signed trail in 2–3 m of water along the coastal reef. The park's islands are home to colonies of sea-lions and penguins and observation cruises are available for wildlife spotting. Mandurah has long been a favourite weekend getaway for boating and fishing enthusiasts, who are drawn to the calm waters of Peel Inlet. Cruises on the local waterways, canals and estuary are popular, as are dolphin and whale watching tours. If you're looking for something different, pay a visit to the Abingdon Miniature Village, a mini-reproduction of the buildings of Abingdon (the oldest inhabited town in the UK) set in spacious landscaped gardens (Husband Rd, Ph: (08) 9534 9079).

Bunbury & Busselton

Bunbury is the State's second-largest population centre and a major southern port. Many visitors come to meet the friendly Bottlenose Dolphins that live close to shore at Koombana Beach. The Dolphin Discovery Centre is located on Koombana Drive and offers eco-cruises and seasonal "swimming with dolphins" tours (November to April, Ph: (08) 9791 3088). If you prefer to swim alone, the Back Beach on Ocean Drive is one of Bunbury's best. Excellent panoramas of the coast and port can be seen from Baulters Heights (off Stirling Street), which also features a 26 m artificial waterfall built in 1966 to commemorate the visit of the Queen Mother. The streets of Bunbury are crowded with beautifully kept historic buildings, churches and hotels and the town's 16 km heritage trail takes in no less than 50 sites of interest — the Stirling Street Historic Precinct is a highlight. Busselton, facing north on Geographe Bay, is one of Western Australia's most charming (and visited) towns. With its broad streets, friendly atmosphere, sandy white beaches (over 30 km worth) and close proximity to other regional attractions, Busselton is a great base for exploring Australia's south-west corner. Though its name may suggest otherwise, it enjoys a gentler pace than most tourist towns, and features some superbly refined seaside architecture, a number of excellent restaurants and abundant accommodation options. Visit Wonnerup House (classified by the National Trust of Australia) — a remarkable window on the lives of early settlers set in magnificent gardens and situated 10 km north of town off Tuart Forest Scenic Drive. Continue along the drive through stands of giant Tuart trees, past Wonnerup Beach to the Port Geographe marina development.

Downtown Bunbury Western Australia's second-largest centre and a major southern port.

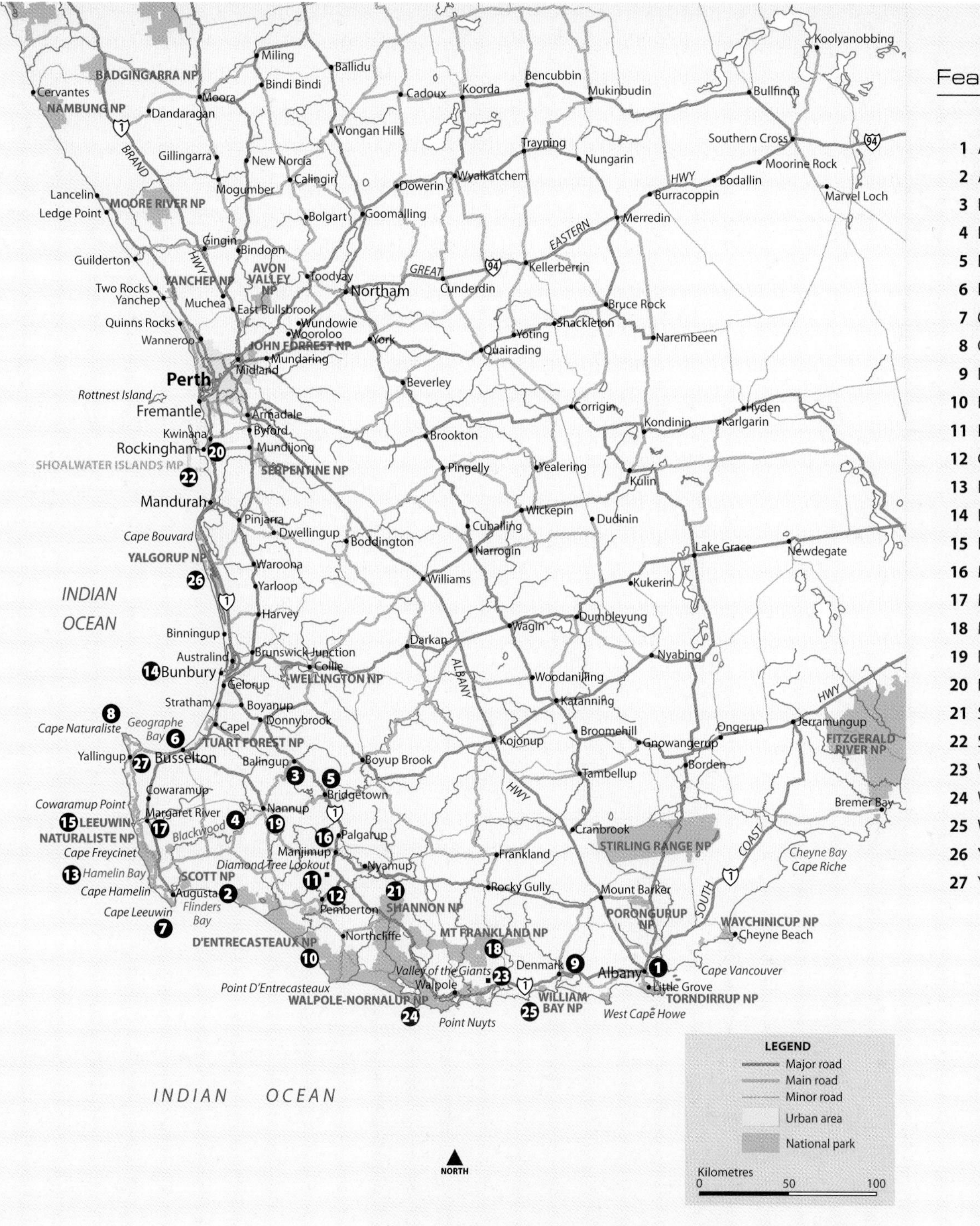

Feature Localities

1 Albany
2 Augusta
3 Balingup
4 Blackwood River
5 Bridgetown
6 Busselton Jetty, Busselton
7 Cape Leeuwin
8 Cape Naturaliste
9 Denmark
10 D'Entrecasteaux National Park
11 Diamond Tree Lookout
12 Gloucester Tree, Pemberton
13 Hamelin Bay
14 Koombana Beach, Bunbury
15 Leeuwin–Naturaliste NP
16 Manjimup
17 Margaret River
18 Mount Frankland National Park
19 Nannup
20 Rockingham
21 Shannon National Park
22 Shoalwater Islands Marine Park
23 Valley of the Giants
24 Walpole–Nornalup National Park
25 William Bay National Park
26 Yalgorup National Park
27 Yallingup Caves, Yallingup

A Walk on the Water

Busselton is famed for its wooden jetty (*left*), which was once used for loading ships but is now reserved for strolling and sightseeing. This remarkable 2 km structure took 95 years to complete and now features an underwater observatory. This installation provides glimpses of the marine creatures that inhabit Busselton's artificial reef at a depth of 8 m.

River of Vines

The vine-clad Margaret River region is renowned for its award-winning wineries, which produce millions of bottles of fine table wine each year. The high rainfall, nutrient-rich soil and cooler coastal temperatures are ideally suited to producing outstanding grape yields. Wine production only commenced in the region in the 1970s, but now the 100-odd wineries scattered around the countryside are responsible for producing over 15% of Australia's premium wine. Many also offer gourmet dining experiences, tours and concerts set in the vineyards.

Sensational Surf

Both Yallingup and Margaret River are famed for their superb surf breaks and both amateur and professional surfers from around the world make the pilgrimage here to pit themselves against the spectacular Indian Ocean waves. Several major world surfing events (including the prestigious Margaret River Pro) are held here each year. Size up the breaks and catch the action (if not a wave) at Prevelly Park, Surfers Point, Three Bears, Yallingup or Injidup.

Cape Naturaliste to Cape Leeuwin

Leeuwin–Naturaliste National Park protects almost the entire length of coast between the capes. More than 360 limestone caves and tunnels lie beneath the flowering heath-covered headlands. Many distinctive rock formations jut from the ocean waters between the capes, including Sugarloaf Rock — a popular vantage for observing seabirds and thought to be the only place in the South West where the Red-tailed Tropicbird comes to rest. The park's southern region is characterised by gangling Karri trees. Both Cape Leeuwin and Cape Naturaliste have historic lighthouses — the light at Cape Leeuwin marks the extreme south-west point of Australia.

Coastal Towns of the South West

A short distance west of Busselton on the edge of the national park are the towns of Dunsborough and Yallingup. Dunsborough is perched at the western end of Geographe Bay toward Cape Naturaliste and divers are attracted here by the chance to dive upon the wreck of the HMAS *Swan*, a 120 m destroyer scuttled by the navy in 1997. It is thought to be the largest accessible dive wreck in the Southern Hemisphere. The nearby beaches of Meelup, Eagle Bay and Bunker Bay are also popular and wining and dining options are plentiful. Yallingup, ten minutes south-west, first became a popular tourist destination over a century ago, largely due to its proximity to the various caves (including Ngilgi Cave) in the region. It is now a major surfing and holiday destination. The Art Deco-styled Caves House and its 4.5 ha of gardens have long been a romantic retreat and "Sunday sessions" at the garden view bar are a local tradition (Yallingup Beach Rd, Ph: (08) 9750 1500). Both Dunsborough and Yallingup have many interesting art and craft galleries to explore.

Most famous of the "cape towns" is Margaret River. This high-traffic tourism centre has somehow managed to retain an enormous amount of charm, probably due to its unrivalled location between vines, forest, national park and ocean. Within just a few square kilometres there are a glut of accommodation and dining choices, beaches to stroll and surf and a myriad of local wineries to explore. The Margaret River Wine Region Festival is held in November each year. With Leeuwin–Naturaliste National Park on the doorstep, Margaret River also offers a wide variety of outdoor activities, including caving and canoeing on the Margaret River. Contact Margaret River Visitor Centre for information on regional tours and activities (cnr Bussell Highway and Tunbridge St, Ph: (08) 9780 5911). Eleven kilometres from town, Prevelly Park (at the mouth of Margaret River) is a modern seaside resort offering reef diving and snorkelling, surfing and fishing as well as excellent swimming at Gnarabup Beach.

Toward Cape Leeuwin are the township of Karridale and Hamelin Bay. Karridale is a historically interesting one-time timber town at the edge of Boranup Karri Forest. This forest of Karri trees was comprehensively milled during the boom of the late 1800s, but even after only a century of re-growth these timber titans already reach for the skies. Hamelin Bay boasts remnants of a wooden jetty that once served sailing ships, as well as one of the most beautiful beaches on the coast.

Caves Between the Capes

Within the Leeuwin–Naturaliste Ridge are a series of spectacular caves formed by water seeping through the soft limestone. Many of the larger caves (including Calgardup, Giants, Ngilgi, Mammoth and Jewel Caves) are accessible to the public and showcase some of Australia's most compelling underground scenery.

Giants Cave, 575 m long and descending to a depth of 86 m, offers a real sense of adventure as you climb unaccompanied down stairways and ladders through narrow crevices into subterranean chambers filled with strange beauty. There is a lake at the bottom of Calgardup Cave and gum tree roots penetrate through the cave roof. Helmets and torches are provided and the Calgardup Cave Office has maps and other information (Ph: (08) 9757 7422). Both Calgardup and Giants Cave are a short distance south of Margaret River off Caves Road.

Sugarloaf Rock Leeuwin-Naturaliste National Park

Top to bottom: Cape Naturaliste Lighthouse; Fascinating rock formations and flora.

Leeuwin-Naturaliste National Park

Phone Ranger: (08) 9752 1677

Stretching over 120 km between Bunker Bay in the north and Augusta in the south, Leeuwin-Naturaliste National Park features windswept, rugged coastlines, secluded bays and impressive granite outcrops. Some of Australia's most beautiful caves also lie within the park (*see box on facing page*). The world's third-tallest tree, the Karri, grows in the Boranup Karri Forest in the south of the park between Caves Road and the coast. There are excellent lookouts dotting the coast and Humpback and Southern Right Whales can often be observed from these vantage points. Bushwalking is extremely popular as is salmon fishing and surfing. Ellensbrook Homestead, a historic National Trust property, also lies within the park.

Walks in the Park: If you have the time, fitness, experience and energy it is possible to walk the entire 140 km distance from Cape Naturaliste to Cape Leeuwin on the Cape to Cape Walking Track. For lesser mortals, the trek can be broken into more easily conquered sections. At Cape Naturaliste there is a medium grade, 1–1.5 hour walk through small limestone pinnacles to a panoramic whale lookout. A medium grade, 2 hour walk from the car park on Canal Rocks Road offers excellent views en route to Wyadup. The 1 hour Water Wheel to Skippy Rock Track commences at the Leeuwin Waterwheel, near the Cape Leeuwin Lighthouse in Augusta. There is also a walking track from Ellensbrook Homestead leading to the picturesque Meekadarabee Falls, known to Aboriginals as "the bathing place of the moon".

Access: The park can be entered at many points along the coast from Cape Naturaliste to Augusta. Roads are mostly sealed and gravel roads are generally accessible to 2WD vehicles. Ellensbrook Homestead is off Caves Road, 9 km from Margaret River.

Camping: National park camping areas with good facilities (including toilets and water) are available at Conto campground (turn off onto Conto Road from Caves Road), Point Road campground (first track to the right from the northern end of Boranup Drive — 4WD recommended) and Boranup campground (off the southern end of Boranup Drive).

Left to right: Driving through Karri forest; Leeuwin-Naturaliste National Park has an extensive wild sea coast; Cape Leeuwin Lighthouse.

Cape Leeuwin to Albany

Top Things to Do

1. Wander the gardens and historic streets of Nannup, Balingup and Bridgetown.
2. Climb to the top of the 61 m tall Gloucester Tree (pegged for easy ascension).
3. Ride a steam train through ancient forest in Pemberton.
4. Walk in the treetops at the Valley of the Giants near Nornalup.

Augusta

The Augusta area was first sighted by the Dutch in 1622, but even after the English arrived 200 years later it took several attempts before a town was eventually established. It developed slowly, boosted by post-war soldier settlement and today is a small but pleasant place popular as a base for exploring the neighbouring attractions. Cape Leeuwin, where the Indian and Southern Oceans merge, is only 8 km south of Augusta. Visit the century old lighthouse and imagine Matthew Flinders' joy at sighting this tiny corner of land before mapping Australia's entire southern coast aboard the *Investigator* in 1801. Nearby Jewel Cave and the Shipwreck Trail at Hamelin Bay should also be explored while visiting the area.

Denmark

This Great Southern town is located on the banks of the Denmark River. The neighbouring coast is etched with inlets, coves and bays, which make it an ideal destination for fishing, boating and swimming.

Cape Leeuwin to Albany

Inland from the south-west corner at Augusta is the heart of Karri country. These stately old eucalypts grow throughout the region alongside their relatives the Marri, Jarrah and Tingle. In Walpole–Nornalup National Park, unique conditions have produced the huge Red Tingle trees of the Valley of the Giants. Several other major national parks protect the region's forest and coast. These include D'Entrecasteaux, Mount Frankland, Shannon and William Bay National Parks. The inland towns of Pemberton, Nannup and Manjimup reflect their origins as timber centres while Walpole and Denmark are perfectly situated coastal retreats.

Into the Forest

The Brockman Highway commences at Karridale and leads east to Nannup at the western corner of a heavily wooded region, bordered by the towns of Bridgetown and Balingup, known as the "golden triangle". Nannup's houses, gardens and roadside planter boxes overflow with flowering plants, providing kaleidoscopic displays in spring and summer. Timber remains the dominant industry in these parts and the town's arboretum at the end of the main street (on a bend of the Blackwood River) is certainly worth visiting.

The short (and scenic) road north-east to Balingup winds up the Darling Escarpment to offer panoramic views of the region. Balingup itself is a tiny village that features a variety of gourmet food outlets, including a French restaurant and an attractive stone tavern. After local industry began to struggle in the 1970s, Balingup was given a fillip by the arrival of "alternative lifestylers". Together with their modern day counterparts, the "tree-changers", they have played a large role in rejuvenating the town with a range of art, craft and unique local festivals — including a Mediaeval Carnivale staged each August. This entertaining fair coincides with the annual garden and flower festival at Nannup. Bridgetown, on the banks of the Blackwood River, is the largest of the area's three towns and also boasts a botanic atmosphere. It's collection of well preserved heritage buildings have earned it classification as a historic town by the National Trust. An impressively long Jarrah bridge crosses the river, which is also the venue for the Blackwood Classic Powerboat Race (reputedly the world's longest event of its kind). Puzzle freaks will revel in the town's jigsaw gallery and museum.

The highway continues south to Manjimup and Pemberton, the "capitals" of the southern forest region. Around Manjimup are numerous tree-oriented attractions, including: the 51 m Diamond Tree Lookout (complete with wooden viewing platform); the remarkable 600-year-old King Jarrah on Perup Road; and the pretty, historic swimming area and gardens of Fonty's Pool (10 km south on Seven Day Road). Nearby Deanmill is an old sawmill town and tours of the old local mills are available. A 19 km forest drive west of the highway leads to Pemberton, at the middle of a ring of small yet fascinating national parks. The town's name recalls one of the area's early farming settlers, Pemberton Walcott, but has operated as a timber centre since the early 1900s. Signs from the main street lead to the Gloucester Tree, a famous local attraction that offers the opportunity to scale a series of ladders to a platform at the tip of a 61 m tree originally used for bushfire detection. One of the best ways to explore the surrounding forest is to take a ride on a steam train operated by the Pemberton Tramway Company over 57 kilometres of rail (Ph: (08) 9776 1322).

Out to the Sea

South of Pemberton the highway twists and turns to the coast through Shannon National Park and onto Walpole and Nornalup on the Nornalup Inlet. Walpole was built during the Great Depression of the 1930s as a new home for dislocated urban workers and is a great place to stay when touring the lower South West. The region's rivers, waterfalls and coastal scenery are particularly attractive and the world famous Valley of the Giants lies just east of Nornalup off the main highway (*see page 200*). Twenty-nine kilometres north of Walpole, Mount Frankland National Park offers superb views from the summit of Mt Frankland as well as stunning mirror-surfaced waterways. The town of Denmark (*see left*) bears no actual relationship to its Scandinavian namesake, but the love of craft, carpentry and furniture-making displayed by the district's denizens would make any Dane proud. There are numerous studios, workshops and galleries here and in the surrounding hinterland — follow the Southern Art and Craft Trail (booklet available at the Denmark Visitor Centre, 60 Strickland St).

D'Entrecasteaux National Park The coastal scenery of D'Entrecasteaux National Park.

Shannon National Park Tall timber dominates the drive through Shannon National Park.

Great Southern National Parks

One of the primary attractions of the lower South West and Great Southern region of Western Australia is its abundance of superb national parks. Commencing from where the Southern Ocean meets Cape Leeuwin, these parks form a near-continuous chain that reaches up through forests of giant trees and stretches along the coast almost all the way to Denmark.

D'Entrecasteaux National Park

Phone Ranger: (08) 9776 1207

This is true coastal wilderness — over 130 km of untouched southern coast featuring massive windblown dunes, high limestone cliffs, wildflower-laden coastal heath, unspoilt rivers flowing to the ocean and groves of Karri forest. These elements combine to create an environment of rare purity. Barring a few isolated campsites and walking tracks, this is pristine territory that nature lovers (and photographers) will find impossible to resist. Behind the coastal cliffs and dunes are several expansive lakes, including Lake Yeagarup and Lake Jasper — the largest in the southern region of Western Australia. There are also vast regions of wetland (known as the Blackwater) and the 10 km long Yeagarup Dune. West of Black Point are a series of hexagonal basalt columns rising out from the shore — the remnants of ancient lava flows now being eroded by sea. Toward Walpole, greeting the mouth of the Shannon River, is Broke Inlet — Western Australia's largest untouched estuary.

Walks in the Park: Walking in D'Entrecasteaux National Park is definitely not for the faint of heart, body or spirit. The wild coastal areas can be extremely windy and steep. A compass and map should be carried by all walkers, together with usual necessities such as water, first aid equipment, torches etc. There is a scenic but steep 1 km track to the summit of Mount Chudalup (dangerous in windy weather). Otherwise the boardwalk and lookouts at Mandalay Beach may prove the better option.

Access: Access is via numerous roads off the Brockman and lower South Western Highway. Windy Harbour, Salmon Beach, and Broke Inlet are the only coastal locations accessible by 2WD vehicle. There are numerous 4WD tracks in the park leading to other coastal fishing and camping spots. Many places, such as the mouth of the Donnelly River, can be reached only by small boat.

Camping: The campground at Lake Jasper has toilets, water and barbecue facilities. Black Point, Moore's Hut, Salmon Beach and Crystal Springs have toilets and barbecue facilities.

Shannon National Park

Phone Ranger: (08) 9776 1207

Shannon National Park borders D'Entrecasteaux between the towns of Northcliffe and Walpole. Its huge tracts of Karri forest make it a superb place to camp, walk or drive. The area remained unlogged until a timber shortage following World War II prompted the government to act. Part of the town that was built to accommodate the timber workers is now used as the park campground. The houses are gone but some remnants of old buildings and railway lines still exist near the Shannon Dam Trail. Aside from a number of worthwhile walking tracks, there is also the spectacular Great Forest Trees Drive, a 48 km loop road that passes through the park commencing from an information shelter and picnic area off the South Western Highway.

Walks in the Park: The Rocks Trail is a medium grade, 5.5 km, 2 hour walk through forest to a granite outcrop overlooking the former Shannon town. Shannon Dam Trail is an easy 3.5 km, 1–1.5 hour return walk. The first 1.5 km is suitable for wheelchairs. Great Forest Trees Walk is a medium, 8 km, 3 hour return walk that follows an old forestry track. It is steep in places, particularly when it crosses the Shannon River (the Shannon can flood, submerging the track). The track commences 4 km north of the Shannon campsite.

Access: Off South Western Highway approximately midway between Manjimup and Walpole.

Camping: The Shannon recreation area off the highway has excellent facilities (including water, toilets and barbecues).

Top to bottom: Towering Karri and Tingle trees in Walpole–Nornalup National Park; The suspended footbridge above the Valley of the Giants.

Top to bottom: Rocky beaches buffeted by wind and wave in William Bay National Park; Coastal heathland clutching at granite tors is a feature of William Bay National Park.

Walpole-Nornalup National Park

Phone Ranger: (08) 9840 1111

This extensive coastal park envelops the towns of Walpole, Nornalup and Peaceful Bay. Coastal inlets and beaches are complemented by vast stands of native forest.

The Valley of the Giants is one of the park's major attractions. Named for the towering Karri and Tingle trees that soar up to 60 m above the valley floor, this magnificent forest can be admired from both below and above. The Treetop Walk rises 38 m into the forest canopy and provides an exhilarating stroll through these leafy altitudes. Below, a boardwalk curls through a grove of 400-year-old Tingle trees branded the Ancient Empire. Three species of Tingle tree are found only in the Walpole area. Viewing platforms and an interpretive centre provide you with a unique opportunity to learn more about some of the world's oldest living plants.

Walks & Canoe Cruises in the Park: At Hilltop and the Knoll, short walking tracks lead through remnant forests to lookouts over the Walpole and Nornalup Inlets. Experienced bushwalkers looking for an extended hike can follow a section of the 960 km Bibbulmun Track along Deep River, then continue west of the inlets to Walpole, and on through the Valley of the Giants. Canoeing is a great way to explore the inlets and lower river reaches. During Spring, when water levels are high, canoeists can travel the Frankland River to Circular Pool, where the river drops into a large rockpool.

Access: Via South Western Highway. Vehicle access to the park's coastline is restricted to the eastern end between Conspicuous Cliff and Peaceful Bay. Boats can be launched from Nornalup Inlet.

Camping: Camping is permitted at some locations in the park, including Crystal Springs (toilets, barbecues and water). There are also commercial campsites at Rest Point, Coalmine Beach and Peaceful Bay.

William Bay National Park

Phone Ranger: (08) 9840 2055

At William Bay, granite tors rise out of the coastal heathland above narrow stretches of rocky beach. In some places, the powerful ocean winds have pushed sand dunes several kilometres inland. These mobile dunes cover up old Karri forest and are themselves re-colonised by shrubs and trees. Galaxies of flowers can be found in the heathland throughout the year but are particularly spectacular from August to October. Between Greens Pool and Madfish Bay, granite rocks probe more than 100 m out to sea. Greens Pool and Madfish Bay are both excellent swimming spots but other areas can be dangerous. There are picnic areas at Elephant Rocks and Waterfall Beach.

Walks in the Park: Take care when exploring the coast as unpredictable ocean surges can flood the rocks. Walk to the lookout at Greens Pool or follow walking tracks through the heathland.

Access: Fifteen kilometres west of Denmark off the South Western Highway.

Camping: Not permitted, however, there is a Walkers Camp on the William Bay section of the Bibbulmun Track (www.bibbulmuntrack.org.au).

Flora of the South West

The unique wildflowers of Western Australia's South West are at their best in spring and early summer. On protected areas of the coast, some species appear throughout the year, while in more arid areas of the region they are at their most spectacular following heavy winter rains. Within the Stirling Range, north of Albany, exist over 1500 species of plant — 87 of which are found nowhere else on Earth. Some are found only on the high peaks where cloud creates a moist, cool environment quite unlike that of the surrounding plains. An incredible 1800 species of flowering plant (15% of all found in the State) grow in Fitzgerald River National Park. The phenomenal floral diversity of the region between Albany and Esperance has led to its listing as a World Biosphere Reserve by UNESCO. Red and Green Kangaroo Paw, Western Australia's striking floral emblem is a feature of the coastal plains (particularly between Shark Bay and Manjimup).

Myriad species of orchid (including the Custard Orchid, Splendid White Spider Orchid and the Queen of Sheba Orchid) bloom around the coast and hinterland to dazzling effect. The distinctive Common Donkey Orchid (with two upper petals resembling donkey ears) is found in the Jarrah forests and woodlands between Dongara and Albany.

Red and Green Kangaroo Paw

Top row, left to right: Pink Fairy Orchid; *Lechenaultia linarioides*; Spider Orchid; *Gompholobium villosum*. **2nd row, left to right:** *Acacia lasiocalyx*; Many-flowered Fringe Lily; *Caladenia flava*; Red Bottlebrush. **3rd row, left to right:** Hairy Jug Flower; *Anigozanthos pulcherrimus*; Mottlecah; *Burchardia umbellata*. **Bottom row, left to right:** *Pimelea ferruginea*; Yellow-eyed Flame Pea; *Diuris corymbosa*; Geraldton Wax.

ALBANY to Norseman

Albany to Port Augusta
Top Things to Do

1 Take in the sweeping views from Mount Clarence over Albany and King George Sound.
2 Tour historic Princess Royal Fortress on Mount Adelaide.
3 Visit the Western Australian Museum, Albany.
4 Explore the early days of whaling and board an old whaling ship at Whale World Museum.
5 Walk among wall-to-wall wildflowers at Stirling Range National Park (October to December is best).
6 Photograph spectacular granite formations at Torndirrup National Park.
7 Wander Western Australia's oldest continually operating farm at Strawberry Hill.

The first European settlement in Western Australia was not Fremantle or the Swan River colony but the southern port town of Albany. Aboriginal sites in the region show that the Aboriginal Mineng people had in fact occupied the area around King George Sound, Princess Royal Harbour and Oyster Harbour for nearly 20,000 years.

After sightings of this coast by Dutch explorers in the early 17th and 18th centuries, Commander George Vancouver arrived at King George Sound in 1791 to chart the coast and take possession of the South West for Britain. A flurry of visitations by both English and French explorers followed. In December 1826, Major Edmund Lockyer arrived from Sydney with a small detachment of soldiers and the intention of establishing the West's first penal colony. The place was named Fredericks Town and operated as a small military outpost for several years before being proclaimed Albany. A small number of convicts were landed but with the development of the Swan River colony, Albany's role as a prison was forgotten. With few prospects for farming (due to poor soil and noxious plants), the town's focus remained firmly on the sea. The presence of large numbers of Humpback and Southern Right Whales around King George Sound had been identified by English whalers in 1800 and whaling gradually became one of Albany's biggest industries. The practice eventually ceased in 1978 due to economic and environmental pressures. With the advent of steam ships, the town became Western Australia's most important international port, before being superseded by Fremantle in the early 1900s. This long maritime tradition has a strong presence in Albany today.

Historic Albany

A good place to begin exploring Albany is at the top of Mount Clarence, where a walking trail provides sweeping views over the city and King George Sound (follow Apex Drive off Marine Drive). There is also an interesting memorial here commemorating the Desert Mounted Corps who fought in the Suez region during World War I. The memorial's granite blocks were originally located in Port Said and bullet marks are still visible on them. Albany was the last port of call for many soldiers bound for Gallipoli and other wartime fronts. Atop the neighbouring peak, Mount Adelaide, stands a historic fort, Princess Royal Fortress, which operated from 1893 to 1956. There is a café on-site and the fort looks down upon Middleton Bay (open daily, follow Forts Road off Marine Drive). A tower on nearby Mount Melville Lookout, know locally as "the spark plug", also offers excellent seaward views.

On the foreshore off Princess Royal Drive is a full-size replica of Edmund Lockyer's brig *Amity* (tours available, Ph: (08) 9841 5403). Overlooking Princess Royal Harbour at the site of his landing is the Western Australian Museum, Albany (Residency Rd, Ph: (08) 9841 4844). Set within a restored 1850s government resident's house, it contains a wide range of social and natural history displays as well as the frighteningly large jaws of a White Shark. The restored former home of the original government resident is located at Strawberry Hill on an 1827 a farm reputed to be the State's oldest farm under continuous use.

Albany – A Harbour City

There can be few prettier sights in the west than to stand in Albany's main streets and take in the panorama of Princess Royal Harbour beyond. You can only imagine Edward Eyre's joy at drinking in this water-filled view after completing his pioneering journey across the bone-dry Nullarbor Plain in 1841. Albany is a town of unsullied environs and intriguing history — wander the Stirling Terrace precinct (*above*) to be instantly transported back to the early years of this picturesque port.

Whale World Museum

This fascinating attraction, situated on the site of Australia's last operating whaling station at Cheyne's Beach, includes tours aboard an authentic decommissioned whale chaser, the *Cheynes IV*.

The museum also offers a huge whale skeleton exhibit entitled Giants of the Sea, a state of the art 3D film theatre and interactive explorations of the world of whaling (Frenchman Bay Road, Ph: (08) 9844 4021).

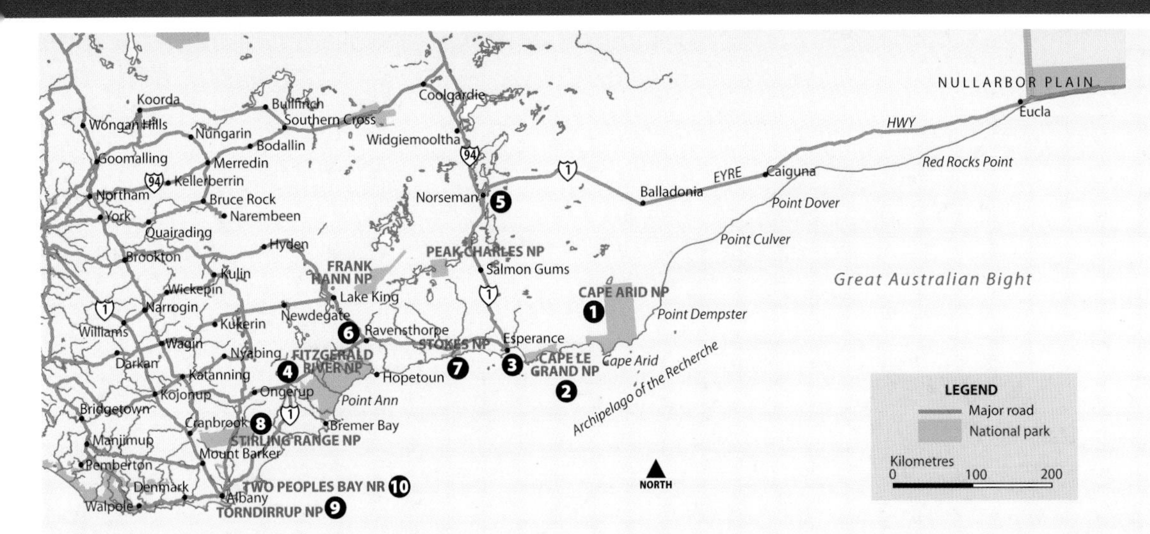

Feature Localities

1. Cape Arid National Park
2. Cape Le Grand National Park
3. Esperance
4. Fitzgerald River National Park
5. Norseman
6. Ravensthorpe
7. Stokes National Park
8. Stirling Range National Park
9. Torndirrup National Park
10. Two Peoples Bay Nature Reserve

Stirling Range National Park

Phone Ranger: (08) 9827 9230

The Stirling Range lies 100 km north-east of Albany and incorporates the 1073 m high Bluff Knoll — the highest peak in the South West. The national park encompasses the entire 65 km extent of this jagged and rocky range. A staggering variety of flora has been identified in the park — more species in fact than can be found in the whole of Britain. The coastal location and elevation of the range have resulted in ideal conditions for the growth of wildflowers — creating a sumptuous floral spectacle to rival anything of its kind in the world (*right*). An amazing 123 orchid species can be found here. Late spring to early summer (October to December) is the best time for seeing and photographing this miraculous display. The park is also notable for unique cloud formations that sometimes form over the range, and for the snow that falls upon its peaks in most winters — a rarity in the west.

Walks in the Park: Numerous walks within the range offer excellent views. Bluff Knoll, Toolbrunup and Mount Magog will all take an experienced walker some 3–4 hours to complete and are all rated as difficult. Talyuberlup (2–3 hours), Mount Hassell (1.5–2 hours) and Mount Trio (1.5–2 hours) are medium grade walks. Walking is not recommended in windy, wet or hot conditions.

Access: Via the town of Cranbrook off the Albany Highway.

Camping: A campground is available at Moingup Springs off Chester Pass Road.

Cranbrook Bell (*left*) & Scarlet Banksia

Torndirrup National Park

Phone Ranger: (08) 9844 4090

One of the State's first national parks, Torndirrup (named after the local Aboriginal clan) protects the Flinders Bay Peninsula 10 km south of Albany between the Southern Ocean and Princess Royal Harbour. On the ocean side, the coastal granite has been carved into spectacular formations. The most impressive of these are the Gap and Natural Bridge (*right*) off Frenchmans Bay Road and the blowholes on Jimmy Newhills Harbour.

Walks in the Park: Short walking trails lead to the park's major features. There is also a 500 m heritage trail leading to lookouts at the park's highest point (at Stony Hill). A much more difficult 6–8 hour trek over Isthmus Hill and Limestone Head finishes at Bald Head on the eastern side of the park.

Access: Follow Frenchmans Bay Road through the park. There are sealed roads to most of the popular natural features.

Camping: There are no camping grounds within the park. The Department of Sport and Recreation runs a recreation and camping facility at the old quarantine station at Quaranup (enquiries and bookings, Ph: (08) 9844 4087).

Albany to Norseman

Top Things to Do

1. See incredible floral displays in Fitzgerald River National Park.
2. Spot the rare Gilbert's Potoroo and Noisy Scrub Bird at Two Peoples Bay Nature Reserve near Albany.
3. Walk through Waychinicup Gorge.
4. Stay at Quaalup Homestead and take a guided nature tour.
5. Spy Australian Sea-lions from the Southern Ocean Discovery Centre in Hopetoun.

Esperance & Surrounds

Esperance is intimately connected with its natural environment. By way of introduction, walk out on Tanker Jetty where a bronze statue honours a local legend by the name of Sammy the Sea-lion (he cruises the waters below, snaffling angler's leftovers). Cruises to the Bay of Isles and the 110 islands of the Recherche Archipelago offer sightseeing, diving and snorkelling. On Woody Island, safari huts and tours permit exploration of an unspoilt island wilderness. East of Esperance are Cape Le Grand and Cape Arid National Parks (*see facing page*).

Albany to Norseman

The coast from east of Albany to Esperance is dominated by heath-covered headlands, snow white beaches and stark granite outcrops. The unparalleled abundance of floral species in this region has led to much of it being declared a World Biosphere Reserve, described by UNESCO as "the most important Mediterranean ecosystem conservation reserve in the world". The area contained within Fitzgerald River National Park has been the subject of international botanical interest since the early 1830s. Several other national parks and reserves protect substantial sections of coastal habitat between Albany and Ravensthorpe. Two Peoples Bay Nature Reserve is a sanctuary for rare and threatened species including Gilbert's Potoroo and the Noisy Scrub Bird (*see facing page*). Nearby Waychinicup National Park comprises a stretch of coastal cliffs, inlets and wooded gullies around Cheyne Beach, Lookout Point and the western end of Hassell Beach. The Waychinicup River and surrounding gorge is particularly scenic, with numerous polished granite formations and boulders scattered across the valley. Wander the short tracks around the Waychinicup River gorge and along the beach.

From Boxwood Hill, Bremer Bay Road diverts east to Bremer Bay and Fitzgerald River National Park. Bremer Bay is a peaceful fishing village whose magnificent coastal assets have made it increasingly popular as a holiday resort. A commercially operated wilderness retreat has also been developed within the national park around historic Quaalup Homestead, built in 1858. The retreat offers accommodation, camping and caravan facilities, home-cooked meals and guided nature tours (Quaalup Homestead, Ph: (08) 9837 4124). The South Coast Highway continues through sheep farming district developed in the 1950s by returned soldiers, reflected in street names like Tobruk, Kokoda and Coral Sea in the town of Jerramungup. North of the highway between Jerramungup and Fitzgerald is Lake Magenta Nature Reserve. The reserve is home to many native animals and has been the focus of efforts to save the Chuditch, Western Australia's largest carnivorous marsupial, from the brink of extinction.

Ravensthorpe & Surrounds

The towns of Ravensthorpe and its coastal neighbour, Hopetoun, sprang to life with the discovery of gold around the Phillips River in 1898. Rich copper reserves were found a few years later and the subsequent establishment of government smelters saw the towns boom. Ravensthorpe's mining heritage continues today with the establishment of a major nickel extraction venture in the region. Wander Morgan Street and visit the Palace Hotel (1907) and Dance Cottage, a 1900 miners' residence that has been meticulously fitted out to reflect the period. The former goldfields port turned holiday town of Hopetoun is the main eastern access point for Fitzgerald River National Park. A modern tourism complex known as The Deck includes the Southern Ocean Discovery Centre, where tele-cameras allow you to observe the activities of Australian Sea-lions just offshore at Seal Island (cnr Clarke and Veal Sts, Ph: (08) 9838 3303). Camping is possible along the coast east of Hopetoun at Jerdacuttup Lakes Nature Reserve, Lake Shaster Nature Reserve and near Stokes Inlet in Stokes National Park (access via the South Coast Highway).

Esperance to Norseman

The Esperance coast, Recherche Archipelago and Bay of Isles were first surveyed by Matthew Flinders in 1802 and whalers and sealers harvested the surrounding Southern Ocean waters throughout the 19th century. The sudden influx of fortune seekers bound for Kalgoorlie and Coolgardie in 1895 transformed the tiny port town of Esperance (*see left*) into a bustling tent city. The 360 km track they trudged north to the Eastern goldfields is now the Coolgardie-Esperance Highway. It passes through sheep and wheatbelt country en route to Norseman. Stop off for a refreshment at the shaded and aptly titled Gibson Soak Hotel, or take the signposted heritage walk around Salmon Gums (named for a large stand of smooth-barked local eucalypts that were once a landmark for goldfields travellers).

East of the highway between here and Norseman lies Lake Dundas, the location of gold strikes in the 1890s. A bronze stallion in town recalls the tale of Norseman — a horse that supposedly made his owner rich when he scraped a gold nugget from the ground with his hoof, thus revealing the location of a major reef and sparking the Norseman rush. The massive granite boulders at Dundas Rocks, 22 km south, are a popular picnicking, photography and camping spot. Bush trails from here explore the old townsite and the 2800-million-year-old rock formations. A lonely timber headstone on a spit of land at the edge of the lake marks the resting place of a baby that died during the boom days in 1897.

Two Peoples Bay Nature Reserve

Phone Ranger: (08) 9841 1088

Two Peoples Bay Nature Reserve, 35 km east of Albany, is an internationally significant protection area for threatened animal species. Its most famous resident is Gilbert's Potoroo, a diminutive relative of the kangaroo that was thought extinct for a century before being re-discovered at Two Peoples Bay. There are thought to be only around 40 of these creatures left in the wild. The rare Noisy Scrub Bird was also considered extinct until found in this area in 1961. Quokkas and Quendas (Southern Brown Bandicoots) are also found in this important habitat.

Walks in the Park: The Two Peoples Bay Heritage Trail is a 2 km nature walk over headlands to the white shores of Little Beach.

Access: From Albany via Two Peoples Road.

Camping: No camping facilities are available in the park.

Fitzgerald River National Park

Phone Ranger: (08) 9835 5043

The steep rocky slopes of the Barren Ranges form the backdrop for a 100 km arc of magnificent coastline featuring low sea cliffs, jagged headlands, pristine beaches and sheltered inlets. Several rivers, including the Fitzgerald and Hamersley, have cut deep valleys between the ranges. At Fitzgerald Inlet, intriguing red and orange striped cliffs of spongolite flank the river. The estuarine lagoon into which it flows is favoured by waterbirds and waders.

Walks in the Park: There are many enjoyable coastal walks ranging from the one hour Point Ann Heritage Trail to a testing 22 kilometre trek from the point to Twin Bays via Fitzgerald Inlet.

Access: Via South Coast Highway to Bremer Bay or Hopetoun.

Camping: Campsites are available at Four Mile Beach, Hamersley Inlet, Twertup, Fitzgerald Inlet & Saint Mary Inlet. Fees apply.

Cape Le Grand National Park

Phone Ranger: (08) 9075 9022

Within easy reach of Esperance, Cape Le Grand National Park is a coastal retreat popular with beach and fishing enthusiasts. There are sheltered bays, sweeping beaches and granite headlands, creating some impressive scenery.

Walks in the Park: The best view of the park and the Recherche Archipelago is from the top of Frenchman's Peak. This easy grade walk takes around two hours and features a huge wave-cut cavern below the 282 m summit. The 15 km Coastal Trail between Le Grand Beach and Rossiter Bay is divided into shorter sections of varying difficulty. There is also a self-guided heritage trail between Lucky Bay and Thistle Cove.

Access: Via Karijini Drive off the Great Northern Highway 35 km south of Munjina Roadhouse.

Camping: There are very well-equipped caravan and camping sites at Cape Le Grand Beach and Lucky Bay (tank water, toilets, solar heated showers, barbecues; no power.)

Cape Arid National Park

Phone Ranger: (08) 9075 0055

Situated on the western edge of the Great Australian Bight, Cape Arid National Park features some of Australia's most dramatic white sandy beaches. The park's granite ridges were once a chain of islands — overhangs and wave-cut platforms just below Mt Ragged's razorback summit mark the ancient sea levels. In spring, a blaze of colour ignites the vast heath plains as tea trees, banksias and myrtle burst into blossom. Whales are often seen in late winter to spring.

Walks in the Park: The Tagon Coastal Walk, a 15 km return trek, offers magnificent views across the headlands to the Recherche Archipelago. The 3 km climb to the summit of Mt Ragged offers panoramic views.

Access: 120 km east of Esperance on unsealed roads to Thomas River and Seal Creek.

Camping: Basic facilities (no power or water) at Thomas River and Seal Creek.

NORSEMAN to Port Augusta

Norseman

A horse with the Midas touch isn't Norseman's only animal sculpture. The corrugated iron camels on Princep Street pay tribute to the camel trains that hauled supplies and mail to and from the town prior to the construction of the railway.

The drive east across the Nullarbor Plain, Australia's ultimate road trip, begins at Norseman. While gold mining still occurs in the region, Norseman benefits from its position as the first (or last) town travellers pass through when crossing the bottom of the continent. Norseman has several unusual features. On display at the historical museum is a fragment of Skylab, the US space station that disintegrated over Western Australia in 1979. Close to town is a giant tailings dump — a white mountain of quartz said to still contain up to $50 million in gold. Before leaving town, be sure to visit the Norseman Tourist Bureau, which offers up-to-date information on the conditions you will encounter and facilities available along the Eyre Highway. It is recommended to book all accommodation in advance before crossing the Nullarbor.

Eyre Highway to Eucla

The Eyre Highway is named for Edward John Eyre, the intrepid explorer who led a tiny expedition party 1900 km around the Great Australian Bight by foot in 1841. Today the Eyre Highway to Port Augusta is more travelled but fuel stops and accommodation remain separated by hundreds of kilometres. The Western Australian section includes Australia's longest stretch of straight road, 146.6 km of unwavering bitumen between Balladonia and Caiguna. Near Cocklebiddy, the Eyre Bird Observatory has been established at the old Eyre Telegraph Station. This isolated coastal retreat offers accommodation and a chance to explore the surrounding Nuytsland Nature Reserve and see some of the 250 bird species recorded here (4WD required, Ph: (08) 9039 3450). Thirteen kilometres from Eucla, over the South Australian border at Border Village Roadhouse, stands a giant kangaroo (dubbed *Rooey II*), along with a signpost displaying the huge distances to various capitals. Over the next 275 km there are only two roadhouses, at Nullarbor and Yalata, but both offer accommodation and operate 24/7.

Eucla

Now semi-submerged in dunes, the Eucla Telegraph Station was the original reason for the town's existence. Together with other town buildings the station was gradually inundated after a rabbit plague in the 1890s destroyed vegetation and destabilised the local sandhills. The site was eventually abandoned and the town moved 5 km east.

Across the Nullarbor

Tourism publications spruik the Nullarbor Plain as the "world's largest single lump of limestone", 50-million-years-old and spreading over 250,000 km^2. The pseudo-latin name roughly translates to "treeless plain", but this only really describes a brief stretch between Nullarbor and Yalata. There is, in fact, over 3 million ha of mallee between Eyre Peninsula and the Western Australian border. The scenery can certainly become hypnotic, if not monotonous in parts, but there are also six magnificent clifftop lookouts perched up to 100 m above the bight between Eucla and Nullarbor. The Bunda Cliffs are reputed to be the longest continuous cliff face in the world and Head of Bight is Australia's best whale watching location (*see facing page*).

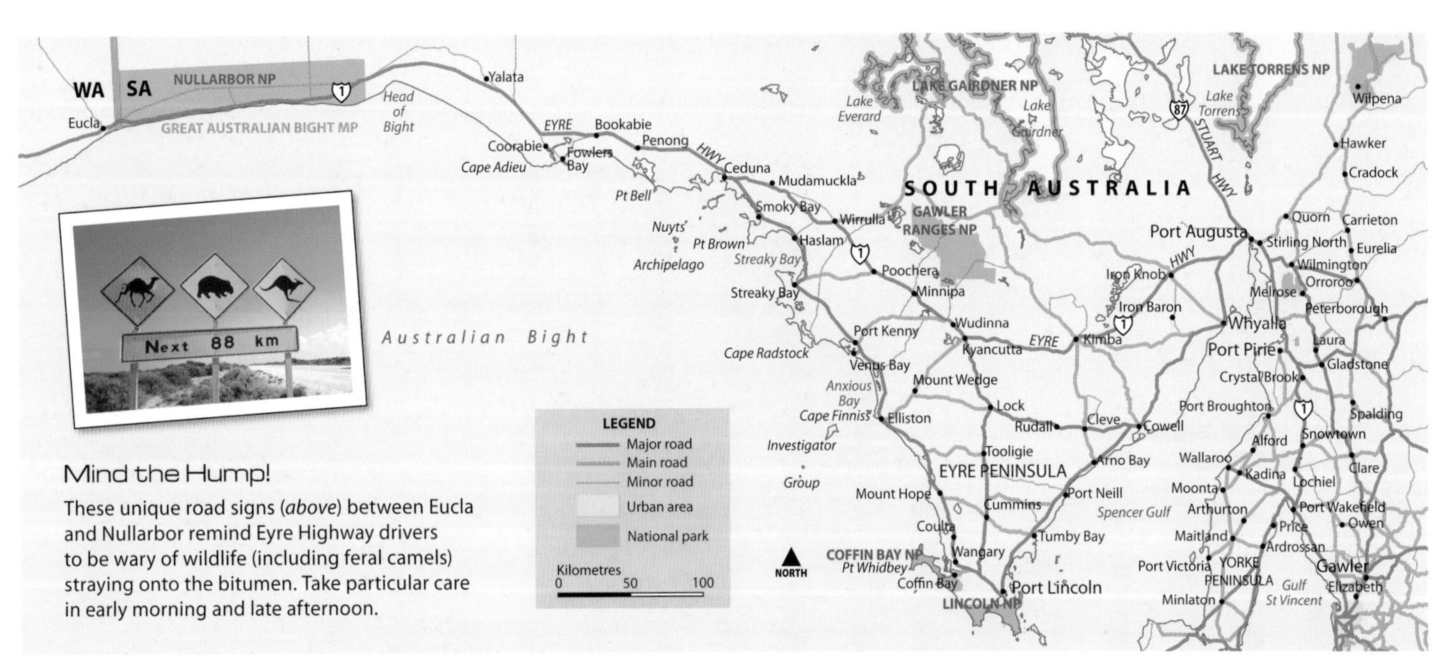

Mind the Hump!

These unique road signs (*above*) between Eucla and Nullarbor remind Eyre Highway drivers to be wary of wildlife (including feral camels) straying onto the bitumen. Take particular care in early morning and late afternoon.

Nullarbor National Park & Great Australian Bight Marine Park

Phone Ranger: (08) 8625 3144

The Great Australian Bight Marine Park is divided into two zones that protect coastal waters east of the Western Australian border. Australia's only mainland sea-lion colonies breed at the base of the Bunda Cliffs and the entire region is a breeding and calving area for the endangered Southern Right Whale (*see below*). Twenty species of whale have been recorded in the region and Bottlenose Dolphins are even more frequently seen. White Sharks maintain a heavy presence here, feeding on sea-lions and New Zealand Fur-seals.

Nullarbor National Park straddles the Eyre Highway and protects the world's largest semi-arid karst (limestone) landscape. Aside from the saltbush and bluebush, the plains may look flat and featureless, but don't be tempted to go for a wander — they conceal deep sinkholes where the roofs of subterranean caverns have collapsed. The region also supports Australia's largest population of Southern Hairy-nosed Wombats as well as endangered bird species (including the Nullarbor Quail-thrush).

Head of Bight Whale Watching

Phone Ranger: (08) 8625 6201

At Head of Bight, whales come close enough to watch their watchers. Surrounded by the Yalata Dunes and Nullarbor Cliffs, observation platforms at Callosity Point provide unparalleled views of Southern Right Whales calving, nursing, breaching and mating, often less than 100 m from the shore. About one-third of all Southern Right Whale calves bred in Australian waters are born here. The whales leave their sub-Antarctic feeding grounds in autumn to journey over thousands of kilometres to the warmer, protected waters of Head of Bight. In 1998, 103 individual whales were observed in a single day. Over 15,000 visitors come to Head of Bight in the main whale watching season (July to October) each year. The Head of Bight is part of Yalata community lands and an interpretative centre provides information on the social and natural history of the area. A permit is required to enter the whale watching area (available from the interpretive centre, open 8 am – 5 pm, May to October). Scenic flights over the Great Australian Bight operate from the Nullarbor Roadhouse (Ph: (08) 8555 4075).

Ceduna

Located 211 km east of Yalata Roadhouse on pretty Murat Bay, Ceduna's name is appropriately derived from an Aboriginal word meaning "resting place". Rest up on the white sandy beaches after your trek across the Nullarbor or try your hand at fishing, crabbing or squidding from the historic jetty at Denial Bay (*above*). If you have no luck, you can always fall back on some fresh oysters from one of the many local growers. A coastal walking and cycling trail leads 3.6 km from Ceduna Sailing Club to Pinky Point Lookout at Thevenard on the tip of the peninsula.

Port Augusta

Directly east of Ceduna across the top of the Eyre Peninsula is Port Augusta, where "the outback meets the sea". Perched at the head of the Spencer Gulf, the town was long a major port for wheat, minerals and wool freighted by rail and road from far across the South Australian outback. The completion of the Trans-Australian Railway line to Kalgoorlie in 1917 joined with the *Ghan* railway to make Port Augusta a major transport nexus. Visit the extensive Wadlata Outback Centre (Flinders Terrace, Ph: (08) 8642 4511) to explore the history of the region or wander through 200 ha of unique desert flora at the Australian Arid Lands Botanic Garden (Stuart Highway, Port Augusta West, Ph: (08) 8641 1049). Boat cruises are also available on the picturesque Spencer Gulf.

Streaky Bay

The Powerhouse Restored Engine Centre in Streaky Bay is a unique museum dedicated to the evolution of stationary engines used in the area from the late 19th century onward. Marvel at the 280 working engines on display and then lunch alfresco at the Streaky Bay Hotel with its panoramic views across the water (corner Alfred Terrace and Bay Road). South of Streaky Bay off the Flinders Highway are a cluster of huge granite boulders (dubbed Murphy's Haystacks), which demand photography (*see right*).

Elliston

Set on the reef-sheltered Waterloo Bay, Elliston is a town proud of its fishing and farming heritage. Australia's largest historical mural adorns the Town Hall (*above*), depicting the Elliston region's evolution from settlement to the present day. An inspiring exhibition of sea-inspired art (entitled *Sculptures on the Cliff*) is staged in even-numbered years.

Eyre Peninsula

The sparsely populated Eyre Peninsula is ruggedly handsome, boasting coastal wilderness, sandy beaches and dramatic seascapes extending along the eastern reaches of the Great Australian Bight. The southern spike is prime farming land, some of which is still bordered by dry stone walls painstakingly constructed by early settlers (*right*). It is also renowned for a thriving seafood industry. Fishing villages and resort towns (as well as some of the country's best surf beaches) line the coast from Ceduna to Port Lincoln. Names like Anxious Bay, Mount Misery and Point Avoid hint at the difficulties endured by early explorers in these parts. Today, Australia's largest commercial fishing fleet plies the Southern Ocean waters off Port Lincoln, famed for its catches of tuna, abalone, prawns and lobsters.

Smoky Bay to Coffin Bay

The Flinders Highway leads south-east from Ceduna to Smoky Bay, a fishing and beach retreat named by Eyre for the smoke he observed rising from local Aborigines' fires. From here, the road follows the curve of Streaky Bay (*see left*) to Haslam (where beachside camping is possible near the jetty). Beach camping is also possible just south of Streaky Bay along a spectacular coastal tourist route known as Westall Way. The sites operate on an honesty payment of just $1 and offer views of the coast's carved granite formations and limestone cliffs. A leisurely low tide wander about the intertidal granite rockpools at Smooth Pool will reveal a thriving community of crabs, fish and starfish. At Point Labatt, a colony of sea-lions have made their home at the base of the cliffs, but binoculars are required for a close-up look from the viewing platform. Sea-lions, dolphins and even the occasional Southern Right Whale can also be seen from the South Head Walking Trail at Venus Bay. Alternatively, take the Talia Caves Tourist Drive 20 km south of Venus Bay and enjoy the sea view from around these unique limestone coastal caves. On Anxious Bay, there are stunning wetland and white dune vistas at Lake Newland Conservation Park (camping permitted, Ph: (08) 8688 3111). South of Elliston (*see bottom left*) camping is possible among the dunes at the salmon fishing haven of Sheringa Beach. Coffin Bay, with its protected marine and coastal parks is the highlight of the Eyre Peninsula's south-west tip (*see facing page*).

Murphy's Haystacks These imposing pink granite sentinels are found south-east of Steaky Bay.

The Spencer Gulf Coast

Port Lincoln nestles below green hills in the crook of Boston Bay. This beautiful natural harbour's attractions are mainly maritime, but Boston Island remains a fully fleeced sheep station. Cruises to the island and a nearby tuna farm run throughout the year (Ph: (08) 8682 6666). Visit the Axel Stenross Maritime Museum (Lincoln Highway), Mill Cottage (Flinders Park) and the Mikkira Station and Koala Park (off Fishery Bay Rd). On the road north to Whyalla are the coastal holiday towns of Tumby Bay, Arno Bay and Cowell. Each offers family-friendly beaches, plentiful accommodation, great fishing and seaside walking trails. Cowell is also famous for its huge deposits of jade, first dug from the Minbrie Ranges in 1965. From here the Lincoln Highway diverts inland to the iron ore rich Middleback Ranges before returning to the coast at Whyalla — the last major town before Port Augusta (*see facing page*).

Coffin Bay National Park

Phone Ranger: (08) 8688 3111

At the eastern end of the Great Australian Bight, Coffin Bay is one of South Australia's best coastal retreats. The sheltered northern shoreline weaves around the bay, creating channels, inlets and broad waterways ideal for boating, fishing, sailboarding and diving. Here is habitat for waders, heathland parrots and seabirds such as albatrosses, petrels and Ospreys. Across the saltpans, heath and shifting dunes lie the wild, exposed south and west coasts. Heavy ocean swells sweep among rocky islands and reefs to shape the park's limestone cliffs, granite shelves and beaches. Swimming and diving are not advisable on this side of the park as local seal colonies attract hungry White Sharks, which have a reputation for aggressive feeding and attacks on humans.

Walks in the Park: There are numerous short walks from the Yangie Bay campground and lookout.

Access: 2WD vehicles can reach the limestone headland at Point Avoid, Almonta Beach, Golden Island Lookout and Yangie Bay.

Camping: Bush camping sites with limited facilities are located around the park (contact ranger for details).

Lincoln National Park

Phone Ranger: (08) 8688 3111

The southernmost tip of the Eyre Peninsula is a contrasting landscape of rugged, ocean-battered cliffs and tranquil bay beaches. Lincoln National Park includes Memory Cove Wilderness Area as well as regions of coastal mallee and extensive sand dunes. Cape Catastrophe was named by Matthew Flinders in 1802 after eight members of his *Investigator* crew were lost to the depths after they set sail in a small cutter in search of fresh water. Flinders erected a memorial tablet in their honour at Memory Cove. Evidence of the region's earliest inhabitants also survives in the form of middens, stone fish traps and working sites. Donington Cottage, on the northern tip of the park, was once part of an 1875 grain growing property and has now been restored as seaside accommodation. Southern Right Whales can sometimes be seen from the ocean side of the park between July and October.

Walks in the Park: There are numerous short walks in the park — including the 45 minute return Stamford Hill Trail, which leads to a lookout with magnificent views over Boston Bay and Port Lincoln.

Access: From Port Lincoln via Tulka.

Camping: There are twelve camping sites with varying facilities within the park (contact park ranger for details).

Port Lincoln

First surveyed by Matthew Flinders and once considered a potential site for South Australia's capital, Port Lincoln instead became Australia's tuna fishing capital. It is home to Tunarama, a fish fest staged in January each year and featuring the inimitable World Champion Tuna Toss Competition.

Whyalla

The discovery of iron ore deposits in the neighbouring Middleback Ranges during the 1890s saw Whyalla grow from a small rural settlement (named Hummock Hill) to a bustling port. BHP Billiton triggered a second boom in 1964 with the development of a major steelworks that still operates today. Tours of the installation can be booked through the Whyalla Visitor Centre (Ph: (08) 8645 7900).

The centre is dwarfed by the adjacent HMAS *Whyalla*, built in 1941 at the Whyalla steel shipyards. Australia's largest landlocked ship, it lies 2 km from the sea and is the centrepiece of the Whyalla Maritime Museum. The museum also displays artefacts and memorabilia relating to the other three ships built in Whyalla during World War II. Guided ship tours are available daily (Lincoln Highway, Ph: (08) 8645 8900).

Hummock Hill Lookout, which served as a wartime gun battery and observation post protecting the shipyards, provides excellent views of the entire Whyalla region. The lookout was developed by BHP as a gift to Whyalla to mark the company's centenary year in 1986 and has sheltered viewing platforms and picnic areas. A sealed road at the eastern end of town leads to the top.

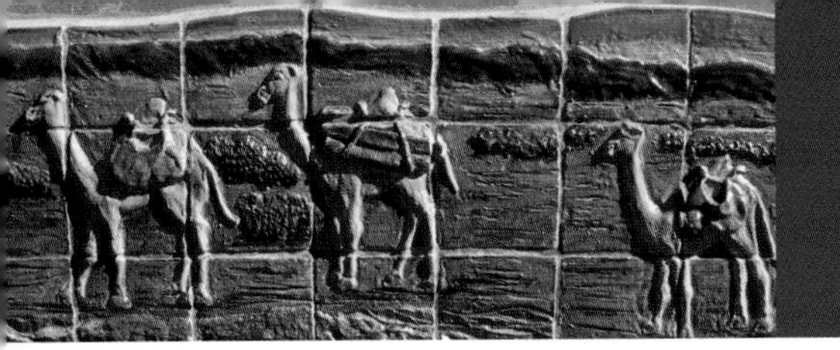

PORT AUGUSTA to Adelaide

Port Augusta to Adelaide
Top Things to Do

1. Explore historic Wilmington in Beautiful Valley.
2. See brilliant views over the Flinders Ranges and Spencer Gulf from Alligator Gorge.
3. Camp at Mambray Creek in Mount Remarkable National Park.
4. Feel your car roll uphill at Magnetic Hill.
5. Visit Steamtown Depot in the railway town of Peterborough.
6. Discover the Port Pirie Regional Tourism and Arts Centre.

Mid North Painterly fields and landscapes abound.

Port Pirie

Port Pirie's striking railway station has been redeveloped as the Port Pirie Regional Tourism and Arts Centre (*above*). Along with some excellent rail-oriented exhibits, it includes the regional art gallery and a replica of the longest White Shark caught off South Australia (open daily, 3 Mary Elie Street).

Port Pirie was South Australia's first provincial city and has been a major port since the 1880s. The rail link with Broken Hill was forged in 1888, leading to the establishment of one of the world's largest lead smelting operations in the town. Railway lines once ran down the main street to the port. Port Pirie is also a major wheat export terminal and huge grain silos dominate the town's skyline.

Travelling from Port Augusta to Adelaide via Highway One involves a journey of just over 300 km, and can be completed in a half a day's drive if desired. However, the Mid North, Yorke Peninsula, and Clare and Barossa Valley regions have an absorbing range of attractions to explore. If time is no obstacle, take a detour north-east to the magnificent Flinders Ranges National Park and Wilpena Pound.

Port Augusta to Port Pirie

South of Port Augusta, the highway stays close to the Spencer Gulf coast, with views of the Flinders Ranges to the east. Flat plains of saltbush and scrub are replaced by wheat fields as the road heads toward Port Pirie. An interesting option is to leave the highway at Winnowie and drive 44 km through Horrocks Pass in the southern Flinders Ranges to Wilmington. John Horrocks was a young pastoralist-cum-explorer who surveyed much of this district in the 1840s. He established the first vineyard in the Clare Valley and imported Australia's first camel for his explorations during 1846. It was an ill-fated move — only six weeks later the camel shied while Horrocks was reloading his rifle, causing injuries that led to his death. This picturesque region was named Beautiful Valley by early settlers and the town of Wilmington has some outstanding stone buildings. The Wilmington Hotel has been in operation since 1876 and the original police station and butter factory in the main street have both been converted to private residences. From Wilmington, roads lead south to Mount Remarkable National Park and east to the historic farm and rail towns of Orroroo and Peterborough.

Mount Remarkable National Park

At Alligator Gorge in Mount Remarkable National Park, steps have been cut into the red quartz rockface allowing you to descend to the gorge floor. There are also easy to moderate walks to lookouts with views over the gorge, ranges and Spencer Gulf. The park has a huge range of longer hiking trails and offers great accommodation — including extensively equipped campsites and cabins at Mambray Creek and a converted ranger's lodge at Alligator Gorge. You may also access the park from Highway One, 45 km north of Port Pirie (Mambray Creek) or the town of Melrose at the foot of Mt Remarkable (Ph: (08) 8634 7068).

Orroroo & Peterborough

Orroroo, 52 km east of Wilmington, has several features worth exploring. Take a walk along Pekina Creek where there are both Aboriginal rock carvings and the rock-engraved poetry of a local resident, Donald McDonald; carved on the eve of his departure in 1896 for America to peddle his unique invention — the crank-driven bicycle. The State's biggest River Red Gum tree stands close by. South of town, off the road to Peterborough, is Magnetic Hill — where (even sober) locals swear a car left in neutral will roll uphill, even if sceptics claim it's simply an optical illusion caused by the angle of the surrounding terrain. Orroroo is perched on Goyder's Line, an imaginary boundary across South Australia laid down by the State's surveyor-general in 1865 to mark the division between fertile and drought-ridden land. Goyder's Line was no illusion — attempts to establish farming properties to its north almost invariably failed due to low rainfall and only homestead ruins remain to tell the tale.

Peterborough was once a major freight train hub, with three different gauge railway lines running through town. Four scale model stream trains greet visitors at each entrance to the town and a restored 1880s locomotive graces the main street. Even the visitor information centre is located in a restored train carriage. At the western end of the street, in the old railway workshops, is Steamtown Depot — a museum dedicated to all things rail, exhibiting early train carriages and the Southern Hemisphere's largest roundhouse (open daily, 9 am – 4 pm). Tiny Terowie, 22 km south of Peterborough, made global headlines in 1942 when General Douglas MacArthur gave a press interview from the station platform after escaping from the Philippines, uttering his famous words, "I came out of Bataan and I shall return". MacArthur never returned to Terowie, but a monument on the station platform honours the historic moment. Jamestown also has a railway museum and its broad main street, the State's widest, is lined with trees planted by a local doctor, John Cockburn, who later became South Australia's premier. Nestled among towering grain silos en route to Port Pirie are the historic farming towns of Gladstone (the childhood home of poet C J Dennis) and pretty Crystal Brook.

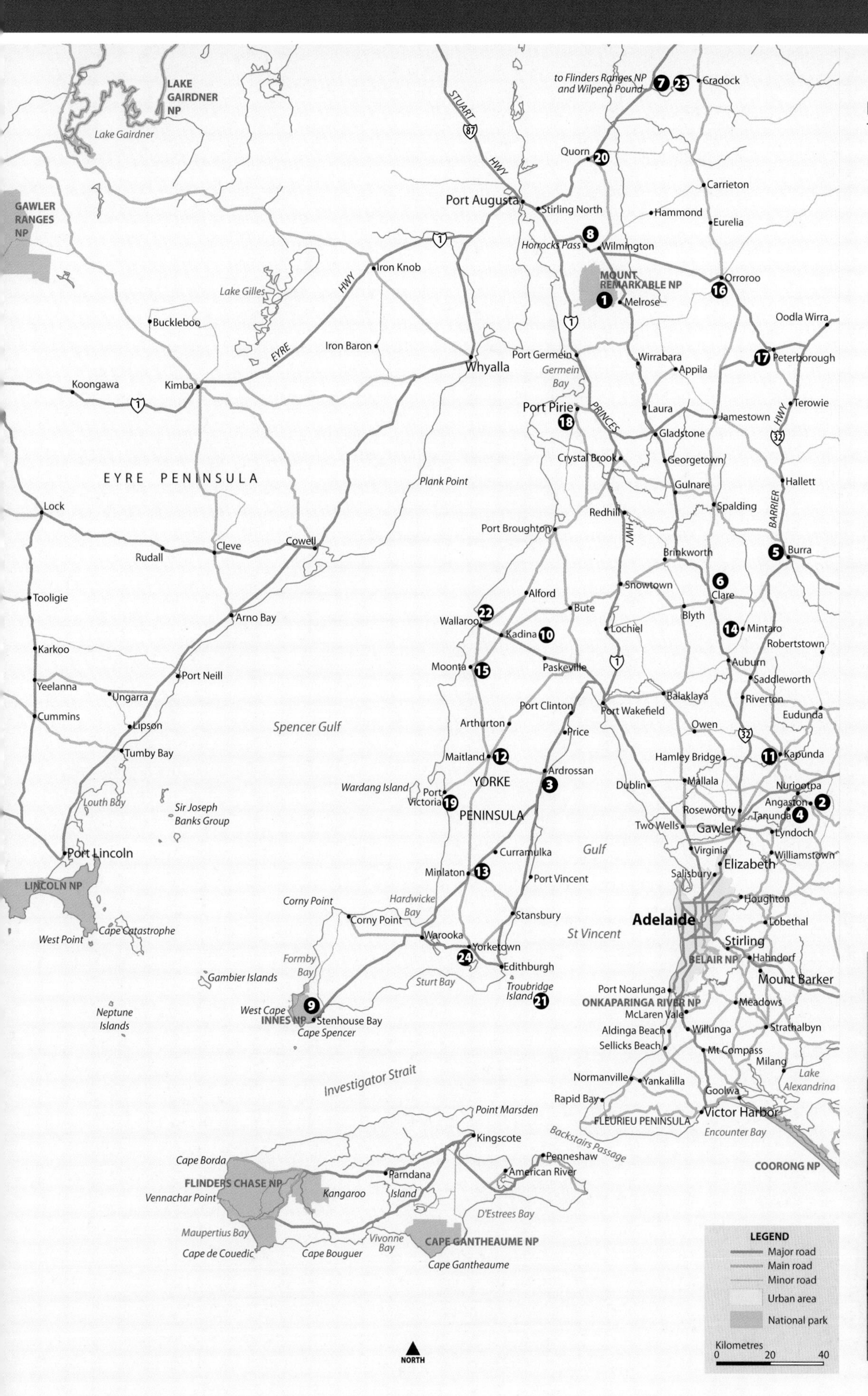

Feature Localities

1. Alligator Gorge, Mount Remarkable National Park
2. Angaston
3. Ardrossan
4. Barossa Valley
5. Burra
6. Clare Valley
7. Flinders Ranges National Park
8. Horrocks Pass
9. Innes National Park
10. Kadina
11. Kapunda
12. Maitland
13. Minlaton
14. Mintaro
15. Moonta
16. Orroroo
17. Peterborough
18. Port Pirie
19. Port Victoria
20. Quorn
21. Troubridge Island
22. Wallaroo
23. Wilpena Pound
24. Yorketown

Flinders Ranges
Top Things to Do

1. Ride the old *Ghan* railway track through Pichi Richi Pass.
2. Explore Quorn's celluloid heritage.
3. See Aboriginal rock art at Youramballa Caves and Arkaroo Rock.
4. Tour the Old Wilpena Station Historic Precinct.
5. Enjoy magnificent views of Wilpena Pound from the Moralana Scenic Drive.
6. Walk the Corridors Through Time Trail at Brachina Gorge.
7. Set out on a desert adventure — follow the old *Ghan* railway past Lake Eyre to Oodnadatta and the Painted Desert.

A Legend of Australian Rail

Construction of the original transcontinental railway commenced in 1878 but lack of funds saw track building stall at Oodnadatta. It is popularly thought that the *Ghan* was named for the Indian (Afghan) cameleers whose teams of camels previously carried freight to Alice Springs and assisted in the building of the track. Quorn locals think otherwise. In 1923, the South Australian Railways added a sleeper car to the train and a crowd gathered at Quorn station to witness its arrival. Legend has it that when the train pulled into Quorn at dusk, an Afghan passenger jumped from the train and ran to a quiet place where he could kneel facing Mecca and recite his evening prayers. A rail worker in attendance joked that if he was the only passenger on the train it should be re-named the *Afghan Express*.

A Detour North – The Flinders Ranges

The Flinders Ranges provide a spectacular window on both the natural and human history of one of Australia's most visually dramatic regions. Massive geological formations, intricate Aboriginal art, historical ruins and stunning landscapes combine to form an irresistible lure for visitors.

Quorn & Hawker Region

Originally a farming town, Quorn's history is inextricably entwined with the development of the famous *Ghan* railway (*see bottom left*). Don't miss the chance to take a ride on one of the superb steamtrains that have been restored to run on the oldest preserved section of the *Ghan* track through Pichi Richi Pass. Four separate steamtrains are in operation, departing Port Augusta and Quorn and some services include meals at the Old Willows Brewery or historic Quorn hotels (bookings, Ph: 1800 440 101). If you prefer a more traditional mode of transport, camel rides and safaris are available through the Flinders Ranges from near Pichi Richi Pass (Pichi Richi Camel Tours, Devils Peak Road, Ph: (08) 8648 6640). The unspoiled beauty, historic buildings and predictably dry climate of the Quorn district have seen it used as a location for numerous iconic Australian films including *Kangaroo, Robbery Under Arms, Sunday Too Far Away* and *Gallipoli*. The Quandong Cafe and Criterion Hotel in Quorn feature displays and photographs relating to its movie heritage.

Several large homestead ruins on the road north to Hawker are a reminder of the accuracy of Goyder's Line. Victims of debilitating drought in the 1860s, Gordon, Simmonston and Kanyaka were once the headquarters of huge sheep runs carrying up to 50,000 sheep. Kanyaka takes its name from a nearby permanent waterhole of importance to local Aborigines and is overshadowed by a large granite outcrop known as Death Rock. Yourambulla Caves, 12 km south of Hawker, conceal some intriguing Aboriginal ceremonial paintings in caves, shelters and overhangs. Walking trails connect the sites. The township of Hawker offers an extensive choice of services and accommodation for visitors to Flinders Ranges National Park.

The Flinders Ranges & Wilpena Pound

The road north from Hawker to Wilpena features excellent views of Rawnsley Bluff, just one of a string of peaks surrounding Wilpena Pound. Take your time to stop at the various lookouts along the way, including a steep walk at Arkaroo Rock that includes Aboriginal painting sites. The ochre and charcoal images depict the creation of Wilpena Pound. The Moralana Scenic Drive follows the southern wall of Wilpena Pound and has brilliant views of the surrounding landscape. Wilpena Pound is a natural rock formation hollowed out by erosion over millions of years. Campsites, accommodation and supplies are available at the Wilpena Pound Resort and there is a multitude of walks to take in and around this breathtaking Flinders Ranges feature (*see facing page*). Near the resort at Old Wilpena Station Historic Precinct are the carefully preserved stone remnants of one of South Australia's oldest pastoral properties. Tours are available daily and the precinct is also the location of the national park headquarters.

Port Augusta to the Red Centre via Oodnadatta & the Painted Desert

If your appetite for Australia's outback has not yet been satiated, the 1400 km journey from Port Augusta out to Oodnadatta and into the Red Centre beckons. Travelling via the Flinders Ranges, this desert adventure offers the opportunity to follow the old *Ghan* rail route past the southern shores of the mighty (but usually empty) Lake Eyre and massive cattle properties to the old railhead of Oodnadatta. Forty-five kilometres south of town near Mt Arckaringa lies the Painted Desert, one of South Australia's most extraordinary landscapes. Created by the erosion of sediments laid down by an inland sea over 80-million-years-ago, and the subsequent leaching of minerals from the rock, these multi-coloured desert hills are the perfect precursor to the wonders of Uluru and Kata Tjuta.

Flinders Ranges National Park Nature is painted in vibrant hues.

Flinders Ranges Silhouette of a grass-tree.

Wilpena Pound The stark and imposing beauty.

Flinders Ranges National Park

Phone Ranger: (08) 8648 0048

Wilpena Pound is the heart of the Flinders Ranges National Park. This vast basin, rimmed by jagged bluffs, rises above grassy plains and cypress-clad foothills. Creeks lined with River Red Gums follow the steep-sided gorges that curve through the ranges. The rich colours of the ranges are an inspiration for the park's many visitors. Spring rains bring a carpet of mauve, red and yellow flowers to the golden grasslands and lower slopes.

Indigenous rock art sites scattered throughout the park are evidence of the area's importance to its traditional custodians, the Adnyamathanha people. Rockpools and waterholes attract frogs, reptiles and birds. Kangaroos graze on the plains, while Yellow-footed Rock-wallabies take refuge in the rocky outcrops of the gorges. Failed wheat and grazing ventures have left their mark among the ruins at Aroona and Wilpena Pound.

Walks in the Park: A network of gravel roads and walking tracks bring the park's natural and cultural features within easy reach, as well as providing access to some challenging treks for experienced bushwalkers. Delightful creekside walks are a feature of Bunyeroo and Brachina Gorges. The Corridors Through Time Trail in the limestone and quartzite gorge at Brachina is a self-guided tour through the park's geological history. Short walks near the southern boundary lead to Aboriginal art sites at Sacred Canyon and Arkaroo where paintings depict the creation of Wilpena Pound. Tracks from Wilpena Pound car park include a 1.5 hour walk to historic Hills Homestead. Add an extra hour to climb Wangara Hill behind the homestead for good views across Wilpena Pound.

Access: Fifty kilometres from Hawker to Wilpena Pound on sealed road. Highway B83 provides access to the western side of the park between Hawker and Parachilna. Gravel roads in the park may be impassable after rain.

Yellow-footed Rock-wallabies may be seen in the Brachina and Wilkawillina Gorges.

Camping: The campground at Wilpena Pound offers powered and non-powered sites and is extensively equipped with toilets, showers, fuel, phone, ATM, internet access, store, swimming pool, bar and restaurant (bookings, Wilpena Pound Visitor Centre, Ph: (08) 8648 0048). A range of other camping sites are available throughout the park.

Mid North & Barossa Valley

The sweeping valleys north of Adelaide have become synonymous with wine production, gourmet foods and vintage villages. Vines were first planted by John Horrocks in the Clare Valley in 1842 and now the region boasts over twenty acclaimed wineries, producing rieslings regarded among the nation's best. Just outside Adelaide, the Barossa Valley is Australia's most famous wine region and its Lutheran heritage towns and hamlets are a fascinating place to stay and explore. Reaching west to the Gulf St Vincent coast are the Adelaide Plains' wheatfields, grazing lands and market gardens.

Clare Valley

The Clare Valley and Mid North remain South Australia's agricultural heartland and produce some of the country's best grain, wool and beef. Set in a landscape of gently rolling hills, Clare is the region's largest town, but Auburn, Mintaro and Burra all provide interesting detours. Clare has an abundance of accommodation (*below*), making it a great base for exploring the local vineyards. There are many organised winery and cellar door tours on offer, but you might just as easily walk, drive or pedal yourself. Just south of Clare at Sevenhill, where Jesuits first produced wine for sacramental purposes in 1851, the priests still produce wine for ceremonial, domestic and international consumption. Take a tour of the winery and neighbouring St Aloysius Church or picnic in the shaded grounds (College Road, Sevenhill, open daily, Ph: (08) 8843 4222). The winery is also part of the Riesling Trail — a 27 km cycling and walking track linking some of the Clare Valley's most interesting wineries and towns. The trail follows a disused railway track and can be toured in sections or small loops. Highlights include the pretty village of Penwortham, pub and gourmet lunches in historic Auburn and dining in the vines at Neagle Rocks Vineyards and Kirrihill Estate. Alternatively, you can rent a bicycle from Clare Valley Cycle for delivery and pick up at any point and they'll even drop off a picnic hamper along the way (24 hours notice required, 32 Victoria Road, Ph: (08) 8842 2782).

West of Clare at Armagh, you can also taste olives and gourmet olive oils direct from the tasting sheds at Valley of Armagh olive groves and the Terrace Gallery at Patly Hill. Drive on to Blyth for brilliant views of the surrounding countryside and Adelaide Plains from Brookes Lookout. Blyth is named for Sir Arthur Blyth, who introduced the bill to South Australian parliament proposing the development of a railway from Adelaide to Darwin in 1875. Little did he know it would take over 130 years to complete.

South to the Barossa

Australia's first great mining rush occurred north-east of Adelaide when copper was discovered at Kapunda in 1842 and Burra in 1845. Cornish, Welsh and German immigrants flocked to the region to work the mines and several museums in the area showcase relics and machinery from the boom era. At Kapunda, this heritage is celebrated at the town entrance by the "Big Miner", an 8 m statue called *Map Kernow* (Cornish dialect for "son of Cornwall"). Kapunda is also renowned as the home of early 20th century cattle king Sir Sidney Kidman, who accumulated 25.8 million ha of grazing lands across Australia and once staged the world's biggest horse sales from behind the existing North Kapunda Hotel. Walk the heritage trail before taking lunch amid walls of local art at the charming Wheatsheaf Hotel (1855) in Allendale, 5 km north of town. As you continue south to the Barossa Valley through the village of Freeling, you may sense you have seen this country before — the region forms the backdrop of the former Australian television series, *McLeod's Daughters*.

Mid North & Barossa Valley

Top Things to Do

1. Hire a bike and ride the Riesling Trail through the Clare Valley.
2. Picnic among vines at the Clare Valley's oldest winery at Sevenhill.
3. Walk the heritage trail at Kapunda and lunch at the Wheatsheaf Hotel in nearby Allendale.
4. Celebrate all things grape at the biennial Barossa Vintage Festival.
5. Sample local produce at the weekly Barossa Farmers Market in Angaston.
6. Take a gourmet tour down Seppeltsfield Road.
7. Explore the Barossa Small Winemakers' Centre in Tanunda.

Valleys of Wheat & Wine

With a Mediterranean climate and steady rainfall, the Clare Valley was first settled as farming land in the late 1830s. Huge holdings, such as Bungaree Station (comprising 700 km^2) occupied most of the Mid North. By the 1860s, the rail system had been established and many of the sheep stations were divided into smaller farms growing cereal crops. Vines were first planted in the fertile valleys north of Adelaide in the 1840s and today it is fine wine production that has put both the Clare Valley and Barossa Valley regions on the international map.

Top to bottom: Château Yaldara; Château Tanunda; Barossa Valley vineyard. **Inset:** Tabor Lutheran Church, Tanunda.

Clockwise from top: Lyndoch Hotel; Angaston; Tanunda Hotel.

Barossa Valley Viticulture

Australia's best-known wine region is also one of the nation's most scenic, with a landscape of vine-clad hills punctuated by charming towns, rustic buildings and grand old wineries. Originally named "Barrosa" by Surveyor-General Colonel William Light, misspelling on Australian maps led to the region becoming known as the Barossa Valley.

By 1842, waves of immigrants from Silesia, Brandenburg, Prussia and Posen (many of them Lutherans escaping religious persecution) had established estates and began making wine and producing food. For more than 150 years, expert vignerons in the region have produced world-renowned wines from shiraz, riesling and semillon grapes (and more recently cabernet sauvignon and chardonnay). Over 500 wine growers supply grapes to more than 80 wineries. Barossa also pleases the palate with excellent local produce such as smoked meats, cheeses, olive oil and delectable German-style pastries.

With a plethora of boutique and luxury accommodation, cellar door restaurants, pubs and historic attractions; the Barossa presents the perfect place to unwind and indulge. Events such as the week-long Barossa Vintage Festival (in April of odd-numbered years), the Barossa International Music Festival (October) and the Barossa Gourmet Weekend (August) attract eager foodies and assorted visitors from near and far.

Touring the Barossa

The Barossa Valley community is proud of its European roots, and towns such as Bethany, Greenock, Lyndoch, Tanunda and Nuriootpa all pay homage to their Germanic past. The architecture is distinctive — solid bluestone buildings and spire-topped Lutheran churches abound. For a great introduction to the area's produce, visit the weekly Saturday morning Barossa Farmers Market in the Vintners Sheds near Angaston. Pick up some local cheeses and delicacies before heading off to find a complementary wine at one of the countless cellar doors. Take a drive down date palm-lined Seppeltsfield Road through countryside dotted with gourmet food outlets (including Maggie Beer's Farm Shop) and vineyards. Tour the famous Seppelts Winery or continue on to Château Tanunda where the Barossa Small Winemakers' Centre showcases the best wines produced by the region's independent wineries. Barossa Visitor Information Centre has maps and complete information on tours, accommodation and trails (Murray St, Tanunda, Ph: (08) 8563 0600).

Yorke Peninsula
Top Things to Do

1. Scoff a traditional Cornish pastie in the historic copper mining town of Kadina.
2. See the landlocked lighthouse in Wallaroo.
3. Ride the Moonta Mines Tourist Train.
4. Dive the 19th century shipwrecks off Wardang Island on the Underwater Heritage Trail.
5. Stay in a lighthouse keeper's cottage on Troubridge Island.

Port Victoria

Port Victoria is known as "the last of the windjammer ports". For 70 years after the jetty was built (in 1878), huge sailing ships (adorned with multiple masts and vast areas of canvas) transported grain from here across the seas to England and Europe. Known as the Great Grain Races, ship's masters pitted their vessels against one another in an effort to reach port quickest and secure the best prices. In 1933, a vessel named the *Parma* completed the voyage from Port Victoria to the English Channel in only 83 days. Photographs and displays relating to this golden age of sailing, as well as shipwreck relics, can be seen at the Port Victoria Maritime Museum (The Esplanade, Port Victoria, Ph: (08) 8834 2202).

Yorketown

The Edithburgh–Yorketown district is dotted with over 200 salt lakes and was once South Australia's major salt producer. Production of salt ceased in the 1950s but the lakes remain. They are occasionally tinged with a pink due to the presence of a pink algae. Yorketown itself is a large rural service centre and an excellent place to obtain supplies before you travel to Innes National Park.

Yorke Peninsula

Roughly the shape of Italy, the boot of Yorke Peninsula is flanked by the waters of Gulf St Vincent to the east and the Spencer Gulf to the west, with Innes National Park at its tip. Its long stretches of coastline are perfect for fishing, surfing and diving; while inland, golden fields of wheat and barley grow in soil once rich with minerals. Seaside resorts now nestle in bays along the coast but it was the discovery of copper ore around the "copper triangle" of Kadina, Wallaroo and Moonta in the 1850s that heralded the Yorke Peninsula's development.

The Copper Triangle

Legend has it that a wombat made the first strike of copper while digging a burrow near Kadina, and the town's Wombat Hotel still stands in tribute to the marsupial's efforts. Kadina quickly became home to over 2000 Cornish men specifically recruited to work the mines and many of the original buildings remain in place. Eat a traditional Cornish pastie here — that trademark crimped "handle" of pastry was supposedly designed to allow miners with dirty hands to grip it without soiling their lunch. Copper ore was smelted at Wallaroo, on the peninsula's north-west coast, and exported from the town's port. It is probably the only place in Australia with a lighthouse in its main street, relocated from Tipara Reef in 2001. It stands adjacent to the Wallaroo Nautical Museum, which presents the port's maritime history and also features George the Giant Squid (Ph: (08) 8823 2366). At Moonta, take a 50 minute ride through the mining heritage area on the Moonta Mines Tourist Train (operates daily from the Moonta Mines Museum, Ph: (08) 8251 1891).

Spencer Gulf Coast

The road from Moonta leads south to Port Victoria via the central town of Maitland. Discover the rural town's early history by walking the heritage trail or simply visit the town hall and peruse the huge bicentennial tapestry, which took over 5000 hours to complete. Port Victoria is set on Victoria Bay and was once a major grain port. Some of the cargo ships never made safe harbour and there is an Underwater Maritime Heritage Trail off nearby Wardang Island where no less than eight wrecks can be dived. Further south, Minlaton has proclaimed itself the "Barley Capital of the World", but the town's most interesting attraction focuses on the daredevil feats of World War I flying ace and local hero Harry Butler. Captain Butler shipped his monoplane, the *Red Devil*, back to Minlaton after the war and once staged an aerobatic display before 20,000 people. His airmail flight from Adelaide to Minlaton in 1919 is credited as the first flight across sea in the State. Butler is celebrated at the Butler Memorial Museum, where the *Red Devil* is exhibited in a hangar. The National Trust Museum also displays Butler-related memorabilia.

Gulf St Vincent Coast

The jagged coastal shoals of the peninsula's south-east tip have claimed many ships and lives. In 1856, after many vessels had already been lost, a cast iron lighthouse was erected on Troubridge Island near Edithburgh. The island is now a conservation park and a popular swimming, snorkelling and birdwatching destination. The lighthouse still stands, having survived an earthquake and fire in 1902, but tidal erosion now threatens its foundations. If you're willing to take the chance it won't topple, accommodation is available in an adjacent keeper's cottage (Troubridge Island Hideaways, Ph: (08) 8852 6290). Many of the coast's seaside towns, including Stansbury, Port Vincent and Port Julia make delightful holiday destinations with protected swimming beaches and superb boating, fishing and crabbing. The major port on this coast is Ardrossan, perched on red-hued cliffs above the Gulf St Vincent. At the town jetty, where horses once dragged trolleys of grain to waiting vessels, locals and visitors now drag Blue Swimmer Crabs from the water with nets (February to April are the best months for crabbing).

Innes National Park

Phone Ranger: (08) 8854 3200

With much of the Yorke Peninsula having been cleared for crop farming in the 19th century, Innes National Park (at the peninsula's tip) is an important conservation reserve. The coastal area features sharply rising cliffs and rocky outcrops sculpted by the ceaseless might of the Southern Ocean.

These treacherous waters are also the final resting place for numerous ships that came to grief in the violent storms and swells that pound the peninsula. At Ethels Beach, the skeletal remains of the *Ethel* and the lonely boiler of the SS *Ferret* are reminders of the perils faced by past sailors on these seas. The park's three lighthouses at Cape Spencer, West Cape and Peter Island were the salvation of many others.

The park's woodlands and coastal heath are significant wildlife habitats. The rare Western Whipbird was thought extinct in this region until re-discovered in the mid-1960s. Western Grey Kangaroos and Emus are also commonly seen as well as pygmy-possums and Bearded Dragons.

Walks in the Park: The West Cape and Cape Spencer Lighthouse Walks, Inneston Village Interpretive Trail and Stenhouse Bay Lookout Walk can all be completed in an hour or less. There are longer walks from Browns Beach to Gym Beach (5 hr return), along an old railway line between Stenhouse Bay and Inneston (3 hr return) and through coastal heath at Royston Head (2 hr return).

Access: Highway B86 via Marion Bay.

Camping: At old Inneston township, one-time gypsum miners' lodges have now been converted into visitor accommodation. Stenhouse Bay has well-equipped caravan and camping sites in close proximity to the visitor centre, store and jetty. There are also numerous other campsites throughout the park and a cottage at Shell Beach.

People of the Peninsula

Cornish and Welsh immigrants provided much of the labour force for the mines of the copper triangle and their cultural influence is still evident. Although mining ceased in the 1920s, 60 years of prosperity left the area with a significant collection of historic buildings and a thriving sense of multiculturalism — to this day the district is referred to as "Little Cornwall" and quantities of Cornish beer (known as "swankie") and Cornish pasties are consumed at the biennial Kernewek Lowender (Cornish Happiness) Festival (staged in May).

Following the cessation of major mining operations, the well-established grain industry, centred around Minlaton, Maitland, Ardrossan, Port Giles and Yorketown sustained the economy. The lucrative grain export trade turned the peninsula's ports into high-traffic shipping centres, but the toll on vessels and crew plying the Gulf waters was also high — an extraordinary 85 shipwrecks are scattered around the Yorke Peninsula coastline.

Wildlife of the Peninsula

One of Australia's quirkiest birds, the vulnerable Malleefowl (*above*) can frequently be seen near Inneston in Innes National Park. This flightless bird constructs massive incubation mounds that can reach up to 1.5 m high and 6 m wide by persistently scratching at the surrounding leaf litter, sand and rocks. Ospreys, White-faced Herons, White-bellied Sea-Eagles and Emus are also found in the park. Rare Australian Sea-lions live on the peninsula's offshore islands, pods of dolphins swim near the coast and endangered Leafy Seadragons live camouflaged among seaweed meadows.

THE RED CE

& THE JOURNEY NORTH & SOUTH

7

There can be few places in the world where the ancient nature of our planet is as powerfully evident as in the Red Centre. Gigantic rocky monoliths erupt from bare desert plains; remnants of rainforest shelter under steepling gorge walls and the mysterious motifs of the land's first inhabitants are found engraved in rock. The memories of the hardships of their descendants are also found in these sands, along with the tracks of desert-defying 19th century pioneers and a telegraph wire that connected colonial Australia to the world. While in the presence of Uluru or Kata Tjuta, it is easy to forget just which century you are in — the experience is without doubt one of the highlights of any Red Centre journey. But while their cultural importance, fame and sheer size may overshadow the centre's other attractions, there are myriad other memorable experiences on offer. Alice Springs came to life with the construction of the *Ghan* railway — named in tribute to Afghan cameleers who ferried provisions to the desert settlers. Ride aboard an old *Ghan* train or visit the original bush hospital established by Flying Doctor service founder John Flynn. The Red Centre is also a focal point for Indigenous art, with many galleries in Alice Springs showcasing works by artists residing in the region. The works of their ancestors remain on view — at Ewaninga, intriguing petroglyphs sacred to the Arrernte people and dating back millennia are carved into the sandstone.

Left: Uluru typifies the majesty and mythology of Australia's Red Centre. **Above:** The MacDonnell Ranges contain some of the Red Centre's most inspiring scenery.

PORT AUGUSTA to Yulara

Port Augusta to Yulara

Top Things to Do

1. Visit Woomera, site of the world's largest land-based rocket testing range.
2. Wander Woomera's Missile Park.
3. Explore the Woomera Heritage Centre.
4. Tour an underground house in Coober Pedy.
5. Play nine holes at the grassless Coober Pedy golf course.
6. Photograph the Painted Desert and Moon Plain.
7. Noodle (fossick) for outback opals.
8. Dine in an underground café.
9. Tour a subterranean church.
10. Take in views of the giant table-topped mesa, Mt Conner.

Coober Pedy & Woomera

Visiting the South Australian outback towns of Coober Pedy (*top*) and Woomera (*above*) is a highlight of any journey to the Red Centre. Coober Pedy's underground houses, surreal landscape and opal mining heritage make for a fascinating stopover. Woomera (derived from the Aboriginal word for a spear thrower) is headquarters for the world's largest land-based aerospace and rocket testing range. Gaze skyward at the rockets and aircraft displayed in Missile Park before exploring the Woomera Heritage Centre.

The 1276 km journey from Port Augusta to the Red Centre commences in the footsteps of John McDouall Stuart, the never-say-die Scottish explorer who was perhaps the most famous (and successful) of all the country's inland explorers. His remarkable south–north transcontinental expedition (1861–1862) paved the way for the Overland Telegraph Line (1872), connecting Australia with the rest of the world. The road that now follows much of his route is named the Stuart Highway and, as you travel the southern section to Eridunda, the landscape that Stuart traversed on foot lies largely unchanged. Despite his various travails (which included temporary blindness, scurvy and paralysis), this son of a Scottish port worker still managed to see such beauty in his desert environs as to call it: "wonderful country ... scarcely to be believed".

The Stuart Highway (via Coober Pedy)

This section of South Australian outback is a vision of red and brown — ruddy soil, saltbush and drought-adapted trees and plants. East of the highway lie a chain of salt pans leading north to the vast Lake Torrens. The term "lake" is used loosely here — the 250 km lake bed has only filled with water once since Stuart's time. There are no towns between Port Augusta and Pimba, only old railway sidings at Hesso and Bookaloo built to service the district's sheep farms. Today, the *Ghan* (Adelaide–Darwin) and *Indian Pacific* (Adelaide–Perth) passenger trains run on these rails beside the Stuart Highway. Pimba, another former siding, owes its survival not to sheep but rockets. Due to its isolation and proximity to the rail line, nearby Woomera was chosen as the location for a British long-range rocket testing centre in 1946. Over its history, the facility has been instrumental in testing defence rockets, tracking space missions and launching satellites. A 127,000 km^2 region around Woomera remains an active aerospace testing and defence exercise zone. Once a closed, secretive town with a military population of 6000, Woomera Village is now home to around 300 people and tourists are encouraged (*see bottom left*).

Painted Desert Sandstone formations rise from the plains at Breakaways Reserve near Coober Pedy.

A teenager's lucky strike in 1915 sparked an opal industry around Coober Pedy that now produces over 80% of the world's opals. The town's underground homes were not constructed as shelters from wayward Woomera rockets. Instead, returned WWI soldiers settling in the relentlessly hot area imported the practice of building "dugouts" from the trenches of France. The name Coober Pedy is reputed to derive from Aboriginal words meaning "white man in a hole". Consequently, there are many subterranean attractions (including art galleries, hotels, cafés and even churches). Test your skill at Coober Pedy's unique grass-free golf course or simply explore the incredible apocalyptic landscape of Painted Desert, Moon Plain and Breakaways Reserve. Tourists be advised — between Coober Pedy and the Northern Territory border there are only two fuel, accommodation and supply stops (Cadney Homestead and Marla). At Kulgera, just over the border, is a roadhouse and police station.

Lasseter Highway – Heading West to Yulara

The Lasseter Highway commences 74 km north of Kulgera at Eridunda and is the main route to Yulara and Uluṟu–Kata Tjuṯa. Forty-one kilometres east of Curtin Springs, Luritja Road diverts north to Watarrka National Park, the location of beautiful Kings Canyon. Closer to Curtin Springs, a lookout provides views of Mt Conner — a huge table-topped mesa that is often (understandably) confused for Uluṟu.

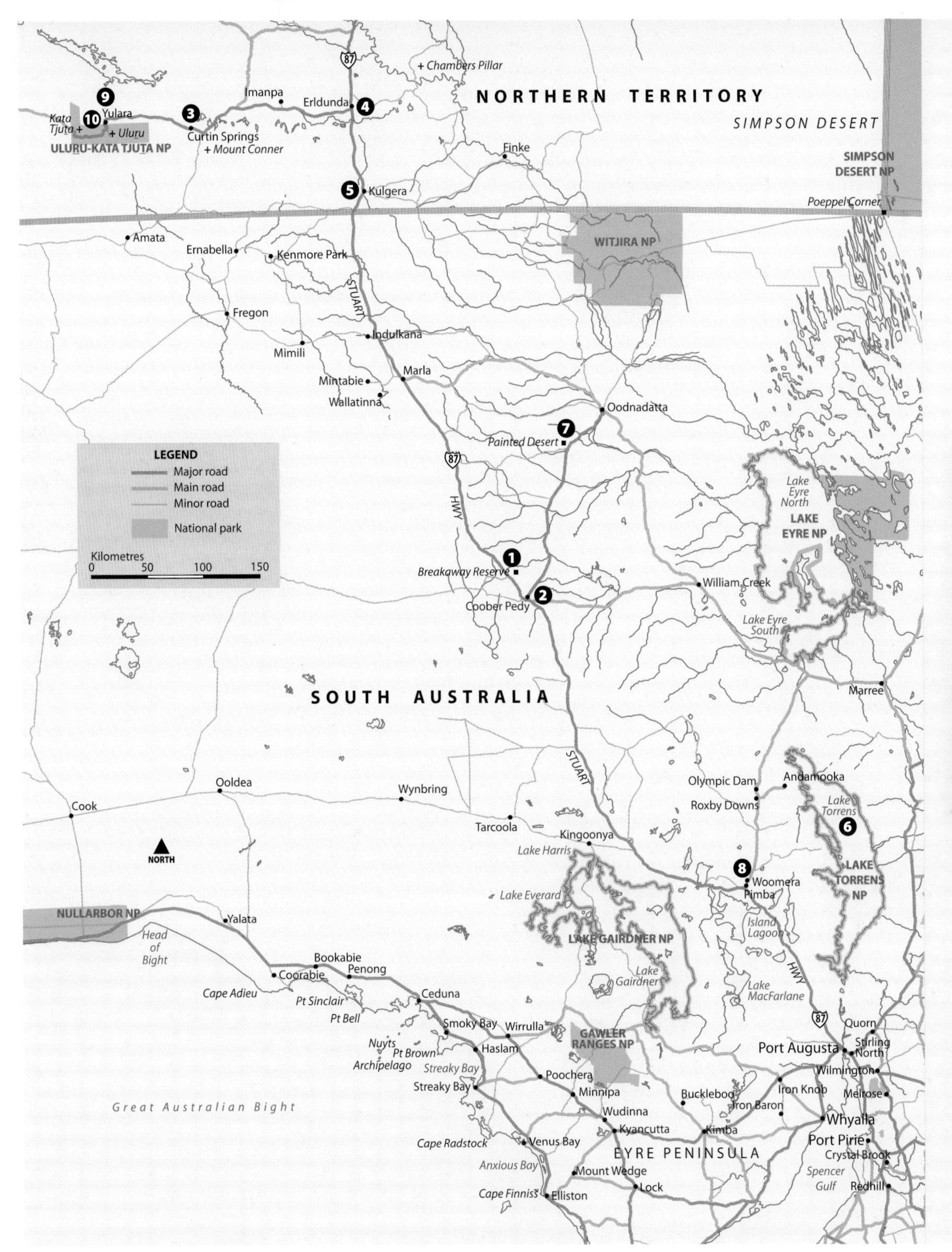

Feature Localities

1 Breakaways Reserve
2 Coober Pedy
3 Curtin Springs
4 Erldunda
5 Kulgera
6 Lake Torrens
7 Painted Desert
8 Woomera
9 Yulara
10 Uluru–Kata Tjuta National Park

The Hardy Ghost Gum

Australia has over 700 eucalypt species. Found in virtually every type of habitat, the hardy gum tree has become characteristic of the country's landscape.

In central Australia, the Ghost Gum (*Eucalyptus papuana*) is arguably the most distinctive species. Growing up to 18 m high, the texture of its smooth, pale white bark adds a stunning contrast to the hardened, red-brown country.

Local Aborigines traditionally crushed the sickle-like leaves of the Ghost Gum to use as a fish poison in desert waterholes.

Look Out for the Devil!

One of the great attractions of travelling to the Red Centre is the opportunity to see the unique native wildlife that call the desert regions home. The Thorny Devil (*Moloch horridus*), with its protective spiky skin and prehistoric profile, is one of the most striking creatures you may encounter. Known to the Anangu people as *Ngiya,* the Thorny Devil (*right*) survives on a diet of ants and has the capacity to camouflage itself by changing colour to match the surrounding soil. It also features a remarkable false head on the back of its neck, designed to deceive predators. The Thorny Devil lives throughout the arid spinifex sandplains of central Australia and is not restricted to national park areas. Look for it in roadside scrub. Despite its fearsome looks, the Thorny Devil is harmless and grows to around 20 cm long.

The Red Centre Circuit
Top Things to Do

1 See Uluṟu and Kata Tjuṯa from the window of a fixed-wing plane.
2 Walk around the base of Uluṟu.
3 Photograph Uluṟu at dawn and dusk.
4 Visit the Cultural Centre at Uluṟu.
5 Take a walking tour of Uluṟu with an Aṉangu guide.
6 Explore the Aboriginal rock art of Uluṟu on the Mala and Kuniya Walks.
7 Photograph Kata Tjuṯa from the dune viewing area.
8 Look for desert creatures on the Walpa Gorge Walk at Kata Tjuṯa.
9 Walk through the Valley of the Winds at Kata Tjuṯa.

Aboriginal Lands

The entire region around the Red Centre is the traditional land of numerous Indigenous peoples including the Pitjantjajara, Yankuntajatjara and Luritja. Many still practise their cultural traditions in the area. All their sacred sites are protected by Commonwealth and Northern Territory legislation and hunting and foraging rights are protected under lease agreements with the director of national parks. Remember that you are a guest of these traditional owners — pay proper respect to their beliefs, sites and traditions.

Uluṟu is the uncontested superstar of the Red Centre, but any itinerary that did not include the other outstanding geological and cultural wonders of the region would result in an incomplete inland experience. Kata Tjuṯa (the Olgas), Kings Canyon and Finke Gorge are just a few of the remarkable features to be found within easy touring distance of Uluṟu. It would be easy to spend a month exploring central Australia's national parks and immersing yourself in the region's cultural history, but even several days can suffice to see the highlights. The key is to properly plan your trip around the Red Centre circuit in advance. Otherwise, it's all too easy to get caught up in the charismatic presence of Uluṟu, and become awestruck by its ever-changing moods.

Desert Safety

Even in such a heavily touristed area as the Red Centre, it is important to take proper precautions to make sure you enjoy your visit in safety and comfort. Despite the fact that many of the region's biggest attractions are excellently managed, with signposted tracks and experienced rangers on site, the Red Centre remains a desert wilderness that demands you pay attention to weather conditions and potential dangers. Never walk alone or divert from designated trails and always wear proper clothing (long sleeves recommended) and footwear (sturdy rubber-soled boots or shoes). Carry more than adequate first aid, water and food supplies. It is advised to carry at least a litre of water for each hour you walk or climb. A hat with a strap, sunscreen and insect repellent are essential. Don't walk or climb in the heat of the day and observe all safety signs. Avoid strenuous climbs or walks if you have high or low blood pressure, heart or breathing problems, a fear of heights or if you are not reasonably fit. Never try to retrieve an item (no matter how precious!) that has been blown or dropped away from a climbing track. Camp only in designated areas and register where necessary. Before setting out to explore, remember also to secure your personal belongings and vehicle. Always inform a responsible person or ranger of your planned route and anticipated time of return.

Indigenous Culture & Photography

The primary rule for photographing Indigenous people and their ceremonies is to always ask first. By doing this you will avoid causing most of the problems or offence that might otherwise arise. In the case of many communities and ceremonies, however, you will need the written permission of a specific Aboriginal elder. For sacred sites (like those found at Uluṟu and Kata Tjuṯa), the simple rule is NO PHOTOGRAPHY at all. It is acceptable to photograph some ceremonial re-enactments staged as tourist attractions, but always remember to ask first.

Planning Your Trip

The best time to visit the Red Centre will depend on your overall itinerary, but in general it is best to avoid the excessive heat from October to February. Wildflowers bloom after heavy rains from July onward. Allow at least two days to explore Uluṟu and one full day for driving to and exploring Kata Tjuṯa — these are only the bare minimums, the longer the better. If budget allows, try to include a scenic flight over the region from Yulara in your plans.

Mt Conner

Despite playing second fiddle to Uluṟu, this giant table-topped sandstone mesa can hold its own. It may not have the same celebrity status, but Mt Conner is three times larger in area than Uluṟu and also changes colour with the sunlight. Commercial operators offer tours and climbs.

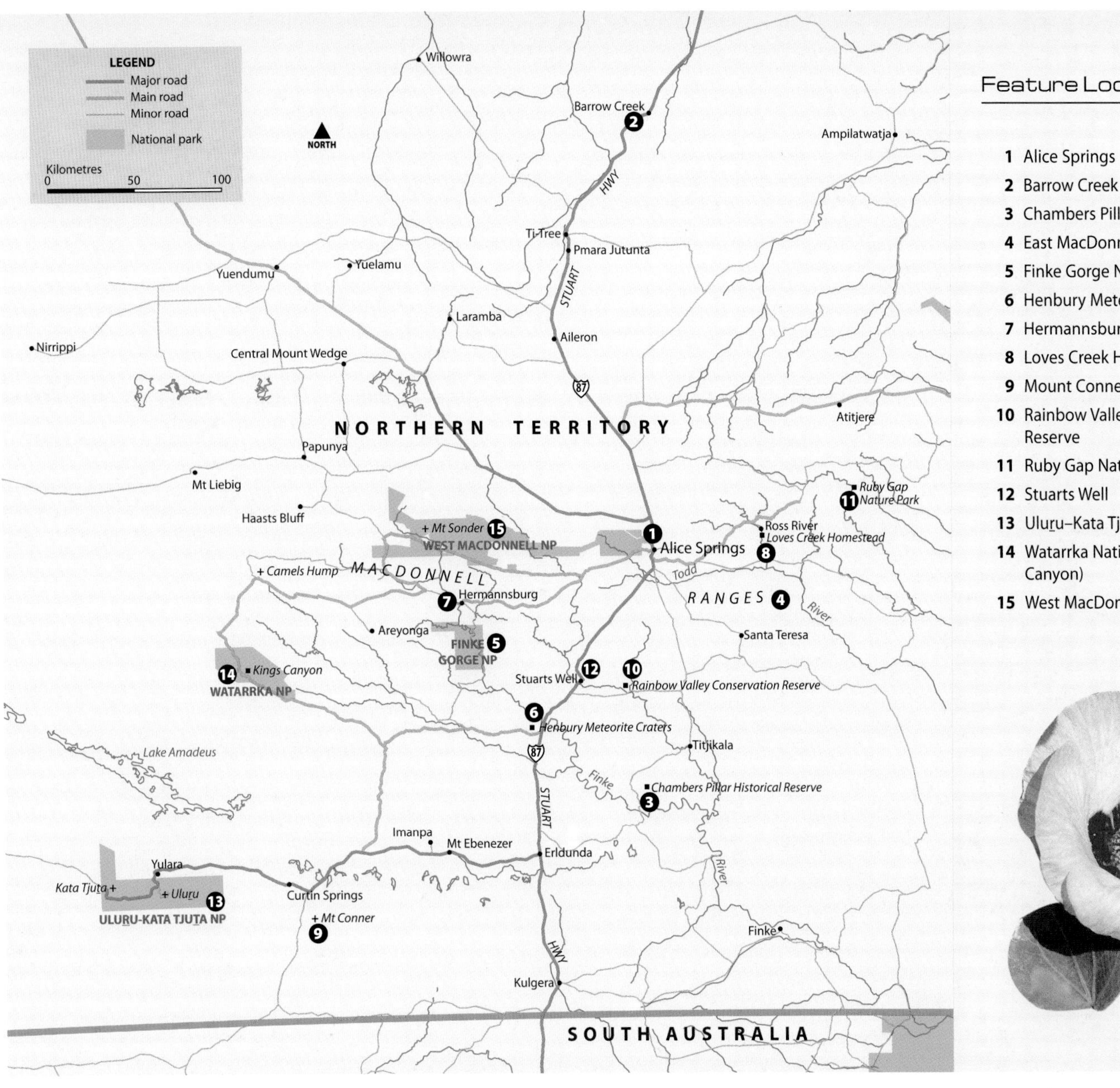

Feature Localities

1. Alice Springs
2. Barrow Creek
3. Chambers Pillar Historical Reserve
4. East MacDonnell Ranges
5. Finke Gorge National Park
6. Henbury Meteorite Craters
7. Hermannsburg
8. Loves Creek Homestead
9. Mount Conner
10. Rainbow Valley Conservation Reserve
11. Ruby Gap Nature Park
12. Stuarts Well
13. Uluru–Kata Tjuta National Park
14. Watarrka National Park (Kings Canyon)
15. West MacDonnell National Park

Sturt's Desert Rose, floral emblem of the Northern Territory

Seasons of the Red Centre

The desert landscape around Uluru–Kata Tjuta changes dramatically according to the time of year. Anangu people define their seasons by the effect the changing climate has on the region's plants and animals.

Aug-Sept *Piriyakutu/piriya piriya*
Dry with warm winds. Plants flower. Animals breed and reptiles abound.

Nov-Dec *Mai wiyaringkupai/kuli*
Hot, dry and stormy. Little food from plants.

Jan-Mar *Itjanu/inuntji*
Hot, cloudy and rainy. Food plants in flower.

Apr-May *Wanitjunkupai*
Cooler and drier. Reptiles hibernate.

June-July *Wari*
Cool nights and frosty mornings. Dry.

Uluru-Kata Tjuta National Park

Zebra Finch

There can be few Australian experiences to rival viewing Uluru and Kata Tjuta for the first time. It is not only the incredible spectacle of these unique geological features rising out of the red desert sand that has such an impact, but also the knowledge that they have played a vital role in the beliefs of their traditional Indigenous owners for tens of thousands of years. The Yankuntajatjara and Pitjantjatjara peoples (known collectively as Anangu) perceive themselves as direct descendants of the very beings who created the land during the *Tjukurpa* (creation time). After nearly 30 years of government control of the Uluru–Kata Tjuta region, and increasing pressure from Aboriginal leaders, the title deeds were handed back to the Anangu by Australia's governor-general in 1985. They subsequently leased the land back to the federal government for 99 years and a joint management scheme was initiated between the Anangu and Parks Australia, which continues today. The cultural and natural values of the entire national park were recognised in its listing as a World Heritage Area in 1987. Visit the Cultural Centre at Uluru before travelling further into the national park — it will only enhance your understanding of the region's significance and will definitely increase your enjoyment in exploring Uluru Kata-Tjuta (13 km inside the park entrance, open daily, 7 am – 6 pm).

Yulara

Most of the township of Yulara is occupied by the huge multi-facility Ayers Rock Resort (*see below left*). The town was first gazetted in 1976 and has the specific purpose of providing services and accommodation to tourists visiting the Uluru–Kata Tjuta region. Yulara's location, only 20 km from Uluru and 50 km from Kata Tjuta, make it the perfect base. Nearly everything you could possibly desire while staying in the Red Centre can be found here, but resort prices apply so beware of monolith-sized bills. Yulara has a permanent population of around 1000, but during the height of tourist season, over 4000 people visit the town daily. Direct flights from capital cities around Australia arrive at Yulara's Connellan Airport.

Driving in the Park

All main roads in the park are sealed and accessible to 2WD vehicles. Drivers are advised that they must stay on the bitumen roads and within the designated car parks. Take care as these roads are often extremely busy and are used by many forms of transport, from bicycles and motorbikes to large tourist coaches. The return journey from Yulara to Kata Tjuta is approximately 110 km.

Ways of Seeing Uluru-Kata Tjuta

The means by which you can experience the national park are ever expanding. Join a minibus tour, take a scenic flight, ride a camel or be chauffeured on a Harley. If you can squeeze it into the budget, the view from the air by helicopter or light plane is nothing less than stunning. Walk Uluru or Kata Tjuta with an Anangu guide (Ph: (08) 8956 2123), or circumnavigate the rock yourself via the 9.8 km track around the base.

Yulara Accommodation

In Yulara, hotels with names such as Sails in the Desert (*above*), Desert Gardens and The Lost Camel leave no doubt that you have arrived in a commercially oriented desert oasis. While not quite on the same scale as that famous casino town in Nevada, Yulara does offer a variety of luxury accommodation and activities not normally associated with remote outback Australian towns. The hotels are contained within a single resort complex and, with no accommodation permitted in Uluru–Kata Tjuta National Park itself, the operators have a somewhat captive market. While some consider it a blight on the landscape, others simply relax and welcome the restaurants, swimming pools and tennis courts. There are also self-catering accommodation and camping/caravan facilities at Ayers Rock campground (Ph: (08) 8957 7001).

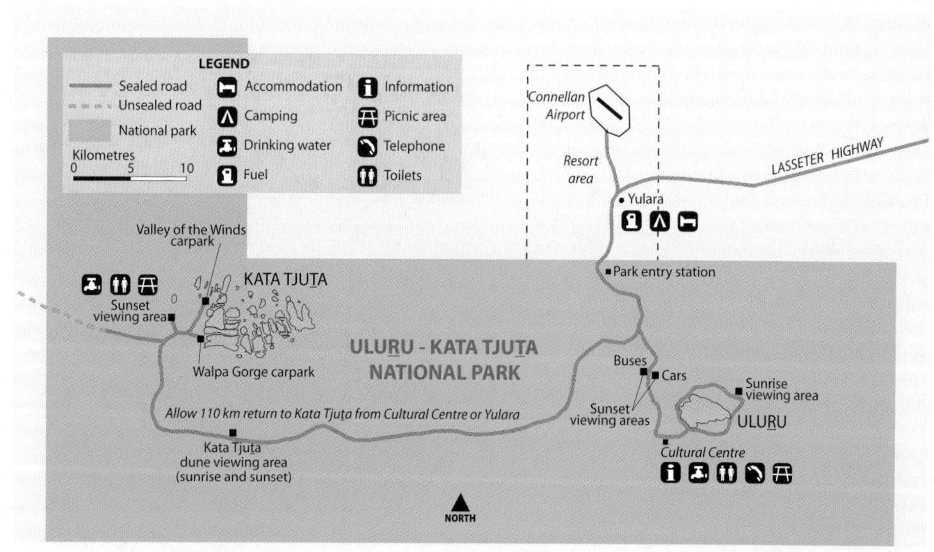

Clockwise from left: The 9.8 km walk around Uluṟu takes 3–4 hours; Uluṟu's sunset viewing area; The loop road around the rock.

Clockwise from top: Moonrise over Uluṟu; A red iron oxide coating covers the rock; Water-worn ridges ripple the flanks of Uluṟu.

Uluṟu-Kata Tjuṯa National Park – Uluṟu Section

Phone Ranger: (08) 8956 1100

While you can appreciate Uluṟu without going any further than the sunrise and sunset view car parks, there are several walking trails designed to enlighten visitors about the rock's cultural and geological history. Depending on the weather conditions (and your own level of fitness), circumnavigating the rock by foot can be one of the best ways to gain a closer appreciation of its true immensity and import.

Climbing Uluṟu: Although it is possible to climb Uluṟu, the Aṉangu owners of the land request visitors refrain from doing so in respect of their traditional laws and culture. The climb path follows a traditional route taken by Mala men upon their arrival at Uluṟu. If you still choose to climb, be aware that it is physically demanding (*see safety advice on page 222*) and can be dangerous.

Walks in the Park: Remember to set out early on any Uluṟu walk to avoid the hottest part of the day. The 2 km Liru Track from the Cultural Centre leads directly to the base of the rock through mulga (and, after rain, wildflowers). From here, the 1.5 km Mala Walk, which includes some excellent examples of Aṉangu rock art, continues clockwise around the rock. If you have come prepared for a 3–4 hour walk, you can then tackle the 9.8 km Base Walk that encircles Uluṟu. The 1 km (return) Kuniya Walk commences from the Kuniya car park and leads around the rock to a waterhole (home of *Waṉampi*, an ancestral watersnake) and an Aboriginal shelter decorated with rock art. Ranger-guided tours of the Mala Walk (departing from the Mala Walk sign are available from October to April (8 am) and May to September (10 am). All walks except the Base Walk are wheelchair accessible in dry weather.

Camping: Not permitted in the park.

The Birth of Uluṟu

The scientific view of the geology of Uluṟu differs from the perspective of the Aṉangu people. Geologists describe the rock as having formed from alluvial deposits that were once covered by sediments in a shallow inland sea. These deposits were compressed into a type of sandstone known as arkose. The rock is about 348 m high but most actually lies below the surface, reaching a depth of up to 6 km. Uluṟu is mainly composed of a mineral known as feldspar and its red colour derives from a coating of iron oxide (which rusts with exposure). According to the Aṉangu, nothing existed on earth until their ancestors (in the forms of people, plants and animals) travelled across the land and created the world as we know it.

Sunrise & Sunset Viewing – Different Moods

The reflecting rays of the rising and setting sun have a dramatic effect on the appearance of Uluṟu and Kata Tjuṯa. When photographing the monoliths at sunset, do not leave until at least 20 minutes after the sun has sunk below the horizon. It is during this twilight period, especially if there are clouds, that both Uluṟu and Kata Tjuṯa will glow bright red. The sunrise and sunset parking areas near both monoliths are positioned to provide the best possible views. You can also view the sunrise from the Dune Walk, which is accessible all day until an hour before sunset (when it is reserved for bus groups).

Uluṟu–Kata Tjuṯa National Park Moods and colours constantly change.

The Geology of Kata Tjuṯa

Kata Tjuṯa (the Olgas) is home to many creation stories and is as sacred to the Aṉangu as Uluṟu.

Like Uluṟu, geologists describe Kata Tjuṯa as being composed of sedimentary rock. As is evident from close inspection, however, the type of rock is quite different. The rock at Kata Tjuṯa is a coarse gravel conglomerate consisting of other rocks, pebbles and boulders glued together by sand and mud. It is riddled with iron oxide impurities (providing the red colouring). The deep valleys between the domes have been caused by chemical erosion processes initiated by rainwater. Between Uluṟu and Kata Tjuṯa is a 65-million-year-old valley now filled with sand and mineral deposits up to 100 m thick.

Kata Tjuṯa (the Olgas)

Kata Tjuṯa (a Pitjantjatjara phrase meaning "many heads") is a distinctive series of 28 smooth, domed peaks divided by cavernous valleys and canyons. At its highest point it reaches 545 m (197 m taller than Uluṟu). The formation covers an area of nearly 22 km^2 and numerous clusters of smaller domes rise out of the dunes in its vicinity. The first European to sight Kata Tjuṯa was Ernest Giles. The Bristol-born explorer was leading an expedition searching for a route from the Overland Telegraph Line to Australia's west coast in 1872 when he saw the monolith from near King's Canyon (Watarrka). He described the formation as: "an exceedingly high and abruptly ending mountain" but his attempts to explore it further were frustrated by an impassable, mud-filled salt pan lying between his party and Kata Tjuṯa. He named it Mount Olga, after a German queen who had made his expeditionary patron Ferdinand von Mueller a baron the previous year.

Wa̱lpa Gorge The walk.

Clockwise from top: Late afternoon from the sunset viewing area; A magnificent view from the Kata Tjuṯa dune viewing area; Kata Tjuṯa in mid-morning from the lookout at Yulara village; Kata Tjuṯa dune viewing platform.

Uluṟu-Kata Tjuṯa National Park – Kata Tjuṯa Section

Phone Ranger: (08) 8956 1100

As with Uluṟu, it is possible to simply drive and walk to the viewing areas at Kata Tjuṯa and enjoy the spectacle without venturing any further. Twenty-six kilometres along the road from Uluṟu, an easy 600 m walk (wheelchair accessible) leads to the excellent dune viewing area (shaded platforms with seating). Uluṟu can also be seen from here in the distance.

The sunset viewing area is close to the western side of Kata Tjuṯa near the end of the main road (and includes the only toilets in this section of the park). Nearby are car parks that serve walkers to Wa̱lpa Gorge and the Valley of the Winds.

Walks in the Park: There are two main walks at Kata Tjuṯa — the Wa̱lpa Gorge Walk and the Valley of the Winds Walk. Both are spectacular but the latter is considerably steeper and longer. The 2.6 km Wa̱lpa Gorge Walk winds through a long gully below sheer dome walls. This moist valley is a haven for hardy desert plants and animals.

The 7.4 km Valley of the Winds Walk leads through stone country to the Karingana (2nd) Lookout. It takes about 3 hours to complete but is closed at 11 am on days when the temperature is forecast to exceed 36 °C.

Access: The dune viewing area is 26 km from Uluṟu on the main park road. The sunset viewing area is approximately 15 km further on.

Camping: No camping is permitted in the park. Camping and other accommodation is available at Yulara.

Peregrine Falcon

Hermannsburg

The establishment of a Lutheran mission at Hermannsburg in 1877 had a dramatic impact on the local Arrernte people. In return for shelter, health and education services, many were persuaded to give up their traditional beliefs in favour of Christianity. Albert Namatjira, who revealed the hidden beauty of the Red Centre through his watercolour paintings and became Australia's most famous Indigenous artist, was born and lived at Hermannsburg. The mission buildings and potters' gallery are open to the public.

Gosse Bluff

A sacred site to the local western Arrente people, the massive crater in Tnorala Conservation Reserve is thought by scientists to have been caused by a comet crashing into Earth 142 million years ago. The crater was named Gosse Bluff by Ernest Giles in 1872 and is approximately 5 km in diameter. There are walking tracks to views over the crater and a picnic area for visitors.

Yulara to Alice Springs

(via Luritja Road & Hermannsburg)

North-east of Uluru–Kata Tjuta National Park are Watarrka National Park and Finke Gorge National Park. It is possible to visit both these parks and the historic mission town of Hermannsburg by travelling in a 587 km wide loop that terminates at Alice Springs. The majority of the route is on sealed road but the 197 km Mereenie Loop section from Kings Canyon to Hermannsburg is dirt road only. Fuel, camping facilities and accommodation are available en route. Coach and 4WD tours also travel to these captivating regions from Yulara and Alice Springs.

Commencing at Yulara, drive 136 km east on the Lasseter Highway before turning north onto the Luritja Road. Continue beyond the junction with Ernest Giles Road to the eastern entrance of the Watarrka National Park near Kings Creek Station. The station was established in 1982 as a combined cattle, camel and tourist property and is now Australia's largest exporter of wild camels. It has fuel, supplies, cabins and camping facilities as well as a boisterous live camel handling and whipcracking show at the Stockcamp (Ph: (08) 8956 7474).

Watarrka National Park & Kings Canyon

The gaping sandstone vault of Kings Canyon is the highlight of Watarrka National Park. As you drive into the park, you will notice the change in habitat from scrubby red desert to green vegetated rocky range. A car park at the commencement of the pleasant Kathleen Springs Walk and the longer Giles Track is signposted to the right. Further along the park road another track diverts to the parking areas for the Kings Creek Walk and the Canyon Walk. Near the end of the sealed road is Kings Canyon Resort, an upmarket desert retreat with spa suites and a restaurant that also caters to more budget-conscious travellers (*see facing page*).

Kings Canyon to Tnorala

After Kings Canyon Resort, the comfort ends and the dirt Mereenie Loop road begins. It leads north out of the park past the Mereenie gas and oil fields, from where a pipeline runs all the way to Darwin. The road veers east near Camels Hump, a peak in the Gardiner Range just to the north. Eighty-six kilometres further on is Tnorala Conservation Reserve — the location of the remarkable crater named Gosse Bluff by Ernest Giles and sacred site known to Aborigines as Tnorala (*see left*).

Finke Gorge & Palm Valley

South of the Aboriginal community of Hermannsburg, Finke Gorge National Park has numerous fascinating features. The entirely unexpected oasis of Palm Valley contains plants of great rarity and beauty (including the Red Cabbage Palm), while a 4WD track along the Finke River bed to the southern section of the park leads to lookouts and the historical ruins of Boggy Hole police camp (*see facing page*).

Wildlife by the Roadside

The Red Centre may look like a tough environment in which to live but it is home to a huge proliferation of wildlife. When driving throughout the region, look out for Emus running through the scrub (*right*) and Red Kangaroos bounding in the open (*far right*). Numerous species of lizard live here (though many stay motionless in the heat of the day and blend in so well with their surroundings that they can be difficult to spot). Stay alert for the Red Centre's most distinctive looking resident, the Thorny Devil and Australia's largest lizard, the Perentie (*Varanus giganteus*) (*above*) which can grow to over 2.5 m in length.

Kings Canyon Looking into and across to the plateau of domes around its rim.

Clockwise from top left: The Garden of Eden; Kings Canyon; The Lost City; Kings Canyon.

Left to right: The desert oasis of Palm Valley; Red Cabbage Palm in Finke Gorge National Park.

Watarrka National Park–Kings Canyon

Phone Ranger: (08) 8951 8250

Protecting spectacular gorges at the western end of the George Gill Range, Watarrka National Park's sheltered gullies are also a refuge for plants and animals. The 100 m deep Kings Canyon offers the most vertigo-inducing views, but there are also several excellent walks leading to permanent waterholes and leafy glades. The park is open all-year-round, but the cooler months (April to September) are more comfortable for walking.

Walks & Tours in the Park: The two most popular scenic walks are the Canyon Walk, around the rim of Kings Canyon, (6 km, 3–4 hr return) and the Kings Creek Walk (2.6 km, 1 hr return). Check the temperature gauge at the start of these tracks before setting out and follow the markers — orange for the creek walk and blue for the rim walk. The Kathleen Springs Walk in the east of the park is an easy 1.5 hour return walk to a spring-fed waterhole. The nearby Giles Track (22 km) follows the top of the range to Kings Canyon and takes two days to complete. It should only be attempted by experienced, fit bushwalkers. Helicopter and motorcycle tours of the park are available from Kings Creek Station (helicopter tours, Ph: (08) 8956 7474; Chrome Saddle Tours, Ph: (08) 8955 8082).

Camping: Luxurious commercial accommodation is available at Kings Canyon Resort. The resort also has budget facilities, including share-facility lodge rooms and powered and non-powered camping sites (booking required for rooms and powered sites, Ph: 1300 669 051).

Finke Gorge National Park

Phone Ranger: (08) 8951 8211

The most popular (and most easily reached) section of the park is Palm Valley with its impressive stands of rare Red Cabbage Palms.

Walks & Cruises in the Park: There are numerous walks off the Palm Valley Road. From the Kalaranga car park take the 45 minute return track to the lookout with its glorious views over a natural rock amphitheatre. Two tracks lead through Palm Valley — the Arankaia Walk (2 km, 1 hr return) and the longer Mpulungkinya Walk (5 km, 2 hr return).

Camping: A campground near the Kalaranga car park has toilets, showers and gas barbecues.

Camel Country

Although there may be more comfortable modes of transport, there is no better way to experience the pioneering desert life than by heading out across the sands aboard a camel (Dromedary, to be exact).

The introduction of camels as beasts of burden in Australia dates back to 1840. Their ability to carry large amounts of cargo across vast distances on minimal water supplies made them the preferred companion of 19th century desert explorers, including Burke and Wills and Ernest Giles. Experienced cameleers from Egypt, India and Asia emigrated to Australia to drive the beasts and the camel was instrumental in assisting with the construction of the Territory's railway line, the *Ghan*. There are now thought to be over 500,000 feral camels wandering the Australian outback in herds.

Camels are bred and farmed for live export and tourism activities in the Red Centre. Numerous tour operators offer camel riding experiences ranging from five minute joyrides to five-day treks. At Stuart's Well, Camels Australia conduct multi-day safaris from April to September (Ph: (08) 8956) 0925).

Yulara to Alice Springs

(via Stuart Highway)

The slightly less adventurous route from Yulara to Alice Springs via the Stuart Highway has the advantage of being a sealed road and a few hundred kilometres shorter than its alternative. It is not without its own attractions — including meteorite craters, aboriginal carvings and stark beauty. The traffic is heavier but, should the urge arise, you can always escape by swapping the car for a camel and venturing out on humpback to explore the desert. And if the idea of travelling on bitumen road surfaces seems out of kilter with your idea of a desert experience (or you just wish to avoid backtracking over the route to Uluṟu) you can take the Luritja Road to its junction with Ernest Giles Road and then follow this gravel track 90 km east to Henbury Meteorite Conservation Park and the Stuart Highway.

Henbury Meteorite Craters

If you are approaching from Erldunda, travel 69 km up the Stuart Highway to Ernest Giles Road. The craters lie within a small conservation reserve reached via a track 8 km down the road on your right. The twelve meteorite craters range in size from 6–180 m in diameter and 15 m deep. The fragments of meteorites responsible for gouging out these holes are estimated to have collided with the planet around 4700 years ago at speeds of up to 40,000 km/h. The craters are best photographed in the early morning or late afternoon and there is a self-guided walking track with information signs detailing their geological and Aboriginal history. There is also a basic campground with pit toilets (but no drinking water or firewood) adjacent to the reserve's car park.

Stuart's Well

When explorer John McDouall Stuart reached the dry Hugh River bed on his expedition north in 1862, his party's battle with thirst was threatening continuation of the journey. He dug a hole in the cracked earth and was relieved to discover water lying below. Today the Stuart's Well roadhouse, known as Jim's Place (and home to Dinky Di, the world's only song and dance Dingo) provides a more convenient source of refreshment. Stuart's Well is also famous for its desert camel safaris, operated by Camels Australia (*see left*).

Rainbow Valley & Chambers Pillar

Eleven kilometres north of Stuart's Well, a track diverts from the highway east to Rainbow Valley Conservation Reserve. The main feature is a striking multi-coloured sandstone bluff that forms part of the James Range (*see facing page*). Close to Alice Springs, an unsealed road following the old *Ghan* railway line departs south from the Stuart Highway. It may be tempting to simply continue on to the Alice, but the magnificent Ewaninga rock carvings (26 km from the highway) and historically significant Chambers Pillar (151 km via Maryvale Station) reward the effort.

Ewaninga Rock Carvings

Phone Ranger: (08) 8951 8211

These age-old petroglyphs (rock engravings) feature a wide variety of symbols and motifs created by Arrernte people. They have been carved in soft sandstone near a claypan that once served as a watering hole and refuge for desert wildlife. The meaning of the petroglyphs is considered by Arrernte elders to be too sacred and dangerous to reveal to those not initiated into Aboriginal law.

Walks in the Park: Follow the 680 m walking track around the rock carving site, but do not walk on or touch the rocks themselves.

Camping: No camping is permitted.

Rainbow Valley The dramatic landscape inspires photography.

Clockwise from left: Sand drifts below the rock face; Colours change with the sunlight; Ancient boulders cluster around the base.

Rainbow Valley Conservation Reserve

Phone Ranger: (08) 8951 8211

The multi-coloured, saw-toothed ridge for which this reserve is named may be one of the Territory's less promoted features, but it is also one of its most spectacular. The dramatic shape and red, orange and white bands running through the stone create a landscape that seems at first glance to have been created by a Hollywood production unit. But nature has been the director here, with water eroding the surface and drought causing red oxide to leach from the layers of sandstone below. It all makes for a photographer's dream, particularly in the glow of sunrise and sunset. After rain, the whole scene is brilliantly reflected by water collected in the claypan below the bluff.

Aboriginal carvings and paintings are found around the range. A large rock outcrop (known as *Ewerre*) to the south of the main bluffs is an Aboriginal sacred site. The black rocks at the base of the northern section of the main formation are also a significant site to the southern Arrente people and should not be moved.

Walks in the Park: There is a walking track to Mushroom Rock, a sandstone formation that is home to Fairy Martins — white-breasted birds that feed on flying insects and build their nests in the cliff crevices. There are unmarked trails around the bluff and into the James Range but extreme caution should be taken when moving away from the main reserve areas.

Camping: There is a campground with pit toilets, picnic tables and wood and gas barbecues. Fees payable on site.

Left to right: Castle Rock; Chambers Pillar.

Chambers Pillar Historical Reserve

Phone Ranger: (08) 8951 8211

Chambers Pillar, a 50 m sandstone tower rising out of plains 160 km south of Alice Springs, was used by early explorers as a navigational landmark. Stuart named the pillar for one of his expedition patrons, James Chambers, and numerous 19th century explorers etched their names into the soft rockface. The reserve is accessible only by 4WD from the Maryvale turn-off.

Walks in the Park: There are walking tracks around Chambers Pillar and Castle Rock. A viewing platform has been established at the base of the pillar to protect the rock from damage or erosion.

Camping: There is a campground with pit toilets, picnic tables and gas barbecues. Fees payable on site.

Alice Springs

On 22 April 1860, John McDouall Stuart inscribed in his journal, "Today I find from my observations of the sun ... that I am now camped in the centre of Australia. I have marked a tree and planted the British flag there." Stuart's location was 140 km north of Alice Springs, but for most Australians, the town itself is now synonymous with the nation's heart. Long celebrated in book, song and film, the Alice is a place of historical fascination. It also has a long history of hardship (for Aborigines and settlers alike) and, despite incessant tourism since the early 1960s, remains filled with reminders of its remoteness and connections with the past.

After its first 50 years of existence, the permanent population of Alice Springs had not grown beyond 50 people. Trains and war changed that. The town came of age with the opening of the Central Australian Railway from Adelaide in 1929, which became known as the *Ghan* (*see facing page*). A military base established during World War II saw over 200,000 people, including American troops, pass through Alice Springs and the town's services rapidly expanded. The American presence continues today with the stationing of large numbers of US military personnel in the Alice Springs region to operate the joint defence facility at nearby Pine Gap. Alice Springs' current population (just over 30,000 people) is inflated by more than 500,000 visitors each year, providing a strong economic base and support for a broad spectrum of cultural activities.

The Alice is directly associated with two pioneering innovations that revolutionised life in the desert — the Royal Flying Doctor Service of Australia (founded by Rev Dr John Flynn) and the School of the Air. Both were made possible by Alfred Traeger's 1928 invention of the pedal radio, enabling communication with people on remote pastoral properties and missions. Today, several streets and the main sports grounds in Alice Springs are named for Traeger.

The Town Centre

Alice Springs is located on the banks of the Todd River below the MacDonnell Ranges. Since 1962, the river bed has been the venue for the world's driest boat race, the Henley-on-Todd. The pedestrian precinct of Todd Mall is the town's retail heart and contains an interesting mix of shops and restaurants. Sunday markets are staged in the mall every two weeks (9 am to 1 pm, weekly during July). The mall is also the location of John Flynn Memorial Church — walk through into the courtyard where a large mural honours Flynn's work. Next door is Alice Springs' second-oldest building, Adelaide House, where Flynn established central Australia's first bush hospital. It is now a museum that includes displays of Flynn's journals, photographs and some of the early radio equipment (open Mon–Fri, 10 am – 4 pm; Sat, 10 am – 12 pm). The oldest building in the town is the original gaol, built in 1909. Roofing iron was transported by camel from the Oodnadatta railhead and the two gaol cells still retain the original metal rings used to shackle prisoners (Parsons St, open Mon–Fri, 10 am – 12.30 pm; Sat, 9.30 am – 12.30 pm). One of the town's early guest houses has since been converted into Alice Springs' most popular (if somewhat contrived) pub, the saloon-styled Bojangles. Eat and drink on cowhide seats at sturdy tables built from original *Ghan* railway sleepers but mind you don't become the meal for Jangles, the hotel's resident 2.5 m Carpet Python (80 Todd Street, Ph: (08) 8953 5102).

The Telegraph Station

The restored Alice Springs Telegraph Station (*above, left and right*) was the site of the first white settlement in the region. It is the best preserved of the twelve original repeater stations along the line to Darwin. The first telegraph message was conveyed from here to Adelaide in January 1872 (Stuart Highway, guided tours, Ph: (08) 8952 3993).

A Town Called Alice

Alice Springs entered existence as a repeater station on the Overland Telegraph Line, helping to forge a link with the world beyond the colonies. The town was originally named Stuart (in honour of the inland explorer), but was officially re-named Alice Springs in 1933. Alice was the wife of South Australian Postmaster General Charles Todd, who was one of the driving forces behind the telegraph line. The actual springs lie north-east of town. The traditional Arrernte name for the area is *Mparntwe* (pronounced "Mbarn-twa").

Indigenous Heritage

The Arrernte (pronounced "Arrunda") people are the traditional owners of Alice Springs and there are many significant sites in the area, including *Anthwerrke* (Emily Gap), *Akeyulerre* (Billy Goat Hill), *Ntaripe* (Heavitree Gap), *Atnelkentyarliweke* (Anzac Hill) and *Alhekulyele* (Mt Gillen). Speakers of more than a dozen Indigenous languages live in and visit the region. Since the early 1970s, the town of Alice Springs has also been a focus of activity for Indigenous artists from all over central Australia.

Above, clockwise from top left: Vintage transport memorabilia is a feature of both the National Road Transport Hall of Fame and the Old Ghan Museum in Alice Springs.

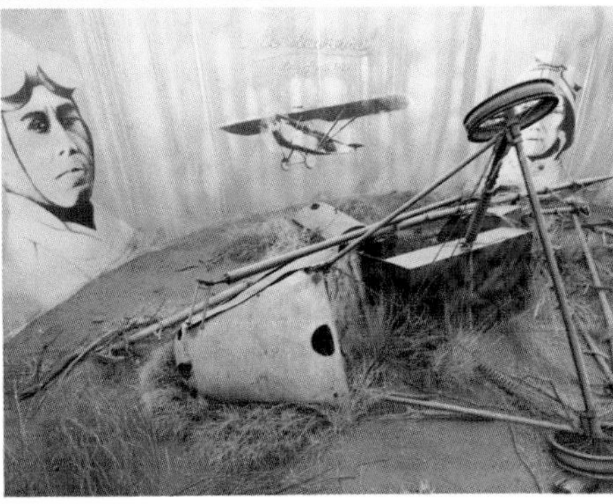

Clockwise from top left: *Yeperenye* sculpture; Prehistoric exhibits inside the Strehlow Research Centre; Royal Flying Doctor Service aircraft on display at the Alice Springs Cultural Precinct; *Kookaburra* memorial.

Central Australian Transport Heritage Precinct

Alice Springs' isolation was only overcome by the introduction of long-distance railway line and road connecting the country's heart with Port Augusta and Adelaide. These transport arteries and their development form a major part of the history of settlement in central Australia and are the focus of the Transport Heritage Precinct (located just south of the town centre).

Old Ghan Museum & Heritage Railway

The Old Ghan Museum has been developed around the original MacDonnell siding. This $7 million dollar restoration project included the construction of the Stuart Station, which had been planned as Alice Springs main rail hub in 1930 but was never built. The highlight is a journey on an old *Ghan* locomotive and carriages over a 30 km preserved section of the original *Ghan* rail line to Ewaninga siding. At Ewaninga an old settler's cottage has also been restored and there are gardens and barbecue facilities. Tearooms operate at MacDonnell. The train departs from MacDonnell each Sunday at 11 am and returns from Ewaninga at 12.30 pm (MacDonnell Siding, Norris Bell Avenue, Alice Springs, Ph: (08) 8955 5047).

National Road Transport Hall of Fame

Adjacent to the Old Ghan Museum is Australia's only hall of fame dedicated to road transport vehicles. Alice Springs is known as the birthplace of the road train, a multi-trailer, long-range truck developed by Kurt Johannsen to haul freight up the Stuart Highway after World War II. The road train is on display as well as a wide variety of early vehicles from motorbikes to touring cars.

Alice Springs Cultural Precinct

Performance spaces, galleries, historic sites and museums combine to form the Alice Springs Cultural Precinct. This vast complex is surrounded by native gardens and includes the Araluen Centre for Arts and Entertainment, Namatjira Gallery, *Yeperenye* sculpture, Museum of Central Australia, the Strehlow Research Centre, Central Australian Aviation Museum, Territory Craft and the Memorial Cemetery. Walk around the grounds and discover the characters who contributed to the development of Alice Springs. There are also seven sacred sites and trees of significance (part of the Two Women Dreaming Track). Albert Namatjira is buried within the cemetery and there is a special section for Afghan cameleers. Aviation also has a home in the precinct. The restored Connellan Homestead was built for the family of Eddie Conellan, who established the Territory's first aviation services in Alice Springs (and for whom the airport is now named at Uluṟu). Two Royal Flying Doctor Service planes are displayed at the Aviation Museum in Connellan Hangar. The *Kookaburra* memorial pays tribute to two pilots who perished in the Tanami Desert in 1929 while searching for lost aviators Charles Kingsford Smith and Charles Ulm.

Clockwise from top left: Crimson Chat; Australian Ringneck; Orange Chat.

Left to right: Masked Woodswallows; Rainbow Bee-eater; Hooded Robin; White-winged Fairy-wren.

Clockwise from top left: Mulgara; Plains Rat; Black-footed Rock-wallaby; Common Wallaroo.

Flora & Fauna of the Red Centre

While there are numerous species of flora and fauna found in the sandplain and dune areas, animal and plant life is generally more prolific in localised "refuges" (such as permanent waterholes, rock crevices and sheltered gorges). Sadly, an estimated 40% of mammal species have disappeared from the bioregions of the Red Centre since the beginnings of European exploration and pastoral settlement 150 years ago.

The introduction of exotic animals such as dogs, camels, house mice, foxes, rabbits and horses has caused the loss of species through predation and habitat degradation. Weed infestation has also promoted changes in flora. These issues remain a threat to key Red Centre fauna such as the Australian Bustard, Emu, Fawn Hopping-mouse, Plains Rat, Mulgara, Southern Marsupial Mole and Black-footed Rock-wallaby.

The Mala (or Rufous Hare-wallaby), an important A̱nangu creation being, has now been rendered extinct in the wild, but 25 individuals reared in Watarrka National Park were provided with a 170 ha feral-proof enclosure at Uluṟu–Kata Tjuṯa National Park in 2005.

Despite its share of noxious weeds, many of the Red Centre's unique plants have survived, including 40 rare and relict species in the MacDonnell Ranges area alone.

Birds

The Red Centre is home to a huge variety of birds but their numbers are completely dependent on the level of rainfall received over any given period. Many of the birds have evolved to cope with the toughest drought conditions, but others simply migrate elsewhere when the desert region becomes too dry.

Nonetheless, it is possible to see many rare birds (including the Peregrine Falcon, Dusky Grasswren and Rufous-crowned Emu-wren). At Uluṟu–Kata Tjuṯa, 178 bird species have been identified (including Striated Grasswrens, Grey Honeyeaters and the rare Scarlet-chested Parrot). Carnivorous birds such as hawks, falcons and Nankeen Kestrels hunt from the sky over the rocky outcrops. Their smaller, insectivorous neighbours, Fairy Martins, build nests high in rock crevices. In the woodlands and shrubs, Black-faced Woodswallows feed on insects and extract pollen from flowers with their specially evolved divided tongues. Major Mitchell's Cockatoos and Red-backed Kingfishers are among those found in the dune and grassplain areas.

River Red Gums in the MacDonnell Ranges and around creek beds are home to Ringneck Parrots and melodious butcherbirds. Waterholes within the park attract Zebra Finches, honeyeaters, pigeons, Grey Teals and grebes.

The Finke River and its tributaries also provide a habitat for riverine birds like Ospreys, Australian Pelicans and herons that would not otherwise survive in these harsh arid regions.

Mammals

Much of Red Centre's mammal population is either nocturnal or habitually elusive. Their numbers are in decline — around 46 mammal species were once known to have lived in Uluṟu–Kata Tjuṯa but today the total is estimated to be closer to 20.

The rocky gorges and stone plains are inhabited by Common Wallaroos, Red Kangaroos, Agile Wallabies and Echidnas. The Mulgara, a small sand-burrowing mammal listed as vulnerable, is found in the northern section of the park along with the *Itjaritjari*, the Southern Marsupial Mole. Numerous species of bat live in the rock caverns.

The Black-footed Rock-wallaby, though no longer present at Uluṟu–Kata Tjuṯa, still survives in the George Gill Ranges and MacDonnell Ranges. The ranges are also a refuge for the Common Brushtail Possum and the threatened Central Rock-rat.

Reptiles & Amphibians

The Red Centre's reptiles and amphibians have been highly creative in adapting to local conditions. Skinks burrow into dunes to escape predators and heat while frogs can live below the sand and immerse in creek beds for long periods.

Uluru–Kata Tjuta has a large reptile population, with 73 species identified. After summer rain, frogs abound at the base of Uluru and Kata Tjuta. Goannas, including the Sand Monitor and giant Perentie, are relatively common but the Great Desert Skink is listed as vulnerable (last sighted in 1936 in the MacDonnell Ranges). Snakes such as the Black-headed Python, Woma and the Large Blotched Python inhabit Watarrka and West MacDonnell National Parks.

The Thorny Devil, central Australia's most famous reptile, reaches 20 cm in length but, as with other desert dwellers, its well-camouflaged hide makes it difficult to spot in the wild. If all else fails, you can always visit the Alice Springs Reptile Centre where over 30 species of reptile are on exhibit from skinks to crocs and you can feed a lizard or become entwined with a python (9 Stuart Terrace, Alice Springs, Ph: (08) 8952 8900).

Clockwise from top left: Centralian Rough Knob-tailed Gecko; Stimson's Python; Leopard Skink; Central Netted Dragon.

Left to right: Desert wildflowers in full bloom; Cycad at Trephina Gorge Nature Park.

Left to right: Lipstick Bush; Parakeelya; Yellow Plume Grevillea; Cassia; Sturt's Desert Rose.

Flora

Central Australia is home to a surprising number of unique plants and wildflowers. The West MacDonnell Ranges in particular are a haven for rare and threatened plants. Rare and relict species include the MacDonnell Ranges Cycad, the Maiden Hair Fern, Skeleton Fork Fern, the Mountain Hakea and the Glory of the Centre Wedding Bush. In the delightful oasis of Palm Valley (Finke Gorge National Park) are the world's only known Red Cabbage Palms. The far more common mulga is found throughout the Red Centre and is of traditional value to the local people who use the wood to make implements, boomerangs, spears and shelters. The larger, sand-growing Desert Oak is also prolific, as are the eucalypts — Centralian Bloodwood, River Red Gum and Blue Mallee.

Alice Springs Desert Park

The daunting scale of the Red Centre's landscape can mean that wildlife observation is a hit and miss affair. The multi-award winning Alice Springs Desert Park (*above, top to bottom*) provides an ideal opportunity to observe over 100 species of native animal and learn about their desert environment. Three kilometres of walking paths wind through 1300 ha of desert wilderness, showcasing a variety of habitats. There is also an outdoor Nature Theatre featuring regular wildlife presentations (including birds-of-prey shows) and demonstrations. The large Nocturnal House gives you the chance to see some of the desert's more elusive creatures of the night. The park is adjacent to West MacDonnell National Park and the traditional Arrernte custodians share their intimate knowledge of the region's environment with visitors. Allow plenty of time to tour the park (at least 3–4 hours if possible). There is a licensed café and picnic facilities on site (Larapinta Drive, open daily from 7.30 am, Ph: (08) 8951 8788).

The West MacDonnell Ranges
Top Things to do

1. Hike a section of the Larapinta Trail.
2. Cycle to Simpsons Gap from Flynn's Grave.
3. Camp at Ormiston Gorge.
4. Walk through Standley Chasm.
5. Clean off the desert dust with a swim at Ellery Creek Big Hole.
6. Explore the Ochre Pits.
7. Take a guided walk at Simpsons Gap.
8. See the Caterpillar Dreaming rock art at Emily and Jessie Gaps.
9. Picnic at Trephina Gorge.
10. Explore the ruins at Arltunga Historical Reserve.

Standley Chasm

At Standley Chasm, vertical rock walls flank a narrow creek bed, allowing only the midday sun to reach the canyon floor. Arrive before noon and take a 1.5 km walk through the chasm as the sun gradually illuminates the rock face.

The West MacDonnell Ranges

Extending more than 200 km west of Alice Springs, the West MacDonnell Ranges dominate the Northern Territory's central range country. Great folds of sedimentary rock stand above arid spinifex plains separated by narrow valleys. Ancestral tributaries of the Todd and Finke Rivers have cut through the multi-coloured layers of quartzite, clay, siltstone and coal, leaving steep-walled gaps in the ranges.

Scenic & Cultural Features

Rivers no longer flow through the West MacDonnell Ranges except in times of floods, but deep permanent waterholes are found at the bottom of rock walls that shelter fig trees, cycads and ferns. These pools provide sustenance to aquatic animals, waterbirds and large mammals (such as rock-wallabies and wallaroos). They have also been the meeting places of the Arrernte people for thousands of years. They believe the ranges themselves to have once been giant caterpillars known as *Yeperenye*. At Simpsons Gap (or *Rungutjirpa*), the red cliffs and waterholes are thought to be the home of giant goanna ancestors. Ormiston Gorge, about 130 km west of Alice Springs, is widely considered the park's most spectacular natural feature. River Red Gums shade a series of waterholes beneath rock walls that open to a 10 km wide, cliff-rimmed natural amphitheatre. The main waterhole is a popular swimming spot and only a fifteen minute walk from the car park. Walking trails include the three hour Ormiston Pound Walk that follows the cliff ranges for views over Ormiston Pound, returning to the main rockpool through the basin.

Larapinta Trail

One of the Northern Territory's best (and longest) walking tracks, the Larapinta Trail, is a 223 km long trek across the spine of the West MacDonnell Ranges. Although a high level of fitness is required to walk the entire distance, the trail is broken down into 12 smaller sections. These range from 9 km to 33 km, each a 1–2 day walk. The trail passes through the major features of West MacDonnell National Park, including Simpsons Gap, Ellery Creek Big Hole, Ormiston Gorge and Glen Helen Gorge. It also connects with other park walking tracks, allowing further exploration of the ranges.

The Larapinta Trail begins at the old Alice Springs Telegraph Station and winds through the park to Mt Sonder. Each of the sections can be accessed by car (some by high-clearance 4WD only), so you can start or complete your walk at any of the trailheads. Basic camp sites are provided en route and all trailheads have a water supply. (Visit www.nt.gov.au/nreta/parks/walks/walking.html or Ph: (08) 8951 8250).

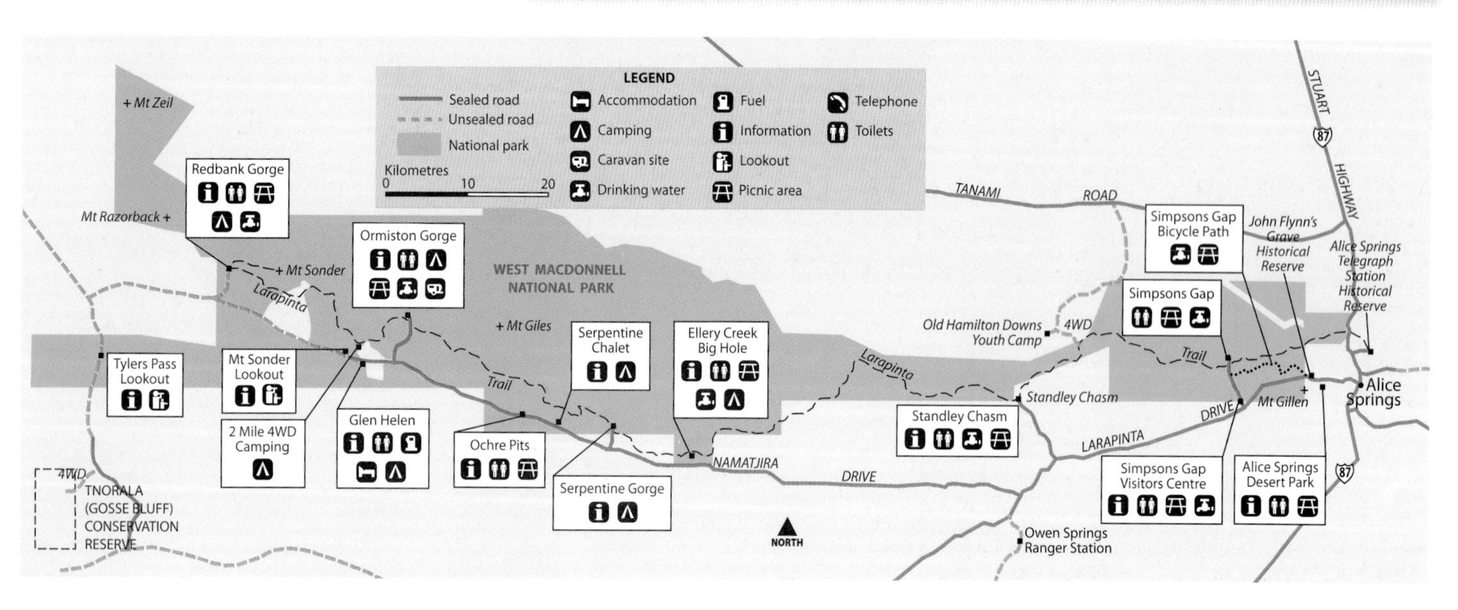

Clockwise from top: West MacDonnell National Park; Ellery Creek Big Hole; Ormiston Gorge.

Clockwise from top left: Glen Helen Gorge; Simpsons Gap; Serpentine Gorge.

West MacDonnell National Park

Phone Ranger: (08) 8951 8211

The magnitude of this national park and the outstanding beauty of its natural features reward either an extended stay or return visits to different sections. Guided walks and interpretative trails provide information about the rich cultural history of the ranges.

Walks & Cycles/Swims in the Park: There is a variety of walking tracks in the park. Many are relatively short, easy tracks leading from car parks to the natural features, gorges and waterholes. If you intend to set out on the Larapinta Trail (or a section of it), remember to register with the Overnight Walker Registration Scheme (Ph: 1300 650 730). The waterholes at Ellery Creek Big Hole, Ormiston Gorge, Glen Helen Gorge and Redbank Gorge are all popular swimming spots (but don't linger too long in the water — it's chilly enough to cause hypothermia, even in summer). There is also an excellent 17 km sealed bicycle path with rest areas and interpretative signs leading from Flynn's Grave in Alice Springs to Simpsons Gap (do not cycle in hot weather).

Access: From Alice Springs via Larapinta and Namatjira Drives (Simpsons Gap is open from 8 am – 8 pm).

Camping: Basic facilities are available at Ellery Creek Big Hole, Redbank Gorge and Serpentine Chalet. Ormiston Gorge has showers and flush toilets. Privately operated facilities at Glen Helen Gorge include caravan sites. A permit is required for bush camping on the Larapinta Trail.

The Ochre Pits

At the Ochre Pits (*above*), 110 km west of Alice Springs, the ravine walls are striped with red, white and yellow soils. These once provided a rich palette of ochres used in ceremonies, body painting and decorating weapons. Ochre was also used for making medicines and in the crafting of magical charms.

Common Bronzewing Birdlife around the waterholes of the Western MacDonnell Ranges is best approached during the cooler hours of dusk and dawn.

Corroboree Rock

Approximately an hour east of Alice Springs off the Ross River Highway, Corroboree Rock is a dark grey dolomite tower of historical importance to the eastern Arrernte people. It is protected by the Corroboree Rock Conservation Reserve and there is a short walk from the car park to the base of the formation. While the rock's precise Aboriginal significance is uncertain, it is no longer believed to be a site for the staging of ceremonies or corroborees, but a place to store weapons. There are picnic facilities and toilets in the reserve but camping is not permitted.

Top to bottom: Historic ruins at Arltunga; Old mine shafts pockmark the area.

Arltunga Historical Reserve

The abandoned ruins of central Australia's original gold town, Arltunga, form the centrepiece of this fascinating reserve. After the discovery of gold in a nearby creek bed in 1887, the area was flooded with prospectors, who often travelled the 600 km from Oodnadatta railhead by foot. Most of the gold was quickly exhausted but the construction of a government battery in 1896 saw the town last another 20 years. Many of Arltunga's stone buildings (including the battery, police station and gaol) are well preserved. There are also several residences, mines and cemeteries in the area. Tours are run from the visitor centre during peak tourist periods (Ph: (08) 8956 9770).

The East MacDonnell Ranges

The East MacDonnell Ranges form an arid, rock and spinifex landscape where tributaries of the Todd and Hale Rivers curve their way through the long ridges along dry creek beds. River Red Gums are a scenic feature of each waterway's voyage, offering shady bowers at permanent waterholes along the river-cut gorges.

Scenic & Cultural Features

The eastern ranges hold great spiritual significance for the Arrernte people. Homesteads and mines also provide evidence of the region's value to Europeans during the search for pastoral and mineral wealth during the late 1800s. Small parks and reserves along the Ross Highway and Arltunga Tourist Drive protect many natural and cultural features in the ranges. Emily and Jessie Gaps Nature Parks, Corroboree Rock, Trephina Gorge Nature Park and N'Dhala Gorge Nature Park all offer spectacular scenery and fascinating walks.

Loves Creek Homestead

Just off the Ross River Highway, 85 km east of Alice Springs, is Ross River Resort — a commercial operation set around the heritage-listed Loves Creek Homestead. The homestead was built on one of the area's original pastoral leases by pioneering cattle farmers in 1898. The resort has cabins, bunk houses and a campground, as well as offering camel and horse rides (Ph: 1800 241 711).

Ruby Gap – A Mining History

When explorer David Lindsay discovered reddish gems in the Hale River bed while digging for water in 1886, he triggered a short-lived "ruby rush" to the region. By 1887 over 200 prospectors were scouring the area for these precious gems, but the venture collapsed a year later when potential purchasers revealed the stones to be far less lucrative garnets. In the meantime, gold had been struck at Paddys Rockhole, 45 km west, giving rise to the more successful Arltunga goldfields (*see bottom left*). The 42 km drive from Arltunga Historical Reserve to Ruby Gap is suitable for high-clearance 4WD vehicles only and may be impassable after heavy rains. At Ruby Gap Nature Park the road follows the river bed for 5 km between steep red gorge walls. A further 2 km walk leads to Glen Annie Gorge. The Northern Territory Parks and Wildlife Service requests that you register with the 4WD Registration Scheme before leaving Arltunga (Ph: 1300 650 730). Camping facilities (and cold beer) are available at the Arltunga Bush Hotel, known as "the pub in the scrub" (Ph: (08) 8956 9797).

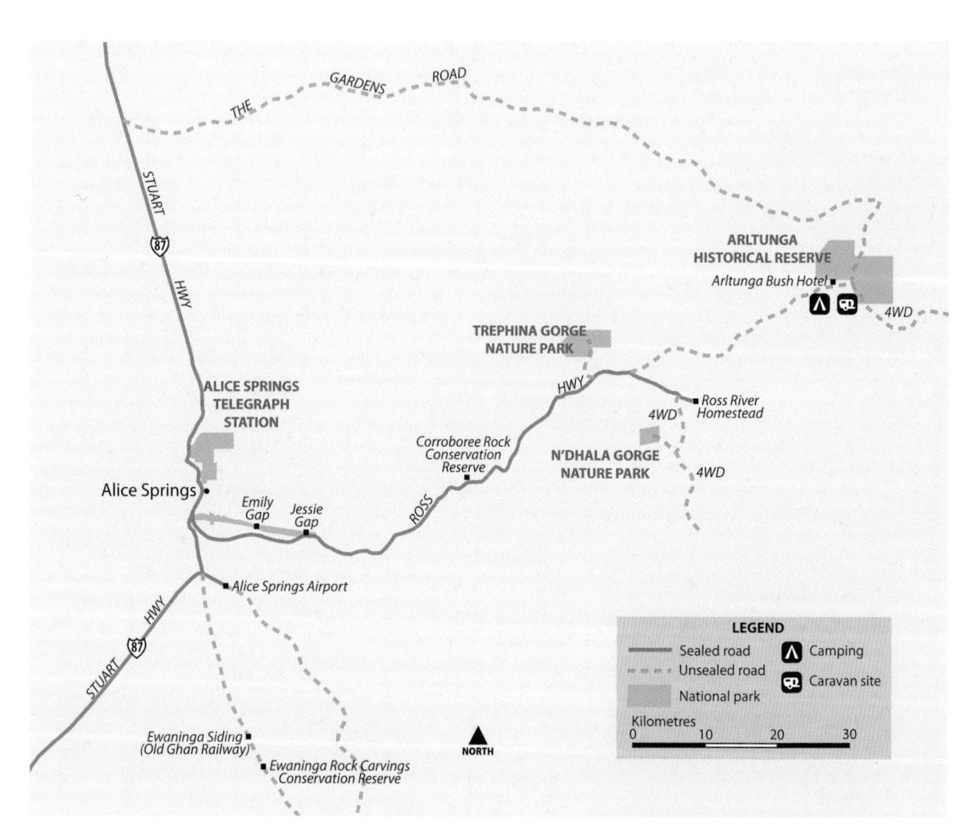

Trephina Gorge The majestic beauty.

Clockwise from top left: The largest Ghost Gum in Central Australia; Rocky outcrops framed by desert eucalypts; Ancient petroglyphs at N'Dhala Gorge Nature Park; N'Dhala Gorge.

Left to right: Emily Gap; Caterpillar Dreaming rock art at Emily Gap.

Trephina Gorge Nature Park

Phone Ranger: (07) 4060 3271

This picturesque park is one of the most popular destinations in the East MacDonnell Ranges. Picnic along the sandy, eucalypt-lined creek bed at Trephina Gorge or walk to John Hayes Rockhole with its stunning sheer cliffs. The waterholes and ridges are a great place to see the Black-footed Rock-wallaby. The park is also home to the Red Centre's tallest Ghost Gum.

Walks in the Park: There are five walks in the park ranging from 45 minutes to over six hours. The 6.5 hour Trephina Ridge Top Trail leads across hilly country to John Hayes Rockhole (also accessible by 4WD). Guided walks are available from June to August (contact ranger).

Access: Turn off the Ross River Highway 85 km east of Alice Springs. From here it is a further 9 km on the 2WD gravel road to Trephina Gorge.

Camping: Excellent camping facilities including pit toilets, drinking water and gas barbecues are available at Trephina Bluff and Trephina Gorge. John Hayes Rockhole campground does not have drinking water.

N'Dhala Gorge Nature Park

Phone Ranger: (08) 8951 8211

The diminutive N'Dhala Gorge Nature Park covers only 501 ha but is the site of nearly 6000 Aboriginal rock engravings, some of which may be up to 10,000-years- old. There are also two scenic gorges.

Walks in the Park: A one hour return interpretative trail leads to the art sites.

Access: Turn off Ross River Highway 90 km east of Alice Springs to the Ross River (Loves Creek) Homestead. The park is a further 11 km of 4WD track.

Camping: Basic bush camping area at the entrance to the park (no water).

Emily & Jessie Gaps Nature Parks

Phone Ranger: (08) 8951 8211

The park includes a sacred site at Emily Gap where there is a large rock painting depicting the Caterpillar Dreaming story.

Walks in the Park: There is a short ridge-top walk between the two gaps where semi-permanent pools lie in sandy creek beds. Euros and rock-wallabies can be seen drinking here at dusk.

Access: 10 km east of Alice Springs along the Ross River Highway.

Camping: Not permitted in the park.

Alice Springs to Tennant Creek

(Linking Map Journey on Page 134)

The Stuart Highway leads north from Alice Springs through arid cattle runs and granite outcrops to the old Overland Telegraph Station of Barrow Creek. To the north and east of the town of Wauchope are the precariously balanced granite boulders known as the Devils Marbles, and Davenport Range National Park respectively (*see facing page*). From Wauchope the highway runs alongside the *Ghan* railway line to the historic mining town of Tennant Creek.

North on the Stuart Highway

While there may be few towns along the Stuart Highway north of Alice Springs, there is no shortage of landmarks, usually accompanied by roadside rest areas. Twenty kilometres north is an unusual stone cairn marking the highest point on the Stuart Highway between Adelaide and Darwin (772 m above sea level). A little further on, a sculpture somewhat resembling an old radio microphone indicates the point where the highway crosses the Tropic of Capricorn. Thirty-one kilometres above this latitude is a memorial to the explorer Peter Warburton who pioneered a route from the Red Centre to the Western Australian coast in 1872. Just south of Aileron Roadhouse stands Ryan Well, one of a series of wells dug under the supervision of Ned Ryan in 1889 as part of a government scheme to attract settlement. It was 25 years, however, before the land was taken up. Glen Maggie Homestead was built nearby in 1918 and its owners sold well water for profit to passing stockmen. The residence also served as a telegraph station and miners' supply store. North of the roadhouse and art gallery at Ti Tree is a memorial to Stuart, who declared nearby Central Mount Stuart the centre of Australia. The Barrow Creek Telegraph Station has been restored — ask for a key at the equally interesting local pub if you would like to take a look inside. Skull Creek, a few kilometres up the highway, was the scene of an Aboriginal massacre in 1874 in reprisal for the deaths of the station master and linesman.

Don't be surprised to be welcomed by aliens at the Wycliffe Well Holiday Park — the region has been famous for UFO sightings since World War II. The pub at Wauchope has been there since before the war when it was built to serve miners in the area. It now offers a campground, accommodation and a swimming pool and does a good trade with visitors to the Devils Marbles (*see facing page*). Tennant Creek (population 3500) is the largest town on the Stuart Highway between Alice Springs and Darwin, but the Barkly region it serves is around the same size as the United Kingdom (or New Zealand). Tennant Creek was the scene of Australia's last goldrush, declared by Prime Minister Joseph Lyons in 1936 to be "the most important goldfield in the Commonwealth". Visit Battery Hill Mining Centre for tours of the battery and old underground mine (Ph: (08) 8962 1281). The town was developed on a site recognised by the Warumungu people as home of the spiky tailed goanna, *Nyinkka*, a powerful ancestral being. The excellent Nyinkka Nyunyu Arts and Cultural Centre is on Paterson Street (Stuart Highway).

Clockwise from top left: Wauchope Hotel, just south of the Devils Marbles; Barrow Creek Telegraph Station; Nyinkka Nyunyu Arts and Culture Centre, Tennant Creek; Glen Maggie Homestead near Wycliffe Well.

Clockwise from top left: A 4WD is essential to explore Davenport Range National Park; Davenport Range National Park is surrounded by rugged ranges; The permanent waterholes are a sanctuary for many bird and fish species.

Clockwise from top left: The Devils Marbles bathed in the soft hues of twilight; The boulders are rounded by natural erosion; A different balancing act from every angle; The formations are a delight for photographers; Cross-country surfers strike camp at Devils Marbles.

Davenport Range National Park

Phone Ranger: (08) 8962 4599

The park protects a region of 1120 square kilometres in the Davenport and Murchison Ranges east of Wauchope. The park's permanent waterholes are a sanctuary for birdlife and fish. Only two sections of the park are accessible — Whistleduck Creek and the Old Police Station Waterhole. A high-clearance 4WD vehicle is essential.

Walks in the Park: There are several short walking tracks around the main camping areas.

Access: From the Stuart Highway turn off at Bonney Well along Kurundi/Epenarra Road or turn off at Taylors Creek along Murray Downs/Hatches Creek Road.

Camping: Basic campgrounds (pit toilets and wood barbecues) are provided at Whistleduck Creek and Old Police Station Waterhole. Fees apply.

Devils Marbles Conservation Reserve

Phone Ranger: (08) 8951 8211

Just north of Wauchope on the Stuart Highway are the famous Devils Marbles. This collection of large rounded granite boulders lies scattered in mounds across a spinifex-studded valley. The boulders were formed by the erosion of sandstone covering slabs of volcanic rock. The Devils Marbles are best photographed in early morning or late afternoon when the reflected sun will accentuate the boulder's red oxide impurities.

Black-headed Monitors and Sand Monitors inhabit the area along with birds such as the Zebra Finch and Painted Finch. Also look out for Fairy Martin nests that cling to the boulders.

Walks in the Park: A 15 minute return track begins at the car park and features information signs. Short tracks lead around the rocks.

Access: Stuart Highway, 9 km north of Wauchope.

Camping: There is a basic bush camping area at the southern end of the reserve with pit toilets and wood fireplaces (no water or firewood).

Wedge-tailed Eagle

ADELAIDE

& THE JOURNEY TO MELBOURNE

8

The city of Adelaide always seems to me to be the perfect starting point for a journey. Radiating out from the city are various routes to desert, riverland, coast and mountain. Within a day's drive are: the grand old mining town of Broken Hill; the wilderness wonders of Kangaroo Island; the ocean-etched sculpture of the Twelve Apostles; the marvellous Murray riverina; and much more. Beyond Broken Hill, the highway ventures east through sheep and wheat farming country to the inland cities of Dubbo and Orange before arriving at the foot of the Blue Mountains outside Sydney. If Melbourne is your destination, the choices are numerous. Follow the trade route of old paddlewheelers along the Murray, and experience the riverboat era at Mannum and the superbly preserved Port of Echuca. Alternatively, head east from Adelaide via Murray Bridge to Gariwerd (the Grampians), where great granite peaks and rock shelters conceal flourishing fauna and some of Australia's best Aboriginal rock art. Along the coast, historic seaports and fishing villages give way to the astonishing limestone formations of the Bay of Islands and Port Campbell National Park. The final leg to Melbourne follows the spectacular Great Ocean Road, courageously carved from cliffs above a raging southern sea by returned WWI soldiers.

Left: An aerial view of "the indented coast" — the key scenic feature of the Great Ocean Road.

ADELAIDE & Surrounds

Adelaide & Surrounds
Top Things to Do

1. Visit the city during the Adelaide Festival of Arts, Adelaide Fringe Festival or WOMADelaide world music & dance festival.
2. Relax on the city's beaches.
3. Explore the Adelaide Hills.
4. Tour the McLaren Vale winery district and the beaches of the Fleurieu Peninsula.
5. Take a trip to Kangaroo Island.

The City of Churches

Adelaide's renown as the "city of churches" is well founded. Some of Australia's best examples of ecclesiastical architecture can be found close to the city centre. On North Terrace, the Anglican Holy Trinity Church is Adelaide's oldest — erected only a short time after first European settlement in 1838. St Peter's Cathedral in North Adelaide was built over 35 years from 1869 and shares a number of architectural features with Paris's celebrated Notre Dame.

A Simple Plan

Adelaide is flanked by wide boulevards, open public spaces and generous gardens. The city's air of graceful harmony is the legacy of Colonel William Light's original vision. Few cities in the world can boast the proportion of parkland to built environment found here. Behind the CBD the Adelaide Hills form a wall of green, enhancing the city's feeling of a close connection to nature.

Originally occupied by the Kaurna people, the coastal region of the Gulf St Vincent in South Australia is distinguished by superb beaches, fertile plains and forested hills. Within this alluring landscape, upon the banks of the River Torrens, lies the meticulously designed city of Adelaide. Governor John Hindmarsh and some 170 free settlers landed at Holdfast Bay, Glenelg, in HMS *Buffalo* on 28 December 1836. Surrounding land was soon sold to free settlers and migrants, artisans, skilled workers and farmers, mostly from the United Kingdom. The city's existing square mile central street grid was set in place almost immediately by colonial Surveyor-General Colonel William Light. As a result, a rare bounty of green space has been preserved within walking distance of the CBD, with gardens and parks forming a natural perimeter on each side. Adelaide also features some of Australia's best examples of colonial architecture. Its array of 19th century public buildings, churches and residences lend it an elegance unparalleled in other Australian cities.

City of Arts

Adelaide is a city with a proud reputation for nurturing the arts, visibly expressed in one of Australia's biggest artistic celebrations, the internationally famed Adelaide Festival of Arts. Inspired by the Edinburgh Festival of Arts, the Adelaide Festival of Arts has been running since 1960 and has presented some of the world's greatest performing artists. It is staged biennially (in even-numbered years) and complemented by the Adelaide Fringe Festival. The WOMADelaide world music and dance festival is held in Botanic Park each March. The River Torrens flows through the city's heart and forms a focus for many of its largest events.

Bound by Nature

Adelaide's natural blessings go beyond the city centre. The city's maritime history is preserved at Port Adelaide, and beautiful Gulf St Vincent beaches (including Glenelg, Henley Beach and Port Noarlunga) lie within easy reach. The neighbouring Adelaide Hills, part of the Mount Lofty Ranges, are scattered with intriguing hamlets and villages whose streets are shaded by deciduous trees. The region was developed by early European settlers, many from Germany, whose heritage remains reflected in the streetscapes and culture. Around the hills are a cluster of conservation parks and botanic gardens, reaching up to the Mount Lofty summit. An easy drive south of the city leads to the vineyard-clad hills of McLaren Vale and the broad, cliff-backed beaches of the Fleurieu Peninsula. Kangaroo Island, west of the peninsula's tip, contains world-renowned wilderness areas and is one of South Australia's most appealing destinations.

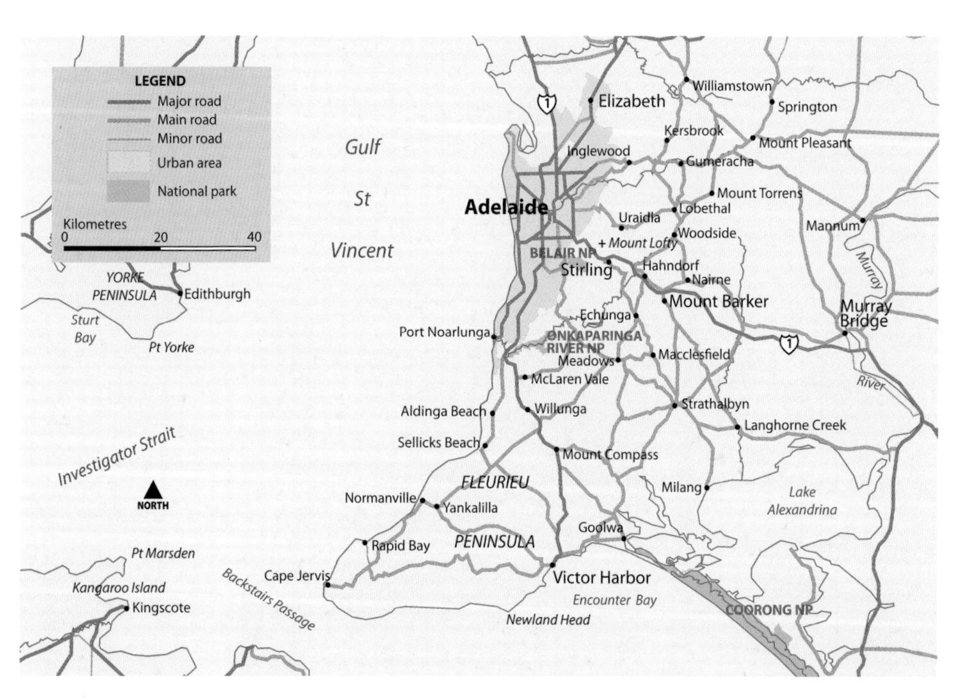

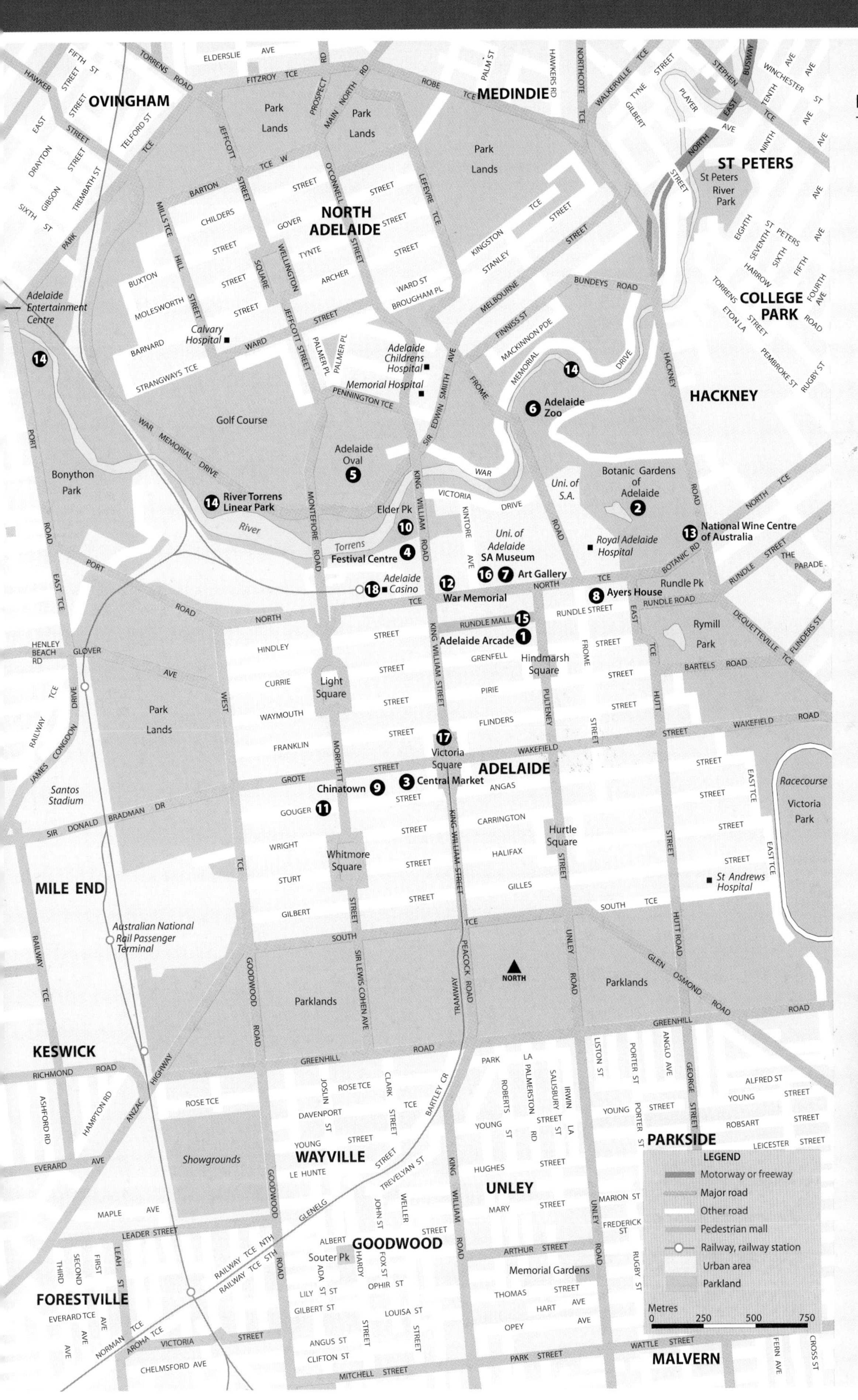

Feature Localities

1. Adelaide Arcade
2. Adelaide Botanic Garden
3. Adelaide Central Market
4. Adelaide Festival Centre
5. Adelaide Oval
6. Adelaide Zoo
7. Art Gallery of South Australia
8. Ayers House
9. Chinatown
10. Elder Park
11. Gouger Street
12. National War Memorial
13. National Wine Centre of Australia
14. River Torrens Linear Park
15. Rundle Mall
16. South Australian Museum
17. Victoria Square
18. *Yerrakartata* Sculpture

Past & Present

Adelaide's modern commercial development has not corrupted Colonel Light's original ambitions for the city. From Montefiore Hill in North Adelaide, a statue of the visionary governor (*above*) overlooks the city he designed.

Adelaide City

Top Things to Do

1 Walk around Victoria Square — birthplace of the Aboriginal flag.

2 Peruse the city's architectural achievements at North Terrace.

3 Visit the South Australian Museum and Art Gallery of South Australia.

4 Have yum cha in Chinatown before shopping at the Adelaide Central Market.

5 Step inside a wine barrel at the National Wine Centre of Australia.

6 Watch an international cricket match at historic Adelaide Oval.

7 Picnic by the Torrens River in Adelaide Botanic Garden.

Adelaide Zoo

Opened in 1885, Adelaide Zoo (*above*) is the nation's second-oldest wildlife sanctuary. The zoo houses more than 3400 animals, both native and exotic with a focus on endangered and rare animals from Australia, South America, Africa and South East Asia (all once part of the supercontinent Gondwana). The zoo also features a reconstruction of Kangaroo Island's Seal Bay (Frome Road, open daily, 9.30 am – 5 pm).

Adelaide City

Where some cities pride themselves on bustle and buzz, Adelaide exudes a more refined charm. From its visionary origins, the city has retained a balance of space and light, resisting the impulse to clutter. The lack of crowding skyscrapers allows sky and sunshine to shine through, shedding generous light on Adelaide's many historic treasures.

At the centre of Adelaide's broad street grid is Victoria Square, known by the Kaurna people as *Tarndanyangga*. It was here at a land rights rally in 1971 that the distinctive red, yellow and black Aboriginal flag was first flown and it now enjoys permanent pride of place here adjacent to the Australian flag. Victoria Square is bordered by some of Adelaide's most important public institutions, including the Supreme Court of South Australia and Federal Court of Australia. *The Three Rivers*, the Victoria Square fountain designed by John S Dowie, pays tribute to Adelaide's triumvirate of major water sources — the Murray, Torrens and Onkaparinga Rivers.

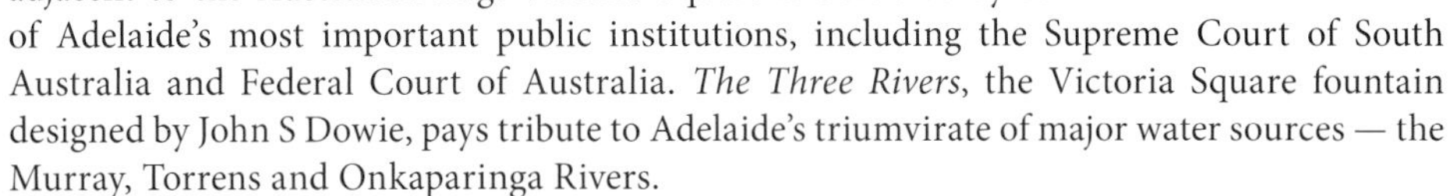

The sublimely elegant North Terrace is home to Adelaide's finest buildings and monuments, including the State Library of South Australia, South Australian Museum, Art Gallery of South Australia and the South Australian National War Memorial. Even the casino meets Adelaide's lofty standards for grace and beauty — its more base attractions being subtly hidden behind the Neo-classical facade of Adelaide Railway Station. Ayers House, the grand former residence of premier Sir Henry Ayers, is a surviving example of the 19th century mansions that once lined North Terrace. The boulevard is also home to a remarkable Indigenous artwork titled *Yerrakartata* (meaning "without design"), occupying the forecourt of the Hyatt Regency Hotel (*detail above right*). This large sculpture and ceramic work, created by Kookatha artist Darryl Pfitzner Milika, Muriel Van Der Byl and Stephen Bower, depicts the seemingly random order of the natural world and represents the land's history.

Adjoining Adelaide's Gouger Street restaurant district in the Adelaide Central Market precinct is Chinatown. Entered via a paifang, or Chinese archway, at either end of Moonta Street, the strip abounds with restaurants, grocery stores and markets. The Adelaide Central Market, between Gouger and Grote Streets, has been in operation since 1869. The market is a sensory extravaganza with stalls lining the aisles selling freshly cut flowers, fruit and vegetables, fish, cheese and imported produce. Surrounding alleys and arcades host cafés, delicatessens, retail outlets and grocery stores.

National Wine Centre

The National Wine Centre (*top and above*), designed to mimic a wooden wine barrel, celebrates South Australia's pre-eminent place in the development of Australia's wine industry. The centre offers tours, a licensed café and even a small vineyard (cnr Botanic and Hackney Rds).

A Sporting City

South Australians love sport. "Aussie Rules" football is closest to their hearts, with two sides, Port Adelaide and the Adelaide Crows, competing in the AFL. International test cricket is staged at elegant Adelaide Oval (*below*) — a lovingly preserved and traditional venue for purists of the sport.

The River Torrens

After meandering down from the Adelaide Hills, the River Torrens springs to life in the city centre providing a focus for arts, recreation and celebration. Adelaide was laid out around the river's banks and the Torrens is now a delightful setting for the city's home of the performing arts (the Adelaide Festival Centre) and the popular Adelaide Festival of Arts.

The distinctive Adelaide Festival Centre was constructed on the riverbank near North Terrace in 1973 — the first such multi-purpose arts centre to be built in Australia. The river is also used for rowing and river cruises; the Henley-on-Torrens, Adelaide's major rowing event, is held in October each year and was first staged in 1911. *Popeye*, a favourite riverboat for many generations of South Australians, cruises from Elder Park to the Adelaide Zoo. Sightseers can also hire pedal boats from near the Adelaide and Victoria Bridges, taking in the River Torrens Linear Park and riverside artworks near the Adelaide Festival Centre. Another option is to pack a picnic and lounge on the terraced lawns flowing down to the riverbanks.

Adelaide Botanic Garden

The 20 ha Adelaide Botanic Garden formed part of Colonel Light's original vision for the city. The intricately detailed, 19th century Palm House (*top*) was imported from Germany in 1875 and restored to its former glory 120 years later. It stands in ornate contrast to the clean modern lines of the Bicentennial Conservatory (*above*) designed by South Australian architect Guy Maron. The conservatory creates a rainforest environment for the cultivation of plants from tropical north Australia, Papua New Guinea, Indonesia and the Pacific Islands.

Rundle Mall

Adelaide's main shopping precinct, Rundle Mall, created in 1976 was Australia's first city street mall. The street is named for John Rundle, director of a London company formed in 1834 to promote settlement in the fledgling colony. The mall is linked to fourteen arcades and shopping centres and is also a forum for performance and street art. Quirky public sculptures, including *Pigs in Space* by Marguerite Derricourt and *Spheres* by Bert Flugelman (*above right*), add a dash of whimsy to this famous shopping zone.

Adelaide Arcade (*above left*), connects Rundle Mall with Grenfell Street and was first developed in the 1880s. It is the city's oldest surviving arcade and adds an air of Victorian charm to the busy streetscape. It was also the first modern retail building in Australia to enjoy electric light. Today its boutique stores offer a stylish old world ambience. Nearby Regent Arcade also boasts a refined interior, showcasing over 30 specialty shops, cafés and eateries.

Museum & Art Gallery

The Art Gallery of South Australia on North Terrace (*above*) holds one of Australia's finest art collections. The adjacent South Australian Museum (*top*) has the world's most extensive collection of Aboriginal artefacts, with more than 3000 items on display in the Australian Aboriginal Cultures Gallery.

Adelaide Coast

Adelaide is blessed with a 60 km strip of stunning metropolitan beaches stretching along the Gulf St Vincent coastline. The city's most popular seaside destination, Glenelg, is a cosmopolitan beachside suburb south-west of the CBD. The 12 km journey from city to sea can be made in leisurely style via a 30 minute tram ride departing from Victoria Square. Adelaide's only remaining tram line first entered service in 1929 and terminates at Moseley Square on the beachfront. On Macfarlane Street stands an old arched gum tree, reputedly the site of the original proclamation of the South Australian colony by Governor Hindmarsh in 1836. Whether the dead gum is in fact the actual tree by which Hindmarsh stood remains the subject of debate, but a re-enactment of the event takes place there on 28 December each year nonetheless. A replica of Hindmarsh's ship, the HMS *Buffalo*, on the Patawalonga Lake waterfront, is definitely not the real thing (which sank off New Zealand). It does, however, have the added attraction of doubling as an award-winning restaurant (cnr Adelphi Avenue and Anzac Highway, Ph: (08) 8294 7000). Salvaged timbers from the wreck of the original *Buffalo* were used in the construction of the Glenelg Mayor's Chair, located in the Town Hall at Moseley Square. The building now houses the Bay Discovery Centre, where a battery of multimedia displays explore Glenelg's past and present. Pick up walking guides to Glenelg's heritage buildings and public art while you are there. In the forecourt, yet another — albeit smaller — replica of the *Buffalo* rests atop the towering Pioneer Memorial.

To the north of Glenelg are West Beach and Henley Beach. In summer people gravitate to Henley Square to dine at outdoor restaurants, listen to live music and laze on the lawns. Half a kilometre north is Grange Jetty where a licensed kiosk also offers shaded open air dining beside the beach and great sunset views over the Gulf. Semaphore is favoured by families and kite flyers, with an International Kite Festival held on the last weekend of March. The vintage carousel on the beachfront is Australia's largest and has been in operation since 1928 when Semaphore was the State's most popular seaside retreat. The historic Semaphore Palais was built as a dance hall and bathing pavilion in 1921.

Port Adelaide lies on the leeward side of the LeFevre Peninsula at the junction of the Port Adelaide River and Barker Inlet. The port was established in 1837 and quickly became Adelaide's major coastal gateway, despite the lack of a wharf — newly arrived immigrants had to trudge through mud and mosquito-infested marshland (granting the port its nickname of Port Misery). By 1900, over 1000 ships used the port annually. Wander among the port's heritage buildings and see the original Port Adelaide Lighthouse at Queens Wharf.

Glenelg

Glenelg's (*above*) picture-perfect beaches have been a favoured Adelaide destination since the mid 19th century. Today, alfresco dining venues, parks, lawns and historic sites lure visitors to the beach all-year-round.

Port Adelaide

One of the city's oldest areas, Port Adelaide was officially proclaimed a harbour in 1837. The waterfront wharves and jetties pre-date much of Adelaide's development and numerous original buildings and relics survive today (*top*). Set on the Port Adelaide River, Port Adelaide remains the city's main service port and its wharves handle many South Australian exports including wine, grain and motor vehicles. A community of resident dolphins (*above*) can often be seen cavorting in the river's lower reaches.

South Australian Maritime Museum

The maritime history collection on exhibit at the South Australian Maritime Museum ranks among the best in Australia. The main exhibition galleries are converted port warehouses (*left*). Permanent exhibitions include explorations of South Australia's immigration history, port life and lobster fishing. Climb aboard the huge replica ketch, *Active II*, in the museum's entrance gallery and experience the life of a 19th century sailor. The museum also houses a database of passenger arrivals in South Australia from 1836–1899 (open daily, 10 am – 5 pm, 126 Lipson Street, Ph: (08) 8207 6255).

National Railway Museum

The National Railway Museum exhibits Australia's largest indoor collection of carriages, engines and locomotives (*left*). It is located on the site of the original Port Dock Station's goods sheds and sidings. See the "tea and sugar" train that once used to freight supplies to residents of the Nullarbor Plain. Working track signals and railway memorabilia are also on display. Steam train rides are available at the museum and along the foreshore from Semaphore to Fort Glanville (September to April). The museum is open daily (10 am – 5 pm, Lipson Street, Ph: (08) 8341 1690).

Adelaide Hills

The beautiful Adelaide Hills provide a picturesque green backdrop to the city centre and conceal villages steeped in European tradition. German heritage and culture is on display in the farmhouses, cafés and shops of historic Hahndorf (*see bottom right*). The Cedars, former studio and residence of famed artist Hans Heysen, is a favourite destination of art lovers. Over 200 of Heysen's original paintings are on display and tours are available of the house and studios. A walking trail around the gardens leads to viewing sites designed to place you before the very scenes that inspired Heysen — compare them with his paintings (Heysen Road, Hahndorf, open Tuesday to Sunday, 10 am – 4.30 pm, Ph: (08) 8388 7277).

Stirling's pretty, tree-lined main street bursts into colour in autumn, while green thumbs will appreciate the floral grandeur of the Wittunga Botanic Garden at Blackwood (*see box below*). Lobethal's old woollen mill and Nairne's original Chapman's factory (home of a famous South Australian luncheon sausage) are both now thriving weekend markets offering a range of local produce and handicrafts.

Gumeracha boasts a giant, slightly scary, 18 m high rocking horse outside a factory selling locally crafted wooden toys. At Easter, real horses take to the track at Oakbank, which hosts Adelaide's most popular Thoroughbred racing carnival, Oakbank Races (featuring the Great Eastern Steeplechase). Birdwood, known for the annual classic car rally, the Bay to Birdwood, attracts car enthusiasts to the National Motor Museum. Like their close neighbour, the Barossa Valley, the Adelaide Hills are also renowned for the finer things in life, such as boutique wineries and gourmet foods. Visit Bridgewater Mill's acclaimed Petaluma winery and restaurant and see the mill's original 1860s waterwheel in action. Further into the hills are prestigious vineyards, cheese makers and olive groves.

Belair National Park in the southern Mount Lofty Ranges combines woodlands, walking trails, recreation facilities and historic sites in a natural bushland setting only 13 km from the city (the main entrance is off Upper Sturt Road). Lunch at one of the numerous picnic grounds (with free gas barbecues) or visit Old Government House, the summer retreat of 19th century South Australian governors. Five walking trails range from 15 minute strolls to longer hikes. Bicycles are also permitted on the park's main sealed roads and a designated shared-use trail. An adventure playground is provided for children and tennis courts are available for hire. Echidnas, Koalas and Western Grey Kangaroos are among the many native species seen in the park. The Eastern Bearded Dragon and slow-moving Shingleback are also frequently encountered (open 8 am – sunset, call bookings office for facility hire, Ph: (08) 8278 8279).

Cleland Conservation Park & Wildlife Park

Set within protected parkland around the Mt Lofty Summit, Cleland Wildlife Park (*right*) is one of the best places to encounter South Australian wildlife. Residents include Australia's most well-known native animals, but the park also protects rarer species such as bettongs and bandicoots. On the park's Yuriddla Trail, Indigenous guides share stories that tell of the importance of wildlife in their culture. See Swamp Wallabies, a Woma Python, Little Penguins and the endangered Yellow-tufted Honeyeater. The park is signposted from the Summit Road (Mt Lofty Scenic Drive).

Wittunga Botanic Garden

Originally established as a formal English garden by Edwin Ashby in 1901, Wittunga Botanic Garden (*right*) has evolved into a fascinating botanical precinct featuring plants from Australia and South Africa. The collection includes natives of the Fleurieu Peninsula, Kangaroo Island and Western Australia. Walk on pathways through the Sandplain and Terrace Gardens or follow the Wittunga Naming Walk, which provides interpretive signs explaining how the various plants have been named (open daily, Shepherds Hill Road, Blackwood).

Mount Lofty Lookout

Mount Lofty (*top and above*) is the most easily identified peak in the Adelaide Hills. Its lookout offers excellent views of the city and surrounds. Picnic by the lake at the nearby Mount Lofty Botanic Gardens or walk through one of the seven "valleys", each dedicated to a specific group of plants. A large collection of ferns is displayed in Fern Gully. Access to the gardens is from Summit Road, Crafers.

Hahndorf

Probably the best known of all Adelaide Hills towns is Hahndorf (*top and above*), which was settled by Prussian Lutherans in 1839. Traditional Teutonic fare can still be enjoyed at the German Arms Hotel and the Hahndorf Inn. Craft shops, stone cottages, floral displays and Plane Trees are all features of the town.

Fleurieu Peninsula

Top Things to Do

1. Snorkel the Port Noarlunga Underwater Reef Trail.
2. Cycle the 34 km Coast to Vines Trail around McLaren Vale.
3. Ride the SteamRanger Cockle Train to Goolwa and Port Elliot.
4. Take a whale cruise from Victor Harbor.
5. Camp on a spectacular coastal ridge high above the ocean at Deep Creek Conservation Park.
6. Spend the night aboard a paddlesteamer at Goolwa.

McLaren Vale Wineries

Located between the Mount Lofty Ranges and Gulf St Vincent, McLaren Vale (*above, top to bottom*) lies at the heart of a wine region that has been producing high quality drops — especially red wine varieties — since the 1890s. The fertile soil is also ideally suited to growing avocados, olives, almonds and stone fruit. A vast patchwork of vineyards covers the famous region and wine tasting attracts hordes of visitors throughout the year. Langhorne Creek, on the opposite side of the peninsula, is watered by the Bremer River — occasional winter flooding sometimes leads to grapes being harvested by boat.

Fleurieu Peninsula

Extending from Adelaide's outer southern suburbs to the Murray River mouth at Lake Alexandrina, the Fleurieu Peninsula is a relaxed holiday region. Scenic coastline, rolling hills and historic towns are complemented by the Southern Vales winery districts. On the peninsula's south-east coast lies Victor Harbor, Goolwa, Middleton and Port Elliot. Goolwa and Port Elliot were first linked by horse-drawn tram and later by rail, capitalising on Murray River boat traffic and port trade. To their north, Strathalbyn has been classified a heritage town and has a fine National Trust museum. The western edge of the Fleurieu Peninsula is hemmed by a strip of beaches and resort towns leading to Cape Jervis and Deep Creek Conservation Park, where the Backstairs Passage separates the peninsula from Kangaroo Island.

The West Coast

Noarlunga is thought to mean "fishing place" in the language of the Kaurna people and the surrounding waters are rich in marine life. Tours operate from Port Noarlunga jetty, taking divers to nearby reefs and wrecks where they can glimpse underwater curiosities, such as the Leafy Seadragon — South Australia's marine emblem. Snorkelling, scuba diving and reef walking are all possible on the shallow reef around the jetty, which forms part of the Port Noarlunga Aquatic Reserve. Plaques along an 800 m underwater trail describe the reef ecosystem, plants and inhabitants.

If you feel like leaving the car and coast behind, the Coast to Vines Trail offers an alternative method of touring the Onkaparinga River and McLaren Vale region. The trail follows 20 km of old railway line from the Onkaparinga estuary to Willunga and can be cycled or walked in sections. En route are the Old Noarlunga township, the beautiful Willunga Hills and the vineyards and village of McLaren Vale.

Maslin Beach, Australia's first legally sanctioned nudist beach, is set below high cliffs and remains popular with McLaren Vale visitors. If you're the bashful type (or maybe if it's just too breezy) head to the clothes non-optional northern end. South of Maslin Beach, divers can explore the underwater cliffs off Aldinga Beach. You can drive the car onto the beach here and at Moana, Sellicks and Silver Sands (but you must buy a visitor's permit from Onkaparinga City Council first).

Toward the south-west tip, Normanville and Carrickalinga are pretty seaside villages with safe beaches and dunes popular with holiday makers. The nearby river town of Yankalilla made international headlines in 1994 when an apparition of the Virgin Mary apparently appeared on the wall of the local Anglican church. Whether you are inclined to believe it or not, the place has now been declared a shrine and attracts visitors from around the world. Rapid Bay to its south-west was the place Colonel William Light first landed in the new colony of South Australia. The colonel marked the moment by carving his initials into a rock which now forms part of a monument on the beachfront. Divers are attracted to Rapid Bay by the opportunity to see marine life around the scuttled HMAS *Hobart*. At nearby Cape Jervis, a vehicular ferry transports passengers daily to Kangaroo Island (*see following pages*).

Heritage Towns

East of McLaren Vale is Strathalbyn, one of the peninsula's best preserved and inviting inland towns. Its Scottish founders laid Strathalbyn out around parkland on the banks of the Angas River. Walk the heritage trail which passes by 30 historic buildings, including St Andrew's Church (*top left*) and the Terminus Hotel, originally located at the end of the old tramway line to Goolwa. The National Trust museum is located in the old court house and police station and features period furnished rooms and a historic yard area.

The main street of the historic slate mining centre of Willunga has changed little since the 1850s. The sandstone Willunga Hotel (*bottom left*), old post and telegraph station, local pug cottages and Old Bush Inn give the town a charming 19th century ambience.

Goolwa

From the mid 19th century, the town of Goolwa (on the final bend of the mighty Murray River) was a bustling riverport.

Visit the River Murray Interpretive Centre on the main wharf to explore the port's history and step aboard the vintage paddlesteamer PS *Oscar W*. If you'd like to spend the night afloat, book a room on the paddlesteamer PS *Goolwa* (*far left*) permanently moored on the river at its own private wharf (Ph: (08) 8555 1733).

Victor Harbor

Victor Harbor on the south-east coast has long been considered the heart of the south coast's tourist region. The site was Governor Hindmarsh's preferred choice of State capital before Colonel Light overruled him in favour of Adelaide. Instead, Victor Harbor became a major port for Murray River trade, transported by rail from Goolwa. Now the SteamRanger Cockle Train uses South Australia's first railway line to carry sightseers along the scenic coastline to Goolwa and Port Elliot.

Granite Island (*left*), just off the coast, was the location of whaling stations until 1872. Southern Right Whales can now be seen close to shore in Encounter Bay between May and October. Take a whale cruise from Granite Island or visit the South Australian Whale Centre in Railway Terrace (Ph: 1900 942 537) for up-to-the-minute information on the best spots for viewing whales. Ride to Granite Island on the horse-drawn tram that once hauled goods across Victoria Pier to waiting vessels (*far left*).

The island is now a nature park and home to a Little Penguin colony. At sunset you can catch penguins returning to shore after a day's fishing (Ph: (08) 8552 7555). An underwater viewing platform at the Below Decks Oceanarium (off the historic screw pile jetty) lets you come face-to-face with sharks, rays and Southern Ocean fish.

Southern Coast

Dramatic folds of rock confront the ocean on the Fleurieu Peninsula's southern coast. Deep Creek Conservation Park (*far left*), 13 km east of Cape Jervis, offers spectacular views across Backstairs Passage to Kangaroo Island, the Pages Islands and into the rugged Deep Creek valley.

The park has five campgrounds and numerous interconnected walking trails. Camp in a stringybark forest near the park entrance or along a coastal ridge with views to the ocean at Tapanappa campground.

The adjacent Talisker Conservation Park protects the ruins of a 19th century Cornish silver–lead mine. An interpretive heritage trail leads through the maze of ruins and mineshafts. For further information, contact the parks office (Ph: (08) 8598 0263).

Kangaroo Island
Top Things to Do

1. Photograph Pennington Bay at sunset.
2. Spend the night in a lighthouse keeper's cottage at Cape du Couedic.
3. Watch Australian Sea-lions at Seal Bay.
4. Swim at Tidal Pool in Kingscote.
5. Climb to Matthew Flinders' original lookout at Prospect Hill.
6. Explore the caves at Kelly Hill.
7. Indulge your inner gastronome on a Kangaroo Island food and wine trail.

Getting to Kangaroo Island

Access to Kangaroo Island is via SeaLink vehicle and passenger ferries from Cape Jervis on the Fleurieu Peninsula (*above*). Two ferries, the *Spirit* and the *Sealion*, operate three return services from Cape Jervis daily with additional services running during peak periods. Cars, boats, caravans, trailers and bicycles can be taken aboard. SeaLink also offers tour packages, including daytrips by coach or self-drive holidays.

Direct flights to Kangaroo Island operate from Adelaide (Air South, Ph: 1800 339 629 or Regional Express, Ph: 13 17 13). The airstrip is at Cygnet River, and a shuttle operates from there to Kingscote (Ph: (08) 8553 2390 for bookings).

Kangaroo Island

Kangaroo Island is situated in the Southern Ocean off the tip of the Fleurieu Peninsula and is reached by vehicular ferry from Cape Jervis or direct flight from Adelaide. Stretching 155 km from east to west and 55 km at its widest point, it is Australia's third-largest island. More than 1600 km of sealed road allow for easy exploration of the island.

Evidence indicates that Aborigines inhabited Kangaroo Island until around 2250 years ago, and it was first explored by Europeans in 1802. Matthew Flinders dubbed it Kangaroo Island after the local marsupial supplied him and his crew with their first fresh meat in nearly six months. By remarkable coincidence, French explorer Nicolas Baudin was also surveying this remote region when he sighted Flinders' ship in what is now known as Encounter Bay.

Sealers and whalers subsequently used the island as a base and Reeves Point, near Kingscote on the island's north-west, became the colony's first settlement in 1836. Fishing and farming later became the island's primary industries. Today, Kangaroo Island exports gourmet foods and boutique wines. Follow the food and wine trails to dairies, cellar doors and honey producers around the towns of Kingscote, Penneshaw, American River, Parndana and Flinders Chase. The magnificent coastal scenery and native wildlife in Kangaroo Island's conservation parks remain its major lure. At Cape de Couedic, a colony of New Zealand Fur-seals lounge on the rocks, while visitors to Seal Bay Conservation Park can take a guided beach tour to view Australian Sea-lions (the country's only endemic seal).

Admirals Arch and Remarkable Rocks, two unusual sculpted stone formations perched precariously above the ocean in Flinders Chase National Park, are reminders of nature's slow power and artistry. At the opposite end of the island, visitors can explore Cape Willoughby and Lesueur Conservation Parks, or climb Prospect Hill's 512 steps to discover spectacular views of Pelican Lagoon and American River — on a clear day even Mount Lofty is visible. Daytrips are possible to Kangaroo Island but its wealth of natural attractions and fascinating heritage sites will make you wish you had stayed longer.

Towns & Accommodation

Penneshaw on the north-west coast is the arrival point for ferries from Cape Jervis. This village of whitewashed houses enveloped in green is one of the island's most charming locations but its most popular attraction is the Little Penguins that live along the shoreline. The adjacent Baudin Conservation Park was private farming land held by the Bates family for 134 years until 1995. Walk along the shore from town and turn onto the bullock track leading to Harry Bates' cottage. At Kingscote on Nepean Bay, explore the island's history at the Hope Cottage Museum or take a swim at Tidal Pool near the jetty. Accommodation on Kangaroo Island is plentiful and ranges from basic campsites in Flinders Chase National Park to guesthouses, luxury apartments, houses and lighthouse keeper's cottages (contact Kangaroo Island Gateway Visitor Information Centre, Howard Drive, Penneshaw, Ph: (08) 8553 1185).

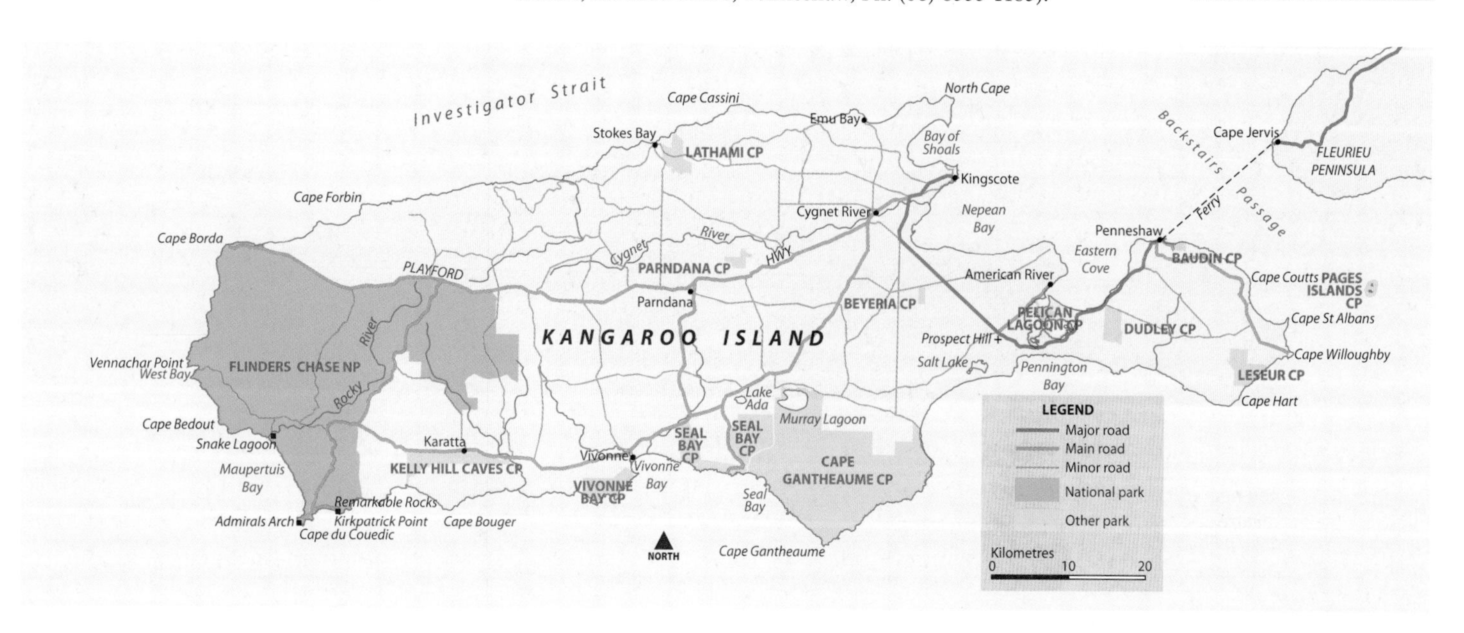

One Island, So Many Great Adventures

There is an embarrassment of natural riches for you to enjoy on Kangaroo Island. Due to its isolation and diversity of habitat, the entire island has become a sanctuary for birds and mammals. The captivating scenery includes ocean-battered headlands, wild beaches and secluded bays. Walk in Flinders Chase National Park, snoop on seals and penguins, explore caves, climb a lighthouse, snorkel, surf and swim — this island overflows with adventurous possibility.

The Penguins of Penneshaw

Take a guided evening tour of the resident Little Penguin colony from the Penneshaw Penguin Centre in Lloyd Collins Reserve. (Tours nightly at dusk, Ph: (08) 8553 1103).

Cape Willoughby Lighthouse

Cape Willoughby's Lighthouse once guided vessels through the waters of Backstairs Passage. Erected in 1852, the lighthouse is the State's oldest. Take a tour to the top (Ph: (08) 8553 1191).

Pennington Bay for Sunset

The glorious vision of sunset from the lookout at Pennington Bay will have you clutching for your camera. This is also a popular surfing and fishing beach, but beware the powerful ocean rips.

Pelican Picnic at Kingscote

The beaks and bellies of Kingscote's Australian Pelicans hold huge meals of fish fetched around the town jetty. Anglers also compete for Tommy Ruff, garfish, King George Whiting and snook.

Explore the Subterranean World

Legend has it that the caves of Kelly Hill were discovered by an unfortunate horse (that fell into one). You can tour these beautiful limestone caves in safety at Kelly Hill Conservation Park.

Vivacious Vivonne Bay

Identified by a Sydney University study as Australia's best beach, Vivonne Bay is the perfect place for swimming, surfing, snorkelling, beachcombing, sea-viewing and sand-lounging.

Sea-lions at Seal Bay

Despite being hunted near to extinction in the 19th century, Australian Sea-lions now live in peace at Seal Bay. Take a guided beach tour or stroll the boardwalk to access viewing platforms (Ph: (08) 8559 4207).

Investigate Island Heritage

Kangaroo Island has an absorbing history. Don't miss seeing the Penneshaw Maritime and Folk Museum (Howard Drive), the Parndana Soldier Settlement Museum (Wedgewood Road) and Matthew Flinders lookout at Prospect Hill.

Cape du Couedic Seals

Walkways around the cliffs at Cape du Couedic afford views of New Zealand Fur-seals resting on the rocks below. Recharge yourself and stay for a night or two in a historic Cape du Couedic lighthouse keeper's cottage.

Flinders Chase National Park

Top Things to Do

1. Comb secluded beaches on the island's western coast.
2. Walk from Cape du Couedic Lighthouse to the granite tunnels of Admirals Arch.
3. Photograph precariously poised boulders at Remarkable Rocks.
4. Follow the Rocky River Trail from Snake Lagoon to waterfalls and sandy beaches.
5. See Little Penguin colonies in the park's limestone caves.
6. Camp among kangaroos and saltwater-drinking Cape Barren Geese.

Marine Mammals

Some of Kangaroo Island's creatures, like the New Zealand Fur-seal, are naturally timid, perhaps wary of humans who hunted their ancestors and nearly rendered them extinct. The seals rest and breed around Admirals Arch in Flinders Chase National Park — look from the viewing platforms for pups playing in the pools. Australian Sea-lions (*left*) also rest and raise pups on the rocks below the sandstone lighthouse at Cape du Couedic.

Flinders Chase National Park

Phone Ranger: (08) 8559 7235

The majority of the western half of Kangaroo Island is protected habitat. Flinders Chase National Park is the largest of Kangaroo Island's many conservation reserves and is best known for its abundant wildlife and striking coastal rock formations.

The park is divided into three sections. The western end of the island's undulating plateau is cloaked in dense, windshorn mallee and heath scrub. Creeks and rivers fringed with eucalypt forest drop from the low plateau to small beaches tucked between eroded granite headlands and limestone cliffs. At Cape du Couedic a historic lighthouse overlooks spectacular cliffs confronting the colossal force of the Southern Ocean. The Cape Borda section includes a historic lightstation, lighthouse keepers' cemetery and original cottages. The Gosse Lands in the north-east are dominated by open mallee country split by streams. The park is well serviced with gravel roads leading to coastal lookouts and walking tracks.

Cape du Couedic Flinders Chase National Park.

Walks in the Park: Flinders Chase National Park offers a variety of walks for all levels of age, fitness and experience. For comprehensive details of the many trails and walking opportunities, obtain a copy of the *Parks of Kangaroo Island* guide from the Flinders Chase Visitors Centre (Ph: (08) 8559 7235 or visit www.parks.sa.gov.au). Short walks include an easy stroll from the lighthouse at Cape du Couedic to the granite tunnel formation of Admirals Arch. A little to the east, the oft-photographed Remarkable Rocks perform a delicate balancing act on Kirkpatrick Point. The 4.5 km Platypus Waterholes Walk (2 hr return) from the visitor centre across Black Swamp to Rocky River is a popular wildlife walk, while the 3 km Rocky River Trail at Snake Lagoon takes in mallee scrub and a delightful waterfall as it follows the river to a small sandy beach. Tracks alongside Sandy Creek and Breakneck River give you the chance to see the park's forest and heathland habitats before emerging onto secluded beaches. The park's longest and most strenuous walk is the 8 km circuit at Ravine des Casoars Wilderness Protection Area. This 3 hour creekside trek through eucalypt forest in the north of the park includes large limestone caves inhabited by Little Penguins.

Access: Western section access via South Coast Highway. Cape Borda section access via Playford Highway. Gosse Lands section access via Playford Highway and West End Highway.

Camping: There are three main campgrounds in Flinders Chase National Park and all are located in the western section. Rocky River campground is the best equipped and is caravan accessible. Hot showers, a telephone and water are also available. Snake Lagoon and West Bay are tent camping sites and have toilets only. Fees, bookings and permits apply. Cottages are also available for hire at Cape du Couedic, Cape Borda and Rocky River (Ph: (08) 8559 7235).

Top to bottom: Typical woodland and low heath at Flinders Chase National Park; Admirals Arch frames the ocean at Cape du Couedic; Granite boulders at Remarkable Rocks.

Kangaroo Island Wildlife

The diversity of Kangaroo Island's wildlife is predominantly due to a lack of feral predators and the introduction of native animals thought to be under threat on the mainland. Over a period of 40 years from 1919, 23 new animal species were released into the park. Koalas, Platypuses and ringtail possums now coexist with original residents, such as the Kangaroo Island Kangaroo, Tammar Wallaby and Short-beaked Echidna.

Wildlife encounters are common on the island. Kangaroos, possums and Cape Barren Geese show no fear of people and haunt picnic and camping areas in search of scraps (although feeding is discouraged by park authorities). Listen at night for the mournful cry of the Bush Stone-curlew.

The name of Ravine Des Casoars Wilderness Protection Park recalls a creature that has become extinct — the Dwarf Emu. Little Penguin colonies are found in many locations around the island's shores, including Penneshaw and Kingscote. They are also habitués of large limestone caves in Flinders Chase National Park. Larger birds such as Ospreys, kites, Wedge-tailed Eagles and White-bellied Sea-Eagles seek their prey from the skies above the island.

The Kangaroo Island Kangaroo (*top*) is frequently seen around the Flinders Chase Visitor Centre, feeding on grass at Black Swamp and at Cape Borda Lightstation. Koalas are also present throughout the island in large numbers. They are often easily visible in the branches of eucalypts around Black Swamp.

The island is also a refuge for the Heath Monitor, which is rarely recorded on the mainland. Watch out for them basking in sunshine on the road and moving across the heath in search of food. Six species of frog can be seen and heard around the island's lagoons and waterways, along with two snake species, the Tiger Snake (normally black, unlike its striped cousin on the mainland) and the rarer Pygmy Copperhead.

Clockwise from top left: Ospreys at their nest; Heath Monitor; New Holland Honeyeater; Short-beaked Echidna.

ADELAIDE to Sydney
(via Broken Hill)

Adelaide to Sydney
Top Things to Do

1 Inspect the historic dug-out homes of Burra.
2 Visit the home of aviator Sir Hubert Wilkins.
3 Go underground at the original BHP mine in Broken Hill.
4 Tour the Royal Flying Doctor Service base.
5 Watch the sun set over the sandstone sculptures of the Living Desert Flora and Fauna Sanctuary.
6 Stay in old shearers' quarters at Kinchega National Park.
7 Browse the art galleries of Silverton.
8 Go on safari at Dubbo's Western Plains Zoo.
9 Photograph the old gold mining towns of Hill End and Sofala.

Bald Hills & Hirsute Sheep

Early South Australian settlers were to discover that Merino sheep bred on the New South Wales tablelands did not cope well with the extreme conditions of the State's semi-arid zones. The tougher South Australian Merino was bred and the colony's flock doubled to 7 million from 1865 to 1890. Many of these were grazed on huge pastoral runs that still operate today between Burra and Broken Hill.

The 1421 km journey from Adelaide through central New South Wales to Sydney includes famous mining centres, expansive sheep grazing properties, classic outback towns and large rural cities. The section along the Barrier Highway to Broken Hill could be undertaken as a singular trip, or perhaps even combined with a dirt road adventure along the Silver City Highway north to the red dunes of Sturt National Park.

Beyond Kapunda and the Clare Valley, the Barrier Highway leads to Burra — a one-time copper mining centre on the desert edge with a fascinating history (*see facing page*). To its north is the township of Mount Bryan, named for Henry Bryan, an English teenager in the party who accompanied Governor Gawler on an exploration of the area in 1839. Bryan tragically disappeared in the bush near the mountain that now bears his name. At 932 m, Mt Bryan is the highest point in the Mount Lofty Ranges and is occasionally dusted with snow. Following Gawler's survey of the region it became home to the colony's richest sheep runs. Hallett was the centre of a property settled by brothers John and Alfred Hallett in 1842 — the town's streets are named for the brothers and their children. Hallett was also the birthplace of the remarkable polar aviator and filmmaker Sir Hubert Wilkins. Wilkins' early career as a newsreel cinematographer led to Arctic aviation expeditions and a failed quest to the North Pole in a World War I submarine in 1931. Wilkins' restored family homestead is open to the public at Mount Bryan East and may be visited by collecting a key from the Hallett general store or pub. Whyte-Yarcowie and Terowie were both once bustling railway hubs, with the latter being "a break of gauge" station where the narrow gauge and broad gauge railways met. It is hard to imagine that more than 600 people were once employed in the transferring of goods from train-to-train and at the town's workshops and sidings. Like Hallett, Terowie also has a film connection — J P McGowan, Australia's earliest Hollywood actor, was born here. Visit the Terowie Information Outlet near the historic railway station for more information.

Just east of Peterborough, the Barrier Highway turns toward Broken Hill. A series of small service towns are scattered along the road to the South Australia–New South Wales border, most boasting populations of fewer than 50 people. Many of the older railway sidings (like Nackara and Paratoo) became virtual ghost towns after the railway was relocated south in the 1960s. Sustained temperatures of over 37 °C are often experienced in these parts. So great was the heat in 1960 that the railway line at Paratoo buckled, causing the derailment of the Adelaide–Broken Hill train and the death of its driver. In the foothills of the southern Flinders Ranges, Oodla Wirra's main reason for existence is a fruit fly inspection point on the edge of the fruit fly exclusion zone straddling the border. Options are to eat your fruit before you get to the boom gates or dump it in the disposal bins provided. The scenery along this stretch is relatively featureless, with the highway bisecting flat-plained sheep stations all the way to the border. Yunta is the largest town before Broken Hill and originated as a watering point for stock drivers on the route to the Terowie railhead in the 1880s. The present day town offers two seven-day service stations, a hotel with accommodation and mercifully in these searing climes, a swimming pool. Mannahill has no fuel but does have the obligatory outback pub and a fine historic rail station. Cockburn, on the South Australian side of the border and its twin town, Burns on the New South Wales side have a pub, internet connection and fuel.

Peterborough – Train Town

Railway lines were the lifeblood of South Australian outback settlers, mining centres and pastoralists. At Peterborough, rail lines leading to Broken Hill, Port Pirie, Port Augusta and Adelaide converged, creating a hectic industry remembered today in the town's many rail memorials and museums. Scale model steam trains stand at each of the town's four main entrances.

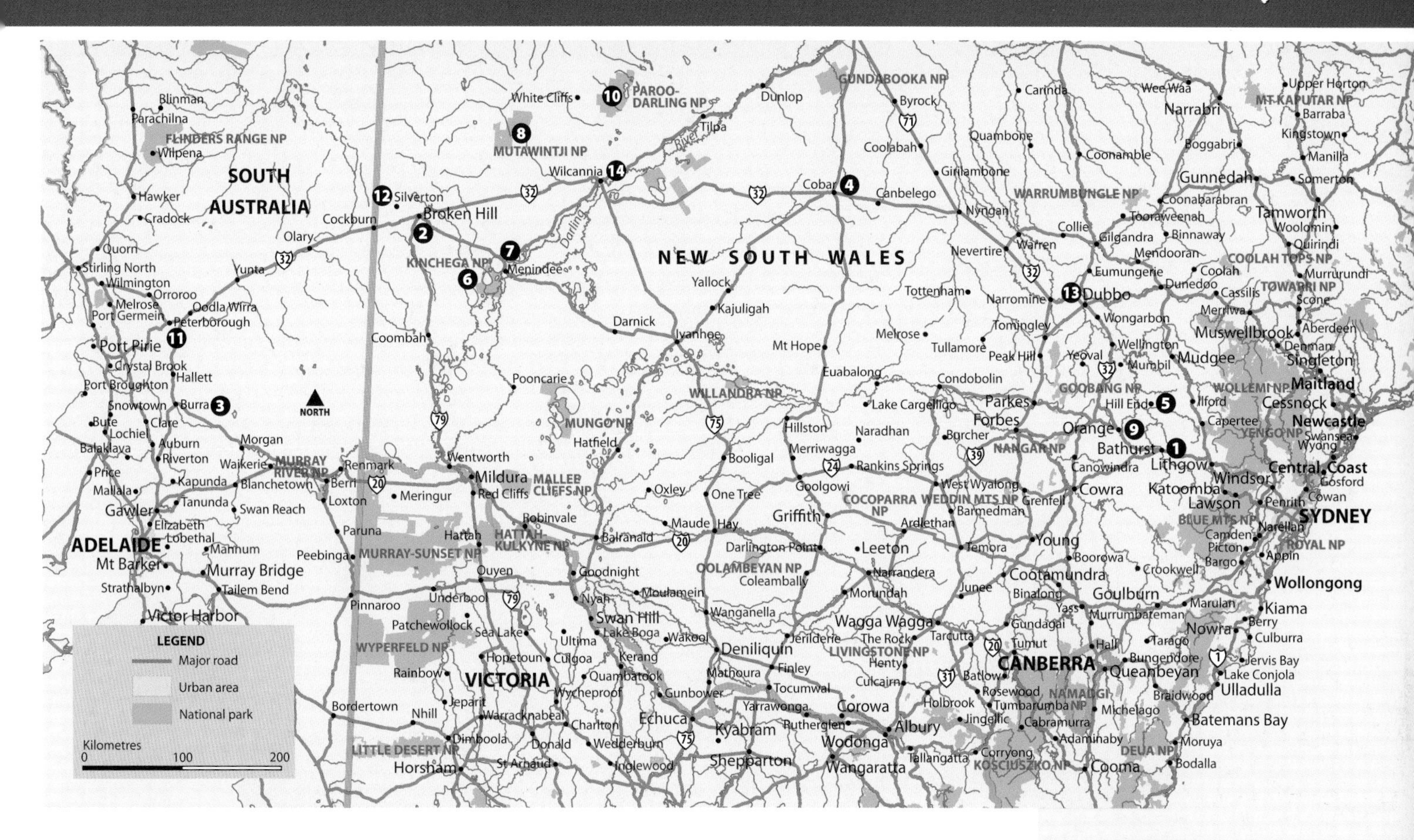

Back in Time – the Burra

Set in the stark landscape of the Bald Hills Range, Burra is a historic copper mining centre. The area is also known as "The Burra", which originally described a collection of mining towns around the mid-north. The district's towns served separate communities of miners — Aberdeen was populated by Scots, Redruth by Cornish, Llwchwr by the Welsh, and Hampton by English miners. The Burra mines generated enormous wealth for the colony from 1845 onward, but many of the miners did not fare as well.

Museums in the town of Burra preserve relics and machinery from pioneering days while Paxton Square miner's cottages provide insight into living conditions in the 1850s. If you think that looks a little too cosy, spare a thought for the estimated 1800 miners whose only home during the early boom years were dugouts along Burra Creek. Several of these dirt houses remain and evidence suggests that many were actually sophisticated dwellings with whitewashed walls, windows and hung doors. Remants of these inventive dugouts can be seen in Blyth Street at the eastern end of town.

Feature Localities

1 Bathurst
2 Broken Hill
3 Burra
4 Cobar
5 Hill End
6 Kinchega National Park
7 Menindee
8 Mutawintji National Park
9 Orange
10 Paroo-Darling National Park
11 Peterborough
12 Silverton
13 Western Plains Zoo, Dubbo
14 Wilcannia

Broken Hill

Broken Hill's more obvious mining heritage is complemented by a trove of unique attractions focusing on nature and the arts. At the Living Desert Flora and Fauna Sanctuary, striking sandstone sculptures (created by twelve international artists in 1993) are arrayed along a desert ridge, producing a brilliant sight at dusk and dawn (*above centre*). The sanctuary also protects wildflowers, an arboretum of endemic plants, a prospector's mine site and desert-hardened wildlife including wallabies and Red Kangaroos. Walk the 2.5 km cultural trail or take a guided Aboriginal tour (Ph: (08) 8088 9700). The sanctuary is located 9 km from the city centre.

Broken Hill & Surrounds

The former mining hub of Broken Hill is the largest regional city in western New South Wales, but in many ways remains South Australian. Clocks are set to South Australian time, South Australian beer is imbibed in the pubs and Adelaide newspapers are read. In fact, the city is nearly 700 km closer to Adelaide than to Sydney. The surrounding landscape is desolate but striking and has long been favoured by artists, photographers and filmmakers (giving Broken Hill an unexpectedly artsy edge). It is this quirky collision of cultural, geographical and historical elements that makes the city such an absorbing place to visit.

History of the Hill

The region was first explored by Charles Sturt, who named the Barrier Ranges and noted in his journal the appearance of a "broken hill". Gold was discovered in the ranges in the 1860s, but it was not until further finds were made in 1875 — during the sinking of a well at Thackaringa Station (40 km west of the present town) — that serious attention was paid to the region's mining potential. Silver was discovered at Silverton and Umberumberka in the early 1880s, luring nearly 2000 prospectors to the area. But this was only the tip of the iceberg — the real population explosion took place after Portuguese-born boundary rider Charles Rasp discovered what he thought was tin at Mount Gipps. The samples turned out to be silver and lead ore, and in 1885 the famous Broken Hill Proprietary Company (BHP) was born. Rasp's discovery had revealed the richest silver, lead and zinc deposits in the world. By 1891, the population of Broken Hill had reached 20,000, making it the third-largest city in New South Wales. However, it was not an easy place to live. Water was in short supply and had to be carted in by train from Silverton. The felling of the region's scarce trees for timber and constant rabbit plagues rid the surrounding hills of vegetation, causing insufferable dust storms. To add to the misery, mine smelters sent clouds of noxious fumes wafting over the town. Conditions improved somewhat with the construction of the nearby Stephens Creek Reservoir in 1891 and after World War II a water pipeline was constructed to Menindee on the Darling River. Today, revegetation and irrigation have reduced the severity of dust storms. BHP ceased mining at Broken Hill in 1940 and there is now only a single mining operator. The city's population peaked at around 30,000 in the 1960s and its present level of around 20,000 is the same as in those heady days of 1891. Towering mullock heaps around the Broken Hill recall the vast mining industry that once supported the town.

Exploring the Hill

The best introduction to this entertaining and history-rich town is to take a guided walking tour (departs visitor information centre, Mon, Wed and Fri at 10 am, Ph: (08) 8088 9700). Underground tours are also available at the original BHP mine on Federation Way (Mon–Fri 10.30 am; Sat 3 pm, Ph: (08) 8088 1604). At the School of the Air, the pioneering outback radio education system has been transformed by the satellite and cyber age, but the centre remains a fascinating place to visit. Sit in on a remote teaching session or explore the school's history (Mon–Fri, sessions 8.30 am – 9.30 am, Lane Street, Ph: (08) 8087 6077). The Royal Flying Doctor Service headquarters and museum (off the road to the airport) also offers tours of this working base (open daily, Ph: (02) 8080 1714). Also in the city are a plethora of art and photographic galleries to explore (featuring both local and internationally acclaimed artists). Pro Hart is the city's most well-known artist and the gallery on Wyman Street exhibits many of his original paintings. At Silver City Mint and Art Centre hangs the largest acrylic painting in the world, measuring a mammoth 12 m x 100 m (66 Chloride Street). Unique crushed mineral collages can be seen at Whites Mineral Art and Living Mining Museum, which also features a walk-in mine (1 Allendale Street). Minerals are also the focus of exhibits at the Broken Hill Geo Centre. Gape at the *Silver Tree* (wrought from 8.5 kg of pure silver) explore the innovative earth science exhibits or view local Indigenous artworks.

As you might expect in such a hot and dusty town, Broken Hill is not short of a pub, but if you prefer something softer, try Bells Milk Bar in Patton Street — a 100-year-old institution that features authentic 1950s soda fountains, murals and memorabilia. Ice-creams also play a part in the town's history — a sculpture of an ice-cream cart at White Rocks (north of town) recalls an incident in World War I when Turkish patriots began shooting from a similar cart at a passing trainload of New Year's Day picnickers. Five townspeople were killed, triggering a riot in the town. It became known as the Battle of Broken Hill and would remain the only World War I enemy attack on Australian soil. Learn more about this and other historic incidents at the Sulphide Street Railway Museum, housed in Broken Hill's original 1900 railway station (open daily, 26 Sulphide Street, Ph: (08) 8088 5961).

Kinchega National Park

Phone Ranger: (08) 8080 3200

The lakes of Kinchega National Park are part of a larger system carrying the overflow of the Darling River as it meanders across the western plains. The area supported a large Aboriginal population 15,000 years ago. By the 1870s the Paakantji people's lifestyle had been taken over by European grazing interests. Menindee and Cawndilla Lakes are now a breeding ground for waterbirds, while Emus and kangaroos roam the sparsely wooded sandhills and grassy plains. The plains are also flooded with wildflowers after winter and spring rains. The lakes are empty during drought conditions.

Walks in the Park: Walking trails and scenic drives follow the Darling River banks and lake shores.

Access: 110 km south-east of Broken Hill on sealed roads.

Camping: Facilities for caravans, tents and camp trailers are available at Lake Cawndilla, Lake Emu and numerous riverside sites. Bunks are also available in shearer's quarters (contact park ranger).

Mutawintji National Park

Phone Ranger: (08) 8080 3200

A protected region of gorges and rockpools containing superb examples of Aboriginal rock art, engraving and stencilling.

Walks in the Park: A range of short walks lead to rockpools, creek beds and art sites

Access: 130 km north-west of Broken Hill on the Tibooburra Road.

Camping: Caravan and tent camping at Homestead Creek (bring firewood and fuel).

Clockwise from top left: A resident kangaroo human-watching in Kinchega National Park; The Kinchega Woolshed, built in 1872; Lakes and waterways concentrate wildlife activity within Kinchega National Park.

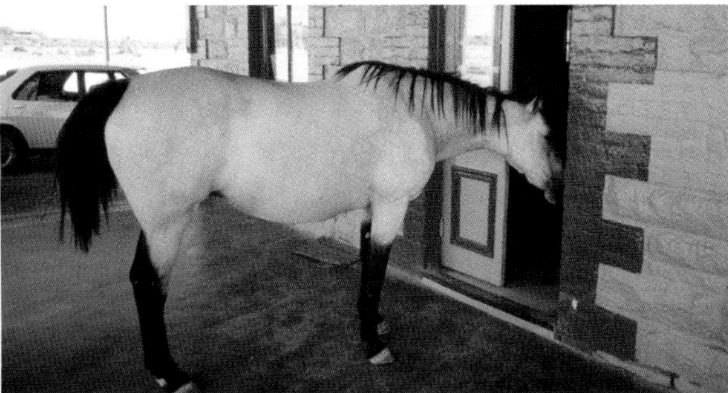

Silverton

This former mining town, encircled by desert, was once connected to Broken Hill by tramway. It has since become a film star, employed as the setting for a swag of well-known films including *Mad Max II, The Adventures of Priscilla, Queen of the Desert* and *Mission Impossible II*. A replica of Mad Max's V8 Interceptor is parked outside the Silverton Hotel, which also houses film memorabilia. Many of the town's original buildings remain, including the Silverton Municipal Chambers (*left bottom*), public school and several churches. The stone gaol has been re-purposed as a local museum. The two hour heritage walking trail takes in Silverton's most significant sites. Like Broken Hill, Silverton has also become a thriving centre for the arts, with numerous galleries exhibiting local works. Look for the painted VW "Beetles" outside the Peter Browne Gallery in Stirling Street (*top right*).

Broken Hill to Sydney

From Broken Hill the Barrier Highway ventures east, crossing the Darling River at the outback town of Wilcannia. The alternative route is to diverge south-east to Menindee and the lakes of Kinchega National Park, before following the Darling River upstream to Wilcannia. The road along the river is little more than a dusty, unsealed red track connecting sheep stations — look for the humorous sculptures on station gates along the way. The Darling River was once the most important inland transport route in New South Wales, with Bourke, Menindee and Wilcannia all home to major ports and busy paddlesteamer trade (*see facing page*). By the early 1880s, Wilcannia was the third-largest port in Australia, known as the "Queen City of the West". The remains of the wharves can still be seen — declining river levels caused by drought in the early 1900s are thought to have contributed to Wilcannia's demise as a port. The area is the traditional home of the Barkindji people and Wilcannia remains home to a large Indigenous community. The town's main street is lined with sandstone buildings — reminders of the rich riverboat era.

Wilcannia to the Mitchell Highway

East of Wilcannia is the Paroo–Darling National Park, protecting the Paroo River wetlands. The Barrier Highway traces the park's southern section, but the main access point is via Wilga on the Bourke Road, 60 km north-east of Wilcannia. Camping is possible at Wilga and there are 75 km of public access roads through the park. When in flood, the Paroo Overflow Lakes are a haven for a host of waterbirds and there are also over 40 species of threatened fauna, including the Brolga, Blue-billed Duck and Large Blotched Python in the vicinity. Thirty kilometres west of Cobar, an unsealed track leads 32 km north from the highway to the Mount Grenfell Historic Site, where hundreds of Aboriginal ochre paintings can be viewed in rock overhangs. These art sites, featuring depictions of humans, mammals, reptiles and Emus made by the Wongaibon people, are a 500 m walk from the car park. The 5 km Ngiyambaa Walkabout Track leads to a lookout with excellent views over the Cobar plains.

Cobar was once the site of Australia's largest copper reserves. In 1870, local Cornish publican Mrs Sidwell Kruge recognised rock samples brought to her by itinerant well-sinkers as copper ore. The knowledge she had gleaned as a "balgal" (ore sorter) in Cornwall, UK, led to the establishment of the Great Cobar Copper Mine (which by 1912 had some 2000 workers). Today, several large mining concerns run open-cut mining operations that are still unearthing gold, silver, lead and zinc in the region. Visit Cobar Miner's Heritage Park where a 2 m bronze statue pays tribute to the miners who lost their lives in the search for ore. Opposite is the Great Cobar Heritage Centre, a museum of interesting relics telling the story of Cobar's Aboriginal, mining and pastoral past. Present-day mining operations can be seen from Fort Bourke Lookout (a great vantage point for photography just east of town) and at the Peak Gold Mine, 8 km south of Cobar on the Kidman Way. The Barrier Highway joins the Mitchell Highway at the town of Nyngan, situated on the Bogan River. It was the scene of major flooding in 1990, which saw the levee overwhelmed and more than 2000 people requiring airlifting by helicopter to safety. Read about this disastrous event, which caused nearly $50 million in damage, at the heritage centre (located in the old railway station on Pangee Street). A helicopter commemorating the rescue efforts stands in adjacent Vanges Park.

Mitchell Highway to the Blue Mountains

From Nyngan to Narromine, the landscape evolves from semi-arid sheep grazing properties to fertile wheatlands, orchards and cotton fields, irrigated by waters from the Macquarie River and Burrendong Dam. Narromine is also famed as the birthplace of Australian cricket legend Glenn McGrath and former Olympic sprinter Melinda Gainsford-Taylor. West of the Blue Mountains are Dubbo, Orange and Bathurst — all major provincial cities with a vast array of cultural and historical attractions to explore. Dubbo's Western Plains Zoo is one of the world's best "open range" wildlife sanctuaries (*see facing page*).

Once known by the decidedly less attractive title of Blackman's Swamp Creek — Orange was the site of gold rushes in the 1850s before becoming an important farming centre. Australia's most famous poet, A B "Banjo" Paterson, was born in Orange in 1864 and a statue and memorial are located in Banjo Paterson Park on Ophir Road. Nearby Mount Canobolas (1395 m) is the highest peak between the Blue Mountains and the Indian Ocean and there are walking tracks and camping areas in the surrounding conservation park. Bathurst, 56 km east of Orange, was proclaimed in 1815 and is Australia's oldest inland settlement. The district yielded Australia's first gold strikes and also became the colony's "experimental farm" where many new crops (including grapes and hops) were first cultivated.

Hill End & Sofala

Two of Australia's best preserved gold mining towns lie north of Bathurst on a 120 km circuit. Sofala (*below*) and its near neighbour Hill End (*above*) are fascinating places to explore and photograph. After Edward Hargraves discovered gold near Bathurst in 1851 the towns did not just boom but fairly exploded into existence. Twenty years later, Hill End was still the largest inland town of New South Wales with over a kilometre of shopfronts (including 27 pubs and an opium den). The gold was eventually exhausted and the town all but deserted. In 1967, it was declared a historic site by the National Parks and Wildlife Service and the process of restoring the town's heritage buildings began. Sofala's golden era was much shorter, lasting only three years, but over 10,000 miners made it their temporary home. Both towns are an outstanding slice of goldfields life and architecture, and have provided inspiration to generations of artists and photographers.

The Darling River

The Darling River is one of Australia's most important waterways, with many thousands of rural properties and communities in New South Wales dependent on the water source for their survival. From its headwaters at the Macintyre River in southern Queensland, the Darling joins the Murray River at Wentworth on the Victorian border.

The Murray–Darling is the nation's longest continuous river system, flowing 3370 km to the Murray mouth on the south-east coast of South Australia. It is approximately half the length of the world's longest river, the Nile, and its drainage basin covers an incredible 14% of Australia.

After the rapid establishment of grazing properties in central and western New South Wales in the mid 19th century, the Darling (*left*) became a critical transport route for wool, meat and goods. Menindee and Wilcannia (*top left*) became flourishing riverports serving properties up to 1.2 million ha in size.

Dubbo & Western Plains Zoo

John Oxley first surveyed the Wiradjuri lands of the Dubbo area in 1817. It became an important goldfields trade route and is today a large rural city with many attractions. Its most famous offering is the spectacular Western Plains Zoo (*left*), an open range sanctuary to over 1000 exotic wildlife species from five continents. Walk, hire a bike, trike or electric cart and prepare for an unforgettable wildlife safari along 15 km of bush trails (open daily, Oxley Rd, Ph: (02) 6881 1400).

Bathurst

Many Australians know Bathurst as the location of the country's most famous motor race, the Bathurst 1000 (staged each October at the foot of Mt Panorama). Car enthusiasts will also get a fuel-injected kick out of the National Motor Museum located at the circuit. Bathurst's colonial history is reflected in its many fine heritage buildings. Visit the Bathurst and District Historical Museum (Russell Street, Ph: (02) 6332 4755) within the grand Bathurst Court House (*left*).

Katoomba

At the western edge of the Blue Mountains lies Katoomba (*left*), a celebrated tourist destination for Sydneysiders since the 1880s. Stay in one of the many restored guesthouses and explore the natural wonders of the region, including the renowned Three Sisters formation. The name Katoomba is derived from Aboriginal words meaning "shining falling waters", aptly describing the many spectacular waterfalls of this beautiful region (*see page 37 for more information*).

ADELAIDE to Melbourne

(via the Murray River)

Adelaide to Melbourne

Top Things to Do

1. See the African wildlife of Monarto Zoological Park at Murray Bridge.
2. Take a night cruise under limestone cliffs at Big Bend.
3. See the Murray's oldest paddlesteamer at Morgan.
4. Camp in Murray River National Park.
5. Cruise aboard the PS *Murray Princess* from Mannum.
6. Drive the Chaffey Trail in Mildura.
7. Step back in time at Swan Hill Pioneer Settlement.
8. See a World War II flying boat at Lake Boga.
9. Relive the days of paddlesteamers and river pirates at the Port of Echuca.
10. Swim on Murray River beaches at Cobram.

Riverlands & Irrigation

The notion of using the Murray waters to create a fertile farming region on the north-western reaches of the river was first conceived in the early 1880s. A long drought in northern Victoria led to Canadian-born brothers and Californian irrigation pioneers William and George Chaffey visiting Australia. They took up crown land and set to the task of creating irrigation colonies near Mildura and Renmark in 1887. Despite early difficulties and political scandal, their pioneering efforts spawned further settlement and the planting of orchards and vines. Despite continuing problems with salinity, the Murray's irrigation areas produce a large proportion of Australia's fruit crop.

The journey to Melbourne from Adelaide via Murray Bridge, Renmark, Echuca and Albury traces the route of Australia's legendary river, the Murray. This vital waterway supported Indigenous peoples for over 20,000 years before being pressed into the service of European settlers. Until the 1890s, paddlewheelers, steamers and barges plied the river; carrying cargoes of wheat, timber and wool. Many of the region's larger towns, such as Mannum and Morgan, preserve historical sites from when "old man Murray" was a hectic river highway. When the rail system was established, the river trade declined, but the development of irrigation colonies paved the way for profitable fruit growing and dairy farming. The river remains one of South Australia's premier aquatic playgrounds. Campsites along the banks attract anglers, kayakers, and wildlife watchers, while nostalgic paddlesteamers and houseboats give you the chance to delve into its reaches.

Murray Bridge to Renmark

Ngaralta people called the area around Murray Bridge *Moop-pol-tha-wong*, meaning "haven for birds". It became known as Edward's Crossing after the district's first European resident and the town developed around the site of the first bridge to span the river in 1879. After a century of service, highway traffic was diverted to cross the Murray at Swanport Bridge, bypassing the city centre. Despite this, Murray Bridge remains a vibrant rural city. There are several excellent wildlife parks in the vicinity, the Monarto Zoological Park (*see facing page*) and Dundee's Hotel and Wildlife Park, where you can pet a python, cradle a croc or converse with a cockatoo (open daily, 10 am – 5 pm, Jervois Road, Ph: (08) 8532 3666).

The Murray's first paddlesteamers were built at Mannum (*see facing page*). Explore their history before browsing the town's antique stores or taking lunch by the river at the historic Pretoria Hotel (50 Randell Street). From Mannum, the Murray meanders north-east to Walker Flat and Swan Reach. The latter only barely survived a series of four floods in the first half of the 20th century, with a final inundation in 1956 washing away much of the main street. The fact that the town is close to the highest cliffs on the entire Murray at Big Bend makes you ponder its vulnerable lowland location. See photos of the floods at the Swan Reach Museum or take a Big Bend by Night tour (Ph: (08) 8570 1097).

From Swan Reach you can detour east and meet the Murray upstream at Loxton, or continue north along its banks to Morgan. At Blanchetown, the Murray's system of locks and weirs begin — excellent views are available of Lock Number One from the town's old bridge. At the former riverport of Morgan, the Murray's oldest paddlesteamer, the PS *Mayflower* is permanently moored in the old wharf precinct. From here east the Murray banks are home to Australia's richest citrus growing areas. The Riverland towns of Berri, Loxton, and Renmark are renowned for vegetable, wine, fruit and fruit juice production. Barmera, on Lake Bonney is a hugely popular holiday town and home to the annual South Australian Country Music Festival (June). Camp at Murray River National Park or hire a houseboat and feast on the local produce. Renmark, largest of the Riverland towns is Australia's oldest irrigation settlement.

Houseboats & Paddlewheelers

The best way to see the Murray is on a leisurely houseboat cruise or aboard one of several chartered tour boats and replica paddlesteamers travelling between Murray Bridge and Morgan. The 67 m long, luxurious PS *Murray Princess* is the largest paddlewheeler built in the Southern Hemisphere (cruises depart Mannum, Ph: 1800 804 843). The floating hotel *Murray River Queen* (Waikerie) offers great river views from its restaurant and café and also offers accommodation.

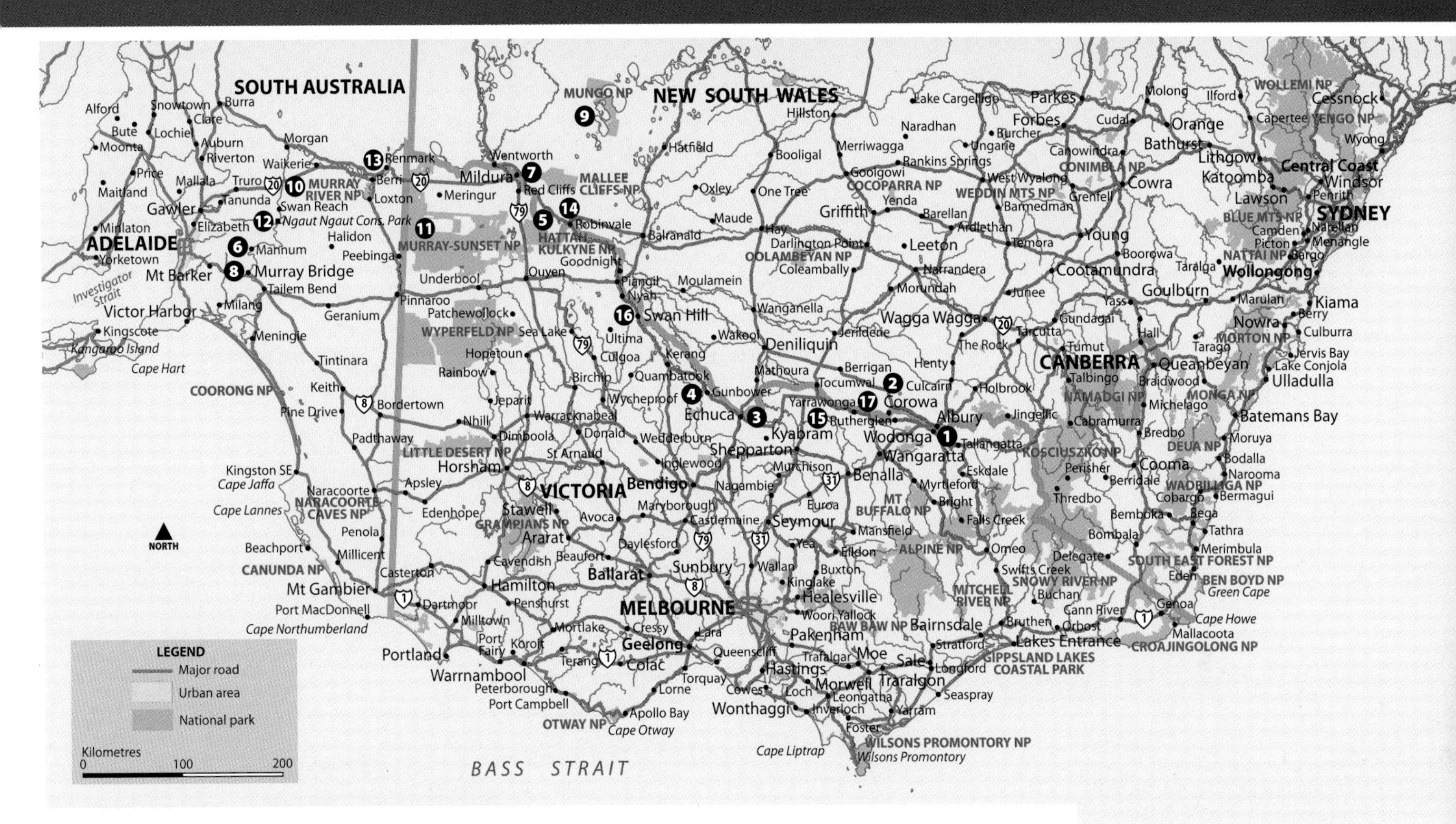

Mannum

Mannum became the birthplace of riverboats on the Murray with the construction of the *Mary Ann* in 1853. A dry dock named for its builder, Captain William Randell was constructed in 1876 and is listed on the National Estate. It now forms part of the Mannum Dock Museum of River History, which also incorporates the visitor centre and the historic PS *Marion*. The vessel still cruises the Murray and is the only original wood-fired paddlesteamer in operation offering overnight accommodation (bookings and enquiries, Ph: (08) 8569 2733).

Walker Flat to Swan Reach

The towering ochre-coloured limestone cliffs along the Murray River between Walker Flat and Swan Reach (*left*) make this a must-see destination for houseboats and river cruises. It is also a great section of the river for birdwatching, fishing and watersports. Near Nildottie is Kroehns Landing and the Ngaut Ngaut Conservation Park, site of the discovery of a 7000 year old skeleton in 1929. Follow the boardwalk leading up through the cliffs or take a tour with local Nganguraku guides. A ferry at Walkers Flat carries passengers over the river to a kiosk and pleasant picnic area.

Renmark

Renmark, is an excellent base for Riverland exploration. Take a cruise on the *Big River Rambler* or visit Ruston's Roses — the Southern Hemisphere's biggest commercial rose garden. Olivewood, original home of the region's irrigation pioneers, the Chaffey brothers, is open to the public (Ph: (08) 8586 6175). The river wetlands and mallee woodland of Chowilla Game Reserve, 50 km north of Renmark, offer some of the most unspoilt habitat along the Murray. Join a bush safari, camp by the riverbank or paddle a canoe along placid floodplains (Ph: (08) 8595 2111).

Feature Localities

1 Albury–Wodonga
2 Corowa
3 Echuca
4 Gunbower Island
5 Hattah-Kulkyne National Park
6 Mannum
7 Mildura
8 Monarto Zoological Park
9 Mungo National Park
10 Murray River National Park
11 Murray-Sunset National Park
12 Ngaut Ngaut Conservation Park
13 Renmark
14 Robinvale
15 Rutherglen
16 Swan Hill
17 Yarrawonga

Camping on the Murray

The Murray banks are one of Australia's best camping locations. There is a huge choice of sites all the way along the river in both South Australia and Victoria. One of the finest spots is Gunbower Island — the country's biggest inland island, which offers riverside sites and is an important refuge for wildlife. The island reaches from Koondrook past Cohuna to Torrumbarry Weir.

Mungo National Park
a World Heritage Area

Phone Ranger: (03) 5021 8900

Approximately 110 km north-east of Mildura, within the magnificent Willandra Lakes World Heritage Area, lies Mungo National Park. The park protects Lake Mungo and its astonishing fossilised dune system that conceals the relics of a past civilisation. Wind and rain have cut into the dunes, unearthing the middens, stone tools and burial sites of the land's original peoples (including the world's oldest human cremation).

Walks & Drives in the Park: Numerous walking trails and a 60 km circuit drive guides visitors through the area's geological and archaeological wonders.

Access: Unsealed roads north-east from Mildura via Arumpo (110 km).

Camping: There are basic campsites at Main Camp and Belah Camp. The visitors centre has flush toilets, hot showers and also sells firewood.

Renmark to Echuca
(via Sturt & Murray Valley Highways)

As you approach Yamba on the Sturt Highway, east of Renmark, a huge tyre-shaped sign arches over the road marking the location of the fruit fly inspection point and bidding you farewell from South Australia's Riverland. The Victorian border lies just east and the highway passes through the northern section of the Murray–Sunset National Park. This is the tip of "Sunset Country", a region of big skies, flat mallee scrub, dunes and sandplains reaching far into eastern Victoria. The river now lies out of view to the north and there are few towns on the 130 km stretch between Yamba and Mildura. Midway is Lake Cullulleraine, a holiday spot with several lakeside caravan parks popular for fishing and watersports.

Just west of Mildura is an interesting detour north off the highway to the town of Merbein. En route is Lake Hawthorn where a fun park features a human-sized snakes and ladders game consisting of huge slides and flying-foxes, along with a unique display of toilets supposedly sat upon by celebrities. Famous flushers aside, the lake is also a popular local picnic and yachting spot. East of Merbein town centre, located on cliffs overlooking the Murray, is Mildara Wines. The Riverina's first major winery was established by the Chaffey brothers as Chateau Mildura in 1887. The winery forms part of a series of historic sites known as the Chaffey Trail, including: William Chaffey's mansion, Rio Vista (now an arts and heritage centre); the National Trust classified Psyche Bend Pumping Station; and the old Mildura Homestead (trail map available from the Mildura Visitor Information Centre, 180–190 Deakin Avenue). A statue of William Chaffey stands among trees planted by the man himself in the central plantation of Deakin Avenue, the town's boulevard-styled main street.

Unlike most Australian settlements, Mildura was a temperance town that had no pub until 1918. Somewhat ironically, the Mildura Working Man's Club would later become famous for possessing the world's longest hotel bar, a T-shaped beer-bearing behemoth measuring 91 m (Deakin Avenue, between 9th and 10th streets). At Mildura's historic wharf, built in 1912, Murray River cruises are available on four original paddlesteamers.

Mildura is the capital of the Sunraysia district and fruit and farm-oriented attractions abound. Orange World includes tractor train tours through the citrus groves and avocado plantations (Silver City Highway, Ph: (03) 5023 5197). Children are very likely to enjoy Humpty Dumpty's Tourist Farm, an eggsellent attraction featuring the world's largest Humpty Dumpty.

Mildura to Swan Hill

The Sturt Highway crosses the river into New South Wales, just north of Mildura before entering Victoria again at Robinvale. On the way into town, visit the nearby Euston Weir where a "fish ladder" has been constructed to help fish swim up to the higher levels of the river. On Robinvale's northern edge, gaze upward at the huge windmill, reputed as the Southern Hemisphere's largest. This pretty fruit farming centre and holiday town is surrounded on three sides by the Murray, providing several perfect picnic spots. Visit Robinswood Homestead, the retirement residence of the town's founder and maintain the spirit of nostalgia by stopping in afterward at the extensive McWilliam's Winery for an old-fashioned cream sherry (the winery's specialty). The Murray Valley Highway commences at Robinvale, and runs parallel with the river as it winds its way south-east to Swan Hill (*see facing page*).

Swan Hill to Echuca

Just outside Swan Hill is the fascinating former flying boat depot of Lake Boga. A Catalina flying boat stationed on the lake's banks in Catalina Park is a memorial to the days of World War II when the aircraft flew to Lake Boga for repair. Discover more about the town's past at the Flying Boat Museum and in the "history room" of the Commercial Hotel. The district was once also the home of 19th century writer T A Browne (aka Rolf Boldrewood), author of the seminal bushranging novel *Robbery Under Arms*. A chain of lakes and waterways leads south from Lake Boga to Kerang on the Loddon River. These superb wetlands are filled with resident and migratory waterbirds and form a playground for a range of human activities. To Kerang's north-east are the twin border towns of Koondrook and Barham on the Murray. Relax by the artificial lakes and beach at Barham Lakes Complex off Murray Street. Cohuna, delightfully situated on the banks of Gunbower Creek opposite Gunbower Island (*see top left*) is a busy service centre for the district. Drive through the Gunbower Island State Forest, hire a canoe and follow the Safes Lagoon Trail past Gunbower Island or test your skill on the island golf course where Australian international golf star Stuart Appleby honed his swing.

Mildura

The Chaffey's original town layout for Mildura included a tramway running down the centre of Deakin Avenue. The trams never ran, but the plan gave Mildura a broad main street that forms a generous entry into town. In line with Chaffey's grand vision, the thoroughfare is 12 km long, making it the longest straight avenue in Australia. The town's cross streets are named with numbers, reflecting the Chaffeys' American background.

Hattah-Kulkyne National Park

Phone Ranger: 13 19 63

Hattah-Kulkyne covers a 48,000 ha region of Murray floodplain, freshwater lakes and creeks 70 km south of Mildura. It is an oasis amid the mallee scrubland where scores of waterbirds arrive seeking mates, food and nesting sites. While the lake system rarely floods, winter rains imbue the mallee with a subtle beauty. Shrubby woodlands of Black Box, Eumong Wattle and bottlebrush rim the floodplains while eucalypts and Cypress Pines dominate the rolling landscape.

Walks in the Park: An introductory nature walk near the park's visitor centre can be combined with a self-guided drive around Lake Hattah or a long circuit walk of the southern lakes.

Access: Via Hattah from Mildura on the Calder Highway.

Camping: Basic facilities at Lake Hattah and Lake Mournpall. Bush camping is also permitted.

Swan Hill

Swan Hill was named by explorer Thomas Mitchell for the noisy Black Swans that kept him from sleep at his campsite. Today the town styles itself as the "Heart of the Murray" and is a magnet for river-based tourism. An 11 m long Murray River Cod in Curlewis Street stands as testament to the legendary fishing to be enjoyed here. It is not the only giant in town — a 44 m wide Moreton Bay Fig in the same street was planted by a local doctor's wife when Burke and Wills passed through town.

Swan Hill Pioneer Settlement Museum

This living history museum complex has been a favourite destination of Victorians for generations. It recreates in authentic detail a riverport town of the paddlesteamer era, including over 50 historic buildings. Take a paddleboat cruise aboard the century old *Pyap* on the Murray River or experience the impressive nightly sound and light show (open Tuesday to Sunday, 9:30 am – 4.00 pm, and daily during public holidays/ school holiday periods, Ph: (03) 5036 2410).

Echuca to Albury-Wodonga

(via Murray Valley Highway)

The Murray River's journey from Echuca to the Australian Alps is punctuated by the former riverports of Yarrawonga and Wodonga. Many of the Murray's Victorian towns (such as Echuca, Cobram and Yarrawonga) have smaller twins across the river border — a legacy of colonial trade and tax collection. The Hume Weir, east of Wodonga was created by flooding the old town of Tallangatta to create a reservoir six times the capacity of Sydney Harbour.

Echuca, once Australia's largest inland port, has been restored to much of its former glory (*see below left*). During holiday periods visitors flock here to see great paddlesteamers of yesteryear thrumming their bladed wheels through the water. There are six authentic paddlesteamers operating as tour vessels from Echuca. The PS *Pevensey* was rebuilt after fire in 1930 and starred in the television mini-series, *All the Rivers Run*. The restored PS *Adelaide*, built in 1866 is the oldest wooden-hulled paddlesteamer operating in the world. Take a cruise or stay landward and purchase a port tour ticket and wander the historic Port of Echuca wharves. Dine within the port precinct at the original Bridge Hotel and Star Hotel, which once served as a "sly grog shop" and features an underground bar and escape tunnel. The Heritage Steam Festival, staged on the river in October each year features a sail-past of paddlewheelers, River of Fire fireworks, live music and heartfelt theatrical performances. The Riverboats, Jazz, Food and Wine Festival is another big crowd-puller and is held in February in venues throughout Echuca and its smaller northern twin Moama.

Echuca to Yarrawonga

At Barmah, on the Murray between Echuca and Tocumwal, 500 year old River Red Gums survive in a forest and floodplain that is home to over 200 bird species as well as numerous mammals, reptiles and amphibians. The area is internationally recognised as a major wetland breeding ground. Camping, canoeing and bushwalking are popular pastimes here and trails lead past several Aboriginal sites. Visitors can learn more about the culture of the Yorta Yorta people at the Dharnya Centre (Sand Ridge Track, Barmah, Ph: (03) 5869 3353).

The Murray Valley Highway rejoins the river at Cobram, 37 km west of Yarrawonga. Here the bends of the Murray boast sandy beaches particularly favoured by locals, campers and anglers. Picnic, canoe or swim at Thompson's Beach north of the bridge to Barooga, or pitch a tent at the campground at Scotts Beach a few kilometres upstream. Alternatively, take a stroll across the bridge to the waterbird habitat of Quinns Island. The River Beaches Festival is held annually on Easter Sunday. Yarrawonga and its New South Welsh cousin Mulwala are famous river holiday retreats (*see facing page*). Their biggest attraction, the boating and fishing paradise of Lake Mulwala was formed by the construction of a weir across the river in the 1930s. Lake cruises depart from the Yarrawonga side (Ph: (03) 5744 1989).

Corowa to Albury-Wodonga

Full of heritage towns and gourmet pleasures, the region between Yarrawonga and Albury-Wodonga is also a hotspot for tourism. Corowa, on the New South Wales side of the river, is a relaxed watersports centre within spitting distance of the Rutherglen wineries. Perhaps surprisingly for an otherwise unassuming town, it also stakes a claim as the "Birthplace of Federation". Members of the 1893 federation conference staged in Corowa courthouse took the momentous decision to draw up a constitution for the new nation. The fact is celebrated by the Federation Bridge (opened in 2005) and the town's Federation Museum (Queen St, Ph: (02) 6033 1568).

Murray River Wildlife

Although at first glance it may not seem overly attractive, the elusive Murray River Cod (*left*) has long been the holy grail of Australian freshwater fishermen. The resident river giant is capable of growing to nearly 2 m and weighing in at over 100 kg. The annual Murray River Cod fishing season officially commences on "cod opening day" (1 Dec). The Murray is also home to an impressive assortment of birdlife — while cruising scan the banks, skies and waters for Sulphur-crested Cockatoos, Black Swans and Australian Pelicans (*right*).

Echuca – History on the River

The wharves, riverboats and streets of this fabulously preserved and restored town tell the saga of Australia's greatest river. Echuca was the largest of all the riverports on the Murray banks and it is easy to stand on the wharves of the Port of Echuca and imagine them teeming with trade. Continuously navigable for most of its length, the Murray was a crucial transport and communications link. Through the Murray–Darling River system, cargo was unloaded in Echuca from as far north as southern Queensland. By the 1880s, hundreds of paddlesteamers and trains of barges carrying passengers, mail, wool, wheat, timber and foodstuffs travelled the Murray. Cruise the river aboard the PS *Emmylou*, a perfectly rendered replica of a wood-fired paddlesteamer that offers day and overnight cruises from Echuca.

Yarrawonga

Walking along the Murray banks gives you the chance to see and photograph thousands of waterbirds amid dramatic stands of River Red Gum. Follow the 3.5 km trail through Yarrawonga Regional Park (a popular camping spot also known as The Common). If you're looking for the ultimate in river adventures, try the Murray Marathon, a 5 day, 400 km paddle that commences in Yarrawonga on December 27 each year and concludes at Swan Hill on New Years Eve.

Corowa

Kids young and old should visit in April when Corowa's (*left*) historic streets are converted into a race circuit for the one and only all ages Australian Billy Cart Championships. While in town, keep your eye on the sky — Corowa is also home to the National Parachute Training Centre and the Australian Soaring Centre, a headquarters for gliding. If you have the nerve, both will let you experience the sensation of unpowered flight over Murray landscapes.

Rutherglen

Mines and vines saw Rutherglen (*left*) prosper from the early 1850s. While only three of the 21 hotels built during the gold rushes survive, many other buildings from Rutherglen's past remain intact. The gold has gone but the grapes grow on, despite an outbreak of phylloxera that destroyed most of north-eastern Victoria's original plantings in the late 1890s. There are seventeen vineyards in the Rutherglen region and the Tastes of Rutherglen food and wine festival is on the menu in March.

Albury-Wodonga

One of Australia's earliest inland cities, Albury was founded as an important trade and transport link between Sydney and Port Phillip. This natural crossing point over the Murray was bolstered by the construction of the railway from Melbourne in 1873 and the restored red and white brick Albury Railway Station stands in proud memory of the city's history. This farming region was also given a boost by the establishment of the migrant reception centre at Bonegilla after World War II.

Today, Albury–Wodonga boasts a population of over 100,000 people. Albury is rich in civic sites and superb riverside parks and gardens. Rising over the city's main street on Monument Hill is a 30 m high glass and stone World War I cenotaph. On the river, the replica paddlesteamer PS *Cumberoona* (*left*) offers daily cruises (September to April) from Noreuil Park (Ph: (03) 5728 2706). Lake Hume, 16 km east of the city, was the largest dam built in the Southern Hemisphere at the time of its completion in 1936.

Albury-Wodonga to Melbourne

(via Victorian High Country, Yarra Ranges & Healesville)

The journey from Albury–Wodonga to Melbourne offers some spectacular sidetrips into the surrounding alpine regions. The Australian Alps are part of the Great Dividing Range, extending south from Canberra into the north-east corner of Victoria. Alpine, Buffalo, Snowy River and Baw Baw National Parks protect much of the region, forming an important natural corridor for flora and fauna. They also offer magnificent mountain scenery and a wealth of opportunities for outdoor activity, including downhill and cross-country skiing, rock climbing, whitewater rafting, bushwalking, horse riding, fishing and trail bike riding.

Alpine National Park

Alpine National Park is Victoria's largest park and one of Australia's grandest. It covers more than 600,000 ha, incorporating vital rivers, snow-frosted mountains, clear lakes and dense forest. It has a rich natural and cultural heritage and the terrain varies from benign areas suited to family pursuits to wild country where none but the most experienced and battle-hardened bushwalkers should venture. Mount Buller, Mount Hotham and Mount Buffalo have long been immensely popular ski resorts and summer retreats (*see boxes left and facing page*).

The High Country

Take the Great Alpine Way from the rural city of Wangaratta through Myrtleford to reach the leafy holiday town of Bright. In autumn, the avenues and gardens are flushed with colour as the foliage of the deciduous trees turns to shades of gold and russet. Bright's delightful setting and fine restaurants make it a popular base from which to journey to Mount Buffalo, Mount Hotham and Falls Creek.

The Bogong High Plains, near Mount Beauty were a traditional grazing area for pioneer cattlemen in the 19th century before becoming a popular ski resort for Victorians in the early 1900s. They incorporate the State's highest peak, Mount Bogong (1986 m) and the Falls Creek Alpine Village. Today the region also attracts visitors in summer, offering bushwalking, mountain biking and horse riding as well as trout fishing in the Rocky Valley Dam and Pretty Valley Pondage. Popular walks include the 5 km moderate trek from Rocky Valley Dam to Ropers Lookout (about 1.5 hours), or if you are really fit, the more difficult day journey along the Mount Bogong Staircase Spur (16 km return, experienced hikers only). South of Rocky Valley Dam is Wallaces Hut, built by the Wallace brothers in 1889. It is the oldest hut still standing in the park. The original Woollybutt roof shingles were replaced by galvanised iron in the 1930s and it is now classified by the National Trust. The hut is not far from the Bogong High Plains Road, near Falls Creek.

Victoria's high country has inspired Australian bush folklore, from Banjo Paterson's epic poem of drovers and wild bush horses, *The Man from Snowy River* to tales of some of Australia's most notorious 19th century bushrangers. Just south of Wangaratta is Glenrowan, scene of Ned Kelly's last stand and the location of numerous Kelly Gang attractions. The bushranger still intimidates visitors to town through his armoured, gun-toting statue in the main street (*top*). In Mansfield, near Mount Buller, a monument commemorates three local policemen shot by the gang in 1878.

Alpine National Park – Mount Buffalo Section

Phone Ranger: (03) 5756 2328

This is the oldest national park in the Victorian Alps, declared in 1898. The chalet at Mount Buffalo Resort was built in 1910 and the resort remains one of the region's most loved retreats.

Walks & Runs in the Park: Mount Buffalo's slopes and cross-country trails are ideal for novice skiers. When the snow is melted, 90 km of walking trails branch off the main park road.

Access: Via B500 then sealed road (C535) from Porepunkah.

Camping: Good facilities at Lake Catani. There is also a choice selection of commercial lodge, chalet and motel-style accommodation in the park and in Bright.

Alpine National Park – Mount Buller Section

Phone Ranger: 1800 039 049

Mount Buller is one of Australia's largest ski resorts. It is also home to the Olympic Winter Institute of Australia. The mountain reaches a height of 1805 m and supports some of the nation's best alpine and sub-alpine terrain.

Walks in the Park: The ski resort has 180 ha of ski trails and 25 lifts. Several walking tracks from the village lead up through Snow Gum forests and snowgrass plains to the summit.

Access: North-east of Melbourne (240 km) via Mansfield.

Accommodation: There are over 7000 beds available at the resort in hotels, chalets, lodges and apartments.

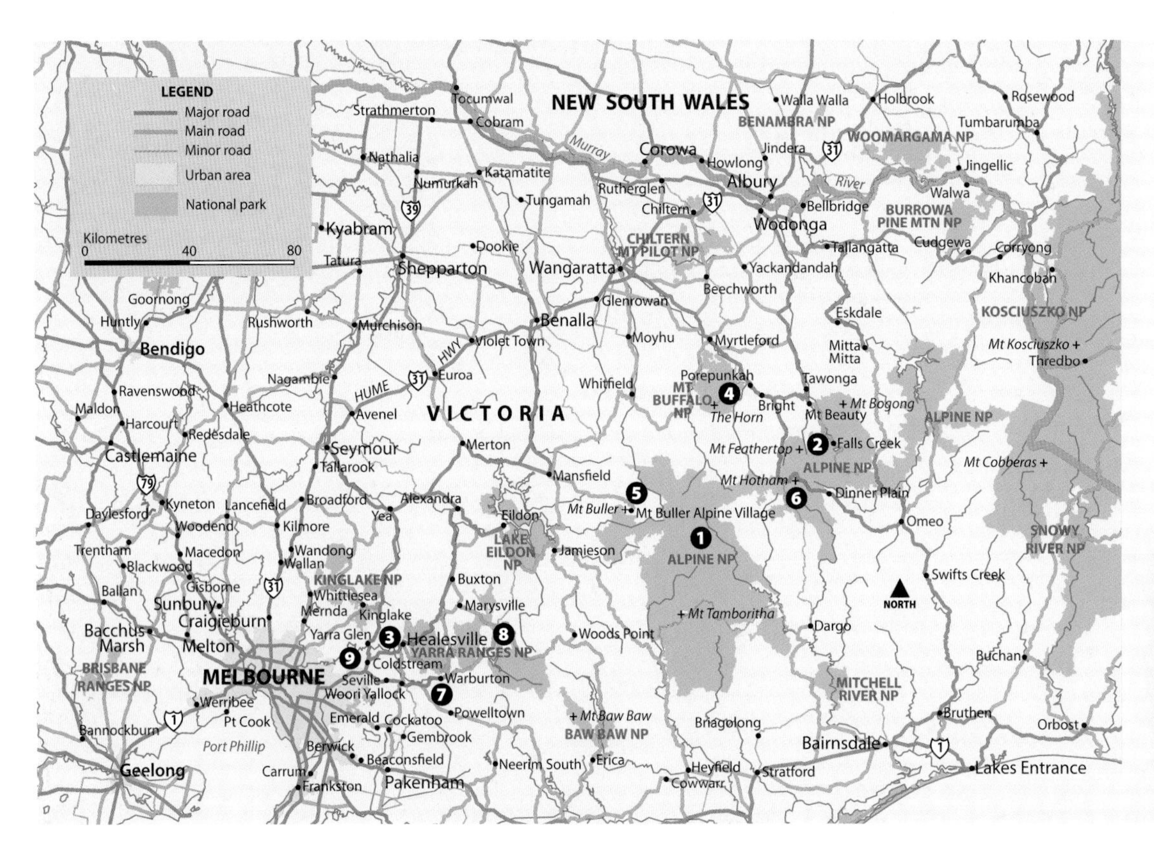

Feature Localities

1. Alpine National Park
2. Falls Creek
3. Healesville Sanctuary, Healesville
4. Mount Buffalo
5. Mount Buller
6. Mount Hotham
7. Warburton
8. Yarra Ranges National Park
9. Yarra Valley

A Blue-billed Duck At Healesville Sanctuary

Alpine National Park – Mount Hotham Section

Phone Ranger: (03) 5759 3550

Situated in the heart of Alpine National Park, this region is best known for its white powder revelry with regular snowfalls on the higher slopes during winter. Mount Feathertop (1922 m) and Mount Hotham (1862 m) are among Victoria's tallest peaks and create the perfect playground for skiers and snowboarders (in winter) and walkers and cyclists (in summer). The Hotham Heights village caters for the downhill skier, while the surrounding mountain ranges are excellent for cross-country enthusiasts, many of whom base themselves at Dinner Plain.

Walks in the Park: Experienced, fit skiers and walkers can tackle the Razorback Trail to Mount Feathertop, an 18 km trek that can be completed in a day; camping at Federation Hut near Mount Feathertop's summit. Walking tracks, best undertaken when the snow melts, abound. The 650 km Australian Alps Walking Track cuts through this region.

Access: Hume Highway via Wangaratta and Bright, or via Albury and Myrtleford. Mount Hotham airport is 20 km from the resort.

Accommodation: Hotels, lodges, self-contained accommodation and chalets at Mount Hotham Alpine Resort and Dinner Plain.

Albury–Wodonga to Melbourne
Top Things to Do

1. Drive a boat, drop a line or pull up a deckchair at Lake Eildon.
2. Walk and camp in scenic Cathedral Range State Park.
3. See the State's highest waterfall, Steavensons Falls, near Marysville.
4. Commune with native animals and visit the famous Platypusary at Healesville Sanctuary.
5. Build an Aussie snowman at Lake Mountain or Mount Donna Buang.
6. Take your motorbike for a strap on the Black Spur (through Yarra Ranges National Park).
7. Stay at a bush resort in Healesville or Warburton.
8. Celebrate in the vines at the Yarra Valley Grape Grazing Festival.

Yarra Valley Wine District

The Yarra Valley region was one of the first viticulture areas in Australia, with the first vines planted on Yering Station in 1838. It became well established but the economic depressions of the 1890s and 1930s bit hard and the vineyards had all been converted to pasture by 1937. Since the 1960s the industry has been revived and there are now nearly 60 wineries operating in the district. Most styles of cool climate grapes are grown and the Yarra Valley's vignerons have gained an international reputation. Many of the wineries operate restaurants and some offer accommodation, but the Yarra Valley is also an easy one hour foray from Melbourne's CBD. The annual Grape Grazing Festival (February) provides an opportunity to wander from vineyard-to-vineyard enjoying superb local produce, wines and entertainment.

Albury–Wodonga to Melbourne

South-west of Mansfield is Lake Eildon, Victoria's largest artificial lake. The dam was originally built in 1952 to irrigate a vast area of northern Victoria and provide hydro-electric power. Some 40,000 people were employed in its construction and it is now a major recreation zone, surrounded by the foothills of the Victorian Alps in Lake Eildon National Park. Camping grounds, picnic areas and walking trails allow visitors to explore the park and also provided is access to the lake where boating, swimming and fishing are all popular. The towns of Bonnie Doon (on the lake's northern shores), Eildon (in the south) and Gough's Bay (across the lake to its east) are traditional Victorian holiday spots.

Yarra Ranges Region

The Maroondah Highway leads west from Eildon to the pretty rural town of Alexandra before heading south past the Cathedral Range State Park. The range is surmounted by a 7 km long rocky ridge. Spectacular peaks, icy mountain streams and walking tracks attract bushwalkers and backpackers to five delightful camping spots.

Turn off the highway at Buxton and drive 11 km to Marysville, the region's mountain-rimmed tourism headquarters. In summer, there are many forest, waterfall and creekside walks ranging from easy strolls to taxing mountain hikes. Highlights include the aptly named Beauty Spot — a picturesque fern glade with trickling stream — and the Trestle Track, which meanders through majestic stands of native trees. Steavensons Falls (at 82 m is the State's highest cascade) has been a favourite of visitors here since the 19th century. At night, the waterfall and adjacent tracks are illuminated by power generated from the falls themselves. In winter, the nearby Lake Mountain, a minor ski field, offers snow cover, tobbogan runs, cross-country skiing and 360° views of the countryside from the tower lookout. This is an area worthy of several days exploration and the shaded, charming town of Marysville offers plentiful hotel, resort and boutique accommodation.

Healesville & Warburton

Below the peak of Mount Rael in the Great Dividing Range is Healesville, a tranquil village that belies its proximity to the busy outer suburbs of Melbourne. The town has several fine restaurants and hotels, but the real attraction lies in the surrounding forest throughout which there is a range of excellent walking trails. Healesville Sanctuary, just north of town, is a world class fauna park (*see facing page*). Nearby Badger Creek is perfect for a relaxed picnic lunch or barbecue, as is Maroondah Reservoir which offers picnic facilities and walk tracks through gardens leading to a lookout with panoramic views. There are a total of nine trails through the catchment area, ranging from 1–21 km in length. Donellys Weir is the terminus for the mind-bogglingly challenging National Trail, which leads from Healesville to Cooktown in far north Queensland. At an incredible 5330 km, this is the longest marked track in the world and was put in place for Australia's Bicentennial Celebrations in 1988. Make sure you have a hearty breakfast by the weir before setting out.

East of Healesville in the foothills of the ranges is Warburton, established after gold strikes in the district in the 1880s. This heavily wooded area is now an urban retreat featuring numerous historic guest houses. Warburton is an ideal launching pad for exploration of the lower Yarra Ranges and an excellent horse riding and bushwalking area.

Yarra Ranges National Park

Phone Ranger: 13 19 63

Yarra Ranges National Park is characterised by its tall Mountain Ash forests (*left*), among which is the 93 m high Big Tree, Victoria's tallest. Tree Ferns (*above*) grow as understorey and cool temperate rainforest harbours ancient Myrtle Beeches. Access to large areas of the forest is restricted due to its importance as part of the Melbourne water catchment. The heights of the park, including Lake Mountain and Mount Donna Buang are cloaked in sub-alpine vegetation and receive regular snowfalls in winter months. Around 40 native mammal species are known to inhabit the park. The large areas of undisturbed forest are particularly important for species that require tree hollows in which to breed, including mammals such as the endangered Leadbeater's Possum, as well as bats, possums and parrots. Among the 120 native bird species are the Sooty, Powerful and Barking Owls.

Walks & Drives in the Park: Drive to the summit of Mount Donna Buang for superb views from the 21 m tower lookout, or the Rainforest Gallery observation platform on the southern side of the slopes. The Acheron Way between Warburton and Marysville, the Black Spur (between Warburton and Narbethong) and the Healesville–Warburton Road also offer brilliant forest scenery and views. Beeches Rainforest Walk on Lady Talbot Drive is an easy 3 km loop walk through pristine ferns and rainforest.

Access: 80 km from Melbourne via the Warburton or Maroondah Highways.

Camping: Campgrounds are located at Upper Yarra Reservoir Park and in the towns of Warburton and Marysville.

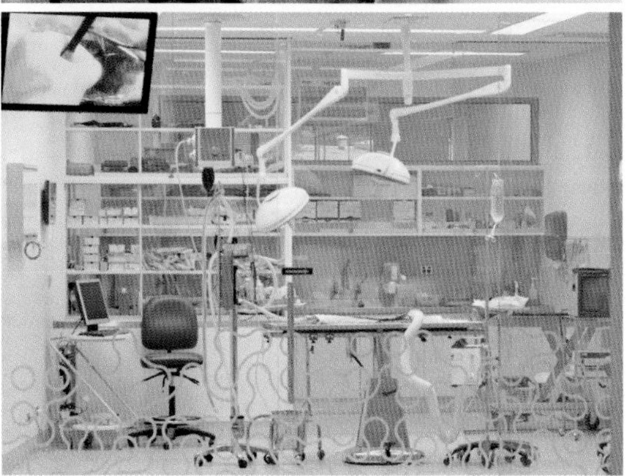

Healesville Sanctuary

Home to bears that are not and egg-laying mammals with duck-like bills, Healesville Sanctuary is an Australian wildlife centre like no other. Nestled in bushland in the foothills of the Yarra Ranges, the sanctuary gives you the chance to observe closely the idiosyncrasies of some of the country's most elusive native creatures. Dingoes, Koalas, kangaroos and Platypuses are just a few of the 200 species of wildlife found here. Focusing on research, conservation and education, Healesville provides insight to a rarely seen world. Highlights include the Birds-of-Prey Flight Presentation and the Sidney Myer World of the Platypus, a unique nocturnal creekside habitat. Until Healesville Sanctuary's world-first success in the 1940s, captive breeding of Platypuses was long considered impossible. In fact, it was another 55 years before that event would be repeated, this time with twins. In 2000, a further baby Platypus was born. The unparalleled success of Healesville's program reflects the sanctuary's precise replication of the Platypus' natural creek habitat. This extraordinary Platypusary reveals the normally secret world of the mysterious monotreme.

The sanctuary also provides a complete animal hospital, the Australian Wildlife Health Centre (*left*), where specialist veterinarians treat sick, injured and orphaned native animals. Healesville Sanctuary is open daily from 9 am to 5 pm and at least two hours should be allowed to fully explore the site. Travel to Healesville from Melbourne via the Eastern Freeway and Maroondah Highway. The sanctuary is off Badger Creek Road just north of the town centre (Ph: (03) 5957 2800).

ADELAIDE to Melbourne

(via Western Highway & Great Ocean Road)

Adelaide to Melbourne

Top Things to Do

1. Walk, drive or camp in Little Desert National Park.
2. Picnic on the Wimmera River in Dimboola or Horsham.
3. Spend at least several days exploring the Grampians (Gariwerd).
4. Pan for gold or watch a spectacular sound and light show at Sovereign Hill, Ballarat.
5. Explore Ballarat's mining history at the Eureka Centre.

Ararat

Ararat, at the foothills of the Grampians was born of a short-lived romance with gold. In 1857, a group of Chinese immigrants on their way from South Australia to the Victorian fields rested near Mount Ararat and while refreshing their water supplies, discovered a rich source of shallow alluvial gold. Today, the Chinese who brought the town into being are remembered by the Gum San Chinese Heritage Centre in Lambert Street.

Ballarat

Located 110 km north-west of Melbourne, Ballarat evolved from a squatter's swampside camp into a goldrush boom town that is now Victoria's largest inland city. Gold's vital role is celebrated through superb historical reconstructions such as Sovereign Hill, the Eureka Centre and the Mining Exchange. Gold was also once won on the waters of Lake Wendouree, which formed an arena for the rowing, kayaking and canoeing events of Melbourne's 1956 Olympics.

Rugged coast or rocky wilderness? Wrecks and relics or gold and green? These are the choices you must make before setting out on the journey from Adelaide to Melbourne. The Western Highway offers the most direct route, leading 729 km past ancient Gariwerd (the Grampians) and through the gold-founded cities of Ararat and Ballarat. The coastal route is longer, but features a seaboard scattered with shipwrecks, historic ports and the visual feast of the famous Twelve Apostles.

Melbourne via Western Highway

From Tailem Bend, just outside Murray Bridge, the Dukes Highway runs parallel with the Adelaide–Melbourne railway line south-east to Bordertown. This grain and grazing shire is promoted as Tatiara, an Aboriginal word meaning "the good country". The town of Keith was once known by the unfortunate name of Mount Monster (in reference to a local granite outcrop). You may also notice a Land Rover atop a pole in the roadside parkland as you are leaving town — it isn't the remnant of some bizarre traffic accident but a memorial to workers who cleared land here for farming in the early 1960s. Down the road in Bordertown, a motorcycle that once belonged to one Bob Hawke is displayed in the lobby of the local council offices (the town was the former prime minister's birthplace). From Keith, it is possible to divert south on the Riddoch Highway to Naracoorte Caves National Park and the acclaimed Coonawarra wine district.

Across the border, the wheat fields and silos of the Wimmera wheat belt flank the Western Highway. In fact, Australia's largest concrete grain silo stands in the town of Nhill (Davis Street), approximately half-way between Adelaide and Melbourne. Much of Nhill was devastated by a tornado in 1897 which, curiously, destroyed every church in the town but left its pubs relatively unscathed. To the south of Nhill lies Little Desert National Park (*see facing page*).

Dimboola was little known to the rest of Australia before a popular play and subsequent film put the town on the map. The Wimmera River flows through town, providing a relaxing eucalypt-shaded setting for lunching, boating and fishing. A walking track from town follows the river some 7 km to Horseshoe Bend in Little Desert National Park. Like Dimboola, Horsham has an attractive river bank setting and the botanic gardens (laid out by Sir William Guilfoyle, curator of Melbourne's Royal Botanic Gardens) are a great place to revive and relax. If you are detouring to Gariwerd National Park (*see following pages*), Horsham's well-equipped retail centre is also the ideal place to stock up on supplies.

Stawell has an international reputation as the home of Australia's most prestigious professional foot race, the Stawell Gift. The event attracts over 15,000 people each Easter. The town grew out of the mid 19th century Victorian gold rushes and remains home to Australia's richest gold mining operations. Just south is Great Western, a town synonymous for many Australians with sparkling wine. Go underground at Seppelt's Great Western cellar door and tour the "drives" that have been used since 1868 to house and mature millions of bottles of sparkling wine. Continuing south-west, the Western Highway passes through the historic gold towns of Ararat and Ballarat (*see boxes left*) on your way into Melbourne.

Sovereign Hill

Victoria's famous goldrush era is revived in authentic detail at Sovereign Hill, Ballarat. Renowned as Australia's best outdoor museum, Sovereign Hill is set on 25 ha of the original alluvial goldfields and presents a complete recreation of 1850s goldfields. Pan for gold at Red Hill Gully Diggings, tour the underground mine and explore the 60-building township. By night, Sovereign Hill is the stage for *Blood on the Southern Cross*, a dramatic show recreating the events of the 1854 Eureka uprising.

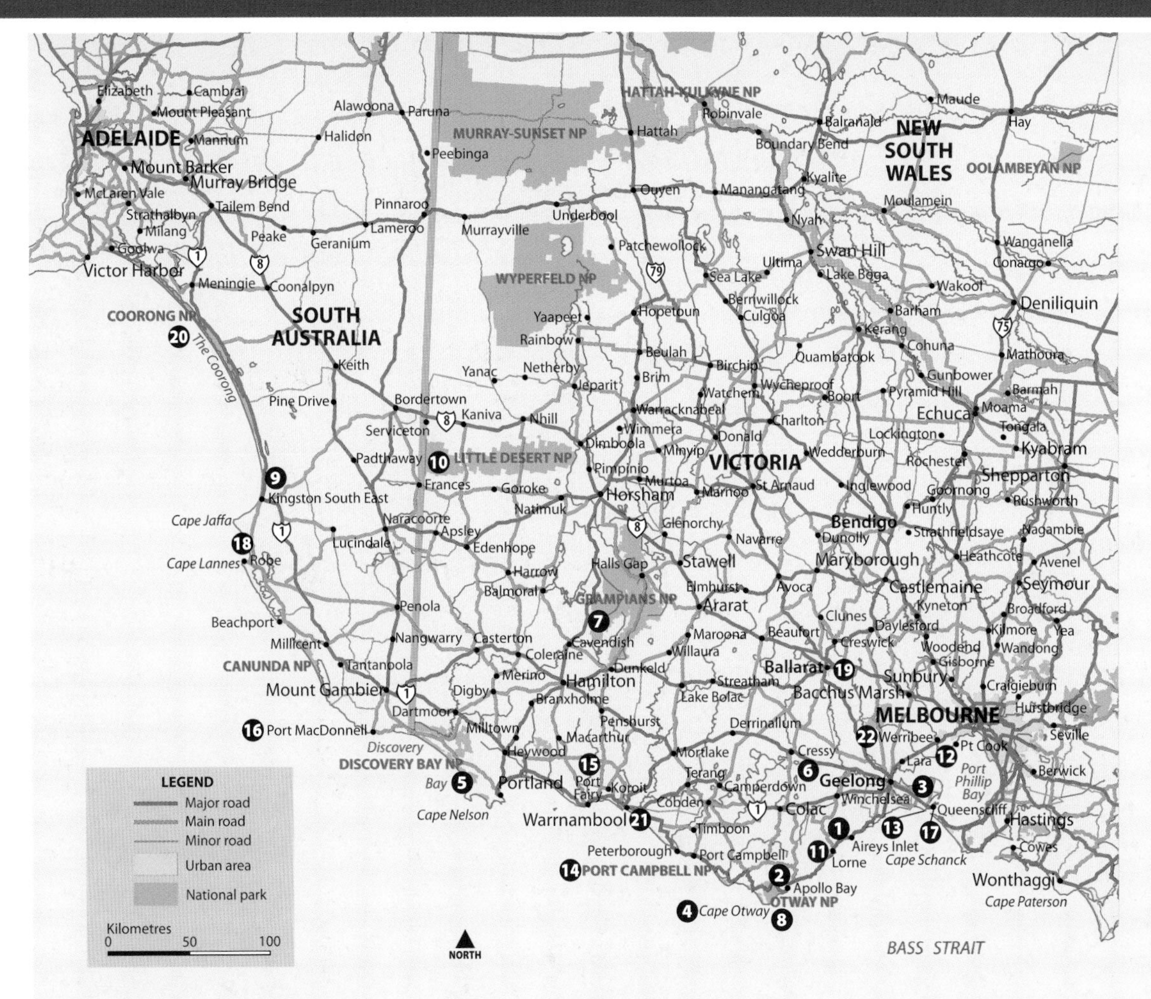

Feature Localities

1. Aireys Inlet
2. Apollo Bay
3. Bellarine Peninsula
4. Cape Otway
5. Discovery Bay National Park
6. Geelong
7. Grampians National Park (Gariwerd)
8. Otway National Park
9. Kingston SE
10. Little Desert National Park
11. Lorne
12. Point Cook
13. Point Lonsdale
14. Port Campbell National Park
15. Port Fairy
16. Port MacDonnell
17. Queenscliff
18. Robe
19. Sovereign Hill, Ballarat
20. The Coorong National Park
21. Warrnambool
22. Werribee

Little Desert National Park

Phone Ranger: 13 19 63

This expanse of river floodplains, claypans and sandplains is not, in fact, a desert. Mild temperatures and moderate winter rainfall support a remarkable number of plant and animal communities. It is also a birdwatcher's paradise with chats, wrens, honeyeaters, finches and the rare Southern Scrub-robin just a handful of the national park's 230 bird species. Ground, mound and tunnel nesters include Emus, Malleefowl, pardalotes and parrots. Wildflowers colour the park in spring with over 50 varieties of orchid spreading across the plains. A 600 km grid system of 4WD tracks overlies the park. Walking trails and camping areas are restricted to the eastern section.

Walks in the Park: Short nature walks provide a good introduction to this fragile ecosystem, starting with the Pomponderoo Hill Lookout over the mallee. Take a spring wildflower stroll on the Stringybark Nature Walk just off the sealed road south of Nhill or search for elusive Malleefowl on the 1 km Sanctuary Nature Walk south of Kiata.

Access: Sealed roads from Kaniva, Nhill and Kiata on the Western Highway.

Camping: Basic facilities at Horsehoe Bend, Ackle Bend and Kiata.

The Grampians National Park
Top Things to Do

1. Explore the Brambuk Aboriginal Culture Centre in Halls Gap prior to departure — this will greatly enhance your understanding of the region and its ancient sites.
2. Picnic with kangaroos at Zumstein on the western edge of the park.
3. Photograph the views from the Pinnacle.
4. Spend at least one night camping in the park — you will be surprised at the range of wildlife you meet.
5. Visit Grand Canyon Gorge, Whale's Mouth and Silent Street in the Wonderland area.
6. Visit MacKenzie Falls.
7. Don't leave without seeing at least several of the superb Aboriginal rock art sites.

The Grampians Walking tracks lead to the Grampians' very edge.

Left to right: A breathtaking panorama from the Pinnacle lookout; Granite peaks rise sharply from the surrounding plain.

Left to right: The plunging waters of MacKenzie Falls; A walk down Silent Street leads to the Pinnacle.

Left to right: Sheer rock walls abutted by dense forest; Nature's balancing act.

The Grampians National Park

Phone Ranger: 13 19 63

Known as *Gariwerd* to the Aboriginal custodians who have lived in the region for thousands of years, the Grampians are a series of dramatic sandstone ranges rising out of the flat lowlands of western Victoria 210 km from Melbourne.

Below these towering peaks are forested slopes, bushland, streams, waterfalls and lakes. Many of the rock formations within the park form settings to the creation stories of local Aboriginals and the region contains more than two-thirds of Victoria's Aboriginal rock art sites. The ranges also present a gallery of bizarre geological features. Great slabs of rock balanced on spindly pedestals or ledges jutting out into thin air simply seem to defy gravity. At MacKenzie Falls, the MacKenzie River plummets from high rock walls into a tranquil pool.

Busy Halls Gap is the Grampians' major township, located in an area known as the Wonderland, which contains numerous nature-sculpted formations (including the Grand Canyon, the Whale's Mouth and Silent Street). The town's well-resourced visitors' centre is an essential starting point, providing comprehensive maps and information on the Grampians' walking tracks, camping and cultural sites, picnic spots and scenic drives. Next stop before venturing into the wilderness is the adjacent Brambuk Aboriginal Culture Centre where multimedia displays, presentations and theatre combine to provide a fascinating introduction to Gariwerd's Indigenous heritage. Local tour operators offer the opportunity to see the Grampians from nearly every imaginable perspective, including hot air balloons, horseback, mountain bikes, Harley Davidson motorcycles and, for the brave of heart, hang gliders.

Walks in the Park: With more than 1000 km of walking tracks and roads winding their way through the park there are simply too many walks to mention, but many popular shorter walks commence at Halls Gap. Venus Baths Loop Walk is an easy 2.3 km wander that starts at the town swimming pool and follows Stony Creek to a natural waterhole. Contact the visitor centre (Ph: 1800 065 599) for walking guides.

Access: Various routes from the Western, Henty and Glenelg Highways.

Camping: There are many excellent camping grounds within the park and all have fireplaces, pit toilets and picnic tables (some sites without water).

Wildlife of the Grampians & Surrounds

The Grampians are alive with wildlife, but much of the fauna is both nocturnal and shy; so camping is certainly the best way to acquaint yourself with the natives. By night, possum, wombats, the Smoky Mouse, Barking Owl and even Platypuses emerge from their well-camouflaged hides to hunt, play, feed and breed. Koalas and kangaroos are also often seen and heard at night. Common Brushtail and Ringtail Possums, tiny Eastern and Little Pygmy-possums, Sugar Gliders and the rarer Squirrel Gliders frequent various Grampians habitats. By day, diurnal birds, reptiles, insects and the occasional mammal keep visitors company. Birds abound, from the elegantly plumed Southern Emu-wren to the sombre-grey Gang-gang Cockatoo with its masquerade red head and crest, to the soaring Peregrine Falcon and Wedge-tailed Eagle. Due to the diverse habitats and varied climate (from the cool south to the warmer, drier north-west), the reptile population is rich in species. The six species of native fish and eleven species of frog might not be visible, but they — and the swimming, crawling, flying and weaving invertebrates — are no less important to this ecosystem than the larger creatures.

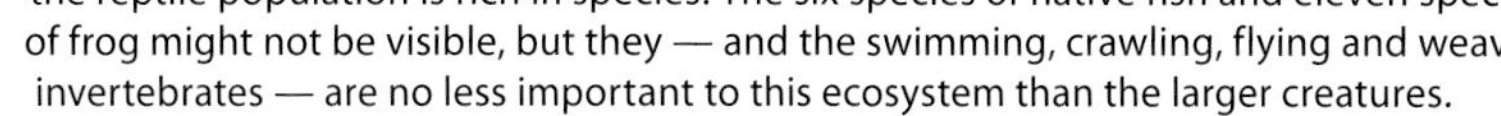

Short-beaked Echidna

Barking Owl

Left to right: Bundled Guinea Flower; Grampians Bauera; Pink Heath; Mountain Grevillea.

Left to right: Red-necked Wallaby, Eastern Grey Kangaroo; Swamp Wallaby.

Left to right: Parrots are the most dominant (and noisiest) of the bird families that inhabit the Grampians area — Rainbow Lorikeet; Gang-gang Cockatoo; Yellow-tailed Black-Cockatoo; Crimson Rosella; Sulphur-crested Cockatoo.

The Grampians' Flora

The Grampians are home to more than 1000 plant species and in spring the whole area is a sea of wildflowers. Plant habitats include heath, wetlands, open woodlands and tree fern gullies; 20 species of these, including the Spectral Duck Orchid, are found nowhere else. Almost one-third of Victoria's native plants thrive here. The forests of eucalypt and wattle, grevillea and banksia are home to abundant birdlife, including waterbirds, songbirds, raptors and parrots. Victoria's floral emblem, the Pink Heath, flourishes alongside many other heathland species.

Meeting the Macropods

More macropod species inhabit the Grampians than anywhere else in Victoria. They will most likely be found in or near open forest and the best time to look for them is when they move out to grasslands from late afternoon to early morning. Eastern Grey Kangaroos live in mobs and tend to spend the day, particularly if it is hot, resting in the shade. The Red-necked Wallaby is the most common large wallaby of the open forests. It lives a mostly solitary life but also grazes in groups on grasses and herbs. The Swamp Wallaby is a browser that eats a large range of vegetation, preferring shrubs and bushes to grasses. Less likely to be seen is the endangered Brush-tailed Rock-wallaby that makes its home on the ledges, caves and crevices of the sandstone ranges.

Boon for Birdwatching

Be sure to take binoculars when you visit the Grampians. Even if birdwatching is not one of your hobbies, Gariwerd's birdlife is so rich that it is impossible not to be fascinated. Emus stalk through the gum trees. Parrots and cockatoos nest in hollow woodland trees. Lorikeets and honeyeaters feed on nectar, pollen and insects. Babblers and choughs forage through the leaf litter for insects, their larvae and other small ground-dwelling prey. In the heathland smaller birds (such as wrens, robins, fantails and whistlers) make their homes. By day, raptors such as the Wedge-tailed Eagle, Peregrine Falcon and threatened Square-tailed Kite patrol the skies. At dusk listen for the boom of the endangered Powerful Owl, and be sure to include owls and the Bush Stone-curlew on your list of creatures to watch out for on a night-time stroll.

Melbourne via Great Ocean Road

Although the coastal journey from Adelaide to Melbourne is longer than the inland route via the Western Highway, it rewards motorists with one of the world's truly great drives. The highlight is, of course, that famous stretch of bitumen known as the Great Ocean Road, which offers exceptional vistas of coastal vegetation and the majesty of the Southern Ocean.

The Coorong to Port Campbell

The coastal route to Melbourne commences with a journey along the Coorong, a shallow saltwater lagoon that hugs the coast for 145 km beginning at the Murray mouth. It is separated from the sea by the massive white dune of the Younghusband Peninsula and is home to over 250 recorded bird species — their habitat guarded by the Coorong National Park (*see below*). South Australia's south-east corner is a major tourism destination, much-loved for its charming beach towns, natural features, seafood and wineries.

Sixty-four national and conservation parks in the region protect an assortment of natural landscapes from the World Heritage Area of Naracoorte Caves to Mount Gambier's Blue Lake (nestled in the crater of an extinct volcano), the steep dunes of Canunda National Park and the underwater secrets of Piccaninnie Ponds Conservation Park.

Mount Gambier, near the Victorian border is the region's largest centre. It is built on the slopes of an extinct volcano and a network of limestone caverns run beneath the town. Smaller coastal towns such as Kingston SE, Robe and Beachport are busy holiday centres. Kingston SE celebrates its status as an important lobster and fishing port with the presence of the Big Lobster, an 18 m high crustacean parked by the highway (*top left*). The pastures of the south-east also produce some of Australia's best lamb and wool and are an important dairy area. Inland, vignerons produce fine table wines around Coonawarra, Australia's most valuable viticultural area. Vines were first planted in the 1800s and today over 20 regional wineries produce wine (including the famous Grange) for domestic consumption and export.

Over the border, south of the highway, the long dune-bordered arc of Discovery Bay National Park follows the coast. Along with the Glenelg River and Lower Glenelg National Park, this is an idyllic camping, canoeing and fishing location favoured by families.

The industrial centre and port of Portland marks the start of a Victorian coastal adventure that includes the historic fishing village of Port Fairy, significant Aboriginal sites, and the maritime intrigues of Warrnambool. On the Shipwreck Coast, the Bay of Islands and Twelve Apostles are rightfully considered some of Australia's greatest natural treasures.

Kingston SE

So named to differentiate it from Kingston on Murray, Kingston SE is a placid holiday and fishing village located at the start of the Limestone Coast. Don't miss the fascinating sundial and sculptures on Maria Creek Island and head south to Cape Jaffa to see the lobster fleet, historic lighthouse (*below*) and winery.

Robe

This traditional seaside retreat attracts vast numbers of holiday visitors, lured by its fine protected beaches and village-like atmosphere. There is a multitude of restaurants and a large choice of accommodation (including historic cottages) but bookings are essential for all holiday periods.

The Coorong National Park

Phone Ranger: (08) 8575 1200

The Coorong is famous for the sheer number and variety of resident and migratory birds that thrive in its wetland habitats. Australian Pelicans, Silver Gulls and Crested Terns in their thousands have established breeding colonies on the lagoon's island sanctuaries. Permanent residents also include egrets, Black Swans (*bottom right*), Black-winged Stilts and many species of duck.

Seeing the Park: Boating and 4WD are the most popular ways of getting around the park and there are several excellent vantage points off the Princes Highway that have views across the haunting dunescapes of Younghusband Peninsula. A 10 minute walk from the Jacks Point car park leads to lookouts over Australian Pelican rookeries.

Access: Numerous access points off the Princes Highway south of Meningie.

Camping: Basic facilities at Barker Knoll, Salt Creek and 42 Mile Crossing.

Beachport

A chain of lakes links Beachport with its northern seaside cousin, Robe and the town is its equal in holiday appeal. Fish off the 700 m long jetty, comb the shores of Beachport Conservation Park or float about in the salt-dense waters of the Pool of Siloam (Scenic Drive). Past the lighthouse, a lookout affords views of Penguin Island, a nesting zone for Little Penguins, Silver Gulls and Crested Terns. Fur-seals can also sometimes be seen resting on the rocks.

Mount Gambier

Mount Gambier, South Australia's second-largest city is a landscape of craters, lakes, caves and underground aquifers. The city is surrounded by the Commonwealth's largest softwood plantation. Wander the boardwalks around Blue Lake (*far left*), go diving under the city streets in EngelBrecht Caves or visit Glencoe Woolshed, which celebrates the area's early pastoral wealth. The visitor centre is built around a replica of the HMS *Lady Nelson*, which charted the nearby coast in 1800.

Port MacDonnell

Port MacDonnell is a proud port and fishing town south of Mount Gambier. Savour fresh seafood or visit the Port MacDonnell Maritime Museum, which displays relics from the 25 ships wrecked off the coast since 1844. A mural on the local community hall (*left*) recalls the port's importance to pastoralists. East of town are the Piccaninnie Ponds — underwater caverns with limpid waters perfect for diving and snorkelling.

Port Fairy

The best surviving example of an original Victorian fishing port is the compellingly enchanting village of Port Fairy. Stand by the historic bluestone walls overlooking the fleet of sail-rigged boats (*far left*) on the Moyne River and you will be instantly immersed in yesteryear. Fifty of the town's buildings are classified by the National Trust (a signposted history walk will lead you past many of them). The Port Fairy Historic Centre (Gipps Street) is also a good place to drop in; it provides a detailed portrait of early port life.

Warrnambool

Warrnambool is steeped in history as deep as the ocean that stretches beyond Lady Bay. Through the persistent puzzle of the Mahogany Ship and 16th century charts detailing this section of coast, it also has credible claims to being the site of Australia's earliest European contact. Warrnambool's more recent maritime past is superbly recalled at the Flagstaff Hill Maritime Museum. Twenty-nine ships lie at the bottom of Lady Bay, but the ocean waters are also a nursery for Southern Right Whales.

Port Campbell National Park
Top Things to Do

1. Stop to view the stranded formations of the Bay of Islands Coastal Park.
2. Learn about the history of the *Loch Ard*.
3. Photograph the Twelve Apostles from the observation decks and boardwalks along the Great Ocean Road.
4. Camp in the face of the Southern Ocean in Port Campbell National Park.
5. Watch out for Little Penguins along the Shipwreck Coast.

The Wreck of the *Loch Ard*

A few kilometres past the Twelve Apostles is the coast's most famous shipwreck site. In 1878, the *Loch Ard*, a clipper nearing the end of its three month voyage from England, became blinded by fog and blundered onto a rocky reef near the cliffs of Mutton Bird Island.

Desperate efforts were made to lower a lifeboat but within only 15 minutes the vessel was lost to the wild sea, taking with her Captain Gibbs and 51 crew and passengers. Only two survived to tell the terrible tale.

Young sailor Tom Pearce was washed into the narrow cove now known as Loch Ard Gorge. Here he was sighted standing on the beach by teenage passenger Eva Carmichael, who had herself survived by clinging to part of the ship's spar. The brave Pearce dived back into the waters and dragged Carmichael ashore where they rested in the shelter of a small cave. After recuperating from his courageous efforts, Pearce scaled the cliffs and was met by a party from nearby Glenample Homestead. The story is now retold on plaques on the paths leading to Wreck Lookout and the gorge. A stairway leads down to the beach.

Port Campbell National Park

Phone Ranger: 13 19 63

Port Campbell National Park is unlike any other coastal region in Australia (or, for that matter, the World). Stretching 27 km from Princetown to Peterborough, its most famous features lie not on the land but stranded in the sea — massive limestone formations severed from the coast by erosion. Along the land's edge, stubborn fingers of remnant rock jut into the ocean, forming a series of coves accessible by boardwalks and tracks. Carved over millennia from sheer cliffs by the relentless swell of the Southern Ocean, the main formations have long been known as the Twelve Apostles. These hauntingly beautiful coastal "orphans", and their neighbouring cousins London Bridge, Mutton Bird Island and the Bakers Oven, are perhaps Victoria's most awe-inspiring natural phenomena. Continuing erosion has seen the original twelve now reduced to just eight. Few would guess that these remarkable pillars of stone were once living creatures. Up to 20 million years ago, below the seabed, the skeletons of countless millions of tiny marine animals broke down and aggregated, slowly forming into limestone. The soft rock was exposed by the retreating ocean, allowing elemental forces (and the slow hand of time) to begin sculpting the compelling shapes we see today.

Though the geological wonders of the coast loom large, Port Campbell National Park is also home to a surprising range of creatures adapted to life on the windswept coast. Peregrine Falcons, Australian Pelicans, gannets and albatrosses survey the sea from above. One of the more remarkable stories of endurance involves Short-tailed Shearwaters, commonly known as "muttonbirds". Every year these birds fly around 30,000 km across the oceans between North America and rookeries in Bass Strait. At Mutton Bird Island, near Loch Ard Gorge thousands of shearwaters nest between October and April. A visitor centre (Ph: (03) 5598 6809) near the Twelve Apostles provides insight into the natural history of the area.

Sights in the Park: Many of the coves and beaches can be reached via boardwalks and stairways. Wooden platforms erected within the heathland provide perfect vantage points to view the sculpted rock and blowholes.

Access: Via Princes Highway between Peterborough and Princetown.

Camping: Commercial caravan and camping sites operate outside the park at Port Campbell and along the coast.

Top to bottom: Both the shape and number of the extraordinary Twelve Apostles are perpetually changing under the ceaseless surge of waves and wind. Once part of the coast, these stacks stand until they too succumb to nature's battering.

The Indented Coast There are many spectacular vantage points.

Twelve Apostles The stacks were once part of the limestone cliffs.

Shipwreck Coast Viewing platforms are dotted along the coast.

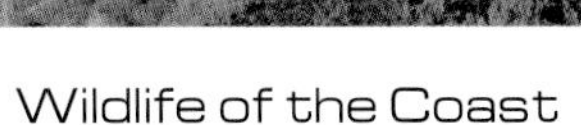

Wildlife of the Coast

There is a great diversity of wildlife concealed within the heathland, dunes, wetland and woodlands of the Shipwreck Coast.

Eighteen mammal species have been observed in the park, and many can be seen before sunrise or sunset, or on nocturnal rambles. Among them are the Southern Brown Bandicoot, Swamp Antechinus, Eastern Grey Kangaroo and Short-beaked Echidna. The area is also rich in birdlife, including the rare Rufous Bristlebird, which lives near the ground among sword grass tussocks and low-growing bushes (its upturned tail may be seen jerking as it runs for cover). Waterbirds abound in the estuaries and wetlands. Hooded Plovers bob their heads and dart about the tide line and several species of albatross can be seen out to sea. These waters are also frequented by the leviathans of the ocean, Humpback and Southern Right Whales, which swim close to shore on their annual journeys to and from warmer waters where they calve and mate (June to October).

Penguins of the Shipwreck Coast

While visiting the Twelve Apostles, keep an eye out for nesting Little Penguins. These avian celebrities may be seen on the beaches at dusk and dawn. Around twilight it is often possible to see the birds returning to shore after a day's fishing. Observation platforms in the area make great penguin-spotting locations.

Port Campbell to Geelong

The stunning vistas of Port Campbell National Park are but an entree to the visual feast of ocean panoramas and mountain wilderness along the Great Ocean Road. This is one of Australia's best coastal drives, a slender winding strip of bitumen barely dividing the treacherous waters of Bass Strait and the Southern Ocean from soaring ranges near the edge of the continent, much of which is protected by national and state parks. Rising up from the lighthouse at Cape Otway are the Otway Ranges. This terrestrial wonderland of temperate rainforest, luxuriant fern gullies and plunging waterfalls is home to a range of flora and fauna.

Great Ocean Road

In times past the only viable route to this coast from Geelong was by sea or horse-drawn coach on often impassable tracks. But returned World War I servicemen, working without the aid of heavy machinery, constructed a spectacular road in memory of the fallen. Their backbreaking labour with pick and shovel left a legacy of astonishing beauty. From Anglesea to Cape Otway, the Great Ocean Road delivers an ever-changing vision of magnificent seascapes.

The Cape Otway Lightstation was built in 1848 to protect passing vessels from the dangers of the narrow entrance to Bass Strait between Cape Otway and King Island, known as the "eye of the needle". Several anchors of ships lost to these waters remain within the park, including that of the *Fiji* at Moonlight Head and a hull section and anchor of *Eric the Red* at the lightstation. A mine laid by an unidentified ship off Cape Otway also claimed the first US naval casualty of World War II — the cargo ship *City of Rayville* in 1940. The lightstation and keepers' quarters are one of mainland Australia's oldest. Thirteen graves in the nearby cemetery form the last resting place of ill-fated sailors.

At Dinosaur Cove near Glenaire, the fossilised remains of herbivorous dinosaurs have been found along with ancient crocodile teeth. The dinos and crocs are long gone, clearing the way for safe and scenic beachside camping at Johanna Beach and Blanket Bay.

When it rains, as it often does in these heights, the Otways spring to life. Melba Gully State Park, north of Apollo Bay via Lavers Hill, is one of the wettest places in Victoria (recording 2000 mm of rainfall annually). It is also one of the best places to see the Otway's full range of vegetation from mosses and fungi to Tree Ferns, as well as a rare carnivorous variety of snail (*Victaphanta compacta*) and the erroneously named glow-worm. Actually a variety of gnat larvae, glow-worms thrive in the dank nooks of the park's many gullies and stream banks. For your best chance of seeing these elusive creatures, remain very quiet on the tracks and don't use torchlight — if disturbed the canny glow-worm will turn off its own light (a luminous part of the abdomen). Tearoom operator Jessie Fry named the park after Australia's famed opera virtuoso Dame Nellie Melba in 1921. The current main picnic area is on the site of her erstwhile tearooms and at the start of the must-do 35 minute Madsen's Track Nature Walk. The (optional) steepish climb to the 300-year-old Big Tree is worth your sweat.

Apollo Bay to Lorne

Apollo Bay was originally known as *Krambruk*, an Aboriginal word thought to mean "sandy place". Its bountiful waters and coastal forests were a rich source of food (shellfish, wallaby and possum) for the original Katabanut people. Whalers found the neighbouring ocean lucrative and European settlement brought fishing and timber milling industries to the area. In 1898, it was dubbed Apollo Bay in honour of a schooner that had once found safe harbour close by. Today Apollo Bay's prosperous fishing fleet, protectively moored behind a large breakwater when not taking their lobster pots, nets and reels to sea, is of great interest to visitors. Sample their daily haul and you will quickly discover why.

Beyond Apollo Bay, the Great Ocean Road passes through the farming and holiday hamlet of Wongarra, where a 30 minute walking track leads to beautiful Carisbrook Falls. The small townships of Wye River and Kennett River were named for their English counterparts in 1846 by surveyor George Smythe and are now popular locations for bushwalking, surfing, fishing and boating. Koalas, kangaroos, dolphins and whales can be seen in the area. The 90 m high lookout at Cape Patton (half-way between Lorne and Apollo Bay) provides a brilliant view of the rocky coast. After the curves and climbs of the Great Ocean Road (made all the more testing by a constant desire to absorb the scenery), Lorne provides you with bountiful rewards. The town is designed for relaxation — cosmopolitan restaurants and cafés, luxury hotels and fashionable shops line the Esplanade. Picnic on the postcard-perfect banks of the Cumberland River or the generous bayside lawns; promenade on the foreshore and dine by the famous pier. Behind town, the waterfall-filled beauty of the Angahook-Lorne State Park awaits.

Port Campbell to Geelong

Top Things to Do

1. Explore Cape Otway Lightstation and its surrounds.
2. Camp by the ocean at Johanna Beach.
3. See glow-worms in Melba Gully State Park.
4. Walk in the forest canopy along the Otway Fly.
5. Relax, dine and refresh in the ocean at Apollo Bay and Lorne.
6. Tour the waterfalls of Great Otway National Park.

Great Ocean Walk

The Great Ocean Walk stretches 91 km from Apollo Bay to Glenample Homestead (near the Twelve Apostles). It follows much of the spectacular coastline, passes through Great Otway National Park and overlooks the marine national park.

The Great Ocean Walk is designed so that walkers can choose between short, day or overnight hikes, completing the trail in sections. Car parks are provided at Shelly Beach, Blanket Bay, Parker Hill, Cape Otway, Aire River and Johanna Beach but there is no car access to "hike-in" bush camps. Walkers are requested to walk the trail from east to west.

Treetop Walk

Fifteen minutes drive from Lavers Hill, near Triplet Falls, a 600 m long elevated walkway known as the Otway Fly offers visitors the chance to stroll among the treetops and survey the surrounding beauty from a 45 m high lookout (open daily, Ph: (03) 5235 9200).

Great Otway National Park

Phone Ranger: 13 19 63

The 103,00 ha Great Otway National Park contains some of Victoria's most compelling (and inaccessible) coastline and the ranges protect vital swathes of native forest. The park is a mix of ancient rainforest (containing some of Victoria's best waterfalls), heathlands, and wet and dry woodlands. Great Otway National Park has tremendous cultural significance, with a rich Indigenous and colonial history.

Walks in the Park: There are over 1000 km of walking tracks and roads through the park (contact the Apollo Bay or Lorne information centres for details).

Access: Via the Great Ocean Road.

Camping: There are a large range of camping opportunities in the park, from well-equipped campgrounds to basic bush camps. Excellent sites with fireplaces and composting toilets are available at Lake Elizabeth — a known habitat of the Platypus.

Angahook-Lorne State Park

Phone Ranger: 13 19 63

Rising up behind the Great Ocean Road from Aireys Inlet to Lorne is Angahook-Lorne State Park (or Great Otway National Park), encompassing wild heathlands, waterfalls and the eastern ranges of the Otways. Hooded Plovers, Koalas, and brushtail and ringtail possums are among a wide variety of animals found in the park.

Walks in the Park: Walking tracks abound, leading to waterfalls, viewing platforms and lookouts surrounded by dense forest and misty fern gullies. For shorter stops on the way to Lorne, well-equipped picnic facilities, short walking tracks and nature trails can be found at Distillery Creek and Moggs Creek close to the coast road.

Access: From Lorne and numerous points along the Great Ocean Road.

Camping: Car-accessible bush camping sites in the north-eastern area at Hammonds Road and around Lorne provide the opportunity to explore the park at length.

Finding the Falls

The Otway Ranges contain some of Victoria's best and biggest waterfalls. Near Lorne, the picturesque Cumberland and Erskine Falls (*above right*) attract a large viewing audience, but there are at least another ten worth the visit.

While some are less accessible than others, the beautiful, fern-enveloped Beauchamp Falls (*far left*) and Hopetoun Falls (*left*) are relatively close to picnic areas and car parking off Aire Valley Road, north-east of Cape Otway.

Apollo Bay

Apollo Bay is a delightful seaside town with an inviting crescent of beach sheltered by Point Bunbury to the south. Twenty-four carved cypress sculptures line the grassy verge overlooking the sand. In summer and school holiday periods the foreshore bustles with activity — an excellent array of restaurants, art galleries and museums can be found here.

Lorne

Nestled in the broad blue lap of Loutit Bay, this perfectly situated seaside retreat has been delighting visitors for more than a century. The sweeping arc of its sheltered beach is complemented by the lush Otways backdrop. The town's Grand Pacific Hotel was the first coastal hotel built in Victoria, completed in 1880 when it could only be reached by ship.

Aireys Inlet

The bright but unassuming beachside town of Aireys Inlet signals the beginning (or end) of the Great Ocean Road's spectacularly curvaceous journey. A tour of the famous "White Lady" (aka Split Point Lighthouse), makes for a pleasant diversion, while surfers will relish the break at Fairhaven Beach.

Geelong & the Bellarine Peninsula

Top Things to Do

1. Wander Geelong's colourful waterfront and visit the National Wool Museum.
2. Spend a night in the historic seaside village of Queenscliff.
3. Watch ships negotiating the heads at Port Phillip Bay from Point Lonsdale.
4. Visit Werribee Park Mansion and stay a night at the adjacent Mansion Hotel.
5. See African wildlife at the Werribee Open Range Zoo.

Silent Statues Telling Tales

Along the Geelong waterfront from Rippleside Park to Limeburners Point and the botanic gardens are artist Jan Mitchell's 104 carved wooden bollards (*above*) — telling the tale of Geelong from its original Wathaurong inhabitants to more contemporary characters. Keep a look out for young ladies in neck-to-knee costumes, sailors, a town band, fishermen and even the great Matthew Flinders.

The National Wool Museum

The National Wool Museum is the only comprehensive museum of wool in Australia. Located in a refurbished bluestone wool store dating from 1872, the museum's displays and tableaux trace the incredible story of the Australian wool industry from its origins to the present day (open Mon–Fri, 9.30 am – 5 pm, Sat–Sun 1 pm – 5 pm, 26 Moorabool Street, Ph: (03) 5227 0701).

Geelong & Bellarine Peninsula

The city of Geelong is the gateway to the historic beach and fishing resorts of the Bellarine Peninsula and the Great Ocean Road. Queenscliff is a holiday village styled in the grand late 19th century tradition and is renowned for its fine food and sophisticated hotels. At the end of the Surf Coast Highway, the benign holiday setting of Torquay gives way to steepling waves, sandy cliffs and striking ocean views.

Geelong

In their epic 1824–25 journey from Sydney, explorers Hume and Hovell recorded the Aboriginal word *Jillong* (translated as "place of the sea bird over the white cliffs") when they reached Corio Bay. Geelong is now Victoria's second-largest city with a population of more than 200,000. Although only a mere 75 km from Melbourne, it has retained its own identity as a dynamic provincial centre. The waterfront, from Cunningham's Pier past the Royal Geelong Yacht Club to Eastern Beach, has undergone modern re-development and includes restaurants, bars and cultural attractions. The landscaped foreshore contains several restored historic buildings, including the National Wool Museum (*see bottom left*) and three buildings behind a single facade containing a university campus and a world-class concert stage (Costa Hall). Motor vehicle assembly has long been a key industry in Geelong and just around the corner is the Ford Discovery Centre, providing a glimpse of cars of yesteryear (cnr Gheringap and Brougham Streets, Ph: (03) 5227 8700). Geelong's commercial and retail district radiates out from Moorabool Street. The western end of Malop Street is the city's cultural precinct with cafés, studios and galleries all within walking distance of the Geelong Performing Arts Centre and the Court House Youth Arts Complex.

Eastern Beach features jetties, a famous Art Deco swimming pool complex, parklands and restaurants. Geelong's history as a seaport is celebrated in the bronze and glass *Cargo Boxes* sculptures representing ships and cargo, in the Customs House Gardens forecourt. Cunningham's Pier, built in the 1880s, was once a busy dock for ships loading with wool and gold. Now home to a restaurant and function complex, it is located on waterfront just a few minutes walk from the CBD. Geelong is also an active sporting centre whose community proudly displays its fiercely parochial support for its local Australian Rules AFL team. Matches at Geelong's Skilled Stadium against other national clubs regularly attract crowds in excess of 30,000 people, no matter what the weather is like. The City's Barwon River has been the scene of important rowing events since the early 1900s.

Surf Coast & Bellarine Peninsula

The pretty seaside villages and resort towns dotted along the Bellarine Peninsula, once an important grain growing region, are now tourism, fishing and watersport centres. The prodigious waves sweeping into Bells Beach and Jan Juc have made them world famous surfing destinations. The car parks and lookouts along the cliffs form ideal observation platforms, particularly during the World Championship Tour Event staged at Easter each year. For a historic perspective on Australia's surfing culture, including 130 boards big and small, visit the Surfworld Museum in Torquay (Beach Rd, Ph: (03) 5261 4606).

Stretching from Jan Juc past Anglesea to Moggs Creek, the 35 km long Surf Coast Walk offers great coastal views as well as rare native birds and wildlife. The offshore waters form part of Point Addis Marine National Park, where fish-rich reefs attract many divers. At peninsula's end Point Lonsdale lighthouse alerts vessels to the perils of the infamous Rip — renowned as one of the most treacherous bay entrances in the world. Below the lighthouse lies a small cave that purportedly once gave shelter to William Buckley, an escaped convict who lived among the Wathaurong people for more than 30 years prior to European settlement.

Clockwise from top left: Grand 19th century homes and hotels in Queenscliff; Marine Discovery Centre, Queenscliff; The Black Lighthouse at Fort Queenscliff; A relaxed place to stroll and fish.

Top to bottom: Point Lonsdale Lighthouse; Wetting a line at Point Lonsdale.

Queenscliff

Historic Queenscliff forever holds a place in Victorians' hearts with its quaint guesthouses, restored boutique hotels and fine dining. The 19th century charm of sandstone buildings and lacework-adorned cottages provides a relaxed seaside atmosphere redolent of bygone days. Overlooking the bay from Shortlands Bluff is Fort Queenscliff, built to protect shipping lanes from attack in the 1850s. Today the old fortification remains complete with cannon, guardroom, cells and even a dry moat. The unique Black Lighthouse is built from Scottish-cut bluestone. But not all is of the past. From Queenscliff Harbour, a modern twin-hull ferry transports visitors and their cars to Sorrento across the bay.

Point Lonsdale

Point Lonsdale is a holiday resort spreading out from the western headland of Port Phillip Bay. The 21 m high lighthouse was built in 1902 and is possibly Australia's last manned station. Standing on the lookout you can watch ships negotiating the Rip as they pass in and out of Port Phillip Bay. This region is protected by Port Phillip Heads Marine National Park, which includes seagrass beds, sheltered mudflats and rocky shores.

Werribee Park Mansion

Werribee Park Mansion is widely considered Victoria's finest colonial homestead. Once Victoria's largest private residence, it is a restored 60-room Italianate home built in the 1870s and set amid extensive formal gardens. The estate formed part of 37,635 ha of prime pastoral land and was home to wealthy Scottish settlers and their retinue of workers. From 1923–1973, the mansion functioned as a priests' seminary before being purchased by the Victorian government. Neighbouring Shadowfax Winery and the luxurious Mansion Hotel complete the experience (open daily, 10 am – 5 pm, off Princes Highway, Ph: (03) 9748 5094).

Werribee Open Range Zoo

Part of Werribee Park was set aside in 1973 to become a wildlife preserve now known as Werribee Open Range Zoo. The zoo's authentic recreation of the native habitat of African, Asian and American species provides a breathtaking experience. Here zebra, giraffes and rhinos wander the savannah, bison browse the prairie and hippos luxuriate at an African waterhole. Slumber safaris enable visitors to spend the night in the company of lions, cheetahs, monkeys and more (open daily, 9 am – 5 pm, Ph: (03) 9731 9600).

Point Cook & Cheetham Wetlands

Point Cook Coastal Park protects grasslands, sedgelands and saltmarshes, the lovely Cheetham Wetlands and one of the last unspoiled reef ecosystems in Port Phillip Bay. As well as being a picnicker's haven, with a swimming beach and walking trails, Point Cook is important for birdlife, which can be observed from Spectacle Lake Bird Hide or from the Cheetham Wetlands Tower. These habitats are visited by the endangered Orange-bellied Parrot, while the Double-banded Plover flies from New Zealand to spend the winter and the heroic Eastern Golden Plover migrates here from Siberia and Alaska. Flyers of another type can be seen at Point Cook RAAF Museum where an impressive collection of aircraft and memorabilia are on display.

HOBART

& THE JOURNEY AROUND TASMANIA

9

An island as varied as the continent itself, Tasmania deceives the first-time visitor with its diminutive size. Although the distances between the major regions are relatively short, there is so much to see and do here that even after several weeks it is easy to depart regretful, wishing for more time to explore. The island's early history — from the proud heritage of its original peoples to the convict era — remains prominent in art, artefacts, brick and stone. So well preserved is much of Tasmania's past that whole towns can appear frozen in time. The ancient past is also visible in Tasmania's renowned national parks. The damming of rivers has been opposed, and dedicated Australians are still working to prevent further logging of old-growth forests, to preserve their unfettered wild beauty for all. The severance of the island from the continental mainland 12,000 years ago created an ark. Many of the plant and animal species found here, such as the Tasmanian Devil and towering Huon Pine, have since evolved and flourished in Tasmania alone. Some, like the Tasmanian Tiger, no longer exist — victims (like the Tasmanian Aborigines themselves) of the European settlers' brutality and folly. Your journey begins in the island's capital, Hobart — a small and serene city spreading out from Mount Wellington along the Derwent River toward the sea. From here explore the remarkable remnants of the Port Arthur penal colony, fly over magnificent South West parks or walk to Wineglass Bay in fabulous Freycinet National Park, but be sure to allow more time than you think you'll need.

Left: Wineglass Bay, Freycinet National Park

TASMANIA the Island

Tasmania
Top Things to Do

1. View Hobart and the Derwent River estuary from Mt Wellington.
2. Walk the ruins of Port Arthur.
3. Catch a ferry to Bruny Island.
4. Spend the night in a convict penitentiary on Maria Island.
5. Hike to Wineglass Bay on the Freycinet Peninsula.
6. Ride the world's longest single span chairlift at Launceston's Cataract Gorge.
7. Climb to the top of the Nut in Stanley.
8. Walk the Overland Track from Cradle Mountain to Lake St Clair.
9. Fish for trout in the Great Lake.
10. Cruise the Gordon River.
11. Fly over Southwest National Park.

An Island in Original Condition

Tasmania's natural and human history is on vivid display nearly everywhere you travel. From the convict prison ruins of Port Arthur to the unforgettable national parks of Southwest, Franklin–Gordon Wild Rivers, Walls of Jerusalem and Cradle Mountain–Lake St Clair; this island is one of Australia's most captivating destinations. It is not only nature that remains unspoiled — in many places, early 19th century buildings, even entire towns, survive in their original condition.

In historical texts, the land that became Tasmania is often described as "the end of the world". Yet in terms of human and natural history, it is more akin to the start of it. Within this island of ancient mountain peaks and glaciers, majestic forests and wild rivers survive two candidates for the oldest living organism and the world's oldest tree (the King's Holly and Huon Pine, respectively), not to mention a menagerie of unique creatures found nowhere else on Earth. Tasmania's superb environment is its greatest asset. At a glance it may appear as a footnote to the map of Australia, but this is an island whose size belies an incredible array of natural and historical wonders.

Early History

Once part of the 60-million-year-old supercontinent known as Gondwana, Tasmania was liberated around 12,000 years ago when rising sea levels (caused by the end of the last Ice Age) flooded the land bridge connecting it to the Australian mainland. From that time until its European settlement, the island's people, flora and fauna lived and evolved in complete isolation. The Aborigines, who first populated Tasmania some 23,000 years earlier, survived in solitude until the land they knew as *Trowenna* was sighted by Dutch explorer Abel Tasman in 1642. Unable to determine if the place was an island or the southern part of New Guinea, Tasman called the place Van Diemen's Land and went ashore on the Forestier Peninsula for supplies. A crew member planted a flag on the soil to claim possession, but the Dutch never returned. Despite a further landing by a French expedition led by Marion Dufresne at Marion Bay in 1772, it was not until Matthew Flinders' and George Bass' circumnavigation in the *Norfolk* in 1798 that Tasmania was proven to be an island.

European Settlement

The British claimed Van Diemen's Land in 1803 and soon after established a penal settlement at the port of Hobart on the Derwent River. Further convict prisons were established at Sarah Island, Maria Island and Port Arthur and a total of 76,000 convicts were transported to the place described by English judges as "beyond the seas" over the following 50 years. Together with free settlers, convicts felled timber, cultivated land and established towns on the east and north coasts; however, European settlement came at the ultimate cost to the island's 5000 original inhabitants. Brutality and introduced diseases caused rapid population decline and Truganini, believed to be the last full blood Tasmanian Aborigine, died in 1876.

After convict transportation ceased in 1853, the island was re-named Tasmania in honour of the first European to lay eyes upon it. Over the next century, timber, shipbuilding, whaling, and the discovery of minerals (including gold and tin) contributed to the island's economy, but even today the State of Tasmania remains less industrially developed than its mainland cousins. Its great wealth is its magnificent natural heritage. One-fifth of the island is World Heritage Area and the national parks of the south and west protect some of the world's greatest natural glories. By virtue of its rich marine resources, pure waterways, fertile soils and temperate climate; Tasmania also boasts seafood and farm produce of the highest quality, much of which is exported around the world. At 68,000 km^2, no coast, park or town is too distant, but regret is assured should you allow only a short time to explore this exceptional land.

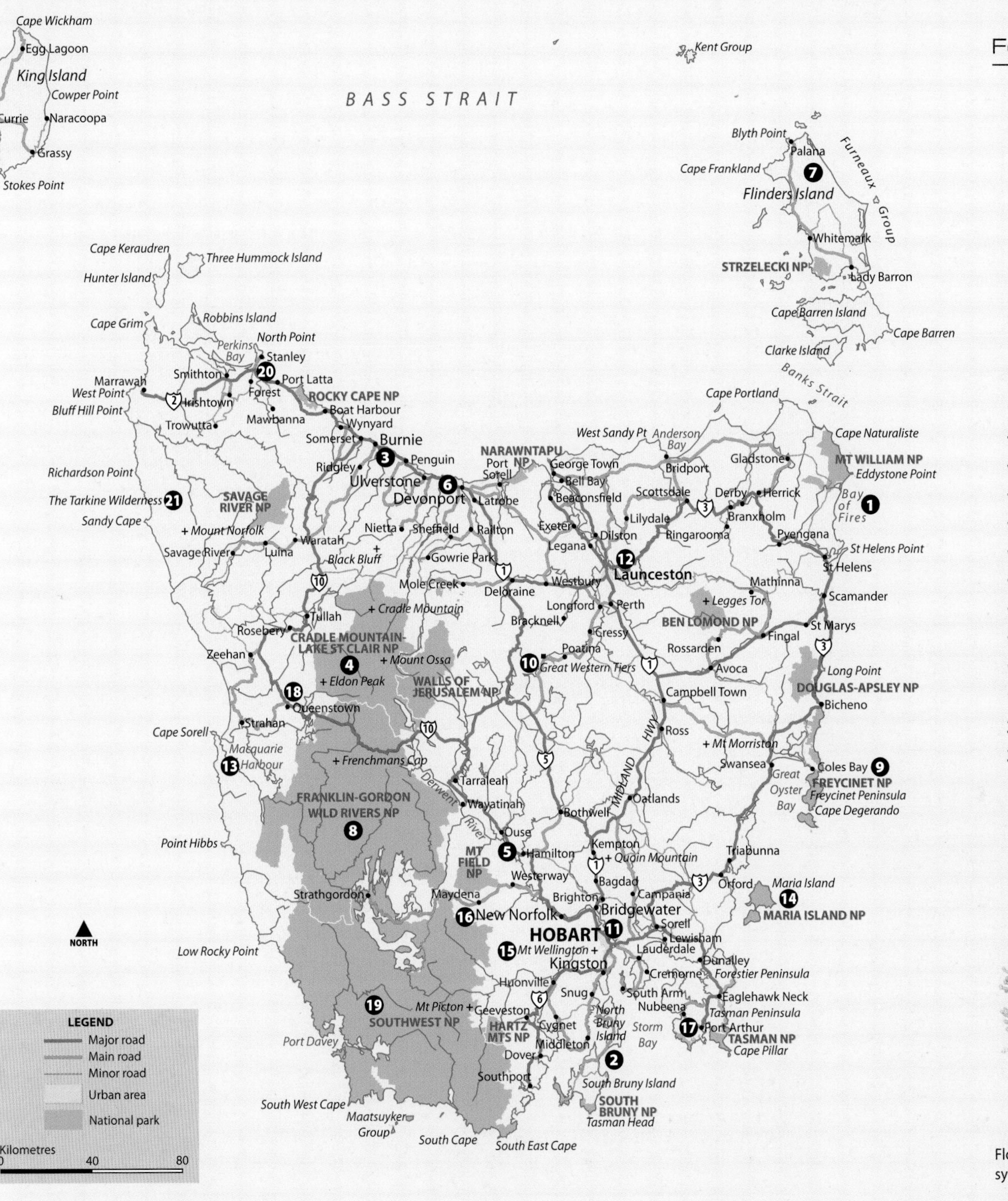

Feature Localities

1 Bay of Fires, Mount William National Park
2 Bruny Island
3 Burnie
4 Cradle Mountain–Lake St Clair National Park
5 Derwent Valley
6 Devonport
7 Flinders Island
8 Franklin-Gordon Wild Rivers National Park
9 Freycinet National Park
10 Great Western Tiers
11 Hobart
12 Launceston
13 Macquarie Harbour
14 Maria Island
15 Mount Wellington
16 New Norfolk
17 Port Arthur, Tasman Peninsula
18 Queenstown
19 Southwest National Park
20 Stanley
21 The Tarkine, Arthur–Pieman Conservation Area

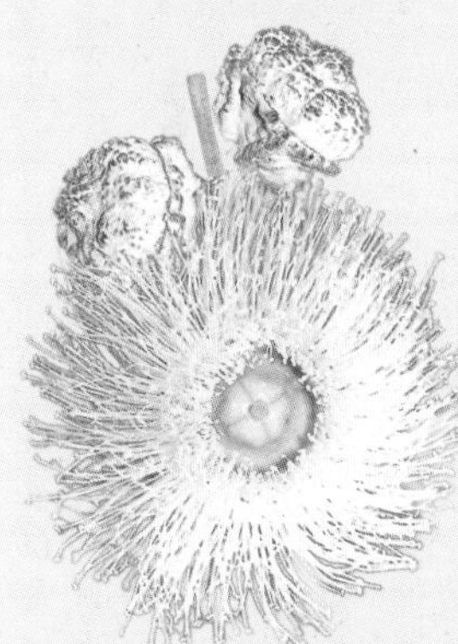

Flower of the Blue Gum — the floral symbol of Tasmania

Getting to Tasmania

While Tasmania's major cities of Hobart and Launceston are less than an hour's flight from Melbourne, you may prefer to extend your island adventure by making the 250 km crossing of Bass Strait aboard the *Spirit of Tasmania*. The large passenger and vehicle ferry (*right*) departs every evening from Melbourne and arrives at Devonport (103 km west of Launceston on Tasmania's north coast) at 7 am. The ferry also carries vehicles at an extra fee, so you may take your car and begin exploring from the moment you arrive.

HOBART & Surrounds

Hobart & Surrounds Top Things to Do

1. Cruise the Derwent River from Brooke Street Pier.
2. See the yachts arrive at Constitution Dock at the end of the Sydney to Hobart Yacht Race.
3. Wander the historic streets of Battery Point.
4. View Hobart from the summit of Mount Wellington.
5. Visit the Salamanca Markets.
6. Tour the famous Cascade Brewery.
7. Dine on Tasmanian delicacies and be entertained at the Hobart Summer Festival.
8. Explore the Tasmanian Museum and Art Gallery.
9. Walk in the Royal Tasmanian Botanical Gardens along the banks of the Derwent.
10. Walk, cycle, horse ride or camp in Wellington Park.

Hobart Looking north over Wrest Point towards the city centre and Tasman Bridge.

Situated on the banks of the Derwent River between the table-topped Mount Wellington in the west and Mount Nelson in the south, Hobart has retained much of its early colonial character. Its physical location, combined with a population no larger than many mainland Australian provincial centres, has had the dual effect of preventing widespread commercial development and preserving much of the city's grace and charm. Around the waterfront many fine examples of 19th century architecture, port buildings and wharves evoke an authentic maritime atmosphere not found elsewhere in Australia. Hobart's unsullied natural surrounds are one of its most striking features. Unlike other cities, it is not office towers but the sharp rise of Mount Wellington that dominates the skyline. Hobart's suburbs flow along both banks of the Derwent River and the sea remains in this venerable port's veins. Each New Year's Eve at Constitution Dock the arrival of a fleet of exhausted sailors — competitors in a gruelling race down Australia's east coast from Sydney — marks the conclusion of the country's most famous sailing event, the Sydney to Hobart Yacht Race.

A History in Buildings

From its convict settlement origins, Hobart developed into a thriving commercial port, first serving the sealing and whaling industries, then shipbuilding and trade; leading to the construction of enduring maritime warehouses, public buildings and housing. Walking through the clusters of authentic 19th century cottages, homes and period gardens of Battery Point transports you to a time when Hobart Town was just beginning to stake its place in the world (*see facing page*). From Battery Point descend Kelly's Steps to Salamanca Place, where the early bond warehouses are now a warren of art and craft galleries, workshops, studios and boutiques, including the Salamanca Art Centre. The city is awash with historic places and structures — over 90 buildings are classified by the National Trust, nearly 60 of which are in Davey and Macquarie Streets alone. Some still serve their original purpose — the Tasmanian Museum (40 Macquarie Street) was established in 1840; the Theatre Royal in Campbell Street (1837) is Australia's oldest continually operating theatre; while the Cascade Brewery (1832) in Cascade Road, South Hobart still produces world-class beer. Hobart's early history is also readily visible in the colonial sandstone architecture of Parliament House (Salamanca Place) and the city's churches. The Holy Trinity Church (Warwick Street) was designed in the Gothic style by convict architect James Blackburn and completed in 1847. Its bells, the oldest in the Southern Hemisphere, were first rung to mark Hobart Regatta Day — an annual tradition to this day.

Left to right: The historic Cascade Brewery in South Hobart; Hobart retains an impressive number of original colonial buildings, including the Hotel Alexandra.

The City Today

Hobart's city centre, a mere five minutes walk from the waterfront, is a relaxed and convenient blend of retail, dining and business facilities, devoid of the hectic pace that dominates many Australian city malls and shopping zones. The pedestrian haven of Elizabeth Street Mall is a great place to meet and eat while Franklin Square (named for Arctic explorer and former Governor Sir John Franklin), offers harbour views and oak-shaded lawns. In summer, cultural festivals enliven the city, including the annual post-Christmas Hobart Summer Festival that features a week of food, performance and arts events staged at Sullivans Cove.

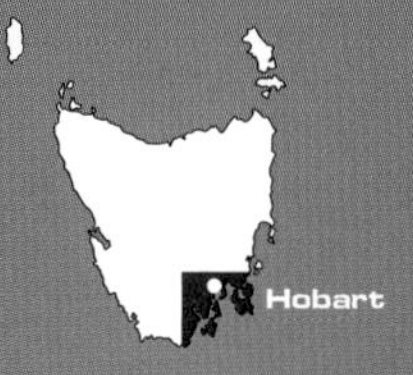

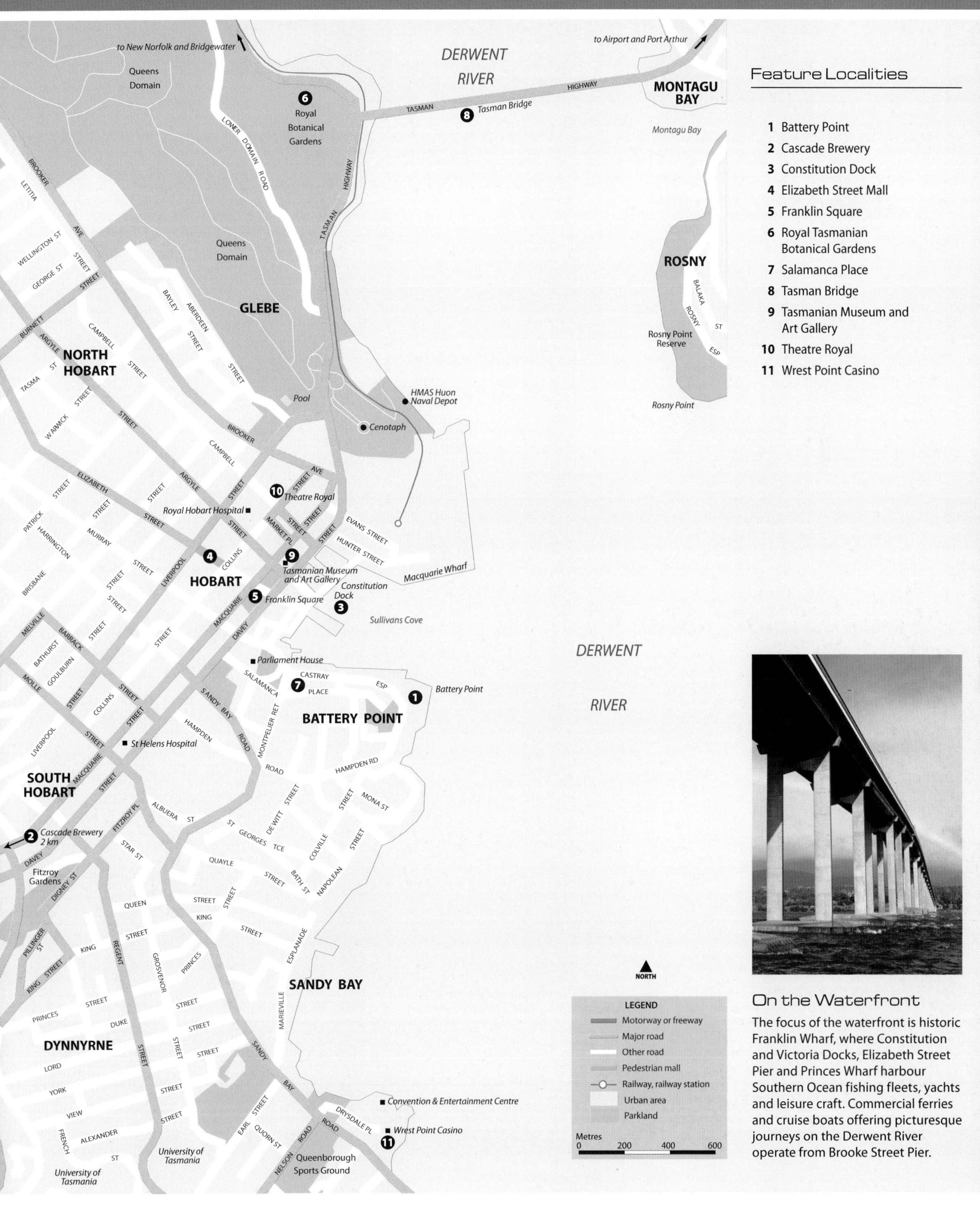

Feature Localities

1 Battery Point
2 Cascade Brewery
3 Constitution Dock
4 Elizabeth Street Mall
5 Franklin Square
6 Royal Tasmanian Botanical Gardens
7 Salamanca Place
8 Tasman Bridge
9 Tasmanian Museum and Art Gallery
10 Theatre Royal
11 Wrest Point Casino

On the Waterfront

The focus of the waterfront is historic Franklin Wharf, where Constitution and Victoria Docks, Elizabeth Street Pier and Princes Wharf harbour Southern Ocean fishing fleets, yachts and leisure craft. Commercial ferries and cruise boats offering picturesque journeys on the Derwent River operate from Brooke Street Pier.

The Mountain City

Hobart reaches out along the banks of the Derwent River from the foothills of Mount Wellington. The mountain was once known by Tasmanian Aborigines as *Unghanyahletta* and was noted on maps made by 18th century European maritime explorers, including Bligh and D'Entrecasteaux. In these latitudes the seasons are sharply defined and the 1271 m mountain both influences the city's weather and acts as a natural barometer, providing residents below with an indication of conditions to come. The mountain is at the eastern edge of Wellington Park, a nature reserve covering 18,250 ha.

Atop Mount Wellington is a lookout affording expansive views across the entire Derwent estuary. A network of walking tracks winding around the slopes below have long been a recreational retreat for Hobart residents. Springs picnic area is close to a cave that once gave refuge to one of Tasmania's most notorious early bushrangers, Rocky Whelan. Pinnacle Road, leading to the mountain summit, can be closed by snow in winter. Call the Council Information Line for road conditions (Ph: (03) 6278 0200).

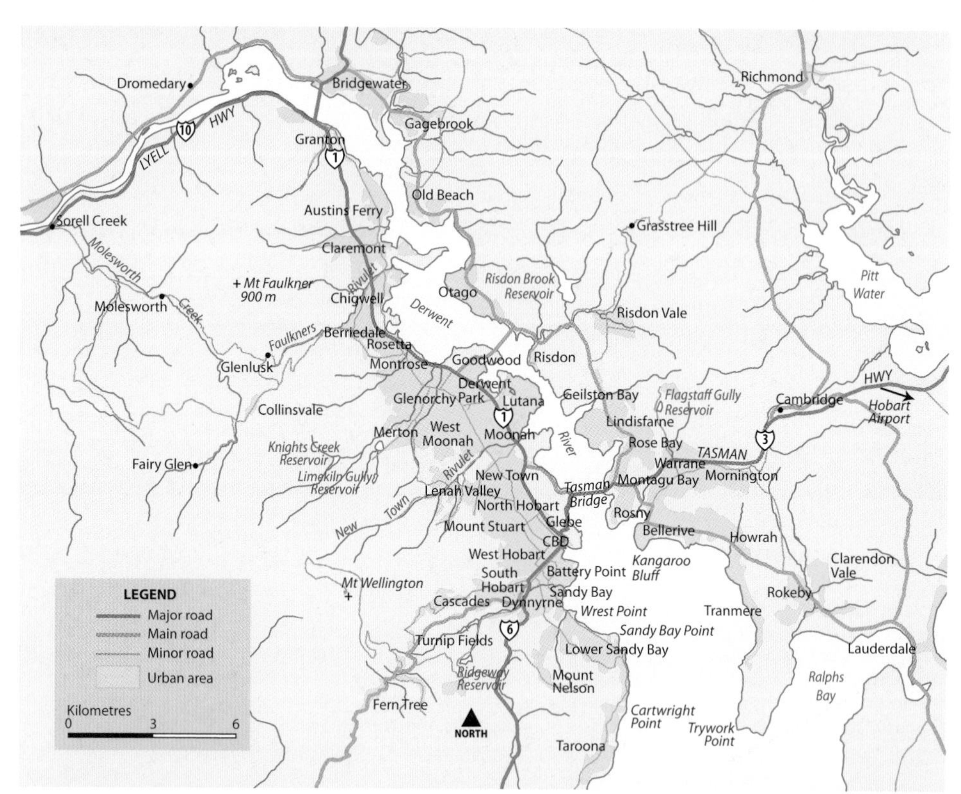

Hanging out in Hobart

Hobart's relaxed city centre provides a pleasant contrast to the pace of other Australian capital cities. Elizabeth Street Mall (*far right*), Franklin Square and the Sullivans Cove waterfront are all great places to eat, meet or stroll. Surprisingly, for a city in these cooler latitudes, Hobart enjoys many days of sunshine and clear skies, allowing for tranquil walks along the Derwent and alfresco dining at the many restaurants and cafés.

A Story on Every Corner

Hobart's modest size conceals a wealth of fascinating tales. Virtually every street around the city is lined with buildings and houses with a story to tell. Hobart's General Post Office (*far right*) was built in 1905 and seven years later became the site of a major historic event. Upon returning from his successful journey to the South Pole, Antarctic explorer Roald Amundsen entered the postal chamber to announce the news of his achievement to the world via telegram.

Salamanca Place

Located just south of the city along the Derwent River near Battery Point, Hobart's Salamanca Place has been a hub of commercial activity for over a century. The long strip of stone warehouses facing the waterfront once served the Port of Hobart and are now a focus for the city's craft industry (*far right*). Each Saturday, Hobart's artists display a rich variety of wares for sale at the colourful Salamanca Markets (*right*).

Battery Point

Deriving its name from guns mounted along the Derwent River promontory in 1818, Battery Point (*far right*) was the original home for many of the sailors and settlers of old Hobart Town. Its superbly preserved streetscapes of quaint workers' cottages, Georgian mansions and English-style village greens recall the backdrops of a land the town's early citizens forever left behind. Savour a true taste of historic Hobart by staying in one of the many houses that have been restored for use as boutique accommodation.

Royal Tasmanian Botanical Gardens & Museum

A short walk through Queens Domain or cruise down the Derwent leads to the Royal Tasmanian Botanical Gardens (*right*). Its parklands, conservatory, native and exotic gardens are set on the river's western bank and a 280 m convict-built stone wall forms part of the eastern boundary. The Tasmanian Museum and Art Gallery (*far right*) is housed in waterfront buildings on Macquarie Street that also date back to the convict era (open daily, admission free).

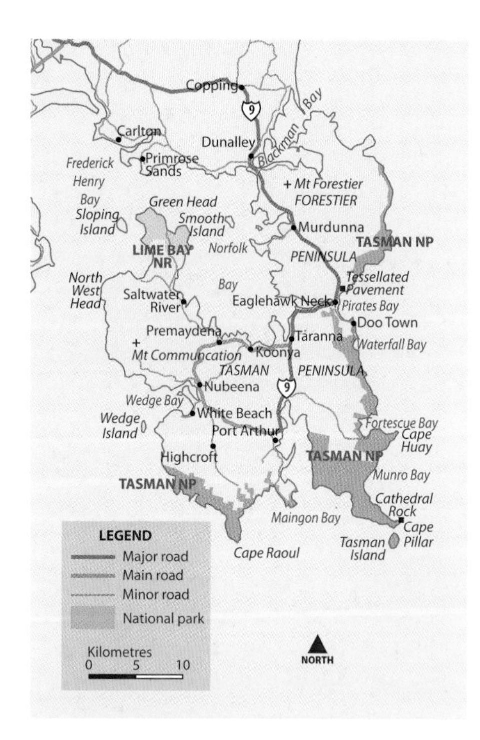

The Tasman Peninsula

It is impossible to talk about the spectacular and rugged peninsula at Tasmania's south-east corner without summoning the image of Port Arthur — the remote penal colony that in its day was feared as one of the most brutal prisons on Earth. But the same geographical isolation and treacherous topography that contributed to Port Arthur's reputation also makes the Tasman Peninsula one of Australia's most scenic (and historically fascinating) destinations. The peninsula maintains its tenuous link with island Tasmania only by virtue of a slender 100 m wide isthmus known as Eaglehawk Neck, making Port Arthur an ideal place for British authorities to establish a near-inescapable prison.

En Route to the Tasman Peninsula

From Hobart, the journey to the Tasman Peninsula commences by crossing the Derwent River on the Tasman Bridge. Re-built since its tragic collapse (after being struck by the *Lake Illawarra* in 1975), the bridge forms the major nexus with Hobart's suburbs along the Derwent's eastern shore. Here Tasmania's major sporting arena, Bellerive Oval, hosts both international cricket and Aussie Rules matches. Across Pitt Water is Sorell, a busy and historic township that was once considered as the site for the colony's first major settlement. From here the Arthur Highway leads south-west through fertile farming land first cultivated only a few years after British possession. Dunalley is located on an isthmus named East Bay Neck at the top of the Forestier Peninsula. This otherwise modest fishing town nevertheless sometimes stops traffic via a bridge over the Denison Canal, which swings open to allow vessels passage from Frederick Henry Bay to the east coast. On the shores of Blackman Bay is the Tasman Monument, commemorating Abel Tasman's landing on nearby shores in 1642 (Imlay Street, Dunalley). The west coast of the Forestier Peninsula is one of several sections (including sections on the Tasman Peninsula) protected by Tasman National Park (*see facing page*).

Exploring the Peninsula

Aside from Eaglehawk Neck's obvious natural attributes for preventing the escape of convicts, it is also surrounded by numerous impressive geological features. Walk from the car park down to the Tesselated Pavement, where neatly (and naturally) cracked lines of flat rocks stretch across the ground like a giant's footpath. A short detour to the eastern coast from Eaglehawk Neck leads through quaintly named Doo Town (where the residents have branded their houses with such witticisms as Doo Little, Love Me Doo and Gunadoo) and on to the Tasman Blowhole, Tasman Arch and Devils Kitchen — huge ocean-sculpted formations wrought from 250-million-year-old rock. The main road route along the eastern side of the peninsula travels through Tasman National Park via Fortescue Bay to Cape Pillar and spectacular Cathedral Rock. The lighthouse-adorned Tasman Island lies just offshore. The main highway ends at Port Arthur (*see facing page*), while unsealed roads continue a short distance south to Palmers Lookout and Remarkable Cave.

Ten minutes drive west of Port Arthur is the tiny coastal town of Nubeena at the head of Wedge Bay. It was originally established as a satellite settlement of Port Arthur but, other than fine fishing and excellent surfing conditions at Roaring Beach and White Beach, the district's greatest attraction lies to its north. Just beyond Saltwater River are the ruins of a coal mining facility once worked by convicts. Many consider these extensive remnants of soldier's barracks and terrifyingly cramped underground cells to be of equal interest to Port Arthur — they are certainly less touristed and, if it is possible, even more isolated. There are no tour facilities or entrance fees — simply wander the ruins at your leisure. Nearby Lime Bay Nature Reserve has basic camping facilities and copious wildflowers bloom here in summer.

Richmond – Frozen in Time

A short diversion north from the Tasman Highway at Cambridge leads to the authentic Georgian village of Richmond. The town was isolated from main traffic routes after the opening of the Sorell Causeway in 1872, freezing development and preserving its many historic treasures, including Australia's first stone-arch bridge, the original gaol, cobbled paths and a fine collection of period buildings.

Tasmanian Devil Conservation Park

The Tasmanian Devil Conservation Park at Taranna is the State's best location for observing these iconic creatures. See the diminutive but feisty meat-eating marsupial in a natural setting and take a "Devil in the Dark" nocturnal tour (Ph: (03) 6250 3230).

Tesselated Pavement These intriguingly geometric rock "tiles" near Eaglehawk Neck were shaped by natural forces.

Eaglehawk Neck Escape from Port Arthur was made even more perilous by the dogs tethered across this narrow point.

Clockwise from top left: Giant kelp forests of Waterfall Bay; Cruiseboats visit the spectacular Cathedral Rock; Tasman Island, with Cape Pillar in the background; Australian Fur-seals breed and rest along the rugged coastline of Tasman National Park.

Tasman National Park

Phone Ranger: (03) 6214 8100

This diverse park protects a series of coastal treasures — towering granite cliffs rising 300 m above the Tasman Sea, ocean-encircled dolerite columns, stacks and pillars, dense underwater forests of giant kelp and wide sandy beaches. The northern section reaches from the Forestier Peninsula down to Waterfall Bay, while the southern section includes Fortescue Bay, Cape Huay and Cape Pillar. To the west a separate region includes Remarkable Cave, Maingon Blowhole and numerous walking tracks along the peninsula's south-west coast.

Walks in the Park: Many of the park's natural features are within walking distance of car parks. There are a variety of longer walks including the Tasman Coastal Track (a 6–8 hr trek from Waterfall Bay to Fortescue Bay). The Devils Kitchen to Waterfall Bay Walk is shorter and easier (1.5–2 hr return) and offers spectacular views.

Access: Via the Port Arthur Highway.

Camping: There are 40 campsites with cold water showers, toilets and barbecues at Fortescue Bay (Ph: (03) 6250 2433).

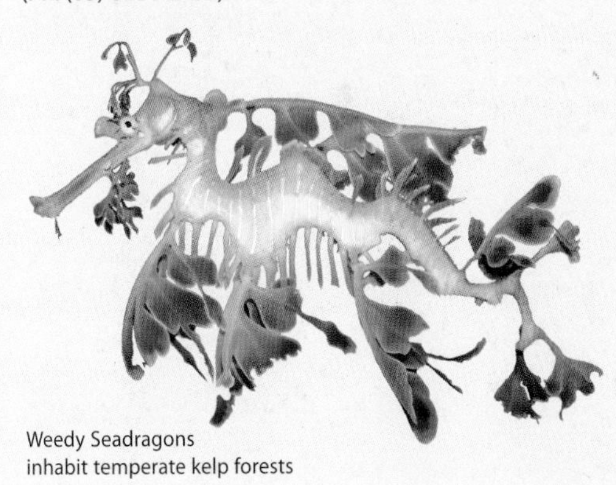

Weedy Seadragons inhabit temperate kelp forests

Port Arthur

The remarkably preserved precinct of Port Arthur is an incredible and unnerving slice of Australia's early European history. Walking among the ruins of this 1830 prison complex provides the most authentic taste of convict life to be experienced anywhere in the country. The history of the convicts and the men who guarded them permeates every sandstone pore. In the bay just off the settlement lies a green island whose tranquillity belies its purpose. On the Isle of the Dead are buried 1769 convicts whose only escape was to the next life; including Australia's first novelist, Henry Savery. Across the Bay at Port Puer is the remains of the juvenile prison that operated between 1834 and 1849. Many of the stones used to build Port Arthur were quarried by these unfortunate boys. That so much of Port Arthur remains standing is testament to the labour and skill of the convict builders themselves. The walls of the imposing Penitentiary remain largely intact and, so too the church and Separate Prison. In fact, more of these buildings might remain if not for major fires in 1895 and 1897. Guided tours, ghost tours and harbour cruises all offer a brilliant, hair-raising insight to Port Arthur, its environs and inhabitants (Ph: 1800 659 101).

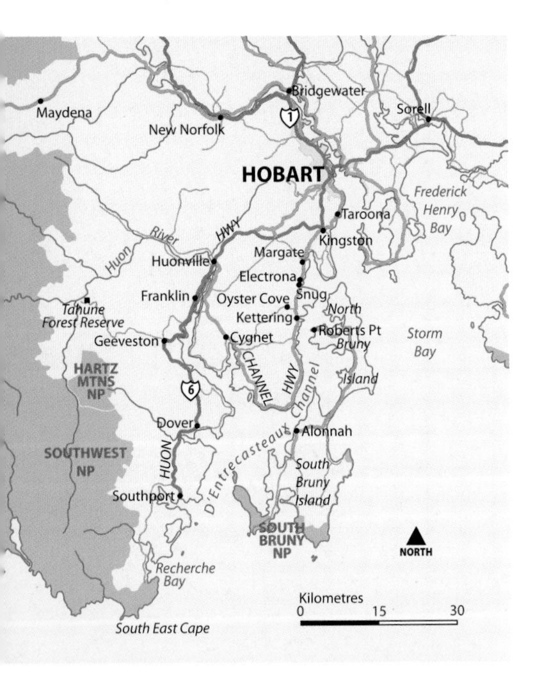

South from Hobart

The bays, channels, coves and islands directly south of the Derwent River were a source of great confusion for European maritime surveyors. This befuddling mosaic of land and water includes the D'Entrecasteaux Channel and Bruny Island, both named for French Rear Admiral Bruny D'Entrecasteaux, who charted the area while searching for lost Pacific explorer La Pérouse in 1792. D'Entrecasteaux actually thought he was surveying adjacent Storm Bay — proof perhaps that even the most accomplished navigators can become distracted by the area's hypnotic beauty.

The coastal journey around the Channel Highway is almost as picturesque. Travel south through Hobart's riverside suburbs and take a detour up to Mount Nelson Signal Station and lookout (with magnificent views over the Derwent) to Tasman Peninsula (follow Nelson Road opposite the Wrest Point Casino in Sandy Bay). Just past Taroona on the suburban fringe is a circular sandstone shot tower, which is believed to be the only one of its type remaining in the world. A 291-step climb to the top is rewarded by stunning views of the Derwent estuary. The Channel Highway leads through Kingston to Margate, passing the Australian Antarctic Division headquarters en route. Established to provide support to Australian Antarctic researchers in the field, the centre's public collection includes expedition photographs and some fascinating artefacts, including Sir Douglas Mawson's sledge (open weekdays, admission free). At Margate, carriages from Tasmania's last passenger train have been transformed into boutique shops and cafés. To its south are two towns of interesting nomenclature — Electrona, named for the electrical systems once used in the local carbide factory and the delightful Snug, reflecting the cosy anchorage that the Snug River provided to sailors. Oyster Cove, just north of Kettering, has a sad place in Tasmanian history. It was here in 1847 that a reserve was established to accommodate the last 47 Tasmanian Aborigines known to exist in the State. The last survivor, Truganini, died less than 30 years later.

Visiting Bruny Island

The southern and northern sections of Bruny Island are connected by a thread of sandy scrub at Adventure Bay. The main island access is via ferry from the small orchard town of Kettering. The vehicular and passenger ferry *Mirambeena* departs from the Bruny D'Entrecasteaux Visitor Information Centre in Ferry Road for Roberts Point on North Bruny Island (services throughout the day, Ph: (03) 6273 6725). The arrival point is approximately midway up the west coast of North Bruny Island and, given the distance to the nearest towns and lack of alternative transport, it is advisable to take a car. Chartered day tours by sea or land are also available, with several departing from and returning to Hobart (Ph: (03) 6267 4494 for further details and bookings). The island's main town is Alonnah on South Bruny.

Huon Valley

South-west of Hobart, the broad Huon River flows through fertile valleys that once were sheltered by towering Huon Pines. These were felled for their valuable and aromatic softwood and the land where they stood cultivated as apple orchards. Hops were also planted to supply Hobart's breweries. Stone fruit, berries and vineyards now flourish in the valley and Atlantic Salmon are farmed. The town of Geeveston (*see facing page*) remains a centre for timber. The river is a focus for recreational craft and fishing, including jet-boat rides through its rapids.

Huonville

Named for the commander of one of D'Entrecasteaux's ships, Huonville is located close to the mouth of the Huon River. It is the major town of a fertile fruit-growing region that forms the core of Tasmania's apple industry (for which the State was given its longstanding sobriquet of the "Apple Isle").

The Huon River

The Huon River flows over 100 km from Lake Pedder to the D'Entrecasteaux Channel. At Franklin, on the river's western bank, the art of wooden boat building is sustained by local artisans employing time-honoured techniques dating back centuries.

Hartz Mountains National Park

Within the most easterly section of Tasmania's World Heritage Wilderness Area near Geeveston is Hartz Mountains National Park. The park centres around the Hartz Range and protects a dolerite plateau of glacial lakes, waterfalls, alpine heath and rainforest. There are breathtaking panoramas from the range peaks over the South West wild. No camping facilities are provided, but bush camping is permitted (Ph: (03) 6264 8460).

Bruny Island Natural History

Early European maritime explorers (including Cook, Furneaux, Bligh and Flinders) all visited Bruny Island in the late 18th century. They anchored at Adventure Bay on South Bruny Island and various memorials, including the Bligh Museum and Captain Cook Monument, have since been established in their honour. Aside from its historical importance, Bruny Island offers many beach and bushwalking opportunities as well as some special wildlife watching experiences. A Little Penguin rookery on the Neck (*far left, top*) offers the chance to observe these alluring creatures as they move from the water up to their nests at dusk (wear dark clothing, do not shine torches and remain on the boardwalk — best viewing is between September and February). Australian Fur-seals (*below*) inhabit rocky coastal outcrops and can be viewed either from land or on deck via a range of cruises (*left*).

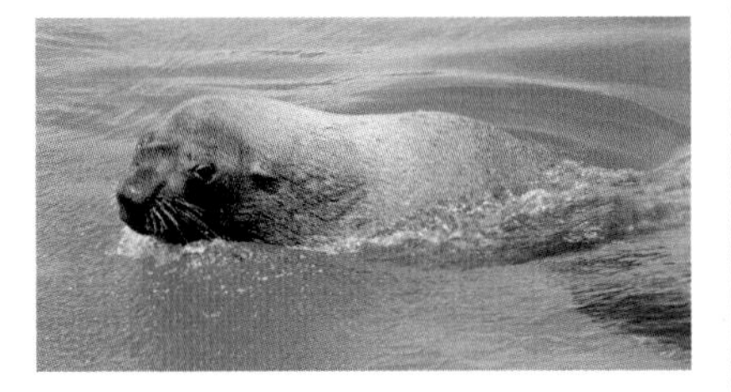

D'Entrecasteaux Channel & Recherche Bay

During their exploration of the south-east coast, Bruny D'Entrecasteaux and his crew made landfall in Recherche Bay at the channel's mouth, where they enjoyed a brief but amiable stay with the local Aborigines. Over the period of a month they planted Tasmania's first European vegetable garden with chicory, cabbage, radish, cress and potatoes, exchanged gifts and shared meals of roasted shellfish. The channel and Huon River estuary have remained one of Tasmania's best regions for seafood (including succulent salmon, oysters, crayfish, scallops and abalone).

Tahune AirWalk

Twenty-eight kilometres north-west of Geeveston is Tahune Forest Reserve — an area of protected woodlands featuring the famous Huon Pine, treasured by early settlers for its value in shipbuilding. While there are several excellent walks that may be enjoyed within the reserve, the undoubted highlight is the Tahune Forest AirWalk. This 597 m elevated walkway rises 20 m into the trees and ascends to a cantilevered section 48 m above river level, providing brilliant views of the forests and confluence of the Picton and Huon Rivers. Camping is possible both along the river and near the visitor centre (open daily, Ph: (03) 6297 0068).

Geeveston

Set on the banks of the Kermandie River, Geeveston is the gateway to the wilderness of the South West. Visit the Geeveston Forest and Heritage Centre where a variety of interactive displays and exhibitions provide a window on forestry in the Huon Valley (open daily, Church Street).

Tahune Forest AirWalk Spectacular views.

Recherche Bay One of Tasmania's best areas for fresh seafood.

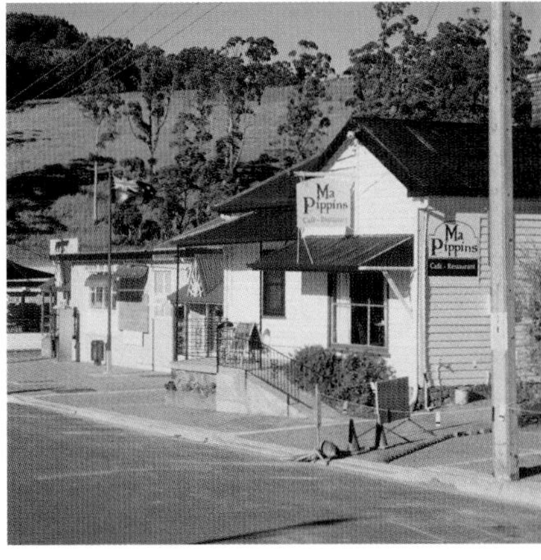

Geeveston Gateway to the South West.

The EAST COAST

A Rugged Coast

The powerful seas that buffet Tasmania's east coast meet their match in imposing granite cliffs and outcrops. South of Bicheno, a spectacular blowhole marks the start of the 3 km Foreshore Footway, leading to Peggy's Point and the Bicheno Sealife Centre.

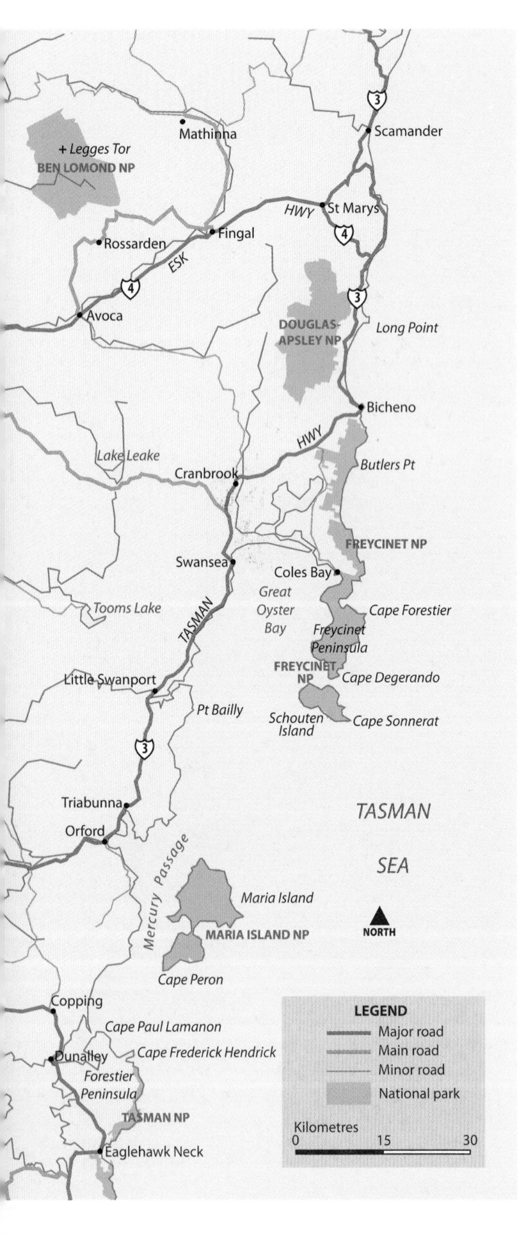

Many first time visitors to Tasmania are surprised to discover the sun, surf and scenery — more commonly associated with the northern parts of Australia's mainland — of the State's east coast. Within easy reach of Hobart are sandy beaches, well-equipped holiday towns, tranquil fishing villages and perfect coastlines. The climate is far less tempestuous than in the island's west; low rainfall and mild temperatures make this a great destination for walking, swimming, touring and relaxing. On Maria Island and the glorious Freycinet Peninsula, opportunities abound for wildlife watching and photography. Head north from Sorell on the Tasman Highway and allow time to explore the region at length — it is possible, but a great shame, to drive to Launceston via the coast in less than half a day.

Maria Island Region

The highway meets the east coast at Orford, a holiday retreat and fishing town at the mouth of the Prosser River. This is a popular place to stay while visiting the national park of Maria Island (*see facing page*) and ferries depart daily from the Eastcoaster Resort (bookings, Ph: (03) 6257 1589). There are great views across the Mercury Passage to the island from Thumbs Lookout, just south of town. A ferry also departs daily from nearby Triabunna to Darlington on the island's north-west corner (bookings advised, Ph: (03) 6227 8900). Campsites are available, but if you crave an authentic encounter with Maria Island's penal colony past, accommodation is also offered in the Old Penitentiary at Darlington. The facilities may seem a little basic (bunk beds, no electricity) but they are luxurious compared to those offered the original occupants and, unlike those poor souls, you can leave whenever you wish (Ph: (03) 6257 1420).

Freycinet Region

Midway up the east coast, 50 km north of Triabunna, is the larger coastal town of Swansea. The town overlooks Great Oyster Bay and, as you might expect, is a great place to enjoy seafood with saltwater views. Across the bay you can also see the rugged topography of Freycinet Peninsula. Once a military outpost, many of Swansea's historic town buildings and homes have been faithfully preserved. Several of these have now been converted to guest accommodation, including Meredith House (15 Noyes Street) and Resthaven (now Oyster Bay Guest House, 10 Franklin Street). On the highway is the Swansea Bark Mill and East Coast Museum, and just south of town is Spiky Bridge, a distinctive stone bridge built by convicts in 1843. In order to reach Freycinet National Park, it is necessary to drive further north on the highway to the top of Moulting Lagoon (a freshwater bird sanctuary and Ramsar site) and turn south from Llandaff. Close to the park entrance, the village of Coles Bay offers numerous accommodation and dining options and is the ideal base for exploration of the wonders of Freycinet (*see facing page*).

Bicheno & St Marys

North of Llandaff the highway returns to the coast at Bicheno (first known as Waub's Harbour), which was used by whalers and sealers as early as 1803, predating the first official settlement near Hobart. The coastal waters, home to kelp forests and marine mammals, are now an internationally popular diving destination. Diamond Island Nature Reserve (with its resident population of Little Penguins) can be reached by foot at low tide. The gorges, waterfalls and forests of Douglas Apsley National Park are only 10 km north of town. Further north, the highway climbs through Elephant Pass to St Marys in the Eastern Highlands. A lookout located at the summit of St Patricks Head, 2 km from town, provides sweeping views of the coast and Fingal Valley (allow an hour each way to walk the track to the summit).

Bicheno Located by a beautiful natural harbour.

Life Fishing and crayfishing is a major part of Bicheno life.

Freycinet National Park

Phone Ranger: (03) 6256 7000

The Freycinet Peninsula region is renowned as the most beautiful section of Tasmania's east coast. Freycinet National Park occupies a large portion of the peninsula and includes the majestic red granite tors known since early seafaring days as the Hazards. Beyond their peaks the rocky slopes descend abruptly to one of Tasmania's most familiar and unforgettable coastal features — the perfect white sand–hemmed arc of Wineglass Bay. The entire peninsula is a haven for creatures, including Tasmanian Pademelons, Bennett's Wallabies and White-bellied Sea-Eagles.

Walks in the Park: There is a huge range of walks possible within Freycinet. The most popular short walks are to Wineglass Bay Lookout (1 hr return, steep in sections) and the Little Gravelly Beach Walk at Sleepy Bay (40 min, clifftops). The complete Wineglass Bay/Hazards Beach Circuit commences at the car park and takes 4–5 hours to complete. Overnight and multi-day treks can include camping at the various beaches, but check in with rangers before departure.

Camping: Year-round campsites are available at Richardsons Beach and Ranger Creek. Sand Dune and Honeymoon Bay are open only over Christmas and Easter periods. Facilities vary but bookings are essential for these periods and a ballot system applies for Christmas campsites.

Clockwise from top: The Friendly Beaches, Freycinet National Park; Trackside gum trees on descent into Wineglass Bay; Wineglass Bay from the air looking north-west; Looking down over Wineglass Bay; Cape Tourville Lighthouse.

Maria Island National Park

Phone Ranger: (03) 6257 1420

The penal settlement ruins at Maria Island are fascinating in themselves, but the national park is also a great place to walk and see wildlife, including Emus and kangaroos. Some of these creatures have been introduced to the island in an effort to conserve threatened species.

Walks in the Park: There are several excellent walks around the historic township of Darlington. Consult national park staff for other walks further afield on the island.

Camping and Accommodation: The Old Penitentiary at Darlington has basic dormitory accommodation (*see opposite page*). The main campground is beside the creek at Darlington and has toilets, showers and fireplaces.

Clockwise from left: Oyster Bay, Maria Island; Historical settlement on Maria Island; Steep western cliffs of Maria Island.

The NORTH EAST

Top to bottom: St Helens; Historical bank in Derby; Bridestowe Estate Lavender Farm, near Scottsdale.

As you travel up the east coast, each new region seems determined to outdo the last in terms of physical beauty, diversity of cuisine and historical interest (not to mention eccentricity of place names). The charming seaside towns and natural attractions of the north-east corner are collected in a single municipality with the entrancing name of Break O'Day. This is one of Tasmania's most visited holiday regions, yet even in busy periods the pace seems unhurried and the biggest crowds to be found are the flocks of migratory seabirds that return regularly to these shores. The far north of the coast, beyond the Bay of Fires, is protected by Mount William National Park — sanctuary to a vast community of native animals, including Tasmanian Devils and Forester Kangaroos.

Camping up the Coast

While there are abundant accommodation options in the north-east, its climate and an array of attractive reserves make it one of Tasmania's best places to camp, particularly out of major holiday periods. The Scamander Forest Reserve has facilities for tents and caravans on the Scamander River. The bream and trout fishing on the river's upper reaches are legendary and there are plenty of shady spots to sit on the bank with a hook or a book. Access the reserve either by boat from Scamander (6 km upriver) or by turning off the Tasman Highway 20 km south of St Helens. Camping is also possible at beach sites all the way up the coast to St Helens. This enviably positioned holiday town is a Tassie favourite and stands at the head of Georges Bay surrounded by coastal nature reserves. Camp among wildflowers at Dora Point or Moulting Bay in the Humbug Point Nature Recreation Area (just north-east of St Helens) or nestle into a spot amid the Peron Dunes on St Helens Point. Walk the beaches or birdwatch but if the lure of the sea proves irresistible, the offshore waters here are also well known for spectacular game fishing. The region north of St Helens from Binalong Bay to Eddystone Point was named the Bay of Fires by explorer Tobias Furneaux in 1773, who observed large numbers of fires lit by Aborigines along the beaches at night. Take Binalong Bay Road and drive up this incredibly photogenic coast of beautiful white sand and lichen-covered granite rock. Swim, dive, snorkel or fish while camping in one of the many sites provided in the Bay of Fires Conservation Area (own water and firewood required). The northern section of the Bay of Fires is bordered by Mount William National Park (*see facing page*).

Around the North East

From St Helens, the Tasman Highway departs the coast for the 163 km journey to Launceston, but if you can find the time there is yet more to explore of the north-east. Around Pyengana, rainforest replaces farmland and a winding road south to Ringarooma (no caravans or trailers) passes two impressive cascades — St Columba Falls (*see facing page*) and Ralph Falls at Mount Victoria Forest Reserve. Further along the A3 is the historic town of Derby on the Ringarooma River. Explore the recreated mining village at the Derby Tin Mine Centre, canoe the Cascade Dam or take tea and scones at one of the town's tearooms. Alternatively, you may prefer to forego waterfalls and mines in favour of the longer, less travelled road to the northern coast. Divert north just after Moorina to Gladstone — main gateway to Mount William National Park. Sixty kilometres further west the road hits the coast and excellent beaches of Bridport. From here, continue west to George Town and the Tamar Valley or head south to rejoin the Tasman Highway at Scottsdale for the more direct drive to Launceston. Scottsdale, enveloped by mountains in a thriving timber and farming district, is a busy commercial hub. Visit the Forest EcoCentre (King Street) to learn everything you ever wanted to know about sustainable forestry in the north-east. Fifteen kilometres west at Nabowla is one of the world's largest lavender farms. Bridestowe Estate's long purple rows of herbs cover 48 ha and form a magnificent sight when in bloom (early December to January). Picnic, sample lavender oil or saunter through the fragrant fields (Ph: (03) 6352 8182).

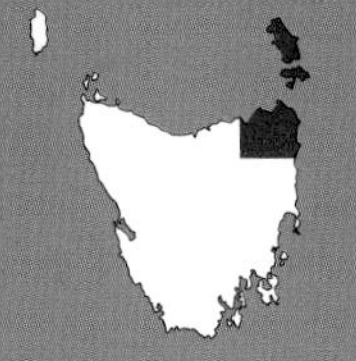

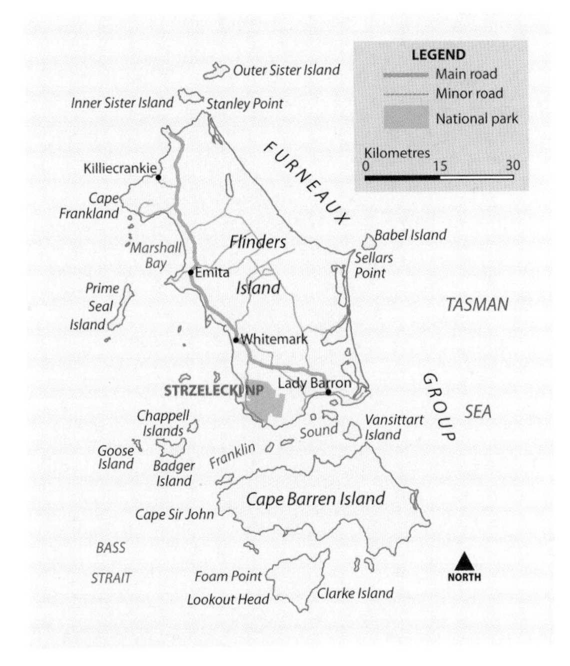

Flinders Island

Remnant of the land bridge that once joined Tasmania to the mainland, Flinders Island rises out of eastern Bass Strait. This island (with a population around 900) is the largest of the Furneaux Group whose 52 islands stretch across the eastern end of Bass Strait. Its granite peaks, rural pasture, coastal dunes and lagoons are home to over 200 bird species (including the rare Cape Barren Goose) and over 800 plant species. Farming, tourism and aquaculture are now the mainstays of the island economy. Flights to Flinders Island from Launceston arrive near the main town of Whitemark, the island's administrative centre, which offers plentiful accommodation and dining. Accommodation is also available at Lady Barron on the south coast and the smaller settlements of Emita and Killecrankie. The island's Strzelecki National Park is a popular bushwalking destination. Dive one of the many shipwrecks or fossick for Killecrankie Diamond — a form of topaz found on beaches.

St Columba Falls State Reserve

Located south of Pyengana, the perpetually flowing St Columba Falls are one of the region's most stunning visions. Waters from a huge catchment area in the Mt Victoria foothills meet to plunge more than 90 m over a granite rockface to the South George River below. Follow St Columba Falls Road from the Tasman Highway and either view the falls from the car park or take the short walking track through myrtle and Sassafrass forest for a closer look. The nearby St Columba Falls Hotel, resembling a farmhouse and known locally as the "pub in the paddock", serves country-sized meals.

Weldborough Pass Rainforest Walk

A short distance further west of the turn-off to St Columba Falls is Weldborough Pass, a region of dense rainforest with views to valley and coast. Pause to admire the forests of myrtle, Blackwood and Giant Tree Ferns and take the 20 minute rainforest walk through the scenic reserve. These scenic, winding forest roads also form part of the challenging Targa Tasmania rally. A little further on is the town of Weldborough, once a vibrant tin mining town with a large Chinese community. The heritage-listed local hotel has displays of historic photographs and memorabilia.

Eddystone Point Mount William National Park.

Mount William National Park

Phone Ranger: (03) 6356 1173

Boasting a granite coastline punctuated by long white sand beaches, Mount William National Park is an important refuge for wildlife (including the Forester Kangaroo, Bennett's Wallaby and Tasmanian Pademelon). Swimming in the bays, beaches and lagoons is popular, as is snorkelling and diving the reefs off Georges Rocks and Eddystone Point.

Walks in the Park: The track to the top of Mt William is an easy 1–1.5 hour return walk. Cobbler Rocks is slightly longer but no more difficult and includes beach, lagoon and bay sections. Due to its exposed position, weather conditions can change quickly in the park. Check forecasts, carry maps and consult rangers before taking long walks.

Camping: Campsites at Musselroe Bay, Deep Creek (near Eddystone Point) and Stumpys Bay. Your own firewood and water must be carried in and fees apply. Fuel stoves are recommended.

Little Penguin

The **MIDLANDS**

Derwent Valley & Central Highlands

East of Lake St Clair, the central region between Launceston and Hobart is known as the Midlands. It enjoys Tasmania's driest climate and is characterised by fertile grazing plains lying between highlands and lake country to the west and low granite ranges to the east. Much of the district was cleared and farmed soon after Hobart's settlement and the Midland Highway (also known as the Heritage Highway) leads through a series of historic towns. In the south-west the Lyell Highway winds through southern lake country before following the banks of the Derwent River as it descends through the Derwent Valley and New Norfolk to Hobart.

Lake Country

The scenic region north and east of Derwent Bridge in the Central Highlands is lake country, a celebrated trout fishing destination and the heart of Tasmania's hydro-electric power scheme. The Marlborough Highway meets the Lake Highway at the southern tip of Great Lake, the largest of a cluster of literally thousands of lakes and natural lagoons of varying size that reach east to Lake Sorell. Small townships are scattered around the lakes with the former hydro-electric workers camp of Poatina being the largest commercial centre in the region. Camping facilities, accommodation, fly fishing tours and boating facilities abound.

Midland Towns

South of Great Lake on the Lake Highway is Bothwell, a historically significant town in the Clyde River Valley whose European settlement was strongly contested by the Big River Aboriginal clan. Inevitably, the original occupants lost out and the town became a trading centre for pastoral interests that took over the region. The local Aborigines' last corroboree was supposedly staged outside the Castle Hotel (Patrick Street) in 1832. In 1842, Australia's first golf course was established at Ratho, now home to the Australasian Golf Museum. You can still play the course (just give way to the sheep, which keep the greens nice and trim). Oatlands, on the shores of Lake Dulverton, is reputed to have the largest number of Georgian sandstone buildings of any Australian town. Nearby Callington Mill is the only tower mill remaining in Australia. Believe it or not, Oatlands was for a time considered a potential State capital. To the north are Ross and Campbell Town (*see left*) — two 19th century convict-built towns, remarkably unsullied by tourism or development. The impressive Ross Bridge was built by the clearly talented convict stonemasons Daniel Herbert and James Colbeck in 1836. In Bond Street, the archaeologically important remains of the Ross Female Factory tell the dark tale of a female convict probation station that operated from 1847–1854. Campbell Town, with its genteel red brick colonial residences set on the banks of the Elizabeth River, could have been conceived by an English landscape painter.

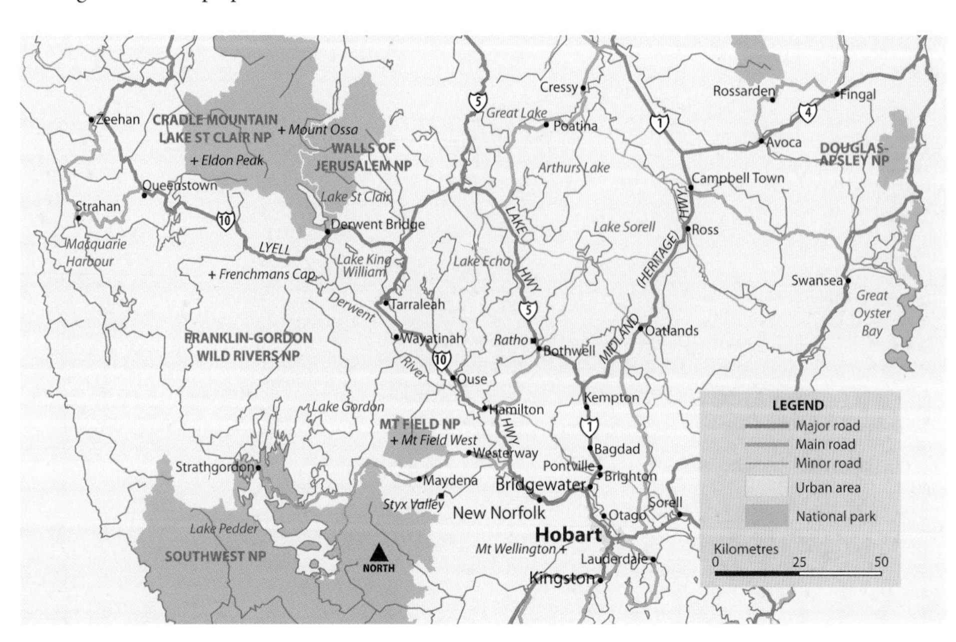

Great Lake

Expanded in 1911 to serve Tasmania's hydro-electric scheme storage needs, Great Lake now covers an area of 164 km^2. This is prime trout territory; Brown Trout were first introduced here in 1870 and their descendants are a huge drawcard for anglers today.

Ross

A Boer War field gun stands at the middle of Ross's main crossroads (*above*). The junction was once known as Temptation, Recreation, Salvation and Damnation for the pub, town hall, church and gaol that occupied the four corners. A stroll down Church Street will reveal many of Ross's best colonial stone buildings.

Campbell Town

Walk into town over the convict-built bridge past the 1840 hotel named the Fox Hunter's Return. A little further down the main street at the town centre is The Grange (*above*), home to a wealthy doctor who reputedly held Australia's first telephone conversation with a friend in Launceston in 1874.

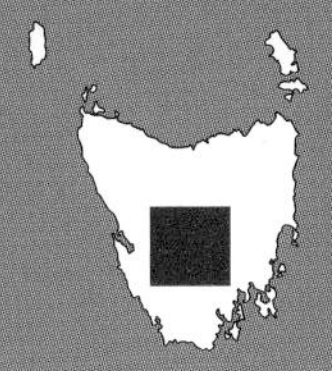

Mount Field National Park

Phone Ranger: (03) 6288 1149

One of the closest national parks to Hobart — and the State's oldest — Mount Field offers a huge diversity of topography, scenery, walks and activities. Russell Falls, near the park entrance, is enveloped by fern and forest featuring the world's tallest flowering tree — the mighty Swamp Gum. Within the central section of the park (near Lake Dobson) is Hobart's closest downhill ski resort.

Short Walks in the Park: Russell Falls are a 10 minute walk from the car park. The walk can be extended through the surrounding forest by following the connecting Horseshoe Falls/Lady Barron Falls/Tall Trees Circuit. The 20 minute Tall Trees walk features majestic Swamp Gums. From the Lake Dobson skifields, the Tarn Shelf Trail leads to a chain of small glacial lakes.

Access: From Hobart travel west on the Brooker Highway (A10) via New Norfolk. Follow the B62 to Westerway and take the sealed road through the township of National Park to the Mt Field entrance. The skifields' car park at Lake Dobson is another 16 km on gravel road (chains may be required, Ph: (03) 6288 1319 to check road conditions before departure).

Camping: Private camping and caravan facilities are available on the Tyenna River near the park entrance (Ph: (03) 6288 1526). There are three basic park-operated cabins at Lake Dobson, which can accommodate six people each (Ph: (03) 6288 1149).

Top to bottom: Russell Falls; A tarn in the high country; A high country lake girt by Giant Pandani heath.

Common Brushtail Possum

Styx Valley

This region of forest south of Mt Field National Park (via the town of Maydena) is home to the tallest hardwood tree on earth. These giant Swamp Gums soar over 95 m upward and can live for more than 400 years. Due to hard fought campaigns by conservation and wilderness movements, parts of this important old growth forest in the Styx Valley are now protected from logging. A new forest reserve, Styx Big Tree Reserve, has been created specifically to protect the tallest member of the Styx Valley giants — a dizzying specimen 97 m tall — and its skyscraping neighbours.

New Norfolk

The capital of the Derwent Valley lies 37 km north-east of Hobart on the Derwent River. First settled by the Irish rebel convict turned police constable, Denis McCarty, New Norfolk subsequently became home to settlers and convicts relocated from Norfolk Island. The planting of hops to supply local breweries led to the construction of the unique Oast Houses — hop processing facilities — still found in the region today (*above*). On the Lyell Highway just south of town, an Oast House that only ceased operation in 1969 has been converted to a museum. Dame Nellie Melba once sang from the balcony of the town's Bush Inn, Australia's oldest continually operating hotel (1815).

Derwent Valley

The picturesque Derwent Valley can be explored by foot, road, rail or river. Derwent Valley Railways operates from New Norfolk and offers short excursions to the Southern Hemisphere's oldest fish hatchery at Salmon Ponds (Ph: (03) 6261 1946). If you're in the mood for something faster, try the *Devil Jet* — a hair raising jet boat ride through the river rapids (Ph: (03) 6261 3460).

LAUNCESTON & Surrounds

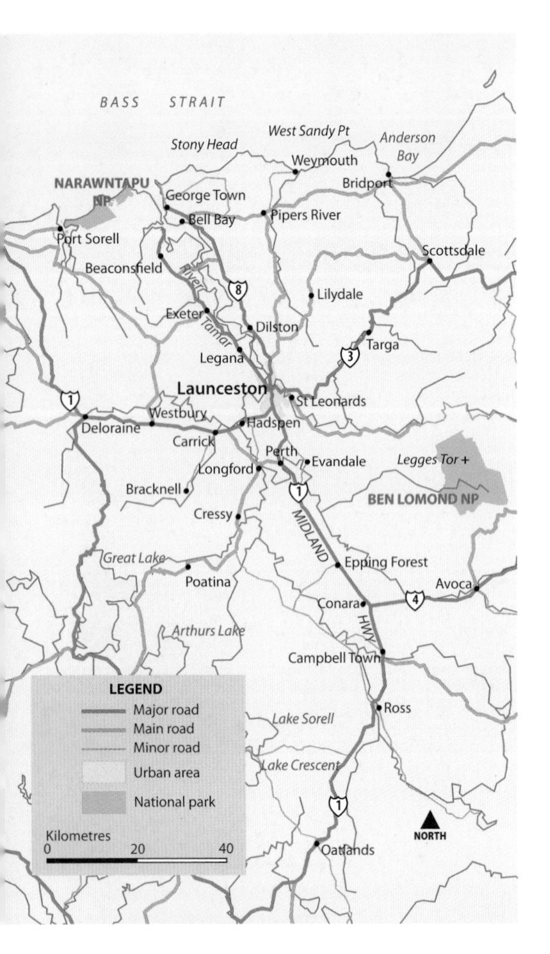

Tasmania's second-largest city was settled a year after Hobart when Governor King dispatched a small expeditionary force from Sydney to survey the Tamar Valley. First camp was made at George Town, but in 1805 the military moved to the present day site of Launceston at the end of the Tamar River's deepwater channel. Launceston still has a decidedly English air and retains a strong romantic attachment to its past. It has numerous superbly preserved Victorian and Georgian streetscapes and is reputed to boast the largest collection of 19th century homes and buildings of any city in Australia.

Launceston City

Launceston's history is visible at every turn but a guided walking tour is a great way to get to know the characters behind the heritage (tours depart the Launceston Travel and Information Centre, 12–16 St John St, 9.45 am, weekdays). If you prefer to go it alone, don't miss visiting the Batman Fawkner Inn (Cameron St) where John Batman and John Fawkner planned an expedition in 1834 across Bass Strait to establish a new colony that would later become Melbourne. The Queen Victoria Museum and Art Gallery has a fascinating collection of colonial paintings and artefacts (open daily, Royal Park, Ph: (03) 6323 3777). Just west of the city at Franklin Village, Franklin House is a meticulously furnished grand Georgian mansion built by convicts for a local brewer in 1838 (413 Hobart Road, open daily, Ph: (03) 6344 6233). The city's parks and gardens are no less grand. Wander City Square with its anachronistic "Monkey Island", conservatory and duck pond or walk the River Edge Trail.

Tamar River

The Tamar River is flanked by highways on both sides, allowing easy exploration of the river and valley north of Launceston to Port Dalrymple. The only crossing point is via the Batman Bridge near Sidmouth, but on each side are lush pastures, orchards and vineyards promising a feast for the soul. This is the heart of Tasmania's cool climate wine-producing area, yielding fine pinots and rieslings primed for tasting at every cellar door.

Tamar River Premium wineries flourish by the Tamar River.

Batman Bridge Spanning the Tamar River.

South of Launceston

Early 19th-century farming towns dot the region immediately south of Launceston. Longford was once known as Norfolk Plain for the pioneers and freed convicts re-settled from Norfolk Island in 1813. Brickendon and Woolmers Estate (*see facing page*) are fabulously preserved examples of the area's first privately owned farms. The bluestone Anglican church on Illawarra Road in Longford is the resting place of acclaimed Australian plein-air artist Tom Roberts.

Penny Royal World

Launceston's English flavour is nowhere better illustrated than at this historic tourist attraction located between Royal Park and Cataract Gorge. A complete replica of a watermill built by English settlers near Launceston in 1825 is the main feature. It is complemented by underground gunpowder mills, an original Launceston electric tram and a huge tower windmill (open daily, 147 Paterson St, Ph: (03) 6334 3975).

Cataract Gorge

Launceston's most scenic spot, Cataract Gorge, was first developed as a pleasure park in 1899. Virtually adjacent to the CBD, the gorge and its environs feature a pretty iron suspension bridge over the South Esk River; the world's longest single span chairlift (with a central span of 308 m), picnic grounds, nature trails, strutting peacocks and a swimming pool complex. Walk to Cataract Gorge via Kings Bridge and take the short cut (Zig Zag Track, 20 min one way) or the full tour (Main Track, 90 min one way). Also within the park are many shorter trails leading to lookouts and historic features. Cruises are a great way to see the gorge and South Esk, North Esk and Tamar Rivers.

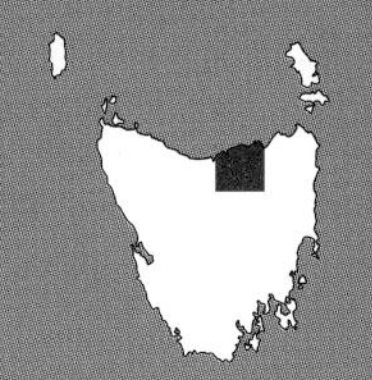

Woolmers Estate

Forty kilometres south of Launceston via the Midlands Highway, Woolmers Estate is one of Australia's oldest farming properties. This historic estate was owned by the Archer family from 1817 to 1994 and features the original homestead and outbuildings. This fascinating complex, with its workers' cottages, chapel, blacksmith's shop, stables, bakehouse, pump house and gardener's cottage resembles a small village. The 2 ha National Rose Garden is a memorable feature of the property (open daily, Ph: (03) 6391 2230).

Beauty Point

Just north of the old gold mining centre of Beaconsfield (the scene of one of Australia's most incredible collapsed mine escapes in 2006) is the port town of Beauty Point. As in much of the Tamar Valley, there is beauty to be found in the scenic river and beaches, but that is not the town's only point. It is also home to two unique wildlife attractions — Seahorse World and Platypus House (both located on Inspection Head Wharf in Flinders St). Seahorse World has its origins in research conducted by the University of Tasmania into the life cycle of the native Pot-bellied Seahorse (*left*). From there it has grown into a major tourist attraction featuring a high-tech seahorse farm and aquarium. Next door, the Platypus House provides a rare opportunity to observe egg-laying monotremes during daylight hours in an indoor setting. The facility's prime objective is to successfully breed the vulnerable Platypus in captivity.

Narawntapu National Park

Phone Ranger: (03) 6428 6277

Dubbed the "Serengeti of Tasmania", Narawntapu National Park is simply a magnificent place to watch native wildlife grazing on coastal grasslands and lagoons. Less than an hour's drive from Launceston, the park also has ongoing links with the Aboriginal community. Aborigines have used the region for more than 20,000 years.

Walks in the Park: Springlawn Nature Walk is a great introduction to the park. This visually arresting 1 hour circuit takes in lagoon, coastal thicket and dune habitat.

Access: Take the West Tamar Highway from Launceston and follow C721 to the park's eastern entrance.

Camping: Excellent camping facilities are provided at Springlawn, Bakers Point and Griffiths Point.

Ben Lomond National Park

Phone Ranger: (03) 6336 5312

Visible from Launceston and the Northern Midlands, Ben Lomond National Park incorporates Tasmania's only fully developed downhill ski resort. The 1572 m Legges Tor, a summit on the Ben Lomond Plateau, is the State's second-highest point. A vast range of alpine plant species are found on the mountain and wildflowers bloom here in summer. In winter, the ski village is visited by many mammals, including Eastern Quolls, Dusky Antechinuses, Bennett's Wallabies and Common Wombats — and, of course, that common beast, the long-footed, goggle-eyed, gore-tex-skinned skier.

Walks & Runs in the Park: The ski season operates from early July to late September but the degree of snow cover is variable (Ph: (03) 6390 6116). It is possible to drive to the plateau and walking is permitted over several of the cross-country ski routes.

Access: Travel south-west of Launceston via St Leonards and White Hills. The Ben Lomond Road turn-off is located 3.5 km before Upper Blessington. Wheel chains must be carried between June and September and anti-freeze should be used.

Camping: There is a single campground (six sites with toilets and water but no power) 1 km inside the park boundary. Bush camping is permitted anywhere in the park but sites must be 500 m from the road. All usual forms of ski accommodation are available in the village.

The CENTRAL NORTH

Even in a State crammed with places of unsurpassed natural beauty, the region west of Launceston stakes its own claim to "must-see" status. From the spectacular bluffs and limestone caves of the Great Western Tiers, to the chain of lakes and rivers flowing down from Cradle Mountain and emptying along wild Bass Strait shores, this unassumingly promoted region should not be overlooked. While many only visit the Central North on their way to the western wilderness, or to Launceston after disembarking the Melbourne ferry at Devonport, there is more than enough here to justify a dedicated journey.

Along the Coast

Devonport, the region's largest coastal town, originated as two separate villages on either side of the Mersey River. They merged in 1890 to capitalise on increased shipping and the port has since grown to become one of the State's most important (*see lower left*). It was for many years the home of the only Tasmanian to become Australian prime minister, Joseph Lyons (1932–1939), and his wife Dame Enid Lyons (who would go on after his death in office to become Australia's first female member of the House of Representatives). Their home and grounds on Home Hill are now a State treasure and are open to the public (66 Middle Rd, open Tuesday to Sunday, 2–4 pm). On the road to the lighthouse at Mersey Bluff is Tiagarra, an Aboriginal cultural and interpretative centre established around a large series of rock carvings re-discovered by a local school headmaster in 1929 (open daily, 9 am–5 pm).

Ulverstone, 19 km west of Devonport, is a tourist town on the Leven River with a variety of attractions including a miniature railway (Maskells Road) and the ornamental Zigzag Garden, which leads to a lookout over the coast (Maud Street). The riverside Anzac Park contains a pine tree grown from a seed brought back from Lone Pine in Gallipoli, along with a "space age" children's playground (replete with rockets). Gunns Plains Caves, 23 km from town, are accessible limestone chambers surrounded by streams that form the homes of Platypus and the world's largest freshwater crayfish. The panoramas across nearby Leven Canyon inspire photography. Twelve kilometres west of Ulverstone, Penguin attracts many visitors to view the colonies of Little Penguins for which the town is named and famed (*see upper left*).

Inland

South of Devonport, the main roads lead through the Mersey and Forth Valleys — a fertile district that accounts for over 40% of Tasmania's vegetable crop. Latrobe, for a time Tasmania's third-largest settlement, is now virtually a satellite suburb of Devonport and home to retiring types — like Platypuses. Look for the oversized specimen clambering up the side of the historic Lucas Hotel, which directs visitors to the Lucas Platypus Experience and details sites where the elusive monotreme might be seen (one of which conveniently happens to be Kings Creek next to the Lucas Hotel). The district around Deloraine to the Cluan Tiers, Great Western Tiers and south-east is some of Tasmania's prettiest countryside. Deloraine, Hagley, Exton and Westbury are particularly well preserved historic towns. English visitors to Westbury, with its authentic village green, Victorian cottages, hedges and maze must have to pinch themselves several times before believing they have not been transported back home.

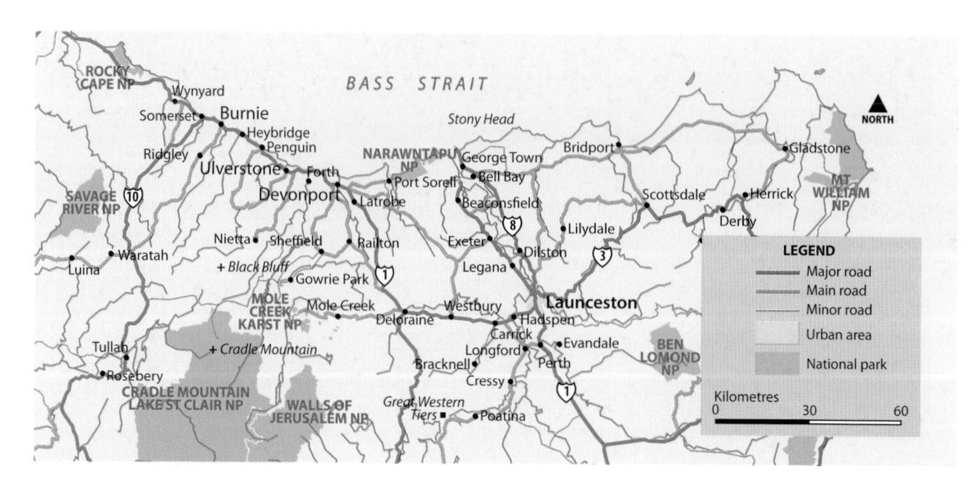

Penguin

Penguins big and small are a common sight in this seaside town near Ulverstone. Little Penguins nest on the town shores between November and March, but the "world's biggest penguin" (*above*) is a permanent fixture.

Sheffield

Centre of the Kentish Plains district, Sheffield is now famous as the "town of murals". Nearly every available blank space — including the town's rubbish bins — has been used as a canvas for paintings depicting scenes from the district's colourful history.

Devonport

Devonport became a key port in the 1880s and the distinctive red and white striped lighthouse on Mersey Bluff (*left*) was built to guide vessels into the deep water harbour of the Mersey River in 1889. It was not always so. Prior to that time, a large sand bar at the river mouth and narrow channels stymied Devonport's development. Today, thanks largely to the arrival of over 500,000 passengers per year on the *Spirit of Tasmania* ferry from Melbourne, Devonport is the gateway to Tasmania. Cargo vessels frequent the busy Bass Strait port, hauling in petroleum, fertiliser and gypsum and shipping out wheat, grain and cement. Forty percent of the State's container goods enter through Devonport.

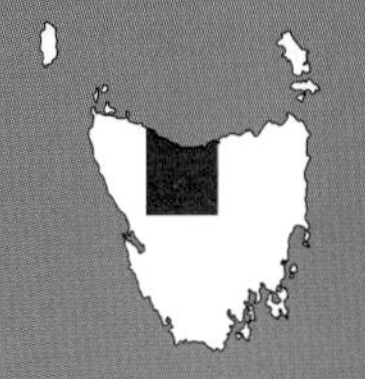

Liffey Falls State Reserve

Phone Ranger: (03) 6424 8388

The gorgeous Liffey Falls are arguably the most picturesque in Tasmania. Set in temperate rainforest on the slopes of the Great Western Tiers, the stepped cascade is surrounded by a series of smaller falls.

Walks in the Park: A 45 minute return walk leads from the picnic area to Liffey Falls, passing Alexandra Falls, Hopetoun Falls, and Albert Falls en route.
Access: Travel south approximately 20 km from Deloraine on the A5 (Lake Highway). The falls road is gravel only.
Camping: Not permitted in the reserve.

Walls of Jerusalem National Park

Phone Ranger: (03) 6363 5133

Located on the eastern edge of Tasmania's World Heritage Wilderness Area, this stunning isolated park protects an alpine plateau of dolerite peaks, tarns and lakes dating from the Jurassic Period (165 million years ago).

Walks in the Park: Only experienced, well-prepared bushwalkers should attempt to walk in the park, which has very few tracks.
Access: The car park is off Mersey Forest Road near Lake Rowallen. A half hour walking trail leads to the park entrance.
Camping: A camping platform is provided at Wild Dog Creek.

Mole Creek Karst National Park

Phone Ranger: (03) 6363 5182

Describing a region where chemical processes have transformed the landscape, "karsts" include limestone caves (such as the spectacular examples found at Mole Creek), and underground springs. There are more than 300 caves and sinkholes in the area — King Solomon and Marakoopa Caves (famed for glow-worms) are open to the public.

Walks in the Park: Guided tours of the caves operate regularly each day (fees apply).
Access: Via the B12 from Deloraine and Mole Creek.
Camping: Not permitted.

Rocky Cape National Park

Phone Ranger: (03) 6452 4998

This is a fascinating area of Aboriginal heritage, dramatic seascapes, warped rock formations, shipwrecks and beaches. Swimming, fishing, boating and beachwalking are popular.

Walks in the Park: There is a huge variety of interesting walks, including beach and rockpool rambles and trails to Aboriginal shelters and caves.
Access: Turn off the Bass Highway (A2) 12 km from Wynyard to Boat Harbour Beach. Turn onto Irby's Road and travel 8 km to Sisters Beach.
Camping: Not permitted within the park.

The Great Western Tiers

Stretching from Tasmania's western wilderness to the Northern Midlands, this dramatic series of peaks, bluffs and forested slopes conceals a stunning region of lakes, caves, rivers and sub-alpine plains.

Tiers Towns

The rural villages of the Tiers district are filled with enchanting character (and characters). Explore homesteads seemingly frozen in time or hunt for treasure at one of the many antique, craft and bric-a-brac stores.

Deloraine

Only 30 minutes west of Launceston, this National Trust classified town is the perfect base for exploring the Great Western Tiers region, Mole Creek caves and the Meander and Liffey Falls areas.

Trowunna Wildlife Park

The main attraction of this well-presented wildlife park near Mole Creek is undoubtedly the Tasmanian Devil (*right*), but a range of native creatures of less demonic demeanour (including kangaroos, quolls, Koalas and reptiles) are also on show (1892 Mole Creek Rd, open daily from 9 am – 5 pm, Ph: (03) 6363 6162).

The NORTH WEST

Burnie

Head up to Roundhill Lookout (near the squat lighthouse known locally as "Blinking Billy") for excellent dawn and dusk panoramas. Platypuses are often seen at Fernglade Reserve and the Little Penguin Observation Centre on Parsonage Point offers a free penguin watching experience.

Table Cape

The region's most prominent natural feature, this flat, grassy promontory lies atop an old volcanic plug with a northern face rising 170 m above sea level. The cape's volcanic soils are regarded as the most fertile in Tasmania. Near Table Cape Light Station are seasonal tulip fields (*above*).

Dip Falls

Located in the Dip River Forest Reserve south of Mawbanna, this two-tiered waterfall features a steep cascade flowing over hexagonal basalt columns. From the car park you can choose to take the steep walk to the base of the falls or cross the bridge to a viewing platform at the top. About a kilometre further on from the car park stands a huge eucalypt known as Big Tree.

The common perception of Tasmania's west is of an inaccessible wilderness of dense forest, rushing rivers and rugged ranges, accessible only to the most intrepid of bushwalkers. While this is an accurate picture of much of the interior, the North West coast is a surprisingly inviting blend of green farmland, flower-filled fields and epic coastal views.

Burnie to Table Cape

Originally a small private port on Emu Bay owned by the Van Diemen's Land Company, Burnie sprang to life with the discovery of massive mineral deposits on the West Coast in the 1880s. Seizing the day, the company built a tramway from the tin mines at Mount Bischoff — then the world's richest — and Burnie was transformed from backwater to boom town. The eventual exhaustion of the underground riches brought recession, but the establishment of one of Australia's largest paper mills in 1938 saw Burnie's population triple in less than ten years. The mill continues to operate (on a scaled-down level) today. Tourism has become an important local money spinner but paper still plays an important role. You can trade your paper currency for handmade paper goods at Creative Paper Tasmania (Old Surrey Road) or walk through the pages of Burnie's history at the Pioneer Village Museum (Little Alexander Street, open Monday to Friday, 9 am–5 pm). Those with a passion for rhododendrons shouldn't miss the 15,000 specimens presented in an amphitheatre setting at Emu Valley Rhododendron Gardens (Breffny Rd, Ph: (03) 6431 6505) and budding fly fishers can apply their piscatorial craft at Natone Hills Fishery (18 km south on Greta Rd).

Fifteen kilometres west of Burnie is Wynyard, a port and beach town at the mouth of the Inglis River, that stages an annual Tulip Festival in October. The flowers are grown in the town, along the beach and in the rich soils of Table Cape (*see left*). Nearby Fossil Bluff was the site of the 19th century discovery of a possum-like marsupial skeleton known as *Wynyardia bassiana*, dated at 19–23 million years old. Many fossils can still be seen encased in the sandstone cliff face. Drive to the car park off Freestone Crescent and study the interpretative display, walk around the bluff at low tide or take the trail to the top for outstanding views of the coast.

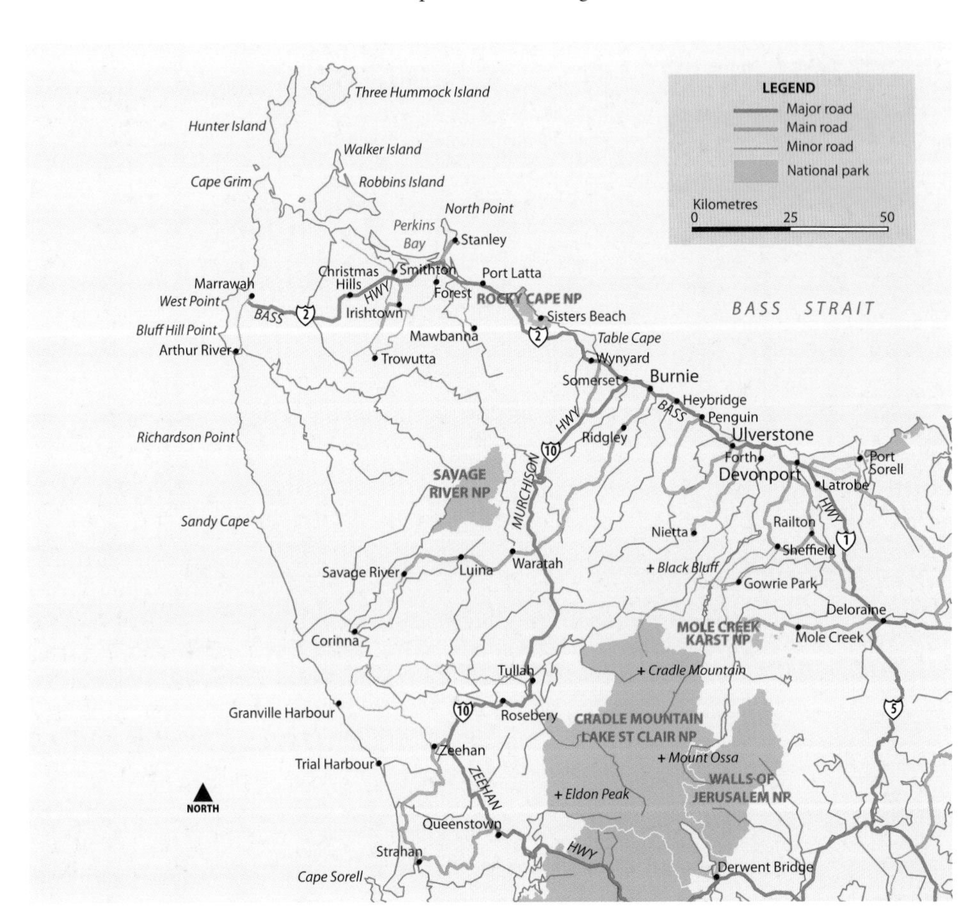

Stanley & Surrounds

When locals in Stanley speak of the Nut, they don't mean the local hermit, but rather a 150 m high table-topped rock formation that rises out of the water above this absorbing town. If you're not feeling like a (very) steep walk to the summit, take the easy way up on the chairlift and enjoy the expansive views over the strait. Stanley began as the headquarters of the Van Diemen's Land Company, a consortium formed in London in 1824, which sought to profit from opening up the North West to Merino sheep farming. The sheep shivered but the company found the land they acquired was suited to agriculture and began to prosper. Several of the company's offices, stores and residences remain prominent in Stanley. The impeccably conserved Highfield House, built in 1832, was once the stately home of the company's chief agent. This utterly fascinating historic site includes an abbey, stables and the ruins of the convict workers quarters (open daily, but closed weekends from June–August, Greenhills Rd, Ph: (03) 6458 1100). The bluestone Touchwood Cottage (1840) was once owned by the company secretary and is now a luxury B&B, café and craft gallery (31 Church Street, Ph: (03) 6458 1348).

Top to bottom: Farmland sweeps down to the sea near the Nut; The ruins of convict quarters at Highfield House.

Stanley Historic timber stores and cottages line the town's main street.

Tiger Country – Stanley to the North West Tip

Dairy farming, fishing and timber are the chief industries of the far North West. The region's main service centre, Smithton, lies 22 km west of Stanley on the Duck River. A huge mill in the town processes timber from forests to the south, once famed as Tasmanian Tiger (Thylacine) country. Several of these forests, including Lake Chisholm, Julius River and Milkshakes Hills, are set aside for walking and wildlife watching. At Dismal Swamp, 40 km west of Smithton off the Bass Highway, is one of the State's most bizarre but enthralling ecotourism attractions. Here you can descend by a 110 m slide, electric buggy or gentle walkway into a truly eerie Blackwood sinkhole where a maze of boardwalks allow you to explore the swamp floor. There are other surprises too, which should be left to those who visit, and a licensed café with viewing deck at the top that will give you the chance to contemplate the strangeness (and beauty) of it all.

The Bass Highway comes to an end at Marrawah, near where the last Tasmanian Tiger was sighted. The extinction of this unique striped carnivore began in 1830 when the Van Diemen's Land Company — which feared the animal would destroy their sheep — began paying a bounty on Thylacine scalps. To the north of Marrawah on the North West tip is Cape Grim and the historic farming property of Woolnorth, owned to this day by the Van Diemen's Land Company. Ironically, the last four Tasmanian Tigers ever captured were found here on the company's property — perhaps they came seeking revenge. Just south of the tip, at Woolnorth, the world's cleanest air drives the turbine blades on one of Australia's biggest wind farms.

Woolnorth The wind farm at Woolnorth is Australia's largest.

The Tarkine

Taking its name from the Tarkiner people who originally inhabited the region, the Tarkine is one of Australia's great wilderness areas. This region of wild rivers, forests and mountains is bordered by the Arthur River in the north, the Pieman River in the south and the Murchison Highway to the east. There are fantastic drives and walks in this region.

Hellyer Gorge State Reserve

This protected region of ferns and rainforest is located approximately midway between Burnie and Rosebery on the Murchison Highway. Walk amid primitive Sassafras, giant Manferns and myrtle trees; even the highway rest area is covered in luminous moss.

Rosebery & Surrounds

Never has the phrase "there's gold in them thar hills" been more apt than in Rosebery. Encircled by mineral-bearing mountains north of Zeehan, the town was founded after the discovery of gold on Mt Black by Tom McDonald in 1893. Today, Rosebery's economy is still founded on mining — Zinifex operates the copper, zinc and lead base mine in the Rosebery valley and the Murchison United underground tin mine at Renison Bell is reputedly the world's largest. Surface tours of the Zinifex mine include a visit to the Rosebery Heritage Centre and various historical sites around town (bookings, Ph: (03) 6473 1247). Experienced walkers can follow tracks to the summit of nearby Mt Farrell for incredible views across to Cradle Mountain–Lake St Clair National Park. Neighbouring Mt Murchison and Mt Read are higher and harder but the views are equally spectacular.

Montezuma Falls is at the end of a 3.5 km track starting at Williamsford and following an old mining railway through rainforest. It is one of Tasmania's most breathtaking (and loud) waterfalls. Take a picnic and admire its sonorous beauty from the viewing platform. The fast-flowing waters of Mackintosh Gorge near Lake Mackintosh are ideal for canoeing, kayaking and rafting. This 30 km^2 human-made lake also provides perfect conditions for boating and fishing (license required, season runs August to May).

Marrawah to Zeehan – an Alternative Adventure

South of Marrawah down Tasmania's west coast is some of Australia's most beautiful wilderness, known as the Tarkine. The settlement of Arthur River signals the start of the Arthur–Pieman Conservation Area but if you wish to travel further than the fishing villages of Couta Creek and Temma, you'll need a 4WD vehicle. While in Arthur River, don't miss the opportunity to cruise up river into the Tarkine rainforest (Arthur River Cruises, Ph: (03) 6457 1158). Canoes and kayaks are also available for hire in the town. From just south of Arthur River the Western Explorer Route begins — a gravel road 4WD adventure through forest and open grasslands along the border of the conservation area to Corinna on the Pieman River nearly 100 km south. The only town en route, Balfour, has been deserted — an overgrown cemetery a reminder of the mining community that once lived amid the rainforest. At Corinna, *Fatman* — a broad vehicular barge — will take you over the Pieman (Ph: (03) 6446 1170). Legend has it that the river was named for a transported convict baker who escaped from Sarah Island and was captured in Corinna in 1823. You can also cruise the Pieman on the charming *Arcadia II* — a 70-year-old vessel, crafted from Huon Pine, which ferries passengers to Pieman Head (Ph: (03) 6446 1170). Stay in an old miner's cabin (don't worry, the old miners are long gone), timber cottage or the historic pub and enjoy the wild pleasures of this eco-friendly township and rainforest region. The fascinating and once even wilder town of Zeehan lies 52 km south. At the height of the silver mining boom, Zeehan was a roaring metropolis boasting its own stock exchange and Australia's largest theatre. Mining is still carried out and much of Zeehan's history remains. Wander among the restored buildings on the main street (including the restored 1000-seat Gaiety Theatre) or visit the excellent Pioneer Memorial Museum (Main Street, Ph: (03) 6471 6225).

Left and right: Much of the coastal hinterland section of the Tarkine is protected by the Arthur–Pieman Conservation Area and the Pieman River State Reserve. Campgrounds are available at Arthur River and Corinna.

Top to bottom: A White-bellied Sea-Eagle fishes at Arthur River; Kayak expeditions are popular on the rivers; *Arcadia II* on the Pieman River; Zeehan.

Clockwise from top left: A 4WD is essential to explore Davenport National Park; Davenport National Park is surrounded by rugged ranges; The permanent waterholes are a sanctuary for many bird and fish species.

The Overland Track

Tracing a spectacular 65 km route through mountains and rainforest from Cradle Mountain to Lake St Clair, the Overland Track is one the world's great wilderness treks. The trail attracts nearly 10,000 bushwalkers every year and takes 6 days (or longer, depending upon weather conditions) to complete.

The main walking season is from 1 November to 30 April. Bookings are required to walk the track during this period (bookings open in July for the following season, Ph: (03) 6233 6047 or visit www.overlandtrack.com.au). While it is possible to walk the track at other times, such practice is only for experienced bushwalkers. All walkers must check in at the Cradle Mountain Visitor Centre before departure.

Camping: There are a series of basic huts along the track that accommodate walkers on a "first-come first-served" basis. They have bunk beds and gas heaters but no cooking facilities or bedding. All walkers must carry a tent. Numerous private tour companies also operate more luxurious huts along the trail and complete guided camping tours are available (see previous website for more details).

Right, top to bottom: Picturesque Kia Ora Hut; Pristine alpine heathland is a feature of the Overland Track; Wooden platforms provide convenient sites for pitching tents.

Cradle Mountain-Lake St Clair National Park – Northern Section

Phone Ranger: (03) 6492 1110

This north-western area of Tasmania's World Heritage wilderness is, for good reason, one of Australia's most beloved bushwalking destinations. The park is effectively split into two sections, with Cradle Mountain in the north and Lake St Clair in the south-east. The Overland Track connects the two (*see below left*). "Doing the track" is the experience many travel here for, but there are a large number of shorter trails in both sections of the park to suit people of all walking levels and ages.

The serrated dolerite peak of Cradle Mountain, dusted with snow in winter (and often shrouded in cloud) is best admired from Dove Lake. Once covered by glaciers, the region remains scattered with glacial features such as moraines, lakes and tarns. The forests are rich in ancient trees such as King Billy and Pencil Pine, Celery Top Pine and Myrtle Beech. Quolls and Tasmanian Devils roam the park, along with Platypuses and echidnas.

Shorter Walks in the Park: Commencing near the Cradle Mountain section entrance, there is a half hour walk through rainforest and moorlands to waterfalls and pools. From the visitor centre a short, wheelchair-accessible boardwalk leads through rainforest to views of Pencil Falls. Near historic Waldheim Chalet, there is a 20 minute forest trail. Visit the chalet and discover the fascinating story of the Weindorfers who constructed the original building in 1912. Don't leave without taking the Dove Lake Loop Track (2 hr) with its vistas across the lake to Cradle Mountain. The national park shop within the visitor centre sells a wide assortment of bushwalking and camping gear.

Access: Access to the Cradle Mountain section from the west and north is via the Murchison Highway and Cradle Link Road (C132). In order to reduce traffic on the park road, a shuttle bus operates from the visitor centre to Dove Lake throughout the day.

Accommodation: Waldheim Cabins at Cradle Mountain (located close to the visitor centre) offer simple and affordable accommodation in close proximity to several excellent walking tracks. There is also commercially operated accommodation and camping at Cosy Cabins Cradle Mountain (Cradle Mountain Link Road, Ph: (03) 6492 1395).

Common Wombats Frequently seen around tracks and cabins in the national park is the Common Wombat.

WEST & South West

Queenstown

The industrially denuded moonscape of Queenstown's hills provides a stark reminder (to locals and visitors alike) of the perils of unchecked environmental destruction.

The West Coast Wilderness Railway

This 35 km railway was built in 1896 to freight loads of copper concentrates to port. Today, the beautifully restored steam train runs from Queenstown to Strahan through dense rainforest and steep gorges.

Sarah Island

For 11 years (1822–1833), Sarah Island in Macquarie Harbour was the site of the most remote and brutal penal colony in Australia. So bad were conditions that, despite its incredible isolation, over 180 escape attempts were made. Amazingly, one group of escapees actually survived to reach Chile in a boat of their own making. Their remarkable story is portrayed in a play entitled *The Ship That Never Was* performed daily at the Strahan Visitor Centre amphitheatre (bookings, Ph: (03) 6471 7622). Sarah Island cruises and tours depart from Strahan.

Tasmania's remote South West is one of Australia's largest areas of pure wilderness. That this is so is mostly due to vociferous campaigning by environmental groups from the 1960s onward. Despite these campaigns, the Tasmanian government chose to dam the Huon and Gordon Rivers in 1972 — forming the State's largest inland water reserve, Lake Pedder. A similar fate was proposed for the Franklin River, but conservationists from around the world rallied to pressure the government into aborting its plans. In 1982, Franklin–Gordon Wild Rivers National Park and Southwest National Park were declared World Heritage Areas, having satisfied more criteria for listing than any other wilderness territory on Earth. Not to be deterred, the Tasmanian Liberal government revoked parts of the national parks, sparking a green blockade on the Gordon River in Strahan at which over 1000 people were arrested. Finally, in 1983, the federal government intervened, taking successful high court action to prevent the dam being built. Struggles between government, environmentalists and industry remain a feature of the Tasmanian political landscape, but today the South West wilderness has greater protection from human interference than ever before. Its magnificent wild rivers, rainforest, mountains and gorges make the South West one of the most scenic regions on the entire planet.

From the East

The Gordon River Road runs 74 km from Maydena (near Mount Field National Park) between Lake Gordon and Lake Pedder to Strathgordon and Gordon Dam. The road enters Southwest National Park at Frodshams Pass, where a gravel road also leads to Scotts Peak and the Huon campground. The journey by car from Hobart takes approximately three hours. Alternatively, it is also possible to enter the park from Cockle Creek, Australia's most southerly town. Take the Huon Highway from Hobart through Geeveston and turn off just prior to Southport on the C635. Turn onto the C636 after Hastings and follow the road to Cockle Creek. The road is rough but can be negotiated with a conventional vehicle. There are also many charter flights and aerial tours over the South West region available from Hobart (*see page 313*).

If you wish to drive through the wilderness to the west coast, the Lyell Highway roughly traces the border between Franklin–Gordon Wild Rivers National Park (to the south) and Cradle Mountain–Lake St Clair National Park (to the north). This scenic journey from Derwent Bridge to Queenstown is a comfortable (but not so tactile) way to view the incredible wilderness landscape. Stop at King William Saddle for views of the surrounding range, Mt Rufus and Frenchmans Cap — a brilliant white quartzite peak. The highway then bends around the southern side of Mt Arrowsmith to valley views from Surprise Lookout. After descending the mountain, you encounter the Franklin River where an easy 1 km interpretive nature trail (wheelchair accessible) provides information on this powerful waterway. A little further on at Donaghys Hill a wilderness trail and lookout offer spectacular views of the Franklin River and Frenchmans Cap. West of here, raft and canoe expeditions commence from the Collingwood River, where there are also basic campsites and fireplaces. Just before Lake Burbury at the bridge over the Nelson River there is an excellent 20 minute return track to Nelson Falls.

Queenstown & Strahan

The scarified, bald hills of Queenstown stand as a disturbing example of what can happen when human industry proceeds without respect for the environment. Once covered by the same lush vegetation found in the wilderness to its immediate east, the forested valley of the Queens River was decimated by logging to feed voracious copper smelters. Sulphur fumes belching from the smelters killed off other plant life, leaving the exposed, rootless topsoil to be washed away by rains. As early as 1900, the virile green valley had started to become dead, bare desert. Mining is still carried out around Queenstown, but it is now predominantly a historic tourist town of museums and mine tours. In 1822, Macquarie Harbour on the west coast became the location of one of Tasmania's most isolated and terrifying convict prisons (*see left*). The town of Strahan was developed 50 years later as the main port servicing the lucrative mining interests at Queenstown and Mt Heemskirk. Today, Strahan is the gateway to the western wilderness. Explore the Wharf Centre on Strahan's boat-bobbing waterfront, walk through Peoples Park to Hogarth Falls or visit the World Heritage Centre at historic Customs House (The Esplanade).

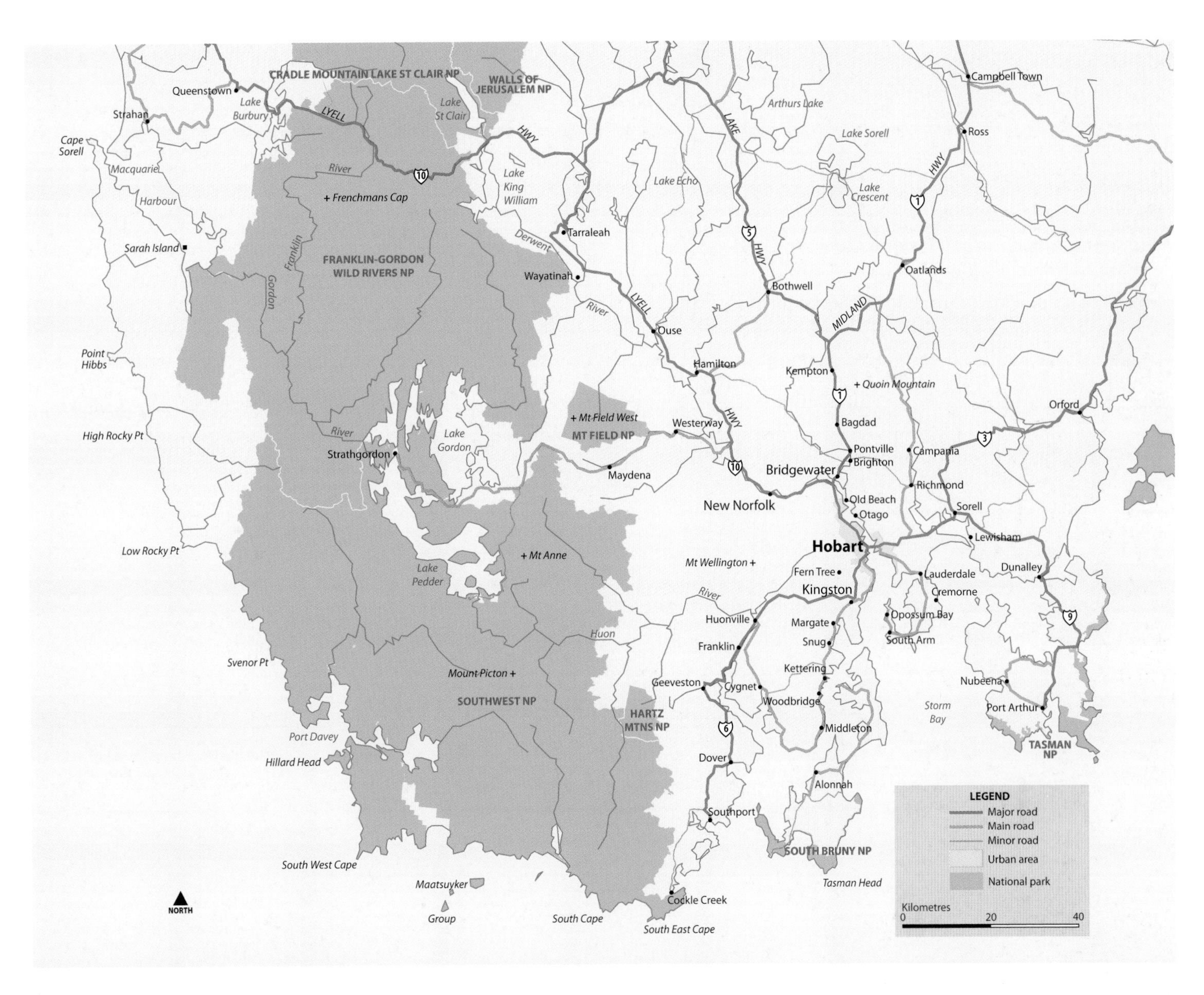

Strahan

Strahan achieved international fame in 1982 as environmentalists flooded in to join the Franklin Dam blockade. Despite government opposition, their efforts (thankfully) eventually succeeded in preventing the proposed Franklin Dam.

Macquarie Harbour

The beauty of this long shallow inlet was long overshadowed by the tales of privation and misery associated with the penal colonies established on its islands and shores. Today its waters are a superb place to cruise and fish.

Gordon River

The lower reaches of the Gordon River were first navigated by Captain James Kelly after he successfully entered Macquarie Harbour in 1815. Cruises on the rainforest-lined Gordon River depart Strahan daily.

Cradle Mountain-Lake St Clair National Park – Southern Section

Phone Ranger: (03) 6289 1172

Lake St Clair, where the Derwent River begins its journey to Hobart, is Australia's deepest freshwater lake. Its 190 m deep basin was carved out over two million years by glacial movement. The impressive Mt Olympus rises over the lake. The Lake St Clair Visitor Centre provides a wealth of information regarding the evolution and exploration of the area.

Walks & Cruises in the Park: Stroll the shores of Lake St Clair at Cynthia Bay. In spring and summer, the Watersmeet Nature Trail (1 hr return) along the crest of a glacial moraine is bordered by wildflowers. From Watersmeet you may continue to Platypus Bay or take the *Larmairremener tabelti* – Aboriginal Cultural Walk. A ferry cruises Lake St Clair from Cynthia Bay to Narcissus Bay. Canoes, bikes and dinghies are available for hire at Cynthia Bay (Ph: (03) 6289 1137). Boat ramps are provided for private craft and trout fishing licences are available from the general store.

Access: Access to the Lake St Clair section of the park is via the Lyell Highway from the west and east. From Derwent Bridge take the 5.5 km park entrance road to Cynthia Bay. Roads may sometimes be closed due to snow in winter.

Lake St Clair The southern end of Lake St Clair.

Camping: At Cynthia Bay there are privately operated camping, hostel and chalet facilities (Ph: (03) 6289 1137). Cynthia Bay also has picnic and barbecue facilities, a restaurant and general store. Commercially operated accommodation is also available at Derwent Bridge.

Franklin-Gordon Wild Rivers National Park

Phone Ranger: (03) 6471 2511, Queenstown Field Office or (03) 6471 7122, Strahan Office

At even the most cursory inspection, it is easy to see why conservationists fought with such conviction to prevent the destruction of any part of this wilderness area. Walking the park tracks, cruising the Gordon River from Strahan or taking a chartered flight over the wild rivers region reveals a landscape of irreplaceable grandeur. From rainforest-fringed rivers to spectacular mountain ranges this is one of Australia's great national parks. It is also one of the least accessible, with most walking tracks only providing access to the northern fringes of the park.

Walks & Cruises in the Park: For most people, the easiest way to explore the park is to travel on the Lyell Highway from Derwent Bridge to Queenstown, allowing time to stop at the numerous trails and lookouts along the way (*see previous page*). If you have time, continue on to Strahan on the west coast and take a boat trip back up the lower reaches of the Gordon, where seeing the adjoining rainforest reflected in waters stained dark with natural tannins is an unforgettable experience. Cruise boats travel up the Gordon River to Heritage Landing from Strahan daily. Flights and helicopter tours are also available (*see facing page*). For fit, experienced bushwalkers there is a 46 km, 3–5 day return walk to the summit of Frenchmans Cap from west of the Franklin Bridge — but beware, it is considered much tougher than the Overland Track from Cradle Mountain to Lake St Clair (see www.parks.tas.gov.au/recreation or call the parks office for further information).

Top to bottom: Nelson Falls (off the Lyell Highway near Lake Burbury); The white quartzite peaks of Frenchmans Cap.

Access: Via the Lyell Highway from the east and west.

Camping: Basic campsites are available at the Collingwood River off the Lyell Highway, approximately midway from Derwent Bridge to Queenstown. Walkers' huts are provided on the Frenchmans Cap Track.

Southwest National Park

Phone Ranger: (03) 6288 1283, Maydena Office or (03) 6264 8460, Cockle Bay Office

Occupying the entire south-west corner of Tasmania, the 600,000 ha Southwest National Park is the island's largest reserve. It also includes Lake Pedder and Lake Gordon, offering unforgettable opportunities for boating and fishing.

Short Walks in the Park: The 20 minute Creepy Crawly Nature Trail (2.5 km down Scotts Peak Road) is an entertaining boardwalk journey through thick rainforest, moss-covered trees and fallen logs — home to a range of Tasmanian invertebrates. From Huon campground, walk up Daveys Track to the forest end (2 hr return) — the track is considerably longer and more difficult beyond this point. The park is also famed for its overnight and multi-day treks (contact ranger for further information).

Access: Via Gordon River Road from Maydena or via Geeveston to Cockle Creek (*see previous pages*). Flights are available to the airstrip at Melaleuca in the far south-west corner where the wild South Coast Track commences.

Camping: There are two campgrounds off the unsealed Scotts Peak Rd, Edgar and Huon, both of which are suitable for tents and caravans (toilets, untreated water, fireplaces with wood supplies). Near Strathgordon at Lake Pedder off the Gordon River Road is Teds Beach campground. These sites are also suitable for caravans and have toilets, untreated water, free electric barbecues and a boat ramp. There are also a wide range of camping facilities around Cockle Bay both on the park border and in the Recherche Bay Recreation Area. There are two bushwalkers huts at Melaleuca.

Lake Pedder Southwest National Park.

Southwest National Park– a Great Place to Fly

Undoubtedly the best way to gain an appreciation of the scale and pristine majesty of Tasmania's South West wilderness is to see it from above. Fares are moderate (from around $170 per adult) and the experience is unforgettable — your holiday snaps from the air over Southwest National Park are guaranteed repeat viewings in years to come. Tasair operates 2 hour and 3 hour return flights from Hobart taking in the magnificent spectacle of Arthur Range, Lake Pedder, Bathurst Harbour, Port Davey and the southern coast. In suitable weather conditions, the flights even include a breathtaking beach landing at Cox Bight. Time is allowed for lunch and a brief land exploration of the region surrounding Melaleuca (Tasair, Ph: (03) 6248 5088). Par-Avion also offers a variety of South West tour packages including flights, boat trips and walking expeditions departing Hobart (Par-Avion, Ph: 1800 144 460).

Left to right: Lake Gordon; Lake Pedder seen over Frankland Range.

Left to right: A tarn on the Arthur Range; Federation Peak, one of the most extreme climbing and bushwalking challenges, Southwest National Park.

Left to right: Bathurst Harbour, Southwest National Park; Looking over Prion Bay towards Precipitous Bluff.

Discovering Tassie Flora

From a wealth of wildflowers to unique orchids and soaring gums, Tasmania is a paradise of forest, fern and flower.

There are at least 2000 species of native flowering plants. Some 20, including the dainty Tasmanian Waratah, grow only in the island State. Sixty species of ground orchid are found in Freycinet National Park alone. The tallest flowering plant in the world, the Swamp Gum (*Eucalyptus regnans*) grows to 100 m high and is found only in Tasmania's forests. Another eucalypt, the Tasmanian Blue Gum (*Eucalyptus globulus*), is the State's floral emblem. This beautiful hardwood is cultivated as a source of timber in Tasmanian plantations as well as many places overseas.

Alpine plants abound during summer in Tasmania's high country, but they are fragile and easily damaged by careless walkers. More easily seen are the wildflowers that grow along the verges of roads and in the bush — plants that bloom at their best when spring and summer bring warm sunshine to complete the work of heavy winter rains.

Tasmania is Australia's largest repository of cool temperate rainforest, which covers a remarkable 10% of the State. Over 40% is in the Tasmanian World Heritage Wilderness Area. High rainfall in mountainous regions creates perfect conditions for the growth of trees like the Huon Pine, Sassafrass, Leatherwood, Celery Top Pine, Pencil Pine and King Billy Pine. This is complemented on the cool, dark forest floor by fungi, mosses and lichen. The State's rainforests contain many ancient species of flora that evolved when Tasmania formed part of the vast continental landmass known as Gondwana some 60 million years ago.

Tasmanian Blue Gum

A Birdwatchers' Paradise

Of all the birds found in Tasmania, none are more colourful than the prolific parrots and cockatoos. The long separation of the island from the rest of Australia has also allowed some species to change enough to be distinct from their mainland relatives. The Green Rosella, which can be seen in large flocks during winter in parks, gardens and heathlands, is one such endemic bird. A more elusive feathered jewel, the Swift Parrot, breeds in Tasmania's eucalypt forests in summer before flying across Bass Strait to winter in warmer climes. The entire population of Swift Parrots is thought to number only around 5000, but the Orange-bellied Parrot is even rarer. Only hundreds of these remain to breed in Tasmania's South West wilderness, before migrating north to spend winter on Victoria's coast.

The islands to the north-east, including Cape Barren and Flinders Islands are the native home of the Cape Barren Goose. Seabirds use the east coast and neighbouring islands as migratory stopovers to destinations as distant as the Arctic circle.

Little Penguins

Giant Pandani The largest heathland plant in the world.

Left to right: *Epacris* sp.; *Banksia* sp.; *Richea* sp.; *Leptospermum* sp.; *Cyathodes* sp.

Left to right: Tasmanian Waratah; *Leptospermum* and *Callistemon* sp.

Left to right: Cormorant rookery; Cape Barren Geese.

Left to right: Australian Shelducks; Swift Parrot; Orange-bellied Parrot; Tasmanian Native-hen; Scarlet Robin.

Left to right: Common Wombat; Tasmanian form of the Short-beaked Echidna.

Left to right: Forester Kangaroo; Cream form of the Common Brushtail Possum; Tasmanian Bettong; Tasmanian Pademelon.

Left to right: Bennett's Wallaby, a Tasmanian subspecies of the Red-necked Wallaby; Eastern Quolls.

Clockwise from top left: Tassie Devil mum with five-month-old cubs; An old male showing the scars of battle; Two male Devils do battle over food; Two males discuss the finer points of dining etiquette while sharing a meal.

Camping with Mammals

Tasmania's national parks are home to a huge population of native mammals. Some, such as the Echidna and Tasmanian Devil, will rapidly retreat if disturbed, often before being seen. Others, like possums, bandicoots, quolls and gliders are more gregarious and are often sighted around campsites.

Eastern Barred Bandicoots

Many of Tasmania's mammals have had the relative luxury of developing and thriving in an environment free of predators. The division of the island from the mainland, the absence of Dingoes and, until recently, foxes, plus the tragic destruction of the Tasmanian Tiger (or Thylacine), created a near threat-free haven. Many, like the Eastern Quoll, Tasmanian Devil, Tasmanian Bettong and Red-bellied Pademelon have disappeared from the mainland but survive in good numbers in Tasmania. The Long-nosed Potoroo and Eastern Barred Bandicoot are following them into exile. Only a few hundred of the latter survive in Victoria. The Forester Kangaroo (known to the rest of Australia as the Eastern Grey Kangaroo) is the largest marsupial in the State, growing up to 2 m tall. It is protected in Tasmania due to its dwindling numbers. Bennett's Wallabies are present throughout Tasmania and are frequently seen in the national parks.

Around 33 native terrestrial mammals and 41 marine mammals are found in the State. As is typical throughout Australia, many of these are marsupials (carrying their young in a pouch). The monotremes, Platypuses and echidnas, are also widespread but the Platypus, in particular, is susceptible to illness. Its nocturnal, reclusive behaviour also makes it difficult to find in the wild — consider it a true privilege if you see one swimming in a bush creek or pool.

The Tasmanian Devil – an Island's Icon

A young Tasmanian Devil yawning

For many visitors, an encounter with a Tasmanian Devil (*Sarcophilus harrisii*) is a defining moment in their journey to Tasmania. Popularised in animated cartoons as a psychotic whirlwind of teeth and claws, the Tassie Devil has a character all its own. Such is the little creature's reputation for ferocity that many expect to encounter a creature the size of a lion. In fact, mature Devils only reach around 30 cm high. Nevertheless, the Tasmanian Devil holds the title of the world's largest carnivorous marsupial.

Early European settlers named the Tasmanian Devil for its netherworld yowl and a daunting gape full of menacing teeth. It is certainly capable of a large amount of noise, particularly when fighting with a fellow Devil over a potential meal. The female Devil carries her young in her pouch until they are old enough to be left in a grass-lined den. The youngsters are highly playful and active, often running back and forth for hours on end. The yawning gape that appears so threatening is usually a sign of fear or uncertainty (or perhaps tiredness!) rather than aggression.

MELBOURNE

& THE JOURNEY TO SYDNEY

10

The journey from Melbourne to Sydney takes in some of the most highly travelled and populous regions of Australia. Most of the intercity traffic travels the ultra-functional Hume Highway, which bypasses nearly every town. Quick it may be — boring it certainly is. This chapter outlines two longer, but infinitely richer, paths to Sydney — an inland adventure via Canberra and a spectacular coastal odyssey. The first trip involves a detour off the Hume to explore the region between highway and coast. East of Albury–Wodonga on the Murray River are the Australian Alps, a spectacular collection of peaks that include the nation's highest, Mt Kosciuszko. The snow that falls in the Alps feeds powerful rivers whose energy has been harnessed by the dams and turbines of the Snowy Mountains Hydro-electric Scheme. The Alps are also a skier's paradise, with major resorts at Thredbo and Perisher linked by an underground train. North of the Alps is Canberra, the sheep pasture that was transformed into Australia's national capital and is now home to some of the country's most important institutions and monuments. The longer, but most scenic, route from Melbourne to Sydney is via the coast. Take the time to visit Phillip Island, trek in Wilsons Promontory, cruise the Gippsland Lakes, go whale watching on the Sapphire Coast or marvel at the marine wonders of Jervis Bay.

Left: Kosciuszko National Park, the largest in New South Wales, offers a snow and eucalypt backdrop to sports during winter, and wildflowers and alpine camping during summer.

MELBOURNE & Surrounds

Melbourne & Surrounds
Top Things to Do

1. View Melbourne and Port Phillip Bay from the observation deck of the Rialto.
2. Visit Melbourne in October for the Melbourne International Arts Festival.
3. Catch the excitement of Australian Rules Football or Test Match Cricket at the MCG.
4. See the world's best musicians at Hamer Hall.
5. Uncover urban secrets within Melbourne's network of lanes and arcades.
6. Dine out in style at one of the city's hundreds of restaurants.
7. Cruise the Yarra River.
8. Photograph Federation Square.
9. Explore the City Heritage Trails.
10. Picnic in Melbourne's magnificent gardens.

Early History

Originally inhabited by the Kulin Aboriginal peoples, formal British settlement of the area around Port Phillip Bay did not occur until the early 1800s. Although explorers had reported fertile land and abundant water, an initial attempt to establish a settlement at Sorrento on the Mornington Peninsula failed.

In 1835, separate parties of free settlers led by John Batman and John Fawkner arrived at Port Phillip from Van Diemen's Land (now Tasmania) and took up land at the mouth of the Yarra River. In March 1837 Governor Bourke christened the township Melbourne in honour of the British prime minister of the time.

When gold was discovered to Melbourne's north in 1851, a massive wave of immigration inflated Victoria's population from 76,000 to 540,000 people in a mere decade. The wealth created by gold ensured Melbourne's future as a major city and financed the construction of housing and public buildings.

At the head of Port Phillip Bay on the banks of the Yarra River lies Melbourne, the capital of Victoria and Australia's second-largest city. Conceived as a village and nourished on the riches of gold in its formative years, Melbourne has matured into a thriving metropolis. While many of Melbourne's assets are on ready display to the first-time visitor, the city handsomely rewards exploration. Stately Victorian architecture is juxtaposed with the unflinchingly modern; skyscrapers give way to parklands and waterfront and a grid of broad open streets is linked by a network of more secretive arcades and lanes.

Modern Melbourne

Twenty-first century Melbourne is a city of more than 3 million people of diverse origins. The CBD is a major corporate and retail hub enveloped by generous public parks and gardens. A proud collection of civic buildings ranges from the Victorian grandeur of Parliament House to the intense modernity of Federation Square. Over generations, Melbourne has meticulously preserved its built heritage while gaining an international reputation as a modern capital of culture, sport, fashion and cuisine. A passion for the arts is reflected in world class galleries, performing arts centres, theatres and concert halls. Each October, the Melbourne International Arts Festival is a focus of artistic celebration.

Sporting Capital

For most Melburnians, sport is life. Melbourne is the birthplace of the nation's only native game, Australian Rules Football, and in September the city pulsates with anticipation of the football season's dramatic conclusion, the Grand Final, staged at the MCG (home of the 1956 Olympics and 2006 Commonwealth Games). The "race that stops a nation", The Melbourne Cup, is run every November, while Formula One's Australian Grand Prix takes centre stage in March. The city also hosts the Australian Open — one of only four international Grand Slam tennis events.

Culture & Cuisine

The city's broad mix of nationalities has produced a smorgasbord of cuisines and cultures. Food from around the globe, from Asia and Europe to Africa and South America, is celebrated in a mouth-watering array of restaurants from formal to alfresco. Generations of migrants and their descendants have also put their own delicious stamp on the city fringe suburbs — look for Italian bistros in Carlton, Vietnamese restaurants in Richmond and Greek tavernas in Collingwood.

Melbourne – Bay City

Melbourne is defined by water. Beyond Southbank, the Yarra merges with the northern edge of Port Phillip Bay. John Murray first entered the bay in 1801 aboard the *Lady Nelson*, before which it was home to the Wurundjeri and Wathaurong peoples. Today popular bayside suburbs spill out from the city around Port Phillip's gentle curve. The 264 km shoreline of Port Phillip Bay is protected from the turbulence of Bass Strait by the Mornington and Bellarine Peninsulas, and is a focal point for swimming, fishing and boating. The city's original docklands area, at the western end of Bourke Sreet, has been re-developed and includes the buoyant NewQuay — a sheltered harbour buzzing with waterside restaurants, hip urban art and trendy apartment complexes.

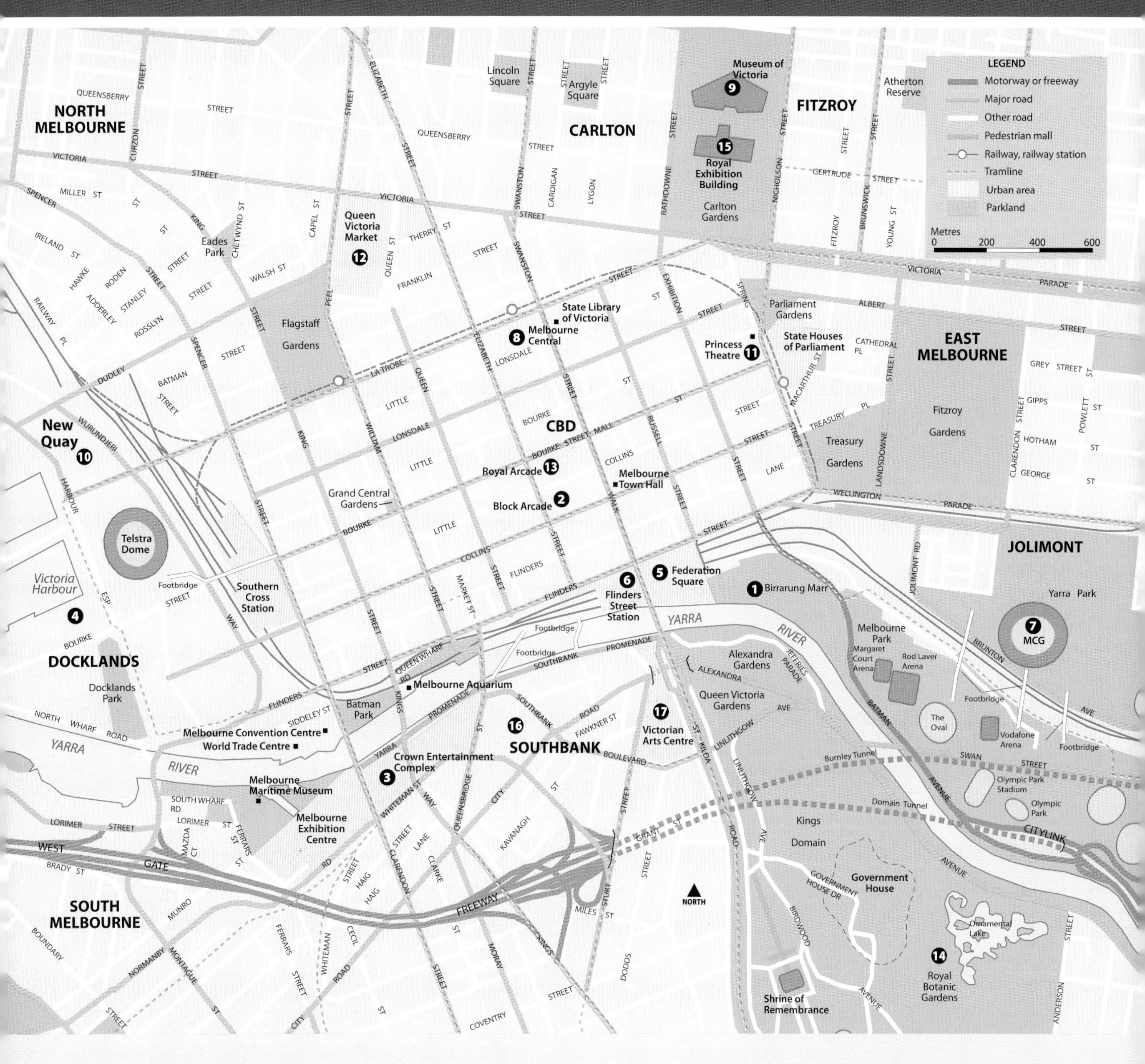

Feature Localities

1 Birrarung Marr
2 Block Arcade
3 Crown Entertainment Complex
4 Docklands
5 Federation Square
6 Flinders Street Station
7 MCG
8 Melbourne Central
9 Museum of Victoria
10 NewQuay
11 Princess Theatre
12 Queen Victoria Market
13 Royal Arcade
14 Royal Botanic Gardens
15 Royal Exhibition Building
16 Southbank
17 Victorian Arts Centre

Melbourne & Surrounds

Top Things to Do

1. Hop on a water taxi and lunch at NewQuay.
2. Engage the city's nightlife at Crown Entertainment Complex.
3. Stroll the Yarra's northern bank past Federation Square to Birrarung Marr.
4. Find a hidden jazz club in the city alleys.
5. Explore the Children's Garden at the Royal Botanic Gardens.
6. Enjoy performing artists and buskers on Southbank.
7. Tour Melbourne's impressive war memorial, the Shrine of Remembrance.
8. Peruse international art exhibitions at NGV International on St Kilda Rd.

Rowing on the River

During the first half of the 20th century, Melbourne's annual spring rowing regatta, the Henley-on-Yarra, was the city's biggest sporting and social event, attracting up to 300,000 people. Today, the city's major rowing clubs still operate from their traditional location on the south bank of the river. The Yarra River has long provided a training base for Australia's Olympic champions in the sport.

The Yarra & Gardens

Where some rivers divide, Melbourne's Yarra unites. It connects the city with its Indigenous past, merges gardens and bay with city bustle, bridges eras and brings together the city's people in a fusion of culture, colour and celebration. The Yarra's ready supply of fresh water was crucial to the survival of both the original Wurundjeri peoples and early European settlers. Waterfalls upstream prevented the saltwater of Port Phillip Bay from rendering the river water undrinkable.

The river's powerful role belies its humble origins as a modest meeting of rivulets and streams far away to the city's north. Over time its eccentric course has been straightened to prevent flooding. Where bridges now stand, punts and ferries once conveyed Melbourne's early inhabitants across the river. Over the past century the Yarra has been the setting for some of Melbourne's most festive moments, including the annual Moomba Waterfest. The development of the Yarra's southern bank beyond historic Princes Bridge has seen the river undergo a remarkable renaissance.

Bridges & Cruises

As the Yarra River nears the end of its 242 km journey from Mt Baw Baw to Port Phillip Bay, the city's bridges reach out to span its waters. Linking the tree-lined boulevard of St Kilda Rd with the central business district is elegant Princes Bridge (*below left*), opened in 1888. Beyond the arched footbridge at Southgate (*below centre*) the twin cantilevers of Bolte Bridge (*below right*) soar majestically out of the Yarra, giving rise to one of the city's main traffic arteries. The Bolte Bridge was completed in 1999 as part of Melbourne's major new freeway system, CityLink. Spanning 490 m with its trademark Gateway Towers rising 140 m above the water, it is a dominant icon. Commercial river cruises, ranging from half-hour sightseeing tours to lavish dining experiences, depart regularly from Southgate. A ferry also operates from the city to Williamstown, and water taxis service the Crown Entertainment Complex and NewQuay. Those seeking a more leisurely Yarra voyage can enjoy a trip on one of Melbourne's historic steam-driven vessels.

Yarra Parks & Gardens

Melbourne's sublime Royal Botanic Gardens are situated on the south side of the Yarra within easy walking distance of the city (*see facing page*). Birrarung Marr is located on the river's northern bank and is Melbourne's newest parkland. The name of the park is a tribute to the Wurundjeri people who originally inhabited the area. *Birrarung* is derived from words meaning "river of mists" and *Marr* "side of the river". The park is adjacent to Federation Square and links the city centre, Yarra River and Melbourne's sporting precinct, including the Melbourne Cricket Ground (MCG). Birrarung Marr is a soothing mix of open spaces, sculpture (such as *Angel* by Deborah Halpern, *top right*) and tree-lined riverbank. At the park's highest point is what looks from afar like a forest of giant ski poles. It is in fact the Federation Bells, 39 individual bells hoisted on metal stands and ranging in weight from tiny to 1.2 tonne. Marking the Centenary of Federation, they are computer-controlled and chime commissioned musical works (at 8 am and 5 pm daily). Cycling and walking tracks and a children's adventure playground are nearby.

Botanic Gardens

Occupying a site on the Yarra River originally selected by Lieutenant-Governor Charles La Trobe, Melbourne's Royal Botanic Gardens were first established in 1846. The design and original plantings were the work of the garden's first two directors, acclaimed botanist Ferdinand von Mueller and William Guilfoyle, who conceived the gardens' stunning landscape. With over 50,000 individual plants, representing more than 10,000 different species, the gardens are home to native wildlife (including Black Swans, bellbirds and kookaburras) as well as Mueller's original National Herbarium of Victoria, an Australian Rainforest Walk and an inspiring Children's Garden. The Ornamental Lake is a popular picnic spot and is adjoined by the Terrace Tea Rooms. A restaurant, outdoor café, Gardens Shop and visitor information centre are located at Observatory Gate. The running track around the garden's perimeter, known locally as "The Tan", is Melbourne's most popular and scenic exercise path. The Royal Botanic Gardens are open daily from 7.30 am to dusk.

Sparkling Southbank

Southbank is a modern shopping and entertainment precinct stretching along the Yarra River south from Princes Bridge directly opposite the Central Business District. Once swampland and river flats, the Yarra's southern bank has been transformed into one of the city's favourite destinations. Near Princes Bridge, Southgate is a diverse complex of shops and restaurants spread over four levels. This colourful riverside venue attracts alfresco diners to its outdoor cafés, while crowds gather to view buskers and performance art (*above right*). A footbridge links the precinct to Flinders Walk and Flinders Street Station, and river cruises and water taxis depart from landings at the water's edge. The Southbank area has become renowned for its presentation of contemporary public sculpture. This open air gallery features work by some of Australia's most critically acclaimed sculptures including Simon Rigg's *The Guardians* on Southbank Promenade (*above left*).

City Nightlife

Unlike some cities, Melbourne's profusion of centrally located restaurants, hotels, theatres, cinemas, bars and nightclubs ensure the CBD remains a vibrant and busy location long after the five o'clock rush. A resurgence in inner city living also breathes life into the CBD after business hours. Nocturnal bars and clubs, unseen by day in the city's lanes, awaken as evening falls. Brilliantly lit streetscapes and riverside promenades signal the transformation of the city's precincts from functional to fun.

Restaurants of every description and style proliferate throughout the CBD, as well as at Southbank, NewQuay and the Crown Entertainment Complex. Chinatown in Little Bourke Street offers a vast choice of Asian cuisine and a Greek quarter features authentic restaurants and taverns near the corner of Lonsdale and Russell streets. King Street boasts a strip of modern nightclubs, several constructed within the old wharfside quarter's restored warehouses.

The Arts Precinct

The Victorian Arts Centre complex comprises four separate theatres and is home to the Melbourne Theatre Company and the Australian Ballet. Hamer Hall is a world-class concert venue hosting the renowned Australian Chamber and Melbourne Symphony Orchestras. The grassed area between the concert hall and theatre complex is utilised for free outdoor concerts and a historic cabaret venue, the dazzling velvet and multi-mirrored Spiegeltent, is erected in warmer months. The adjacent NGV International is regarded as holding Australia's most comprehensive collection of world art and hosts major international touring exhibitions.

Melbourne & Surrounds

Top Things to Do

1. Take tea in historic Royal Arcade.
2. Catch a free City Circle tram around the CBD.
3. Walk the Golden Mile Heritage Trail.
4. Watch a play at the historic Princess Theatre.
5. Visit the Australian Centre for the Moving Image at Federation Square.
6. Explore the Melbourne Museum and Royal Exhibition Building in Carlton Gardens.

Centre Stage

Melbourne's history as a centre for theatre stretches back more than 150 years. The city's first theatre was established in 1841. The Princess Theatre in Spring Street (*above*), built in 1886, is the jewel in the crown of Melbourne's regal performance venues and has presented major international acts from Marlene Dietrich to *The Phantom of the Opera*. Her Majesty's Theatre on Exhibition Street and the Regent Theatre on Collins Street are also heritage theatres still packing in the crowds to musical productions. See the Melbourne Theatre Company's latest productions at Playbox or avant-garde theatre and dance at BlackBox — both within the Victorian Arts Centre.

Dining at Docklands

The re-development of the city's Docklands area has equipped Melbourne with a whole range of waterside dining possibilities. Accessible by tram or via the footbridge from Spencer Street Station, NewQuay is one long strip of indulgence devoted to wining, dining and unwinding by the water. Stylish apartment complexes for a new generation of city dwellers provide the eateries with a trendy local trade. The result is an excellent choice of well-patronised restaurants lapping up the bubbly, near festive, atmosphere, particularly on Friday and Saturday nights. For a real waterside treat, enjoy a pre-dinner drink at Southgate before scooting off on the water taxi to dine at NewQuay.

The Living City

In the second half of the 19th century, the discovery of vast gold deposits in central Victoria delivered a sudden influx of wealth that transformed Melbourne from a ramshackle colonial town to an elegantly attired city. From the early 1850s, gold financed the construction of many civic and commercial buildings that stand today as superb architectural examples of the period. By the 1880s, Melbourne was the second-largest city in the British Empire. Even today, it has the largest number of surviving Victorian-era buildings anywhere in the world outside London. At the northern end of the CBD, on Spring Street, stately Parliament House (the largest 19th century building in Australia) and Old Treasury building (designed by precocious nineteen year old architect John James Clark) watch imperiously over the city. Walk the Golden Mile Heritage Trail, a 4 km journey signposted by brass plaques detailing the history behind many of Melbourne's most significant structures and locations (guided tours and maps available from Melbourne Visitor Centre, Federation Square, Ph: (03) 9658 9658).

The central city area is characterised by two major pedestrian malls, Swanston Walk and Bourke Street Mall, though both continue to allow Melbourne's beloved trams to run down their spines. Without doubt the most startling development of recent times is Federation Square — a head trip of confronting geometry that polarised public opinion when it opened in 2002, but which has rapidly become Melbourne's most distinctive and popular feature.

Trams have been a feature of Melbourne streets since 1887 and remain the most rapid and romantic means of exploring the city. A free City Circle tram painted in cream and burgundy circumnavigates the CBD via Flinders, Latrobe and Spring Streets every 12 minutes and links with trains, buses and light rail services. One of the best vantage points from which to appreciate Melbourne's many facets is the observation deck of the 253 m high Rialto Tower, which offers 360° panoramic views of the city and surrounds. On a clear day, visibility from the tower stretches 60 km to the horizon, taking in the sweeping arc of Port Phillip Bay and the blue of the Dandenong Ranges to the east (525 Collins Street, observation deck open daily).

Melbourne's many lanes and arcades were not always the stylish shopping enclaves they are today. Most simply provided service and drainage access to city buildings and were usually unlit and flooded with water (or worse). Today they are Melbourne's secret treasures, concealing a bevy of designer boutiques, eclectic stores and modish bars. The main arcades have been dubbed the "Magnificent Seven" and run off Little Collins Street between Swanston Walk and Elizabeth Street in the city centre (*see facing page*). Flinders Lane, once the home of Melbourne's rag trade, is perhaps Melbourne's most bohemian quarter, housing within its old warehouses and stores an assortment of craft stores, bars, residential conversions and artists' studios. So where are the some 100 bars located in Melbourne's alleys and lanes? Half the fun is in finding them. Simply follow the crowds at night, or peek within understated doorways and low lit entrances and you'll be surprised what you might discover.

City Icons – Something Old & New

Conceived as a tribute to the first 100 years of Australian nationhood, Melbourne's Federation Square (*top left*) opened in 2002. Situated opposite Flinders Street Station beside the Yarra, its design was the result of an international competition and sparked instant controversy. The spectacularly angled façade of sandstone, glass and zinc makes a striking statement. There are 20 restaurants, cafés and bars throughout the complex and the world's largest collection of Australian art is on display at the Ian Potter Centre: NGV Australia. Federation Square is also home to the Melbourne Visitor Centre, a one-stop info shop for tourists.

Flinders Street Station (*bottom left*) stands on the corner of Flinders and Swanston Streets and has been the hub of the city's rail system since 1854. It has ten platforms, including the 708 m Platform 1 — the fourth longest railway platform in the world. The station's pavilion-like façade resulted from a design competition staged in 1899. It stretches two city blocks to Queen Street and is constructed of granite and basalt. An eight-sided dome rises over the station's main public entrance and the steps below the clocks are a time-honoured meeting place.

Melbourne Shopping

Melbourne is often referred to as the shopping capital of Australia. The city was once divided into several distinct retail precincts — Collins Street for fashion, Bourke Street for household goods and Queen Victoria Market for food. These are still prime shopping zones, but today the city is more akin to a modern bazaar, with fresh possibilities at every turn. The major CBD retail area is bounded by Queen, Flinders, Latrobe and Exhibition Streets. Within this shop-saturated region are Bourke Street Mall with its multi-level department stores, Melbourne Central (*top right*) shopping plaza, the QV "city within a city" complex, Australia on Collins (*top centre*) and many traditional retail arcades.

Royal & Block Arcades

Step into the lavish interior of Melbourne's arcades and you could be in a swank European city quarter of the 19th century. Modelled after the great arcades of London and Paris, the beautiful décor and sublime architectural detail offer a transcendent shopping experience. The Royal Arcade once provided refuge for fashionable lady shoppers escaping the dust and grime of the city streets. For over a century, the arcade has been watched over by statues of the mythical giants Gog and Magog (*top left*), who serve as strikers of Gaunt's Clock. Connecting Collins Street to Little Collins Street, the Block Arcade's elegant shopfronts, etched glass roof, wrought iron and decorative mosaic floor (the country's largest) have lost none of their charm today. Stop for scones at the original Hopetoun Tea Rooms and escape to a more genteel age.

Melbourne Central

Served by its own underground railway station, spreading upward over four levels and across two city blocks, Melbourne Central offers something for everyone. Enter from Swanston Walk or up the escalators from the station and be amazed by the huge and historic brick Shot Tower (*above*) ascending into a glass cone, around which Melbourne Central was built. There are nearly 300 stores here, catering to every desire from food and clothes to jewellery, books, music and toys.

Queen Victoria Market

Melbourne has long been a market town and nothing quite epitomises this tradition as Queen Victoria Market. Bordered by Victoria Street on the northern side of the CBD, this historic market opened officially in 1878 and has become the city's definitive market experience. Featuring a colourful cast of traders, the spirited banter, upbeat energy, competitively priced merchandise and mouth-watering fresh produce create a Melbourne shopping experience unlike any other.

Royal Exhibition Building

The Royal Exhibition Building in Carlton Gardens was purpose-built for Melbourne's International Exhibition of 1880. The building boasts many impressive features including the landmark dome, Great Hall, grand entry portals, internal balconies and manicured gardens. The building and surrounds were the first in Australia to be granted World Heritage status. Prior to the conception of Canberra, the Royal Exhibition Building hosted Australia's first Federal Parliament in 1901.

Melbourne Museum

Located adjacent to the Royal Exhibition Building in Carlton Gardens, Melbourne Museum provides an enthralling perspective on natural sciences, Indigenous cultures, Australian history and cultural heritage. Opened in October 2000, the galleries and exhibition spaces include the Bunjilaka Aboriginal Centre, the Evolution Gallery and Children's Galleries. The 35 m high Forest Gallery is a living interpretation of Victoria's temperate forests incorporating nearly 8000 plants and 20 different vertebrate species, including snakes, birds, fish and frogs. Melbourne Museum also frequently presents major international touring exhibitions. The museum is open 10 am – 5 pm daily (Ph: (03) 8341 7777).

Melbourne Zoo

Spread over 20 ha within Royal Park, Melbourne Zoo is Australia's oldest. Home to over 350 species, the zoo has been meticulously planned to provide its animals with surroundings closely resembling their natural habitat. A magnificent example of the zoo's attention to detail is the Trail of the Elephants, which authentically recreates the environs of a South East Asian village on the fringe of tropical rainforest. The zoo is open 9 am – 5 pm daily (Ph: (03) 9285 9300).

Top Things to Do

1 Shop at St Kilda's Sunday arts and crafts markets on the Upper Esplanade.

2 Cruise the colourful Acland Street strip.

3 Travel by ferry to Williamstown from St Kilda Pier and take in some fresh sea air.

4 Survey the bay from Arthurs Seat.

5 Tour the wineries of the Mornington Peninsula.

6 Laze on the beach at Sorrento.

7 Explore the old fort at Point Nepean.

8 Dine by the bay at Portsea Pub.

9 Surf the longboarding breaks of Shoreham.

Point Nepean

Just a short drive from Portsea is the tip of the Mornington Peninsula at Point Nepean. This slender strip of land just barely protects Port Phillip Bay from the violent swells of Bass Strait. Fort Nepean was built on the point in 1882 to defend Melbourne from a feared attack by the Russians, which never eventuated. Explore the fort's remains, including barracks, gun emplacements, passages and bunkers. Nearby Point Nepean Quarantine Station and Cemetery date from the 1850s. The area was closed to the public for more than a century, but is now part of Mornington Peninsula National Park. A shuttle service operates from Point Nepean Visitor Centre and drops visitors at sites of interest — including Cheviot Beach where Australian Prime Minister Harold Holt disappeared, presumed drowned, while swimming in 1967.

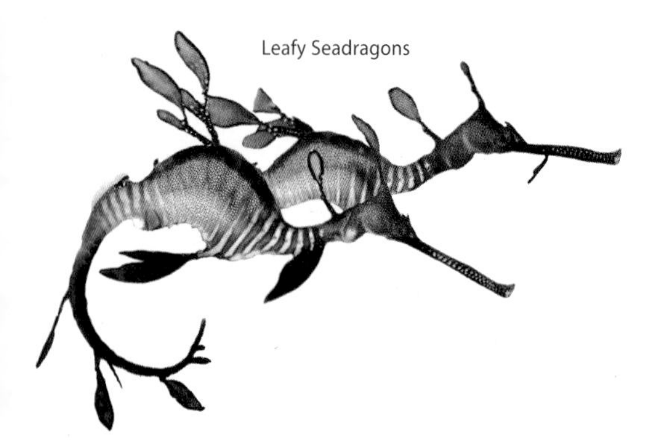
Leafy Seadragons

The Bay & Mornington Peninsula

South of the city along Port Phillip Bay, a single strand of sandy beach links the inner bayside suburbs down to Brighton. The most popular of these is St Kilda. Reborn from a seedy past (a fact that has only fuelled its aura), St Kilda has again become one of the bay's most famous hangouts following its gentrification during the 1990s. Today arty culture and chic urban living collide to create one of Melbourne's most charismatic locations. Along the Upper Esplanade, craft markets draw crowds of Melburnians and beachside visitors. On Acland Street, traditional European cake shops provide a taste of the suburb's multicultural heritage. Backpackers also flock to the seaside area, drawn by the cheapish accommodation, live music and convivial atmosphere. By evening, Fitzroy Street, St Kilda's main thoroughfare, is abuzz with visitors to its popular bars and restaurants. St Kilda Pier juts out into the bay from near the corner of Fitzroy Street and the Esplanade and was first constructed in the 1850s to assist early settlers to receive provisions and timber. The kiosk is a recreation of the original building destroyed by fire in 2003. Ferries and charter boats depart the pier for Williamstown and tours of the remarkably urban Little Penguin colony on St Kilda Breakwater. At Brighton, the pleasures may appear more sedate but at Dendy Street Beach 82 vivaciously decorated and historic bathing boxes give one of the city's most desired addresses a seaside charm of its own.

Mornington Peninsula

The Mornington Peninsula forms the eastern arm of Port Phillip Bay, dividing it from Western Port and hooking round to its tip at Point Nepean. Here, bayside villages include Rosebud, Sorrento and Portsea. On the Western Port side are the small coastal townships of Somers, Shoreham and Flinders. Follow the Nepean Highway or Mornington Peninsula Freeway from Melbourne and plunge into a world of classic seaside getaways. Gently rolling hills, sheltered bay beaches and surfable Bass Strait swells are all found here. Over the last few decades the Peninsula has also fast become recognised as a producer of premium cool-climate wines.

Arthurs Seat

Arthurs Seat, near Dromana, is the highest point on the peninsula — a granite outcrop with an elevation of 304 m set in a state park once home to the Bunurong people. The chairlift (*above*), Seawinds ornamental gardens and Enchanted Maze are highlights. Access is via Nepean Highway and Moorooduc Freeway.

The Briars Park

Within the 240 ha estate of the Briars Park are a faithfully restored 1840s homestead, nature trails, wetlands, birdhides and a restaurant. A surprising bonus when you visit the property is a display of furniture and personal effects once owned by Napoleon Bonaparte (open daily, 9 am – 5 pm, 450 Nepean Highway, Mt Martha, Ph: (03) 5974 3686).

Sorrento

At the turn of the 20th century, Sorrento was a popular seaside retreat and visitors reached Sorrento Back Beach via a steam tram. Today the steam tram has gone, but the beaches, shopping village, restaurants and boutique hotels are more popular than ever. Wander the grass-fringed front beach with its charming jetties or head over to the wild side for bodysurfing and boardriding.

Cape Schank

The southernmost point on the Mornington Peninsula, Cape Schank is a windswept rocky promontory featuring scenic lookouts to Bass Strait and Western Port. Descend the boardwalk to tour the lighthouse (built in 1859) and museum, housed in the old Assistant Lightkeepers Quarters. Accommodation is also available in the keeper's cottage (Ph: 13 19 63).

A Day at the Dandenongs

East of Melbourne on the suburban fringe is a green haven of forested slopes rising up to Mount Dandenong, 700 m above sea level. For thousands of years Aborigines used *Corhanwarrabul*, the Indigenous name for the Dandenong Ranges, as hunting grounds. Following timber felling and clearing in the 1850s, parts of the region were protected. The region became a retreat for the affluent and later — with the advent of the railway and motor car — for the general Melbourne population. Dandenong Ranges National Park was declared in 1987 (*see below right).*

Several excellent drives wind through the Dandenongs and the region's close proximity to Melbourne makes it ideal for daytrips. There are charming villages hidden in the forest and along the ridgetops, as well as numerous walking, cycling and horse riding trails. If you are seeking a longer stay, accommodation in quaint guest houses and luxurious B&Bs is also plentiful. Take the Eastern Freeway from Melbourne to the Maroondah Highway and turn onto Mount Dandenong Road and the Mount Dandenong Tourist Road.

Emerald, at the Dandenong's south-eastern corner, was the first settlement in the ranges. At its heart is a passenger station for the iconic *Puffing Billy* steam train (*see below*). Emerald Lake Park includes two picturesque lakes, lush parklands, picnic grounds, kiosks, paddleboats, a swimming pool and waterslide. Nearby Emerald Lake Model Railway is the Southern Hemisphere's largest working model railway and features 2 km of track (Tues–Sun, 11 am – 4 pm, Ph: (03) 5968 4355). To the north Sassafras, between Ferny Creek and Olinda, is the perfect place to pause for Devonshire tea. At Olinda the acclaimed National Rhododendron Gardens (*see below*) will delight floral aficionados. Further north, head to SkyHigh Mount Dandenong Observatory for brilliant views over Melbourne, Port Phillip Bay and Western Port (Ph: (03) 9751 0443). Alternatively, visit Five Ways Lookout off the Tourist Road at Kalorama with its glorious panorama over the Silvan Reservoir. If you plan to be in the Dandenongs in early March, be sure to explore the Dandenong Ranges Folk Festival, which attracts folk, blues and world music performers.

Puffing Billy

This steam-operated, narrow gauge railway train made its maiden voyage in 1900 and remains a favourite Dandenong attraction. Restaurant cars can mean a scenic luncheon journey through the forest, and children will go nuts over "Thomas the Tank Engine". Operates daily from Belgrave to Emerald and Gembrook (Ph: (03) 9754 6800).

William Ricketts Sanctuary

In the 1930s, Dandenongs resident William Ricketts sculpted these remarkable clay works and carvings in homage to nature's beauty and the original Aboriginal custodians of the land. His property is now a public sanctuary featuring meandering paths through fern gullies and stands of Mountain Ash (open daily, 10 am – 4.30 pm, Ph: 13 19 63).

Mount Dandenong Arboretum

This superb tree conservation reserve near the Mt Dandenong Observatory contains examples of mature deciduous trees and conifers from around the world. The arboretum is a great place to picnic amid the scent of pine needles and views to the Great Dividing Range (Ridge Road, Mt Dandenong, open daily, 10 am – 5 pm, Ph: 13 19 63).

National Rhododendron Gardens

These internationally acclaimed gardens off Georgian Road in Olinda are home to a vast range of brilliant blooms, with plantings of azaleas, camelias, hydrangeas, daffodils and 15,000 rhododendrons. The gardens are framed by stands of the world's tallest flowering plant, the Mountain Ash (open daily, 10 am – 5 pm, Ph: 13 19 63).

Melbourne & Surrounds

Top Things to Do

1. Ride through the Dandenongs on Melbourne's iconic steam train, *Puffing Billy*.
2. Picnic by Emerald Lake.
3. See the city views from the SkyHigh Mount Dandenong Observatory.
4. Have Devonshire tea at Sassafras.
5. Stroll through the National Rhododendron Garden at Olinda.
6. See the intricate sculptures at William Ricketts Sanctuary.
7. Walk or cycle on paths through the ranges.
8. Visit Mount Dandenong Arboretum.

Dandenong Ranges National Park

Visitor Centre: (03) 9758 7522

The park's broad diversity of vegetation includes spectacular Mountain Ash forests (*above*), fern gullies, cool temperate rainforest and woodland. There are also native orchid species throughout the park. The ranges' most famous resident is the Superb Lyrebird (*below*), which lives up to its name by mimicking a huge number of sounds from its environment, including mobile phone ringtones. There are 130 native bird species here including Laughing Kookaburras, Crimson Rosellas and Yellow-faced Honeyeaters. Mammals and reptiles also abound, including some sizeable Lace Monitors.

Walks in the Park: There are over 300 km of tracks in the park. Try the Living Bush Nature Walk or the Ferntree Gully Track in the south-west section of the park.

MELBOURNE to Sydney

Via the Coast or Canberra – The Choice Is Yours

While the quickest route from Melbourne to Sydney is to travel straight up the hectic Hume Highway — around 10 hours drive — there are ample rewards in taking the roads less travelled. Not only will you encounter fewer trucks and less traffic, but the scenic offerings will linger in memory long after your journey is complete — an unlikely event if you stick to the faster (but relatively featureless) Hume. Better to track along the coast on the Princes Highway through Bega or divert from the Hume at Albury–Wodonga and head through the Australian Alps to the nation's capital, Canberra. Australia's incredible topographical diversity is well illustrated by these two contrasting journeys east of the Hume. Both trips are best spread over at least 3–4 days.

Melbourne to Sydney
Top Things to Do

1. Marvel at the technology of the Snowy Mountains Hydro-electric Scheme.
2. Visit Australia's highest town, Cabramurra.
3. Hike or ski among Australia's alps.
4. Match wits with wily trout in Kosciuszko National Park.
5. Tour the museums, galleries and monuments of Australia's capital city, Canberra.
6. Commune with wildlife at Phillip Island.
7. Walk to the end of the continent in Wilsons Promontory National Park.
8. Gear up for game fishing in Merimbula.
9. Discover "surfing kangaroos" on the Clyde Coast.
10. Scuba dive at Jervis Bay National Park.

Sydney via Canberra & the Australian Alps

From Albury–Wodonga, this route heads directly east below the Murray River through Corryong to Khancoban on the western edge of Kosciuszko National Park. This outstanding alpine national park includes Australia's highest peaks and townships, the Thredbo and Perisher Blue ski resorts and regions of completely untouched mountain wilderness. It is traversed by the headwaters of the Snowy River, the heart of the Snowy Mountains Scheme, which diverts water through hydro-electric power stations and then into rivers that irrigate farms west of the Great Dividing Range. Over 100,000 workers from 30 countries were employed on the Scheme from 1949–1974 and several towns in the region, including Cabramurra and Khancoban, were constructed to house them. The old town of Jindabyne was flooded and its community relocated to the new lake shores. The scheme now supplies over 3.5% of Australia's electrical power.

From the major rural centre of Cooma, to Jindabyne's west, the Monaro Highway leads north to Canberra. Australia's capital was also specially constructed to house workers — the members of the nation's federal parliament, public servants and diplomats. Today it is home to many important national institutions, including the Australian War Memorial, National Gallery of Australia, National Library of Australia and National Museum of Australia. From Canberra, the Federal Highway links with the Hume for the final leg through Goulburn to Sydney.

Sydney via the Coast

The Princes Highway leads from Melbourne through the important dairy farming and coal mining region of Gippsland and the Latrobe Valley to the great coastal lakes between Sale and Lakes Entrance. En route, however, there are two essential detours — Phillip Island (holiday retreat and home to seals and penguins at the mouth of Western Port) and Wilsons Promontory (a mountainous national park jutting into Bass Strait). Back on the main route, the highway meets the Snowy River on its way to the ocean near Orbost, before continuing over the Victorian border near Mallacoota. The southern New South Wales coast is lined with historic beach resort and fishing towns from Eden almost all the way to Wollongong. A short distance inland, a continuous chain of national parks protects the flora and fauna of the Great Dividing Range. On the coast east of Nowra, Jervis Bay National Park is one of Australia's best marine diving and photography regions. To the north is the provincial capital of Wollongong and the natural splendour of Royal National Park, Australia's oldest reserve, on Sydney's coastal fringe.

Nature Unbound

From the alpine wilderness of the nation's highest peaks to the picturesque coastline of the eastern seaboard, Australia's south-east region is still dominated by nature. Much of the region's population is concentrated in a thin strip of towns hugging the coast — perfectly positioned bases for exploring both mountains and sea.

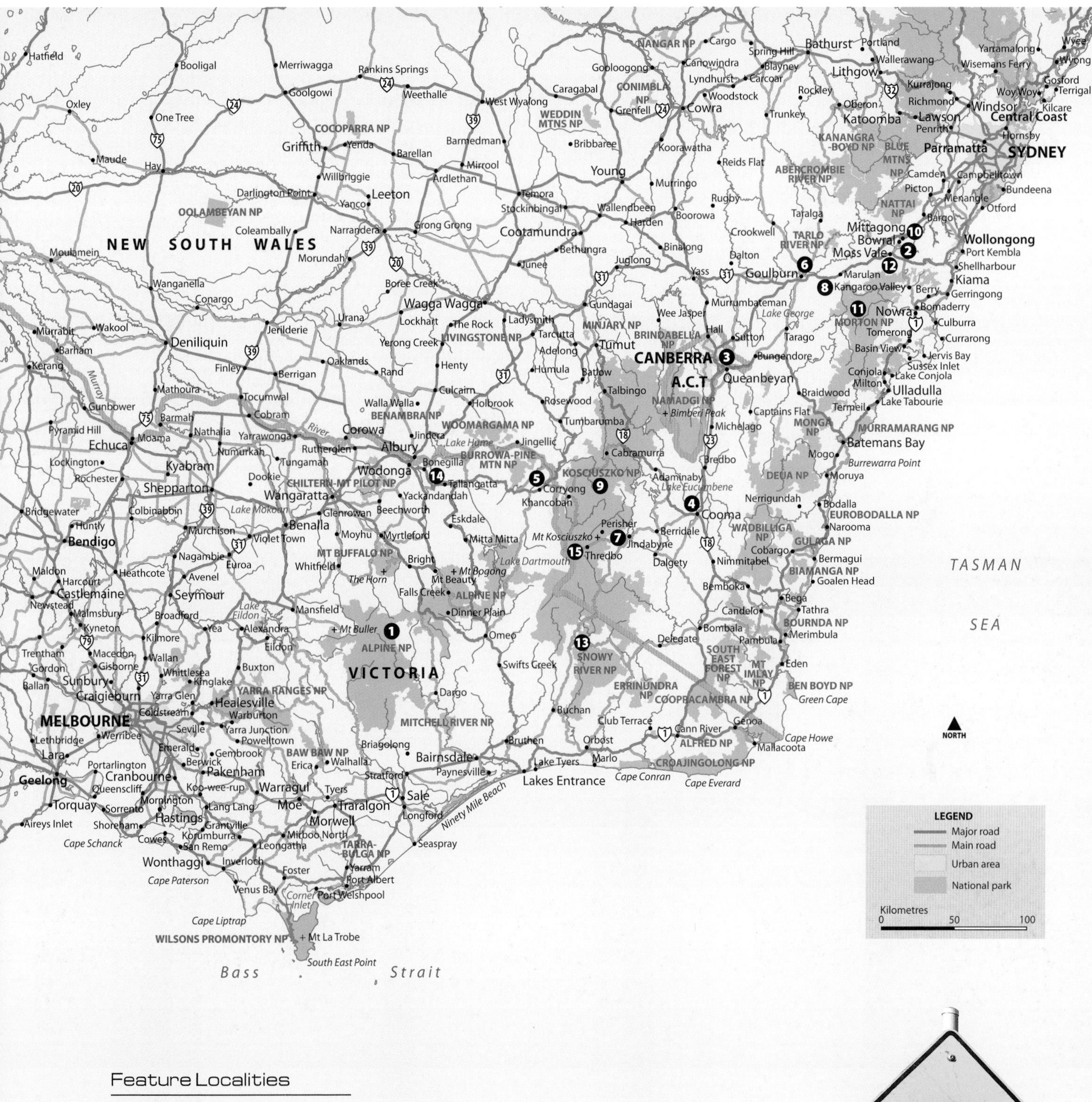

Feature Localities

1 Alpine National Park
2 Bowral
3 Canberra
4 Cooma
5 Corryong
6 Goulburn
7 Jindabyne
8 Kangaroo Valley
9 Kosciuszko National Park
10 Mittagong
11 Morton National Park
12 Moss Vale
13 Snowy River National Park
14 Tallangatta
15 Thredbo

Melbourne to Sydney
Top Things to Do

1. Relive the glory days of *The Man from Snowy River* at Corryong.
2. Get on your bike. Cycle the High Country Rail Trail around Lake Hume to Tallangatta.
3. Strap on your skis and assault the slopes at Thredbo and Perisher Blue.
4. Make tracks in the wild. Go cross-country skiing through the Snowy Mountains.
5. Ride the Skitube to Perisher Valley.
6. Soak up some alpine sun on a summer trek through Kosciuszko National Park.
7. Enjoy the Easter exhibitions of Lake Light Sculpture on the shores of Lake Jindabyne.
8. Uncover Indigenous history with a walk through Lambie Gorge in Cooma.

Where the Rivers Rise

Snow and rain on the peaks of Kosciuszko National Park and adjacent Alpine and Snowy River National Parks feed mountain streams that merge and expand into huge rivers as they descend the high slopes.

In Kosciuszko National Park these fast-flowing waters have been dammed to create reservoirs that include Khancoban Dam, Blowering Reservoir, Talbingo Reservoir, Tantangara Reservoir and the mammoth Lake Eucumbene. The rivers' power is harnessed for hydro-electricity generation and stored water is also re-distributed for regional crop irrigation.

Lake Eucumbene and the upper Murray, Thredbo and Snowy Rivers together comprise some of mainland Australia's most highly regarded fly-fishing destinations.

Albury-Wodonga to Canberra

Beyond Lake Hume, the Murray Valley Highway leads to Tallangatta and Corryong. Tallangatta was originally located 10 km north before the old town was submerged in 1956 to create greater storage capacity in the dam. Tallangatta's river valley surrounds are extremely picturesque but the town's most interesting aspect is that, having been built from scratch in the 1950s, it still seems somewhat frozen in time. This is a fact celebrated by the town in the Tallangatta 50s Festival held on the last Sunday of October each year, when up to 4000 slicked-back rock 'n' rollers cruise into town to shake, rattle and roll. After the juke box stops playing and the hot rods leave town, you might like to hire a bike and cycle the 10 km High Country Rail Trail to the old township and the Lake Hume foreshore.

Corryong is celebrated as the resting place of *The Man from Snowy River*, Jack Riley, about whom Banjo Paterson reputedly wrote his famous poem. Visit *The Man from Snowy River* Museum (103 Hanson Street, Ph: (02) 6076 2600) or see the poem come to life through incredible horse riding feats at *The Man from Snowy River* Bush Festival, staged on the last weekend of March. Khancoban, on the western edge of the Kosciuszko National Park, was built to accommodate workers on the Snowy Mountains Scheme. The town overlooks Khancoban Dam and is a popular trout-fishing base, but despite neatly laid out streets and ample services still has a somewhat temporary feel about it. Cast a fly, visit the nearby Murray 1 Power Station or enjoy the expansive mountain views from Olsens and Scammels Spur Lookouts. South of Khancoban the Alpine Way winds around Mount Kosciuszko through Tom Groggin, another attractive trout-fishing and camping spot on the upper reaches of the Murray River. North, the road leads through Australia's highest town, Cabramurra (1488 m above sea level), to Kiandra on the Snowy Mountains Highway. Now a ghost town, Kiandra became the birthplace of Australian skiing in 1861.

Ski Resorts

Twenty winding kilometres east of Tom Groggin, through Dead Horse Gap, lies the ski village of Thredbo. Drive slowly in winter and on weekends as conditions can be treacherous and traffic heavy on this section of road, particularly around late afternoon. Thredbo generally receives excellent snow coverage from June to October each year and the installation of the Southern Hemisphere's largest remote controlled snow-making system has further extended the annual ski season. Chairlifts were first installed in 1956 and today there are twelve lifts capable of transporting nearly 18,000 skiers per hour to Australia's longest ski runs. In summer there are many fine walking and mountain bike trails throughout the Thredbo region. The "Skitube", a tunnel railway 15 km east of the village, links with Perisher Blue and Blue Cow Mountain to the north, saving skiers from driving through Jindabyne.

Jindabyne & Cooma

Like Tallangatta, and Adaminaby to its north, the original town of Jindabyne was drowned to form a dam. Even now, when the lake level is low, remnants of the old town can still be seen. At half the size of Sydney Harbour, the trout-stocked waters of Lake Jindabyne have become a major fishing, boating and watersport playground. At Easter, an illuminated pathway around the foreshore becomes an outdoor gallery for fantastic displays of sculpture. The surrounding high country is equally compelling. The streams and rivers teem with fit wild salmon and trout. Horse riding and mountain biking are just as popular — you can follow a signed trail from Lake Crackenback through scenic locations featured in the 2006 film *Jindabyne*. For travellers from Sydney and Canberra the town is a gateway to the skifields and Kosciuszko National Park and has a wide range of cosy accommodation options, restaurants and entertainment venues.

Long a sleepy grazing centre, Cooma was thrust into the spotlight when it became the main headquarters for the Snowy Mountains Hydro-electric Scheme in 1949. The sudden melting pot of workers from around the world saw Cooma become Australia's most multicultural town. It remains the home of Snowy Hydro and is the "capital" of the Snowy Mountains. Visit the Snowy Mountains Scheme Information and Education Centre in North Cooma (Monaro Highway, Ph: 1800 623 776) — a state-of-the-art facility with a great exhibition hall, interactive displays and a monument paying tribute to workers who lost their lives on the scheme. Cooma is famed for its memorials, statues and public art, including the historic Avenue of Flags along Sharp Street on Centennial Park. The flags represent the peoples of 28 nations who came to Cooma from 1949–1975. Also in Centennial Park is a statue of *The Man from Snowy River* and the Mosaic Time Walk, a beautiful and detailed collection of ceramic sagas depicting the district's history. Walk historic Lambie Street, take a stroll to nearby Lambie Gorge or enjoy the country views from Nanny Goat Hill.

Clockwise from top left: Forests of Alpine Ash populate the valley floors of Kosciuszko National Park; The broad plateaux are a famous location for cross-country skiing; The park features Australia's highest ski resorts; The region is a superb walking location after the thaw.

Kosciuszko National Park

Phone Ranger: 02 6450 5600

Kosciuszko, the largest national park in NSW, is the main link in a chain of alpine national parks and reserves stretching between the ACT and northern Victoria. A series of worn granite peaks, several exceeding 2000 m, cap this high plateau of rolling meadows. Long narrow valleys and steep western gorges cut into the plateau, carrying rain and melted snow to river systems and reservoirs.

Dense forests with fern gullies and stands of giant Alpine Ash shelter on the valley floors and lower slopes. With increasing altitude, Snow Gums become gnarled, twisted trees marking the edges of alpine plains. From late June through September, the park's Main Range becomes a powder playground for downhill skiers and snowboarders. Thredbo, Perisher and Smiggin Holes attract skiers from around Australia, but resorts and groomed runs occupy less than 1% of the park. The beauty and isolation of the Snowy Mountains' natural snowfields have been luring adventurous cross-country skiers since the 1860s. Flagged trails around the resorts offer great half and full day outings or can be used to launch longer excursions through the back country and lower plains. A popular attraction in the northern section of the park is Yarrangobilly Caves, four of which are open to the public. The thermal pools at Yarrangobilly (with a year-round temperature of 27 °C) provide the perfect remedy for warming chilled bones.

Walks in the Park: By November the snow has melted. Summer brings ideal conditions for walking on Australia's rooftop — an explosion of native wildflowers ignites the meadows and the soothing trickle of pretty glacial lakes can be heard. Numerous alpine tracks of varying length and difficulty feature clear views across barren peaks to distant horizons. Horse riders are also welcome at Kosciuszko, where the Bicentennial Trail picks up some of the old stock routes through high plains country. For experienced walkers, the open country makes map-and-compass navigation easy, but backpackers need to be prepared for wet, cold conditions, even in summer.

Access: From Albury–Wodonga via Khancoban on the Murray Valley Highway. From Canberra via Cooma and Jindabyne.

Camping: Sites and cabins at Sawpit Creek. Basic facilities located along the Alpine Way, Barry Way and the lower Snowy River. Conditions apply to bush camping.

Some Special
Walks to Take

1. The two most popular main trails ascend Mount Kosciuszko via the 25 km circuit from Charlottes Pass or a 13 km return walk from the top of the Crackenback chairlift at Thredbo.
2. Shorter trails taking in cascading mountain creeks and lush forest centre on the Sawpit Creek camping area.
3. Those seeking a journey of epic proportions can tackle all or part of the 650 km Australian Alps Walking Track which runs from Namadgi NP through Kosciuszko to Baw Baw NP.
4. Bushwalkers will find the Main Range area exhilarating.

Nature of the Alps

With most of the continent being relatively flat, the Great Dividing Range is home to wildlife favouring a more mountainous habitat. Over 40 mammal, 200 bird, 30 reptile, 15 amphibian and 14 native fish species are found in the Australian Alps. The wildlife most frequently encountered are birds. Species include the slate-grey Gang-gang Cockatoo (one of only a few native birds to tolerate high altitudes in winter), blue and red Crimson Rosellas and the melodious mainstay of the nation's bird collective, the Australian Magpie.

Patient observers will be rewarded with chance meetings with kangaroos, bats, Echidnas or the Common Wombat, which can be seen foraging at night. There are also some reclusive Emus living in the Alps, but they are rarely seen as they stay out of sight when humans are in the vicinity. Many species of mammal are endemic to the Alps, including the Brush-tailed Rock-wallaby and the Mountain Pygmy-possum — the latter once thought to be extinct.

Alpine Boronia The pink, star-shaped flowers of this small, woody shrub are highly perfumed and appear in late spring and summer in the heathland and dry sclerophyll forests of the Alps.

Snow Gums On the lower alps, larger trees, their branches and trunks twisted low to the ground, shelter beside rocky outcrops. Their roots are protected by an understorey of low woody shrubs and grasses able to tolerate the dry, icy conditions.

Alpine Flora

Alpine flora must weather extremely harsh conditions. Generally, alpine plant communities are made up of species with similar preferences and tolerances for particular environmental conditions. On the lower slopes, the vegetation begins with spaced, low-growing trees that allow sunlight to shine on the forest floors. Interestingly, as the elevation increases, the trees become taller, until a band of tall open forest dominated by Alpine Ash is reached at the treeline. Above this are the subalpine and alpine zones. On the exposed rocky ridges, soil is sparse but scattered shrubby heath, ground-hugging feldmark and snowpatch communities endure.

Snow Myrtle Australia has about 1400 species in the Myrtaceae family. The Snow Myrtle, widespread in the Victorian Alps, has dark-green, heath-like leaves and flowers in spring.

Clockwise from top left: Snow Gums and flowering heath ground cover; *Acacia* species are common in Kosciuszko National Park; Silver Snow Daisies are common and widespread perennial herbs that often form extensive carpets; Candle Heath grows in alpine and subalpine habitats of Kosciuszko National Park; Slender Myoporum, an uncommon Snowy Mountain plant.

Left to right: The Mountain Pygmy-possum is a timid creature that makes its nest among boulders; Common Wombats may be encountered during early morning and late afternoon forays in grassy areas.

Encountering Mammals

Some of the most widespread mammals are large browsing and grazing marsupials such as the Common Wombat, Red-necked Wallaby, Swamp Wallaby and Eastern Grey Kangaroo. The Brush-tailed Rock-wallaby is rare and confined to colonies on rocky cliffs in the Upper Snowy area of the Alps. Look out for smaller mammals living in the forests, including the rare Smoky Mouse, the Long-nosed Bandicoot, and marsupial carnivores such as the Brown and Dusky Antechinus and the Spotted-tailed Quoll. Other marsupials include the tree-dwelling Common Brushtail (*right*), Mountain Brushtail (or Bobuck) and ringtail possums. Diminutive Eastern and Mountain Pygmy-possums and gliders may occasionally be seen. Much less common is the Leadbeater's Possum, found only in mature forests of Mountain and Alpine Ash.

There are also nine species of bat here, including Gould's Wattled Bat, the Lesser Long-eared Bat and the Chocolate Wattled Bat. Few colonies of cave bats are recorded in the Alps and the only fruit-eating bats in the high country are summer visitors.

Left to right: Gang-gang Cockatoo; Scarlet Robin; Australian Magpie.

Birdwatching in the Alps

Birdlife in the Alps is prolific. Open woodlands provide plenty of habitat for birds, including robins, the Eastern Spinebill and White-throated Treecreeper. Common species that make their home in this region include Australian King-Parrots, Superb Lyrebirds, Crimson Rosellas, Laughing Kookaburras, Yellow-faced Honeyeaters, Gang-gang Cockatoos, Fan-tailed Cuckoos and Emus. Birdwatchers will also delight in seeing the country's largest raptor, the imposing Wedge-tailed Eagle, soaring above crags and swooping into valleys. Alpine areas are also important locations for endangered species such as the Barking Owl and Turquoise Parrot. Many birds typical of lowland grasslands and forests are commonly observed in the high Alps during summer. Species seen at the highest elevations include the Flame Robin, Pied Currawong, Grey Currawong, Nankeen Kestrel, Masked Lapwing, Australian Pipit and Little Raven.

Wildlife of the Rivers & Streams

Freshwater crayfish (*above*) and yabbies can be found in the mountain streams. The Mountain Galaxia is a native fish that averages only about 13 cm in length. It survives in the smaller streams above the treeline through its astonishing ability to jump out of the water and clamber up steep rocks and waterfalls. This fragile but acrobatic fish also "walks" over rocks and splashes in shallow pools in order to regulate its body temperature.

Brown Trout and Rainbow Trout were introduced to Australia's alpine waterways in the late 19th century, forcing a retreat of the once prolific galaxia to higher ground.

Reptiles & Amphibians

Some commonly encountered reptiles in the high country include the Alpine Water Skink, McCoy's Skink, Grass Skink, Copperhead (*below*) and Eastern Blue-tongue. Watch also for the Baw Baw Frog (in Victoria) and the strikingly-skinned Corroboree Frog (*above*) in NSW and the ACT. In summer, look for lizards lounging on rocks around alpine summits in the heat of the day.

CANBERRA & the ACT

Canberra & the ACT

Top Things to Do

1 Visit Canberra's original homesteads at Duntroon, Blundell's Cottage and Lanyon Homestead.

2 Stroll the shores of Lake Burley Griffin.

3 Visit the Australian War Memorial.

4 Tour Old Parliament House.

5 Inspect the National Gallery of Australia.

6 Enjoy the fresh air and floral environs of the Australian National Botanic Gardens.

7 Explore history at the National Museum of Australia and National Dinosaur Museum.

8 Check out the Deep Space Communication Complex at Tidbinbilla Nature Reserve.

9 Examine the lay of the land from Mt Ainslie.

Original Homesteads

Prior to being selected as the site for Australia's capital, the Canberra district was renowned as bountiful farmland. In 1911, a former sheep farming estate settled by Scottish emigrant Robert Campbell (in 1825) became the nation's Royal Military College — Duntroon (*above*). Campbell had been granted the land and some 710 sheep in compensation for the loss of his ship *Sydney*, which had been wrecked off the Indian coast while in government service. His son's 1853 homestead, Duntroon House, now serves as the Officer's Mess. Guided tours are available of the military facility.

Blundell's Cottage (*top*) was built around 1858 as the Campbell's ploughman's house and later became home to the family of their bullock driver, George Blundell. It now rests on the shores of Lake Burley Griffin and is open to the public daily.

Bearing a cloak of green and an air of monumental elegance, Canberra — purpose-built as Australia's federal capital — has defied expectations of dour political functionality to become a city of specific interest and unique character. Set amid farmland and native forest at the base of Black Mountain in the Australian Capital Territory, Canberra is affectionately called the "Bush Capital".

Canberra History

Canberra is located on limestone plains beneath the north-eastern slopes of the Australian Alps, part of the ancient lands of the Ngunnawal Aboriginal people. Settlers first visited the area in the 1820s, successfully establishing pastoral properties around where the city now stands. English emigrant Joshua Moore took up a land grant in 1822, naming his stock station "Canberry" based on a Ngunnawal word for the region (later said to mean "meeting place"). The area was first considered as potential site for Australia's capital after a state premiers' meeting in 1899, at which it was agreed that the site should lie within New South Wales, but be at least 100 miles from Sydney. No less than 45 sites were proposed for the capital by the time of federation and over the next 8 years, federal parliament debated the relative merits of locations that included Dalgety, Albury, Tumut, Bombala and Canberra.

In 1911, the Federal Capital Territory (FCT) was formally declared. Canberra's distinctive layout was the vision of innovative Chicago architect Walter Burley Griffin, who won an international design competition staged in 1911. At that time, the fledgling territory had a total population of 1714 non-Indigenous people and over 224,000 sheep. Griffin trumped the other 137 aspiring designers and his original sketches and plans, submitted on cotton cloth, are now preserved in the National Archives of Australia. Griffin's carefully considered "land axis/water axis" design incorporated broad avenues radiating out from Capital Hill to spacious, hexagonally arranged suburbs, all framed by the surrounding ranges.

While numerous commonwealth offices and institutions were founded in the Federal Capital Territory from 1911 onward, federal parliament did not take up its new home until 1927. The parliament convened in Melbourne until Canberra's Parliament House was completed. Disagreements between Griffin and the government, and the intervention of World War I, slowed construction of the city's infrastructure and public buildings. By 1918, the city's population included German nationals confined at the Molonglo internment camp in what is now the suburb of Fyshwick. The camp was later converted to housing for construction workers and their families. The ornamental lake at Canberra's centre, formed by the damming of the Molonglo River, was first suggested in 1908 but not built until 55 years later. Despite Walter Burley Griffin having been removed from his post by Prime Minister Billy Hughes in 1921, the lake was named in the architect's honour. Old Parliament House opened in 1927 (acting as the home of federal parliament until 1988) and in 1938, the Federal Capital Territory became the Australian Capital Territory (ACT).

Event Capital

The national capital hosts a wide range of annual events. See the city burst into bloom during the Floriade Festival (Sept–Oct) or watch hot air balloons lift from the lawns of Old Parliament House during the Canberra Balloon Fiesta (Apr). Music fans luxuriate in the National Folk Festival (Easter), the Canberra International Chamber Music Festival (May) and the Classical Jazz and Ragtime Festival (Nov). Other events of note are Australia's ultimate rev-head show, the Summernats Car Festival (Jan), the city's group hug, Celebrate Canberra (Mar) and the National Multicultural Festival (Feb).

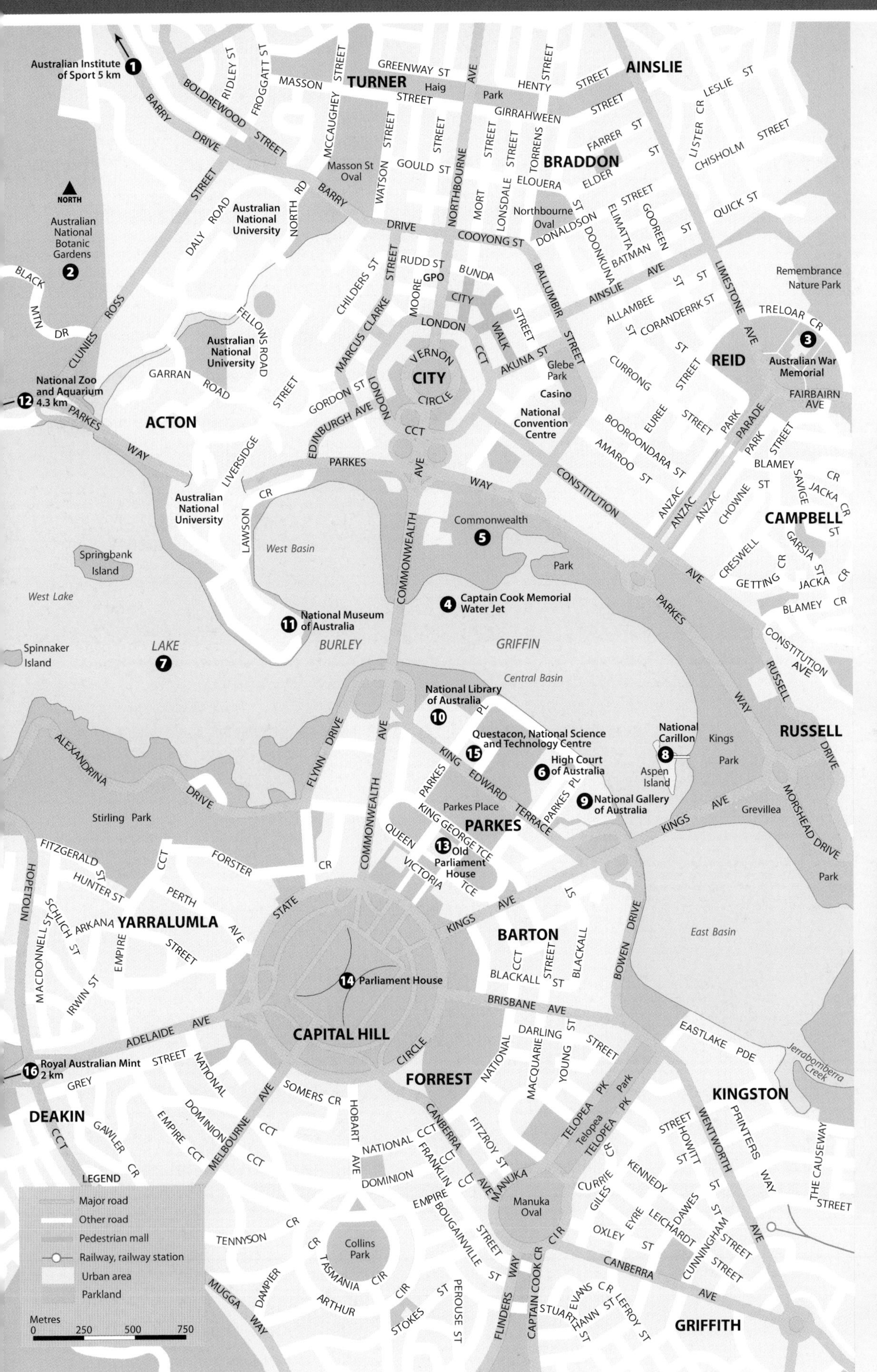

Feature Localities

1. Australian Institute of Sport
2. Australian National Botanic Gardens
3. Australian War Memorial
4. Captain Cook Memorial Water Jet
5. Commonwealth Park
6. High Court of Australia
7. Lake Burley Griffin
8. National Carillon
9. National Gallery of Australia
10. National Library of Australia
11. National Museum of Australia
12. National Zoo and Aquarium
13. Old Parliament House
14. Parliament House
15. Questacon, National Science & Technology Centre
16. Royal Australian Mint

A Federation Flag

Perpetually fluttering above the aluminium flagpole of Parliament House is the symbol of a nation's history and unification. The Australian flag, which combines the British Union Jack with a representation of the Southern Cross and a large "Star of Federation" was selected from more than 30,000 designs in 1901 and became the official flag in 1954.

Tidbinbilla Nature Reserve

A 40 minute drive from Canberra's city centre, Tidbinbilla Nature Reserve is located in a scenic valley lying between the Tidbinbilla and Gibraltar Ranges. Together with Namadgi National Park, Tidbinbilla forms the northern section of the Australian Alps. The mountains surrounding *Tidbinbilla* (derived from an Aboriginal word for "a place where boys are made men") contain numerous Indigenous sites and rock shelters. The 21,000 year old Birrigai Rock Shelter is the ACT's oldest known Aboriginal site. Pioneer houses and other remnants from the area's colonial settlement also survive within Tidbinbilla Valley. Wildlife to watch out for in the reserve includes lyrebirds, kangaroos, possums, wombats, echidnas, Platypuses and Emus. The visitor centre (*above*) has displays that focus on the region's history and also provides walking maps (Ph: (02) 6205 1233).

Tidbinbilla Observatory

The Canberra Deep Space Communication Complex (*above*) is another Tidbinbilla feature. As one of the integral sites of NASA's Deep Space Network, the complex is part of an international network of antennas supporting exploration and scientific research throughout the cosmos.

Lanyon Homestead

This historic homestead, set in pleasure gardens near the Murrumbidgee River, has been faithfully restored and furnished in mid-19th century style. Picnic on the lawns or dine at the café and take a guided tour or wander the beautiful grounds. (Tues–Sun, 10 am – 4 pm, Ph: (02) 6235 5677).

Exploring Canberra & the Australian Capital Territory

Set amid imposing ranges and sprawling native forests, Canberra is a city artfully designed to serve its people. From the shores of Lake Burley Griffin, tree-shaded boulevards lead to leafy suburbs. The city centre merges original 1920s architecture with modern shopping plazas, malls, government offices and corporate headquarters.

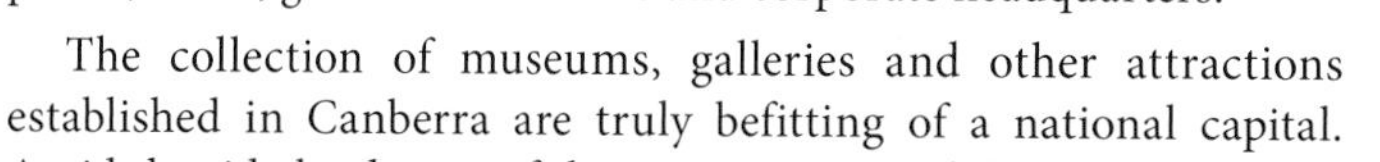

The collection of museums, galleries and other attractions established in Canberra are truly befitting of a national capital. Amid the tidy landscape of this city are some of the country's most revered works of art and historic monuments. The parliament buildings (both old and new) align along an axis with the Australian War Memorial and Mount Ainslie in the south.

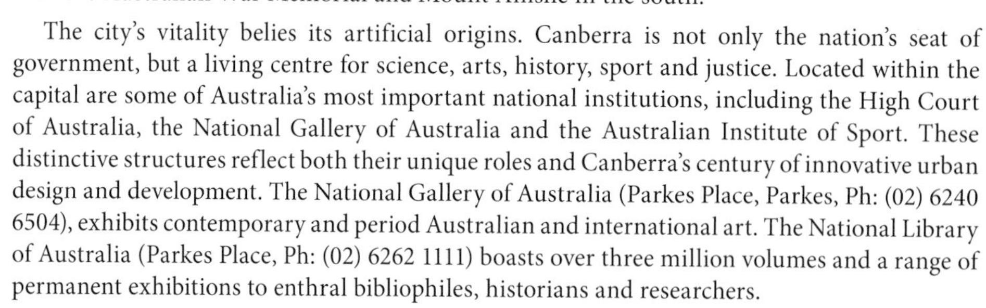

The city's vitality belies its artificial origins. Canberra is not only the nation's seat of government, but a living centre for science, arts, history, sport and justice. Located within the capital are some of Australia's most important national institutions, including the High Court of Australia, the National Gallery of Australia and the Australian Institute of Sport. These distinctive structures reflect both their unique roles and Canberra's century of innovative urban design and development. The National Gallery of Australia (Parkes Place, Parkes, Ph: (02) 6240 6504), exhibits contemporary and period Australian and international art. The National Library of Australia (Parkes Place, Ph: (02) 6262 1111) boasts over three million volumes and a range of permanent exhibitions to enthral bibliophiles, historians and researchers.

Canberra's civic squares, gardens and public spaces are punctuated by monuments, sculptures and impressive displays of public art. Some of the boldest examples of public art are the seventeen large-scale pieces found in the National Gallery of Australia's Sculpture Garden. Here acacias, banksias, eucalypts and other Australian native plants form natural exhibition spaces for works of some of the world's best known sculptors.

Lake Burley Griffin forms the city's geographical centre and is one of the most attractive spots to begin an exploration of the Australian capital. It is around 11 km long, a little over a kilometre wide at its widest point, has 40 km of shoreline and is dotted with six islands. One of the larger islands is Aspen Island, connected to shore by a footbridge. It is the site of the Australian National Carillon, an immense bell tower (with a total of 55 bells) that was presented to the Australian people by the British government to commemorate the 50th anniversary of Canberra as the nation's capital. Also located on the lake is the Captain Cook Memorial Jet, a powerful water fountain that propels regular blasts of water 150 m into the air (*bottom*). The memorial also includes the Terrestrial Globe, which depicts Cook's three major Australian maritime explorations.

Embassies

The embassies are concentrated around the inner lakeside suburbs of Yarralumla, Deakin and O'Malley. The United States established the first embassy in Canberra in 1946 — a classic Virginian mansion styled building on Commonwealth Avenue. There are now over 80 embassies and high commissions based in Canberra. Many, including the Thai, Chinese, Indonesian and Japanese embassies are spectacularly designed to reflect their nation's cultural heritage.

Lake Burley Griffin

Lake Burley Griffin is the capital's focal point for recreation. The artificial lake commemorates the city's designer, American architect Walter Burley Griffin, and provides a tranquil setting for some of Canberra's most significant buildings and monuments. Yachting and hot air ballooning are popular pursuits throughout the year and the lake's shores create a pleasant setting for the city's walkers, runners, cyclists and fitness devotees.

Autumn & Spring

While Canberra experiences bitterly cold and frosty winters, autumn and spring bring milder temperatures and paint the city's leafy environs and gardens with a glorious pallette of colours. Each September, over one million bulbs bloom in Commonwealth Park, signalling the commencement of the Floriade Festival. Four weeks of floral exhibitions and entertainment follow, inspired by the famous Dutch flower festivals.

Memorials to the Fallen

The Australian War Memorial is the nation's grandest tribute to the sacrifices of those who suffered and lost their lives in conflict. Conceived by Australian war historian Charles Bean, and completed in 1941, the sandstone structure set among eucalypts and manicured lawns includes a comprehensive war museum, the Flame of Remembrance and the Tomb of the Unknown Soldier.

Shopping in Canberra

Canberra offers a full complement of shopping experiences. The modern Canberra Centre (Bunda St) has more than 200 retail outlets and department stores. Also explore the range of vintage clothing, bric-a-brac and furniture at the Canberra Antiques Centre (37 Townsville St, Fyshwick). For fresh produce, visit the Belconnen Fresh Food Markets (Lathlain St), or find handicrafts and gourmet food at the excellent Old Bus Depot Markets (Sun, 10 am – 4 pm, Wentworth Ave, Kingston).

Old & New Parliament House

Nowhere is Canberra's contrast of history and modernity more spectacularly illustrated than on Capital Hill. Soaring behind the white facade of the original home of Australia's parliament is the 81 m flagpole of the new Parliament House, opened in 1988. Presiding majestically over Lake Burley Griffin, the buildings align on a land axis linking Canberra's most prominent topographic features. The original Parliament House was designed by Commonwealth Architect John Smith Murdoch and was inaugurated in 1927. It is now a museum and home to the National Portrait Gallery. "New" Parliament House was designed by American-based architects Mitchell, Giurgola and Thorp, and is surrounded by 23 ha of landscaped gardens (open daily for leisurely walks). Guided tours of both buildings are available daily (Old Parliament House, Ph: (02) 6270 8282, Parliament House, Ph: (02) 6277 5399).

Australian War Memorial

The Australian War Memorial is one of the world's great war museums and a national treasure (Treloar Crescent, Campbell, Ph: (02) 6243 4211).

Over the last century, the Australian War Memorial has amassed a vital collection of wartime artefacts and historical pieces. Holdings include official and private records and logs, photographs, heraldry, military technology and family histories relating to Australian servicemen and women. Take a guided tour or peruse the galleries and exhibition rooms at length — half a day will fly by as you explore the vital history on display here.

Mount Ainslie, behind the AWM and accessed via walking tracks at the rear of the building, is an excellent high point overlooking Canberra and affords a splendid view straight down Anzac Parade to Lake Burley Griffin and Parliament House beyond. It provides an ideal aspect for examining the city's land axis — a key feature of Griffin's original plan linking Red Hill and Mt Ainslie. Lake Burley Griffin and the mountain ranges that surround the city are also visible from here and the views of Parliament, Anzac Parade and the AWM are exceptional.

Honouring the Fallen

Canberra's most spectacular vista is the grand Anzac Parade (*above*). Its broad, distinctive red gravel walkway escorts the eye from the Australian War Memorial to Parliament House. Ten memorials are located on the parade, including the New Zealand Memorial (*above top*), the Korean War Memorial (*above, centre*) and the Rats of Tobruk Memorial.

National Zoo & Aquarium

Located just 5 minutes from the city centre, this fascinating sanctuary is Australia's only combined zoo and aquarium. The complex is home to native and exotic animals as well as numerous marine exhibits. The zoo also has a healthy population of big cats, giving you the opportunity to see exotic rarities such as a Tigon or King Cheetah — one of only 20–25 in existence. Thirty-four endangered species are conserved here, with several being the focus of breeding programs (open daily, 10 am – 5 pm, Lady Denman Drive, Ph: (02) 6287 8400).

Australian National Botanic Gardens

Set on a 90 ha tenure at the foot of Black Mountain are the Australian National Botanic Gardens. With both a scientific and aesthetic emphasis on native plants, the Australian National Botanic Gardens contains one of the country's best and most thoughtfully ordered collections of Australian flora. Arranged in taxonomic, geographic or horticultural groups, 99,000 individual plants (from 6800 different species) make up the gardens. Highlights of the gardens are the climatic zones designed to replicate the actual environment of specific plant habitats — desert, rainforest and mountain. Trails follow the landscaped Rainforest Gully, Eucalypt Garden, Rock Garden and Mallee Shrublands (open daily, 8.30 am – 5 pm, extended to 6 pm weekdays and 8 pm weekends in January, Clunies Ross Street, Acton, Ph: (02) 6250 9450).

Cockington Green Gardens

Fifteen kilometres north of Canberra is another artificial town, albeit on a smaller scale than the national capital. This village features miniature buildings (scaled in exacting detail) set within charming landscaped gardens. Visit the Rose Room indoor exhibition, featuring "Waverly", a 34 room dolls house, lunch at the café or pack a picnic. A Miniature Steam Train ride encircles the International Display (open daily, 9.30 am – 5 pm, Gold Creek Road, Nicholls, Ph: 1800 627 273).

Royal Australian Mint

Australia's national mint was established to produce the nation's first batch of decimal coins (introduced in 1966). Since its opening, the mint has produced over eleven billion circulating coins and has the capacity to produce over two million coins per day, or over six hundred million coins per year (open daily, Denison Street, Deakin, Ph: 1300 65 2020).

Questacon – National Science & Technology Centre

Appealing to the science and technology geek in all of us, Questacon takes its visitors on a fascinating journey of discovery, with exhibits that bring the physical world and its natural phenomena within reach of inquisitive minds. Through its entertaining and interactive displays, the institution demonstrates the impact of science and technology on everyday life. Visitors can get close to a lightning bolt, experience an earthquake, watch a tornado rage in a cage or freefall 6 m down a vertical slide, emerging unscathed at the bottom (open daily (except Christmas) 9 am – 5 pm, King Edward Terrace, Ph: 1800 020 603).

Black Mountain Tower

One of the best places from which to survey Canberra's layout is Black Mountain Tower, rising almost 200 m above the surrounding landscape. (Black Mountain Drive, Acton, Canberra, Ph: (02) 6219 6111). The communications tower has two open-air viewing platforms and an enclosed viewing area for 360° panoramic sightseeing. The tower also houses a telecommunications museum, café, gift shop and revolving restaurant. In 1989, the World Federation of Great Towers admitted Black Mountain Tower into a select group of noted architectural structures, which includes London's Blackpool Tower and New York's Empire State Building. Helping visitors keep their bearings, this local landmark has become one of Canberra's most recognisable attractions (open daily, 9 am – 10 pm).

Australian Institute of Sport

Known simply as the AIS or "The Institute", this is Australia's peak facility for elite athletes. Since 1981, the AIS has been at the forefront of sports science and has helped orchestrate the world-beating performances of Australian sportsmen and sportswomen in more than 25 different sports. Major sculptures at the AIS include *Basketballer* by Dominique Sutton (*top*) and *The Acrobats* (*top*) and *Soccer Players* (*above*), both by John Robinson (Leverrier Crescent, Bruce, Ph: (02) 6214 1111).

National Museum of Australia

The National Museum of Australia's five permanent exhibition galleries tell the story of a nation from 50,000 years of Indigenous heritage through European settlement to the present day. Perched on the tip of Acton Peninsula, the building itself is a jigsaw of unexpected angles and visually confronting colours wrapped round a surreal central cultural arena, The Garden of Australian Dreams (*above*) (Lawson Crescent, Acton Peninsula, Ph: (02) 6208 5000).

National Dinosaur Museum

Examine a 150 million year old dinosaur shin bone and learn about the prehistoric evolution of life on Earth through a series of fossil replicas and nearly 400 exhibits at the National Dinosaur Museum (Gold Creek Village, Ph: 1800 356 000).

Canberra to Sydney
Top Things to Do

1. Unlock the secrets of one of Australia's greatest natural enigmas — Lake George.
2. Raise a drink to the spirit of Ben Hall at the notorious Bushranger Hotel in Collector.
3. Tour the open private gardens of the lush Southern Highlands.
4. Visit the Bradman Museum in Bowral.
5. Tiptoe through the tulips at Bowral Tulip Time Festival in September/October.
6. Go waterfall hunting in Morton National Park.
7. Follow heritage trails in the historic townships of Goulburn and Mittagong.

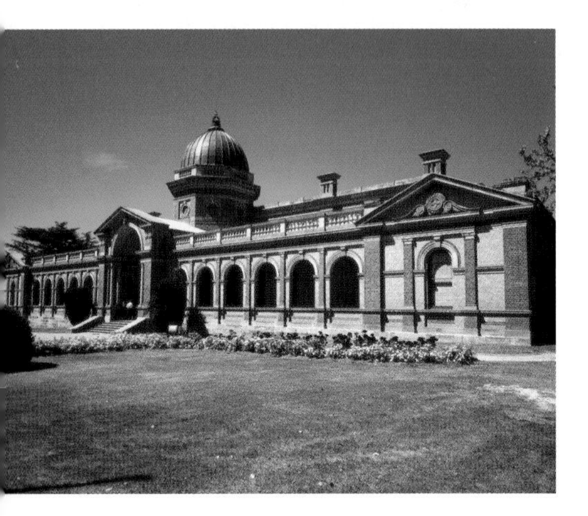

Goulburn

Goulburn was declared Australia's first inland city in 1859 and many fine examples of Victorian architecture remain. The Railway Station (1875) and Post Office (1881), St. Saviour's Cathedral (1884), Court House (*above*, 1887) and the Roman Catholic Cathedral (1890) are superbly preserved monuments to Goulburn's early prosperity.

Mittagong

Just off the Hume Highway, Mittagong was a staging point for Cobb & Co coaches before the advent of the railway in 1867. Mineral discoveries in the area saw a surge in population and created industrial wealth. Visit the area's superb open gardens, including Chinoiserie (off Webb Street) and Kennerton Green (on Bong Bong Road).

Canberra to Sydney
(via Goulburn & Moss Vale)

The 290 km journey from Canberra to Sydney takes in the major rural city of Goulburn and the Southern Highlands towns of Mittagong, Moss Vale and Bowral. Kangaroo Valley and Morton National Park are a short trip south of Moss Vale.

Federal Highway

Depending on when you are driving past, Lake George may or may not exist. This 25 km long, 10 km wide lake north of Canberra was cut off from the Yass River some 27,000 years ago and its highly saline waters gave rise to speculation it was somehow connected underground to the distant sea. Ecologists now believe the salt is blown in by storms from the Pacific. In times of drought the water completely evaporates and the area is barely recognisable as a lake, although a strange mirage effect can be seen from time to time on the dry bed. Explorers Hamilton Hume and William Hovell's pioneering trek to Melbourne commenced from the shores of Lake George in 1824. There is now a cluster of interesting small wineries near the lake not far from the highway (turn off at the Gurney VC rest area). The Federal Highway bypasses the intriguing historical town of Collector, but travellers shouldn't. Divert onto the old highway, which forms the town's main street, and stop for a drink at the Bushranger Hotel, just as notorious highwayman Ben Hall did in 1865. While Hall was whooping it up and raiding the tills inside, his gang's lookout murdered the local constable, who was on his way to investigate. The hotel exhibits a portrait of Hall and a fine collection of antique firearms. If you are passing through at the start of May, be sure not to miss the Collector Pumpkin Festival and Ball.

Goulburn

Since the Hume Highway re-development in 1992, Goulburn has also been bypassed but this traditional rural and commercial centre has continued to prosper. Sheep farming has been the district's economic mainstay since 1825 and the Big Merino still welcomes visitors to town. Since 1875, the town has also been the location for a major gaol facility that operates to this day (Maude Street). Behind the gaol is the old St Saviours Cemetery, resting place of William Hovell and First Fleet convict Mary Martin. Also located in Maude Street is Riversdale, a National Trust property, once home to New South Wales Surveyor-General Edward Twynam. The adjacent barn is Goulburn's oldest stone building, built in 1833. A 20 m tower lookout at the Rocky Hill War Memorial provides sweeping views of Goulburn (open daily, 7 am – 5 pm). The old caretaker's cottage nearby is now a World War I museum (open weekends).

The Southern Highlands

This is one of New South Wales' oldest settled regions. The development of Southern Highland towns was spurred on by the construction of the Great Southern Railway. Designed to link Sydney and Melbourne, the railway reached Mittagong in 1867 before being extended through Bowral and Moss Vale to Goulburn. Today this cool and tranquil highland district is rich in historical interest and famous for the beauty of its private and public gardens.

Bowral

Bowral is celebrated as the birthplace of cricket's greatest player, Sir Donald Bradman, and a pilgrimage to the Bradman Museum is a must for diehard cricket fans. The town is also famed for its spectacular floral displays. Tens of thousands of tulips bloom in Corbett Gardens during the town's famous Tulip Time festival (September/October).

Moss Vale

Moss Vale was once the transfer point for the NSW governor on the way to his summer residence some 8 km south at Sutton Forest. The railway station's vice regal suite no longer operates, but trains still stop here en route to Sydney. Take an open garden tour in autumn or spring or see one of NSW's largest country shows each March.

A Detour through Kangaroo Valley & Morton National Park

(Links with page 356 for an alternative route to Sydney via Wollongong on the Princes Highway)

From Moss Vale, it is possible to turn south and explore the northern section of Morton National Park and Kangaroo Valley. This scenic detour can be extended by linking up with the Princes Highway north of Nowra and following the coastal route to Sydney via Wollongong. Allow plenty of time to walk and gawk at the magnificent Fitzroy Falls on the northern edge of Morton Park. Here in Kangaroo Valley stands one of Australia's great colonial relics — Hampden Bridge. This castellated bridge was officially opened in 1898 and is an enduring marvel of 19th-century engineering. Spanning 77 m the bridge is built from local sandstone, hardwood trusses and steel cable. It is the only surviving suspension bridge from Australia's colonial days — testimony to the high quality of design and construction performed more than a century ago.

Hampden Bridge The historic relic found in Kangaroo Valley.

Left to right: Fitzroy Falls; Tianjara Falls; Belmore Falls; Carrington Falls (just outside Morton National Park).

Morton National Park

Phone Ranger: (02) 4887 7270

This extensive national park extends south from the Southern Highlands east of Goulburn into the Shoalhaven and Clyde Coast regions west of Ulladulla. Morton is a great bushwalking challenge and provides magnificent views of the Budawang Range. Cliff-rimmed gorges, sandstone tableland, untouched wilderness, rainforest gullies and plunging waterfalls are just some of the park's wild features. From the summit of Pigeon House Mountain (inland from Ulladulla) there are superb views of the Budawangs.

Walks in the Park: If you are feeling fit, try the 3 km ladder-assisted climb to the summit of Pigeon House Mountain near Ulladulla, which overlooks the coast and ranges. In the northern section of the park, easy grade trails along clifftops at Fitzroy and Belmore Falls provide striking views of Shoalhaven River tributaries tripping down layers of sandstone blocks into narrow gorges. A little further west, at Gambells Rest, a network of roads and walking tracks leads to waterfalls, fern gullies, and cliffside lookouts over Bundanoon Valley.

Access: Northern section from Nowra, Kangaroo Valley, Moss Vale and Bundanoon. Central and southern sections from Braidwood and the Princes Highway.

Camping: Fees charged and bookings apply at Gambells Rest. Bush camping permitted but conditions apply.

The Waratah is the floral emblem of NSW

National Parks Close to Morton NP

- Budawang National Park
- Budderoo National Park
- Bungonia State Conservation Area
- Cecil Hoskins Nature Reserve
- Comerong Island Nature Reserve
- Conjola National Park
- Jervis Bay Marine Park
- Jervis Bay National Park
- Macquarie Pass National Park
- Narrawallee Creek Nature Reserve
- Seven Mile Beach National Park
- Tallaganda National Park

MELBOURNE to Sydney

Via the Coast (Part One – Melbourne to Bega)

Melbourne to Sydney Top Things to Do

1. Indulge your gastronomic urges in South Gippsland's Gourmet Deli Region.
2. Explore mainland Australia's southern coast.
3. Walk the Bataluk Cultural Trail in East Gippsland.
4. Tour the countryside of the Latrobe Valley.
5. Spend a night in the historic gold mining town of Walhalla.
6. Bushwalk in Tarra-Bulga National Park.
7. Shop for bric-a-brac in Yarragon.
8. Fly-fish for trout at the foothills of the Great Divide in beautiful "escape country".
9. Take a heritage tour of the historic coal mining country around Wonthaggi.

Hunting for History?

Trailblazing explorers Angus McMillan and Count Pawel Strzelecki paved the way for settlement of the Gippsland area from 1839, after which time settlers gradually arrived and began to clear the prevailing swampland, transforming it into highly productive dairying land. Several historic buildings and sites remain as a tribute to the region's past. In the tiny town of Yarram, nestled deep amid the lush pastures, are notable historic edifices such as the Old Courthouse (*above*) and Regent Theatre (built in 1930). Further north, towards Baw Baw National Park, visitors can revisit gold rush days at the historic town of Walhalla. More than 4000 people occupied this town between 1885 and 1890, all vying for a share of the 74 tonne of gold found here over that time. Several old buildings and stores remain and the Walhalla Museum is open daily. To the north-east of this region, Sale was once a thriving port and maintains 19th-century architecture. Indigenous history can also be explored from Sale via the Bataluk Cultural Trail into East Gippsland.

The coastal route from Melbourne to Sydney along the Princes Highway is 170 km longer than the inland route. Unlike the Hume Highway, the coast road also leads directly through many minor and major towns, making this a driving journey best spread over a number of days (at least two). This potential disadvantage in terms of time taken to travel between the capital cities is more than offset by the abundance of natural features encountered along the way. Expansive national parks and conservation reserves provide superb camping and walking opportunities almost all the way from Orbost on the south-east Victorian coast to Nowra near Wollongong. Closer to Melbourne is the bushwalker's paradise of Wilsons Promontory and the penguin haven of Phillip Island.

South Gippsland

Beyond the Dandenongs and Melbourne's outer south-eastern suburbs, the South Gippsland district stretches 140 km along the crest of the mountainous Strzeleckis from Poowong in the east to Tarra-Bulga National Park. Expect to see even more cows than cars along the Princes and South Gippsland Highways — this lush pasture land is a traditional dairy farming region and if you travel the smaller local roads you may still be pleasantly delayed by farmers driving cows across the road from paddock to paddock. Around Neerim South is the Gourmet Deli Region where cheese makers, berry farmers and meat smokers peddle their produce to the public through farm outlets, local shops and markets.

Further inland is the Latrobe Valley, stretching from historic Yarragon (a great destination for antiques and bric-a-brac shopping) to Traralgon. At the heart of the region lies one of the world's largest brown coal deposits. Major plants near Morwell and Yallourn convert this resource into electricity that supplies 85% of the State's power. Travel via Moe to the area known as "escape country", at the foothills of the Great Divide. It is characterised by dense forests, great camping spots and mountain streams dearly cherished by trout anglers. History buffs will also appreciate the town of Walhalla, once a major mining centre, but now a well-preserved window to a period when Victoria was gripped by gold fever. Stay in one of the local boutique hotels, wander the tree-lined streets in crisp mountain air and take a mine tunnel tour.

West of Phillip Island (*see following pages*) is South Gippsland's largest town, Wonthaggi. It was first settled as a "tent town" in 1909 after the State government established coal mines to fill the supply gap caused by industrial unrest in the coal fields of New South Wales. The State Coal Mine became the main supplier of coal to Victorian Railways but closed in 1968. Visit the State Coal Mine Heritage Property and Historic Park and tour the Museum of Mining Activities.

Feature Localities

1. Baw Baw National Park
2. Bega
3. Ben Boyd National Park
4. Croajingolong National Park
5. Eden
6. Gippsland Lakes
7. Gourmet Deli Region, Neerim South
8. Lakes Entrance
9. Mallacoota
10. Merimbula
11. Mitchell River National Park
12. Ninety Mile Beach
13. Phillip Island
14. Sale
15. South East Forest National Park
16. Tarra-Bulga National Park
17. Tathra
18. The Lakes National Park
19. Walhalla
20. Wilsons Promontory
21. Wonthaggi

Melbourne to Sydney
Top Things to Do

1. View the famous Penguin Parade on Phillip Island's Summerland Beach.
2. See Australian Fur-seal colonies at the Nobbies in Wilsons Promontory National Park.
3. Get close to a Koala at the Koala Conservation Centre.
4. Enjoy a seaside picnic at Cowes.
5. Stay in a lighthouse keeper's cottage at Wilsons Promontory.
6. Spend a couple of nights camping at Tidal River and exploring the national park.
7. Watch international superbike riders negotiate the Phillip Island racing circuit.
8. See towering Mountain Ash, the world's tallest flowering plant, in Tarra-Bulga National Park.

Tarra-Bulga National Park

Phone Ranger: (03) 5146 3204

Tarra-Bulga is a small national park tucked away on the southern side of the Strzelecki Ranges. Sheltered slopes and deep valleys nurture stands of cool temperate rainforest. Around 39 species of fern grow in the park's damp gullies, which channel sparkling mountain creeks over mossy boulders southwards to the coast. The moss-festooned trunks of ancient Myrtle Beech rise above smaller Sassafrass along the creeks. On the ridges, towering Mountain Ash dominate the forest canopy and the beech becomes part of the understorey.

Walks in the Park: In the Bulga Section, visitors can stroll over a suspended walkway into the canopy and over a fern-filled gully.

Access: Thirty-five kilometres south of Traralgon.

Camping: No camping in the park. Privately owned guest house at Balook. Commercial caravan parks south of the park on Tarra Valley Road.

A Detour to Phillip Island & Wilsons Promontory

Phillip Island and Wilsons Promontory are two of the Gippsland region's major drawcards. From Melbourne, the South Gippsland Highway traces the shoreline of Western Port Bay, connecting with the Bass Highway for the journey to Phillip Island. This popular holiday retreat is linked to the mainland via a road bridge at San Remo.

While there are excellent surf beaches on the island's southern side and safe swimming beaches near the main town of Cowes, it is the resident colonies of Little Penguins that are the island's stellar attraction. Every evening, the penguins expertly ride waves ashore at Summerland Beach and begin their ungainly waddle up the strand to their burrows, seemingly unfazed by the expectant throng of humans awaiting their arrival. The island's main shopping village and accommodation are at Cowes, which, despite a major population explosion in holiday periods, retains a relaxed air. Walk the jetty, eat at one of the many outdoor cafés or visit the interesting Clock Museum and Gallery (1 Findlay Street, Ph: (03) 5952 2856). Nearby is the Phillip Island Grand Prix Circuit — stage for the World Superbike Championships in April and the Australian Motorcycle Grand Prix in November.

Wilsons Promontory

Wilsons Promontory, at the southernmost tip of the Australian mainland, is one of Victoria's largest and most spectacular national parks. Known as *Yiruk* or *Wamoom* by Aboriginal custodians (whose occupation dates back at least 6500 years and for whom the area was an abundant source of seafood), Wilsons Promontory was first seen with European eyes when George Bass and Matthew Flinders explored the area in 1798. Sealers Cove, on the east coast, was soon established and the commercial exploitation of seals, whales and timber continued for almost a century. These waters are now a marine park.

Phillip Island

Some 30,000 Little Penguins live in the waters around Phillip Island and about 3000 make their burrows around the Penguin Parade precinct. Many return nightly for their floodlit trip up the beach, which you can observe from viewing platforms and boardwalks. The Penguin Parade Visitor Centre also allows you to view penguins in nesting boxes and get a glimpse of life in the burrows. (The parade is nightly, arrive an hour before sunset and wear warm clothing, Ph: (03) 5951 2800). Seal Rocks, home to a colony of Australian Fur-seals, is a group of isolated rocky outcrops off the Nobbies — the headland at Phillip Island's western tip. A viewing station at the Nobbies Centre, boardwalks, and cruise boats from Cowes and Stony Point give you the chance to see these seals up close (Ph: (03) 5951 2800). Just off Phillip Island Road is the Koala Conservation Centre, where treetop boardwalks bring you nose-to-nose with the island's leaf-chewing locals (open 10 am – 5 pm, Ph: (03) 5952 1307).

Top to bottom: Wilsons Promontory Lighthouse, built in 1859 to ensure the safety of vessels in Bass Strait; Tidal River, the Prom's major settlement, seen from Mt Oberon.

Clockwise from top left: Bushwalker's payoff — the view from Mt Oberon; The fern-lined beauty of Lilly Pilly Gully; Granite outcrops overlook the beach; The photogenic beauty of Whisky Bay.

Wilsons Promontory National Park

Phone Ranger: 1800 350 552

Comprising more than 50,000 ha, much of the park was reserved in 1898 with more land being added in 1908 and the 1960s. Wilsons Promontory is an extraordinary blend of rugged seascapes, dense forests, weathered granite outcrops, rocky coastal terrain and secluded beaches. Its varied landscape and rewarding views make the park ideal for bushwalking. The heathlands are especially rich in bird species, and the tidal mudflats around Corner Inlet, a marine and coastal park, are home to numerous migratory waders. Flocks of lorikeets and rosellas are commonly seen gathering around the main store at Tidal River village, as are Laughing Kookaburras and Superb Fairy-wrens. Emus often feed unperturbed on the open heath along the road verges at the park's entrance around Yanakie Isthmus, while kangaroos and wallabies seem entirely unafraid of human observers. At night, wombat spotting by torchlight is a popular pastime. At Tidal River there is a concentration of amenities and accommodation (including camping and caravan sites), as well as the visitor centre and park office. It is recommended to book ahead at all times of year.

Walks in the Park: Almost 30 walks utilise 130 km of tracks in the Prom, ranging from the wheelchair-friendly Loo-Errn Track (which follows the banks of the Tidal River) to the Prom Circuit Walk, a 2–3 day hike. Experienced bushwalkers should also inquire about the long, but thoroughly rewarding, Lighthouse Walk.

Access: Two hundred kilometres south-east of Melbourne via Meeniyan on the South Gippsland Highway.

Camping: At Tidal River choose from environmentally friendly self-contained cabins, motel-style accommodation, huts with bunks, group lodges or one of 480 unpowered camping sites with communal facilities. If this sounds too close to civilisation, consider walking the 19.1 km to the Wilsons Promontory Lighthouse, where you can stay in a cottage on the jutting headland (bookings required). There is also remote outstation camping in eleven areas, including camping from boats.

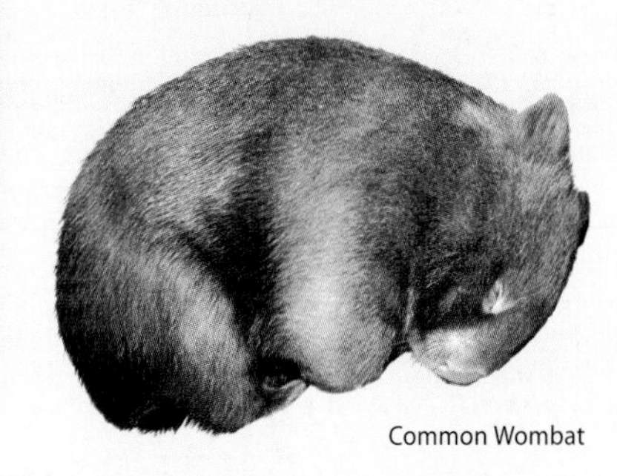

Common Wombat

Melbourne to Sydney

Top Things to Do

1. Explore the Gippsland Lakes by boat.
2. Rent a holiday house at Metung or Paynesville.
3. Feel the sand beneath your feet. Take a walk along Ninety Mile Beach.
4. Camp at the mouth of the Snowy River at Marlo. The Mulloway fishing here is some of the best in Australia.
5. Dine at a waterfront restaurant in Lakes Entrance.
6. Visit the Eden Killer Whale Museum.
7. Sample the local cheeses of Bega or Bodalla.
8. Dangle a line off Merimbula wharf.
9. Cruise Mogareeka Inlet at Tathra.
10. Visit any or all of south-eastern Australia's pristine national parks.

Sale & the Gippsland Region

Central Gippsland stretches from the High Country to the Gippsland Lakes and Ninety Mile Beach. Sale (*top and above*) became a major port for steamers using the 400 km^2 lakes system in 1888 when a canal was cut linking the town with the Thomson River. A swing bridge was built to accommodate the passage of larger vessels into the port — it still operates today and can be seen 5 km south of the city off the South Gippsland Highway.

Sale to Bega

A journey of just under 500 km, the Princes Highway from Sale to Bega connects the perennially popular fishing and boating regions of Ninety Mile Beach and the Gippsland Lakes with the glorious coastal towns of southern New South Wales.

Gippsland Lakes & Ninety Mile Beach

Commencing 15 km east of Sale is a continuous chain of coastal lakes — Lake Wellington, Lake Victoria and Lake King. Known collectively as the Gippsland Lakes and protected by The Lakes National Park, this is the largest navigable inland waterway system in Australia. The region attracts scores of holidaymakers taking advantage of the superb boating conditions, fishing and camping opportunities. Holiday houses, self-contained accommodation and campgrounds abound in the lakeside retreats of Paynesville, Metung, Loch Sport, Rotamah Island, Golden Beach, Seaspray and Holland Landing. The whole Gippsland Lakes region is blessed by natural beauty. The wetlands and waterways are a haven for waterbird rookeries, while spring brings a spectacular explosion of wildflowers and one of Australia's best displays of native orchids. The lakes are divided from the ocean by the slender sandy arc of Ninety Mile Beach, running north-east from Seaspray to Lakes Entrance. The region's major town is Bairnsdale — an excellent base and supply centre for exploration of the lakes and beaches.

Lakes Entrance to Eden

Located at the point where the Gippsland Lakes meet the Southern Ocean, Lakes Entrance has been a popular holiday destination for more than a century. Approximately 4 hours drive from Melbourne, it is also home to one of the largest fishing fleets in the Southern Hemisphere, making it the perfect place to dine on fresh seafood. A footbridge links the town with the lifesaver-patrolled strand of Ninety Mile Beach. Take a chartered cruise on the lakes or hire a paddleboat or catamaran. Back on dry land, visit Jemmy's Point Lookout, which offers brilliant views of the coast, lakes and town. The beautiful Lake Tyers is only 11 km east and features scenic walks and drives through the Lake Tyers Forest Park.

South of Orbost, the Snowy River completes its marathon journey from Mount Kosciuszko to the ocean at the peaceful riverside village of Marlo, another great place to camp, boat and fish. The Princes Highway continues east through Cann River to the New South Wales border, but unless you are in a hurry, it is worth spending time exploring the superb coastal environs of Croajingolong National Park (*see following page*), Gipsy Point and Mallacoota. Wonboyn Lake, just over the border on the edge of Ben Boyd National Park, and the surrounding coast is also an excellent retreat for fishing, boating and simple solitude. The highway meets the coast again at Eden on Twofold Bay (*see facing page*).

Eden to Bega

The southern New South Wales coast has an embarrassment of seaside riches. Choose, if you can, between the tranquil beach villages of Pambula Beach and Tura Beach and the larger holiday towns of Merimbula and Tathra. This whole region is enveloped by national parks and there is a surfeit of accommodation and camping spots to select from. Bega, the capital of the south coast, is at the centre of a famous cheese making district. Visit and tour the Bega Cheese Heritage Centre on the banks of the Bega River just north of town (open daily, 9 am – 5 pm, Ph: (02) 6491 7777).

Lakes Entrance

The rows of fishing trawlers (*left*) moored at Lakes Entrance tell the tale of a town famed as Australia's fishing capital. Positioned between ocean and lakes, there can be few better places in the country to hoist a rod, dunk a line or simply savour the success of other anglers' efforts. Some visitors to Lakes Entrance leave the water only to replenish supplies for their continued voyages on the Gippsland Lakes. If you prefer to stay on land, dine at a waterfront restaurant or wander the jetties as the boats return laden with catch.

Eden

Eden (*left*) originated as an important whaling port. Shore-based whaling in Twofold Bay was so successful that it continued for over 100 years before finally ceasing in 1930. Ironically, whales themselves played an instrumental role in the industry's success. Local Killer Whales would herd migrating whales into the bay where harpooners would lie in wait. Often, Killer Whales would help disable the quarry and were rewarded with the lips and tongues of the catch. The skeleton of one of these deadly accomplices, Old Tom, is exhibited in the Eden Killer Whale Museum (open daily, Ph: (02) 6496 2094).

Merimbula

The largest holiday resort town on the Sapphire Coast, Merimbula (*left*) curls around the edge of several tidal lakes. The lakes provide perfect safe swimming zones for families while the unprotected beaches beyond provide ideal surfing conditions year round. Anglers will enjoy the opportunity to experience deep sea fishing without the need for a boat off Merimbula wharf, while bushwalkers, canoeists and picnickers will enjoy the picturesque coastal surrounds of Bournda National Park. Oh, and for the kids there's Magic Mountain — a water-based theme park with giant slides and a rollercoaster.

Tathra

Set between Mimosa Rocks National Park to the north and Bournda National Park to the south, Tathra (*far left*) is blessed with copious natural attractions. Look for fur-seals and Little Penguins in the water around the wharf. Dolphins are also often seen off Tathra's beautiful 3 km beach. Mogareeka Inlet is popular for its safe swimming beaches and for the cagey flathead that lure fishermen upstream on the river. The surrounding forest resounds with birdlife, so take your binoculars and camera if you plan on boating up river.

Melbourne to Bega – National Parks

The national parks that lie between Melbourne and Bega preserve a huge variety of landscapes — from snow-covered mountains to coastal lakes, temperate rainforests and boulder-strewn beaches. The northern Gippsland region features Baw Baw and Mitchell River National Parks, while the southern region includes Wilsons Promontory National Park, Gippsland Lakes Coastal Park and the extensive Croajingalong National Park.

Across the border in New South Wales, South East Forest National Park protects large sections of the Great Dividing Range behind the coastal towns of Eden, Merimbula and Bega, while Ben Boyd National Park conserves the seascapes around Twofold Bay. You could spend months (or a lifetime) walking, boating, relaxing and camping in these superb parks — if you only have a few days, explore the coastal parks close to the Princes Highway to get a good idea of the incredible coast and country in this part of the world.

The Lakes National Park A family of Australian Shelducks.

Baw Baw National Park Home to an unobtrusive ski resort.

Mitchell River National Park Riding the Rapids.

Baw Baw National Park

Phone Ranger: 13 19 63

Baw Baw National Park protects 13,300 ha of the Baw Baw Plateau and parts of the Thomson and Aberfeldy River valleys. Used by many as a low-key ski resort, Baw Baw's elevation features superb views, sub-alpine vegetation (wildflowers in spring and early summer) and Snow Gum woodlands. Scenic drives and walks cut through the park.

Walks in the Park: Many walks start from the Mount St Gwinear car park, Mount Erica car park and the Baw Baw Alpine Village. The vista from View Point on Mount St Gwinear includes the Thomson and Aberfeldy River valleys. There is an easy Beech Gully Nature Walk (400 m) at Mount Erica. Ski hire, accommodation and all snow facilities (including chairlifts) are available at the Alpine Village in snow season (June to September).

Access: From Latrobe Valley via Traralgon and Moe.

Camping: Basic facilities at Aberfeldy River, Eastern Tyers River and Walhalla.

Mitchell River National Park

Phone Ranger: 13 19 63

Located 50 km north-west of Bairnsdale off the Dargo Road, Mitchell River National Park features gorges carved by the spectacular Mitchell River and impressive Gippsland forests. Walk along Kanooka (Water Gum) banks, and visit the Aboriginal cave known as the Den of Nargun. Intrepid canoeists can negotiate rapids and whitewater all the way along the Mitchell River and emerge at the Gippsland Lakes.

Walks in the Park: If you have the stamina (and several days) try the 18 km Mitchell River Walking Track, which traverses the bank through the main gorge to the Den of Nargun. Walking tracks from the Den of Nargun car park and picnic area lead to the cave. There is also a circuit walk to Bluff Lookout and the Mitchell River.

Access: Via Bairnsdale (Dargo Road from the Princes Highway).

Camping: Basic facilities at Angusvale camp. There is also a commercial caravan park off Dunbar Road near the Den of Nargun car park.

The Lakes National Park

Phone Ranger: 13 19 63

The Lakes National Park is a swampy stretch of sand lying in the midst of the Gippsland Lakes. The 2830 ha national park, consisting of Sperm Whale Head Peninsula and Rotamah and Little Rotamah Islands, is a haven for wildlife. Scrubby woodlands, swamps, coastal heath and salt marshes create habitats for a variety of mammals (including kangaroos, wallabies, possums, gliders and the rare New Holland Mouse). An abundance of habitats also helps support over 190 bird species. Birds Australia runs a bird observatory and nature study courses on Rotamah Island.

Walks in the Park: Well-marked walking tracks traverse the park and are dotted with hides for observing waterbird behaviour. Footbridges from the island cross Lake Reeve to Ninety Mile Beach.

Access: Five kilometres by boat from Paynesville.

Camping: Group camp sites on Rotamah Island, accommodation for birdwatchers at the observatory.

Long-nosed Potoroo

South East Forest National Park

Phone Ranger: (07) 4097 1485

The park is an important conservation area for old-growth forests and protects crucial habitat for several endangered species, including the Long-footed Potoroo, Smoky Mouse, Powerful Owl and Olive Whistler. There are at least 48 mammal species in the park and 115 bird species.

Walks in the Park: This is a great park for those who prefer their walks short. There are six main walks here, and all are less than 2 km in length. Try the Goodenia Rainforest Walk (1.2 km) through coastal temperate rainforest, which leads through fern gullies and lilly pillies. The 500 m Wolumla Peak Walk is slightly tougher than it sounds but offers brilliant views.

Listen out for the sharp cracking call of the Eastern Whipbird and the amazing mimicry of the Superb Lyrebird. The Six Mile Creek Walk (300 m) is short but leads to a tumbling cascade and the Pipers Lookout Walk (500 m) has great views and is wheelchair accessible.

Access: South from Merimbula or Pambula on the Princes Highway then turn off at the Wyndham Road or further west towards Bombala.

Camping: Basic camping facilities at Six Mile Creek, Postman's camping area, Waratah Gully and Nunnock camping ground.

Ben Boyd National Park A sight to behold from the air.

Ben Boyd National Park

Phone Ranger: (07) 4097 1485

Named for a south coast whaling pioneer, Ben Boyd National Park protects the headlands around Twofold Bay near Eden. There are broad surf beaches and rocky bays, sheltered inlets, historic monuments and lighthouses. Birds and mammals found in the park include: the Eastern Bristlebird; Ground Parrot; Hooded Plover; Yellow-bellied Glider and Long-nosed Potoroo. A tower on the southern headland of Twofold Bay was originally constructed by Ben Boyd for whale-spotting.

Walks in the Park: There are many short walks leading to feature locations along with a 3 day trek from Boyd's Tower to Green Cape.

Access: Southern section via Edrom Rd from the Princes Highway. Northern section via Pambula Beach Rd or Haycock Rd.

Camping: Good facilities at Bittangabee Bay and Saltwater Creek in the southern section of the park (no showers, BYO firewood). Lighthouse keepers' cottages at Green Cape.

Croajingolong National Park

Phone Ranger: 13 19 63

This is one of the finest coastal parks in south-eastern Australia. Mountain-fed rivers run through unspoilt forest valleys and designated wilderness areas to a superb coastline featuring tranquil inlets, immense dunes, long beaches and rocky headlands. It is also a biological treasure trove with a thousand species of native plants creating diverse habitats ranging from windshorn heath to hidden rainforest gullies.

Walks in the Park: Three short nature walks introduce visitors to the park's main habitats. The Double Creek Loop Trail, just outside Mallacoota, takes in warm temperate rainforest and eucalypt woodland. Wetlands and heath feature on the Wingan Nature Walk, while the Dunes Walk from the Thurra camping area traverses woodlands and expansive sand dunes.

Access: Via Princes Highway and Mallacoota.

Camping: Basic facilities at Shipwreck Creek, Wingan Inlet and Peachtree Creek Reserve.

South East Forest National Park Old growth forest.

MELBOURNE to Sydney

Via the Coast (Part Two – Bega to Sydney)

Melbourne to Sydney
Top Things to Do

1. Camp by the beach in Mimosa Rocks National Park.
2. Absorb Sapphire Coast panoramas from Lerner Lookout near Bermagui.
3. Visit Tathra's wharf and maritime museum.
4. Swim in Bermagui's saltwater Blue Pool.
5. Go boating on Wallaga Lake.
6. Walk in Wadbilliga National Park and Deua National Park.
7. Look out for Humpback Whales off Merimbula (September to November).
8. Visit historic Central Tilba and the Foxglove Spires Open Garden at Tilba Tilba.
9. Battle giant Yellowfin Tuna offshore.
10. Lie on the beach and read Zane Grey.

Wallaga Lakes National Park

Close to the coastal splendour of Bermagui are two not-to-be-missed natural wilderness areas — Wallaga Lakes National Park and Mimosa Rocks National Park. In Wallaga Lakes National Park, an 8 km coastal walk winds through fauna and flora reserves established in some places over the old diggings of the Montreal Goldfields. The jewel in the national park's crown is Wallaga Lake, and much of the park is best accessed by boat. Boats can be hired from Beauty Point and Regatta Point. For more intrepid adventurers, there are good walking paths although many cover steep terrain, such as the one that leads to the peak of Mt Dromedary. Aboriginal culture tours are also available in the park and are run by the traditional Yuin owners from the nearby Umballa Cultural Centre. The tours, and associated activities, include Aboriginal Dreaming stories of plants, animals and locations, as well as bark-hut building, boomerang throwing and ochre painting lessons (Ph: (02) 4473 7232 to book).

The highway from Bega to Nowra travels along the Sapphire, Eurobodalla, Clyde and Shoalhaven Coasts. These well-populated regions feature a string of towns, seaside villages and busy camping spots overlooking the Tasman Sea. Five major National Parks — Wadbilliga, Deua, Monga, Clyde River and Budawang — protect large regions of the hinterland ranges.

Bega to Eurobodalla National Park

A better alternative to the Princes Highway east of Bega is the old coastal road connecting Tathra to Bermagui and Wallaga Lake. Before heading out of Tathra, visit the Tathra Maritime Museum in the Old Cargo Shed on Wharf Road, which features exhibits recalling the days of steamships. It stands at the only timber sea wharf remaining in southern New South Wales (open daily, Ph: (02) 6494 4062). The coast road leads through Mimosa Rocks National Park, where ancient volcanic rocks have been spectacularly stranded in the ocean by rising sea levels. High granite ridges and dunes provide perfect viewing platforms and there are also several excellent walks through rainforest and open woodland. Four beachside campgrounds — at Aragunnu, Middle Beach, Gilliards Beach and Picnic Point provide an opportunity to walk, fish, swim and surf at your leisure. The Mimosa Rocks formations are a short walk from the Aragunnu campground, north of Wapengo. Aragunnu itself is an important Aboriginal site (the first to be gazetted) and boardwalks lead past a large midden.

Bermagui & Surrounds

Just south of Bermagui (*left*), stop and admire the view from Lerner Lookout. Michael Lerner was a friend of the American western writer and game fisherman Zane Grey, who popularised sportfishing in the region. Legend has it that Lerner is the only man to have hooked two Blue Marlins on a single line. Sportfishing remains one of the Sapphire Coast's major lures today and charter boats and deep sea fishing cruises operate from Bermagui. Leaf through Grey's 1937 book *An American Angler in Australia* and the memorabilia in the local pub before heading out. South of Lerner Lookout, Cuttagee Lake, at the northern end of Cuttagee Beach, offers safe family swimming. Locals have also traditionally swum in the Blue Pool, a natural saltwater swimming hole off Scenic Drive on the southern headland that was extended in the 1940s by blasting. North of Bermagui is Wallaga Lake, a traditional Aboriginal area that is now popular for fishing and boating. Inland, on the Princes Highway, Tilba Tilba and Central Tilba are wonderfully preserved heritage towns demanding exploration.

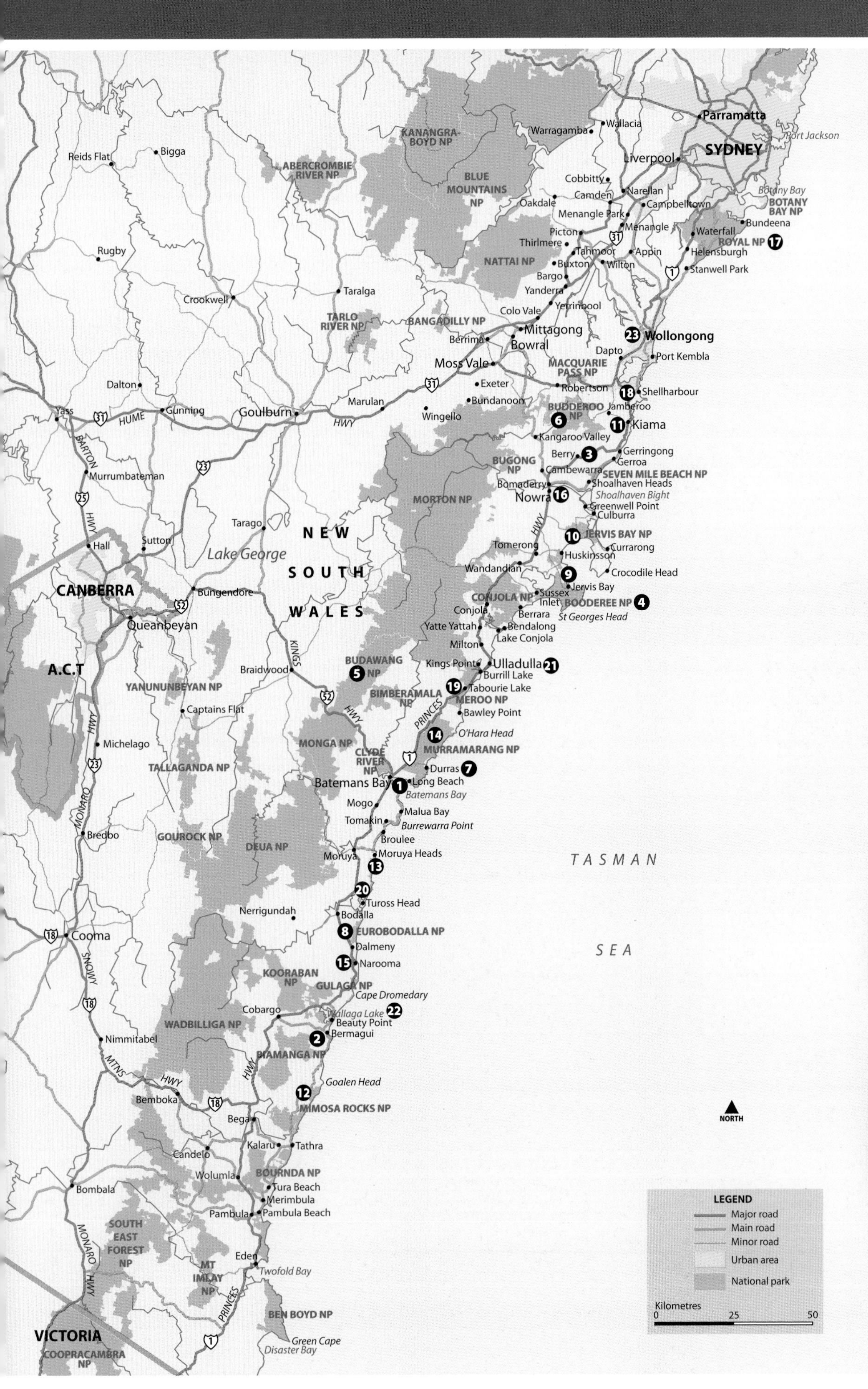

Feature Localities

1 Batemans Bay
2 Bermagui
3 Berry
4 Booderee National Park
5 Budawang National Park
6 Budderoo National Park
7 Durras
8 Eurobodalla National Park
9 Jervis Bay
10 Jervis Bay National Park
11 Kiama
12 Mimosa Rocks National Park
13 Moruya Heads
14 Murramarang National Park
15 Narooma
16 Nowra
17 Royal National Park
18 Shellharbour
19 Tabourie Lake
20 Tuross Head
21 Ulladulla
22 Wallaga Lake
23 Wollongong

Mimosa Rocks

Mimosa Rocks and the surrounding national park are named for a vessel, the SS *Mimosa*, which was wrecked on the rocks off Aragunnu (an Aboriginal sacred site within the park) in 1867.

Top Things to Do

1. Cruise to Montague Island off Merimbula and view the local wildlife (including sea birds and fur-seals).
2. Camp at Congo Point in Eurobodalla National Park.
3. Laze on the beach at Tuross Heads.
4. Stay a few days at Ulladulla or Mollymook.
5. Spot dolphins and whales in Jervis Bay.
6. Go bushwalking in the forests around Batemans Bay.
7. Meet an Eastern Grey Kangaroo in Murramarang National Park.
8. Tour Bundanon, home of Australian artist Arthur Boyd, near Nowra.

Budawang National Park

Phone Ranger: (02) 4887 7270

Approximately 50 km west of Ulladulla lies Budawang National Park. This rugged and remote region is predominantly a declared wilderness area, therefore vehicular access is limited. The park is a mixture of Ironwood and temperate rainforest that is a sanctuary for marsupial species, including the Swamp Wallaby and Common Wombat, as well as the elusive Greater Glider. The summit of Mount Budawang is a worthy challenge, with views of the Southern Highlands that are nothing short of sensational.

Walks in the Park: For accomplished and hardy trekkers, Budawang provides a serious bushwalking experience into unforgiving and unforgettable country.

Access: Via the Braidwood to Mongarlowe Road where a signed track leads to Mount Budawang.

Camping: Bush camping only.

Narooma to Nowra

Narooma, at the southern end of the Eurobodalla Coast, is delightfully set on the Wagonga River estuary with Gulaga (Mount Dromedary) rising in the background. The name *Narooma* derives from an Aboriginal word meaning "clear blue water" and even in this picturesque region there are few more attractive seaside locations. The town originated as a port and shipbuilding centre but has been a popular holiday destination for over a century. Montague Island, 15 km directly east of Narooma in the Tasman Sea, is a nature reserve protecting colonies of Little Penguins, New Zealand and Australian Fur-seals and sea birds. Dolphins, turtles and whales are also often seen in the surrounding waters and cruises can be booked from the Narooma Visitor Information Centre. A replica of the island's lighthouse stands outside the centre (Princes Highway, Ph: (02) 4476 2881).

Between Narooma and Batemans Bay lies the northern section of Eurobodalla National Park. Camp at Congo Point and enjoy surf fishing or long walks on the beach in this unspoilt coastal paradise (but note that swimming can be dangerous due to unpredictable swells, rips and currents). Tuross Head, south of Moruya and only a short distance east of the Princes Highway, is a small but well-equipped hideaway with excellent beaches lined with Norfolk Pines. It is located on a finger of land pointing into the sea between two coastal lakes. A little further north, Moruya Heads at the mouth of the Moruya River is also surrounded by fine sandy beaches. Visit the Eurobodalla Historic Museum in the larger township of Moruya for a journey through the region's lively gold rush history.

Batemans Bay to Nowra

The expansive waterway of Batemans Bay is at the mouth of the Clyde River, 280 km south of Sydney. First surveyed, and named, by James Cook in 1770, the bay is the largest on the New South Wales south coast. Despite the town's rapid growth as a tourism centre in the latter part of the 20th century, Batemans Bay has managed to maintain a friendly village-like feel. It bears the name of Nathaniel Bateman, fellow seaman and colleague of James Cook. The northern points of the Clyde Coast include beautiful Durras, Pretty Beach and Pebbly Beach as well as Murramarang National Park (*see facing page*). Ulladulla and neighbouring Mollymook are also popular holiday spots with sandy swimming beaches and coastal dunes. Between here and Nowra is Jervis Bay (*see below*), one of Australia's most precious marine treasures.

Jervis Bay

Jervis Bay, reached via Huskisson *(above)*, has some of the whitest sands and clearest waters in the world and is frequented by dolphins, whales and myriad marine invertebrates, all protected within the marine park environment. The HMAS *Creswell* site (Jervis Bay Rd, Jervis Bay, Ph: (02) 4429 7900), located on the south-west shores of Jervis Bay in Booderee National Park, was placed on the register of the National Estate by the Australian Heritage Commission in 1981. One of the region's most intriguing sites is the ruins of the Cape St George Lighthouse, a now-disused lighthouse built in 1860. The location of the lighthouse was ill-considered and almost two dozen ships sank around Jervis Bay's waters in the late 1800s.

In 1889 a new lighthouse was constructed at Point Perpendicular and the Cape St George site was used for target practice by the Australian Navy following WWI. Little is left. The lighthouse's tower was destroyed and its beacon light used for the Crookhaven Heads Lighthouse.

Narooma

Narooma's tranquil waterfront setting belies a history of shipwrecks during the 19th century. Sailing and cruising these sparkling waters is safer today and there are numerous cruise choices available to tourists — from bobbing around placid Wagonga Inlet to cruising the offshore wildlife haven of Montague Island. Diving and snorkelling on the reefs is also popular and offshore anglers target game fish such as Yellowtail Kingfish, Blue Marlin and Yellowfin Tuna, as well as many reef species. Mid-September to mid-November is whale watching season, with Humpback, Southern Right, Fin, Bryde's Whales, Sei, Blue and Killer Whales all frequently seen. Contact Narooma Visitor Information Centre for cruise bookings (Princes Highway, Ph: (02) 4476 2881).

Batemans Bay

Batemans Bay has a great range of scenic drives, elevated vantages and bushwalking trails. The Clyde Coast region is blessed with several State forests, including those of Mogo, Boyne, Benandarah, and Buckenbowra. Observation Point has good views of Batemans Bay, overlooking other local landmarks such as North Head and Malua Bay. Round Hill Fire Tower Lookout is located on the Princes Highway, 2 km south of Batemans Bay. Any visit to Batemans Bay should include a trip to Nelligen (10 km upstream on a quiet stretch of the Clyde River). The Batemans Bay Tourist Information Centre (corner of the Princes Highway and Beach Road, Batemans Bay, Ph: (02) 4472 6900 or freecall 1800 802 528) provides detailed maps and information for visitors to the area.

Murramarang National Park

Phone Ranger: (02) 4478 6582

A 40 km drive north of Batemans Bay leads to Murramarang National Park, with its fine beaches, gorgeous lakes and outstanding views up and down the coast. The park is home to impressive forests of native Spotted Gum, some of the largest stands in New South Wales. The park's most popular attraction is Pebbly Beach (*left*), where Eastern Grey Kangaroos lead a leisurely existence while ogled by adoring tourists. The Murramarang Aboriginal Area is a place of spiritual significance. It contains a number of burial sites and perhaps the largest midden pile on the Shoalhaven Coast — several hectares of stone artefacts and scattered deposits from various tribes who lived in the area up to 12,000 years ago.

Walks in the Park: There are numerous rainforest and beach walks in the park — contact the national park office for details.

Access: From Princes Highway between Ulladulla and Batemans Bay.

Camping: Fully equipped campgrounds are located at Pebbly Beach, Pretty Beach and Depot Beach.

Ulladulla

Ulladulla, on the southern Shoalhaven Coast, is primarily a holiday town. The region's first settler, Reverend Thomas Kendall, was drowned when his boat was wrecked in Jervis Bay, but his grandson Henry Kendall lived to become one of Australia's most popular early poets. Inland from Ulladulla are Morton National Park, Pigeon House Mountain and the rugged environs of Budawang National Park. A short drive south of Ulladulla is Burrill Lake, a popular waterway suitable for a variety of aquatic pursuits including swimming, canoeing, windsurfing, fishing and water skiing. Natural landmarks around the lake include Kings Point and Dolphin Point, ideal for picnicking or simply relaxing and savouring the sights. Lake Tabourie, just over 10 km south of Ulladulla, has a well-appointed museum featuring examples of native creepy crawlies, displays of Aboriginal and European history, and period pieces illustrating the region's past.

Nowra

Nowra, to the north of Jervis Bay, lies at the mouth of the Shoalhaven River. The smaller twin town of Bomaderry is situated across the bridge on the opposite bank. There are several excellent nature walks in the vicinity, including Ben's Walk from the showgrounds along the Shoalhaven River (1 hr return). The longer Bomaderry Creek Walking Track is also worth exploring (2 hr return). Nowra is also home to the Australian Museum of Flight at the HMAS *Albatross* site, on Nowra's Albatross Road (Ph: (02) 4424 1920). The museum has a large collection of naval aircraft ranging from helicopters to folding-wing aeroplanes and general-purpose aircraft. Nearby Bundanon was home to the celebrated Australian artist Arthur Boyd and his studios and homestead are now open for public viewing (13.5 km west of Nowra on Illaroo Road, Sundays, 10.30 am – 4 pm, Ph: (02) 4422 2103).

Melbourne to Sydney
Top Things to Do

1. Take a morning or afternoon stroll in Booderee Botanic Gardens near Jervis Bay.
2. View the bay from national park lookouts.
3. Pack a picnic hamper and head for Jervis Bay National Park.
4. Take the White Sands Walk — a round trip from Greenfield Beach to Hyams Beach.
5. Camp or caravan overnight at Green Patch in Booderee National Park.
6. Dive, cruise or snorkel the reefs of Jervis Bay Marine Park.

Booderee Botanic Gardens

With its focus on coastal plants of south-eastern Australia, the Booderee Botanic Gardens comprise some 80 ha of natural bushland and cultivated areas encircling the dark brown waters of Lake McKenzie. Both the national park and botanic gardens were handed back to the Wreck Bay Aboriginal community in 1995.

There are numerous walks throughout Booderee Botanic Gardens, marked with arrows on wooden posts for ease of exploration. Expect a pleasant mix of regional environments from heathland and rainforest vegetation to dunes and sandstone outcrops.

Booderee National Park

Phone Ranger: (02) 4443 0977

Booderee National Park reaches out from the Illawarra coastline, casting a protective arm around the crystalline waters of southern Jervis Bay. Battered seacliffs, rocky platforms, tranquil coves and beaches shape the peninsula's shore. Jervis Bay, known as *Booderee* (meaning "bay of plenty") to the local Aborigines, is on the eastern side of the park. Booderee's beauty extends inland through estuarine and freshwater wetlands, coastal heaths, woodlands and remnant rainforest. Over 180 bird species find food and shelter within the park, along with many different mammals (including possums, gliders and kangaroos). The park is separated into two sections well serviced by roads and walking tracks. In the western section, Wreck Bay Beach stretches down to Sussex Inlet, a narrow twisting estuary leading to the shallow waters of St Georges Basin. Between the two lies an old dune system that supports banksia woodland, eucalypt forest and some interesting freshwater lakes. Booderee Botanic Gardens, just off Cave Beach Road, were set up in 1951 as an offshoot to the Australian National Botanic Gardens. The 80-ha gardens surround Lake McKenzie with a mix of natural bushland and cultivated native plants. The eastern section provides access to Jervis Bay and the rugged coastal cliffs.

Walks in the Park: Short walks through the gardens feature information displays, a rainforest gully and heathland. Lookouts and clifftop circuit trails at Jervis Bay offer excellent views.

Access: Twenty-eight kilometres south-east of Nowra via the Princes Highway and Jervis Bay Road.

Camping: Good facilities with unpowered tent and caravan sites at Green Patch. Basic facilities for tents only at Bristol Point and Cave Beach.

Jervis Bay National Park

Phone Ranger: (02) 4423 2170

Jervis Bay National Park preserves globally important plant and animal habitats. Rocky reefs, sand and seagrass beds support a wealth of marine life. Plants and animals crowd together in these southern waters, covering all available surfaces and filling every nook and cranny. The tranquillity of the national park is best experienced in its secluded beaches, coves, bays and forests — all good spots for swimming, bushwalking and birdwatching. The popular Greenfield Beach has a great selection of picnic and electric barbecue sites.

Walks in the Park: The park's White Sands Walk, a round trip along the coast from Greenfield Beach to Hyams Beach and back through the Scribbly Gum Track, is a perennial park favourite. Popular picnicking spots include Hammerhead Point and Red Point near Callala Bay, which is on the far northern side of Jervis Bay.

Access: Via Nowra on the Princes Highway.

Camping: Visitor camping is not permitted at Jervis Bay National Park. Honeymoon Bay, on the northern side of Jervis Bay, has camping facilities.

Bowen Island Murrays Beach and Booderee National Park beyond.

Point Perpendicular Point Perpendicular Lighthouse.

Steamers Beach, Booderee National Park A glorious, white-sanded escape.

Jervis Bay National Park Features endless stretches of beachside serenity.

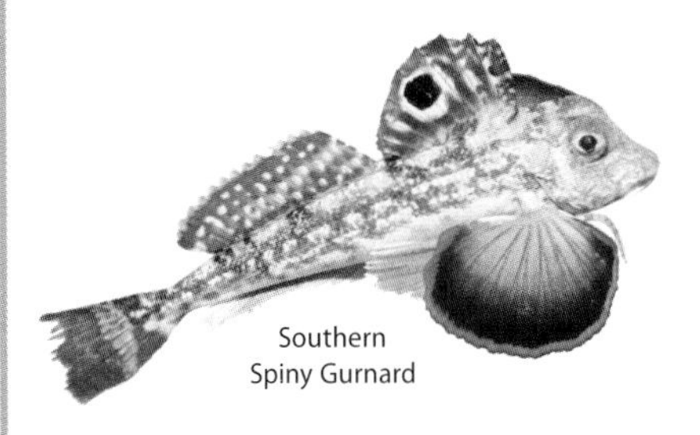

Southern Spiny Gurnard

Marine Life in Jervis Bay

Jervis Bay Marine Park is a world-renowned conservation area that spans over 100 km of coastline and covers almost 22,000 ha. The park supports many marine habitats (sandy beaches, mangroves, estuaries, seagrass flats, and subtidal and deep reefs) and is a hotbed of oceanic biodiversity.

The bay's marine life includes Bottlenose Dolphins, Humpback Whales, Australian Fur-seals, stingrays, wobbegongs and Port Jackson Sharks, different kinds of seahorses (and their fascinating relative, the Weedy Seadragon), as well as numerous types of soft and hard corals, cone shells, anemones, sponges and sea urchins.

The entire park is brimming with weird and wonderful varieties of fish, including wrasse, pigfish, goatfish, seaperch and lionfish, all of which make their homes around Jervis Bay's subtidal reefs.

Southern Roughy

Marine Life Outside Jervis Bay – the Deep Reefs

The outer reefs of Jervis Bay Marine Park contain some spectacular diving and fishing locations. The area has powerful currents and steep, shelving drop-offs, as well as many different varieties of marine life not likely to be encountered closer to shore.

A number of pelagic species frequent these environs and attract recreational anglers from all around the world. The fish targeted include powerhouse pelagics such as kingfish, marlin, and tuna. On the reefs Nannygai, Giant Boarfish, and John Dory are among the most prized catches.

The deep, temperate waters contain impressive underwater caves and rock formations. The labyrinth of nooks, crannies and underwater lairs hide canny and secretive fish species, such as the Eastern Blue Groper — once overfished but now fully protected in New South Wales.

One of the rarest and most unusual visitors to this area is the Mola Mola or Oceanic Sunfish. These gentle behemoths are truly awesome creatures — growing to over 3 m in length and weighing more than 2000 kg. Mola Mola will visit "cleaning stations" in the area, where small wrasse remove parasites that attach themselves to the giant fish's gills and mouth.

Top to bottom: Volute (a predatory gastropod); Bigbelly Seahorse; Sea anemones; Schooling Hussar; Eastern Blue Devil.

Melbourne to Sydney

Top Things to Do

1. Drive to Saddleback Mountain Lookout near Kiama.
2. Swim or surf the beaches of Killalea State Park.
3. Picnic at Jerrara Dam Arboretum.
4. Travel aboard a steam train at the Illawarra Light Railway Museum.
5. Explore the rainforest canopy at Minnamurra Rainforest Centre.
6. See water surge from the spectacular Kiama Blowhole.
7. Walk above Wollongong at Mount Keira.

Budderoo National Park

Rainforest Centre: (02) 4236 0469

Minnamurra Rainforest Centre in Budderoo National Park west of Kiama is a must-see attraction. A 1.6 km elevated timber walkway takes visitors high into the rainforest canopy. The centre has a café and is located in a sandstone canyon featuring a wide variety of rainforest habitat. Eastern Water Dragons and a multitude of birds (including Superb Lyrebirds) are present in the area.

Walks in the Park: Take the Rainforest Loop Walk, a suspended boardwalk that leads through subtropical and temperate rainforests. The walkway connects with a circuit to Minnamurra Falls.

Access: West of Kiama via the Jamberoo Road and Minnamurra Falls Road.

Camping: Not permitted in the rainforest area. Bush camping is only permitted on the Budderoo Plateau.

Nowra to Sydney

Beyond Nowra, the Princes Highway leads to Wollongong via Berry (*see below*), Kiama and Shellharbour. En route from Kiama to Shellharbour are the dramatic Cathedral Rocks. These steepling, eroded sea stacks have attracted sightseers since the late 19th century.

The region inland from Kiama also contains many scenic highlights. Visit Jerrara Dam Arboretum and Wetlands, situated 5 km west of Kiama on the banks of the dam that once served as Kiama's main water supply. Here, there is a pleasant picnic area surrounded by rainforest and freshwater wetlands.

South-west of Kiama is Saddleback Mountain Lookout. At a towering 600 m above sea level, the lookout is a prime vantage point for views of Sydney's southern beaches to the north and the Shoalhaven coast to the south. The lookout car park is the starting point for a 7 km walk along Hoddle's Trail. The track heads west and follows the route trod by colonial surveyor Robert Hoddle in the 1820s. Highlights include a walk-through rainforest and Noorinan Mountain. Half-way along Hoddle's Trail, the path heads south-west through woodland to a spectacular lookout point with vistas south to Foxground and back in the direction of Saddleback.

Killalea State Park, 90 km south of Sydney, has 8 km of beautiful coastline, including Mystics and The Farm — two popular spots for surfing and swimming. Killalea contains a total of some 250 ha of nature reserve, including areas of rainforest and bird-filled wetlands. Barbecue and picnic areas are also available for hungry daytrippers. The walks through Killalea's forested areas are particularly attractive. There are also some fine walking tracks passing through sea bird nesting areas.

The nearby Illawarra Light Railway Museum (Tongarra Rd, Albion Park, north of Kiama, Ph: (02) 4256 4627) is another of the area's best attractions, offering steam train and tram rides in an appealing historic setting. There is an assortment of vintage carriages and steam engines on display in the museum (including the restored *Kiama*, dating back to the early 1900s). The ticket office is built into the original rail terminus of the South Coast railway (designed in the 1800s). Bushrangers Bay at Bass Point, 5 km south of Shellharbour on the south coast, was declared an aquatic reserve in 1982 and is renowned as one of the best scuba diving and snorkelling areas in New South Wales.

Berry

Berry promotes itself as the first truly rural town south of Sydney and has plenty to offer by way of country hospitality. Visit in time for the Berry country markets (first Sunday of each month), the Berry Show (first weekend in February), the Berry Musicale (May and June), the Shoalhaven Coast Wine Festival (June) or the Garden Festival in October. There are more than a dozen boutique wineries in the area, dotted around a painterly landscape of rolling hills and flowing creeks. Berry began as a private town on the country estate of its first major settler, Alexander Berry. It evolved into the commercial centre for a vibrant dairy and timber district and its streetscapes are laden with historic buildings, many now housing cafés, antique stores and craft galleries.

Kiama

The Kiama Blowhole is a celebrated local spectacle, sending towering jets of water skyward. At Blowhole Point (near the visitor centre) Kiama's maritime and regional museum, the Pilots Cottage Museum (Ph: (02) 4232 1001), preserves the area's history in a restored cottage. The Spring Creek Bird Hide at Kiama's Glenbrook Drive is a birdwatching "hide" that permits up-close and unobstructed views of local waterbirds including thornbills, cormorants and swans. Nearby Budderoo National Park includes Carrington Falls, a dramatic 50 m waterfall.

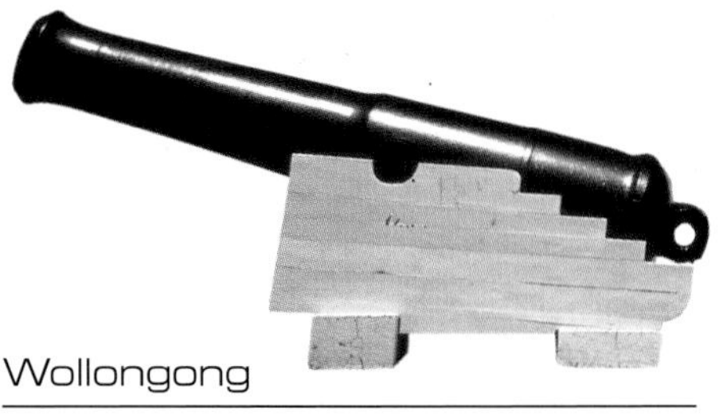

Wollongong

Wollongong is only an hour south of Sydney's city centre and 45 minutes from the Southern Highlands. Centred on an attractive harbour, Wollongong is a blend of residential suburbia, shipping, shopping, industry, education and colonial heritage. Mount Keira is an ideal vantage point for surveying the area — its elevated position permits panoramic views and scenic walks in the surrounding landscape. Wollongong Harbour is a tightly enclosed, circular harbour with two long stretches of beach — North Wollongong and City Beach — stretching directly north and south from the heads. The scenic coastal drive along Cliff Road into outer Sydney includes the picturesque seaside suburbs of Stanwell Park, Thirroul and Bulli.

Royal National Park

Phone Ranger: (02) 9542 0648

On a clear day in central Sydney, the wide green expanses of Royal National Park can be seen from the observation deck of Sydney Tower. Situated some 32 km south of the city, between Loftus and Stanwell Tops, Royal is Australia's oldest national park and the world's second-oldest (after Yellowstone in the USA), having been first established in 1879. It remains a popular destination for thousands of backpackers, campers, and daytrippers from Sydney and beyond each year. The park contains landscapes ranging from classic Australian bush to dunes and rocky coastal escarpments, and protects almost 250 species of animal.

Surfing beaches in Royal National Park include Garie, North Era, South Era and Burning Palms — they are all found along the park's southern coastline. For boating opportunities try the hiring service from Audley Boat Shed (Ph: (02) 9545 4967), a good place from which to head upstream towards one of several popular picnic spots.

Walks in the Park: Many trails make their way to secluded beaches, picnic spots and camping areas. Some are especially popular, including the 8 km trek to the pretty beach at Burning Palms. An elegant, Victorian-era feel is found in the spectacular Lady Carrington Walk and at Audley where, in 1887, some 3700 ornamental trees were planted. There are also Spotlight Safaris where visitors can join a ranger and roam the rainforest at night trying to find elusive nocturnal animals like the Eastern Pygmy-possum.

Access: Forty-seven kilometres north of Wollongong on the Princes Highway.

Camping: There are camping and caravan sites at Bonnie Vale as well as a huge range of accommodation possibilities in adjoining suburbs. Conditions and permits apply to bush camping.

PHOTOGRAPHING AUSTRALIA

CREATING A RECORD OF YOUR JOURNEY

11

We are living at a time when creating photographs, whether as a record of memories or a process of self-expression, has never been more controllable by the photographer. When I first starting using digital cameras, the transformation was unlike anything I would have imagined. Digital technology has obvious benefits, allowing the photographer to view work in progress and the luxury of checking capture quality while still in the field. It generously provides latitude for exposure errors and (at the top of my list) allows you to change the ISO rating on individual shots (in terms of film and its speed or sensitivity). Of course, once you get your camera back home and hooked up to your computer, there are a raft of other benefits as well.

However, it has been my experience that while so many avid photographers are revelling in their new-found digital freedom, they are also finding that digital image-making has neither improved the appeal of their photographs nor necessarily saved them time or money. A computer, expensive software for image management and filing, hard drives for picture storage, and so on, are not essential in the world of film and prints. In summary, I would emphasise that if you have not gone beyond a film camera and a book of prints, do not be concerned that the photographs you take on your trip will be any less appealing than those made on a digital camera. The age-old adage that, "cameras do not take photographs, people do" applies to every single photograph made. Although, I would add that in the world of nature photography the appeal of a photograph is also greatly enhanced by the light (as can be seen opposite), and also the subject material. Achieving a good angle of view, perspective, composition, and colour management — to mention just a few aspects of picture-taking — call the individual's creative skills into play.

This section has been created to give you a helping hand in taking the step from a part-time happy-snapper to a creative, thinking photographer. The following photographic tips cover the primary subjects that you will encounter as you wend your way around the enormous island of Australia.

Left: The photographs opposite were all taken at Cape Leeuwin — the south-west extremity of Australia. Facing west, and with the sun rising from the east, I simply made a series of images with the best of the changing light. The series perfectly illustrates how important it is to be up and about when light is fast changing, which — in most cases — is during the times of dawn and dusk. It also enabled me to give you the tip that "hanging about" at the same spot is the single best piece of advice I could ever give a photographer.

Australia – a Different Light

Working with Australia's many types of natural light is a challenge to photographers. It can cause aggravation, particularly when all the elements of a stunning picture are in front of you ... all, that is, except the "right" light. Serious photographers spend a lot of time sky-watching, because the sky conditions play an important role in all natural light photography, especially if the sky itself is to be included in the photograph. If the sky is featureless, then you may need to crop much of it out by composing the image to include more foreground — although empty space can create a great photograph. You will find that there are few immutable laws in photography — there are exceptions to most rules of thumb.

In Australia, from the tropical north to the temperate south, there is a vast array of weather conditions. Light is directly affected by the weather, which, in turn, is influenced by topography, latitude and longitude, and season. Over the many years during which I have worked with natural light, I have learned to defuse my aggravation and instead broaden my preparedness to work with varying light conditions. I have discovered that different subjects are best shot in different lights; and that angle of view, choice of ISO (film speed) setting, lens selection, perspective, and so on, all play a role in shifting emphasis away from "bad" light.

Different kinds of weather suit different kinds of photographic subjects. Overcast weather that doesn't throw dense shadows is ideal for photographing in the rainforest. On a bright sunny day, you might change your plans and head for the coast. If, having arrived at the coast you find that clouds have sprung up and the sky is overcast after all, try wandering the streets of coastal towns. There's no point in shaking your fist at the sky. Turn the negative to positive and you'll get some great shots, even if they weren't what you originally planned.

Harsh Midday Light

The main problem associated with working while the sun is high is contrast in light and shade, which can produce deep, dark, unattractive shadows and colours with little tonal variation.

I must admit that for many years I avoided shooting in the middle of the day or in harshly lit situations, preferring to shoot in the softer, warmer light of early morning and late afternoon. However, I have found that if I work throughout the day, carefully choosing my subject, lens and angle of view, I can extend my working time. This is important when I'm on the move because I can get impatient with the delays and frustrations of waiting for light to be "right". Depending on the type of shooting, bright days can produce benefits:

Tripod. A small aperture results in increased depth of field, which means a hand-held camera doesn't need a tripod.

Shutter speed. Higher shutter speeds are great for freezing action.

Light. In some circumstances, light penetrates best in the middle of the day. Underwater photography and working in gorges with parallel high walls are two such circumstances.

If the light is too bright for your corresponding ISO setting, it may be necessary to use either polaroid or neutral density filters to reduce light. These, and ultra-violet filters, will also assist in reducing haze.

Diffused Light

When cloud cover, mist, dust or some other sort of haze is diffusing the light, don't despair. This type of light is perfect for a wide range of photographic subjects. Fine particles in the air soften the landscape, and, in certain circumstances, can enhance the mood in an image. I find misty and hazy days beneficial for close-up or telephoto work with wildflowers and wildlife, or when shooting inside a forest. In these instances, harsh sunlight creates dark shadows that can make a photograph unappealing; whereas light filtered and reflected from fine particles can gently illuminate even the darkest areas.

Overcast weather bringing cooler conditions can cause wildlife to become more active. Nocturnal mammals may remain out and about, or emerge for their night activities earlier, due to the lowered light level and associated cooler weather. Birds also become more active during the middle of a sunless day. An added benefit of cloudy weather is that it softens the light to the extent that details like fur and feathers become far more defined.

Another effect of diffused light is intensified colour. This effect can be seen when bright areas of sky are excluded from the frame. As a result of the lack of shadow and contrast, colours appear more tonally varied and fine textures are visible. The subject's form is more likely to be enhanced in diffused light, especially if the photographic angle is varied. To select the best angle, simply try moving around your subject (if you can).

Top to bottom: The MacDonnell Ranges of the Northern Territory; Featuring a series of thirteen gorges, Katherine Gorge is a must-see; Light filters through a fan palm forest in the Daintree National Park.

Reflected Natural Light

Apart from shooting in the diffused light of an overcast or misty day, another way of achieving softer, more evenly lit photographs on normal sunny days is to try and position, or choose, subjects that can be illuminated by light reflected from nearby surfaces. If the light level is very low, requiring a slow shutter speed, below say 1/30 of a second then a tripod may be needed to hold the camera steady. In most instances, however, ISO 100 film combined with an aperture above f5.6, or even wider, will suffice.

In certain circumstances (close-ups for example) a hand-held reflector can be used to either add more light or fill in shadows. In public spaces, like shopping malls, gallery foyers, outdoor eating areas, and so on, there is often enough reflected light to make a photograph with a hand-held camera. If the day is bright overcast, hazy or misty, then the amount of reflected light available in shaded areas is likely to increase. When photographing people during the day, I sometimes ask them to move or subtly manoeuvre them into an area where reflected light exists (such as beside a light-coloured wall).

As a general rule, if photographs are composed tightly with an eye on the aesthetic appeal and the relationship that the background has with the subject, shooting in and around reflected light can produce some very appealing photographs — even if the light is harsh and full of contrast. Of course, when all else fails, there is always fill-in flash. Remember to calculate exposure in areas that represent the focal point of interest.

The Glow of Sunrise & Sunset

In the glow that accompanies many sunrises and sunsets, colours are usually warmer and wild creatures are more likely to be out and about. The beginning and end of the day are my favourite times and they are times I often wish would last forever.

Haze, welcome at these times of day and shunned otherwise, and the angle of the rising or setting sun, can produce some spectacular pictures. The photographs may be of any subject — cityscapes, people, animals, wildflowers or insect close-ups and, especially, natural and rural landscapes — all will be particularly attractive in light that has such special qualities. At dawn, the sun's rays may have to penetrate fog, producing wonderfully soft images when the sun is included in the composition. At sunset, the day's dust reflects the dying light and softens the world's hard edges. Water, wet sand or wet mud reflections can add to the drama of a picture and, depending on your angle of view to the sun, there may be some fine silhouettes that can be composed as photographs.

Storms

I love the time just after a violent storm when the sky is spectacular and light streams through breaks in the clouds. Australia has some marvellous storms, especially in the tropics at the end of the dry season. Similarly, I have seen some of the most spectacular skies in southern Australia — usually as a storm builds or just after it has passed.

Clouds often help make a picture that is otherwise not much of a picture at all. Some of my favourite images are interesting only because of the sky colours and cloud formations. To heighten the effects of sky and clouds you might try using a Polaroid filter, particularly if the sky is very bright and sunny. Alternatively, try under-exposing by one or two f-stops as this will accentuate sky colours and give contrast between them and the clouds. Because there can be several f-stops between the sky and the ground it is also a good idea to bracket exposures if you feel unsure. Bracketing exposures means taking a series of shots of the same subject at different exposures. You may even choose to use one of the many filters available that create sky colour effects. If you have advanced skills in digital image management then bracketing may not be necessary because there is considerable exposure flexibility.

Top to bottom: In public places there is often enough reflected light to get a good shot; Kata Tjuṯa's ever-changing moods; Boab trees make a stark contrast against the sunset in the Kimberleys; Wildflowers bloom in Uluṟu-Kata Tjuṯa NP.

Top to bottom: A Green Tree-frog, found in all States except Tasmania and Victoria; The mass flowering of Sturt's Desert Pea has brought many a traveller to a standstill; An Assassin Bug ambushes a Ladybird.

Tips for Photographing Plants, Animals & Landscapes

Australia is home to a spectacular variety of animals and plants that will fill you with awe as you travel. Of course, what species you encounter depends not only upon your location, but also upon the type of habitat you are travelling through, the time of year, the season and, of course, the amount of rain that has recently fallen. The latter is particularly important because rainfall has a vital effect on all living things. I know that even on my urban block, drought causes a standstill, but when it rains the property explodes with birds, insects, spiders, mammals, frogs and reptiles — all in some way attracted to the fresh flowering blooms, which either form a source of food or are a place to hunt for prey.

Apart from the specific topical tips listed on the following pages, the very best advice I can give the travelling nature photographer falls into three general categories:

Planning. Research your trip to follow the very best regional seasons.

Study. Read about the sorts of animals and plants you are likely to encounter. In saying that, you don't need to become a scientist, just an aware observer.

Attitude. Do yourself a big favour and take time on your trip to be alone with nature — slowly walking, quietly sitting, practising patience and being at one with your surrounds. Be warned though, you may well find a new life direction! Photographing nature is an extremely addictive hobby.

Photographing Wildflowers

- An SLR camera is much better for wildflower photography than a point-and-shoot-style camera, as it is far easier, looking through the lens, to focus on the subject and control the "look" of the background through depth-of-field control.
- Macro lenses give much better results than close-up filter attachments. The best focal lengths for flowers are between 100 mm and 200 mm.
- Master fill-in flash photography, as this will be of considerable benefit, particularly to maximise the number of species you record. You can use either a macro ring-flash or a single flash attached to your hot shoe.
- Research is your best friend. The internet is chock-full of information. There are also a number of excellent reference books available on the subject of Australian wildflowers.
- Most botanic gardens have either wildflower sections or entire gardens devoted to native flowers. The Australian National Botanic Gardens in Canberra and Kings Park in Perth are but two of the many public gardens around the country that have excellent native wildflower displays. They are ideal for recording species in top condition and offer easy access to subjects as you develop your flower photography skills.

Photographing Spiders & Insects

- An SLR camera is best for invertebrate photography, preferably (but not essentially) with a motor drive and automatic metering system.
- These are small animals, so I suggest a macro lens, preferably 105 mm or, even better, a 200 mm macro lens. For very small insects you may need to add close-up lens attachments or extension bellows. An electronic flash system is also essential.
- Creepy crawlies may be encountered day or night, although night-time lighting draws them in, and can be a great place to find an abundance of species.
- Management of depth-of-field and selective focus is the same for close-ups as through any lens; however, the focus with extreme close-ups may be even more critical, and understanding the relationships between apertures and shutter speeds is essential.
- Watch your backgrounds. Aesthetic backgrounds will enhance your spider and insect photos. If you use light to attract insects at night, you will get black backgrounds.
- As you travel around Australia you will discover that some areas are more prolific with insects than others. This also applies to seasons. For example, spring flowering (wherever you are in Australia) is best for insects.
- Remember that invertebrates can be habitat-specific, so be careful about moving them.

Photographing Mammals

- For mammal photography, an SLR camera is best, although point-and-shoot cameras can suffice. For daylight work on kangaroos and marine mammals, use 400–600 mm lenses. For night work on animals like possums, rodents, dasyurids and bandicoots I use the 80–200 mm zoom with a power flash, or sometimes two, depending on the subject.
- Apart from kangaroos, wallabies and the marine mammals, most mammals are very shy and are rarely seen in wild areas (where they may not have encountered humans). Many smaller mammals are photographed either in captivity or in areas where they have developed tolerance of, or curiosity about, humans.
- Small mammals (e.g. dasyurids, bandicoots and rodents) are nocturnally active, so a head torch and a focus lantern are essential accessories.
- While auto-focus does work at night, I sometimes prefer to focus manually.
- Watch your backgrounds. Aesthetically pleasing backgrounds will enhance your images.

Photographing Birds

- An SLR is the best camera for bird photography, preferably with a motor drive and automatic metering system; however, the latter two are not essential. I have seen some stunning bird photos taken with point-and-shoot cameras, but these are usually wider shots where exact focus is not as important.
- Lenses from 300–600 mm are ideal. I use 300 mm and a 70–400 mm zoom for close work with small bush birds in shrubs, with an automatic flash for fill-in if necessary. Use a 500–600 mm lens for water and sea birds (you may even choose to use a tele-converter).
- A tripod is essential, especially in low light when a slow shutter speed is required.
- You will need to be patient and calm. Any anxiety or noise will cause your highly sensitive and acutely aware quarry to take flight.
- As with all subjects, the foreground and background are almost as important as the primary subject. A little computer editing might prove necessary, at a later date, to remove ugly and intrusive elements.
- Sea birds are common residents of Australia's coastal environments. It is important not to disturb these animals during their nesting season; if you scare away the parent birds, you may endanger the chicks or the eggs by exposing them to predators. Give rookeries a wide berth — observe and photograph them from a safe distance.
- Birds of prey, parrots and all those delightful small wrens, warblers, finches and so on, are very sensitive around their nesting areas and may abandon their chicks if disturbed. I tend to keep away from nests and concentrate on birds' many other fascinating behaviours. If nesting birds are your objective, work from a hide or blind, and find out as much as you can about the bird's behaviour and sensitivities before you start.
- Water birds, if disturbed during nesting, may also abandon their chicks and, like sea birds, they may nest in large colonies. Again, learn as much as you can before going near a colony. If there are marauding gulls around, stay well away.

Photographing Frogs & Reptiles

- An SLR camera is best, although point-and-shoot cameras can achieve good results with reptile photography. Preferable (although not essential) is a camera with a motor drive and automatic metering system.
- Because reptiles range in size from tiny geckoes to giant crocodiles there are no ideal lenses — the full range of focal lengths will be useful. For the majority of small skinks, frogs, geckoes, dragons, and snakes, a 50 mm, 105 mm or 200 mm macro lens is, in my opinion, ideal. For full-body shots of snakes (non-venomous, of course), I would choose a moderately wide-angle lens, such as 35 mm. Zoom lenses may be easier, because you can move from a full-body shot to a portrait with just a flip of the wrist.
- Reptiles are more likely to be active when it is warm — day or night. On warm nights, I recommend you carry a powerful electronic flash with automatic flash-fill.
- If you wish to photograph reptiles, I strongly advise you to do your research. Reptiles are usually secretive and, being cryptically coloured, are not easy to find in the wild.
- Take care with dangerous snakes.
- It is illegal to capture and transport reptiles without a permit in all Australian States.

Top to bottom: Black-footed Rock-wallabies are easily photographed in many places in the MacDonnell Ranges; Egrets feeding beside the road in the Top End; A Velvet Gecko photographed in the Pilbara.

Top to bottom: Sunlight shafting through the rainforest; A waterfall photographed with a slow shutter speed; A Boab tree bathed in late afternoon light. Note how the low angle of the sun also helps create a three-dimensional effect.

Photographing Wet Forests

Wet forests, perhaps more than most environments, provide a multi-sensory experience involving touch, sight, sound and smell. Being in the dense forest can be a profound experience. It envelops the soul, taking you to a peaceful place where emotions are not easily communicated through a photograph.

The best conditions for photographing inside dark forests are either bright overcast or misty days. The shafts of light that fill the forest create a spectacular effect. The reason for preferring overcast weather is that the water particles in cloud and mist diffuse the light, allowing it to penetrate into even the darkest areas of forest. With a camera mounted on a tripod, a wide-angle lens, and a cable release attached to your camera (to reduce any movement), you will be amazed at the results you will get even under what may appear to be quite dark conditions. Depending on the sophistication of your digital camera, you may not need a tripod as the wide range of ISO settings may enable you to arrange your camera settings to suit the conditions. The trick is to avoid large areas of sky in the picture — they will overwhelm the forest, making it appear darker and filled with shadow. Follow these tips for photographing wet forests:

- Get as much information as you can about conditions and scenic/botanical attractions.
- Always pack for a day's outing. Even if you are planning a half-day, you never know what delights may be encountered.
- Pack wet-weather protection for your equipment; it's not called wet forest for nothing! Take insect repellent, and wear leggings and watertight boots, particularly during the wet season in the tropics — the leeches will get you where you least expect, you can be sure of that.
- Walk quietly — wet forest birds and mammals do not like sudden noises. Try to pick times when other people are less likely to visit so noise is minimised.
- An SLR, wide-angle, close-up lens, flash and medium telephoto lens are great tools.

Photographing Waterfalls

Some of the most appealing images to come out of a wet forest are of waterfalls, especially after recent heavy rain when falls are exploding with water. The overall appeal of the image is intensified if the light is diffused by water particles from either cloud or mist. Bright overcast weather with a touch of mist is ideal, but not always possible.

To further enhance a waterfall photograph, use a slow shutter speed, say 1/30 of a second, and preferably even slower — around 1/15, 1/10 or 1/5 of a second or even slower. This effectively blurs the water, creating a sense of movement. You might like to try several shutter speeds then judge the result. If the light is too bright you can reduce the light level by attaching a neutral density filter. To ensure a sharp image, attach your camera to a tripod and use either the delay timer on your camera or a cable release to prevent movement.

Photographing Trees

Trees are an excellent subject when you are new to photography. They present a perfect opportunity for you to develop your skills in vital areas like light management, perspective control, balance and viewpoint.

First, find a tree that you want to work with. Then, camera in hand, work your way around the tree, framing it without taking any pictures. Study each viewpoint, frame it loose and tight, move around close to its trunk and see what interesting relationships might exist between the branches and the surrounding landscape. You can see an example of this in the photograph of the grand old Boab on the left. When I first encountered this tree, it was about a kilometre from the road. I could see the interesting landscape on my right and wondered if there was a composition that would bring the tree and the landscape together. I decided to come back when the light was warmer later in the day, hoping that the angle of light would be right. I returned some hours later and fortunately all the elements came together. See how the light has given dimension and form to both the tree and the distant escarpment? Light from behind my viewpoint would have flattened the tree and the landscape.

- Apart from being the centre of interest, trees can also provide a vital element of contrast in what may otherwise be a bland landscape — against a setting sun, for example. In such cases your meter reading should be taken on the sky.
- Trees, particularly when they are isolated against a clear unbroken horizon, can provide the perfect key element in a sunset shot. As you drive, start looking for solitary trees. Once you have found a target, study it closely. Take your time — it will not go away. Watch the weather, and then choose your moment.

Photographing Landscapes

Australia has amazingly varied landscapes, from spacious, open, arid dunes and grasslands with dead-flat horizons to precipitous alpine peaks. These extremes are often a short drive from most urban centres and, with camera in hand, it is easy to get lost in landscape magic. Regardless of the format of your camera, or what lenses you have, most important in photographing a landscape are content, mood and design. I find the initials CMD a useful reminder of these three primary elements:

Content. The content of a landscape scene — this refers to the land itself.

Mood. Mood is a combination of light and other natural elements.

Design. Design is multifaceted, involving the successful marriage of elements such as composition, planes, angles of view and colour.

Every time I approach a landscape, I consider all of these. It reminds me to capture each place in different styles for different applications — in documentary or artistic styles. Explore and work with content, mood and design. The more you explore landscape with your body, mind and soul, the better you will connect with the subject and, consequently, the more powerful your images will be.

Where applicable to the scene, I shoot landscape in several formats — horizontal, vertical, loose and tight. To maintain high resolution, nice sharp pictures that are suitable for enlargement, I use prime (fixed focal length lenses as opposed to zoom) and low ISO settings in digital work. In the past I have used medium-format cameras and film; however, I now find digital formats, used with care, produce very similar results. As far as lenses are concerned, there is no such thing as a perfect focal length for landscape. In my own work I have used everything from 10 mm ultra-wide to 500 mm — it all depends on the landscape and which elements you wish to isolate to tell your story.

- An SLR camera is excellent for landscape photography. Ideal lenses are 20 mm and 35 mm, or a short zoom; however, any lens can be used to photograph trees and determining focal length depends entirely on the perspective you seek.
- All weather is good. Try using the prevailing conditions as an integral part of your picture. For example, if the weather is moody and you feel moody, shoot a moody picture! If you need specific conditions for a particular shot then you will just have to wait. Remember, of course, that there is always much to do while waiting.
- All lenses and all formats are excellent for landscape photography. The equipment/formats available to you may limit the sort of things you can communicate, but they will not stop you communicating.
- The best way to educate yourself about the emotional interpretation of landscape is to study the works of renowned landscape artists — particularly abstract painters. They have learned to paint their feelings.
- Keep the initials CMD (content, mood and design) in mind. They are the three primary elements that must be considered in the construction of every image you make.
- Film types and formats, camera brands, accessories and so on, are the means of constructing images, not the ends in themselves. For example, an expensive camera does not equal good landscape photography — results usually have more to do with the imagination of the photographer.

Getting Back to Basics

I recommend the following as basic landscape photography techniques and suggest that you modify them as you gain experience:

- Take care when composing your images.
- Take both horizontal and vertical shots.
- Include clouds in your shots if there are any.
- Shoot in the early morning and late afternoon.
- Don't stop shooting when the sun goes down; work with the twilight as well.
- Stop down the aperture in most cases.
- Use a variety of lenses and vary your point of view.
- Look for interest in the foreground.

Top to bottom: All five of these images illustrate just how relevant content, mood and design are in creating an effective picture.

Photographing Australia's Built Environment

When photographing Australia's built environment you are making images of places familiar to many, so your challenge is to engage and hold people's attention. That is a big goal, and one that I constantly remind myself of when confronted with re-photographing a building for the 20th time. A question I always ask myself is, how can I make these images different? The approach is similar to photographing natural landscape — use the formulas with which we started this section, considering content, mood and design. I'll explain them in reverse order.

Design

Angle of view is the key component of design, as is the overall composition of the image, including issues such as the magnification of perspective that can occur when you are photographing a tall, square-edged object. When the photograph includes a subject with vertical edges the problem of parallax distortion is introduced. This is particularly accentuated by a wide-angle lens, and is worse if the angle of view is low to the building (which it will be if you are standing on the ground) and angled upwards.

There are several ways to overcome the problem of parallels. First, you can use a camera with the facility for correcting parallax by tilting. Second, you can find a vantage point as high as about halfway up the building. Third, and this is less likely in the closed environment of a city, you can take a more distant viewpoint and use a longer lens. It is possible to correct parallax distortion (to a degree) in photo-editing software on a computer. Finally, you can choose to ignore the accentuated parallax distortion and accept it as being part of the overall design of the photograph. Unless you are a purist who sees distortion as a fault, you will probably accept, and sometimes even admire, the effect (as most people invariably do).

Mood

Consider carefully the mood you wish to convey. Harsh shadows and contrast will add impact, and, if that is your aim, a bright sunny day is the best time to work. If the building is illuminated at night and there is an opportunity to frame the structure somewhat loosely (maybe to include twilight sky colours), you will have to find out when the lights come on and when the sun sets and hope that they coincide. There is not much use in having the lights come on an hour after sunset as the sky will be pitch black and an important effect in the image will be lost. Mist can be effective, as can a bright overcast day. The latter is particularly useful if the buildings have verandas or deep recesses that will be illuminated in overcast conditions.

Content

If a building is the main feature of your photograph, decide on your primary objectives. For example, is the image to stand alone, or is it to be part of a series? If this is the case, are there several angles to consider? If the building has a textured surface you wish to accentuate, then the angle of the light will have to be considered. If the building has any signs that would date the shot, you may have to come back when the banners are removed, or consider having the images scanned at a high resolution so the signage can be edited out on computer.

Top to bottom: The repetitive design of Parliament House reflected in the pool gives this picture its effect; Melbourne in twilight helps create an all over effect to this picture; A hotel in Rockhampton, Queensland, illustrates how important it is to use shadow to help give dimension to your pictures; A rustic corrugated iron house in Queensland's outback shows how dramatic simple, graphic lines can help with the design of a photograph.

- While 35 mm SLR cameras are adequate for making images of architecture, I personally use 6 x 7 format cameras — both range-finder and SLR. The best cameras are those with a tilting back or front, enabling parallax correction. Parallax distortion is commonly seen when buildings are photographed (particularly in close-up with a wide-angle lens). Some of the better brands of 35 mm lenses, which can sometimes be picked up second-hand at a reasonable price, offer vertical and horizontal movements and will correct this distortion.
- A tripod with an easily adjustable head is an important aid in architectural photography.
- The right quality of light is vital with urban images, particularly when buildings are your primary focus. The golden colours of dawn and dusk, or the softness of twilight, can enhance the appeal of your photographs.
- A "familiarising visit" before a shoot may pay dividends.
- If you intend to shoot in twilight, take a tripod and cable release, as shutter speeds may need to be slow. Slow shutter speeds can be effective in street scenes that involve the headlights and tail lights of passing vehicles. Shutter speeds of 1/15 to 1/8 of a second give excellent results.
- For artificial light outdoors, you may choose to use filters, but (apart from where there is heavy use of fluorescent lighting) it is generally not necessary to change film or use filters.

Photographing Australians

Photographing Your Subjects "Aware"

The top four photographs on this page were taken with the subject being aware of my intention to photograph them. Photographs in which your subject is aware of your presence can have their own magic because they are engaging directly with the viewer of the photograph. Understandably, there are degrees of subject "awareness", which are as variable as the many different facial expressions shown by different subjects.

Photographing Your Subjects "Unaware"

Hanging around small towns, camps, communities and cattle stations in the Australian outback, "fitting in" as best you can (even though you stick out like a sore thumb), is one way to make candid shots. The other is to travel the back streets of towns and country roads searching out unusual photographs of people going about their daily lives. Rodeos, horse races or anything organised by the locals for the locals offer the best possibilities for photos.

If you find yourself in a major outback centre (e.g. in a town the size of Kalgoorlie, Alice Springs, Mount Isa or Longreach), you might try joining the locals and doing what they are doing. Spend time with your prospective subjects. The more time you invest and the more interest you show, the more you are likely to connect with the people around you. Above all else, talk to them. Look for character, watch for body language and have fun. The very best results are achieved when you are accepted as part of a community. For that to happen, you will need time.

- If you are working on a project, go without your camera, maybe when you wouldn't be shooting anyway, and talk to people about what you would like to do. This strategy can work well in small communities — a cattle camp, a homestead or an Aboriginal community. When you do pick up your camera, you will probably be ignored and able to photograph without feeling you are invading people's personal space.
- Be very selective. Look for interesting faces, people who look as if they belong to the place you are in. Unguarded, not posed, expressions usually work best (although people aware can also be fun).
- Trust your instincts. If something looks and feels good, shoot it and think later. Spontaneity is crucial! I have a memory full of missed prize-winners!
- I don't usually ask permission in a very public place. I try and blend in by being casual and not dressing like a professional photographer. In those instances, I certainly don't carry lots of photographic equipment.
- Don't move on from a shoot until you have tried every possible angle. If you began taking shots of people unaware, maybe talk to your subject and make them aware of the camera.
- Don't be a tourist. Be yourself and, above all, be interested enough to stop and sit a while. To make excellent pictures of people, it is essential that you connect — maybe not with the individual but certainly with their culture and traditions. Try reversing the situation in your mind. How would you feel if someone shoved a camera in your face? How would you like to be treated?
- Flashes and tripods are a big put-off. Keep the gear simple — for example, an SLR with a zoom lens but without a motor drive. Even better is a simple rangefinder camera.
- If your target is a trader, try discussing their wares first. Then go for a wander, and come back when your presence has been forgotten.
- Do not stint on film, if you still use it. It's cheap. With digital images, memory cards are also an even cheaper alternative.
- Watch the body language of your subject; it is far more important than the surrounds.
- Most people like being photographed and some will even volunteer.
- Consider how you may like to use the pictures of people that you are creating. For example, the gun shearer sleeping on a pile of wool clippings (*right*) was initially part of a story on shearing. To go with this photograph I made images of shearing, the wool sheds, the transport trucks, shepherds at work and so on.

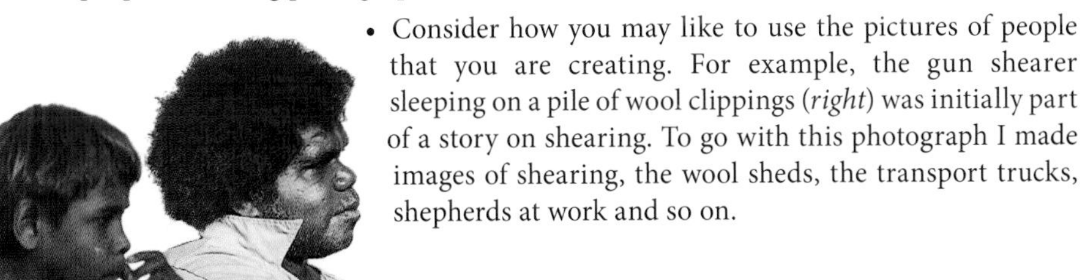

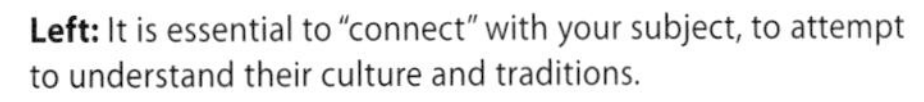

Left: It is essential to "connect" with your subject, to attempt to understand their culture and traditions.

Top to bottom: The top four pictures illustrate subject "aware", while the next five illustrate subject "unaware".

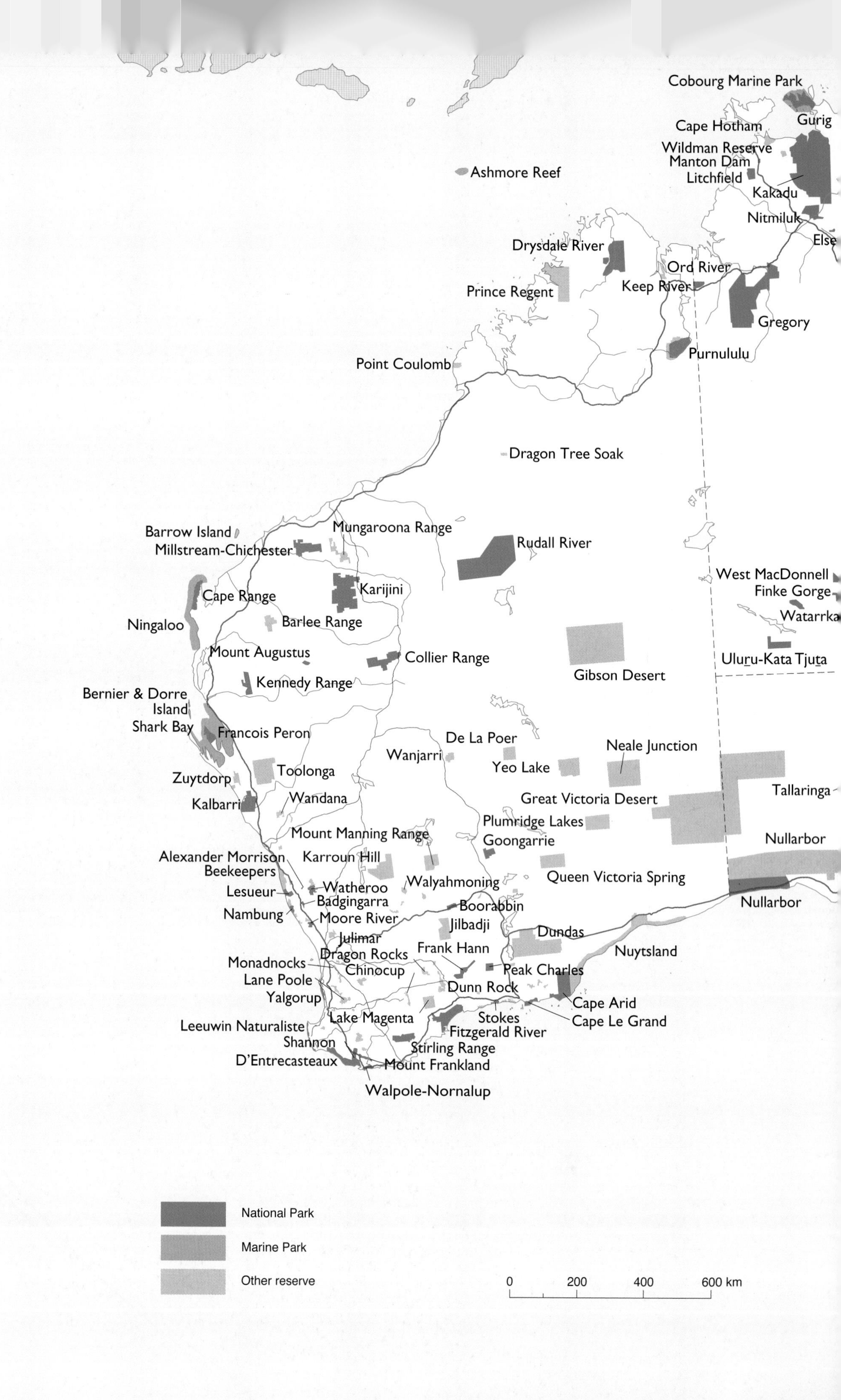
Cobourg Marine Park
Gurig
Cape Hotham
Wildman Reserve
Manton Dam
Litchfield
Kakadu
Nitmiluk
Else
Ashmore Reef
Drysdale River
Ord River
Keep River
Prince Regent
Gregory
Purnululu
Point Coulomb
Dragon Tree Soak
Barrow Island
Mungaroona Range
Millstream-Chichester
Rudall River
Karijini
Cape Range
West MacDonnell
Finke Gorge
Ningaloo
Barlee Range
Watarrka
Mount Augustus
Collier Range
Uluru-Kata Tjuta
Gibson Desert
Kennedy Range
Bernier & Dorre
Island
Shark Bay
Francois Peron
De La Poer
Neale Junction
Wanjarri
Yeo Lake
Toolonga
Zuytdorp
Tallaringa
Great Victoria Desert
Wandana
Kalbarri
Plumridge Lakes
Mount Manning Range
Goongarrie
Nullarbor
Alexander Morrison
Karroun Hill
Beekeepers
Queen Victoria Spring
Walyahmoning
Watheroo
Lesueur
Nullarbor
Badgingarra
Boorabbin
Nambung
Moore River
Jilbadji
Dundas
Julimar
Frank Hann
Nuytsland
Dragon Rocks
Monadnocks
Chinocup
Peak Charles
Lane Poole
Dunn Rock
Yalgorup
Cape Arid
Stokes
Lake Magenta
Cape Le Grand
Leeuwin Naturaliste
Fitzgerald River
Shannon
Stirling Range
D'Entrecasteaux
Mount Frankland
Walpole-Nornalup
National Park
Marine Park
Other reserve
0
200
400
600 km

Jardine River
Great Barrier Reef
Iron Range
Mungkan Kandju
Cape Melville
Lakefield
Barranyi
Mitchell and
Alice Rivers
Great Barrier Reef
Daintree
Staaten River
Coringa-Herald
Wooroonooran
Bulleringa
Lihou Reef
Hinchinbrook Island
Connells Lagoon
Undara Volcanic
Lawn Hill
Lumholtz
Mt Spec
Bowling Green Bay
Camooweal Caves
Great Basalt Wall
Conway
White Mountains
Repulse
Eungella
Moorrinya
Great Barrier Reef
Bladensburg
Broad Sound
Arltunga
Ruby Gap
Diamantina
Goneaway
Goodedulla
Blackdown Tableland
Lochern
Kroombit Tops
Idalia
Welford
Carnarvon
Palmgrove
Simpson Desert
Great Sandy
Expedition
Burrum Coast
Mariala
Simpson
Desert
Maaroom
Witjira
Chesterton Range
Innamincka
Bunya Mountains
Lake Eyre
Thrushton
Mount Mistake
Moreton Island
Southwood
Currawinya
Main Range
Lamington
Elliot Price
Culgoa
Floodplain
Border Ranges
Bundjalung
Bald Rock
Strzelecki
Sturt
Washpool
Gibraltar Range
Gammon Ranges
Kings Plains
Nymboida
Lake Torrens
Lake Frome
Mount Kaputar
Yuraygir
Cathedral Rock
Dorrigo
Guy Fawkes River
Mootwingee
New England
Flinders
Range
Warrumbungle
Hat Head
Werrikimbe
Oxley Wild Rivers
Lake Gairdner
Pinkawillinie
Lake Gilles
Woko
Kinchega
Goulburn River
Crowdy Bay
Mount Remarkable
Yathong
Barrington Tops
Wollemi
Willandra
Bascombe
Well
Danggali
Blue Mountains
Yengo
Myall Lakes
Lord Howe Island
Mallee Cliffs
Murray River
Conimbla
Dharug
Mungo
Weddin Mts.
Hincks
Brisbane Water
Coffin
Bay
Hattah-Kulkyne
Cocoparra
Kanangra-Boyd
Ku-ring-gai Chase
Tarlo River
Royal
Billiatt
Murray-Sunset
Lincoln
Innes
Nattai
Marramarra
Ngarkat
Wyperfeld
Flinders
Morton
Budderoo
Chase
Big Desert
Kosciuszko
Budawang
Cape Gantheaume
Little Desert
Alpine
Deua
Coorong
Wadbilliga
Mount Buffalo
Grampians
Mimosa Rocks
Canunda
Kinglake
Ben Boyd
Brisbane Ranges
Nungatta
Lower Glenelg
Coopracambra
Angahook-Lorne
Baw Baw
Croajingolong
Otway
Mitchell River
Errinundra
Wilsons Promontory
Snowy River
Lavinia
Central
Plateau
Waterhouse
Mount William
Arthur-Pieman
Ben Lomond
Cradle Mtn-Lake St Clair
Douglas-Apsley
Walls of Jerusalem
Freycinet
Franklin-Lower Gordon
Wild Rivers
Maria Island
Mount Field
Hartz Mountains
Southwest

A

B

C

F

G

L

M

T

U

V

W

Y

Z

Published by Steve Parish Publishing Pty Ltd
PO Box 1058, Archerfield, Queensland 4108 Australia

www.steveparish.com.au

ISBN 978174193226 3

First published 2008

Text: Rod Howard

Principal photographer: Steve Parish

Photographic assistance: Emma Harm, SPP: pp. 32 (centre left), 63 (bottom left), 340 (bottom right) & 357 (Sea Cliff Bridge, Stanwell Park & Hacking River, Royal National Park); Greg Harm, SPP: pp. 271 (handler with Wedge-tailed Eagle) & 278 (top right); Darran Leal: pp. 14 (woman with pram, Brisbane) & 23 (king parrot & bottom right); Ian Roberts: pp. 321 (hydrangeas & bottom left)

Additional photography: Yaa Asantwaa Eleanor Adjei: p. 60 (Auditorium, City Hall); Cyril Webster/ANTPhoto.com: p. 176 (centre); Jean-Paul Ferrero/ Auscape: p. 159 (bottom); Fred Kamphues/Auscape: p. 161 (Manning Gorge & Galvans Gorge); Wayne Lawler/Auscape: p. 161 (top right); Cameron Britt: p. 286 (top left); Michael Cermak: pp. 25 (bottom left) & 132 (bottom left); Robin Chok: p. 248 (top left); Allan Fox: pp. 329 (bottom left) & 330 (bottom right); Emma Harm: pp. 13 (top right), 58 (top left), 59, 91 (camping, Hook Island) & 92 (centre left); Greg Harm: pp. 60 (State Library of QLD), 90 (bottom left), 91 (bottom right) & 330 (bottom centre); Courtesy Historic Photographs www.historicphotographs.com.au: p. 318 (bottom left); Paul Kent: p. 309 (the Overland Track); Courtesy Melbourne Zoo: p. 32 (top left); M & I Morcombe: p. 194 (centre left); Ian Morris: pp. 53 (Brush-tailed Phascogale & Freckled Monitor), 123 (Saw-shelled Turtle, Stoney Creek Frog & Ornate Burrowing Frog), 131 (Northern Snapping Turtle), 132 (top right, Great Bowerbird, Tornier's Frog & Northern Death Adder), 133 (Comb-crested Jacana, Short-eared Rock-wallabies & Rock Ringtail Possum), 149 (right), 157 (top insert); 163, 228 (top left) & 279 (Blue-tongue Lizard); Rodney Start/ Museum Victoria: p. 323 (centre right); Melanie Newton: p. 78 (top); Gary Bell/OceanwideImages.com: pp. 24 (great white shark), 126 (bottom left) & 293 (top left); SATC: p. 216 (bottom right); Courtesy Sea World: p. 48 (bottom left); Jamie Seymour: p. 24 (top & centre left); Peter Slater: p. 224 (top right); Len H. Smith: p. 52 (top left); Gary Steer: pp. 222 (centre & bottom left) & 232 (bottom left); Ron & Valerie Taylor: pp. 74 (centre left), 207 (bottom left) & 209 (insert); Geoff Murray/Tourism Tasmania: p. 305 (Walls of Jerusalem NP); Courtesy Voyages Hotels and Resorts: p. 154 (centre left); Justine Walpole: p. 60 (Concert Hall, QPAC); Martin Willis: pp. 93 (Allied Rock-wallaby) & 122 (Golden Bowerbird, Noisy Pitta & Victoria's Riflebird)

Front cover, top to bottom: Wildflowers frame Mount Augustus, WA; Sydney Harbour Bridge and climbers with a view to the Opera House (Photo: Phillip Hayson); Dove Lake and Cradle Mountain, Cradle Mountain–Lake St Clair National Park, Tas; Russell Island with Normanby Island beyond, in Queensland's Frankland Islands.

Back cover, clockwise from top: Warrumbungle National Park, NSW; The Twelve Apostles standing along the Great Ocean Road, Vic; The vibrant face of Uluṟu, Uluṟu–Kata Tjuṯa National Park, NT; Researching the journey is half the fun: a map of Queensland's Wet Tropics World Heritage Area; Fraser Island in Queensland; A trip to the Low Isles, just offshore from Port Douglas, Queensland.

Title page: Kata Tjuṯa, Uluṟu-Kata Tjuṯa National Park, NT

Pages 2-3: Flinders Ranges National Park, SA

Page 4: Fitzroy Island, Qld

Page 5: Uluṟu, Uluṟu-Kata Tjuṯa National Park, NT

Page 7: Yarra Ranges, Vic

Editing: Ted Lewis, Helen Anderson, Michele Perry, Sarah Lowe, SPP
Design: Leanne Nobilio, SPP
Image Library: Emma Harm, Greg Harm, Heather Elson, SPP
Production: Tina Brewster, SPP

Maps by MAPgraphics Pty Ltd, Brisbane, Australia

Prepress by Colour Chiefs Digital Imaging, Brisbane, Australia
Printed in China by Imago

Produced in Australia at the Steve Parish Publishing Studios